Lecture Notes in Computer Science 3785

Commenced Publication in 1973
Founding and Former Series Editors:
Gerhard Goos, Juris Hartmanis, and Jan van Leeuwen

Kung-Kiu Lau   Richard Banach (Eds.)

Formal Methods and Software Engineering

7th International Conference
on Formal Engineering Methods, ICFEM 2005
Manchester, UK, November 1-4, 2005
Proceedings

 Springer

Volume Editors

Kung-Kiu Lau
Richard Banach
University of Manchester
School of Computer Science
Oxford Road, Manchester M13 9PL, UK
E-mail: {kung-kiu,banach}@cs.man.ac.uk

Library of Congress Control Number: 2005934587

CR Subject Classification (1998): D.2.4, D.2, D.3, F.3

ISSN   0302-9743
ISBN-10   3-540-29797-9 Springer Berlin Heidelberg New York
ISBN-13   978-3-540-29797-0 Springer Berlin Heidelberg New York

Springer is a part of Springer Science+Business Media

springeronline.com

© Springer-Verlag Berlin Heidelberg 2005
Printed in Germany

Typesetting: Camera-ready by author, data conversion by Scientific Publishing Services, Chennai, India
Printed on acid-free paper   SPIN: 11576280   06/3142   5 4 3 2 1 0

Preface

This volume contains papers presented at the 7th International Conference on Formal Engineering Methods (ICFEM 2005), 1–4 November 2005, Manchester, UK.

Formal engineering methods are changing the way that systems are developed. With language and tool support, these methods are being used for semi-automatic code generation, and for the automatic abstraction and checking of implementations. In the future, they will be used at every stage of development: requirements, specification, design, implementation, testing, and documentation.

The aim of ICFEM 2005 was to bring together those interested in the application of formal engineering methods to computer systems. Researchers and practitioners, from industry, academia, and government, were encouraged to attend, and to help advance the state of the art.

The conference was supported by sponsorships from Microsoft Research, USA, the Software Engineers Association of Japan, the University of Manchester, Manchester City Council, Formal Methods Europe (FME) and the British Computer Society Formal Aspects of Computing Specialist Group (BCS-FACS). We wish to thank these sponsors for their generosity.

The final programme consisted of 3 invited talks and 30 technical papers selected from a total of 74 submissions. The invited speakers were: Anthony Hall, independent consultant, UK; Egon Börger, University of Pisa, Italy; John Rushby, SRI, USA. Their talks were sponsored by BCS-FACS, Microsoft Research and FME respectively. We wish to thank the invited speakers for their inspiring talks.

Our heartfelt thanks go to all the members of the Programme Committee for their hard and conscientious work in reviewing and selecting the papers at various stages. I would also like to thank all the additional reviewers for their efforts and professionalism.

For organizing ICFEM 2005, we would like to thank the workshops and tutorials chair Mike Poppleton, the publicity chair Kenji Taguchi, the local organization chair Dave Lester, and the web-masters Elton Ballhysa and Faris Taweel. Their efforts were pivotal for the success of ICFEM 2005.

Finally, we would like to thank all the authors who submitted papers and all the conference attendees.

September 2005   Kung-Kiu Lau and Richard Banach
Manchester

Organization

Conference Chair

Richard Banach   University of Manchester, UK

Programme Chair

Kung-Kiu Lau   University of Manchester, UK

Programme Committee

Farhad Arbab	CWI and Leiden University, The Netherlands; University of Waterloo, Canada
Richard Banach	University of Manchester, UK
Luıs Soares Barbosa	Minho University, Portugal
Mike Barnett	Microsoft Research, USA
Eerke Boiten	University of Kent, UK
Tommaso Bolognesi	CNR-ISTI, Italy
Marcello Bonsangue	Leiden University, The Netherlands
Jonathan P. Bowen	London South Bank University, UK
Manfred Broy	Technische Universität München, Germany
Bettina Buth	HAW Hamburg, Germany
Ana Cavalcanti	University of York, UK
Michel Charpentier	University of New Hampshire, USA
Jim Davies	University of Oxford, UK
Jin Song Dong	National University of Singapore, Singapore
Kai Engelhardt	University of New South Wales and NICTA, Australia
Colin Fidge	Queensland University of Technology, Australia
Mamoun Filali Amine	Université Paul Sabatier, France
John Fitzgerald	University of Newcastle upon Tyne, UK
Marc Frappier	Université de Sherbrooke, Canada
Dimitra Giannakopoulou	USRA/NASA Ames, USA
Chris George	United Nations University, China
Wolfgang Grieskamp	Microsoft Research, USA
Lindsay Groves	Victoria University of Wellington, New Zealand
Henri Habrias	Université de Nantes, France
Andrew Ireland	Heriot-Watt University, UK
Thomas Jensen	IRISA/CNRS, France
Soon-Kyeong Kim	University of Queensland, Australia
Steve King	University of York, UK
Rom Langerak	University of Twente, The Netherlands
James Larus	Microsoft Research, USA
Kung-Kiu Lau	University of Manchester, UK

Mark Lawford	McMaster University, Canada
Yves Ledru	LSR/IMAG, Domaine Universitaire, France
Peter A. Lindsay	University of Queensland, Australia
Shaoying Liu	Hosei University, Japan
Zhiming Liu	UNU-IIST, China
Brendan Mahony	Defence Science and Technology Organisation, Australia
Tiziana Margaria	University of Göttingen, Germany
Brad Martin	US Department of Defense, USA
Dominique Mery	Université Henri Poincaré Nancy 1, France
Huaikou Miao	Shanghai University, China
Alexandre Mota	Federal University of Pernambuco, Brazil
David Naumann	Stevens Institute of Technology, USA
Richard Paige	University of York, UK
Iman Poernomo	King's College London, UK
Fiona Polack	University of York, UK
Michael Poppleton	University of Southampton, UK
Steve Reeves	University of Waikato, New Zealand
Ken Robinson	University of New South Wales, Australia
Abhik Roychoudhury	National University of Singapore, Singapore
Harald Ruess	SRI International, USA
Motoshi Saeki	Tokyo Institute of Technology, Japan
Thomas Santen	Technische Universität Berlin, Germany
Klaus-Dieter Schewe	Massey University, New Zealand
Wolfram Schulte	Microsoft Research, USA
Kaisa Sere	Åbo Akademi University, Finland
Paul Strooper	University of Queensland, Australia
Asuman Suenbuel	SAP Research, USA
Paul A. Swatman	University of South Australia, Australia
Kenji Taguchi	National Institute of Informatics, Tokyo, Japan
Sofiene Tahar	Concordia University, Canada
Tetsuo Tamai	University of Tokyo, Japan
T.H. Tse	University of Hong Kong, China
Margus Veanes	Microsoft Research, USA
Charles Wallace	Michigan Technological University, USA
Farn Wang	National Taiwan University, Taiwan
Wang Yi	Uppsala University, Sweden
Jim Woodcock	University of York, UK

Additional Referees

Pascal André	Jean-Paul Bodeveix	Manuela Xavier
Marcelo Arenas	Jeremy Bryans	Robert Colvin
Christian Attiogbé	Michael Butler	Hugo ter Doest

Yuzhang Feng
David Faitelson
Benoit Fraikin
Amjad Gawanmeh
Frédéric Gervais
Irina Mariuca
  Gheorghita
Ben Gorry
Jens Grabowski
Olga Grinchtein
Juan Guillen-Scholten
Neil Henderson
Lutz Kettner
Bas Luttik
Tom Maibaum

Frank Marschall
Tim McComb
Sun Meng
Haja Moinudeen
Shin Nakamima
O. Nasr
Lemai Nguyen
Corina Pasareanu
Pascal Poizat
M. Rached
Rodrigo Ramos
Pritam Roy
Johann Schumann
Emil Sekerinski
Qin Shengchao

Rakesh Shukla
Colin Snook
Maria Sorea
Graham Steel
Bernhard Steffen
Jing Sun
Willem Visser
Nabil Wageeh
Marina Waldén
Geoffrey Watson
James Welch
Mohamed Zaki
Sergiy Zlatkin

Table of Contents

Communication

Development

Testing

Verification

Tools

Realising the Benefits of Formal Methods

Anthony Hall

22 Hayward Road, Oxford OX2 8LW, UK
anthony@anthonyhall.org

I keep six honest serving-men
(They taught me all I knew);
Their names are What and Why and When
And How and Where and Who.

Rudyard Kipling

Abstract. The web site for this conference states that: "The challenge now is to achieve general acceptance of formal methods as a part of industrial development of high quality systems, particularly trusted systems." We are all going to be discussing How to achieve this, but before that we should maybe ask the other questions: What are the real benefits of formal methods and Why should we care about them? When and Where should we expect to use them, and Who should be involved? I will suggest some answers to those questions and then describe some ways that the benefits are being realised in practice, and what I think needs to happen for them to become more widespread.

1 What Have Formal Methods Ever Done for Us?

Formal methods consist of writing formal descriptions, analyzing those descriptions and in some cases producing new descriptions – for example refinements – from them. In what way is this a useful activity? First, experience shows that the very act of writing the formal description is of benefit: it forces the writer to ask all sorts of questions that would otherwise be postponed until coding. Of course, that's no help if the problem is so simple that one can write the code straight away, but in the vast majority of systems the code is far too big and detailed to be a useful description of the system for any human purpose. A formal specification, on the other hand, is a description that is abstract, precise and in some senses complete. The abstraction allows a human reader to understand the big picture; the precision forces ambiguities to be questioned and removed; and the completeness means that all aspects of behaviour - for example error cases - are described and understood.

Second, the formality of the description allows us to carry out rigorous analysis. By looking at a single description one can determine useful properties such as consistency or deadlock-freedom. By writing different descriptions from different points of view one can determine important properties such as satisfaction of high level requirements or correctness of a proposed design.

K.-K. Lau and R. Banach (Eds.): ICFEM 2005, LNCS 3785, pp. 1–4, 2005.

There are, however, stronger claims sometimes made for formal methods that are not, in my opinion, justified. The whole notion of proof as qualitatively superior to other analysis methods seems to me wrong: proof is no more a guarantee of correctness than testing, and in many cases far less of one. Furthermore, formal methods are descriptive and analytic: they are not creative. There is no such thing as a formal design process, only formal ways of describing and analyzing designs. So we must combine formal methods with other approaches if we actually want to build a real system.

2   Why Bother?

There sometimes seems to be a belief that formal methods are somehow morally better than other approaches to software development, and that they can lead to the holy grail of zero defect software. This is nonsense, and the fact that it's so obviously untrue is part of the reason for the strong backlash against formal methods. What is true, however, is that formal methods contribute to demonstrably cost-effective development of software with very low defect rates. It is economically perverse to try to develop such software without using them.

Furthermore, formal methods provide, for free, the kind of evidence that is needed in heavily regulated industries such as aviation. They demonstrate responsible engineering and give solid reasons for trust in the product. As more and more industries demand such trust, formal methods become increasingly attractive.

In trying to realise the benefits, therefore, we should be looking at cost-effective methods that address the major risks and that provide tangible evidence of trustworthiness. That is not the same as looking for perfection or proving every single piece of code.

3   When Do Formal Methods Bring Benefit?

It is well known that the early activities in the lifecycle are the most important. It follows that the most effective use of formal methods is at these early stages: requirements analysis, specification, high-level design. In contrast, a lot of research in formal methods has concentrated on low-level design and programming. The early use of formal methods does pose challenges: we need better notations and tools to address large scale specification issues.

As well as concentrating on the early lifecycle, formal methods need to be used from the start of each activity, not as a check at the end. We should concentrate, I believe, on correct construction rather than post-hoc analysis. Lots of experience with analysis tools tells us that it is far easier and more effective to demonstrate the correctness of a well constructed program than to analyse a poorly constructed one to find the numerous flaws that it contains. However, there is a real human problem in persuading people to think carefully rather than adopting the classic hack and test approach to programming.

4   Where Are They Best Used?

Formal methods traditionally live in a ghetto where they are applied to critical parts of critical systems. While I don't believe that they will ever be widely applied to fast-moving software such as web pages where the occasional failure is tolerated or even expected, there is an increasing amount of software where failure is becoming unacceptable and costly, and we need to extend the reach of formal methods to a wide range of systems such as banks, cars, telecommunications and domestic appliances.

Even where they have been used, formal methods have often been seen as a specialist activity divorced from the main development. Although there are some successful projects that have followed this approach, it is not a viable approach for most organisations. I believe strongly that formal methods will only be accepted when they clearly add value to mainstream development and verification activities.

5   Who Uses Formal Methods?

It follows from the previous point that everyone on a project needs to come into contact with formal methods. This is clearly a challenge: current formal notations are notoriously opaque, and formal methods tools are almost all hard to use. We need two things to happen.

First, there needs to be a change in attitude among developers, to accept that like engineers in any other discipline they need to use relevant mathematics as a daily part of their job.

Second, we need to make the mathematics more relevant and palatable, and integrate it better into the other less frightening notations that people are used to.

6   How Can We Realise the Benefits?

The previous sections have provided a pretty challenging list of issues for formal methods practitioners and researchers. In this section I will describe one process, Correctness by Construction (CbyC), which I believe starts to address these issues. CbyC aims to be a Lean Development process: there are, remarkably, commonalities between its philosophy and that of many so-called Agile processes. In particular it is strongly risk-driven, demands that all activities add value to the final product, and is based on tight feedback at every stage. Its big difference is the use of the most rigorous practical notation for each artifact, giving the maximum opportunity for analysis.

CbyC has some successful projects under its belt, but there is a long way to go before it or anything like it is a mainstream process. I will conclude by looking at the challenges for formal methods researchers and tool developers if they are going to support a practical process on a large scale in industry. Here are some examples of questions that need to be answered:

- How can we write perspicuous yet analysable descriptions of large systems without getting bogged down in detail?
- How can we validate formal descriptions with end users and other stakeholders?
- How can we integrate formal notations with more conventional notations like class diagrams, sequence diagrams or deployment diagrams?
- How can formal methods tools interwork with informal documents, requirements management tools, CASE tools, test generators, change and configuration management systems?
- How can we describe and prove refinements on to distributed, asynchronous, multiprocessing platforms that use COTS middleware?
- How can we use formal descriptions to generate system tests automatically?
- How can we automate other verification methods such as model checking and proof?

All these are practical, important questions. Some of them require research; many of them require collaboration between practitioners and researchers to put into practice ideas that we have all been developing for many years.

A Compositional Framework for Service Interaction Patterns and Interaction Flows

Alistair Barros[1] and Egon Börger[2]

[1] SAP Research Centre Brisbane, Australia
alistair.barros@sap.com
[2] Università di Pisa, Dipartimento di Informatica,
I-56125 Pisa, Italy
boerger@di.unipi.it

Abstract. We provide precise high-level models for eight fundamental service interaction patterns, together with schemes for their composition into complex service-based business process interconnections and interaction flows, supporting software-engineered business process management in multi-party collaborative environments. The mathematical nature of our models provides a basis for a rigorous execution-platform-independent analysis, in particular for benchmarking web services functionality. The models can also serve as accurate standard specifications, subject to further design leading by stepwise refinement to implementations.

We begin by defining succinct rigorous models to mathematically capture the behavioral meaning of four basic bilateral business process interaction patterns (Sect. 1), together with their refinements to four basic multilateral interaction patterns (Sect. 2). We then illustrate with characteristic examples how by appropriate combinations and refinements of these eight fundamental patterns one can define arbitrarily complex interaction patterns of distributed service-based business processes that go beyond simple request-response sequences and may involve a dynamically evolving number of participants. This leads to a definition of the concept of process interaction flow or conversation, namely via multi-agent distributed interaction pattern runs (Sect. 3). We point to various examples in the literature on web-service-oriented business process management, which illustrate the models and concepts defined here.

We start from the informal business process interaction pattern descriptions in [2][1], streamlining, generalizing or unifying them where the formalization suggested to do so. Our models provide for them an accurate high-level view one can consider as *ground model* (blueprint) definition, in the sense defined in [4], clarifying open issues and apt to direct the further detailing, by stepwise refinement in the sense defined in [5], to an executable version as for example BPEL code. Since for the semantics of the forthcoming BPEL standard a formal model has been provided in [15,24,13,14], such refinements can be mathematically investigated to *prove* their correctness with respect to the ground model, thus preparing for the application of verifying compiler techniques [17,10].

---

[1] All the not furthermore qualified quotes in this paper are from there.

K.-K. Lau and R. Banach (Eds.): ICFEM 2005, LNCS 3785, pp. 5–35, 2005.
© Springer-Verlag Berlin Heidelberg 2005

For the modeling we use the Abstract State Machines (ASMs) method with its ASM ground model and ASM refinement techniques, extending the pattern description scheme outlined in [8,9]. The support the ASM notion offers to express the dynamics of abstract state changes allows us to provide a high-level state-based view of service inter-*action* patterns, where the behavioral interface is defined through pattern actions performed by submachines, which remain largely abstract due to the intention to leave the design space open for further refinements to concrete pattern instantiations. Most of what we use below to model service interaction patterns by ASMs is self-explanatory, given the semantically well-founded pseudo-code character of ASMs, an extension of Finite State Machines (FSMs) by a general notion of state. For the sake of completeness we sketch in the appendix (Section 5) what is needed for a correct understanding: the simple semantics of ASMs as extension of FSMs by generalized memory locations together with the ASM classification of locations and functions that supports modularity in high-level system descriptions. A recent tutorial introduction into the ASM method for high-level system design and analysis is available in [7]. For a more detailed textbook presentation of the method see the AsmBook [12].

1   Basic Components of Bilateral Interaction Patterns

The basic bilateral (one-to-one) interaction patterns we have identified are characterized by four component type ASMs, refinements of which suffice to compose any other bilateral interaction pattern of whatever structural complexity: *Send* and *Receive* and their sequential combinations *SendReceive* (for sending a request followed by receiving a response) and *ReceiveSend* (for receiving a request followed by sending a response). Each of these pattern components describes one side of an interaction, as illustrated in Figure 1, so that all the basic bilateral interaction pattern ASMs we define in this section are mono-agent machines or modules.

1.1   Pattern Send

Different versions for sending are considered, depending on whether the delivery is reliable (guaranteed) or not and whether, in case of reliable delivery, the action is blocking or non-blocking. Also the possibility is contemplated that the send action may result in a fault message in response or that a periodic resending of a message is performed.

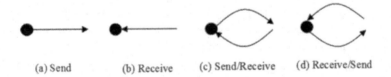

(a) Send   (b) Receive   (c) Send/Receive   (d) Receive/Send

Fig. 1. Basic Bilateral Interaction Pattern Types

For each version it is required that the counter-party may or may not be known at design time. This is reflected by the following possibly dynamic function, associating a recipient to each message. In case the recipient depends on further parameters, one has to refine $recipient(m)$ by adding those parameters to the function to determine $recipient(m, param)$.

$recipient$: $Message \rightarrow Recipient$
$recipient$: $Message \times Param \rightarrow Recipient$

All considered types of the send pattern use an abstract machine BASICSEND (m) with the intended interpretation that message m is sent to $recipient(m)$, or to $recipient(m, param)$ in case some additional recipient $param$eters are given by the context. Some patterns also use the notation BASICSEND(m, r) where $r =$ $recipient(m, param)$. This abstraction will be refined below, e.g. to capture broadcasting instead of bilateral sending. It also reflects that the underlying message delivery system is deliberately left unspecified.

To indicate that a faulty behavior has happened at the receiver's side as result of sending message m, we use an abstract monitored predicate $Faulty(m)$ with the intended interpretation that a fault message in response has arrived. Possible faults originating at the sender's side, during an attempt to send a message m, are captured by a SENDFAULTHANDLER, typically triggered by a condition **not** $OkSend(m)$. A typical refinement of $OkSend(m)$ would be that there exists a channel, connecting the sender to the recipient, which is open to send m.

We therefore have two abstract methods, a machine which does a FIRSTSEND (m) without further resending and a machine to HANDLESENDFAULT(m). These two machines use, as guards for being triggered, abstract monitored predicates $SendMode(m)$ respectively $SendFaultMode(m)$. A typical assumption on the underlying scheduler for calling these machines will be that for each m, $SendFaultMode(m)$ can become true only after $SendMode(m)$ has been true.

To formalize sending messages whose delivery is requested to be guaranteed by an acknowledgement, a machine SETWAITCONDITION will typically INITIALIZE a shared predicate $WaitingFor(m)$, whose role is to record that the sender is still waiting for an acknowledgement which informs that m has been delivered. In case of a $BlockingSend(m)$, the $blocking$ effect is formalized by setting $status := blocked(m)$. Here $status$ itself is not parameterized by m given that its role is to possibly block the SEND machine from further sending out other messages (see below the discussion of the blocking case).

FIRSTSEND$(m) =$ **if** $SendMode(m)$ **then** [2]
  if $OkSend(m)$ **then**
    BASICSEND(m)

---

[2] For notational succinctness we assume the firing of this rule to be preemptive. This means that when the rule is applied because $SendMode(m)$ became true, $SendMode(m)$ becomes false as a result of this application. Usually such an preemptiveness assumption is automatically guaranteed through further refinement steps.

> **if** $AckRequested(m)$ **then** SETWAITCONDITION(m)
> **if** $BlockingSend(m)$ **then** $status := blocked(m)$

HANDLESENDFAULT(m) = **if** $SendFaultMode(m)$ **then**
SENDFAULTHANDLER(m)[3]

As typical assumption $SendMode(m)$ **and not** $OkSend(m)$ implies $SendFault\ Mode(m) = true$.

SEND&CHECK = {FIRSTSEND(m), HANDLESENDFAULT(m)}[4]

Send Without Guaranteed Delivery. For the instantiation of SEND&CHECK to SEND$_{noAck}$ it suffices to require $AckRequested$ and $BlockingSend$ to be always false.

> *MODULE* SEND$_{noAck}$ = SEND&CHECK
> **where** [5] **forall** m $AckRequested(m) = BlockingSend(m) = false$

Guaranteed Non-blocking Send. For the instantiation of SEND&CHECK to SEND$_{ackNonBlocking}$ with guaranteed delivery, but without blocking effect, it suffices to require $AckRequested$ to be always true resp. $BlockingSend$ to be always false and to further detail the abstract submachine SETWAITCONDITION(m). This machine has to SET various deadlines and to INITIALIZE the predicate $WaitingFor(m)$,[6] which is reset to $false$ typically through an action of the $recipient(m)$ upon receipt of m, e.g. by sending an acknowledgement message under a reliable messaging protocol[7]. Among the various deadlines occurring in different patterns we mention here $deadline(m)$ and $sendTime(m)$, which are typically used to define $Timeout(m)$ by $(now - sendTime(m) > deadline(m))$, using a system time function now to which $sendTime(m)$ is set in SET. We also mention a function $frequency(m)$ which will help to define the frequency of events expected by the sender, e.g. the arrival of response messages or the $ResendTime(m)$ at which m has to be resent periodically (see below). A frequent requirement on the scheduler is that $SendFaultMode(m)$ is implied by a $Timeout(m)$, although some patterns come with Timeout concepts which are not related to faulty message sending and therefore trigger other machines than TIMEOUTFAULTHANDLERS.

---

[3] As for FIRSTSEND(m) we assume also the firing of HANDLESENDFAULT(m) to be preemptive.

[4] By this notation we indicate that SEND&CHECK consists of the two methods FIRSTSEND and HANDLESENDFAULT, callable for any legal call parameter m, whatever may be the parameter passing mechanism.

[5] Notationally we use unrestricted quantifiers, assuming that their underlying range is clear from the context.

[6] This predicate reflects the not furthermore specified message delivery system. In some cases below it will be refined by providing further details for its definition.

[7] The limit case is possible that INITIALIZE($WaitingFor(m)$) sets $WaitingFor(m) := false$ in case of immediate and safe delivery.

$MODULE$ SEND$_{ackNonBlocking}$ = SEND&CHECK
where
  forall m $AckRequested(m) = true$ **and** $BlockingSend(m) = false$
  SETWAITCONDITION$(m) =$
    INITIALIZE($WaitingFor(m)$)
    SET($deadline(m), sendTime(m), frequency(m), \ldots$)

Guaranteed Blocking Send. For the instantiation of SEND&CHECK to SEND$_{ackBlocking}$ with guaranteed delivery and *blocking* effect, we require both *AckRequested* and *BlockingSend* to be always true, refine *SendMode(m)* to *status = readyToSend* and add a submachine UNBLOCKSEND(m). Its role is to switch back from *blocked(m)* to an unblocked status, typically *readyToSend*, and to PERFORMACTION(m) to be taken upon the end of the waiting period.[8]

For a succinct formulation of the refinement of SETWAITCONDITION we use the following notation introduced in [6]: M **addRule** R denotes the parallel composition of M and R.

M **addRule** $R =$
  M
  R

To avoid confusion among different machines, which occur as submachine of machines N, N' but within those machines carry the same name M, we use indexing and write M_N respectively $M_{N'}$.

$MODULE$ SEND$_{ackBlocking}$ = SEND&CHECK $\cup$ {UNBLOCKSEND(m)}
where
  forall m $AckRequested(m) = BlockingSend(m) = true$
  $SendMode(m) = (status = readyToSend)$
  SETWAITCONDITION$(m) =$ SETWAITCONDITION$_{\text{SEND}_{ackNonBlocking}}(m)$
    addRule $status := blocked(m)$
  UNBLOCKSEND$(m) =$ **if** $UnblockMode(m)$ **then**
    UNBLOCK($status$)
    PERFORMACTION(m)
  $UnblockMode(m) = (status = blocked(m)$ **and not** $WaitingFor(m))$
  $SendFaultMode(m) = (Faulty(m)$ **and** $status = blocked(m)$ **and**
  $WaitingFor(m))$

Send with Resending. In case one wants a still not delivered message to be resent from time to time, it suffices to periodically trigger an additional machine RESEND(m) [9] until the $WaitingFor(m)$ value has changed to *false*—or

---

[8] We use here an abstract machine UNBLOCK($status$) instead of $status :=$ *readyToSend* to be prepared for further refinements of PERFORMACTION which could include *status* updates, in coordination with a corresponding refinement of UNBLOCK($status$).

[9] The period is determined by a predicate $ResendTime(m)$, which typically is defined in terms of the function $lastSendTime(m)$ and the monitored system time *now*.

a *Faulty*(*m*) event triggers HANDLESENDFAULT(*m*), which typically is assumed to stop RESENDing. We write the pattern for any *SendType* considered above, namely $t \in \{noAck, ackNonBlocking, ackBlocking\}$. We foresee that message copies are variations *newVersion*(*m*, *now*) of the original *m*, where the variation may depend on the current time *now*.

$MODULE$ SEND$_{tResend}$ = SEND$_t$ $\cup$ {RESEND(*m*)}
where
  RESEND(*m*) = **if** *ResendMode*(*m*) **then**
    BASICSEND(*newVersion*(*m*, *now*))
    lastSendTime(*m*) := *now*
  ResendMode(*m*) = *ResendTime*(*m*) **and** *WaitingFor*(*m*)

For a pictorial representation of SEND$_{ackBlockingResend}$ see Figure 2. It generalizes the Alternating Bit Sender control state ASM diagram in [p.243][12].

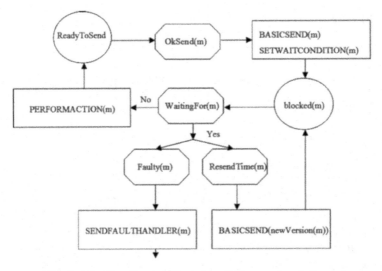

Fig. 2. Blocking Send with Acknowledgement and Resend

We reassume here the definition of the set of *SendType*s considered in this paper:

SendType = {*noAck*, *ackNonBlocking*, *ackBlocking*}
  ∪{*noAckResend*, *ackNonBlockingResend*, *ackBlockingResend*}

1.2   Pattern Receive

We formalize a general form for receiving messages, which can be instantiated to the different versions discussed in [2], depending on whether the action is blocking or non-blocking, whether messages which upon arrival cannot be received are buffered for further consumption or discarded and whether an acknowledgement is required or not. Also the possibility is contemplated that the receive action may result in a fault message.

For each version it is required that the party from which the message will be received may or may not be known at design time. This is reflected by the following possibly dynamic function, associating a sender to each message.

sender: *Message* → *Sender*

We use abstract predicates checking whether a message m is $Arriving$[10] and *ToBeAcknowledged* and whether our machine is *ReadyToReceive*(m) and in case it is not whether the message is *ToBeDiscarded* or *ToBeBuffered*, in which cases the action is described by abstract machines to CONSUME(m), DISCARD(m), BUFFER(m) or to send an $Ack(m)$ message or a *faultMsg*(m) to the *sender*(m). For the buffering submachine we also forsee the possibility that upon *DequeueTime*, which is typically defined in terms of the *enqueueTime* of messages, a DEQUEUE action is required. We leave it as part of the here not furthermore specified submachines DISCARD(m) and ENQUEUE(m) to acknowledge by BASICSEND(*discardOrBufferMsg*(m), *sender*(m)) a received but discarded or buffered message m where required. Similarly one may consider sending a further acknowledgement as part of the DEQUEUE submachine.

RECEIVE(m) = **if** $Arriving(m)$ **then**
  if $ReadyToReceive(m)$ **then**
    CONSUME(m)
    if $ToBeAcknowledged(m)$ **then** BASICSEND$(Ack(m), sender(m))$
  elseif $ToBeDiscarded(m)$ **then**
    DISCARD(m)
  else BUFFER(m)
  where BUFFER(m) =
  if $ToBeBuffered(m)$ **then**
    ENQUEUE(m)
    $enqueueTime(m) := now$
  if $DequeueTime$ **then** DEQUEUE

Remark. Note that CONSUME and DISCARD are typically realized at the application (e.g. BPEL) level, whereas BUFFER(m) belongs to the system level and is usually realized through lower level middleware functionality.

Instances of RECEIVE(m). It is now easy to define special versions of RECEIVE by restricting some of the abstract guards.

RECEIVE$_{blocking}$ can be defined as RECEIVE where no message is discarded or buffered, so that for an $Arriving(m)$ that is not $ReadyToReceive(m)$, the machine is 'blocked' (read: cannot fire its rule for this m) until it becomes $ReadyToReceive(m)$, formally speaking where there is no $DequeueTime$ and for each message m holds:

---

[10] The intended interpretation of $Arriving(m)$ is that m is in the message channel or in the message buffer.

$$ToBeDiscarded(m) = false = ToBeBuffered(m).$$

RECEIVE$_{discard}$ can be defined similarly as RECEIVE where arriving messages, if they cannot be received at arrival time, are discarded, so that for each message m holds:

$$ReadyToReceive(m) = false \Rightarrow ToBeDiscarded(m) = true.$$

RECEIVE$_{buffer}$ can be defined as RECEIVE where arriving messages, if they cannot be received at arrival time, are buffered, formally where for each message m holds:

$$ReadyToReceive(m) = false \Rightarrow$$
$$ToBeDiscarded(m) = false\, ToBeBuffered(m) = true.$$

For each of the preceding RECEIVE instances one can define a version RECEIVE$_{ack}$ with acknowledgement, namely by requiring that for each message m it holds that $ToBeAcknowledged(m) = true$; analogously for a version RECEIVE$_{noAck}$ without acknowledgement, where it is required that $ToBeAcknowledged(m) = false$ holds for each message m.

We reassume here the definition of the set of *ReceiveTypes* considered above, where we add the distinction among those with and those without acknowledgement, depending on whether $ToBeAcknowledged(m)$ is true or not for every m:

$$ReceiveType = \{blocking, buffer, discard\} \cup$$
$$\{noAckBlocking, noAckBuffer, ackBlocking, ackBuffer\}$$

1.3 Pattern Send/Receive

This pattern is about receiving a response to a previously sent request. One can define this pattern as a combination of the machines for the send and the receive pattern. The requirement of "a common item of information in the request and the response that allows these two messages to be unequivocally related to one another" is captured by two dynamic predicates[11] *RequestMsg* and *ResponseMsg* with a function *requestMsg*, which identifies for every $m \in ResponseMsg$ the $requestMsg(m) \in RequestMsg$ to which m is the *responseMsg*.[12]

For the non-blocking version of the pattern, sending a request message is made to precede the call of RECEIVE for the response message m by refining the RECEIVE-guard $Arriving(m)$ through the condition that the message which *Arrived* is a *ResponseMsg*. If no acknowledgement of the response is requested, it suffices to require $ToBeAcknowledged(m) = false$ for each m. Another natural assumption is that after having INITIALIZEd $WaitingFor(m)$ through FIRSTSEND(m), $WaitingFor(m)$ is set at the $recipient(m)$ to *false* in the moment $responseMsg(m)$ is defined. For the blocking version this assumption guarantees that both RECEIVE and UNBLOCKSEND can be called for the $responseMsg(m)$. We formulate the Send/Receive pattern for any pair (s, t) of *SendType* and *ReceiveType*.

---

[11] We identify sets with unary predicates.

[12] This view of *ResponseMsg* can be turned into a refined view by distinguishing at each agent *ReceivedResponseMsg*es from *ToBeSentResponseMsg*es.

$MODULE$ SENDRECEIVE$_{s,t}$ = SEND$_s$ $\cup$ {RECEIVE$_t(m)$}
where
  $Arriving(m) = Arrived(m)$ **and** $m \in ResponseMsg$
  $ResponseMsg = \{m \mid m = responseMsg(requestMsg(m))\}$

1.4   Pattern Receive/Send

This pattern is a dual to the Send/Receive pattern and in fact can be composed out of the same constituents, but with different refinements for some of the abstract predicates to let receiving a request precede sending the answer. The different versions of the pattern are reflected by the different versions for the constituent machines for the Receive or Send pattern. The refinement of $SendMode(m)$ by adding the condition $m \in ResponseMsg$ guarantees that sending out an answer message is preceded by having received a corresponding request message, a condition which is represented by a predicate $ReceivedMsg$.

$MODULE$ RECEIVESEND$_{t,s}$ = {RECEIVE$_t(m)$} $\cup$ SEND$_s$
where
  $SendMode(m) = SendMode_t(m)$ **and** $m \in ResponseMsg$
  $ResponseMsg = \{responseMsg(m) \mid ReceivedMsg(m)\}$

An example of this bilateral service interaction pattern appears in the web service mediator model defined in [1], namely in the pair of machines to RECEIVE REQUESTS and to SENDANSWERS.

2   Basic Multilateral Interaction Patterns (Composition of Basic Bilateral Interaction Patterns)

In this section four basic multi-party interaction patterns are identified for each of the four basic bilateral interaction pattern ASMs of the previous section, namely by allowing multiple recipients or senders: *Send* messages (representing requests or responses) to multiple recipients, *Receive* responses or requests from multiple senders, *SendReceive* to send requests to multiple interaction partners followed by receiving responses from them, similarly *ReceiveSend* to receive requests from multiple interaction partners followed by sending responses to them.

Each of these patterns describes one side of the interaction, as illustrated in Figure 3, so that all the components we define in this section are mono-agent ASM machines or modules. Refinements of the identified basic multilateral interaction pattern ASMs suffice to compose any other multilateral interaction pattern of whatever structural complexity.

2.1   One-to-Many Send Pattern

This pattern describes a broadcast action where one agent sends messages to several recipients. The requirement that the number of parties to whom a message is sent may or may not be known at design time is reflected by having a dynamic set *Recipient*. The condition that the message contents may differ from

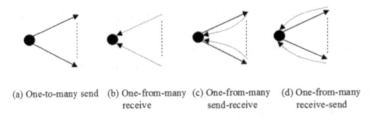

(a) One-to-many send   (b) One-from-many   (c) One-from-many   (d) One-from-many
                             receive   send-receive   receive-send

Fig. 3. Basic Multilateral Interaction Pattern Types

one recipient to another can be captured by a dynamic function $msgContent$ for "instantiating a template with data that varies from one party to another".

$$msgContent\colon MsgTemplate \times Recipient \to Message$$

Variations of the pattern can be captured by refining the abstract predicates like $FaultMode(m)$ or $SendMode(m)$ accordingly[13] and refining the BASICSEND component by **forall** $r \in Recipient$ **do** ATOMICSEND$_{type(m,r)}(msgContent(m,r))$, where the new abstract machine ATOMICSEND plays the role of the atomic sending mechanism for broadcasting messages to multiple recipients. We forsee that it can be of a *type* which depends on messages m and their recipients r.

> ONETOMANYSEND$_s$ = SEND$_s$
> **where**
> > BASICSEND(m) = **forall** $r \in Recipient(m)$ **do**
> > ATOMICSEND$_{type(m,r)}(msgContent(m,r))$

2.2   One-from-Many Receive Pattern

This pattern describes correlating messages, received from autonomous multiple parties, into groups of given types, whose consolidation may complete successfully, e.g. into a single logical request, or trigger a failure process. "The arrival of messages needs to be *timely* enough for their correlation as a single logical request." The pattern can be defined by adding to a refinement of RECEIVE a new module GROUPRULES whose components manipulate groups by creating, consolidating and closing them.

The refinement of RECEIVE consists first of all in adapting the predicate $ReadyToReceive(m)$ to mean that the current state is *Accepting* the type of arriving message. The $type(m)$ serves to "determine which incoming messages should be grouped together". The machine CONSUME(m) is detailed to mean that m is accepted by and put into its current (possibly newly created) correlation group $currGroup$, which depends on the $type(m)$. By the constraint that

---

[13] For example $SendMode(m)$ could be refined for the guaranteed blocking send by stipulating $SendMode(m) \equiv status =$ **forall** $r \in Recipient$ $ReadyToSendTo(m,r)$ and refining $WaitingFor(m)$ to **forall** $r \in RecipientExpectedToAnswer(m)$ $WaitingFor(m,r)$ or to **forsome** $r \in RecipientExpectedToAnswer(m)$ $WaitingFor(m,r)$.

a message, to be inserted into its correlation group, has to be accepted by its *currGroup*, we reflect a stop condition, which is needed because in the pattern "the number of messages to be received is not necessarily known in advance". The definition of *ToBeDiscarded(m)* as the negation of *Accepting(m)* reflects that no buffering is foreseen in this scheme.

The machine CREATEGROUP(*type*) to create a correlation group of the given *type* reflects that following the pattern requirements, groups can be created not only upon receipt of a first message (namely as part of CONSUME), but "this can occur at any time". To INITIALIZEGROUP for a newly created element $g \in Group(t)$ comes up to make it the *currGroup* of $type(g) = t$, *Accepting* and with the *timer(g)* set to the current system time *now*.

The group closure machines CLOSECURRGROUP and CLOSEGROUP reset *Accepting* for their argument (namely *currGroup* or a group type) to *false* in case a *Timeout*, imposed on the correlation process, or a group completion event respectively a *ClosureEvent* for a correlation type does occur.

To CONSOLIDATE a group g upon its completion into a single result, the two cases are forseen that the correlation "may complete successfully or not depending on the set of messages gathered" in g, wherefore we use abstract machines to PROCESSSUCCESS(*g*) or PROCESSFAILURE(*g*).

MODULE ONEFROMMANYRECEIVE$_t$ = {RECEIVE$_t$} ∪ GROUPRULES
where
ReadyToReceive(m) = *Accepting(type(m))*
CONSUME(*m*) =
  let $t = type(m)$ **in**
    if *Accepting(currGroup(t))*
      then insert m into *currGroup(t)*
      else INITINSERT(*m, new(Group(t))*)
INITINSERT(*m, g*) =
  INITIALIZEGROUP(*g*)
  insert m into g
ToBeDiscarded(m) = **not** *Accepting(type(m))*
GROUPRULES = {CREATEGROUP(*type*), CONSOLIDATE(*group*),
  CLOSECURRGROUP(*type*), CLOSEGROUP(*type*)}

CREATEGROUP(*type*) = **if** *GroupCreationEvent(type)* **then**
  let $g = new(Group(type))$ **in** INITIALIZEGROUP(*g*)
INITIALIZEGROUP(*g*) =
  Accepting(g) := *true*
  currGroup(type(g)) := g
  timer(g) := *now*

CONSOLIDATE(*group*) = **if** *Completed(group)* **then**
  if *Success(group)*
    then PROCESSSUCCESS(*group*)
    else PROCESSFAILURE(*group*)

CLOSECURRGROUP($type$) =
   if $Timeout(currGroup(type))$ **or** $Completed(currGroup(type))$
      then $Accepting(currGroup(type)) := false$
CLOSEGROUP($type$) =
   if $ClosureEvent(type)$ **then** $Accepting(type) := false$

This formalization permits to have at each moment more than one correlation group open, namely one *currGroup* per message type. It also permits to have at each moment messages of different types to arrive simultaneously. It assumes however that per message type at each moment only one message is arriving. If this assumption cannot be guaranteed, one has to refine the CONSUME machine to consider completing a group by say m_1 of m simultaneously arriving messages and to create a new group for the remaining $m - m_1$ ones (unless the completion of a group triggers the closure of the group type).

2.3 One-to-Many Send/Receive Pattern

This pattern is about sending a message to multiple recipients from where responses are expected within a given timeframe. Some parties may not respond at all or may not respond in time. The pattern can be composed out of the machine ONETOMANYSEND and the module ONEFROMMANYRECEIVE, similarly to the composition of the SENDRECEIVE modules out of SEND and RECEIVE. For this purpose the sending machine used in ONETOMANYSEND is assumed to contain the SETWAITCONDITION submachine to initialize $sendTime(m) :=$ *now*. This value is needed to determine the *Accepting* predicate in the module ONEFROMMANYRECEIVE to reflect that "responses are expected within a given timeframe". Remember that the refinement of the RECEIVE-guard $Arriving(m)$ guarantees that ONETOMANYSEND has been called for $requestMsg(m)$ before ONEFROMMANYRECEIVE is called to RECEIVE(m).

MODULE ONETOMANYSENDRECEIVE$_{s,t}$ =
   ONETOMANYSEND$_s$ ∪ ONEFROMMANYRECEIVE$_t$
    where
      $Arriving(m) = Arrived(m)$ **and** $m \in ResponseMsg$

An instance of this multilateral service interaction pattern appears in the web service mediator model defined in [1], realized by the machine pair FEEDSEND REQ and RECEIVEANSW. The former is an instance of ONETOMANYSEND, the latter is used as a ONEFROMMANYRECEIVE until all expected answers have been received.

2.4 One-from-Many Receive/Send Pattern

This pattern is symmetric to ONETOMANYSENDRECEIVE and can be similarly composed out of ONETOMANYSEND and ONEFROMMANYRECEIVE but with a different refinement, namely of the *SendMode* predicate, which guarantees that in any round, sent messages are responses to completed groups of received requests. Since several received messages are correlated into a single response message, which is then sent to multiple recipients, *responseMsg* is defined not on received messages, but on correlation groups of such, formed by ONEFROMMANYRECEIVE.

$MODULE$ ONEFROMMANYRECEIVESEND$_{t,s}$ =
ONEFROMMANYRECEIVE$_t$ $\cup$ ONETOMANYSEND$_s$
    where $SendMode(m)$ =
        $SendMode(m)_s$ **and** $m = responseMsg(g)$ for some $g \in Group$ **with**
        $Completed(g)$

This pattern generalizes the abstract communication model for distributed systems proposed in [16] as a description of how communicators route messages through a network, namely by forwarding into the mailboxes of the *Recipients* (read: via ONETOMANYSEND) the messages found in the communicator's mailbox (read: via ONEFROMMANYRECEIVE). The core of this communicator model is the ASM defined in [16, Sect.3.4], which exhibits "the common part of all message-based communication networks" and is reported to have been applied to model several distributed communication architectures.

3   Composition of Basic Interaction Patterns

In this section we illustrate how to build complex business process interaction patterns, both mono-agent (bilateral and multilateral) and asynchronous multi-agent patterns, from the eight basic interaction pattern ASMs defined in the preceding sections. There are two ways to define such patterns: one approach focusses on refinements of the interaction rules to tailor them to the needs of particular interaction steps; the other approach investigates the order and timing of single interaction steps in (typically longer lasting) runs of interacting agents.

To illustrate the possibilities for refinements of basic interaction pattern ASMs, which exploit the power of the general ASM refinement notion [5], we define two bilateral mono-agent patterns, namely an instance COMPETINGRECEIVE of RECEIVE and a refinement MULTIRESPONSE of the bilateral SENDRECEIVE. We define TRANSACTIONALMULTICASTNOTIFICATION, a mono-agent multilateral instance of the multilateral ONETOMANYSENDRECEIVE and a generalization of the well-known Master-Slave network protocol. We define MULTIROUND ONETOMANYSENDRECEIVE, an iterated version of ONETOMANYSEND RECEIVE. As examples for asynchronous multi-agent patterns we define four patterns: Request with Referral, Request with Referral and Notification, Relayed Request, Dynamic Routing.

The list can be extended as needed to include any complex or specialized monoagent or multiagent interaction pattern, by defining combinations of refinements of the eight basic bilateral and multilateral interaction pattern ASMs identified in the preceding sections.

At the end of this section we shortly discuss the investigation of interaction pattern ASM runs and link the management of such runs to the study of current thread handling disciplines.

3.1 Competing Receive Pattern

This pattern describes a racing between incoming messages of various types, where exactly one among multiple received messages will be chosen for a special CONTINUATION of the underlying process. The normal pattern action is guarded by *waitingForResponses* contained in expected messages of different types, belonging to a set *Type*; otherwise an abstract submachine will be called to PROCESSLATERESPONSES. The CONTINUATION submachine is called for only one *ReceivedResponse*(*Type*), i.e. one *response* of some type $t \in$ *Type*, and is executed in parallel with another submachine to PROCESSREMAININGRESPonses. The interaction is closed by updating *waitingForResponse* to *false*. The choice among the competing types of received response events is expressed by a possibly dynamic and here not furthermore specified *selection* function to select one received *response* of some type. An abstract machine ESCALATIONPROCEDURE is foreseen in case of a *Timeout* (which appears here as a monitored predicate). It is natural to assume that ESCALATIONPROCEDURE changes *waitingForResponse* (*Type*) from *true* to *false*. Apparently no buffering is foreseen in this pattern, so that *ToBeDiscarded*(*m*) is defined as negation of *ReadyToReceive*(*m*).

An ASM with this behavior can be defined as a refinement of RECEIVE(*m*) as follows. We define *ReadyToReceive*(*m*) to mean that up to now *waitingForResponse*(*Type*) holds and no *Timeout* occurred. This notion of *ReadyToReceive*(*m*) describes a guard for executing RECEIVE which does not depend on *m*. In fact we have to make COMPETINGRECEIVE work independently of whether a message arrived or not, in particular upon a *Timeout*. Therefore also *Arriving*(*m*) has to be adapted not to depend on *m*, e.g. by defining it to be always true.[14] The submachine CONSUME is refined to formalize the normal pattern action described above (which may be parameterized by *m* or not), whereas *ToBeDiscarded*(*m*) describes that either a *Timeout* happened or the system is not *waitingForResponse* (*Type*) any more, in which case DISCARD formalizes the abnormal pattern behavior invoking ESCALATIONPROCEDURE or PROCESSLATERESPONSES.

> COMPETINGRECEIVE = RECEIVE
> **where**
>   *Arriving*(*m*) = *true*
>   *ReadyToReceive*(*m*) =
>   *waitingForResponse*(*Type*) **and not** *Timeout*
>   CONSUME =
>   **let** *ReceivedResponse*(*Type*) = {*r* | *Received*(*r*) **and** *Response*(*r*, *t*)
>   **forsome** *t* ∈ *Type*}
>   **if** *ReceivedResponse*(*Type*) ≠ ∅ **then**
>   **let** *resp* = *select*(*ReceivedResponse*(*Type*))
>   CONTINUATION(*resp*)
>   PROCESSREMAININGRESP(*ReceivedResponse*(*Type*) \ {*resp*})

---

[14] These stipulations mean that the scheduler will call COMPETINGRECEIVE independently of any message parameter, which is a consequence of the above stated requirements.

$waitingForResponse(Type) := false$
$ToBeDiscarded(m) = Timeout$ **or not** $waitingForResponse(Type)$
DISCARD $=$
    if not $waitingForResponse(Type)$ **then** PROCESSLATERESPONSES
    if $Timeout$ **then** ESCALATIONPROCEDURE

3.2 Contingent Request

This pattern has multiple interpretations. It can be defined as an instance of SENDRECEIVE, where the SEND(m) comes with the RESEND submachine to re-send m (maybe to a new recipient) if no response is received from the previous recipient within a given timeframe. I can also be defined as a combination of COMPETINGRECEIVE with RESEND. In both cases the function $newVersion$ reflects that the recipient of that version may be different from the recipient of the original.

3.3 Multi-response Pattern

This pattern is a multi-transmission instance of the SENDRECEIVE pattern, where the requester may receive multiple responses from the recipient "until no further responses are required". It suffices to refine the RECEIVE-guard $readyToReceive$ according to the requirements for what may cause that no further responses r will be accepted (and presumably discarded) for the request m, namely (a response) triggering to reset $FurtherResponseExpected(m)$ to $false$ or a $Timeout(m)$ due to the expiry of either the request $deadline(m)$ (time elapsed since the $sendTime(m)$, set in SETWAITCONDITION(m) when the request m was sent) or a $lastResponseDeadline(m)$ (time that elapsed since the last response to request message m has been received).

To make this work, SETWAITCONDITION(m) has to be refined by adding the initialization rule $FurtherResponseExpected(m) := true$. To RECEIVE response messages m, CONSUME(m) has to be refined by adding the rule $lastResponseTime\ (requestMsg(m)) := now$, so that the timeout predicate $Expired(lastResponse\ Deadline(m))$ can be defined with the help of $lastResponseTime(m)$. For the refinement of SETWAITCONDITION and CONSUME we use the notation M **addRule** R from [6] to denote the parallel composition of M and R.

$MODULE$ MULTIRESPONSE$_{s,t}$ = SENDRECEIVE$_{s,t}$
where
    SETWAITCONDITION(m) = SETWAITCONDITION$_{\text{SENDRECEIVE}_{s,t}}$($m$)
      addRule $FurtherResponseExpected(m) := true$
    $ReadyToReceive(m) = FurtherResponseExpected(requestMsg(m))$ **and**
    not $Timeout(requestMsg(m))$
    CONSUME(m) = CONSUME$_{\text{SENDRECEIVE}_{s,t}}$($m$)
      addRule $lastResponseTime(requestMsg(m)) := now$
    $ToBeDiscarded(m) =$ **not** $ReadyToReceive(m)$
    $Timeout(m) = Expired(deadline(m))$ **or**
    $Expired(lastResponseDeadline(m))$

3.4 Transactional Multicast Notification

This pattern generalizes the well-known Master-Slave network protocol investigated in [19,12]. In each round a notification m is sent to each recipient in a possibly dynamic set $Recipient(m)$. The elements of $Recipient(m)$ are arranged in groups, allowing in groups also further groups as members, yielding a possibly arbitrary nesting of groups. Within each group g a certain number of members, typically between a minimum $acceptMin(m, g)$ and a maximum $acceptMax(m, g)$ number, are expected to "accept" the request m within a certain timeframe $Timeout(m)$. Recipients "accept" m by sending back an $AcceptMsg$ to the master.

The pattern description given below defines the master program in the master-slave protocol, whereas in applications it is typically assumed that each slave uses a blocking SEND machine. The master ASM can be defined as a refinement of the ONETOMANYSENDRECEIVE pattern with blocking SEND. $WaitingFor(m)$ is refined to **not** $Timeout(m)$, so that the blocking condition $status = blocked(m)$ appears as waiting mode for receiving $AcceptMsges$ from $Recipients$ in response to the notification m. The nested group structure is represented as a $recipientTree(m)$ whose nodes (except the root) stand for groups or recipients. The set $Leaves(reci-\ pientTree(m))$ of its leaves defines the set $Recipient(m)$; for each tree node n which is not a leaf the set $children(n)$ represents a group. Since for each inner node there is only one such group, we keep every corresponding $currGroup(t)$ open by defining it as $Accepting$. We can define $type(r) = r$ so that $currGroup(r)$ for any response message r collects all the $AcceptMsgs$ which are received from brothers of $sender(r)$.

SETWAITCONDITION(m) is extended by a máchine to INITIALIZEMINMAX (m) and a machine to INITIALIZECURRGROUP(m) for each group. The $Accept$ance notion for tree nodes has to be computed by the master itself, namely as part of PERFORMACTION (m). We abstract from the underlying tree walk algorithm by defining $Accept$ as a derived predicate, namely by recursion on the $recipientTree(m)$ as follows, starting from the $AcceptMsg$ concept of response messages accepting the notification m. By $|\ X\ |$ we denote the cardinality of the set X.

$Accept(n) \Leftrightarrow acceptMin(m, children(n)) \leq|\ \{c \in children(n)\ |\ Accept(c)\}\ |$
$Accept(leaf) \Leftrightarrow$ some $r \in ResponseMsg(m)$ with $AcceptMsg(r)$
was received from $leaf$

It may happen that at $Timeout(m)$ more than $acceptMax(m, g)$ accepting messages did arrive. Then a "priority" function $chooseAccChildren$ is used to choose an appropriate set of accepting children among the elements of $g = children(n)$. The elements of all these chosen sets constitute the set $chosenAcc\ Party(root)$ of recipients chosen among those who accepted the notification m. Both functions are defined as derived functions by a recursion on the $recipientTree\ (m)$ as follows:

$$chooseAccChildren(n) =$$
$$\begin{cases} \emptyset & \text{if } |\, AcceptChildren(n)\, | < acceptMin(m, children(n)) \\ \subseteq_{min,max} AcceptChildren(n) & \text{else} \end{cases}$$
where

$AcceptChildren(n) = \{c \in children(n) \mid Accept(n)\}$

$min = acceptMin(m, children(n))$

$max = acceptMax(m, children(n))$

$A \subseteq_{l,h} B \Leftrightarrow A \subseteq B$ **and** $l \leq |\, A\, | \leq h$

$$chosenAccParty(leaf) = \begin{cases} \{n\} \text{ if } Accept(n) \\ \emptyset \quad\ \text{else} \end{cases}$$
$$chosenAccParty(n) = \bigcup\nolimits_{c \in chooseAccChildren(n)} chosenAccParty(c)$$

The submachine PERFORMACTION(m), which in case that $Accept(root(recipientTree(m)))$ holds is executed in $UnblockMode(m)$, PROCESSES the $fullRequest(m)$ for the $chosenAccParty$ at the $root(recipientTree(m))$, taking into account also the other recipients. Otherwise a REJECTPROCESS is called.

To formulate the refinement of SETWAITCONDITION we use again the notation M **addRule** R from [6] to denote the parallel composition of M and R. $OTMSR$ stands as abbreviation for ONETOMANYSENDRECEIVE$_{ackBlocking,t}$.

$MODULE$ TRANSACTIONALMULTICASTNOTIFY$_t$ =

ONETOMANYSENDRECEIVE$_{ackBlocking,t}$

where [15]

$WaitingFor(m) =$ **not** $Timeout(m)$

SETWAITCONDITION(m) = SETWAITCONDITION$_{OTMSR}(m)$

  addRule

    INITIALIZEMINMAX(m)

    INITIALIZECURRGROUP(m)

      where

      INITIALIZEMINMAX(m) = **forall** $g = children(n) \in recipientTree(m)$

        INITIALIZE($acceptMin(m, g), acceptMax(m, g)$)

      INITIALIZECURRGROUP(m) = **forall** $r \in Recipient(m)$

      $currGroup(r) := \emptyset$

$type(response) = response$

$Accepting(response) = response \in AcceptMsg$ **and not** $Timeout(requestMsg(response))$

$currGroup(response) = currGroup(sender(response))$

$currGroup(recipient) = brothers\&sisters(recipient) \cap \{leaf \mid Accept(leaf)\}$

$Accepting(currGroup(r)) =$ true

PERFORMACTION(m) =

  if $Accept(root(recipientTree(m)))$ **then**

    let

    $accParty = chosenAccParty(root(recipientTree(m)))$

    $others = Leaves(recipientTree(m)) \setminus accParty$ **in**

---

[15] One could probably delete the GROUPRULES since they are not used by this pattern.

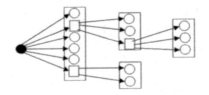

Fig. 4. Transactional Multicast Notify

PROCESS(*fullRequest*(*m*), *accParty*, *others*)
   else REJECTPROCESS(*m*)

For a pictorial representation of TRANSACTIONALMULTICASTNOTIFY (without arrows for the responses) see Figure 4, where the leaves are represented by circles and the groups by rectangles.

3.5   Multi-round One-to-Many Send/ReceivePattern

This pattern can be described as an iteration of (a refinement of) the ONETO MANYSENDRECEIVE components ONETOMANYSEND and ONEFROMMANY RECEIVE. The number of one-to-many sends followed by one-from-many receives is left unspecified; to make it configurable one can introduce a corresponding *roundNumber* counter (into the *SendMode* guard and the SETWAITCONDITION).

The dynamic set *Recipient* guarantees that the number of parties where successive requests are sent to, and from where multiple responses to the current or any previous request may be received by the sender, may be bounded or unbounded. There is also no a priori bound on the number of previous requests, which are collected into a dynamic set *ReqHistory*.

The main refinement on sending concerns the submachine SETWAIT CONDITION, which has to be adapted to the fact that *WaitingFor*, *sendTime* and *blocked* may depend on both the message template *m* and the recipient *r*. Furthermore this submachine has to record the message template as new *currRequest* and to store the old *currReq* into the *ReqHistory*, since incoming responses may be responses to previous request versions. The pattern description speaks about responses to "the request" for each request version, so that we use the request template *m* to define *currRequest* (and *Group* types below)[16]. Also the guard *SendMode*(*m*) is refined to express (in addition to the possible *status* condition) that **forall** $r \in Recipient(m)$ a predicate *ReadyToSendTo*(*m*, *r*) holds, where this predicate is intended to depend on the responses returned so far (defined below as a derived set *ResponseSoFar*).

The main refinement on receiving concerns the definition of *type*(*m*) for any $m \in ResponseMsg$ as the *requestMsg*(*m*) that triggered the response *m*. This reflects that each response message is assumed to be a response to (exactly) one of the sent requests. However, every request *r* is allowed to trigger more than one response *m* from each recipient (apparently without limit), so that the function *responseMsg* is generalized to a relation *responseMsg*(*m*, *r*).

---

[16] Otherwise one could define *currReq*(*r*) := *msgContent*(*m*, *r*) for each recipient *r*.

Therefore $currGroup(request)$ represents the current collection of responses received to the *request*. It remains to reflect the condition that "the latest response ... overrides the latest status of the data ... provided, although previous states are also maintained". Since the pattern description contains no further requirements on the underlying state notion, we formulate the condition by the derived set *ResponseSoFar* defined below and by adding to CONSUME an abstract machine MAINTAINDATASTATUS to allow one to keep track of the *dataStatus* of previous states, for any request. *OTMSR* stands as abbreviation for ONETOMANYSENDRECEIVE.

> *MODULE* MULTIROUNDONETOMANYSENDRECEIVE = ONETOMANYSENDRECEIVE
> **where**
> $SendMode(m) = SendMode(m)_{OTMSR}$ **and**
>   **forall** $r \in Recipient(m)$ $ReadyToSendTo(m, r)$
> SETWAITCONDITION$(m) =$
>   **forall** $r \in Recipient(m)$
>   INITIALIZE$(WaitingFor(m, r))$
> $sendTime(m, r) := now$
> $status := blocked(m, r)$
>   insert $currRequest$ into $ReqHistory$
> $currRequest := m$
> $type(m) = requestMsg(m)$
> CONSUME$(m) =$ CONSUME$(m)_{OTMSR}$
>   **addRule** MAINTAINDATASTATUS$(Group(requestMsg(m)))$

$ResponseSoFar = \bigcup\{Group(m) \mid m \in ReqHistory\} \cup \{currGroup(currReq)\}$

3.6   Request With Referral

This pattern involves two agents, namely a sender of requests and a receiver from where "any follow-up response should be sent to a number of other parties ...", in particular faults, which however "could alternatively be sent to another nominated party or in fact to the sender". Apparently sending is understood without any reliability assumption, so that the sender is simply formalized by the module SEND$_{noAck}$. For referring sent requests, the appropriate version of the RECEIVE machine is used, with the submachine CONSUME refined to contain ONETOMANYSEND for the set $Recipient(m)$ encoded as set of *followUpResponseAddr*essees extracted from m. As stated in the requirement for the pattern, *followUpResponseAddr* may be split into disjoint subsets *failureAddr* and *normalAddr*. Since the follow-up response parties (read: $Recipient(m)$) may be chosen depending on the evaluation of certain conditions, *followUpResponseAddr* can be thought of as a set of pairs of form $(cond, adr)$ where *cond* enters the definition of $SendMode(m)$.

> 2-Agent ASM REQUESTREFERRAL =
>   Sender agent with module SEND$_{noAck}$
>   Referral agent with module RECEIVE

where
$\text{CONSUME}(m) = \text{ONETOMANYSEND}(Recipient(m))$
$Recipient(m) = followUpResponseAddr(m)$

For a pictorial representation of REQUESTREFERRAL see Figure 5.

Fig. 5. Request with Referral and Advanced Notification

A refinement of REQUESTREFERRAL has the additional requirement of an advanced notification, sent by the original sender to the other parties and informing them that the request will be serviced by the original receiver. This requirement comes with the further requirement that the sender may first send his request m to the receiver and only later inform the receiver (and the to-be-notified other parties) about $Recipient(m)$. These two additional requirements can be obtained by refining in REQUESTREFERRAL the SEND_{noAck} by a machine with blocking acknowledgment—where $WaitingFor(m)$ means that $Recipient(m)$ is not yet known and that $Timeout(m)$ has not yet happened—and the PERFORMACTION(m) submachine as a ONETOMANYSEND of the notification guarded by $known(Recipient(m))$.

2-Agent ASM NOTIFIEDREQUESTREFERRAL =
　　Sender agent with module $\text{SEND}_{ackBlocking} \cup \{\text{ONETOMANYSEND}\}$
　　　where
　　　　$WaitingFor(m)\ = \textbf{not}\ known(Recipient(m))\ \textbf{and not}\ Timeout(m)$
　　　　PERFORMACTION(m) =
　　　　　if not $known(Recipient(m))$ **then** SENDFAILURE(m)
　　　　　else ONETOMANYSEND($advancedNotif(m)$)
　　Referral agent with module RECEIVE
　　　where
　　　　$\text{CONSUME}(m) = \text{ONETOMANYSEND}(Recipient(m))$
　　　　$Recipient(m) = followUpResponseAddr(m)$

3.7　Relayed Request Pattern

The RELAYEDREQUEST pattern extends Request Referral by the additional requirement that the other parties continue interacting with the original sender and that the original receiver "observes a "view" of the interactions including faults" and that the interacting parties are aware of this "view". To capture this we refine REQUESTREFERRAL by equipping the sender also with a machine to RECEIVE messages from third parties and by introducing a set *Server* of third party agents, each of with is equipped with two machines RECEIVE and

SEND&AUDIT where the latter is a refinement of SEND by the required observer mechanism.

For a pictorial representation of RELAYEDREQUEST see Figure 6.

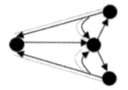

Fig. 6. Relayed Request

n+2-Agent ASM RELAYEDREQUEST =
  2-Agent ASM REQUESTREFERRAL
    where *module*(*Sender*) =
      *module*_{REQUESTREFERRAL}(*Sender*) ∪ {RECEIVE}
  n Server agents with module {RECEIVE, SEND&AUDIT}
    where
    SEND&AUDIT = SEND$_s$ **with**
      BASICSEND = BASICSEND$_s$ ∪
        {**if** *AuditCondition*(*m*) **then** BASICSEND$_s$(*filtered*(*m*))}

Using as subcomponent NOTIFIEDREQUESTREFERRAL yields NOTIFIED RELAYEDREQUEST.

3.8 Dynamic Routing

This pattern comes with a dynamic set of agents: a first party which "sends out requests to other parties" (an instance of ONETOMANYSEND) but with the additional requirement that "these parties receive the request in a certain order encoded in the request. When a party finishes processing its part of the overall request, it sends it to a number of other parties depending on the "routing slip" attached or contained in the request. This routing slip can incorporate dynamic conditions based on data contained in the original request or obtained in one of the "intermediate steps"."

In this way the third parties become additional pattern agents to receive requests, process them and forward them to the next set of recipients. Furthermore, this set of agents is dynamic: "The set of parties through which the request should circulate might not be known in advance. Moreover, these parties may not know each other at design/build time."

We therefore have a first *sender* agent with module ONETOMANYSEND concerning its set *Recipient*(*sender*). We then have a dynamic set of *RoutingAgents* which can RECEIVE request messages *m* with *routingSlip*(*m*) and CONSUME requests by first PROCESSING them and then forwarding a *furtherRequest* (*m*, *currState*(*router*)), which may depend not only on the received (and thereby without loss of generality of the original) request message, but also on data in the router state $currState(router)$ after message processing. Thus also the $routingSlip(m, currState(router))$ may depend on the original request and router data. The *Recipient* set depends on the *router* agent and on the *routingSlip* information. For the intrinsically sequential behavior we make use of the **seq** operator defined for ASMs in [11] (see also [12]).

Multi-Agent ASM DYNAMICROUTING =
   Agent *sender* with module ONETOMANYSEND($Recipient(sender)$)
   Agents *router* ∈ *RouterAgent* each with module RECEIVE
   where
   CONSUME(m) =
      PROCESS(m) **seq** ONETOMANYSEND($furtherRequest(m, currState(router))$)
      ($Recipient(router, routingSlip(m, currState(router)))$)

3.9 Defining Interaction Flows (Conversations)

In the preceding section the focus for the composition of basic interaction patterns into more complex ones was on combination and refinement of basic interaction pattern ASMs, i.e. on how the interaction rules (read: the programs) executed by the communicating agents can be adapted to the patterns under consideration. An equally important different view of interaction patterns is focussed instead on the run scenarios, that is to say on when and in which order the participating agents perform interaction steps by applying their interaction rules. This view is particularly important for the study of interaction structures which occur in long running processes, whose collaborations involve complex combinations of basic bilateral or multilateral interaction pattern ASM moves.

As an example for an interaction structure in a long running process consider a one-to-many-send-receive to short-list candidate service providers, which may be followed by a transactional multi-cast to issue service requests to selected providers, where finally individual providers may use relayed requests for outsourcing the work.

An elementary example is the well-known corouting pattern, which is characterized by two agents a_1 and a_2 each equipped with a SEND$_{noAck}$ and a RECEIVE module. The typical scenario is a distributed run where an application of SEND$_{noAck}$ by a_1 precedes firing RECEIVE by a_2, which (as consequence of the execution of CONSUME at a_2) is followed by an application of SEND$_{noAck}$ by a_2 and eventually triggers an execution of RECEIVE at a_1.

Such interactions structures resemble *conversations* or *interaction flows* between collaborating parties. This concept is captured by the notion of asynchronous runs of multi-agent service interaction pattern ASMs, i.e. ASMs whose rules consist of some of the basic or composed service interaction pattern ASMs defined in the preceding sections. Such runs, also called distributed runs, are partial orders of moves of the participating agents, each of which is (read: executes) a sequential ASM, constrained by a natural condition which guarantees that independent moves can be put into an arbitrary execution order without changing the semantical effect. [17] We therefore define a *conversation* or *interaction flow* to be a run of an asynchronous service interaction pattern ASM, where such an ASM is formally defined by a set of agents each of which is equipped with some (basic or complex, bilateral or multilateral) service interaction pattern modules defined in the previous sections.

A theory of such interaction flow patterns is needed, which builds upon the knowledge of classical workflow analysis [25]. A satisfactory theory should also provide possibilities to study the effect of allowing some agents to START or SUSPEND or RESUME or STOP such collaborations (or parts of them), the effect such conversation management actions have for example on security policies, etc. This naturally leads to investigate the impact of current thread handling methods (see for example [26,23,22]) on business process interaction management.

4   Conclusion and Outlook

We would like to see the ASM models provided here (or modified versions thereof) be implemented in a provably correct way, e.g. by BPEL programs, and be used as benchmarks for existing implementations. We would also like to see other interaction patterns be defined as combinations of refinements of the eight basic bilateral and multilateral service interaction pattern ASMs defined here. In particular we suggest the study of conversation patterns (business process interaction flows), viewed as runs of asynchronous multi-agent interaction pattern ASMs.

5   Appendix: The Ingredients of the ASM Method

The ASM method for high-level system design and analysis (see the Asm-Book [12]) comes with a simple mathematical foundation for its three constituents: the notion of *ASM*, the concept of *ASM ground model* and the notion of *ASM refinement*. For an understanding of this paper only the concept of ASM and that of ASM refinement have to be grasped,[18] whose definitions support the intuitive understanding of the involved concepts. We use here the definitions first presented in [7,3] and [5].

5.1   ASMs = FSMs with Arbitrary Locations

The instructions of an FSM program are pictorially depicted in Fig. 7, where $i, j_1,$ $\ldots, j_n$ are internal (control) states, $cond_\nu$ (for $1 \leq \nu \leq n$) represents the input condition $in = a_\nu$ (reading input a_ν) and $rule_\nu$ the output action $out := b_\nu$ (yielding output b_ν), which goes together with the ctl_state update to j_ν. Control state ASMs have the same form of programs and the same notion of run, but the underlying notion of state is extended from the following three locations:

---

[17] Details on this definition of partial order ASM run can be found in [12, pg.208].

[18] For the concept of ASM ground model (read: mathematical system blueprint) see [4].

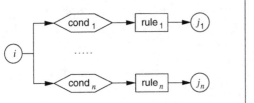
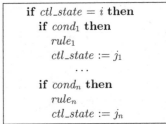

Fig. 7. Viewing FSM instructions as control state ASM rules

- a single internal *ctl_state* that assumes values in a not furthermore structured finite set
- two input and output locations *in*, *out* that assume values in a finite alphabet

to a *set of possibly parameterized locations holding values of whatever types*. Any desired level of abstraction can be achieved by permitting to hold values of arbitrary complexity, whether atomic or structured: objects, sets, lists, tables, trees, graphs, whatever comes natural at the considered level of abstraction. As a consequence an FSM step, consisting of the simultaneous update of the *ctl_state* and of the *out*put location, is turned into an ASM step consisting of the simultaneous update of a set of locations, namely via multiple assignments of the form $loc(x_1, \ldots, x_n) := val$, yielding a new ASM state.

This simple change of view of what a state is yields machines whose states can be arbitrary *multisorted structures*, i.e. domains of whatever objects coming with predicates (attributes) and functions defined on them, structures programmers nowadays are used to from object-oriented programming. In fact such a memory structure is easily obtained from the flat location view of abstract machine memory by grouping subsets of data into tables (arrays), via an association of a value to each table entry $(f, (a_1, \ldots, a_n))$. Here f plays the role of the name of the table, the sequence $(a_1, \ldots, a_n)$ the role of a table entry, $f(a_1, \ldots, a_n)$ denotes the value currently contained in the location $(f, (a_1, \ldots, a_n))$. Such a table represents an array variable f of dimension n, which can be viewed as the current interpretation of an n-ary "dynamic" function or predicate (boolean-valued function). This allows one to structure an ASM state as a set of tables and thus as a multisorted structure in the sense of mathematics.

In accordance with the extension of unstructured FSM control states to ASM states representing arbitrarily rich structures, the FSM-input *condition* is extended to arbitrary ASM-state expressions, namely formulae in the signature of the ASM states. They are called *guards* since they determine whether the updates they are guarding are executed.[19] In addition, the usual non-deterministic interpretation, in case more than one FSM-instruction can be executed, is replaced by the parallel interpretation that in each ASM state, the machine executes simultaneously all the updates which are guarded by a condition that is true in this state. This *synchronous parallelism*, which yields a clear concept of

---

[19] For the special role of *in/out*put locations see below the classification of locations.

locally described global state change, helps to abstract for high-level modeling from irrelevant sequentiality (read: an ordering of actions that are independent of each other in the intended design) and supports refinements to parallel or distributed implementations.

Including in Fig. 7 *ctl_state* = *i* into the guard and *ctl_state* := *j* into the multiple assignments of the rules, we obtain the definition of a *basic ASM* as a set of instructions of the following form, called ASM *rules* to stress the distinction between the parallel execution model for basic ASMs and the sequential single-instruction-execution model for traditional programs:

if *cond* **then** *Updates*

where *Updates* stands for a set of *function updates* $f(t_1, \ldots, f_n) := t$ built from expressions t_i, t and an n-ary function symbol f. The notion of run is the same as for FSMs and for transition systems in general, taking into account the synchronous parallel interpretation.[20] Extending the notion of mono-agent sequential runs to asynchronous (also called partially ordered) multi-agent runs turns FSMs into globally asynchronous, locally synchronous Codesign-FSMs [18] and similarly basic ASMs into *asynchronous ASMs* (see [12, Ch.6.1] for a detailed definition).

The synchronous parallelism (over a finite number of rules each with a finite number of to-be-updated locations of basic ASMs) is often further extended by a synchronization over arbitrary many objects in a given *Set*, which satisfy a certain (possibly runtime) *Property*:

forall $x \in Set$ **with** *Property*(*x*) **do**
   rule(*x*)

standing for the execution of *rule* for every object *x*, which is element of *Set* and satisfies *Property*. Sometimes we omit the key word **do**. The parts $\in Set$ and **with** *Property*(*x*) are optional.

ASM Modules. Standard module concepts can be adopted to syntactically structure large ASMs, where the module interface for the communication with other modules names the ASMs which are imported from other modules or exported to other modules. We limit ourselves here to consider an ASM module as a pair consisting of *Header* and *Body*. A module header consists of the name of the module, its (possibly empty) import and export clauses, and its signature. As explained above, the signature of a module determines its notion of state and thus contains all the basic functions occurring in the module and all the functions which appear in the parameters of any of the imported modules. The body of

---

[20] More precisely: to execute one step of an ASM in a given state S determine all the fireable rules in S (s.t. *cond* is true in S), compute all expressions t_i, t in S occuring in the updates $f(t_1, \ldots, t_n) := t$ of those rules and then perform simultaneously all these location updates if they are consistent. In the case of inconsistency, the run is considered as interrupted if no other stipulation is made, like calling an exception handling procedure or choosing a compatible update set.

an ASM module consists of declarations (definitions) of functions and rules. An ASM is then a module together with an optional characterization of the class of initial states and with a compulsory additional (the main) rule. Executing an ASM means executing its main rule. When the context is clear enough to avoid any confusion, we sometimes speak of an ASM when what is really meant is an ASM module, a collection of named rules, without a main rule.

ASM Classification of Locations and Functions. The ASM method imposes no a priori restriction neither on the abstraction level nor on the complexity nor on the means of definition of the functions used to compute the arguments and the new value denoted by t_i, t in function updates. In support of the principles of separation of concerns, information hiding, data abstraction, modularization and stepwise refinement, the ASM method exploits, however, the following distinctions reflecting the different roles these functions (and more generally locations) can assume in a given machine, as illustrated by Figure 8 and extending the different roles of *in*, *out*, *ctl_state* in FSMs.

A function f is classified as being of a given type if in every state, every location $(f, (a_1, \ldots, a_n))$ consisting of the function name f and an argument $(a_1, \ldots, a_n)$ is of this type, for every argument $(a_1, \ldots, a_n)$ the function f can take in this state.

Semantically speaking, the major distinction is between static and dynamic locations. Static locations are locations whose values do not depend on the dynamics of states and can be determined by any form of satisfactory state-independent (e.g. equational or axiomatic) definitions. The further classification of dynamic locations with respect to a given machine M supports to distinguish between the roles different 'agents' (e.g. the system and its environment) play in using (providing or updating the values of) dynamic locations. It is defined as follows:

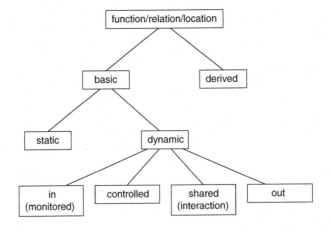

Fig. 8. Classification of ASM functions, relations, locations

- *controlled* locations are readable and writable by M,
- *monitored* locations are for M only readable, but they may be writable by some other machine,
- *output* locations are by M only writable, but they may be readable by some other machine,
- *shared* locations are readable/writable by M as well as by some other machine, so that a protocol will be needed to guarantee the consistency of writing.

Monitored and shared locations represent an abstract mechanism to specify communication types between different agents, each executing a basic ASM. *Derived* locations are those whose definition in terms of locations declared as basic is fixed and may be given separately, e.g. in some other part ("module" or "class") of the system to be built. The distinction of derived from basic locations implies that a derived location can in particular not be updated by any rule of the considered machine. It represents the input-output behavior performed by an independent computation. For details see the AsmBook [12, Ch.2.2.3] from where Figure 8 is taken.

A particularly important class of monitored locations are selection locations, which are frequently used to abstractly describe scheduling mechanisms. The following notation makes the inherent non-determinism explicit in case one does not want to commit to a particular selection scheme.

choose $x \in Set$ **with** $Property(x)$ **do**
$rule(x)$

This stands for the ASM executing $rule(x)$ for some element x, which is arbitrarily chosen among those which are element of Set and satisfy the selection criterion $Property$. Sometimes we omit the key word **do**. The parts $\in Set$ and **with** $Property(x)$ are optional.

We freely use common notations like **let** $x = t$ **in** R, **if** $cond$ **then** R **else** S, etc. When refining machines by adding new rules, we use the following notation introduced in [6]: M **addRule** R denotes the parallel composition of M and R. Similarly M **minusRule** R denotes N for $M = N, R$. To avoid confusion among different machines, which occur as submachine of machines N, N' but within those machines carry the same name M, we use indexing and write M_N respectively $M_{N'}$.

Non-determinism, Selection and Scheduling Functions. It is adequate to use the **choose** construct of ASMs if one wants to leave it completely unspecified who is performing the choice and based upon which selection criterion. The only thing the semantics of this operator guarantees is that each time one element of the set of objects to choose from will be chosen. Different instances of a selection, even for the same set in the same state, may provide the same element or maybe not. If one wants to further analyze variations of the type of choices and of who is performing them, one better declares a $Selection$ function, to select an element from the underlying set of $Candidates$, and writes instead of **choose** $c \in Cand$ **do** $R(c)$ as follows, where R is any ASM rule:

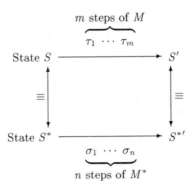

$\equiv$ is an equivalence notion between data
in locations of interest in corresponding states.

Fig. 9. The ASM refinement scheme

let $c = Select(Cand)$ **in** $R(c)$

The functionality of *Select* guarantees that exactly one element is chosen. The
let construct guarantees that the choice is fixed in the binding range of the **let**.
Declaring such a function as dynamic guarantees that the selection function applied to the same set in different states may return different elements. Declaring
such a function as controlled or monitored provides different ownership schemes.
Naming these selection functions allows the designer in particular to analyze and
play with variations of the selection mechanisms due to different interpretations
of the functions.

5.2   ASM Refinement Concept

The ASM refinement concept is a generalization of the familiar commutative
diagram for refinement steps, as illustrated in Figure 9.

For an ASM refinement of an ASM M to an ASM M^*, as designer one has
the freedom to tailor the following "handles" to the needs for detailing the design
decision which leeds from M to M':

- a notion of *refined state*,
- a notion of *states of interest* and of *correspondence* between M-states S and
  M^*-states S^* of interest, i.e. the pairs of states in the runs one wants to relate
  through the refinement, including usually the correspondence of initial and
  (if there are any) of final states,
- a notion of abstract *computation segments* $\tau_1, \ldots, \tau_m$, where each τ_i represents a single M-step, and of corresponding refined computation segments
  $\sigma_1, \ldots, \sigma_n$, of single M^*-steps σ_j, which in given runs lead from corresponding states of interest to (usually the next) corresponding states of inter-
  est (the resulting diagrams are called (m, n)-diagrams and the refinements
  (m, n)-refinements),

- a notion of *locations of interest* and of *corresponding locations*, i.e. pairs of (possibly sets of) locations one wants to relate in corresponding states, where locations represent abstract containers for data,
- a notion of *equivalence* $\equiv$ of the data in the locations of interest; these local data equivalences usually accumulate to a notion of equivalence of corresponding states of interest.

The scheme shows that an ASM refinement allows one to combine in a natural way a change of the signature (through the definition of states and of their correspondence, of corresponding locations and of the equivalence of data) with a change of the control (defining the "flow of operations" appearing in the corresponding computation segments).

Once the notions of corresponding states and of their equivalence have been determined, one can define that M^* is a correct refinement of M if and only if every (infinite) refined run simulates an (infinite) abstract run with equivalent corresponding states, as is made precise by the following definition. By this definition, refinement correctness implies for the special case of terminating runs the inclusion of the input/output behavior of the abstract and the refined machine.

Definition Fix any notions $\equiv$ of equivalence of states and of initial and final states. An ASM M^* is called a *correct refinement* of an ASM M if and only if for each M^*-run $S_0^*, S_1^*, \ldots$ there is an M-run $S_0, S_1, \ldots$ and sequences $i_0 < i_1 < \ldots, j_0 < j_1 < \ldots$ such that $i_0 = j_0 = 0$ and $S_{i_k} \equiv S_{j_k}^*$ for each k and either

- both runs terminate and their final states are the last pair of equivalent states, or
- both runs and both sequences $i_0 < i_1 < \ldots, j_0 < j_1 < \ldots$ are infinite.

Often the M^*-run $S_0^*, S_1^*, \ldots$ is said to simulate the M-run $S_0, S_1, \ldots$. The states $S_{i_k}, S_{j_k}^*$ are the corresponding states of interest. They represent the end points of the corresponding computation segments (those of interest) in Figure 9, for which the equivalence is defined in terms of a relation between their corresponding locations (those of interest). Sometimes it is convenient to assume that terminating runs are extended to infinite sequences which become constant at the final state.

M^* is called a *complete refinement* of M if and only if M is a correct refinement of M^*.

This definition of ASM refinement underlies numerous successful applications of ASMs to high-level system desing and analysis (see the survey in the history chapter in [12]) and generalizes and integrates well-known more specific notions of refinement (see [20,21] for a detailed analysis).

Acknowledgement. The bulk of the work on this paper was done when the second author was on sabbatical leave at SAP Research, Karlsruhe, Germany. We thank M. Altenhofen and W. Reisig for critical comments on earlier versions of this paper.

References

1. M. Altenhofen, E. Börger, and J. Lemcke. An abstract model for process mediation. In R. Banach, editor, *Proc. 7th International Conference on Formal Engineering Methods (ICFEM 2005)*, LNCS. Springer, 2005.
2. A. Barros, M. Dumas, and A. ter Hofstede. Service interaction patterns: Towards a reference framework for service-based business process interconnection. Technical Report FIT-TR-2005-02 (To be presented at BPM'2005, Third International Conference on Business Process Management 2005, September 2005, Nancy, France), Faculty of Information Technology, Queensland University of Technology, Brisbane (Australia), March 2005.
3. E. Börger. High-level system design and analysis using Abstract State Machines. In D. Hutter, W. Stephan, P. Traverso, and M. Ullmann, editors, *Current Trends in Applied Formal Methods (FM-Trends 98)*, volume 1641 of *Lecture Notes in Computer Science*, pages 1–43. Springer-Verlag, 1999.
4. E. Börger. The ASM ground model method as a foundation of requirements engineering. In N.Dershowitz, editor, *Verification: Theory and Practice*, volume 2772 of *LNCS*, pages 145–160. Springer-Verlag, 2003.
5. E. Börger. The ASM refinement method. *Formal Aspects of Computing*, 15:237–257, 2003.
6. E. Börger. Linking architectural and component level system views by abstract state machines. In C. Grimm, editor, *Languages for System Specification and Verification*, CHDL, pages 247–269. Kluwer, 2004.
7. E. Börger. The ASM method for system design and analysis. A tutorial introduction. In B. Gramlich, editor, *FroCoS 2005*, volume 3717 of *Lecture Notes in Artificial Intelligence*, pages 264–283. Springer, 2005.
8. E. Börger. Design pattern abstractions and Abstract State Machines. In D. Beauquier, E. Börger, and A. Slissenko, editors, *Proc.ASM05*, pages 91–100. Université de Paris 12, 2005.
9. E. Börger. From finite state machines to virtual machines (Illustrating design patterns and event-B models). In E. Cohors-Fresenborg and I. Schwank, editors, *Präzisionswerkzeug Logik–Gedenkschrift zu Ehren von Dieter Rödding*. Forschungsinstitut für Mathematikdidaktik Osnabrück, 2005. ISBN 3-925386-56-4.
10. E. Börger. Linking content definition and analysis to what the compiler can verify. In *Proc.IFIP WG Conference on Verified Software: Tools, Techniques, and Experiments*, Lecture Notes in Computer Science, Zurich (Switzerland), October 2005. Springer.
11. E. Börger and J. Schmid. Composition and submachine concepts for sequential ASMs. In P. Clote and H. Schwichtenberg, editors, *Computer Science Logic (Proceedings of CSL 2000)*, volume 1862 of *Lecture Notes in Computer Science*, pages 41–60. Springer-Verlag, 2000.
12. E. Börger and R. F. Stärk. *Abstract State Machines. A Method for High-Level System Design and Analysis*. Springer, 2003.
13. R. Farahbod. Extending and refining an abstract operational semantics of the web services architecture for the business process execution language. Master's thesis, Simon Fraser University, Burnaby, Canada, July 2004.
14. R. Farahbod, U. Glässer, and M. Vajihollahi. Abstract operational semantics of the Business Process Execution Language for web services. Technical Report SFU-CMPT-TR 2004-03, Simon Fraser University School of Computing Science, April 2004.

15. R. Farahbod, U. Glässer, and M. Vajihollahi. Specification and validation of the Business Process Execution Language for web services. In W. Zimmermann and B. Thalheim, editors, *Abstract Sate Machines 2004*, volume 3052 of *Lecture Notes in Computer Science*, pages 78–94. Springer-Verlag, 2004.
16. U. Glässer, Y. Gurevich, and M. Veanes. Abstract communication model for distributed systems. *IEEE Transactions on Software Engineering*, 30(7):1–15, July 2004.
17. C. A. R. Hoare. The verifying compiler: A grand challenge for computing research. *J. ACM*, 50(1):63–69, 2003.
18. L. Lavagno, A. Sangiovanni-Vincentelli, and E. M. Sentovitch. Models of computation for system design. In E. Börger, editor, *Architecture Design and Validation Methods*, pages 243–295. Springer-Verlag, 2000.
19. W. Reisig. *Elements of Distributed Algorithms*. Springer-Verlag, 1998.
20. G. Schellhorn. Verification of ASM refinements using generalized forward simulation. *J. Universal Computer Science*, 7(11):952–979, 2001.
21. G. Schellhorn. ASM refinement and generalizations of forward simulation in data refinement: A comparison. *Theoretical Computer Science*, 336(2-3):403–436, 2005.
22. R. F. Stärk. Formal specification and verification of the C# thread model. *Theoretical Computer Science*, 2005. To appear.
23. R. F. Stärk and E. Börger. An ASM specification of C# threads and the .NET memory model. In W. Zimmermann and B. Thalheim, editors, *Abstract State Machines 2004*, volume 3052 of *Lecture Notes in Computer Science*, pages 38–60. Springer-Verlag, 2004.
24. M. Vajihollahi. High level specification and validation of the Business Process Execution Language for web services. Master's thesis, School of Computing Science at Simon Fraser University, April 2004.
25. W. M. van der Aalst, A. ter Hofstede, B. Kiepuszewski, and A. Barros. Workflow patterns. *Distributed and Parallel Databases*, 14(3):5–51, July 2003.
26. C. Wallace, G. Tremblay, and J. N. Amaral. An Abstract State Machine specification and verification of the location consistency memory model and cache protocol. *J. Universal Computer Science*, 7(11):1089–1113, 2001.

An Evidential Tool Bus

John Rushby

Computer Science Laboratory, SRI International,
333 Ravenswood Ave, Menlo Park California 94025, USA
Rushby@csl.sri.com

Abstract. Theorem provers, model checkers, static analyzers, test generators...all of these and many other kinds of formal methods tools can contribute to the analysis and development of computer systems and software. It is already quite common to use several kinds of tools in a loose combination: for example, we might use static analysis and then model checking to help find and eliminate design flaws prior to undertaking formal verification with a theorem prover. And some modern tools, such as test generators, are built using model checkers, predicate abstractors, decision procedures and constraint solvers as components in tight combination.

But we can foresee a different kind of combination where many tools and methods are used in ad hoc combination within a single analysis. For example, static analysis might yield invariants that enable decision procedures to build a predicate abstraction whose reachable states are calculated as a BDD and then concretized to yield a strong invariant for the original system; the invariant then enables properties of the original system to be verified by highly automated theorem proving.

This sort of combination clearly requires an integrating platform – a tool bus – to connect the various tools together; but the capabilities required go beyond those of platforms such as Eclipse. The entities exchanged among clients of the bus – proofs, counterexamples, specifications, theoreems, counterexamples, abstractions – have logical content, and the overall purpose of the bus is to gather and integrate *evidence* for verification or refutation.

In this paper I propose requirements for such an "evidential tool bus," and sketch a possible architecture.

K.-K. Lau and R. Banach (Eds.): ICFEM 2005, LNCS 3785, p. 36, 2005.

Derivation of UML Class Diagrams as Static Views of Formal B Developments*

Akram Idani, Yves Ledru, and Didier Bert

Laboratoire Logiciels, Systèmes, Réseaux - IMAG,
B.P. 72 - F-38402 - Saint Martin d'Hères Cedex - France
{Akram.Idani, Yves.Ledru, Didier.Bert}@imag.fr

Abstract. Although formal methods provide excellent techniques for the precise description of systems, understanding these descriptions is often restricted to experts. This paper investigates a practical solution to assist the understanding of a formal specification, written in B, by providing a complementary view of the specification as UML class diagram. Our technique improves the state of the art by taking into account operations in the construction of the diagram, through the use of concept formation techniques. A documentation tool automates the approach. It has been applied to several specifications built independently of the tool.

Keywords: Method integration, B, UML, Formal concept analysis.

1 Introduction

Formal methods are nowadays the most rigorous way to produce software. Several safety critical industries, like the railway industry, have perceived the benefits of such approaches and significant developments like the Paris Meteor subway have been partially performed using formal methods [2]. Companies like Siemens Transport [2], Clearsy [15], or Gemplus [6] have used B [1] as the central method for either code or model developments. Still, while formal methods provide solutions to the verification problem ("do the system right"), the validation problem ("do the right system") remains a major challenge for formal methods engineers.

In the last decade, graphical specification techniques such as UML [5] have become a widespread communication support for software projects. A study [16], which compared the use of the B method and the use of UML on the same project, concluded that B led to better precision than UML while UML produced more intuitive and readable documents. The authors advocated a combination of both methods.

In the area of model-based specification techniques, efforts have been devoted to translating annotated UML diagrams into B [11,13,12] and Z or Object-Z [7,10] specifications. Such approaches are useful to give a semantics to the graphical diagrams, but the generated formal text obeys strict translation rules which do not always fit the needs of formal methods engineers.

---

* This work is partially supported by the EDEMOI project of the French national ACI Sécurité informatique.

K.-K. Lau and R. Banach (Eds.): ICFEM 2005, LNCS 3785, pp. 37–51, 2005.
© Springer-Verlag Berlin Heidelberg 2005

This paper investigates the reverse approach, trying to give some ways to extract UML class diagrams from B specifications. The goal is to provide a (partial) documentation of existing B specifications. Fig. 1 shows how our documentation activities are integrated with the overall B development process. The bottom of the figure shows a classical B development. The B developer builds the initial B specification from the customer needs, and then constructs and proves a series of refinements until he reaches an implementation. On top of the figure, the documentation process presented in this paper builds UML views from the various formal documents (abstract specification and refinements) produced during the development. They are intended to be read by the customer, or by some certification authority, to validate that the B development fits with the customer needs. This validation process favours the involvement of users who are not trained in formal methods, but still get a semi-formal and partial view on the contents of the actual formal development.

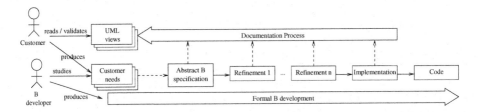

Fig. 1. The proposed documentation process

Early work in the production of UML documentation from B specifications includes [17,8] which define sets of rules in order to construct static views, such as class diagrams, from the analysis of the data structures of the B specification. Other efforts extract the behaviour of a specification to represent it as a state transition diagram [4] or as a set of scenarios [14]. Our approach adds two significant improvements to the early works in this domain.

- Existing approaches [17,8] construct a class diagram from the analysis of the data modeled in the specification. Operations modeled in the specification are not taken into account in this construction. In [9], we proposed to improve the existing approaches by applying concept formation techniques. These techniques take into account the links between data and operations to identify relevant classes. This paper builds on the principles of [9] but introduces a new notion, named pertinent context, and an algorithm that improves the potential for automation.
- A tool has been built on the basis of these notions and algorithm. The tool automates the production of UML diagrams as much as possible and reduces the interaction with its user to the sole identification of a target for each operation. This paper also evaluates the approach by reporting on the application of the tool to several B specifications.

2   A Simple Example

Several formal specifications of this paper are taken from the EDEMOI project[1] which aims at modeling airport security. They give a formal model of security procedures applied to passengers and their luggage in an airport. Example 1 shows a specification which abstracts from passengers and luggage and only considers the objects carried by passengers or included in their luggage. It models how objects are loaded either in the cabin or in the hold luggage compartment of an airplane. Objects which are loaded in the cabin transit through a boarding room and may only leave it when the gate is open.

Graphical Documentation. Before we present the formal specification in detail, let us have a look at the class diagram generated by our tool (Fig. 2)[2]. The B specification corresponds to two classes: *Objects* and *BoardingRoom*.

Some objects may be used to attack an airplane. Two boolean attributes (*unauthorized_in_cabin* and *unauthorized_in_hold*) are used to qualify such objects. *unauthorized_in_cabin* marks the objects that passengers may not bring in the aircraft cabin (e.g. bombs or weapons), *unauthorized_in_hold* marks those objects that may not be carried in the hold luggage (e.g. bombs). Since hold luggage is not accessible to passengers during the flight some objects that are dangerous in the cabin are authorized in the hold luggage (e.g. a razor).

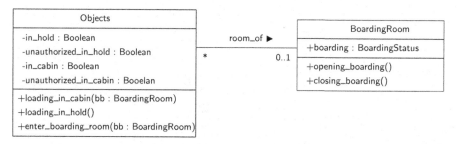

Fig. 2. Class diagram generated by our approach (case 1 of Fig. 5)

Two additional attributes (*in_cabin* and *in_hold*) record if the object has been effectively loaded in either the cabin or in the hold compartment of some aircraft[3]. Operations *loading_in_hold* and *loading_in_cabin* are used to modify the values of these attributes.

Objects which are intended to be loaded in the cabin must go through a boarding room before being brought on-board. They must wait in the boarding room until it becomes open. Operation *enter_boarding_room* modifies the association *room_of* to link an object to a boarding room. Class *Boarding_Room*

---

[1] http://www-lsr.imag.fr/EDEMOI/

[2] The rest of the paper details how we build this diagram from the B specification.

[3] In this model, the cabins of all aircrafts are abstracted as a single cabin, and similarly for the hold luggage compartments.

includes a single attribute *boarding*, which denotes the current status of the room (open or closed), and two operations to change the value of this attribute.

Formal Specification. The B specification was written before the production of the UML diagram. Three constant sets are introduced: the set of all objects (*Objects*), the set of all boarding rooms (*BoardingRoom*), and an enumerated set which gives the possible status of a boarding gate (*open* or *closed*).

The objects which are not authorized in the cabin or in the hold compartment are modelled as two constant subsets of *Objects*. Similarly, the objects actually loaded in some cabin or hold compartment are modelled as variable subsets of *Objects*. Invariant properties mandate that these sets do not include unauthorized objects. Variable *boarding* is a function which gives the status of the gate associated to a boarding room, and *room_of* associates a boarding room to objects. An invariant property constrains the domain of this function to objects which are authorized in a cabin.

The rest of the specification includes the initialisation (all variable sets are empty and all gates are closed), and the associated operations. The *PRE* field of these operations specifies a pre-condition, i.e. an assertion which must be true at the initial state of the operation (e.g. the precondition of *enter_boarding_room* checks that the object is authorized in cabin). The non-deterministic statement *ANY v WHERE Q THEN A END* means that action *A* is performed for an arbitrary value *v* that satisfies predicate *Q*. For example, *loading_in_hold* loads in some hold compartment, an arbitrary authorized object.

Example 1.

```
MACHINE SecureFlight
SETS
    Objects;
    BoardingRoom;
    BoardingStatus = {open,closed}
CONCRETE_CONSTANTS
    unauthorized_in_cabin,
    unauthorized_in_hold
PROPERTIES
    unauthorized_in_cabin ⊆ Objects ∧
    unauthorized_in_hold ⊆ Objects
VARIABLES
    in_cabin, in_hold, boarding, room_of
INVARIANT
    in_cabin ⊆ Objects ∧ in_hold ⊆ Objects ∧
    in_hold ∩ unauthorized_in_hold = ∅ ∧
    in_cabin ∩ unauthorized_in_cabin = ∅ ∧
    boarding ∈
        BoardingRoom → BoardingStatus ∧
    room_of ∈ Objects ⇸ BoardingRoom ∧
    dom(room_of) ∩
        unauthorized_in_cabin = ∅
INITIALISATION
    in_cabin, in_hold, room_of := ∅ , ∅ , ∅ ||
    boarding := BoardingRoom × {closed}
OPERATIONS
    enter_boarding_room(oo,bb) =
    PRE
        oo ∈ Objects ∧ bb ∈ BoardingRoom ∧
        oo ∉ unauthorized_in_cabin ∧
```

```
        oo ∉ dom(room_of)
    THEN room_of := room_of ∪ {oo ↦ bb}
    END;
opening_boarding (bb)=
PRE bb ∈ BoardingRoom ∧
        boarding(bb) = closed
    THEN boarding(bb) := open
    END ;
closing_boarding (bb)=
PRE bb ∈ BoardingRoom ∧
        boarding(bb) = open
    THEN boarding(bb) := closed
    END ;
loading_in_cabin =
ANY bb WHERE
bb ∈ BoardingRoom ∧ boarding(bb) = open
THEN
        ANY oo WHERE
        oo ∈ Objects ∧ bb = room_of(bb)
        THEN
            in_cabin := in_cabin ∪ {oo}
        END
    END ;
loading_in_hold =
ANY oo WHERE
        oo ⊆ Objects ∧
        oo ∩ unauthorized_in_hold= ∅
    THEN in_hold := in_hold ∪ oo
    END
END
```

Short Comparison of the UML and B Specifications. As we can see, the UML specification does not include all the information conveyed in the B specification: invariant properties and the detailed description of operations are missing. Still the graphical description provides the overall structure of the specification by listing the main classes and relations, and linking operations to these classes.

By presenting the UML diagram first, we focus on a global synthetic view of the specification, then we can go into details by browsing the B specification.

3   A Concept Formation Technique

3.1   Identifying Class Candidates

The data of B specifications, declared in sections SETS, CONSTANTS and VARI-ABLES, and which are sets or relations, are called "data concepts". In the example, data concepts correspond to every abstract set (*Objects, BoardingRoom, BoardingStatus*), or subset (*in_cabin, in_hold, unauthorized_in_cabin, unauthorized_in_hold*) and relation (*boarding, room_of*). A data concept d represents the B object denoted by $\mathcal{B}(d)$. Each data concept ($\mathcal{D}ata$) is associated to a "type" by function $Type$:

$$Type \in \mathcal{D}ata \rightarrow \{Set, \ SubSet, \ Relation\}$$

In our approach, the goal of the first step is to identify the data concepts which are candidate to become classes in the UML diagrams derived from the B specifications. The analysis is based on the links between data concepts and operations of the specification. So, we define a **data concept dependence relation** $\mathcal{I}$ between data concepts $\mathcal{D}ata$ and operations $\mathcal{O}$:

Definition 1. *A data concept dependence relation is $\mathcal{I} \in \mathcal{D}ata \leftrightarrow \mathcal{O}$, where $(d, o) \in \mathcal{I}$ means that data concept d is used by operation o. We denote by $\mathcal{D}$ the set of data concepts which are actually used by at least one operation, i.e. $\mathcal{D} = dom(\mathcal{I})$.*

One could consider three kinds of "use" modes: read access, write access (modification of the data) and require access (access in operation precondition). In this paper, we choose to only take into account the occurrences of data concepts in the body of the operations (uniformly read and write accesses).

In our example, $\mathcal{D}$ includes all the concepts listed above, except *BoardingStatus*. Fig. 3 displays $\mathcal{I}$ for the example.

Given a set of data concepts $\mathcal{S}$, $Op(\mathcal{S})$ denotes the set of operations common to all data concepts in $\mathcal{S}$:

$$Op(\mathcal{S}) \,\widehat{=}\, \{o \mid o \in \mathcal{O} \wedge \forall d \cdot (d \in \mathcal{S} \Rightarrow (d, o) \in \mathcal{I})\}$$

For example, $Op(\{room\_of, Objects\}) = \{loading\_in\_cabin, enter\_boarding\_room\}$. The UML diagrams express encapsulation of operations in classes. Amongst the data concepts, some are associated to more operations than others, for example,

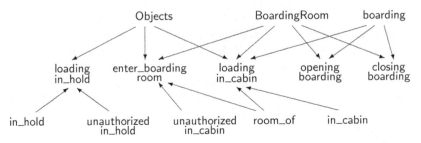

Fig. 3. A bipartite graph showing the relation $\mathcal{I}$ for the SecureFlight System

$Op(\{room\_of\}) \subset Op(\{Objects\})$. Therefore, $Objects$ can be considered as a better class candidate than $room\_of$.

In the following, in order to identify the best class candidates, we introduce the notion of **maximal data concept** and the notion of **class concept**. A data concept d is maximal, if for any other data concept s in the specification, the set of operations using d is not strictly included in the set of operations using s.

Definition 2. *For a data concept dependence relation $\mathcal{I}$ and $d \in \mathcal{D}$:*

$$maximal(d) \Leftrightarrow \forall s \cdot (s \in \mathcal{D} - \{d\} \Rightarrow Op(\{d\}) \not\subset Op(\{s\}))$$

We call $max(\mathcal{I})$ the set of all maximal concepts of $\mathcal{I}$.

In our example, $max(\mathcal{I}) = \{Objects, BoardingRoom\}$. Both maximal concepts are of type Set, but it may happen that subsets or relations correspond to maximal concepts.

We consider the relation $Incl$ between data concepts, which refers to the inclusion property on the B objects they represent.

Definition 3. *Relation $Incl \in Data \leftrightarrow Data$ is such that for all d where $Type(d) = Set$ or $Subset$:*

$$
\begin{aligned}
(d',d) \in Incl &\Leftarrow Type(d') = Relation \wedge dom(\mathcal{B}(d')) \subseteq \mathcal{B}(d)\\
(d',d) \in Incl &\Leftarrow Type(d') = Relation \wedge ran(\mathcal{B}(d')) \subseteq \mathcal{B}(d)\\
(d',d) \in Incl &\Leftarrow Type(d') = Subset \wedge \mathcal{B}(d') \subseteq \mathcal{B}(d)
\end{aligned}
$$

We say that a data concept is a class concept if it is a maximal set or subset concept, or if it relates by relation $Incl^+$ to a maximal data concept.

Definition 4. *For a data concept dependence relation $\mathcal{I}$, for data concepts d of type Set or $SubSet$, then $d \in Classes(\mathcal{I})$ iff one of the following items inductively holds: 1. $maximal(d)$*
*   2. $\neg maximal(d) \wedge \exists d' \cdot (d' \in Data \wedge (d',d) \in Incl \wedge d' \in Classes(\mathcal{I}))$*

Notice that data concepts c that are in $Classes(\mathcal{I})$ are not necessarily in $\mathcal{D}$. For these data concepts, obviously, $Op(c)$ is empty. In example 1, we obtain $max(\mathcal{I}) = Classes(\mathcal{I}) = \{Objects, BoardingRoom\}$. This means that the two data concepts $Objects$ and $BoardingRoom$ may be converted into UML classes.

The set of **private operations** of a class concept c is the set of operations using c and not shared by any other class concept c':

$$\mathcal{O}_{Private}(c) \hat{=} \{o \mid \forall c' \cdot (c' \in Classes(\mathcal{I}) \wedge c' \neq c \Rightarrow o \in Op(\{c\}) - Op(\{c'\}))\}$$

3.2   Grouping Data Concepts and Operations into Contexts

The second step of our approach builds the class candidates by grouping the remaining data concepts and the operations around the class concepts.

The following definition is inspired by [3]. It introduces the notion of **context** which gathers a set of data concepts, where at least one is a class concept, together with a set of operations, each of them using at least one data concept of the context.

Definition 5. *A **context** of the data concept dependence relation $\mathcal{I}$ is a pair $\mathcal{F} = (\mathcal{D}', \mathcal{O}')$ with:* $\mathcal{D}' \subseteq Data$ *and* $\mathcal{D}' \cap Classes(\mathcal{I}) \neq \emptyset$
$$\mathcal{O}' \subseteq \mathcal{O} \quad and \quad \mathcal{O}' \subseteq \mathcal{I}[\mathcal{D}']^4$$

We introduce the notion of **pertinent context** which is commented below:

Definition 6. *A **pertinent context** of $\mathcal{I}$ is a context $\mathcal{F} = (\mathcal{D}', \mathcal{O}')$*
with: $\forall c \cdot (c \in \mathcal{D}' \wedge c \in Classes(\mathcal{I}) \Rightarrow \mathcal{O}_{Private}(c) \subseteq \mathcal{O}')$
$\forall d \cdot (d \in \mathcal{D}' \wedge d \notin Classes(\mathcal{I}) \Rightarrow \mathcal{I}[\{d\}] \cap \mathcal{O}' \neq \emptyset)$

The first rule mandates that private operations are encapsulated with their corresponding class, because there is no other place to store them. For example, $\mathcal{O}_{Private}(Objects) = \{loading\_in\_hold\}$, which means that a context which includes the class concept $Objects$ is pertinent if it includes $loading\_in\_hold$.

Non-class concepts of a context will end up as attributes of the class. The second rule is motivated by the fact that each attribute of the class should be manipulated by at least one operation of the class.

The set of pertinent contexts partition the set of class concepts and the set of operations, so that each class and each operation appears only once in the class diagram. The following section will give an algorithm to build such a set of pertinent contexts.

4   An Algorithm to Identify a Set of Pertinent Contexts

4.1   Description of the Algorithm

Our algorithm is built on relation $\mathcal{J} \in (\mathcal{O} \cup Data) \leftrightarrow Data$, which is defined as $\mathcal{I}^{-1} \cup Incl$. Its graph is refered to as a *concept network*. A concept network relates the considered operations to their data concepts (relation $\mathcal{I}^{-1}$), and the data concepts themselves (sets, sub-sets and relations) by relation $Incl$. The concept network issued from the specification of example 1 is represented in Fig. 4. For the sake of readability, the machine name is put over the operations.

---

[4] $R[S]$ is the image of set S by relation R.

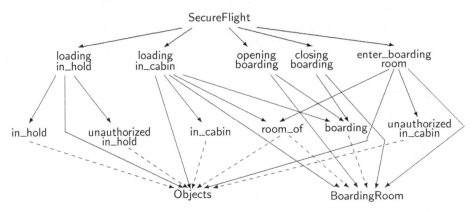

Fig. 4. The concept network derived from the SecureFlight System

The algorithm consists of three steps:

(i) For each operation o, choose a class concept c ($c \in Classes(\mathcal{I})$) such that there exists a path from o to c in the concept network. c is said to be the target of o. So, function $Target$, given by the user, is a total function from the operations to the class concepts:

$$Target \in \mathcal{O} \to Classes(\mathcal{I})$$

(ii) For each class concept c such that $c \in ran(Target)$, form a context $\mathcal{F} = (\mathcal{D}', \mathcal{O}')$ defined by: $\mathcal{O}' = Target^{-1}(c)$
$$\mathcal{D}' = \{c\} \cup (\mathcal{J}^+[\mathcal{O}'] \cap ((\mathcal{J}^{-1})^+[\{c\}]))$$
The set $\mathcal{D}'$ contains the data concepts which are used by operations $\mathcal{O}'$ (through $\mathcal{I}^{-1}[\mathcal{O}']$) and which include theses data (transitively by $Incl$), but also which are transitively included in the class concept c.

(iii) Check that all the data concepts in $\mathcal{D}$ are member of a context. If some data concept $d' \in \mathcal{D}$ does not belong to a context, then place d' in a context which contains at least one operation which uses d'.

The algorithm contains two levels of non-determinism: the choice of the $Target$ function (step (i)) and the choice of the context, for data concepts which are not in $(\mathcal{J}^+[\mathcal{O}'] \cap ((\mathcal{J}^{-1})^+[\{c\}]))$ for any element c of the target (step (iii)). Given a target function, the algorithm can list all the possible assignments for the second non-determinism, so providing a way for the user to determine the good choice between them, or to change its target function if no choice is adequate.

4.2   Validation of the Algorithm

We can prove that the contexts built by this algorithm are pertinent.

1. The contexts built by the algorithm satisfy the properties of contexts: each context includes a class concept, and the operations of the context are members of $Op(\mathcal{D}')$. This second property results from the formation of the

data elements of the context: for each o in a context c, $\{c\} \cup (\mathcal{J}^+[\{o\}] \cap ((\mathcal{J}^{-1})^+[\{c\}]))$ is not empty, because $Target$ is a total function[5].

2. All private operations of a class concept c have necessarily this class concept as their only possible target and are included in the context built from c if c is the target, or from a superset of c.

3. If a data concept appears in a context, then there is an operation which uses it, either at step (ii) or step (iii).

It can be noticed that all operations and all data concepts of relation $\mathcal{I}$ belong to the contexts built by the algorithm. However, not all the class concepts are necessarily put in these contexts. The final choice of the user can determine a grouping which fits well to the visualization of the notions involved in the specification.

4.3   Application of the Algorithm to the Example

The concept network of Fig. 4 has the following properties:

- It features two class concepts: $Classes(\mathcal{I}) = \{Objects, BoardingRoom\}$
- For each operation, we can list the possible targets:
  - $Target(loading\_in\_hold) \in \{Objects\}$
  - $Target(loading\_in\_cabin) \in \{Objects, BoardingRoom\}$
  - $Target(enter\_boarding\_room) \in \{Objects, BoardingRoom\}$
  - $Target(opening\_boarding) \in \{BoardingRoom\}$
  - $Target(closing\_boarding) \in \{BoardingRoom\}$

In the first step of the algorithm, we choose a target for each operation. Three private operations ($loading\_in\_hold$, $opening\_boarding$, $closing\_boarding$) have only one possible target. We have two choices for the targets of operations $loading\_in\_cabin$ and $enter\_boarding\_room$. Let us choose $Objects$ as the target of both operations[6].

In the second step, we build two contexts, one for each class concept.

- The context associated to $BoardingRoom$ has operations $opening\_boarding$, $closing\_boarding$. It also includes the $boarding$ concept which is in $\mathcal{J}^+[opening\_boarding, closing\_boarding] \cap ((\mathcal{J}^{-1})^+[\{BoardingRoom\}])$.
- The other context is associated to $Objects$. It includes the private operation $loading\_in\_hold$, and operations $loading\_in\_cabin$ and $enter\_boarding\_room$. It also includes data concepts: in_hold, $unauthorized\_in\_hold$, in_cabin, $room\_of$, and $unauthorized\_in\_cabin$ in the same way.

The third step verifies that all data concepts are taken into account which is the case here. Let an other choice of the target function be with $loading\_in\_cabin$ and $enter\_boarding\_room$ with $BoardingRoom$.

---

[5] Totality of the function is actually enforced by the tool.

[6] This choice may result from modeling concerns such as the fact that the user feels that $Objects$ play a central role in this specification, and that most operations should be associated to this class.

$$Target(loading\_in\_cabin) = Objects$$
$$Target(enter\_boarding\_room) = Objects$$

class concept	Objects	
	Concept	Type
concepts	in_hold	SubSet
	unauthorized_in_hold	SubSet
	in_cabin	SubSet
	room_of	Relation
	unauthorized_in_cabin	SubSet
operations	loading_in_hold	
	loading_in_cabin	
	enter_boarding_room	

class concept	BoardingRoom	
	Concept	Type
concepts	boarding	Relation
Operations	opening_boarding	
	closing_boarding	

$$Target(loading\_in\_cabin) = BoardingRoom$$
$$Target(enter\_boarding\_room) = BoardingRoom$$

class concept	Objects	
	Concept	Type
concepts	in_hold	SubSet
	unauthorized_in_hold	SubSet
operations	loading_in_hold	

class concept	BoardingRoom	
	Concept	Type
concepts	boarding	Relation
	in_cabin	SubSet
	room_of	Relation
	unauthorized_in_cabin	SubSet
Operations	opening_boarding	
	closing_boarding	
	enter_boarding_room	
	loading_in_cabin	

Fig. 5. Two possible contexts from the SecureFlight System

After step (ii), data concepts *in_hold,unauthorized_in_hold* are in the context of *Objects*, while *room_of* and *boarding* are in the context of *BoardingRoom*. Data concepts *in_cabin* and *unauthorized_in_cabin* are not assigned to. At step (iii), they become elements of context *BoardingRoom*, because they are used by operations of this context.

Fig. 4 can lead to four different sets of contexts, depending on the choices of the targets for non-private operations. In Fig. 5, we show the two possible configurations explained above.

5   Contexts Transformation Rules

5.1   From Contexts to Classes

The last step of our approach transforms the contexts into classes. We have defined a set of rules to support this transformation, but for space and clarity reasons, we will give an informal presentation of these rules. Fig. 2 and 6 give the class diagrams for both contexts of Fig. 5.

Each context is transformed into a class whose name is the class concept which is at the origin of the context, and whose operations are the operations of the context. All operations are declared as "public" by default, including the ones appearing in $\mathcal{O}_{private}$. This is motivated by observing that operations that set or get some attribute of the class need to be public although they only access information of a single class and appear in $\mathcal{O}_{private}$. Operations *opening_boarding* and *closing_boarding* fall into this category.

The other concepts of a context will be translated into class attributes or associations between classes.

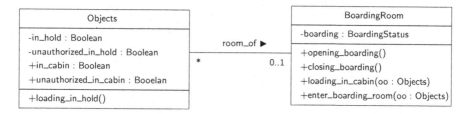

Fig. 6. The derived class diagram for case 2 of Fig. 5

Concepts of type *Relation* are transformed into UML associations if they link two classes. For example, *room_of* is defined between concepts *Objects* and *BoardingRoom*, and is translated into a UML association. Some relations do not link a pair of class concepts, they are then translated as attributes of the class corresponding to their context, or may lead to the creation of new classes. For example, *boarding* links *BoardingRoom* to *BoardingStatus*, which is not a class concept. It is translated into an attribute of type *BoardingStatus* in class *BoardingRoom*.

Attributes of type *Subset* are translated into boolean attributes if they correspond to subsets of their class. For example, *in_hold* is a subset of *Objects* and it is translated as a boolean attribute. By default, all attributes are private to the class (denoted by a "-" sign).

Another interesting case is when an attribute has few connections to the class concept. For example, in the second set of contexts, where *BoardingRoom* is the target of non-private operations, *in_cabin* is in the context of *BoardingRoom* but has no direct link to it. The reason why it is located in this context is that it is used by *loading_in_cabin*. A naive, and erroneous, translation would turn it into an attribute *in_cabin : Objects*[*][7]. This translation is erroneous because it defines a functional dependency between a boarding room and its associated set *in_cabin*; as a result there would be several sets of *in_cabin* objects, one set per boarding room. One way to solve this problem is to declare *in_cabin* as a static attribute of *BoardingRoom*. Another way is to translate it as a public attribute of class *Object* and make sure that there exist an association (here *room_of*) which allows *loading_in_cabin* to have access to this information.

Other rules, allow the creation of subclasses, such as *admittedP* in Fig. 8.

5.2 Discussion

This paper has proposed an approach to represent a B specification as a class diagram. From a B specification, we construct a set of pertinent contexts, which are then translated into the class diagram. Compared to our previous proposal [9], the current approach builds on the same principles but introduces the notion of pertinent context and richer translation rules.

– The approach is automated and requires only a few user interaction. On the one hand, in the construction of pertinent contexts, the only activity left

---

[7] The attribute *in_cabin* is a set-valued attribute of type *Objects*.

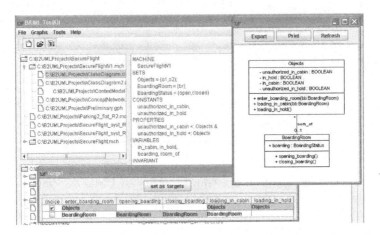

Fig. 7. The B/UML Tool

to the user is the choice of the *Target* function. On the other hand, the translation of pertinent contexts into classes builds on very systematic rules, which require no user input.

- The translation rules bring more flexibility in the construction of subclasses. In our previous approach, each subset led to a subclass. In our example, the four attributes of *Objects* would have led to four subclasses, which tends to make the class diagram more complex.

Both improvements, reduction of user interaction and lower number of sub-classes, are motivated by our wish to scale up the approach to larger specifications. Reduction of user interaction is a trivial requirement when large specifications are considered. The careful treatment of subclasses appeared as another requirement when we tried to apply our approach to larger examples, such as those presented in the next section.

6   The B/UML Tool

6.1   Overview of the Tool

In order to automatically generate the graphs and class diagrams presented in the previous sections, we built a tool based on the algorithm of Sect. 4. Fig. 7, shows a class diagram derived by the tool from the SecureFlight machine. Several class diagrams can be produced from the SecureFlight machine depending on the choice of targets of operations. In the "target" window, the user selects the set of targets corresponding to the operations and the tool automatically generates the corresponding class diagram. Optionally, graphs such as the data concept dependance relation and the concept network are also displayed by the tool. They can be useful to understand precisely how the tool came to a given result.

6.2   Evaluation

The tool was used experimentally on several specifications either taken from the examples of the ProB tool [14] (BookStore and TravelAgency) or developed independently in our laboratory (Parking and SecureFlight). Two specifications (Parking and SecureFlight) involve refinement steps. We produced a single B machine for each refinement step by manually flattening the specifications. Table 1 gives several measures of the input specifications (number of data concepts and operations, number of lines), and of the resulting diagrams (percentage of data concepts and operations represented, number of diagrams that can be generated depending on the choice of targets).

These experiments show that the tool can be applied to non trivial specifications (see Fig. 8). The diagrams generated for all specifications but "Parking" cover 100% of the data concepts and operations. For Parking, coverage is partial because the specification features a significant number of data concepts which are not sets, subsets or relations, but are typically integer variables. Further work is needed to broaden the scope of our method and address such variables.

The last column gives the number of class diagrams which can be constructed for each specification. This number increases with the number of class concepts and operations, because it allows a wider variety of *Target* functions. As this number increases for developments which involve a large number of refinement steps, further help should be provided by the tool to help selecting the right targets, and keep this selection consistent through the refinement steps.

6.3   Comparison with Other Approaches

Our tool gives comparable or better results than the existing approaches [17,8]. In [17], Tatibouet et al generate a class for every machine, set and relation. In fact, applying these rules to the SecureFlight machine of example 2 leads to 10 classes linked by numerous associations to a central class which contains all operations of the specification. For SecureFlight4, our tool generates at most 7 classes (Fig. 8), while the approach of Tatibouet et al leads to 26 classes. We believe that our diagrams are simpler and therefore more readable.

In [8], Fekih et al have proposed a more flexible approach based on the application of rules selected by the user. These rules are quite informal and further work is needed to reach a sufficient level of formality to allow some tool

Table 1. Case studies

	Data concepts	Operations	Source lines	Operation coverage	Concept coverage	Class Diagrams
BookStore	5	6	119	100%	100%	1
TravelAgency	23	10	296	100%	100%	1
Parking1	22	20	364	20%	64%	2
Parking2	25	24	462	21%	64%	2
SecureFlight0	5	2	80	100%	100%	1
SecureFlight1	10	2	142	100%	100%	3
SecureFlight2	12	3	158	100%	100%	8
SecureFlight3	15	4	192	100%	100%	16
SecureFlight4	17	6	222	100%	100%	108

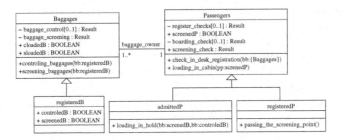

Fig. 8. A class diagram issued from the SecureFlight4 machine

support for their approach. We believe that a careful application of their rules can lead to similar class diagrams as the ones we produce. But this requires a lot more involvement of the user than the single selection of targets.

Compared to these existing works, our approach based on concept formation features a better treatment of operations. In Tatibouet's approach, all operations are grouped in a single class, while in Fekih's approach the distribution of operations into classes is left to the choice of the user, without specific rules.

7   Conclusion and Perspectives

Graphical formalisms are often considered as the most efficient techniques to describe complex systems in an understandable way, while formal techniques offer excellent tools to prepare precise and consistent specifications. This paper has proposed an original approach and its tool support for the construction of class diagrams from a formal analysis of B specifications. First, a concept network is built in order to find groups of concepts called formal contexts. Then, these are translated into class diagrams. Still, our approach suffers several limitations:

- The major limit of the resulting diagrams is that they give a less complete information than that which could be expressed in a formal specification. Other views, such as the dynamic views are needed to provide a more complete graphical documentation of the B specification. Early work in this direction includes [4] which proposed a tool to produce state-transition diagrams from formal B specifications.
- The approach does not support all types that appear in B specifications. Function $Type$ (Sect. 3), is neither defined for basic types such as integer variables nor for complex structures such as power sets or relations which link relations. Further work is needed to explore ways to translate such structures.
- Another limit is the support of specification composition constructs, i.e. IN-CLUDES, IMPORTS and SEES and the support for refinement. As far as refinements and INCLUDES are concerned, developments are manually flattened into a single B machine. We are developing a tool that automates this flattening.

These limitations offer thus interesting research perspectives. We are also conscious that the quality of the graphical descriptions produced from a B specification needs to be evaluated through carefully designed experiments.

The B method has received a lot of interest in the last decade from the scientific community. We hope that the technique described in this paper will contribute to its integration outside of the traditional formal method community.

References

1. J.-R. Abrial. *The B-book: assigning programs to meanings.* Cambridge University Press, 1996.
2. P. Behm, P. Benoit, A. Faivre, and J.-M. Meynadier. METEOR: A successful application of B in a large project. In *Proc. of FM'99: World Congress on Formal Methods*, volume 1709 of *LNCS*, pages 369–387. Springer-Verlag, 1999.
3. G. Bernhard and W. Rudolf. *Formal concept analysis.* Springer, 1999.
4. D. Bert, M.-L. Potet, and N. Stouls. GeneSyst: a tool to reason about behavioral aspects of B event specifications. Application to security properties. In *Proc. of ZB2005*, volume 3455 of *LNCS*. Springer-Verlag, 2005.
5. G. Booch, J. Rumbaugh, and I. Jacobson. *The Unified Modeling Language user guide.* Addison Wesley Longman Publishing Co., Inc., 1999.
6. L. Casset. Development of an embedded verifier for java card byte code using formal methods. In *FME'02*, volume 2391 of *LNCS*. Springer-Verlag, 2002.
7. S. Dupuy, Y. Ledru, and M. Chabre-Peccoud. An Overview of RoZ : a Tool for Integrating UML and Z Specifications. In *12th Conf. on Advanced information Systems Engineering-CAiSE'2000*, volume 1789 of *LNCS*. Springer-Verlag, 2000.
8. H. Fekih, L. Jemni, and S. Merz. Transformation des spécifications B en des diagrammes UML. In *AFADL : Approches Formelles dans l'Assistance au Développement de Logiciels*, 2004.
9. A. Idani and Y. Ledru. Object Oriented Concepts Identification from Formal B Specifications. In *Proc. of 9th Int. Workshop on Formal Methods for Industrial Critical Systems*, volume 133 of *ENTCS*, pages 159–174. Elsevier, 2005.
10. S.-K. Kim and D. Carrington. Formalizing the UML class diagram using object-z. In *UML'99 - The Unified Modeling Language. Beyond the Standard. 2nd Int. Conf., Fort Collins, CO, USA*, volume 1723 of *LNCS*, pages 83–98. Springer-Verlag, 1999.
11. R. Laleau and F. Polack. Coming and going from UML to B: A proposal to support traceability in rigorous IS development. In *ZB'2002 – Formal Specification and Development in Z and B*, LNCS 2272, pages 517–534. Springer-Verlag, 2002.
12. K. Lano. *Formal object-oriented development.* Springer-Verlag, 1995.
13. H. Ledang and J. Souquières. Contributions for modelling UML state-charts in B. In *Integrated Formal Methods, IFM 2002*, volume 2335 of *LNCS*, 2002.
14. M. Leuschel and M. Butler. ProB: A Model Checker for B. In *FME 2003: Formal Methods*, LNCS 2805, pages 855–874. Springer-Verlag, 2003.
15. G. Pouzancre. How to Diagnose a Modern Car with a Formal B Model? In *ZB 2003: Formal Specification and Development in Z and B*. Springer-Verlag, 2003.
16. M. Satpathy, R. Harrison, C. Snook, and M. Butler. A Comparative Study of Formal and Informal Specifications through an Industrial Case Study. In *FSCBS'01: IEEE/ IFIP Wkshp on Formal Specification of Computer-Based Systems*, 2001.
17. B. Tatibouet, A. Hammad, and J.C. Voisinet. From an abstract B specification to UML class diagrams. In *2nd IEEE Int. Symposium on Signal Processing and Information Technology (ISSPIT'2002)*, Morocco, December 2002.

29 New Unclarities in the Semantics of UML 2.0 State Machines*

Harald Fecher, Jens Schönborn, Marcel Kyas, and Willem-Paul de Roever

Christian-Albrechts-Universität zu Kiel, Germany
{hf,jes,mky,wpr}@informatik.uni-kiel.de

Abstract. UML 2.0, which is the standard modeling language for object-oriented systems, has only an informally given semantics. This is in particular the case for UML 2.0 state machines, which are widely used for modeling the reactive behavior of objects. In this paper, a list of 29 newly detected trouble spots consisting of ambiguities, inconsistencies, and unnecessarily strong restrictions of UML 2.0 state machines is given and illustrated using 6 state machines having a problematic meaning; suggestions for improvement are presented. In particular, we show that the concepts of history, priority, and entry/exit points have to be reconsidered.

1 Introduction

UML has become the standard modeling language for object-oriented systems. UML state machines are one of the most important constituents of UML, since they are widely used for modeling the reactive behavior of objects. UML state machines have evolved from Harel's statecharts [4] and their object-oriented version [5]. The fact that the semantics of UML is only informally described leads to many ambiguities and inconsistencies in earlier versions of UML, see for example [9,11]. Many of the detected ambiguities and inconsistencies are ruled out in UML 2.0 [8], but new ones are added.

We present a list of 29 newly detected ambiguities, inconsistencies and unnecessarily strong restrictions of UML 2.0 (behavioral) state machines [8, p. 573–639], which we found during an attempt to define their formal semantics [10]. These unclarities are illustrated on 6 state machines, which are legal according to [8] but having a problematic meaning. Some of the listed unclarities are serious, i.e., they cannot straightforwardly be eliminated. This holds, e.g., for the concepts of history, priority, and entry/exit points, which are discussed in Subsection 3.1 till Subsection 3.3, where also suggestions for improvement are given. Our suggestions for improving UML state machines lead to a simplified and less ambiguous semantics, in particular, all serious unclarities are eliminated.

---

* Part of this work has been financially supported by IST project Omega (IST-2001-33522) and NWO/DFG project Mobi-J (RO 1122/9-1, RO 1122/9-2).

K.-K. Lau and R. Banach (Eds.): ICFEM 2005, LNCS 3785, pp. 52–65, 2005.

2 UML 2.0 State Machines

The basic concepts of UML 2.0 state machines are states and transitions between them. A state may contain regions[1] (called direct subregions of that state) and a region must contain states (called direct substates of that region) such that this hierarchy yields a tree structure. States that contain at least one region are called composite states, otherwise, they are called simple states. For example state 1 in Fig. 1 is a simple state, state 3 is a composite state containing one region, and state 0 is a composite state containing two regions.

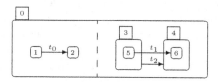

Fig. 1. State machine

A configuration describes the currently active states, where exactly one direct substate of an active region must be active and all regions of an active state must be active. For example, $\{0, 1, 3, 5\}$ is a configuration in Fig. 1. A state may have associated an entry behavior (evoked when the state becomes active), an exit behavior (evoked when the state becomes deactivated), and a doActivity behavior (sequence of actions, which may be (partially) executed when the state is active). In the following, to execute doActivities means the partial execution of such action sequences.

The environment may send events to the state machine. These events are collected in the event pool of the state machine. A state machine may either execute doActivities of active states or may dispatch a single event from its event pool to trigger transitions.

Beside its source and target, a transition consists of an event, a guard (a boolean expression), and an action sequence. A transition is enabled if its source state is currently active, its event is dispatched from the event pool, and its guard evaluates to true. Among the enabled transitions, those are fired which belong to a maximal set whose elements are pairwise conflict-free. Two transitions are in conflict if the intersection of the set of states that will be left by the firing of these transitions is non empty. A state s will be left by the firing of transitions t if it is active and either a substate of the source state of t or, roughly spoken, the transition points outside the border of s. For example, state 3 and 5 have to be left in Fig. 1 by the firing of transition t_1 or by the firing of t_2. Hence, t_1 and t_2 are in conflict.

The firing of transition t leads, in this order, (i) to the deactivation of the states that will be left by the firing of t together with the execution of the exit behavior of these states, (ii) the execution of the actions of t (which we simply call the execution of t), and (iii) the activation of its target states (the transition's

---

[1] Multiple regions of a state are separated by a dashed line.

target state together with the non-active states 'crossed' by the transition and some substates of the target state via a default mechanism) together with the execution of the entry behavior of these states. UML state machines follow the *run-to-completion* assumption, i.e., "an event occurrence can only be taken from the pool and dispatched if the processing of the previous current occurrence is fully completed" [8, p. 617].

There also exist different kinds of additional pseudostates, which are not allowed to occur in configurations, and which have special interpretations. For example, a choice pseudostate, which is depicted by a diamond-shaped symbol (see Fig. 5), leads to a new decision concerning which of its outgoing transitions will be fired without completing the run-to-completion step. In other words, the guards of transition leaving a choice pseudostate are evaluated when the choice pseudostate is left, contrary to guards of other transitions, which are evaluated when an event is dispatched. Further pseudostates are described in the next section. Transitions may also have pseudostates as their sources or targets. A compound transition is, roughly spoken, a transition obtained by subsuming transitions involving pseudostates. In particular, one (single) transition between states is also a compound transition. The semantics of firing transitions is defined on compound transitions.

3   Semantical Unclarities of UML 2.0 State Machines

The unclarities discussed here are categorized as:

Incompleteness: meaning that no clear statement is made.
Inconsistency: meaning that parts are in contradiction with other parts.
Ambiguity: meaning that interpretations in more than one way are possible.
Equivocality: meaning that it is unclear whether the implicitly given interpretation is the intended one.

3.1   History Pseudostates

An initial pseudostate of composite state s indicates how the substates of s are entered if a transition t with target state s was fired: after firing t, the unique transition leaving the initial pseudostate of s, called initial transition, will be fired. A history pseudostate of a region r is used to activate those substates of r that were active when r was the last time active. The shallow history concept considers only the direct substates of r, whereas that of deep history considers also deeper nested substates. In case r was not active before or the last active direct substate of r is a final state, the history default transition, which is the unique transition leaving the history pseudostate, is fired instead. Final states are special simple states. Initial pseudostates are depicted by a solid filled circle, a deep history pseudostate by a circle containing an 'H*', and a final state by a circle surrounding a solid filled circle, see, e.g., Fig. 2.

Inconsistency 1. *On the one hand, history pseudostates belong to regions [8, p. 598]. On the other hand, the semantics of a history pseudostate is defined for its containing state [8, p. 591] and, therefore, no meaning of history pseudostates belonging to multiple regions of a composite state is defined.*

We proceed by applying the definition of its semantics to its containing region.

Incompleteness 2. *The firing of transitions is only defined for compound transitions, which do not include history or initial pseudostates [8, p. 625]. Hence, the semantics of firing transitions that point to history pseudostates (or initial pseudostates) is not defined.*

The solution to allow also history and initial pseudostates as targets of a compound transition does not eliminate all unclarities:

Incompleteness 3. *May a transition to a history pseudostate be fired if the guard of the history default transition evaluates to false and either the corresponding region was not visited before or a final state of the corresponding region was last active?*

UML 2.0 only mentions implicitly that initial transitions and history default transitions have to point to default states [8, p. 591], thus:

Equivocality 4. *Is it really the case that transitions from initial pseudostates or from history pseudostates may not point to pseudostates (such as a choice pseudostate)?*

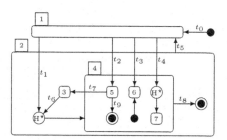

Fig. 2. History illustration

Improvement: *Interpret history and initial pseudostates as choice points with additional semantics. Then more than one transition may leave a history or a initial pseudostate, and may point to pseudostates; the model is ill-formed (i.e., any behavior is possible) when a history (or initial) pseudostate is reached and all guards of the outgoing transitions evaluate to false.*

Ambiguity 5. *The semantical behavior of transitions that point to a deep history pseudostate from inside the region containing the history pseudostate is not clear.*

Consider, e.g., the firing sequence $(t_0, t_3, t_5, t_2, t_7, t_6)$ in Fig. 2. Then which one of the states 3,5,6,7 is active? The comment given at [8, p. 591], which concerns the last active configuration before exiting, favors state 6, whereas the recursive application of the shallow history rule [8, p. 606] favors state 5, and when 'last active' does not correspond to the exiting of the state then state 3 would be active.

Furthermore, the recursive application approach mentioned leads to the following unclarities:

Equivocality 6. *Is it really the case that also the deeper nested final states will not be activated in case of a deep history activation?*

Consider, e.g., the firing sequence $(t_0, t_2, t_9, t_5, t_1)$ in Fig. 2. Then state 7 is active and not the final state that is contained in state 4.

Ambiguity 7. *How is the default activation for nested substates determined in case of deep history activation. Are they determined by the initial transitions or are they determined by the default history states of the corresponding regions?*

Consider, e.g., the firing sequence (t_0, t_1) in Fig. 2. Then, is state 6 or state 7 active?

Ambiguity 8. *How is the history information reset when a final state is reached? Are only the direct substates reset or are all substates reset?*

Consider, e.g., the firing sequence $(t_0, t_2, t_8, t_5, t_4)$ in Fig. 2. Then state 7 is active if the firing of t_6 also resets state 4. Otherwise, state 5 is active.

Improvement: *We suggest to store the history information at the point in time when the region is left. The 'last active' direct substate, instead of the 'last active' subconfiguration, is stored (deep history will use this information recursively), which reduces the complexity. The history information of region r is set to a 'not-visited' value, whenever (i) r was not visited before, or (ii) r or an outer region of r was exited after a final state was reached there. The firing of a transition pointing to a deep history pseudostate h of region r (i) fires the default history transition of h (where a default entering determined by the initial transitions takes place in its target) if the history information of r yields the 'non-visited' value, or (ii) recursively activates the states stored in the history information (also the stored final states) otherwise.*

Our suggestion has the advantage that (a) no configuration that partly consist of history information and partly consist of default information is generated; (b) a default history entering just corresponds to the firing of the corresponding history default transition; and (c) entering a region where a final state was last active has the same behavior as if the region was not visited before.

Concerning our examples this suggestions yields that (i) state 5 is active after the firing of $(t_0, t_3, t_5, t_2, t_7, t_6)$ in Fig. 2; (ii) the final state contained in state 4 is active after $(t_0, t_2, t_9, t_5, t_1)$; (iii) state 6 is active after (t_0, t_1); and (iv) state 7 is active after $(t_0, t_2, t_8, t_5, t_4)$.

3.2 Priority

Priority between transitions is used to rule out some nondeterminism in determining the set of transitions that may fire. "By definition, a transition originating from a substate has higher priority than a conflicting transition originating from any of its containing states" [8, p. 618]. Join pseudostates define a set of states, rather than a single state, as source of a compound transition. Fork pseudostates define a set of states, rather to a single state as target of a compound transition. Join and also fork pseudostates are depicted by a short heavy bar as, e.g., illustrated in Fig. 3.

Inconsistency 9. *The definition of priority of joined transition ("The priority of joined transitions is based on the priority of the transition with the most transitively nested source state" [8, p. 618]) is not well defined and in contradiction to the algorithm describing the determination of the sets of transitions that will be fired [8, p. 618].*

The priority definition for join transitions is not well defined, since the 'most transitively nested source state' (the state that has the the greatest distance to the outermost region) cannot be uniquely determined and, therefore, the priority between transitions cannot be uniquely determined. For example, it is not clear if transition t_0 in Fig. 3 has priority over t_1 or not. The contradiction between

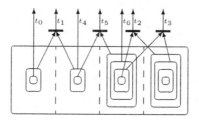

Fig. 3. Priority illustration

the priority definition for join transitions and the algorithm is illustrated on the following example: In Fig. 3, transition t_2 has priority over t_3 with respect to the priority definition for joined transition, but t_3 has priority over t_2 with respect to the algorithm.

The algorithm mentioned contains the sentence: "For each state at a given level, all originating transitions are evaluated to determine if they are enabled" [8, p. 618].

Ambiguity 10. *The interpretation of level is not clear. Does it correspond to the maximal distance to a simple state or does it correspond to the distance to the outermost region?*

For example, if level corresponds to the maximal distance to a simple state, then in Fig. 3 transition t_4 has priority over t_5 and over t_6, and t_6 has priority over t_5.

On the other hand, if level corresponds to the distance to the outermost region, then t_6 has priority over t_4 and over t_5, and no priority between t_4 and t_5 exists.

Improvement: *Use the definition given by the algorithm except that level is ignored[2]: t has priority over t' if every source state of t is a substate of a source state of t' and one is a proper one. Then in Fig. 3 transition t_6 has priority over t_4 and no further priorities exist between t_4, t_5, and t_6. The advantage of this definition is that the priority relation is completely determined by the source states (e.g., further substates are irrelevant, which is not the case if level is interpreted as distance to simple states).*

3.3   Entry/Exit Points

Another unclarity concerns entry/exit points. Entry/exit points are pseudostates that belong to state machines or to composite states. "An entry pseudostate [and symmetrically, an exit pseudostate] is used to join an external transition terminating on that entry point to an internal transition emanating from that entry point" [8, p. 601]. Entry (exit) points are depicted by a small circle (respectively, by a small circle with a cross) on the border of the state machine or composite state.

Inconsistency 11. *Is it really the case that entry points (respectively, exit points) only exist at the topmost region of a state machine [8, p. 591] (i.e., cannot belong to composite state), since entry points (respectively, exit points) belonging to composite states are explicitly discussed at [8, pp. 592,594,603].*

In the following, we assume that entry/exit points are also allowed at composite states. Junction pseudostates describe sets of transitions obtained by combining any incoming transition with an outgoing transition.

Inconsistency 12. *On the one hand, the entry (exit) behavior of a state is executed between the transition pointing to an entry (respectively, exit) point and the transition leaving that entry (exit) point [8, pp. 601,606] (e.g., the entry behavior of state 0 in Fig. 4 is executed in between transitions t_0 and t_1). On the other hand, entry (exit) pseudostates are considered as junction pseudostates [8, pp. 607-608] and, therefore, the entry behavior of state 0 is executed after the execution of transitions t_0 and t_1 [8, pp. 625-628].*

The approach to drop the correspondence to junction pseudostates does not eliminate all unclarities as illustrated in the following:

Incompleteness 13. *How is the behavior defined if an exit point is reached that does not have an outgoing transition? Is this an ill-formed situation?*

---

[2] Ignoring level yields less priorities and, therefore, the approaches where level is interpreted can be considered as a refinement step in the sense that less executions are allowed.

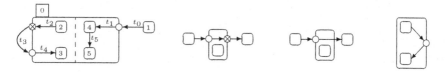

Fig. 4. Entry/exit point illustration

Incompleteness 14. *It is not explicitly mentioned that the invocation of the exit (entry) behavior of a state enforced through an exit (respectively, entry) point corresponds to the point in time when the state is exited (respectively, entered). Furthermore, it is not even clear if the state is always exited in this situation.*

For example, consider Fig. 4. Suppose the compound transition consisting of t_2, t_3, t_4 is fired. Is then only the exit (respectively, entry) behavior of state 0 executed without exiting state 0? This question is essential for execution of doActivities and conflict determination.

In the following, we assume that a state is immediately left after executing its exit behavior and that a state is immediately entered before executing its entry behavior.

Equivocality 15. *The deepest state (or region) containing the source and target state of a transition (called the least common ancestor of the transition) is not sufficient to determine the conflict relation.*

For example, in Fig. 4 the compound transition consisting of t_2, t_3, t_4 is in conflict with transition t_5, since the firing of each transition will exit state 4 (if a composite state, like 0, is exited all its substates have to be exited). But the least common ancestor of these transition yields different subregions of state 0.

Incompleteness 16. *May transitions (or transition paths on pseudostates) point from entry points to exit points as, e.g., depicted in the second picture of Fig. 4?*

More problematic, transitions from an entry point belonging to state s may point outside s (probably by using pseudostates in between), which contradicts the invariant that after a run-to-completion step a configuration will be reached [8, p. 617]. Furthermore, transitions pointing from inside state s to an entry point belonging to s would execute the entry behavior of an already active state. Therefore:

Incompleteness 17. *The following restrictions are needed: Every transition path on pseudostates starting at an entry (exit) point of a composite state s may only leave (respectively, enter) that state through an exit (respectively, entry) point of s.*
Any transition path on pseudostates starting from outside (inside) a composite state s or from an exit (respectively, entry) point of s and which (i.e., that path) does not contain an entry (respectively, exit) point of s may not end at an exit (entry) point of s.

For example, the third and the fourth state machine of Fig. 4 should be not allowed.

Inconsistency 18. *Consider the state machine of Fig. 5. Suppose t_0 will be fired. Then state 0 has to be left (independent whether transition t_1 or t_3 will be taken). But if t_1 will be fired, state 0 is left after the execution of t_1 (and, therefore, after t_0) by the semantics of exit points [8, p. 606]. On the other hand, if t_3 will be fired, then state 0 has to be left before transition t_0 is executed, since states have to be left before the compound transition is executed [8, pp. 627].*

In particular, no allowed execution order exists if the execution of the exit behavior of state 0 changes the evaluation of the guard of t_1 to true and of t_2 to false.

Fig. 5. Entry/exit point illustration (2)

Inconsistency 19. *Consider the state machine of Fig. 5. On the one hand, by the semantics of exit pseudostates state 6 has to be left after the execution of t_5. On the other hand, state 4 has to be exited before transition t_5 is executed, since states have to be left before the compound transition is executed [8, pp. 627]. Furthermore, state 4 may only be exited if all its active substates are exited, hence state 6 has to be exited before t_5 is executed.*

Equivocality 20. *Transitions from fork pseudostates may not point to entry points or to history pseudostates, since transitions from fork pseudostates may not point to pseudostates [8, p. 624].*

Equivocality 21. *Transitions from exit points may not point to join pseudostates, since transitions pointing to join pseudostates may not have pseudostates as their sources [8, p. 624].*

Improvement: *Many unclarities can be avoided by forbidding transitions crossing state borders. Instead, use always entry/exit points. This has the consequence that only the substates of the source (target) states of a compound transition are exited (respectively, entered) before (respectively, after) the transition is executed; all other states are exited (respectively, entered) in between the execution of the transition.*

Furthermore, exit (entry) points should be considered as join (respectively, fork) pseudostates, where the source of a transition pointing to an exit point of state s has to be a direct substate of s or an exit point of a direct substate of s. The same holds, for transitions leaving entry points of s, except that they may also point to direct subpseudostates of s. Note that in this approach no explicit join or fork pseudostates are needed.

3.4 Transitions

It is unclear whether the default state (the target of an initial transition) has to be a direct substate. More problematic is that an initial transition may point outside its region, which contradicts, similarly to Incompleteness 17, the invariant that after a run-to-completion step a configuration will be reached [8, p. 617]. Therefore:

Incompleteness 22. *The following restriction is needed: Transitions from initial pseudostates or from history pseudostates may only point to substates of the region that directly contains the corresponding pseudostate.*

For example, the state machine on the left hand side of Fig. 6 should not be allowed, since if state 0 is entered by default then states 0 and 1 become active. The reason is that these states are direct substates of the same region and that only one direct substate of a region may be active [8, p. 605].

Fig. 6. Disallowed and allowed state machines

Another restriction, which is necessary to guarantee the above mentioned configuration invariant, concerns local transitions, i.e., transitions with transition kind 'local'. A local transition differs from a normal (i.e., external) transition in the sense that if it is fired, its source state is not exited (only the substates of the source state) [8, p. 634].

Incompleteness 23. *The following restriction is needed: A local transition may only point to its source state or to substates (properly reached through a fork pseudostate) of its source state.*

For example, the second state machine of Fig. 6 is not allowed, since if the local transition[3] fires, then state 3 remains active and state 5 becomes active, which is forbidden, as explained before. On the other hand, the third state machine of Fig. 6 does not yield any semantical problems.

Inconsistency 24. *Transitions crossing regions, as illustrated in the fourth picture of Fig. 6, are forbidden [8, p. 627], but their meaning is explicitly described [8, p. 627].*

If guards with side effects are used [8, p. 624,627], an ill-formed situation occurs and therefore no behavior can be guaranteed.

Incompleteness 25. *How should it be ensured that the evaluation of guards does not need time, which is a side effect?*

---

[3] Local transitions are illustrated by the attached symbol *.

Improvement: *One possibility is to make the observable time steps so coarse that the execution time of the guards cannot be observed.*

Another possibility is to allow only guards that depend on single boolean attributes, which are, e.g., calculated by the entry behavior. In order to obtain a dynamic dependency, these boolean attributes can be updated by doActivities.

3.5 Nondeterminism

The determination of the set of firing transitions is not completely deterministic [8, pp. 618], since not always a priority between conflicting transitions exist. Suppose transitions t_0 and t_1 are enabled in Fig. 7, then either t_0 or t_1 fires.

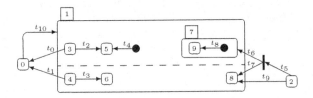

Fig. 7. Illustration of a state machine for nondeterminism

UML 2.0 seems to enforce at least determinism between the selection of transitions that have the same source state: "Each event name may appear more than once per state if the guard conditions are different" [8, p. 609].

Ambiguity 26. *What does different guard conditions mean? Does it mean that for each pair of guards, there exists a situation where one of the guards is true and the other is false? Does different guards mean mutually exclusive guard conditions (i.e., no two guards may be true at the same time), as enforced for completion transitions[4] [8, p. 626]?*

The order in which transitions of a compound transition fire is not completely deterministic. More precisely, transitions to a join pseudostate (respectively, leaving a fork pseudostate) can be fired in any order. In UML 2.0, there is a contradiction in the definition of the execution order of the initial transition of a composite state that is a target of a firing transition (such as t_4 after firing t_{10}):

Inconsistency 27. *"The entry behavior of the composite state is executed before the behavior associated with the initial transition" [8, p. 605] is in contradiction to the fact that "A transition to the enclosing state represents a transition to the initial pseudostate in each region" [8, p. 600] and that actions corresponding to a compound transition are executed before entry behaviors [8, p. 627-628].*

---

[4] Completion transitions are transitions that do not have an explicit trigger. They are triggered if their source states are completed. Roughly spoken, a state is completed if its doActivities are terminated and their direct subregions, if existing, have reached a final state.

For example, after firing transition t_{10} in Fig. 7, must the entry behavior of state 1 be executed before transition t_4 or must transition t_4 be executed before the entry behavior of state 1?

Ambiguity 28. *Suppose transitions to the enclosing state represent transitions to the initial pseudostate: In which order are actions of transitions from fork pseudostates and actions of the enabled initial transitions executed? Is there a depth-first or branching-first strategy? Is the order completely nondeterministic (except for the fact that actions of transitions to outer states have to be executed first)?*

For example, if t_5 fires in Fig. 7, then it is not clear which of the execution sequences (t_6, t_7, t_8), (t_6, t_8, t_7), (t_7, t_6, t_8) are allowed.

Equivocality 29. *Is it really the case that the actions of the initial transition do not have to be executed before the entry behavior of the target state of the initial transition, in case of default entry?*

For example, after the firing of t_9 in Fig. 7, it is not clear whether t_4 may also be executed after the entry behavior of state 5.

4   Conclusion and Related Work

We have presented 29 inconsistencies, ambiguities, forgotten restrictions, and unnecessary strong restrictions in UML 2.0 state machines. Some of the unclarities are serious, i.e., their elimination is not straightforward. This holds for history pseudostates, priority, exit/entry points, and assuring side-effect-free guards. The serious problems are eliminated by our improvements.

Many of the detected unclarities also exist in earlier versions of UML. In particular, most unclarities concerning history pseudostates[5] (Unclarities 2-5 and 7), all unclarities concerning priority, and the assurance of side-effect-free guards also exists in UML 1.5 [7]. Entry/exit points do not exist in UML 1.5. The semantics of history and priority with respect to join pseudostates in UML 1.x are defined in the literature as follows:

In the work of van der Beeck [12], concerning history, 'last active' does not correspond to the exiting of the state. Furthermore, a transition t has priority over t' if the least common ancestor of t is below the least common ancestor of t', i.e., this yields a weaker priority concept concerning join pseudostates.

The history information in the work of Börger et al. [1] corresponds to the 'last active configuration'. Furthermore, when a state is entered via history, the history information is forgotten, i.e., in this case the semantics of transitions pointing to the history pseudostates from inside the region is unclear. Join pseudostates are encoded by completion transitions and, therefore, a priority principle similar to the one in [12] is used.

---

[5] Note that final states do not reset the history information in UML 1.5.

In [3], where no history pseudostates are considered, priority is handled as a variation point. Nevertheless, the authors make the suggestion that a transition t has lesser or equal priority than t' if every source state of t is below a source state of t'. This differs from our suggestion, e.g., in Fig. 3 transition t_4 has priority over t_1 in their suggestion, whereas no priority between t_4 and t_1 exists in our suggestion.

In [2], priority is also handled as variation point and in [6] join transitions are compiled away, but an exact definition of the transformation is missing and, therefore, the used priority schema is unclear. Both works do not consider history pseudostates. Most of the other works on the semantics of UML 1.x state machines, see, e.g., the references given in [10], do not consider join or history pseudostates and, therefore, do not cover the related problems. We are not aware of works different from ours [10] that define formal semantics of UML 2.0 state machines.

Future work is to define a precise formal semantics with respect to all the suggested improvements, e.g., our semantics [10] does not handle entry/exit points and choice pseudostates. The redefinition concept in UML 2.0 state machines has to be examined, e.g., to clarify to which extent redefinition corresponds to a refinement concept.

References

1. E. Börger, A. Cavarra, and E. Riccobene. Modeling the Dynamics of UML State Machines. In Y. Gurevich, P. Kutter, M. Odersky, and L. Thiele, editors, *Abstract State Machines: Theory and Applications*, volume 1912 of *LNCS*, pages 223–241. Springer-Verlag, 2000.
2. R. Eshuis, D. N. Jansen, and R. Wieringa. Requirements-level semantics and model checking of object-oriented statecharts. *Requirements Engineering Journal*, 7:243–263, 2002.
3. S. Gnesi, D. Latella, and M. Massink. Modular semantics for a uml statechart diagrams kernel and its extension to multicharts and branching time model-checking. *The Journal of Logic and Algebraic Programming*, 51(1):43–75, 2002.
4. D. Harel. Statecharts: A visual formalism for complex systems. *Science of Computer Programming*, 8(3):231–274, July 1987.
5. D. Harel and E. Gery. Executable object modeling with statecharts. *Computer*, 30(7):31–42, July 1997.
6. J. Lilius and I. P. Paltor. Formalising UML state machines for model checking. In R. France and B. Rumpe, editors, *UML*, volume 1723 of *LNCS*, pages 430–445. Springer-Verlag, 1999.
7. Object Management Group. *OMG Unified Modeling Language Specification, Version 1.5*, 2003. http://www.omg.org/cgi-bin/doc?formal/03-03-01.
8. Object Management Group. *UML 2.0 Superstructure Specification*, Oct. 2004. (updated version). http://www.omg.org/cgi-bin/doc?ptc/2004-10-02.
9. G. Reggio and R. Wieringa. Thirty one problems in the semantics of uml 1.3 dynamics. In *OOPSLA'99 workshop, Rigorous Modelling and Analysis of the UML: Challenges and Limitations*, 1999.

10. J. Schönborn. Formal semantics of UML 2.0 behavioral state machines. Master's thesis, Christian-Albrechts Universität zu Kiel, 2005. `http://www.informatik.uni-kiel.de/ jes/jsFsemUMLsm.pdf`.
11. A. J. H. Simons and I. Graham. 30 things that go wrong in object modelling with uml 1.3. In H. Kilov, B. Rumpe, and I. Simmonds, editors, *Behavioral Specifications of Businesses and Systems*, pages 237–257. Kluwer Academic, 1999.
12. M. von der Beeck. A structured operational semantics for UML-statecharts. *Software and System Modeling*, 1(2):130–141, 2002.

The Semantics and Tool Support of OZTA

Jin Song Dong[1], Ping Hao[1,*], Shengchao Qin[2], and Xian Zhang[1]

[1] National University of Singapore
{dongjs, haoping, zhangxi5}@comp.nus.edu.sg
[2] University of Durham, UK
shengchao.qin@durham.ac.uk

Abstract. In this work, we firstly enhance OZTA, a combination of Object-Z and Timed Automata, by introducing a set of timed patterns as language constructs that can specify the dynamic and timing features of complex real-time systems in a systematic way. Then we present the formal semantics in Unifying Theories of Programming for the enhanced OZTA. Furthermore, we develop an OZTA tool which can support editing, type-checking of OZTA models as well as projecting OZTA models into TA models so that we can utilize TA model checkers, e.g., Uppaal for verification.

Keywords: Timed Patterns, Semantics, Tool and Verification.

1 Introduction

The specification of complex real-time systems requires powerful mechanisms for modelling state, concurrency and real-time behavior. Integrated formal methods are well suited for presenting complete and coherent requirement models for complex systems. This research area has been active for a number of years (e.g. [4, 3]) with a particular focus on integrating state based and event based formalisms (e.g. [9, 18]). However, the challenge is how to provide a systematical semantic model for the integrated formal languages, and how to analyze and verify these models with tool support? For the first issue, we believe Unifying Theories of Programming (UTP) [13] is particularly well suited for giving formal semantics for the integrated specification languages and it has been used to define other integrated formalisms [12, 13]. For the second issue, we believe one effective approach is to project the integrated requirement models into multiple domains so that existing specialized tools in these corresponding domains can be utilized to perform the checking and analyzing tasks.

OZTA [6] is an integrated formal language which builds on the strengths of Object-Z (OZ) [8, 15] and Timed Automata (TA) [1, 19] in order to provide a single notation for modelling the static, dynamic and timing aspects of complex systems as well as for verifying system properties by reusing Timed Automata's tool support. One novel aspect of OZTA is its communication mechanism which supports partial and sometime synchronization [6].

The basic OZTA notation has been briefly described in an introductory paper [6] and this paper enhances the OZTA notation by extending its automaton part with time

---

* Author for correspondence: haoping@comp.nus.edu.sg

K.-K. Lau and R. Banach (Eds.): ICFEM 2005, LNCS 3785, pp. 66–80, 2005.

pattern structures. However the main purpose of this paper is to formalize the semantics of OZTA and present an OZTA tool we developed for its editing, type-checking and projection.

The rest of the paper is organized as follows, section 2 presents syntax of OZTA with extension of timed patterns; section 3 provides semantics of OZTA; section 4 shows the tool support of OZTA; and lastly section 5 gives the conclusion.

2 Extending OZTA with Timed Patterns

OZTA specifications are combinations of Object-Z schemas with Timed automatons. Timed Automata, with powerful mechanisms for designing real-time models using multiple clocks, has well developed automatic tool support. However, if TA is considered to be used to capture real-time requirements, then one often need to manually cast those timing patterns into a set of clock variables with carefully calculated clock constraints, which is a process that is close to design rather than specification. In our previous paper [7], we studied time automata patterns and found that a set of common timed patterns, such as *deadline, timeout, waituntil*, can be used to facilitate TA design in a systematic way. In this paper before presenting the semantics of OZTA, we firstly give a full version of the OZTA syntax, in which the automaton part of the the OZTA notation is extended with timed pattern structures. The enhanced specification of OZTA syntax with the notion of timed patterns is presented as follows:

$Specification ::= CDecl; ...; CDecl$
$CDecl ::= \lceil Visiblist; InheritC; StateSch; INIT; StaOp; [TADecl]$
$Visiblist ::= VisibAttr; VisibOp$
$InheritC ::= InheritCName$
$StateSch ::= CVarDecl$
$CVarDecl ::= v : T$
$StaOp ::= \Delta(AttrName \mid ActName), CVarDecl \bullet Pred(u, v')$
$TADecl ::= ClockDecl; TA$
$ClockDecl ::= x : Clock$
$TA ::= State \mid State \bullet Inv(x, n) \mid [(Event)][(Reset(x))][(Guard(x, n))] \bullet TA \mid Wait (x, n)$
$\quad \mid TA \bullet Deadline (x, n) \mid TA \bullet WaitUntil (x, n) \mid TA \bullet Timeout(x, n) \bullet TA$
$\quad \mid TA; TA \mid TA \square TA \mid TA \sqcap TA \mid \mu X \bullet TA(X) \mid TA_1 \parallel TA_2 \bullet S$
$State ::= StaOp \mid StaCtr$
$Event ::= Event \mid Event! \mid Event?$
$Reset ::= (\_ := \_) \langle\langle Clock \times N \rangle\rangle$
$Guard ::= (\_ <= \_) \langle\langle Clock \times N \rangle\rangle \mid (\_ >= \_) \langle\langle Clock \times N \rangle\rangle \mid (\_ < \_) \langle\langle Clock \times N \rangle\rangle$
$\quad \mid (\_ > \_) \langle\langle Clock \times N \rangle\rangle \mid (\_ \wedge \_) \langle\langle \Phi \times \Phi \rangle\rangle \mid true$
$Invar ::= (\_ <= \_) \langle\langle Clock \times N \rangle\rangle \mid (\_ < \_) \langle\langle Clock \times N \rangle\rangle \mid true$
$S ::= \{\_ \leftrightarrow \_\} \langle\langle Event \times Event \rangle\rangle \mid \{\_ \leftrightarrow \_\} \langle\langle Event \times Event \rangle\rangle \mid \{\_ \rightarrow \_\} \langle\langle Event \times Event \rangle\rangle$

in which, the argument x represents a certain clock, and n is a natural number; *StaCtr* represents a control state and *StaOp* is an operation state corresponding to an Object-Z operation; $State \bullet Inv(x, n)$ specifies a state with a local invariant; *Event, Reset(x)*, *Guard(x, n)* are transition labels, which respectively specifies event (Event! is an output

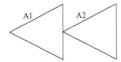

Fig. 1. Sequential Composition ';'

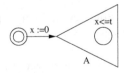

Fig. 2. Deadline 'Deadline(x, t)'

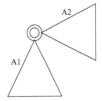

Fig. 3. External Choice '□'

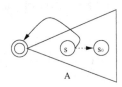

Fig. 4. Recursion '$u\ s_0 \bullet A(s_0)$'

event, Event? is an input event), clock reset and clock constraint; the three branches of S respectively represent the construct of handshaking synchronization, partial synchronization and sometime synchronization; the rest of the TA expressions are the timed automata patterns which can be directly utilized to construct timed automata.

2.1 The Pattern Structure

Each of the pattern expressions has a graphic presentation and the semantics of these expressions will be examined later. One related work is Wafula and Swatmanon's work on a diagrammatic illustration of Object-Z Specifications [17]. Some TA patterns are presented in Figure 1 - 4, the rest can be found in [7]. In these graphical TA patterns, an automaton A is abstracted as a triangle, the left vertex of this triangle or a circle attached to the left vertex represents the initial state of A, and the right edge represents the terminal state of A. For example, Figure 1 demonstrates how two timed automatons can be sequentially composed. By linking the terminal state of A_1 with the initial state of A_2, the resultant automaton passes control from A_1 to A_2 when A_1 goes to its terminal state. Figure 2 shows one of the common timing constraint patterns – *deadline*. There is a single clock x. When the system switches to the automaton A, the clock x gets reset to 0. The local invariant $x <= t$ covers each state of the timed automaton A and specifies the requirement that a switch must occur before t time unit for every state of A. Thus the timing constraint expressed by this automaton is that A should terminate no later than t time units. Figure 3 shows the external choice pattern of two timed automatons A_1 and A_2 which share an initial state, and the environment has the choice to trigger one of them by different external events. Figure 4 illustrates the *recursion* pattern of a timed automaton A, s_0 is the fixed point, The recursion is achieved by diverting all the transitions from pointing to s_0 to the initial state of A.

2.2 An Example: Frog Puzzle Game

A traditional frogs puzzle game is that: given seven stones, three white frogs at left facing right and three black frogs at right facing left. A frog can move in the direction

it is facing to an empty stone, which is adjacent or is reached by jumping over a frog on an adjacent stone. To complex the puzzle, we add some timing constraints to the moves of frogs, i.e., each frog takes at least 1 time units but no more than 2 time units to move to its next position. We define that the puzzle is solved if a sequence of moves can be found that will exchange the positions of the black and white frogs within 30 time units. The OZTA model of this frog puzzle is given as follow,

$Posn == 1..7$

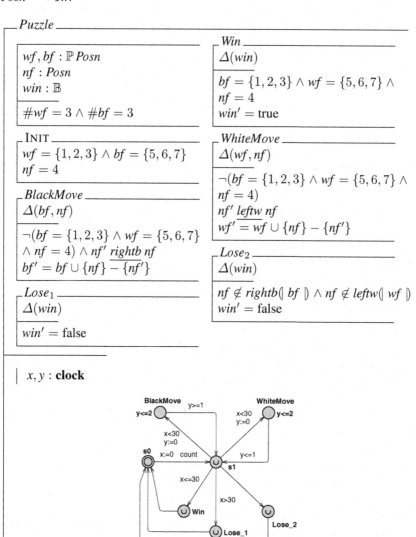

$$\frac{rightb : Posn \leftrightarrow Posn}{\begin{array}{l} \forall i,j : Posn \bullet \\ i\ \underline{rightb}\ j \Leftrightarrow i = j+1 \vee i = j+2 \end{array}} \qquad \frac{leftw : Posn \leftrightarrow Posn}{\begin{array}{l} \forall i,j : Posn \bullet \\ i\ \underline{leftw}\ j \Leftrightarrow i = j-1 \vee i = j-2 \end{array}}$$

In this model, we define the empty stone also as a frog object *nf*. *BlackMove* captures the position exchanges between the black frogs and the empty stone; same for *WhiteMove*; *Win* defines the situation when the puzzle is solved. The game begins with a *count* event after its initial state; player will lose the game when the time is out as described by $(x > 30) \bullet Lose_1$ or whenever the frogs are all jammed by each other in the middle way as described by $Lose_2$. The graphical TA part of the model can be derived from the following textual specification according to the *sequential composition*, *external choice*, *deadline*, *waituntil*, and *recursion* patterns:

$$
\begin{aligned}
TA \;\widehat{=}\; &\mu\, Y \bullet (x := 0)(count) \bullet \\
&\quad \mu X \bullet ((x < 30) \bullet BlackMove \bullet Deadline(y,2) \bullet WaitUntil(y,1);\ X) \\
&\quad \Box\ ((x < 30) \bullet WhiteMove \bullet WaitUntil(y,1) \bullet Deadline(y,2);\ X) \\
&\quad \Box\ ((x <= 30) \bullet Win;\ Y)\ \Box\ ((x > 30) \bullet Lose_1;\ Y)\ \Box\ (Lose_2;\ Y)
\end{aligned}
$$

To illustrate the synchronization mechanism of OZTA, we consider several puzzle-solving competition systems:

The handshaking synchronization operator $\leftrightarrow$ indicates that the two switches labelled *count* in the objects of $p0$, $p1$ were identical, i.e., the automata must synchronize on these switches, as illustrated in Figure 5(1). The product of the two timed automata effectively ensures that the two puzzles start to be solved at same time point in the competition while operating independently and concurrently.

PuzzleC₁

$p0, p1 : Puzzle$

$(p0 \parallel p1) \bullet \{p0.count \leftrightarrow p1.count\}$

The partial synchronization operator $\rightarrow$ indicates that whenever the $p0.count$ is taken, then there must be synchronization with the switch $p1.count$. However, the switch $p1.count$ can occur independent of the switch $p0.count$. The partial synchronization between $p0$ and $p1$ is illustrated in Figure 5(2).

PuzzleC₂

$p0, p1 : Puzzle$

$(p0 \parallel p1) \bullet \{p0.count \rightarrow p1.count\}$

The sometime synchronization operator $\leftrightarrow\!\!\!\!\cdot$ indicates that when any of the switches $p0.count$ or $p1.count$ is taken there may or may not be synchronization with the switch $p1.count$ or $p0.count$ respectively. The sometime synchronization between $p0$ and $p1$ is illustrated in Figure 5(3).

PuzzleC₃

$p0, p1 : Puzzle$

$(p0 \parallel p1) \bullet \{p0.count \leftrightarrow\!\!\!\!\cdot\ p1.count\}$

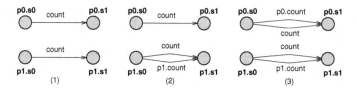

Fig. 5. Handshaking, Partial and Sometime Synchronization

3   The Semantics of OZTA

Before building the semantic model for OZTA, we need to choose an appropriate model of time. There are two typical time models: a discrete model and a continuous model. The current semantic model for OZTA [6] is a primitive operational semantics based on continuous time without pattern features. To make our model with the extension of timed patterns and more apt for exploration of algebraic refinement laws, we choose the discrete model. The discrete time model has also been adopted by the Sherif and He's work [14] on the semantics for time Circus [12] and Qin, Dong and Chin's work [13] on the semantics for TCOZ.

3.1   The Automata Model

The following meta variables are introduced in the alphabet of the observations of the OZTA automata behavior, some of which are similar to those in the previous UTP semantic frameworks [13]. The key difference is that we now take consideration of clock variable updates.

- ok, ok': *Boolean*. These two variables are introduced to denote the observations of automaton initiation and termination. ok records the observation that the automaton has started. When ok is false, the automaton has not started, so no observation can be made. ok' records the observation that the automaton has terminated or has reached an intermediate stable state. The automaton is *deadlock* when ok' is false.

- $wait, wait'$: *Boolean*. When $wait$ is true, it states that the automaton starts in an intermediate state. When $wait'$ is true, the automaton has not terminated; when it is false, it indicates a final observation.

- $state, state'$: *Var* → *Value*. In order to record the state of data variables(class attributes and local variables) that occur in an automaton, these two variables are introduced to map each variable to a value in the corresponding observations.

- tr, tr': seq(seq *Event* × ℙ*Event*). The two variables are introduced to record the sequence of observations on the interactions between an automaton and its environment. tr records the observations that occurred before the automaton starts and tr' records the final observation. Each element of the sequence represents an observation over one time unit. Each observation element is composed of a tuple, where the first element of the tuple is the sequence of events that occurred during the time unit, and the second one is the associated set of refusals at the end of the same time unit. The set *Event* denotes all possible communicating events.

– *trace*: seq *Event*. This variable is used to record a sequence of events that take place so far since the last observation. It can be derived from tr, tr' as the following:

$$flat(tr) \frown trace = flat(tr')$$

where $\frown$ is a concatenation operator and flat :

$$\text{seq}(\text{seq}(Event \times \mathbb{P}Event) \rightarrow \text{seq}\,Event$$

$$flat(\langle\rangle) \,\widehat{=}\, \langle\rangle \qquad flat(\langle(es, ref)\rangle \frown tr) \,\widehat{=}\, es \frown flat(tr)$$

– *cval*, *cval'*: *Clock* $\rightarrow N \cup \{NULL\}$. Among which *Clock* denotes all clock variables; N is the set of natural number; *NULL* is a number of no meaning, denoting the situation that the clock has not been enabled yet.

Some other definitions are given to facilitate the description of OZTA semantics.

– The predicate *no_interact*(*trace*) denotes that there are no communication events recorded in *trace*.

$$no\_interact(s) \,\widehat{=}\, s = \langle\rangle$$

– The operator ∘ is the composition of two sequentially made observations. For two observation predicate $P(v, v')$, $Q(v, v')$, where v, v' represents respectively the initial and final versions of all observation variables, the composition of them is:

$$P(v, v') \circ Q(v, v') \,\widehat{=}\, \exists v_0 \bullet P(v, v_0) \wedge Q(v_0, v')$$

– A binary relation $\preceq$ is the ordinary subsequence relation between sequences of the same type.
– The predicate *clock_update*(x, n) denotes that the value of clock variable x is updated to a natural number n.

$$clock\_update(x, n) \,\widehat{=}\, cval' = cval \oplus \{x \mapsto n\}$$

3.2 The Semantics of Automata with Patterns

In this section, the observation model for OZTA automata is developed. We use *TA* to stand for the semantics of an automaton *TA* instead of the term $[\![TA]\!]$ in UTP. Before we go into the detail of the semantics for each Automata expressions, A healthiness condition **R** must be satisfied by the semantics predicate TA for any automaton, which is defined as,

$$\mathbf{R}(TA) \,\widehat{=}\, TA = (TA \wedge tr \overset{t}{\preceq} tr')$$

$tr \overset{t}{\preceq} tr'$ states that, given two timed traces, tr and tr', tr' is an expansion of tr [13].

State and Control Operation.

- State Operation

  $StaOp \cong \Delta(b), a : T \bullet Pred(u, v') \cong ok' \land \neg wait' \land no\_interact(trace) \land$
  $(\forall x : dom\, cval \mid cval(x) \neq NULL \bullet clock\_update(x, \#tr' - \#tr)) \land ((\exists val_1 \bullet$
  $state' = state \oplus \{a \mapsto val_1\}) \circ (\exists val \bullet state' = state \oplus \{a \mapsto val\} \land Pred$
  $(state(u), state'(v'))))$

  In an operation state, time may progress, no event occurs, state will be updated.
  NULL means the clock has no value, and it has not been initialized yet.

- Control Operation

  $StaCtr \cong ok' \land \neg wait' \land no\_interact(trace) \land (\forall x : dom\, cval \mid cval(x) \neq$
  $NULL \bullet clock\_update(x, \#tr' - \#tr))$

  In a control state, time may progress, no event occurs and no state updates.

- Urgent state

  $StaU \cong (StatOP \lor StaCtr) \land \#tr' = \#tr$

  The semantics of an urgent state is that the automaton will pass the control from
  the urgent state to a next state without delay.

- Init State

  $StaI \cong ok' \land \neg wait' \land tr = \langle \rangle \land no\_interact(trace) \land \forall x : dom\, cval \bullet cval(x) = NULL)$

  The sequence of observations of an OZTA model starts from an initial state. The
  value of each clock variable is initially set to *NULL*.

Local Invariant. In verification tools, e.g. Uppaal, local invariants are often restricted
to constraints that are downwards closed, i.e., in the form: $x < n$ or $x \leq n$, where n is
natural number.

$State \bullet (x < n) \cong x \in dom\, cval \land (State \land (cval(x) + \#tr' - \#tr) < n \land (\forall c : dom\, cval \mid cval(c) \neq NULL \bullet clock\_update(x, cval(c) + \#tr' - \#tr)) \lor Stop)$

$State \bullet (x <= n) \cong x \in dom\, cval \land (State \land (cval(x) + \#tr' - \#tr) \leq n \land (\forall c : dom\, cval \mid cval(c) \neq NULL \bullet clock\_update(x, cval(c) + \#tr' - \#tr)) \lor Stop)$

Clock Reset. $Reset(x) \cong ok' \land \neg wait' \land \#tr' = \#tr \land state' = state \land x \in dom\, cval \land clock\_update(x, 0)$

It can also be described in this way,

$Reset(x) \bullet TA \cong Reset(x); TA$

Consecutive clock reset operations are combined into one atomic reset operation.

Event. $Event \cong ok' \land \neg wait' \land trace = \langle Event \rangle \land state' = state \land \#tr' = \#tr$

It can also be described in this way,

$Event \bullet TA \cong Event; TA$

Clock Constraint. An automaton can be guarded by clock constraints. The clock-
guarded automaton $Guard(x, n) \bullet TA$ behaves as *TA* if the condition $Guard(x, n)$ is
initially satisfied.

$Guard(x, n) \bullet TA \cong (\exists x : Clock \bullet x \in dom\, cval) \land (Guard(x, n) \land TA \lor$
$\neg\, Guard(x, n)$
$\land Stop)$

It enjoys the following properties:

- $false \bullet TA = Stop$
- $true \bullet TA = TA$
- $Guard(x, n) \bullet Stop = Stop$
- $Guard_1(x_1, n_1) \bullet (Guard_2(x_2, n_2) \bullet TA) =$
  $(Guard_1(x_1, n_1) \wedge Guard_2(x_2, n_2)) \bullet TA$
- $Guard(x, n) \bullet (TA_1; \; TA_2) = (Guard(x, n) \bullet TA_1); \; \bullet TA_2$

Wait. The Wait construct specifies an automaton in which time idles for n time units then terminates.

$Wait(x, n) \; \hat{=} \; ok' \wedge \neg \; wait' \wedge \#tr' - \#tr = n \wedge (\forall i : \#tr' < i < \#tr \bullet$
$no\_interact(\pi_1(tr'(i))))$

It is subjected to the following laws.

- WAIT n_1; WAIT $n_2 =$ WAIT$(n_1 + n_2)$
- STOP $\bullet$ $Timeout(x, n) \bullet TA =$ WAIT n; TA

Deadline. The Deadline construct $TA \bullet Deadline$ imposes a timing constraint on a timed automaton, which requires that TA should terminate no later than n time units.

$TA \bullet Deadline(x, n) \; \hat{=} \; (ok \wedge x \in \text{dom} \, cval \wedge clock\_update(x, 0)) \circ (TA \wedge \#tr' - \#tr \leq n)$

WaitUntil. The WaitUntil construct $TA \bullet WaitUntil(x, n)$ constrains automation TA to finish its process no less than n time units.

$TA \bullet WaitUntil(x, n) \; \hat{=} \; (TA \wedge (\#tr' - \#tr \geq n)) \vee ((\exists tr_o \bullet tr \preceq tr_o \preceq tr' \wedge \#tr_o - \#tr < n) \wedge ((ok \wedge x \in \text{dom} \, cval \wedge clock\_update(x, 0)) \circ TA[tr_o/tr', true/ok', false/wait'] \circ Wait(x, n - (\#tr_o - \#tr))[tr_o/tr]))$

Timeout. The Timeout construct $TA_1 \bullet Timeout(x, n) \bullet TA_2$ specifies that if no transition has been triggered for n time units in timed automaton TA_1, then TA_1 will be timeout and the control will be passed to TA_2.

$TA_1 \bullet Timeout(x, n) \bullet TA_2 \; \hat{=} \; (ok \wedge x \in \text{dom} \, cval \wedge clock\_update(x, 0)) \circ ((TA_1 \wedge no\_interact(trace) \wedge \#tr' - \#tr \leq n) \vee (\exists k : \#tr < k \leq tr + n, \exists tr_o \bullet \pi_1(tr'(k)) \neq \langle \rangle \wedge tr \preceq tr_o \wedge \#tr_o - \#tr = k \wedge (\forall i : \#tr < i < \#tr + k \bullet no\_interact(\pi_1(tr'(i))) \wedge tr_o(i) = tr'(i)) \wedge TA_1[tr_o/tr]) \vee (\exists tr_o \bullet tr \preceq tr_o \wedge \#tr_o - \#tr = n \wedge (\forall i : \#tr < i < \#tr + n \bullet no\_interact(\pi_1(tr'(i))) \wedge tr_o(i) = tr'(i)) \wedge TA_2[tr_o/tr]))$

Recursion. We define the semantics of recursion same as [13],

$\mu X \bullet TA(X) \; \hat{=} \; \sqcap \{X \mid X \sqsupseteq TA(X)\}$, where X is the fixed point.

Parallel Composition. The parallel composition of two automatons represents all the possible behaviors of both automatons which are synchronized on a specific set of events and on the time when the events occur.

In addition to the handshake synchronization, OZTA also supports other two synchronization mechanisms, namely, partial synchronization and sometime synchronization.

Given a parallel composition $TA_1 \; ||[E]|| \; TA_2 \bullet S$, where E denotes the set of events that TA_1 and TA_2 will communicate with, and S contains elements of the form $a \rightarrow b$, $a \leftrightarrow b$ ($E \cap event(S) = \varnothing$), the notation $a \rightarrow b \in S$ simply indicates that event a from TA_1 must be synchronized with event b from TA_2, but event b can occur independently of a. Given $a \leftrightarrow b \in S$, it indicates that event a from TA_1 and b from TA_2 may synchronize with each other, or occur independently.

This parallel composition is defined in terms of the general parallel merge operator $||_M$ in UTP [10]:

$$A_1 \; ||[E]|| \; A_2 \bullet S \cong (((A_1; \; idle) \; ||_M \; A_2) \vee (A_1 \; ||_M \; (A_2; \; idle)));$$
$$((ok \Rightarrow \text{SKIP}) \wedge (\neg ok \Rightarrow tr \preceq^t tr'))$$

Take note that SKIP is a semantic predicate which preserves the observations, that is, $\text{SKIP} \cong (obs' = obs)$, where obs denotes all observables.

An *idle* process, which may either wait or terminate, follows after each of the two automatons. This is to allow each of the automatons to wait for its partner to terminate.

$$idle \cong ok' \wedge no\_interact(trace) \wedge state' = state$$

The merge predicate M is defined as,

$M \cong ok' = (0.ok \wedge 1.ok) \wedge wait' = (0.wait \vee 1.wait) \wedge state' = (0.state \oplus 1.state) \wedge tr' \in syn(0.tr, 1.tr, E, S) \wedge \#tr' = \#0.tr = \#1.tr \wedge cval' = 0.cval \oplus 1.cval$

Given two timed traces tr_1, tr_2, and a set of events E, and a set of pairs of partial/sometime synchronizations S, the set $syn(tr_1, tr_2, E, S)$ is defined inductively as follows.

$$syn(tr_1, tr_2, E, \varnothing) \cong syn(tr_2, tr_1, E, \varnothing)$$
$$syn(\langle \rangle, \langle \rangle, E, S) \cong \{\langle \rangle\}$$
$$syn(\langle (t, r) \rangle, \langle \rangle, E, S) \cong \{\langle (t', r) \rangle \mid t' \in (t \; \|_{E \; S} \; \langle \rangle)\}$$
$$syn(\langle \rangle, \langle (t, r) \rangle, E, S) \cong \{\langle (t', r) \rangle \mid t' \in (\langle \rangle \; \|_{E \; S} \; t)\}$$
$$syn(\langle (t_1, r_1) \rangle \frown tr_1, \langle (t_2, r_2) \rangle \frown tr_2, E, S) \cong$$
$$\{\langle (t', r') \rangle \frown u \mid t' \in (t_1 \; \|_{E \; S} \; t_2) \wedge r' = r_1 \cup r_2 \wedge$$
$$u \in syn(tr_1, tr_2, E, S)\}$$

$s \; \|_{E \; S} \; t$ is used to merge untimed traces s and t into one untimed trace, where E is the set of events to be synchronized, S is the set of partial/sometime synchronization pairs.

In the following clauses, e, e_1 are representative elements of E (events), x, x_1 represent communication events not residing in E or S, $a \rightarrow b$, $a_1 \rightarrow b_1$ are representative partial synchronization pairs from S, while $c \leftrightarrow d, c_1 \leftrightarrow d_1$ are representative sometime synchronization pairs from S. Let $y, y_1, y_2 \in \{x, x_1, b, b_1, c, d, c_1, d_1\}$.

Let $z, z_1, z_2 \in \{e, a, e_1, a_1\}$. Moreover, we use $k(a, b)$ to denote the synchronization of a and b.

$$s \underset{E\ \varnothing}{\|}\ t \cong t \underset{E\ \varnothing}{\|}\ s \qquad \langle\rangle \underset{E\ S}{\|}\ \langle\rangle \cong \{\langle\rangle\}$$

$$\langle z\rangle \underset{E\ S}{\|}\ \langle\rangle \cong \langle\rangle \underset{E\ S}{\|}\ \langle z\rangle \cong \{\}$$

$$\langle y\rangle \underset{E\ S}{\|}\ \langle\rangle \cong \langle\rangle \underset{E\ S}{\|}\ \langle y\rangle \cong \{\langle y\rangle\}$$

$$\langle y\rangle^\frown s \underset{E\ S}{\|}\ \langle z\rangle^\frown t \cong \{\langle y\rangle^\frown l \mid l \in (s \underset{E\ S}{\|}\ \langle z\rangle^\frown t)\},\ z \to y \notin S$$

$$\langle z\rangle^\frown s \underset{E\ S}{\|}\ \langle y\rangle^\frown t \cong \{\langle y\rangle^\frown l \mid l \in (\langle z\rangle^\frown s \underset{E\ S}{\|}\ t)\},\ z \to y \notin S$$

$$\langle e\rangle^\frown s \underset{E\ S}{\|}\ \langle e\rangle^\frown t \cong \{\langle e\rangle^\frown l \mid l \in (s \underset{E\ S}{\|}\ t)\}$$

$$\langle z_1\rangle^\frown s \underset{E\ S}{\|}\ \langle z_2\rangle^\frown t \cong \{\},\ \text{where } z_1 \neq z_2$$

$$\langle y_1\rangle^\frown s \underset{E\ S}{\|}\ \langle y_2\rangle^\frown t \cong \{\langle y_1\rangle^\frown l \mid l \in (s \underset{E\ S}{\|}\ \langle y_2\rangle^\frown t)\} \cup$$
$$\{\langle y_2\rangle^\frown l \mid l \in (\langle y_1\rangle^\frown s \underset{E\ S}{\|}\ t)\},\ \text{where } y_1 \leftrightarrow y_2 \notin S$$

$$\langle a\rangle^\frown s \underset{E\ S}{\|}\ \langle b\rangle^\frown t \cong \{\langle k(a,b)\rangle^\frown l \mid l \in (s \underset{E\ S}{\|}\ t)\} \cup$$
$$\{\langle b\rangle^\frown l \mid l \in (\langle a\rangle^\frown s \underset{E\ S}{\|}\ t)\}$$

$$\langle b\rangle^\frown s \underset{E\ S}{\|}\ \langle a\rangle^\frown t \cong \{\langle k(a,b)\rangle^\frown l \mid l \in (s \underset{E\ S}{\|}\ t)\} \cup$$
$$\{\langle b\rangle^\frown l \mid l \in (s \underset{E\ S}{\|}\ \langle a\rangle^\frown t)\}$$

$$\langle c\rangle^\frown s \underset{E\ S}{\|}\ \langle d\rangle^\frown t \cong \{\langle k(c,d)\rangle^\frown l \mid l \in (s \underset{E\ S}{\|}\ t)\} \cup$$
$$\{\langle c\rangle^\frown l \mid l \in (s \underset{E\ S}{\|}\ \langle d\rangle^\frown t)\} \cup \{\langle d\rangle^\frown l \mid l \in (\langle c\rangle^\frown s \underset{E\ S}{\|}\ t)\}$$

A network of timed automata is the parallel composition $A_1 \parallel A_2 \parallel ... \parallel A_n$ of a set of timed automata $A_1, A_2, ..., A_n$.

3.3   The Semantics of Class

OZTA has two kinds of classes, active and passive ones. The behavior of (an object of) an active class can be specified by a record of its continuous interactions with its environment via its time automaton specifications, whereby any update on its data state is hidden. Passive class does not have its own thread of control and its state and operations (processes) are available for use by its controlling object.

In order to address issues like class encapsulation and dynamic typing that are essential for object-orientation, a class model is established which is very similar with [13, 11] except that the Timed Communicating Sequential Process (TCSP) operations are replaced with timed automatons. More detailed information on the semantics of class model can be referred to [13].

4   OZTA Tool

This section introduces the tool **OZTA** we developed for OZTA notation.

OZTA is a tool for modelling, type-checking and projecting complex real-time systems. It mainly consists of four components, i.e., a GUI editor, a type checker, a

LaTeX code generator and a model translator to Uppaal [2] for verification. The input language is based on the syntax and semantics we presented in the previous sections. The output of **OZTA** can either be LaTeX source files of OZTA models or an XML representation of OZTA models (Similar work on the XML representation of Z language family can be found in [16]); **OZTA** can also generate projections of OZTA models which is ready to be taken as input for simulation and verification in Uppaal.

Figure 6 provides an overview of **OZTA**:

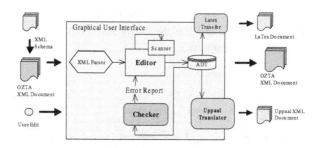

Fig. 6. Class Diagram of **OZTA**

4.1   GUI Editor with Pattern Support

The graphical editor has a main editing panel which consists of a schema editing part and a timed automaton editing part. Implemented with the timed patterns, the editor can support a more systematic design of timed automata. Automatons are generated in a top-down way. Firstly an abstracted default automaton $\mathcal{A}$ of an external choice pattern is automatically generated on the TA editing panel according to its established schema part of the model. Each branch of $\mathcal{A}$ is also an abstracted automaton and respectively represents one of the operation schemas defined on the schema editing panel. The designer can later embody these branches by recursively applying certain patterns until the behavior of the automaton meets its requirements.

4.2   Type Checker

The major functionalities of our **OZTA** type checker are to check syntax errors and to check static semantic errors in the OZTA specification. A full set of type checking rules can be found in our technical report [5].

4.3   LaTeX Code Generator

This generator outputs the LaTeX source file and EPS files for an OZTA model, which can be directly complied and viewed in LaTeX tools such as WinEdt.

4.4   Translator

A model translator is developed and integrated with **OZTA**. It extracts TA and state variables information from OZTA notation and generates an XML representation of Uppaal model for further embodiment and verification.

OZTA to Uppaal. Uppaal is a useful integrated tool for modelling, simulation and verification of real-time systems. The simulation in Uppaal enables examination of possible dynamic executions of a system during early design (or modelling) stages and thus provides an inexpensive mean of fault detection prior to verification by the model checker which covers the exhaustive dynamic behavior of the system. Its model checker is to check invariant and bounded liveness properties by exploring the symbolic state space of a system, i.e., reachability analysis in terms of symbolic states represented by constraints. The description language of Uppaal is a timed automaton extended with a set of locally declared clocks, variables and constants. By projecting an OZTA model to a TA model, we can reuse Uppaal to simulate the dynamic behaviors the OZTA model and verify its various kinds of properties.

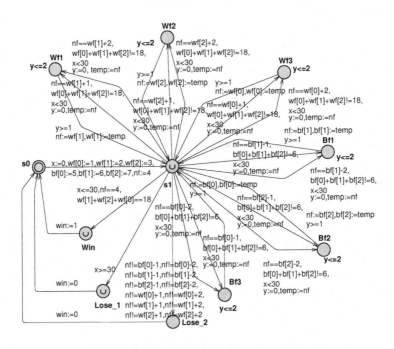

Fig. 7. Frog Puzzle Model in Uppaal

Coupled with operation schema predicates and data structures, the semantics of operation states in the TA part of an OZTA model is slightly different from those of states in Uppaal. However, the main structure of the OZTA automata model is still consistent with that of Uppaal model by regarding the OZTA operation states as abstracted automatons which need further implementation. This gap between the OZTA's TA model and Uppaal's TA model can be remedied by some manual work on the operation states, namely, to further embody these abstracted automatons by adding the data information.

For example, in the frog puzzle game, we map the state variables bf, wf, nf of its OZTA model to the Uppaal model as global *int* variables $bf[3], wf[3], nf$. Due to the limited expressiveness for data manipulation in Uppaal, we need to respectively expand

BlackMove and *WhiteMove* into three branches. The predicates in the operation schemas of the OZTA model are projected as guards on the corresponded transitions. The final Uppaal model can be generated in this way as shown in Figure 7.

Although our projection can handle most of the TA information of an OZTA model, one limitation needed to be pointed out is that, there is no verification tool yet which can support checking the properties related with the partial synchronization and sometime synchronization due to the novelty of this concept.

Model-Checking OZTA Models. To find the solution of this frog puzzle, we can check the following property in Uppaal.

$$E <> P.Win$$

which means that there exists a sequence of moves that will exchange the positions of the black and white frogs within 30 time units.

Uppaal verified that this property actually holds for this given model. Solutions of the puzzle can be visualized in Uppaal's simulator by running its diagnostics trace.

5   Conclusion

The contributions of the paper are listed as follows:

- We enhanced OZTA notation by introducing a set of timed patterns as language construct that can specify the dynamic and timing features of complex real-time systems in a systematic way.
- We presented a semantic model of OZTA in Unifying Theories of Programming which provides the semantic foundation for language understanding, reasoning and tool construction.
- We constructed an OZTA tool which can support editing, type-checking OZTA models as well as transforming OZTA models into TA models so that we can utilize TA model-checkers, e.g., Uppaal for verification.

In our future work, we plan to further enhance our **OZTA** tool by extending the current set of TA patterns into a dynamic pattern library so that new patterns can be defined by system designers and added into the pattern library for future reuse. We are also interested to study other projections, e.g., OZTA to Alloy, so that various properties of an OZTA model can be analyzed in the projected domains. Another future research work would be develop our own verification tool which based on constraint logic programming.

Acknowledgement

We would like to thank Chen Qian, and He Kang for their part of work on the coding of the OZTA tool.

References

1. R. Alur and D. L. Dill. A theory of timed automata. *Theoretical Computer Science*, 126:183–235, 1994.
2. J. Bengtsson, K. G. Larsen, F. Larsson, and P. Pettersson avd W. Yi. UPPAAL - a tool suite for automatic verification of real-time systems. In *Hybrid Systems III: Verification and Control*, pages 232–243. Springer, 1996.
3. E. Boiten, J. Derrick, and G. Smith, editors. *IFM'04: Integrated Formal Methods*, Lect. Notes in Comput. Sci. Springer-Verlag, April 2004.
4. M. Butler, L. Petre, and K. Sere, editors. *IFM'02: Integrated Formal Methods*, Lect. Notes in Comput. Sci. Springer-Verlag, October 2002.
5. J. S. Dong, P. Hao, S. C. Qin, and X. Zhang. OZTA. Technical report TRC6/05, School of Computing, National University of Singapore, 2005.
6. J.S. Dong, R. Duke, and P. Hao. Integrating Object-Z with Timed Automata. In *The 10th IEEE International Conference on Engineering of Complex Computer System*, Shanghai, China, 2005.
7. J.S. Dong, P. Hao, S.C. Qin, J. Sun, and W. Yi. Timed Patterns: TCOZ to Timed Automata. In *The 6th IEEE International Conference on Formal Engineering Methods*, Seattle, 2004.
8. R. Duke and G. Rose. *Formal Object Oriented Specification Using Object-Z*. Cornerstones of Computing. Macmillan, March 2000.
9. C. Fischer and H. Wehrheim. Model-Checking CSP-OZ Specifications with FDR. In *IFM'99: Integrated Formal Methods, York, UK*. Springer-Verlag, June 1999.
10. C.A.R. Hoare and J. He. *Unifying Theories of Programming*. Prentice-Hall, 1998.
11. Z. Liu J. He and X. Li. A relational model for specification of object-oriented systems. Technical report 262, UNU/IIST, 2002.
12. A. Cavalcanti J. Woodcock. The Semantics of Circus. In *The 2th International Conference on Z and B*, LNCS 2272, pages 184–203. Springer-Verlag, 2002.
13. S. C. Qin, J. S. Dong, and W. N. Chin. A Semantic Foundation of TCOZ in Unifying Theory of Programming. In *Formal Methods(FM'03)*, LNCS 2805, pages 321–340. Springer-Verlag, 2003.
14. A. Sherif and J. He. Towards a Timed Model for Circus. In *The 2th IEEE International Conference on Formal Engineering Methods*, Shanghai, 2002.
15. G. Smith. *The Object-Z Specification Language*. Advances in Formal Methods. Kluwer Academic Publishers, 2000.
16. M. Utting, I. Toyn, J. Sun, A. Martin, J. S. Dong, N. Daley, and D. Currie. Zml: Xml support for standard Z. In *3nd International Conference of Z and B Users (ZB'03)*, LNCS. Springer, June 2003.
17. E. N. Wafula and P. A. Swatman. FOOM: A Diagrammatic Illustration of Inter-Object Communication in Object-Z Specifications. In *The 1995 Asia-Pacific Software Engineering Conference (APSEC'95)*. IEEE Press, December 1995.
18. J. Woodcock and A. Cavalcanti. The Semantics of Circus. In *2nd International Conference on Z and B*, volume 2272 of *Lect. Notes in Comput. Sci.*, pages 184–203. Springer-Verlag, 2002.
19. X.Nicollin, J.Sifakis, and S.Yovine. Compiling Real-time Specifications into Extended Autoamta. In *IEEE TSE Special Issue on Real-Time Systems*, volume 18(9), pages 794–804, 1999.

An Abstract Model for Process Mediation*

Michael Altenhofen[1], Egon Börger[2], and Jens Lemcke[1]

[1] SAP Research, Karlsruhe, Germany
{michael.altenhofen, jens.lemcke}@sap.com
[2] Università di Pisa, Dipartimento di Informatica, I-56125 Pisa, Italy
boerger@di.unipi.it
On sabbatical leave at SAP Research, Karlsruhe, Germany
egon.boerger@sap.com

Abstract. We define a high-level model to mathematically capture the behavioural interface of abstract Virtual Providers (VP), their refinements and their composition into rich mediator structures. We show for a Virtual Internet Service Provider example how to use such a model for rigorously formulating and proving properties of interest.

1 Introduction

For the configuration [1] and composition [2,3] of Web services in interaction protocols, a central role is played by process mediation (see MIBIA [4], WSMF [5], WebTransact [6]). We propose here an abstract model for mediators (Sects. 2, 3), viewed as Virtual Providers (VP). The model supports provably correct mediator composition and the definition of appropriate equivalence concepts (Sect. 4), which underlay algorithms for the discovery and run-time selection of services satisfying given requests. In Sect. 5 we illustrate our definitions by a Virtual Internet Service Provider (VISP) case study.

We start with a simple interaction model where each single request receives a single answer from the VP, with no need to relate multiple requests. However, to process single requests the VP has a hierarchical structure at its disposition: Each request arriving at VP is viewed as root of a so-called *seq/par tree* of further requests, which are forwarded to other providers. The children of a request node represent subrequests which are elaborated in sequence. Each subrequest node may have in turn children representing multiple subsubrequests, which are elaborated independently of each other. Nestings of such alternating seq/par trees and other more sophisticated hierarchical subrequest structures can be obtained by appropriate compositions of VPs as defined in Sect. 4.1.

The compositionality of our mediator model stems from an explicit separation of its tree processing component from its communication interfaces for sending and receiving requests and answers. This separation, defined in Sect. 2 on the basis of an abstract message passing system, supports a flexible definition of the service behaviour of VPs and of their behavioural equivalence (Sect. 4), which

---

* Work on this paper was partly funded by the EU-project DIP.

K.-K. Lau and R. Banach (Eds.): ICFEM 2005, LNCS 3785, pp. 81–95, 2005.

also allows one to clearly identify the place of data mediation during the discovery and runtime selection of providers able to satisfy given requests. Furthermore, the separation of communication from proper request processing supports a smooth integration of a variety of workflow and interaction patterns [7,8].

In Sect. 2.3 the single-request oriented model is refined by a notion of internal state, so that the relevant information about previous requests, which may be related to an incoming request, can be extracted from the internal state — in practical Web applications typically by a wrapping session handling module. This refinement step is only a tiny illustration of much more one can do to turn our abstract VP model in a faithful way into fully developed mediator code.

As modelling framework we use Abstract State Machines (ASM),[1] a form of pseudo-code working on arbitrary structures. An introduction into the ASM method for high-level system design and analysis is available in textbook form in [9], but most of what we use here is self-explanatory. The various refinements used are instances of the general ASM refinement concept defined in [10].

2   The Communication Interface of VIRTUALPROVIDERs

We see a Virtual Provider as an interface (technically speaking as an ASM module VIRTUALPROVIDER) providing the following five methods (read: ASMs):

- RECEIVEREQ for receiving request messages (elements of a set *InReqMssg* of legal incoming request messages) from clients,[2]
- SENDANSW for sending answer messages (elements of a set *OutAnswMssg*) back to clients,
- PROCESS to handle request objects, elements of a set *ReqObj* of internal representations of *ReceivedReq*uests, typically by sending to providers a series of subrequests to service the currently handled request *currReqObj*,[3]
- SENDREQ for sending request messages (elements of a set *OutReqMssg*) to providers (possibly other VPs, see the VP composition in Sect. 4.1),
- RECEIVEANSW for receiving incoming answer messages (elements of a set *InAnswMssg*) from providers.

This module view of VIRTUALPROVIDER — as a collection of defined and callable machines, without a main ASM defining the execution flow — separates the specification of the functionality of VP components from that of their schedulers. The underlying architecture is illustrated in Fig. 1.

---

[1] This is not the place for a systematic comparison of different methods. The model developed in this paper starts from scratch, which explains that, besides what is cited in Sect. 6, there is no other related work we used.

[2] Since instances of VIRTUALPROVIDER can be composed (see Sect. 4.1), such a client can be another VP' asking for servicing a subrequest of a received request.

[3] Since the underlying message passing system is abstract, VIRTUALPROVIDER can be instantiated in such a way that also PROCESS itself can be a provider and thus service a subrequest 'internally'. This reflects that the mediation role for a request is different from the role of actually servicing it.

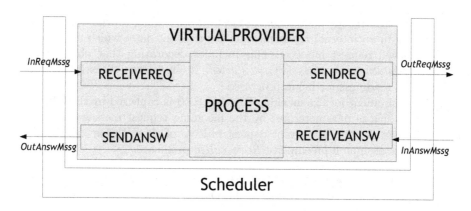

Fig. 1. Architecture

MODULE VIRTUALPROVIDER =
RECEIVEREQ SENDANSW PROCESS SENDREQ RECEIVEANSW

2.1 Abstract Message Passing

For sending and receiving request and answer messages we abstract from a concrete message passing system by using abstract communication interfaces (predicates) for mail boxes of incoming and outgoing messages.

- *ReceivedReq* in RECEIVEREQ expresses that an incoming request message has been received from some client (supposed to be encoded into the message).
- *ReceivedAnsw* in RECEIVEANSW expresses that an answer message (to a previously sent supposed to be retrievable request message) has been received.
- An abstract machine SEND is used a) by SENDANSW for sending out answer messages to requests back to the clients where the requests originated, b) by SENDREQ for sending out requests to providers. We assume the addressees to be encoded into messages.

We separate the internal preparation of outgoing messages in PROCESS from their actual sending in SEND by using the following abstract predicates for mail boxes of outgoing mail:

- *SentAnswToMailer* expresses that an outgoing answer message (elaborated from a PROCESS internal representation of an answer) was passed to SEND.
- *SentReqToMailer* expresses that an outgoing request message (corresponding to an internal representation of a request) has been passed to SEND.

2.2 The SEND and RECEIVE Submachines

The interaction between a client and a VIRTUALPROVIDER, which is triggered by the arrival of a client's request message so that *ReceivedReq(inReqMsg)* becomes true, is characterized by creating a request object (a request ID, say element r of a set *ReqObj* of currently alive request objects), which is appropriately initialized by recording in an internal representation the relevant data, which are encoded in the received request message. This includes decorating that object by an appropriate *status*, say $status(r) := started$, to signal to (the scheduler for) PROCESS its readiness for being processed.

This requirement for the machine RECEIVEREQ is captured by the following definition, which is parameterized by the incoming request message *inReqMsg* and by the set *ReqObj* of current request objects of the VP. For simplicity of exposition we assume a preemptive *ReceivedReq* predicate.[4]

> RECEIVEREQ(*inReqMsg, ReqObj*) = **if** *ReceivedReq*(*inReqMsg*) **then**
>   CREATENEWREQOBJ(*inReqMsg, ReqObj*)
> **where** CREATENEWREQOBJ(*m, R*) =
>   **let** $r = new(R)$[5] **in** INITIALIZE(*r, m*)

The inverse interaction between a VP and a client, which consists in sending back a message providing an answer to a previous request of the client, is characterized by the underlying request object having reached, through further PROCESSing, a *status* where a call to SENDANSW with corresponding parameter *outAnswMsg* has been internally prepared by PROCESS — namely by setting the answer-mailbox predicate *SentAnswToMailer* for this argument to *true*. Thus one can specify SENDANSW, and symmetrically SENDREQ with the request-mailbox predicate *SentReqToMailer*, as follows:

> SENDANSW(*outAnswMsg, SentAnswToMailer*) =
>   **if** *SentAnswToMailer*(*outAnswMsg*) **then** SEND(*outAnswMsg*)

> SENDREQ(*outReqMsg, SentReqToMailer*) =
>   **if** *SentReqToMailer*(*outReqMsg*) **then** SEND(*outReqMsg*)

For the definition of RECEIVEANSW we use as parameter the *AnswerSet* function which provides for every *requester* r, which may have triggered sending some subrequests to subproviders, the *AnswerSet*(r), where to insert (the internal representation of) each *answer* contained in the incoming answer message.[6]

> RECEIVEANSW(*inAnswMsg, AnswerSet*)[7] =
>   **if** *ReceivedAnsw*(*inAnswMsg*) **then**
>   insert *answer*(*inAnswMsg*) into *AnswerSet*(*requester*(*inAnswMsg*))

---

[4] Otherwise a DELETE(*inReqMsg*) has to be added, so that the execution of RECEIVEREQ(*inReqMsg, ReqObj*) switches *ReceivedReq*(*inReqMsg*) to *false*.

[5] *new* is assumed to provide at each application a sufficiently fresh element.

[6] The function *requester*(*inAnswMsg*) is defined below to denote the value of *seqSubReq* in the state when the request message *outReq2Msg*(*s*) for the parallel subrequest *s* was sent out to which the *inAnswMsg* is received now.

[7] Without loss of generality we assume this machine to be preemptive (i. e. *ReceivedAnsw*(*inAnswMsg*) gets false by firing RECEIVEANSW for *inAnswMsg*).

Behavioural Interface Types. Through the definitions below, we link calls of RECEIVEREQ and SENDANSW by the *status* function value for a *currReqObj*. Thus the considered communication interface is of the "provided behavioural interface" type, discussed in [11]: The RECEIVEREQ action corresponds to receive an incoming request, through which a new *reqObj* is created, and occurs before the corresponding SENDANSW action, which happens after the outgoing answer message in question has been *SentAnswToMailer* when *reqObj* was reaching the *status deliver*. The pair of machines SENDREQ and RECEIVEANSW in PROCESS realizes the symmetric "required behavioural interface" communication interface type, where the SEND actions correspond to outgoing requests and thus occur before the corresponding RECEIVEANSW actions of the incoming answers to those requests.

2.3   Refinement by a "State" Component

It is easy to extend RECEIVEREQ to equip VIRTUALPROVIDERs with some state for recording information on previously received requests, to be recognized when for such a request at a later stage some additional service is requested. The changes on the side of PROCESS defined below concern the inner structure of that machine and its refined notion of state and state actions. We concentrate our attention here on the refinement of the RECEIVEREQ machine. This refinement is a simple case of the general ASM refinement concept in [10].

The first addition needed for RECEIVEREQ is a predicate *NewRequest* to check, when an *inReqMsg* is received, whether that message contains a new request, or whether it is about an already previously received request. In the first case, CREATENEWREQOBJ as defined above is called. In the second case, instead of creating a new request object, the already previously created request object corresponding to the incoming request message has to be retrieved, using some function *prevReqObj(inReqMsg)*, to REFRESHREQOBJ by the additional information on the newly arriving further service request. In particular, a decision has to be taken upon how to update the *status(prevReqObj(inReqMsg))*, which depends on how one wants the processing *status* of the original request to be influenced by the additional request or information presented through *inReqMsg*. Since we want to keep the scheme general, we assume that an external scheduling function *refreshStatus* is used in an update $status(r) := refreshStatus(r, inReqMsg)$.[8] This leads to the following refinement of RECEIVEREQ (we skip the parameters *ReqObj*, *prevReqObj*):

RECEIVEREQ(*inReqMsg*) = **if** *ReceivedReq(inReqMsg)* **then**
   if *NewRequest(inReqMsg)* **then**
      CREATENEWREQOBJ(*inReqMsg, ReqObj*)
   else let $r = prevReqObj(inReqMsg)$ **in** REFRESHREQOBJ(*r, inReqMsg*)

---

[8] What if *status(prevReqObj(inReqMsg))* is simultaneously updated by the refined RECEIVEREQ and by PROCESS as defined below? In case of a conflicting update attempt the ASM framework stops the computation; At runtime such an inconsistency is notified by ASM execution engines. Implementations will have to solve this problem in the scheduler of VP.

3   The PROCESSing Submachine of VIRTUALPROVIDERs

In this section we define the signature and the transition rules of the
ASM PROCESS for the processing kernel of a VIRTUALPROVIDER. The definition
provides a schema, which is to be instantiated for each particular PROCESSing
kernel of a concrete VP by giving concrete definitions for the abstract functions
and machines we are going to introduce. For an example see Sect. 5.

Since we want to abstract from the scheduler, which calls PROCESS for
particular current request objects *currReqObj*, we describe the machine as
parametrized by a global instance variable *currReqObj* $\in$ *ReqObj*. The definition
is given in Fig. 2 in terms of control state ASMs, using the standard graphical
representation of finite automata or flowcharts as graphs with circles (for the
internal states, here to be interpreted as current value of *status(currReqObj)*),
rhombuses (for test predicates) and rectangles (for actions).

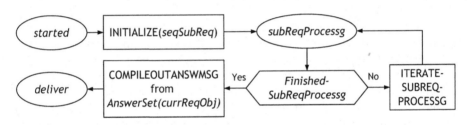

Fig. 2. PROCESSing(*currReqObj*)

Figure 2 expresses that each PROCESSing call for a *started* request object *currReqObj* triggers to INITIALIZE an iterative sequential subrequest processing, namely of the immediate subrequests of this *currReqObj*, in the order defined
by an iterator over a set *SeqSubReq(currReqObj)*. This reflects the first part of
the hierarchical VP request processing view, namely that each incoming (top
level) request object *currReqObj* triggers the sequential elaboration of a finite
number of immediate subrequests, members of a set *SeqSubReq(currReqObj)*,
called sequential subrequests. As explained below, each sequential subrequest
may trigger a finite number of further subsubrequests, which are sent to external providers where they are elaborated independently of each other, so that we
call them parallel subrequests of the sequential subrequest.

PROCESS uses for the elaboration of the sequential subrequests of *currReqObj*
a submachine ITERATESUBREQPROCESSG specified below. Once PROCESS has
FinishedSubReqProcessg, it compiles from *currReqObj* (which allows to access
AnswerSet(currReqObj)) an answer, say *outAnswer(currReqObj)*, and transforms the internal answer information *a* into an element of *OutAnswMssg* using
an abstract function *outAnsw2Msg(a)*. We guard this answer compilation by a
check whether *AnswToBeSent* for the *currReqObj* evaluates to true.

For the sake of illustration we also provide here the textual definition of the
machine defined in Fig. 2. For this purpose we use a function *initStatus* to yield

for a control state ASM its initial control status, which is hidden in the graphical representation. The function $seqSubReq(currReqObj)$ denotes the current item of the iterator submachine ITERATESUBREQPROCESSG defined below.

PROCESS($currReqObj$) =
   if $status(currReqObj) = started$ **then**
      INITIALIZE($seqSubReq(currReqObj)$)
      $status(currReqObj) := subReqProcessg$
   if $status(currReqObj) = subReqProcessg$ **then**
      if $FinishedSubReqProcessg$ **then**
         COMPILEOUTANSWMSG from $currReqObj$
         $status(currReqObj) := deliver$
      else
         $StartNextRound$(ITERATESUBREQPROCESSG)
  where
     COMPILEOUTANSWMSG from o = **if** $AnswToBeSent(o)$ **then**
     $SentAnswToMailer(outAnsw2Msg(outAnswer(o))) := true$
     $StartNextRound(\mathrm{M}) = (status(currReqObj) := initStatus(\mathrm{M}))$

The submachine to ITERATESUBREQPROCESSG is an iterator machine defined in Fig. 3. For every current item $seqSubReq$, it starts to FEEDSENDREQ with a request message to be sent out for every immediate subsubrequest s of the current $seqSubReq$, namely by setting $SentReqToMailer(outReq2Msg(s))$ to $true$. Here $outReq2Msg(s)$ transforms the outgoing request into the format for an outgoing request message, which has to be an element of $OutReqMssg$. Since those immediate subsubrequests, elements of a set $ParSubReq(seqSubReq)$, are assumed to be processable by other providers independently of each other, FEEDSENDREQ elaborates simultaneously for each s an $outReqMsg(s)$.

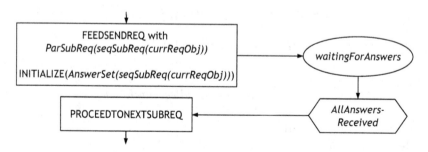

Fig. 3. ITERATESUBREQPROCESSG

Simultaneously ITERATESUBREQPROCESSG also INITIALIZEs the to be computed $AnswerSet(seqSubReq)$ before assuming $status$ value $waitingForAnswers$, where it remains until $AllAnswersReceived$. When $AllAnswersReceived$, the machine ITERATESUBREQPROCESSG will PROCEEDTONEXTSUBREQ.

As long as during *waitingForAnswers*, *AllAnswersReceived* is not yet true, RECEIVEANSW inserts for every *ReceivedAnsw(inAnswMsg)* the retrieved internal *answer(inAnswMsg)* representation into *AnswerSet(seqSubReq)* of the currently processed sequential subrequest *seqSubReq*, which is supposed to be retrievable as *requester* of the incoming answer message.

ITERATESUBREQPROCESSG =
 if *status(currReqObj)* = *initStatus*(ITERATESUBREQPROCESSG) **then**
  FEEDSENDREQ with *ParSubReq(seqSubReq(currReqObj))*
  INITIALIZE(*AnswerSet(seqSubReq(currReqObj))*)
  status(currReqObj) := *waitingForAnswers*
 if *status(currReqObj)* = *waitingForAnswers* **then**
  if *AllAnswersReceived* **then**
   PROCEEDTONEXTSUBREQ
   status(currReqObj) := *subReqProcessg*
 where FEEDSENDREQ with *ParSubReq(seqSubReq)* =
 forall $s \in ParSubReq(seqSubReq)$
  SentReqToMailer(outReq2Msg(s)) := *true*

For the sake of completeness we now define the remaining macros used in Fig. 3, though their intended meaning should be clear from the chosen names. The **Iterator Pattern on** *SeqSubReq* is defined by the following items:

- *seqSubReq*, denoting the current item in the underlying set *SeqSubReq* $\cup$ { *Done(SeqSubReq(currReqObj))* },
- The functions *FstSubReq* and *NxtSubReq* operating on the set *SeqSubReq* and *NxtSubReq* also on *AnswerSet(currReqObj)*,
- The stop element *Done(SeqSubReq(currReqObj))*, constrained by not being an element of any set *SeqSubReq*.

INITIALIZE(*seqSubReq*) = **let** $r = FstSubReq(SeqSubReq(currReqObj))$ **in**
 seqSubReq := r
 ParSubReq(r) := *FstParReq(r, currReqObj)*

FinishedSubReqProcessg =
 seqSubReq(currReqObj) = *Done(SeqSubReq(currReqObj))*

PROCEEDTONEXTSUBREQ =
 let $o = currReqObj$
  $s = NxtSubReq(SeqSubReq(o), seqSubReq(o), AnswerSet(o))$ **in**
  seqSubReq(o) := s
  ParSubReq(s) := *NxtParReq(s, o, AnswerSet(o))*

This iterator pattern foresees that *NxtSubReq* and *NxtParReq* may be determined in terms of the answers accumulated so far for the overall request object, i. e. taking into account the answers obtained for preceding subrequests.

INITIALIZE$(AnswerSet(seqSubReq)) = (AnswerSet(seqSubReq) := \emptyset)$

$AllAnswersReceived = $ **let** $seqSubReq = seqSubReq(currReqObj)$ **in**
for each $req \in ToBeAnswered(ParSubReq(seqSubReq))$
there is some $answ \in AnswerSet(seqSubReq)$

The definition foresees the possibility that some of the parallel subrequest messages, which are sent out to providers, may not necessitate an answer for the VP: A function $ToBeAnswered$ filters them out from the condition $waitingForAnswers$ to leave the current iteration round.

The answer set of any main request object can be defined as a derived function of the answer sets of its sequential subrequests:

$$AnswerSet(reqObj) = Combine(\{AnswerSet(s) \mid s \in SeqSubReq(reqObj)\})$$

4   Mediator Composition and Equivalence Notions

We show how to combine VIRTUALPROVIDERs and how to define their service behaviour, which allows one to define rigorous equivalence notions for VPs one can use a) to formulate algorithms for the discovery and runtime selection of providers suitable to satisfy given requests, and b) to prove VP runtime properties of interest.

4.1   Composing VIRTUALPROVIDERs

Instances $VP_1, \ldots, VP_n$ of VIRTUALPROVIDER can be configured into a sequence with a first VIRTUALPROVIDER VP_1 involving a subprovider VP_2, which involves a subprovider VP_3, etc. For such a composition it suffices to connect the communication interfaces in the appropriate way (see Fig. 1):

- SENDREQ of VP_i with the RECEIVEREQ of VP_{i+1}, which implies that in the message passing environment, the types of the sets $OutReqMssg$ of VP_i and $InReqMssg$ of VP_{i+1} match (via some data mediation).
- SENDANSW of VP_{i+1} with the RECEIVEANSW of VP_i, which implies that in the message passing environment, the types of the sets $OutAnswMssg$ of VP_{i+1} and $InAnswMssg$ of VP_i match (via some data mediation).

Such a sequential composition allows one to configure mediator schemes (see Fig. 4) where each element seq_1 of a sequential subrequest set $SeqSubReq_1$ of an initial request can trigger a set $ParSubReq(seq_1)$ of parallel subrequests par_1, each of which can trigger a set $SeqSubReq_2$ of further sequential subrequests seq_2 of par_1, each of which again can trigger a set $ParSubReq(seq_2)$ of further parallel subrequests, etc. This provides the possibility of unfolding arbitrary alternating seq/par trees. More complex composition schemes can be defined similarly.

4.2   Defining Equivalence Notions for VIRTUALPROVIDERs

To be able to speak about the relation between incoming requests and outgoing answers, one has to relate the elements of the corresponding sets $InReqMssg$ and $OutAnswMssg$ on the provider side (the left hand side in Fig. 1) or

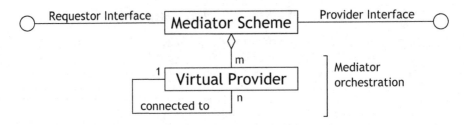

Fig. 4. Mediator Scheme

OutReqMssg and *InAnswMssg* on the requester side of a VIRTUALPROVIDER (the right hand side in Fig. 1). In the first case this comes up to unfold the function *originator*, which for an *outAnswMsg* yields the *inReqMsg* to which *outAnswMsg* represents the answer. In fact this information is retrievable by COMPILEOUTANSWMSG from the *currReqObj*, if it was recorded there by CREATENEWREQOBJ(*inReqMsg*, *ReqObj*) as part of INITIALIZE.

One can then define the *ServiceBehaviour(VP)* of a Virtual Provider *VP* = VIRTUALPROVIDER as (based upon) the correspondence between any *inReqMsg* and the *outAnswMsg* related to it by the *originator* function:

$$originator(outAnswMsg) = inReqMsg$$

Two VIRTUALPROVIDERs *VP*, *VP'* can be considered equivalent if an equivalence relation *ServiceBehaviour(VP)* ≡ *ServiceBehaviour(VP')* holds between their service behaviours. To concretely define such an equivalence involves detailing of the meaning of service 'requests' and provided 'answers', which comes up to providing further detail of the abstract VP model in such a way that the intended 'service' features and how they are 'provided' by VP become visible in concrete locations.

On the basis of such definitions one can then formally define different VPs to be alternatives for a Strategy pattern [12, p. 315] for providing requested services. For the run-time selection of mediators, any suitable provider interface can be viewed as one of the implementations ("mediator orchestration") of a Strategy pattern assigned to a requester interface. This provides the basis for investigating questions like: How can one assure that a provider interface matches the Strategy pattern of the requester? How and starting from which information can one build automatically the Strategy pattern implementations?

5   Illustration: Virtual Internet Service Provider

One of the use cases in the DIP project (see http://dip.semanticweb.org) deals with a *Virtual Internet Service Provider* (VISP). A VISP resells products that are bundled from offerings of different providers. A typical example for such a product bundle is an *Internet presence* including a personal Web server and a personal e-mail address, both bound to a dedicated, user-specific domain name,

e. g. `michael-altenhofen.de`. Such an Internet presence would require this domain name to be registered (at a central registry, e. g. DENIC).

Ideally, the VISP wants to handle domain name registrations in a unified manner using a fixed interface. We assume now that this interface contains only one request message *RegisterDomain*, requiring four input parameters:

- `DomainName`, the name of the new domain that should be registered
- `DomainHolderName`, the name of the domain owner
- `AdministrativeContactName` the name of the domain administrator
- `TechnicalContactName`, the name of the technical contact

On successful registration, the answer will contain four so-called RIPE-Handles,[9] uniquely identifying in the RIPE database the four names provided in the request message. We skip the obvious instantiation of VIRTUALPROVIDER to formalize this VISP.

5.1   A Possible VIRTUALPROVIDER Refinement for *RegisterDomain*

We now consider the case that the VISP is extending it's business into a new country whose domain name registry authority implements a different interface for registering new domain names, say consisting of four request messages:

- *RegisterDH* (`DomainHolderName`),
- *RegisterAC* (`AdministrativeContactName`),
- *RegisterTC* (`TechnicalContactName`),
- *RegisterDN* (`DomainName,DO-RIPE-Handle,AC-RIPE-Handle,`
  `TC-RIPE-Handle`).

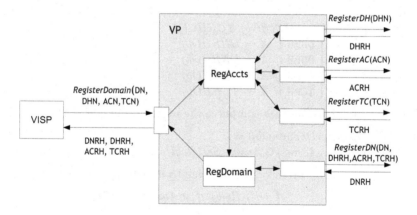

Fig. 5. VIRTUALPROVIDER Instance

A VP instance for that scenario is depicted in Fig. 5.[10] Within this VP, the incoming request *RegisterDomain* is split into a sequence of two subrequests. The

---

[9] RIPE stands for "Réseaux IP Européens", see http://ripe.net.
[10] We use mnemonic abbreviations for the request message and parameter names.

first subrequest is further divided into three parallel subrequests, each registering one of the contacts. Once all answers for these parallel subrequests have been received, the second sequential subrequest can be performed, whose outgoing request message is constructed from the answers of the previous subrequest and the DomainName parameter from the incoming request.

Using the notational convention of appending *Obj* when referring to the internal representations of the different requests, we formalize this VP instance by the following stipulations. We start with refining the INITIALIZE ASM:

INITIALIZE(*RegisterDomainObj, RegisterDomain*(DN, DHN, ACN, TCN) =
   $params(RegisterDomainObj) := \{DN, DHN, ACN, TCN\}$
   $SeqSubReq(RegisterDomainObj) := \{RegAccnts, RegDomain\}$
   $FstSubReq(\{RegAccnts, RegDomain\}) := RegAccnts$
   $NxtSubReq(\{RegAccnts, RegDomain\}, RegAccnts, \_\_) := RegDomain$
   $NxtSubReq(\{RegAccnts, RegDomain\}, RegDomain, \_\_) := nil$
   $FstParReq(RegAccnts, RegisterDomainObj) :=$
       $\{RegisterDH($DHN$), RegisterAC($ACN$),$
       $RegisterTC($TCN$)\}$
   $NxtParReq(RegDomain, RegisterDomainObj, AS) :=$
       $\{RegisterDN($DN$, handle(DHRHObj),$
       $handle(ACRHObj), handle(TCRHObj)\}$
   $AnswToBeSent(RegisterDomainObj) := true$
   $ToBeAnswered(\{RegisterDH, RegisterAC, RegisterTC\}) :=$
       $\{RegisterDH, RegisterAC, RegisterTC\}$
   $ToBeAnswered(\{RegisterDN\}) := \{RegisterDN\}$
   $status(RegisterDomainObj) := started$
where
   $AS = \{DHRHObj, ACRHObj, TCRHObj\}$
   $handle(X) = \begin{cases} \text{DHRH} & \textit{if } X = DHRHObj \\ \text{DNRH} & \textit{if } X = DNRHObj \\ \text{ACRH} & \textit{if } X = ACRHObj \\ \text{TCRH} & \textit{if } X = TCRHObj \end{cases}$

The derived function *Combine* computes the union of the two answer sets:

   $Combine(RegisterDomainObj) =$
   $AnswerSet(RegAccnts) \cup AnswerSet(RegDomain)$

Function *answer* maps an incoming message to its internal representation:

   $answer(inAnswMsg) = \begin{cases} DHRHObj & \textit{if } inAnswMsg = \text{DHRH} \\ DNRHObj & \textit{if } inAnswMsg = \text{DNRH} \\ ACRHObj & \textit{if } inAnswMsg = \text{ACRH} \\ TCRHObj & \textit{if } inAnswMsg = \text{TCRH} \end{cases}$

The abstract function *Formatted* is used to transform the parameters into the format expected by the requester, in our case the VISP:

   $outAnsw2Msg(\{DHRHObj, DNRHObj, ACRHObj, TCRHObj\}) =$
   $Formatted(\{$DNRH, DHRH, ACRH, TCRH$\})$

In [13] we give five other simple examples for refinements of VP to capture the execution semantics of some workflow patterns discussed in [14].

5.2   Proving Properties for VirtualProviders

Once one has a mathematical model of VPs, this can be used to prove properties of interest for the model and its refinements to executable code. We illustrate this by a proof sketch that the two VISPs defined above are equivalent.

The claim follows if we can show the correctness of both VPs with respect to the requested service, namely that any successful initial *inReqMsg* to *RegisterDomain(DN, DHN, ACN, TCN)* will receive an *outAnswMsg* containing four RIPE-Handles, one for each of the *RegisterDomain(DN, DHN, ACN, TCN)* parameters. For the first VP this is trivial under the assumption that the (sub)provider provides real RIPE handles as answers to *RegisterDomain(DN, DHN, ACN, TCN)* requests. For the refined VP, the claim can be stated more precisely by saying that the following holds for every successful pair of *inReqMsg* and corresponding *outAnswMsg* (the correspondence is formally established by their belonging to one *reqObj* in VP; successful refers to the fact that in the example VP we consider only the case of successful registrations, without further interaction between requester and mediator):

Correctness Lemma

For corresponding successful *inReqMsg*, *outAnswMsg* holds :

$RIPE\text{-}Handle(DomainName(inReqMsg)) =$
$DomainNameRipeHan(outAnswMsg)$
$RIPE\text{-}Handle(DomainHolderName(inReqMsg)) =$
$DomHolderNameRipeHan(outAnswMsg)$
$RIPE\text{-}Handle(AdminContactName(inReqMsg)) =$
$AdmContactNameRipeHan(outAnswMsg)$
$RIPE\text{-}Handle(TecContactName(inReqMsg)) =$
$TecContactNameRipeHan(outAnswMsg)$

Here the function *RIPE-Handle* denotes a real-life RIPE handle, which uniquely identifies its argument name in the RIPE database. *DomainNameRipeHan*, etc. denote projection functions, which extract the corresponding information from the *outAnswMsg = Formatted({*DNRH, DHRH, ACRH, TCRH*})*.

Proof. A simple analysis of VISP runs shows that an incoming request message *RegisterDomain(DN, DHN, ACN, TCN)* triggers VP to Send first three subrequests *RegisterDH(DHN)*, *RegisterAC(ACN)*, *RegisterTC(TCN)*, which are (assumed to be) answered by RIPE handles *DHRH, ACRH, TCRH*. Then VP Sends the subrequest *RegisterDN(DN, DHRH, ACRH, TCRH)*, which is (assumed to be) answered by a domain name ripe handle *DNRH*. By definition of the *answer* function, the *outAnswMsg* contains a *Formatted* version of the four RIPE handles obtained for the parameters in the *inReqMsg*, from where the projection functions extract these RIPE handles.

We want to stress that the proof works only under the assumption that the subproviders work correctly, i. e. that they provide upon request ripe handles for domain holder names, administrative contact names, technical contact names and domain names. This is the best one can prove for VP, which is only a mediator and relies for the correctness of the provided service upon the correctness of its subproviders.

6   Conclusions and Future Work

Our formal, high-level ASM model of process mediation provides a basis for *"communicating and documenting design ideas"* and supports *"an accurate and checkable overall understanding"* of the controversially discussed topic of process mediation, a part of the Semantic Web services (SWS) usage process [4,5,6]. ASM models can help to provide *explicit, exact and formal specifications* with an accurate meaning of all underlying terms, needed to produce a consistent view of the general SWS usage process. Furthermore, the ASM method allows to *"isolate the hard part of a system"* [9, p. 14-15] and thus to concentrate on the essential parts for refinement, targeted at bridging controversial approaches, like dynamic composition vs. static composition, through explicitly showing their differences by deriving them as different refinements of the same abstractions. We look for more involved practical instantiations of VIRTUALPROVIDER than the simple one illustrated in Sect. 5. Another direction of research concerns replacing the simple communication patterns used by VP by more complex ones. RECEIVEREQ and SENDANSW are identified in [15] as basic bilateral service interaction patterns, namely as mono-agent ASM modules RECEIVE and SEND; The FEEDSENDREQ submachine together with SENDREQ in PROCESS realize an instance of the basic multilateral mono-agent service interaction pattern called ONETOMANYSEND in [15], whereas the execution of RECEIVEANSW in ITERATESUBREQPROCESSG until *AllAnswersReceived* is an instance of the basic multilateral mono-agent ONEFROMMANYRECEIVE pattern from [15]. One can refine VP to concrete business process applications by enriching the communication flow structure built from basic service interaction patterns as analysed in [15].

Besides the mediation and composition topics, VP has proven to be useful as a basis for formal specifications of distributed semantic discovery frameworks. As shown in [16], only minor changes on the VP structure are required in order to specify a formal, high-level ASM model of distributed semantic discovery services. The different distribution and semantic matchmaking strategies, depending on the technology used for an implementation of a discovery service, can be derived as different refinements of the same abstractions.

References

1. Stumptner, M.: Configuring web services. In: Proceedings of the Configuration Workshop at the 16th European Conference on Artificial Intelligence (ECAI). (2004) 10–1/10–6
2. Pistore, M., Barbon, F., Bertoli, P., Shaparau, D., Traverso, P.: Planning and monitoring web service composition. In: AIMSA. (2004) 106–115

3. Lee, Y., Patel, C., Chun, S.A., Geller, J.: Compositional knowledge management for medical services on semantic web. In: WWW (Alternate Track Papers & Posters). (2004) 498–499
4. Bornhövd, C., Buchmann, A.: Semantically meaningful data exchange in loosely coupled environments. In: Proceedings of the International Conference on Information Systems Analysis and Synthesis (ISAS). (2000)
5. Fensel, D., Bussler, C.: The web service modeling framework wsmf. Electronic Commerce Research and Applications **1** (2002) 113–137
6. Pires, P.F., Benevides, M.R.F., Mattoso, M.: Building reliable web services compositions. In: Web, Web-Services, and Database Systems. (2002) 59–72
7. van der Aalst, W.M.P., ter Hofstede, A.H.M., Kiepuszewski, B., Barros, A.P.: Workflow patterns. Distributed and Parallel Databases **14** (2003) 5–51
8. Barros, A., Dumas, M., ter Hofstede, A.: Service interaction patterns: Towards a reference framework for service-based business process interconnection. Technical report, Faculty of IT, Queensland University of Technology (2005)
9. Börger, E., Stärk, R.F.: Abstract State Machines. A Method for High-Level System Design and Analysis. Springer (2003)
10. Börger, E.: The ASM refinement method. Formal Aspects of Computing **15** (2003) 237–257
11. Barros, A., Dumas, M., Oaks, P.: A critical overview of the web services choreography description language (WS-CDL). White paper (2005)
12. Gamma, E., Helm, R., Johnson, R., Vlissides, J.: Design patterns: elements of reusable object-oriented software. Addison-Wesley Longman Publishing Co., Inc., Boston, MA, USA (1995)
13. Altenhofen, M., Börger, E., Lemcke, J.: An execution semantics for mediation patterns. In: Proc. of 2nd WSMO Implementation Workshop WIW'2005, Innsbruck, Austria, CEUR Workshop Proceedings (2005) ISSN 1613-0073, online CEUR-WS.org/Vol-134/lemcke-wiw05.pdf.
14. Cimpian, E., Mocan, A.: D13.7 v0.1 Process mediation in WSMX – WSMX working draft (2005) http://www.wsmo.org/TR/d13/d13.7/v0.1/.
15. Barros, A., Börger., E.: A compositional framework for service interaction patterns and communication flows. In: Proc. 7th International Conference on Formal Engineering Methods (ICFEM). LNCS, Springer (2005)
16. Friesen, A.: A high-level specification for semantic web service discovery framework. In preparation (2005)

How Symbolic Animation Can Help Designing an Efficient Formal Model

Fabrice Bouquet, Frédéric Dadeau, and Bruno Legeard

Laboratoire d'Informatique (LIFC),
Université de Franche-Comté, CNRS - INRIA,
16, route de Gray - 25030 Besançon cedex, France
{bouquet, dadeau, legeard}@lifc.univ-fcomte.fr

Abstract. This paper presents a non-conventional application of symbolic animation. We propose to assist the modeller in building an efficient formal model, by automatically detecting potential weaknesses or imprecisions in the model. We propose to detect inconsistencies within the formal models written with pre- and postconditions, and to point out unusual model properties, such as a weak invariant or unreachable effects. Our approach is based on constraint solving technologies to perform the animation and to detect the various problems.

Keywords: Symbolic animation, properties detection, weak invariant, strong preconditions, unreachable effects, constraints.

1 Introduction

The use of formal models is widely spread in the software design process. A large variety of formal languages is available for formalizing specifications. Each notation is most of the time well tool-supported, providing proof or model-checking techniques to verify the model, to ensure that no invariants are violated and so on. Apart from this *verification* process, there exists a need to build the most complete model possible, which can not be done using verification. To illustrate this statement, it is obvious to see that a model can be proved with respect to its invariant if the latter contains only weak properties.

The *validation* phase consists in checking the conformance of the model w.r.t. initial requirements usually written in natural language. One of the most important techniques for validating a model is to animate it. Unlike many kinds of animation, which require human intervention to select which operation to activate and which input values to provide, we have chosen to use symbolic animation, relying on a constraint solver, to perform the animation. The principle of symbolic animation is to gather the system states within a constraint system, and to consider the execution of an operation as solving a Constraint Satisfaction Problem (CSP). As a consequence, the user no longer has to provide input values when invoking each operation; inputs are constrained by their definition domain and the operation's preconditions.

K.-K. Lau and R. Banach (Eds.): ICFEM 2005, LNCS 3785, pp. 96–110, 2005.

In this paper, we propose a way to assist the modeller when writing a formal model. We focus on models expressed using a pre- and postcondition semantics, and we illustrate this approach using B abstract machines [1]. We perform symbolic animation with customized algorithms to point out potential problems that may occur in the model, and help the modeller in designing an efficient model. By "efficient" we mean that we want the model not only to respect its invariant, but to contain no unintended behaviour such as deadlocks, weak invariant, unactivable operations, etc. This is different from the model checking point of view, since we propose to assist the modeller in the validation of the formal model, by looking for specific imprecisions. Moreover, this process does not require any human assistance and has therefore been fully automated, with interesting results. In addition, this approach is complementary to the model proof, since proof can lead to undecidability or non-termination problems. Our proposal is to point out *"warnings"*, resulting of model's imprecisions. The modeller is then free to consider them or not, since the problems which have raised warnings may be intended or not.

The paper is organized as follows. Section 2 gives an overview of the formal notation. It also introduces a running example. Section 3 presents the symbolic animation and the way it realized within our framework. Section 4 gives the formal definitions that will be used in Section 5 to describe the kind of properties we propose to detect. Section 6 presents the algorithms and techniques employed. Finally, Section 7 presents the related work, and Section 8 concludes.

2 Formal Modeling

We use the B abstract machine notation [1], as a formal specification language for our study. This section introduces the notation and an example which will be used throughout the remainder of the paper.

2.1 The B Abstract Machine Notation

The B Abstract Machine Notation (AMN) has been introduced by J.-R. Abrial. It consists of a language for expressing models as "machines", which are the highest level of abstraction existing within the B method. This notation makes it possible to express abstract data types, such as sets, and provides a wide syntax for expressing predicates with first order logic enriched by set and relational/functional symbols.

The AMN describes a system in terms of several clauses, each one representing a specific part of the system, expressed either by predicates, for the static part (constants, assertions, invariant, etc.), or by generalized substitutions for the dynamic part (variables, initialization and operations). The operational semantics is given by a Labeled Transition System (LTS), where the transition between the states are given by the operations.

A machine is proved if the invariant properties are established by the initialization and preserved through the execution of an operation.

```
MACHINE
    scheduler

SETS
    PID = {p1,p2,p3,p4,p5}

VARIABLES
    active, ready, waiting

INVARIANT
    active ⊆ PID ∧
    ready ⊆ PID ∧
    waiting ⊆ PID ∧
    waiting ∩ ready = ∅ ∧
    active ∩ ready = ∅ ∧
    active ∩ waiting = ∅ ∧
    card(active) ≤ 1

INITIALIZATION
    active, ready, waiting := ∅,∅,∅

OPERATIONS
    new(pp) ≙ PRE pp ∈ PID ∧
                 pp ∉ active ∧
                 pp ∉ ready ∧
                 pp ∉ waiting ∧
             THEN
                 waiting := waiting ∪ {pp}
             END;
```

```
    del(pp) ≙ PRE pp ∈ waiting THEN
                  waiting := waiting \ {pp}
              END;

    ready(pp) ≙ PRE pp ∈ waiting THEN
                    waiting := waiting \ {pp} ||
                    IF (active = ∅) THEN
                        active := active ∪ {pp}
                    ELSE
                        ready := ready ∪ {pp}
                    END
                END;

    swap(pp) ≙ PRE pp ∈ active THEN
                   waiting := waiting ∪ {pp} ||
                   IF (ready = ∅) THEN
                       active := ∅
                   ELSE
                       ANY pp1 WHERE
                           pp1 ∈ ready
                       THEN
                           active := {pp1} ||
                           ready := ready \ {pp1}
                       END
                   END
               END
END
```

Fig. 1. The B machine of the process Scheduler

Definition 1 (B Machine Proof Obligations). *Let $\mathcal{I}nv$ be the invariant predicate and Init be the initialization substitution, the following predicate has to be proved, to ensure that the initialization establishes the invariant:*

$$[Init]\mathcal{I}nv \tag{1}$$

In order to prove that the preservation of the invariant by the different operations, the following predicate has to hold for each operation Op of the machine:

$$\mathcal{I}nv \Rightarrow [Op]\mathcal{I}nv \tag{2}$$

Remark: In these equations, we denote by $[S]P$ the application of the generalized substitution S to the predicate P, as described in [1].

2.2   Running Example

Figure 1 presents the example which will be used throughout the remainder of the paper. This example describes a simple process scheduler [4], and their access to a shared resource. Each process is identified by a Process Identifier (PID). Each process may be either active, when it accesses the resource, ready, when it is asking for the resource but another process is already active, or waiting, when the process is done with the resource. The set of process identifiers is a constant, with a given value.

The model presents four operations. The first one, *new*, creates a new process from the set of available processes, and puts it in the waiting state. On the other hand, the *del* operation deletes a waiting process. The *ready* operation moves a waiting process to the active state, if no other process is currently active, or to the ready state otherwise. Finally, the *swap* operation makes the active process return to the waiting state, and a non-deterministic choice is made among the ready processes to select the new active process. At the initial state, there are no processes in the system.

3   Symbolic Animation

The symbolic animation is performed using an underlying constraint solver which makes it possible to gather the system states within a constraint store. Expressing the operations in terms of before-after predicates leads to considering the execution of an operation as a Constraint Satisfaction Problem between variables from both before and after states. In order to express the operations as before-after predicates, we translate the generalized B substitutions according to [1] (p. 262) into predicates. Moreover, we decompose these predicates into *effect predicates* (called *effects*) which can be considered as a Disjunctive Normal Form of the before-after predicates, onto which factorizing and re-ordering have been applied, named the EDNF and described in [3].

Definition 2 (Effects). *An effect is a subpart of an operation. It is denoted by $effect_N(Op)$, where N is the number of the effect and Op is the name of the operation.*

$$op \in \mathcal{O} \Rightarrow op = effect_1(op) \; [] \ldots [] \; effect_N(op) \qquad (3)$$

We express with the $[]$ operator the choice between different effects.

Throughout the remainder of the paper, we denote by $\mathcal{E}\!f\!f$ the set of effects that can be extracted from all the operations of the considered machine.

Extracting an Effect. Effects are extracted from the EDNF of a before-after predicate representing an operation. The variable assignments are expressed by equalities between the primed version of the variable –representing the after-value– and its new value. We introduce a choice operator $[]$ to symbolize a choice-point within the predicate.

Example 1 (Computation of the effects from example's operation). The effects extracted from the different operations of the example are given in Fig. 2. In this figure, the *skip* operation states that the unmodified variables remain at the same value. For space reasons, the state variables `active`, `ready` and `waiting` are represented by their first letter (a, r, w respectively).

Note that the IF...THEN...ELSE...END structure is expressed as a choice-point between two mutually exclusive predicates, and the ANY...WHERE...THEN...END structure is expressed as an existential quantification.

Fig. 2. Effects extracted from the operations of the Scheduler example

Operation	Effect
new	$pp \in PID \wedge pp \notin (a \cup r \cup w) \wedge w' = w \cup \{pp\} \wedge skip$
del	$pp \in w \wedge w' = w\backslash\{pp\} \wedge skip$
ready	$pp \in w \wedge w' = w \setminus \{pp\} \wedge a = \emptyset \wedge a' = a \cup \{pp\} \wedge skip$
	$pp \in w \wedge w' = w \setminus \{pp\} \wedge a \neq \emptyset \wedge r' = r \cup \{pp\} \wedge skip$
swap	$pp \in a \wedge w' = w \cup \{pp\} \wedge r = \emptyset \wedge a = \emptyset \wedge skip$
	$pp \in a \wedge w' = w \cup \{pp\} \wedge r \neq \emptyset \wedge$
	$(\exists\, pp_1.pp_1 \in r \wedge a' = \{pp_1\} \wedge r' = r\backslash\{pp_1\}) \wedge skip$

4   Preliminary Definitions

This section gives the preliminary definitions that will be used through the remainder of the paper.

Definition 3 (System States). *Let $\mathcal{V}$ be the set of system variables, and $\mathcal{D_V}$ be the set of variable domains of $\mathcal{V}$. A system state is an instantiation of the state variables according to their domain. The set of system states is denoted by $\mathcal{S}$, and we have:*

$$\mathcal{S} = \mathcal{V} \rightarrow \mathcal{D_V} \tag{4}$$

The state space is built on the Cartesian product of the state variables' domains. Notice that the variable's domains have to be known and finite.

Example 2. In our example $\mathcal{S}$ is defined by:

$$S = \{ (active = X, ready = Y, waiting = Z) \mid$$
$$(X, Y, Z) \in \mathbb{P}(PID) \times \mathbb{P}(PID) \times \mathbb{P}(PID) \}$$

4.1   Systems Transitions

A transition between two system states is defined by the activation of an effect. The effects are extracted from the operations. An operation is defined by a 4-tuple $\langle O, L, Pre, Post \rangle$, where O is the operation name, L is the set of local variables, Pre is the precondition of the operation, and $Post$ is its postcondition, expressed as a before-after predicate.

In the remainder of the paper, we will denote by $Pre(T)$, the precondition component of the transition T (either an effect or an operation). By extension, we will also denote by $Pre(T)(s)$ the evaluation of the precondition of the transition T within the system state defined by s.

Definition 4 (Effect Activation). *Let s_1 and s_2 be two system states from $\mathcal{S}$, let eff be an effect from the set of effects $\mathcal{Eff}$. The activation of the effect eff between s_1 and s_2 is possible if and only if the effect's predicates are satisfiable.*

$$s_1 \xrightarrow{\text{eff}} s_2 \Leftrightarrow Pre(\text{eff})(s_1) \wedge Post(\text{eff})(s_1, s_2) \text{ holds} \tag{5}$$

An operation is called "executable" if and only if one of its effects can be activated from the considered state.

Definition 5 (Reachable States). *A reachable state is a system state that can be reached from one of the initial states and through a sequence of effect activations. We denote by $\mathcal{R}(s)$ the fact that s is a reachable state, and we have:*

$$\forall s \in \mathcal{S} . \ Init(s) \Rightarrow \mathcal{R}(s) \tag{6}$$

$$\forall s_1, s_2 \in \mathcal{S} . \ (\mathcal{R}(s_1) \wedge \exists \ eff \in \mathcal{E}ff \ / \ s_1 \xrightarrow{eff} s_2) \Rightarrow \mathcal{R}(s_2) \tag{7}$$

We propose to replace the reachable states, which may only be known by computing the complete reachability graph, with the virtually reachable states.

Definition 6 (Virtually Reachable States). *A virtually reachable state is a system state that can be reached by activating an effect from any states of the system. We denote by $\mathcal{VR}(s)$ the fact that s is virtually reachable, and we have:*

$$\mathcal{VR}(s) \Leftrightarrow \exists \ s_1 \in \mathcal{S} \ / \ (\exists \ eff \in \mathcal{E}ff / s_1 \xrightarrow{eff} s) \tag{8}$$

4.2 Using Symbolic Animation

The use of symbolic animation induces the gathering of several states within a single constrained state. As a consequence, and considering a constraint store $\mathcal{C}$, the concrete states associated to $\mathcal{C}$, denoted by $S_{\mathcal{C}}$ is defined by:

$$S_{\mathcal{C}} = \{s \in \mathcal{S} \mid \mathcal{C}(s)\} \tag{9}$$

where $\mathcal{C}(s)$ means that the variables in state s satisfy the constraints of $\mathcal{C}$.

Thus, activating an effect means moving from one constraint system to another, which is the addition of the effect predicate to the original constraint system. The consistency of the resulting constraint system determines whether the effect is activable or not. The activation of effects from a constrained environment is defined by:

$$S_{\mathcal{C}_1} \xrightarrow{eff_i(op)} S_{\mathcal{C}_2} \tag{10}$$

Example 3 (Illustration of the activation of an effect). Consider the example in Fig. 1, the activation of the effect from the **new** operation from a constraint system $S_{\mathcal{C}_1} = \{(active = A, ready = R, waiting = W) \mid P_1(A, R, W)\}$ leads to a constraint system $S_{\mathcal{C}_2}$ defined by:

$$S_{\mathcal{C}_2} = \{(active = A', ready = R', waiting = W') \mid$$
$$(P_1(A, R, W) \wedge pp \in PID \wedge pp \notin (A \cup R \cup W)$$
$$W' = W \cup \{pp\} \wedge A' = A \wedge R' = R)\}$$

Symbolic animation is an efficient and powerful means to perform animation, by gathering many "concrete" states under the scope of one constraint system. As a consequence, this reduces the reachability graph size and leaves the user free to instantiate or not the parameters of the operation.

4.3   System States and Invariant

The system states are given by the typing information. In the formal model this information is given by the data types, or by a specific part of the invariant.

We propose to detect properties w.r.t. the set of states respecting the invariant. We call invariant the properties, written by the modeller, that the system has to preserve at each state of the system. The invariant is presented as a set of states, subset of the system states, as illustrated hereby.

System states   Invariant

Example 4 (Illustration of the Invariant State Space). Consider the example given in Fig 1. The invariant state space, denoted by $\mathcal{I}nv_{xmpl}$, is given by:

$$
\begin{aligned}
\mathcal{I}nv_{xmpl} = \{&(active = A, ready = R, waiting = W) \mid \\
&(A \subseteq \{p1, p2, p3, p4, p5\} \wedge R \subseteq \{p1, p2, p3, p4, p5\} \wedge \\
&W \subseteq \{p1, p2, p3, p4, p5\} \wedge A \cap R = \emptyset \wedge R \cap W = \emptyset \wedge \\
&A \cap W = \emptyset \wedge card(A) \leq 1)\}
\end{aligned} \tag{11}
$$

5   Characterization of the Properties to Detect

This section presents the different properties we want to detect using the symbolic animation. We suppose that the model has been proved (automatically or interactively), i.e., that the invariant is established by the initialization and preserved by the execution of the different operations.

Some of the properties that are presented here can be checked statically, other may only be checked dynamically, by activating successive effects of the system operations.

5.1   Statically Detectable Properties

We describe here the static properties we intend to detect. These properties will concern the system states as well as the system transitions.

Definition 7 (Deadlock State). *A deadlock state is defined as a state from which no effect precondition holds.*

$$
\exists\, s \in \mathcal{S} \wedge \forall\, eff \in \mathcal{E}ff \; . \; \neg Pre(eff)(s) \tag{12}
$$

The deadlock property is directly inspired from the model-checking techniques. The consequence of reaching a deadlock state is that the system can not evolve, and remains in this given state.

Definition 8 (Light Invariant Weakness). *An invariant is said to be lightly weak if and only if there exists states that satisfy the invariant without being virtually reachable.*

$$
\exists\, s \in \mathcal{S}/Inv(s) \wedge \neg \mathcal{VR}(s) \tag{13}
$$

If the model is proved, then we have the guarantee that the reachable states satisfy the invariant. Reasoning on the state spaces, the set of reachable states is included within the set of states respecting the invariant. Nevertheless, if the invariant is (too) weak, then there may exist a large state space that satisfies the invariant without being reachable, as displayed hereby. The objective is to help the modeller in refining the model's invariant so that the reachable system states and the invariant are the tightest possible.

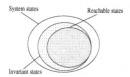

Thus, without performing any animation, it is possible to have a first idea of the presence of a weak invariant. This statement has to be refined later using the symbolic animation, to compute on-the-fly the unreachable states.

Definition 9 (Effect Inconsistency). *An effect eff is said to be inconsistent if and only if there exists no state from which the effect can be activated.*

$$\forall s_1 \in \mathcal{S} \, . \, (\neg \exists s_2 \in \mathcal{S}/s_1 \overset{eff}{\to} s_2) \tag{14}$$

We can notice that inconsistent effects are easily discarded by a proof engine, since they directly lead the proof obligation to be obviously true. Nevertheless, such a mistake, made by the modeller, may have important consequences, since the model is "proved" for wrong reasons!

Definition 10 (General Effect Activability). *An effect eff is said to be generally activable if and only if there exists a state in which its preconditions are true.*

$$\exists s \in \mathcal{S}/Pre(eff)(s) \tag{15}$$

The general effect activability property gives the modeller a first indication on the executability of its operation. If no effect from a given operation can be activated, then we can conclude that the operation can never be executed.

Definition 11 (Weak Preconditions). *The precondition of the operation is said to be weak if and only if the set of system states from which the operation effects can be activated is a strict subset of the system states satisfying the preconditions of the considered operation.*

Weak preconditions detection is similar to comparing the weakest precondition of the operation –computed by *wp*-calculus– and the actual precondition of the operation. It helps detecting the state variables values, but also the input values, which satisfy the preconditions, but are "filtered" for the execution of the operation itself, and so, are obsolete.

Determining potential error statically is interesting, but not really sufficient in the actual process. Therefore, we propose to refine our detections to put them in a dynamic context, in order to get more accurate results.

5.2   Dynamically Detectable Properties

We describe here the properties we intend to detect using an automatically-driven symbolic animation engine. The properties described here are already checkable from the static point of view, but they bring more accurate results when checked dynamically.

Definition 12 (Effect Activability). *An effect is said to be activable if and only if there exists a reachable state in which the precondition of the effect is true.*

$$\exists\, s \in \mathcal{S} \ /\ \mathcal{R}(s) \ \wedge \ Pre(\mathit{eff})(s) \tag{16}$$

where eff is the considered effect. By extension, the non-activability of an effect is detected if and only if there is no reachable state that satisfy the preconditions of the effect.

$$\forall\, s \in \mathcal{S} \ .\mathcal{R}(s) \Rightarrow \neg Pre(\mathit{eff})(s) \tag{17}$$

The detection of never activated effects leads –in practice– to pointing out potentially too strong preconditions, that may be unintended by the modeller. Since effects can be activable in a general context, an animation may detect that, for a given search-depth, certain effect may never be activated.

Definition 13 (Weak Invariant). *A weak invariant is detected when there exists unreachable system states that satisfy the invariant.*

$$\exists\, s \in S \ /\ \mathcal{I}nv(s) \wedge \neg \mathcal{R}(s) \tag{18}$$

The invariant weakness detection refines the light invariant weakness detection in the sense that it focuses on the actual unreachable states that satisfy the invariant.

Definition 14 (Reachable Deadlock). *A reachable deadlock is detected when there exists a reachable system state that does not satisfy any effect precondition.*

$$\exists\, s \in S \ /\ (\mathcal{R}(s) \wedge \forall\, \mathit{eff} \in \mathcal{E}\mathit{ff} \ . \ \neg Pre(\mathit{eff})(s)) \tag{19}$$

The general deadlock detection, working on the whole system state space, is refined by the dynamic detection of deadlocks. If a deadlock is detected by the previous method, the dynamic detection is in charge of checking whether or not the deadlock states can be reached from the initial state.

After having characterized the properties we propose to check, we present how these properties can be detected using CSP-solving and symbolic animation.

6   Processing the Detections

Our main contribution on these problems is the use of symbolic animation to process these detections. The detections are processed using the BZ-Testing-Tools [2] technology, which provides a symbolic animation engine and customized constraint solvers. After a short discussion on our process relevance, this section presents the verification principles used for each detection, based on the definitions given in the previous section.

6.1   Preliminary Discussion

Since the reachability problem is undecidable, we have chosen to bound our researches to a certain depth, which may guarantee the termination of our algorithms. Usually, when looking for errors, such as breaking invariants and so on, we can not ensure that if no error is found, then there actually is are errors. On the other hand, if an error is found, we guarantee its existence, as explained in [8]. In this particular case of potential error detections, it is the opposite.

When a problem is found, because of the search-depth limitation there is no guarantee that this problem may still occur with a deeper search. On the contrary, when no errors are found (e.g. all effects are activable) we have this guarantee. We believe this is a real assistance to the modeller, despite the depth limitation, since it can (i) improve the quality of the model, (ii) guarantee that certain effects are reachable and consistent (which allows the modeller to focus on the remaining effects), and (iii) help to explain why automated test generation tools can not produce test cases for one particular operation/effect.

6.2   Processing Static Detections

Static detections are performed from the largest possible set of states. This is represented by the typing invariant or the data typing. In practice, this set of states is expressed by a constraint system, which only assigns the domains of the state variables. On the example, it is given by the $\mathcal{S}_{xmpl}$ constraint system. Most of the properties detection is then considered as a constraint satisfaction problem (CSP).

Detecting Deadlocks. Deadlocks can be detected by checking the non-satisfiability of all the effects preconditions within the constraint system representing the state space to consider. Nevertheless, we can refine this process by considering the virtually reachable state space $\mathcal{VR}$. In this case, each effect is activated from the state space constraint system, creating a new constraint system which represents a subset of the virtually reachable states for the considered effect. We can then perform the same verification. Restricted to a smaller set of states, the results will be more accurate.

Let $\mathcal{S}_{C_{VR}} = \{X \mid VR(X)\}$ be the constraint system representing the virtually reachable state space. The goal is then to find the values of the state variables X that satisfy the constraint $VR(X) \wedge \forall\, eff \in \mathcal{E}ff.\neg Pre(eff)$. The solutions to this CSP presents a counter-example representing a concrete deadlock state.

Detecting Light Invariant Weakness. A light invariant weakness is detected by checking the satisfiability of the constraint systems representing the invariant state space, $\mathcal{S}_{C_{inv}} = \{X \mid Inv(X)\}$ and and the refutation of the constraint system representing the virtually reachable state space $\mathcal{S}_{C_{VR}} = \{X \mid VR(X)\}$.

The goal is to find the values of the state variables X that satisfy the constraint $Inv(X) \wedge \neg VR(X)$. The solutions to this CSP presents a counter-example illustrating the weakness of the invariant.

Detecting Effect Inconsistencies. Effect inconsistencies are deduced by *reducing* the effect predicate within the constraint system representing the state space. If the resulting store is inconsistent, then the effect is also inconsistent.

Example 5. Considering the Scheduler example in Fig. 1 and its state space defined by $\mathcal{S}_{xmpl}$ described in example 4. By modifying the **new** operation, we may have:

```
new(pp) ≙ PRE pp ∈ PID ∧ pp ∉ active ∧ pp ∉ ready ∧ pp ∉ waiting
         THEN
                 IF (pp ∈ waiting) THEN
                    skip
                 ELSE
                    waiting := waiting ∪ {pp}
                 END
         END;
```

which is not a mistake, but this may produce the following inconsistent effect predicate, if we consider the IF...THEN branch:

$$pp \in PID \land pp \notin a \land pp \notin r \land pp \notin w \land pp \in w \land w' = w \land a' = a \land r' = r \quad (20)$$

We detect an obvious inconsistency between $pp \notin waiting \land pp \in waiting$. As a consequence, the skip statement located in the IF...THEN branch is unreachable.

This kind of errors is classic, in models as well as in programs, especially when encapsulating IF...THEN...ELSE structures. Notice that this kind of error can not be detected by the proof, since it simplifies the proof obligation formula which becomes obviously true.

In case of parallel composition of substitutions, such as in B, the combination of parallel predicates frequently creates inconsistent effects. Reporting them is can be seen as insignificant, since it may represent "false negatives", but it can also be seen as an indication that the operation was not written in the most efficient way, introducing contradictory predicates, as in the previous example.

Detecting General Effect Inactivability. Effects can be considered as inactivable if the precondition of the effect can never be satisfied in any state of the system. Once again, if the system's invariant preservation is proved then we can reason from the invariant state space.

We process the detection by *reducing* the effect preconditions within the constraint system representing either the complete state space, or the invariant state space.

Example 6 (Detecting an Inactivable Effect). Consider the example given in Fig. 1. By modifying the precondition of the **del** operation, we may have:

```
del(pp) ≙ PRE pp ∈ waiting ∧ pp ∈ ready THEN
              waiting := waiting \ {pp}
          END;
```

By trying to reduce this predicate within the constraint system representing the invariant state space, we get an inconsistency between $pp \in waiting \land pp \in ready$ (in the operation) and $waiting \cap ready = \emptyset$ (in the invariant).

This kind of error may also be found in multiple IF...THEN...ELSE...END structures. Once again, proof is unable to detect this kind of mistake, for the same reasons.

Detecting Weak Preconditions. Weak preconditions are detected by reducing the precondition of the operation within the constraint system S_C representing the state space S. In parallel, we activate all the possible effects from the S_C constraint system. As a consequence, new constraint systems, denoted by S_{C_1}, ..., S_{C_N} and representing the new states after the activation of N effects, extracted from the considered operation, are created. In these constraint systems, the values of the variables before and the inputs are still available, and can then be extracted. By refuting the constraints in S_C with regard to constraints stored in the S_{C_i}, we are able to exhibit values for inputs and state variables which are allowed by the precondition of the operation, but are useless for the operation. This indicates a weak precondition.

Example 7. Consider the following B operation, admitting one integer parameter:

```
weak_pre(ii) ≙ PRE ii ∈ -100..100 THEN  IF (ii > 0) THEN xx := ii END  END;
```

The constraint system associated with the precondition is
$$S_{C_x} = \{xx = X, ii = I \mid X \in dom(xx) \land I \in -100..100\}$$
The constraint system resulting from the activation of the effect of `weak_pre` is
$$S_{C_{\mathit{eff}}} = \{xx' = X, ii = I \mid X = I \land I \in 0..100\}$$
We can then deduce a range of values for the parameter `ii` that are not used:
$$ii \in -100.. - 1.$$

6.3   Processing Detections Dynamically

We describe here the detections that are performed dynamically, i.e., by using a symbolic animation mechanism. The basic idea is to perform a depth-first search algorithm, and to perform verifications at each step of the animation. Operation parameters are left unknown, and their value is constrained by the precondition of the operation. Only the activable effects for a given state are considered. All the algorithms work on this principle. The animation ends when the maximal depth is reached.

The complexity of all these detection algorithms is, in the worst case, n^d where n is the number of effects, and d is the user-defined depth.

Detecting Never Activated Effects. The idea of this algorithm is to manage a list of unactivated effects, initialized by all the effects extracted from all the specification. Each time an effect is activated, it is removed from the list. When the computation is over, the remaining list gives the never activated effects for the specified depth.

Example 8 (Illustrating the Detection of a Never Activated Effect). Consider the example given in figure 1. Suppose we add an operation that is consistent, even w.r.t. the invariant, but which can never be activated.

```
test_op(pp) ≙ PRE pp ∈ ready ∧ active = ∅ THEN
                 ready := ready \ {pp} ‖ active := {pp}
           END;
```

With a depth of 5, the effect extracted from this operation can never be activated. So, a warning is raised.

Detecting a Reachable Deadlock. At each step of the execution, we perform the same verification as for the general deadlock detection. Thus, we refine this latter by considering the reachable deadlocks, for a given depth. Once the deadlock is detected, a labeling provides a reachable execution sequence that leads to this deadlock.

Example 9 (Illustrating a Deadlock Detection). By adding the following operation to the example in Fig. 1

```
create_deadlock(pp) ≙ PRE pp ∈ waiting ∧ ready = ∅ ∧ active = ∅ THEN
                         ready := ready ∪ {pp}
                     END;
```

Once the after-state of this operation/effect is reached, no operation can be executed. The detection of this deadlock is performed within a few seconds, with only a depth of 2, and a counter-example is generated, providing a path to this state: `Init ⟶ new(p1) ⟶ create_deadlock(p1)`

Detecting a Weak Invariant. The detection of a weak invariant is based on the parallel management of a constraint system, denoted by $\mathcal{S}_{unrea}$, dedicated to the representation of the unreached states. At each step of the animation, the new resulting constraints are refuted in the $\mathcal{S}_{unrea}$ constraint system, to symbolize that the unreachable states do not contain the current state.

Once the $\mathcal{S}_{unrea}$ constraint system becomes inconsistent, we can be sure that all the invariant states are reachable and that the invariant is not weak. Otherwise, a labeling of the constraint system provides a counter-example which illustrates the invariant weakness.

Example 10 (Illustration of Weak Invariant Detection). On the example in Fig. 1, a counter-example is generated, that indicates a weak invariant, with the search-depth of 5: $active = \emptyset \wedge ready = \{p1\} \wedge waiting = \emptyset$.

By analyzing this counter-example, and by restoring its original meaning, it states that there may exist processes that are ready –asking for the resource– whereas there are no processes currently using the resource. This is a complete nonsense w.r.t. the initial requirements, since we easily imagine that if a process is asking for a free resource, then it should obviously have it. These cases can be avoided by strengthening the invariant with: $active = \emptyset \Rightarrow ready = \emptyset$.

7   Related Work

Among the symbolic animators, there exists ProB [6]. ProB is a model-checker for B specifications. It also relies on a constraint solver, and performs a variety of detections on the models, such as unreachable operations, non-deterministic operations, deadlocks, non-resetable states, and so on. The main difference with our approach is that the constraints in ProB are only used to step through a transition. When the transition has been executed, a labeling is performed to extract all the concrete states and go on with the animation. This allows to perform model-checking, but the major restriction is the combinatorial explosion which restrains ProB to be used for small systems. On the contrary, by focusing only on the constraints, without performing any labeling during the animation, it is certainly impossible to perform model-checking, but the approach is perfectly scalable since the BZ-Testing-Tools animation engine has been designed and optimized for large-scale specifications. Moreover, we propose new kinds of model properties, that could be adapted within the ProB model-checking system. In addition, we do not restrict to B machines, since our internal format can be used to express a variety of before-after semantics notations, such as Z, UML/OCL, JML [5] or Statecharts.

Another close work is done by Miller and Strooper in [8]. In this context, they use test-graphs to exhibit errors similar to the ones described here, within Z models. Test-graphs partially model the states and the transitions of a specification being tested, representing states by nodes and transitions by arcs. The main difficulty in this work is to derive a relevant test-graph. In our approach, we replace test-graphs by the use of constraints to represent system states and their transitions. This considerably simplifies the error detection process, and more accurate results can be obtained.

Our approach seems also close to Symbolic Model Checking (SMC), presented by Clarke et al. [9]. If the principle is similar, the purpose is different since model checking aims at checking properties and not detecting potential weaknesses in the model. Moreover, model checking needs the user to intervene to formalize the (temporal) properties he wants to check. On the contrary, our approach is fully automated and does not require additional effort from the modeller.

8   Conclusion

We have presented in this paper a way to use symbolic animation to detect potential errors in a formal model written by a modeller. We have implemented it in a specific module, which uses the symbolic animation engine of the BZ-Testing-Tools framework. In this context, we are able to deal with all the input languages of this framework to perform our detection. We have shown in this paper the application to the B abstract machine notation, and we have illustrated this approach on an example. First experimentats on mutual exclusion protocols gave us an interesting feedback.

We believe that detecting potential model weaknesses is important because it is an important help for the modeller to write an accurate model and properties, especially the invariant. This approach is complementary to the proof verification step, since a weak invariant (e.g. containing only typing information) can be proved without any difficulties, but this success is not really sufficient, and does not guarantee that the model actually does fit the initial requirements. The importance of having strongest possible invariant is growing especially with the new modeling languages which consists of assertions within the implementation, such as JML [5] or SPEC# [7]. When performing runtime assertion checking, we expect more possible errors to be found by this testing phase.

For the future, we plan to try our approach on industrial cases. This is the current challenge for this kind of verification. Therefore, we will have to filter the possible "false negatives", so that our results are the most relevant possible. We would also like to apply these detections to other modeling languages. This step should be straightforward, since the animation engine of the BZ-Testing-Tools technology works with an intermediate format, into which all the supported languages are translated.

References

1. J.-R. Abrial. *The B-book: assigning programs to meanings.* Cambridge University Press, 1996.
2. F. Ambert, F. Bouquet, S. Chemin, S. Guenaud, B. Legeard, F. Peureux, N. Vacelet, and M. Utting. BZ-TT: A tool-set for test generation from Z and B using contraint logic programming. In Robert Hierons and Thierry Jerron, editors, *Formal Approaches to Testing of Software, FATES 2002 workshop of CONCUR'02*, pages 105–120. INRIA Report, August 2002.
3. F. Bouquet, B. Legeard, N. Vacelet, and M. Utting. Faster Analysis of Formal Specifications. In *Proceedings of the 6th International Conference on Formal Engineering Methods (ICFEM'04)*, LNCS, pages 239–258, Seattle, USA, November 2004. Springer-Verlag.
4. J. Dick and A. Faivre. Automating the generation and sequencing of test cases from model-based specifications. In *Proceedings of the International Conference on Formal Methods Europe (FME'93)*, volume 670 of *LNCS*, pages 268–284. Springer-Verlag, April 1993.
5. G.T. Leavens, A.L. Baker, and C. Ruby. JML: a Java Modeling Language. In *Formal Underpinnings of Java Workshop (at OOPSLA '98)*, October 1998.
6. M. Leuschel and M. Butler. ProB: A model checker for B. In Keijiro Araki, Stefania Gnesi, and Dino Mandrioli, editors, *FME 2003: Formal Methods*, LNCS 2805, pages 855–874. Springer-Verlag, 2003.
7. K.R.M. Leino M. Barnett and W. Schulte. The Spec# Programming System: An Overview. In *Proceedings of the International Workshop on Construction and Analysis of Safe, Secure and Interoperable Smart devices (CASSIS'04)*, volume 3362 of *LNCS*, pages 49–69, Marseille, France, March 2004. Springer-Verlag.
8. Tim Miller and Paul A. Strooper. Animation can show only the presence of errors, never their absence. In *Australian Software Engineering Conference*, pages 76–88, 2001.
9. P. F. Williams, A. Biere, E. M. Clarke, and A. Gupta. Combining decision diagrams and SAT procedures for efficient symbolic model checking. In *Proc. Computer Aided Verification (CAV)*, volume 1855 of *Lecture Notes in Computer Science*, Chicago, U.S.A., July 2000. Springer-Verlag.

A Theory of Secure Control Flow

Martín Abadi[1], Mihai Budiu[2], Úlfar Erlingsson[2], and Jay Ligatti[3]

[1] Computer Science Department, University of California, Santa Cruz
[2] Microsoft Research, Silicon Valley
[3] Computer Science Department, Princeton University

Abstract. Control-Flow Integrity (CFI) means that the execution of a program dynamically follows only certain paths, in accordance with a static policy. CFI can prevent attacks that, by exploiting buffer overflows and other vulnerabilities, attempt to control program behavior. This paper develops the basic theory that underlies two practical techniques for CFI enforcement, with precise formulations of hypotheses and guarantees.

1 Introduction

Many modern attacks against computers take advantage of software flaws, such as buffer-overflow or integer-overflow vulnerabilities. The abundance of software flaws, and the corresponding success of the attacks, has motivated substantial defensive efforts. These efforts include systematic attempts to eliminate those flaws from legacy software and to avoid them in new software, relying on programmer education and security reviews. Although these attempts have been at least partly fruitful, one might be concerned about their cost, and also about the possibility that they will not remove all flaws. Therefore, complementary approaches have also been considered and sometimes adopted.

One such approach is the use of various mitigation tools. These tools can be applied to code, more or less automatically, in order to reduce or eliminate the effects of certain vulnerabilities. The goals of these tools include runtime detection of buffer overflows [4, 13], randomization and artificial heterogeneity [11, 20], and tainting of suspect data [17]. Unfortunately, these tools often target only specific classes of vulnerabilities. For example, stack canaries [4] address only certain buffer overflows in the stack (and none in the heap). Moreover, these tools offer imperfect, hard-to-define safeguards, which determined attackers can defeat or circumvent [12, 14, 19].

Another approach is the adoption of high-level, type-safe languages, such as Java and C#. These languages aim to guarantee general, fundamental properties that can be defined precisely and proved rigorously, in particular memory safety. These properties contribute greatly to program security. Unfortunately, implementation flaws and interoperation with low-level code can weaken the guarantees. Furthermore, it is questionable whether every piece of software will be written or rewritten in these languages. For instance, media codecs, automatic

K.-K. Lau and R. Banach (Eds.): ICFEM 2005, LNCS 3785, pp. 111–124, 2005.

memory management, and operating-system interrupt dispatching typically rely on hand-written, optimized machine code; it seems unlikely that they will enjoy the full benefits of high-level languages, even in new systems.

A third approach, which we advocate, is the enforcement of *Control-Flow Integrity* (CFI). CFI means that program execution dynamically follows only certain paths, in accordance with a statically specified policy given as a control-flow graph (CFG). Many attacks aim to subvert execution and control software behavior. For instance, a buffer overflow in an application may result in a call to a sensitive system function, possibly a function that the application was never meant to use [12]. An attack may also cause a jump into the middle of a function body, or even into the middle of a multi-byte machine-code instruction (triggering the execution of a different instruction). The resulting behavior, while allowed at the hardware level, is in contradiction with programmer intent. Since these attacks invariably affect control flow, CFI can prevent them.

Like various mitigation tools, CFI enforcement can be applied to existing source code and binaries. At the same time, CFI has much in common with the properties guaranteed by high-level, type-safe languages. In particular, as we demonstrate, CFI can be defined precisely and proved rigorously. In these respects, CFI enforcement resembles the use of proof-carrying code (PCC) [10]. (Indeed, although research on PCC has emphasized memory safety, PCC could be used for proving CFI, even under weak assumptions on memory.)

In a companion paper [2], we explore the benefits of CFI and present an implementation. The implementation relies on machine-code rewriting that instruments software with runtime checks; it applies to legacy systems (e.g., code compiled from C and C++ on x86 Windows) with only a modest performance overhead. We also validate, experimentally, that CFI thwarts many types of exploits and several documented past attacks. Finally, we show that CFI can help in the enforcement of additional security properties.

The CFG on which CFI relies should be designed to exclude unwanted software behavior. Even a coarse CFG that prevents jumps into the middle of function bodies can be useful; such a coarse CFG is easy to obtain. A more precise CFG, of the sort that could be derived by source-code analysis, might also prevent certain dangerous sequences of system calls. Our machine-code rewriting aims to guarantee CFI with respect to the CFG, whatever it is. Simple static verification can ensure that the rewriting achieves the specified effect. This verification can be seen as a special case of PCC proof-checking, while the rewriting obviates the need for explicit logical proofs. Only the verification is required for establishing CFI; design or implementation flaws in the rewriting do not compromise security.

This paper is concerned with the foundations of CFI. It develops the basic theory that underlies our strategy for CFI enforcement. It includes a detailed semantics for programs, definitions for program instrumentation (focusing on its verification), and theorems about the executions of instrumented programs. We regard this basic theory as central to our approach. The precise formulation of hypotheses, guarantees, and proofs is a major difference between our approach and those based on previous mitigation tools, and an important similarity with research on high-level, type-safe languages. Furthermore, a formal approach is useful not only for elucidating hypotheses and guarantees, but also as a guide in the design and development of techniques. Indeed, in the course of our work, we rejected several alternatives that made unclear assumptions or that offered protection only in hard-to-define circumstances.

The main theorems of the paper establish that CFI holds for programs processed according to either of two enforcement techniques, even with respect to a powerful attacker that controls data memory. Although both techniques employ machine-code rewriting, they differ in their specifics and their assumptions. Most noticeably, one technique requires that data memory not be executable. This assumption, which we call NXD, thwarts some attacks on its own, but not those that exploit unintended control transfers in pre-existing code, such as "jump-to-libc" attacks [12]. Some architectures support NXD, and recent versions of Windows use it [8]. NXD can also be implemented in software, with support from the underlying operating system [11]. The second technique is a refinement of the first with a built-in, inline implementation of NXD.

This second technique relies on a generalization of *Software Fault Isolation* (SFI) [18] that we call *Software Memory Access Control* (SMAC). SFI provides multiple domains of memory protection within a single address space. For SFI, code inserted before each memory access ensures that the target memory address is within a certain range. For SMAC, more generally, each instruction that may perform a memory access is constrained to a particular range of addresses, potentially a different one per instruction. CFI can facilitate the implementation of SMAC for irregular architectures, such as the x86, on which traditional SFI has been problematic [5]. One of the goals of this paper is to show that this cooperation between CFI and SMAC is real, rather than an incorrect result of informal circular reasoning.

Section 2 defines the setting for our work: a simple machine model and a corresponding machine language. Section 3 discusses CFGs. Section 4 describes and analyzes the first technique for CFI enforcement. Section 5 concerns the second technique, in which CFI enforcement is combined with SMAC. Section 6 concludes. Some details of proofs and additional material can be found at our website [3].

2   The Setting: Programs and Their Semantics

The machine model and the programs that we define in this section are typical of formal studies in programming-language theory. For the sake of simplicity, we work with a basic machine model and a small set of machine instructions which enable us to study CFI but exclude virtual memory, dynamic linking, threading, and other sophisticated features found in actual systems. Essentially, our language is a minor variant of that of Hamid et al. [6]. We have yet to attempt a similar investigation for the full x86 architecture and for the x86 code sequences that our instrumentation inserts. We believe that such an investigation would be feasible, particularly because of the similarities between our x86 code sequences and those studied in this paper; on the other hand, the investigation would certainly be laborious and may yield diminishing returns.

2.1 Machine Model

For our machine model, we define words, memories, register files, and states as follows:

$$Word = \{0, 1, ...\}$$
$$Mem = Word \rightarrow Word$$
$$Regnum = \{0, 1, ..., 31\}$$
$$Regfile = Regnum \rightarrow Word$$
$$State = Mem \times Regfile \times Word$$

We often adopt the notations w and pc for elements of $Word$, and M, R, and S for elements of Mem, $Regfile$, and $State$, respectively. When S is a state, we may write $S.M$, $S.R$, and $S.pc$ for the Mem component, the $Regfile$ component, and the pc in S, respectively.

We further distinguish between code memory (M_c) and data memory (M_d), so we split memories into two functions with disjoint domains, each of them contiguous. We assume that a statically defined program that comprises $n > 0$ instructions always occupies memory locations 0 to $n - 1$, with the first instruction of the program located at address 0. When we split a memory M into M_c and M_d, we write $M = M_c | M_d$, provided M_c contains $n > 0$ instructions and the following constraints hold: $\mathrm{dom}(M_c) = \{0..(n-1)\}$, and $\mathrm{dom}(M_d) = \mathrm{dom}(M) - \mathrm{dom}(M_c)$, and $M_c(a) = M(a)$ for all $a \in \mathrm{dom}(M_c)$, and $M_d(a) = M(a)$ for all $a \in \mathrm{dom}(M_d)$. We consider only states whose memory is partitioned in this way. We write $S.M_c$ to indicate the code memory of state S, and $S.M_d$ for the data memory.

Similarly, we split register files into distinguished and general registers. When we split R into R_{0-2} and R_{3-31}, we write $R = R_{0-2} | R_{3-31}$ provided the following constraints hold: $\mathrm{dom}(R_{0-2}) = \{r_0, r_1, r_2\}$, and $\mathrm{dom}(R_{3-31}) = \{r_3..r_{31}\}$, and $R_{0-2}(r) = R(r)$ for all $r \in \mathrm{dom}(R_{0-2})$, and $R_{3-31}(r) = R(r)$ for all $r \in \mathrm{dom}(R_{3-31})$. We distinguish the registers r_0, r_1, and r_2 because we assume that they are used only in CFI enforcement code. (In fact, in our x86 implementation, we need only one distinguished register and only at certain program points. This feature is important in practice, since the x86 architecture has few registers. While permanently reserving many registers for a special use is difficult, finding a free register now and then is easy.)

2.2 Instructions

Our language is that of Hamid et al. [6] plus a *label* instruction in which an immediate value can be embedded and which behaves like a nop. (It is not too hard to implement such a *label* instruction on common architectures.) The set of instructions is:

If $Dc(M_c(pc))=$	then $(M_c|M_d, R, pc) \to_n$
label w	$(M_c|M_d, R, pc + 1)$, when $pc + 1 \in \mathrm{dom}(M_c)$
add r_d, r_s, r_t	$(M_c|M_d, R\{r_d \mapsto R(r_s) + R(r_t)\}, pc + 1)$, when $pc + 1 \in \mathrm{dom}(M_c)$
addi r_d, r_s, w	$(M_c|M_d, R\{r_d \mapsto R(r_s) + w\}, pc + 1)$, when $pc + 1 \in \mathrm{dom}(M_c)$
movi r_d, w	$(M_c|M_d, R\{r_d \mapsto w\}, pc + 1)$, when $pc + 1 \in \mathrm{dom}(M_c)$
bgt r_s, r_t, w	$(M_c|M_d, R, w)$, when $R(r_s) > R(r_t) \wedge w \in \mathrm{dom}(M_c)$ $(M_c|M_d, R, pc + 1)$, when $R(r_s) \leq R(r_t) \wedge pc + 1 \in \mathrm{dom}(M_c)$
jd w	$(M_c|M_d, R, w)$, when $w \in \mathrm{dom}(M_c)$
jmp r_s	$(M_c|M_d, R, R(r_s))$, when $R(r_s) \in \mathrm{dom}(M_c)$
ld $r_d, r_s(w)$	$(M_c|M_d, R\{r_d \mapsto M(R(r_s) + w)\}, pc + 1)$, when $pc + 1 \in \mathrm{dom}(M_c)$
st $r_d(w), r_s$	$(M_c|M_d\{R(r_d) + w \mapsto R(r_s)\}, R, pc + 1)$, when $R(r_d) + w \in \mathrm{dom}(M_d) \wedge pc + 1 \in \mathrm{dom}(M_c)$

Fig. 1. Normal steps

$Instr ::=$	instructions
label w	label (with embedded constant)
add r_d, r_s, r_t	add registers
addi r_d, r_s, w	add register and word
movi r_d, w	move word into register
bgt r_s, r_t, w	branch-greater-than
jd w	jump
jmp r_s	computed jump
ld $r_d, r_s(w)$	load
st $r_d(w), r_s$	store
illegal	illegal

where w is a word and r_s, r_t, and r_d are registers. Thus, instructions may contain words. Like Hamid et al., we omit the routine details of instruction storage and decoding. We assume a function $Dc : Word \to Instr$ that decodes words into instructions.

2.3   A Semantics of Programs Under Attack

In this section we give a first semantics for instructions. Figures 1 and 2 define two binary relations on states, $\to_n$ and $\to_a$.

- The relation $\to_n$ models normal small steps of execution, that is, those steps that may occur in the absence of an attacker. This relation is deliberately

$$(M_c|M_d, R_{0-2}|R_{3-31}, pc) \rightarrow_a (M_c|M_d', R_{0-2}|R_{3-31}', pc)$$

Fig. 2. Attacker steps

If $Dc(M(pc))=$	then $(M, R, pc) \rightarrow_n$
$label\ w$	$(M, R, pc + 1)$
$add\ r_d, r_s, r_t$	$(M, R\{r_d \mapsto R(r_s) + R(r_t)\}, pc + 1)$
$addi\ r_d, r_s, w$	$(M, R\{r_d \mapsto R(r_s) + w\}, pc + 1)$
$movi\ r_d, w$	$(M, R\{r_d \mapsto w\}, pc + 1)$
$bgt\ r_s, r_t, w$	(M, R, w), when $R(r_s) > R(r_t)$
	$(M, R, pc + 1)$, when $R(r_s) \leq R(r_t)$
$jd\ w$	(M, R, w)
$jmp\ r_s$	$(M, R, R(r_s))$
$ld\ r_d, r_s(w)$	$(M, R\{r_d \mapsto M(R(r_s) + w)\}, pc + 1)$
$st\ r_d(w), r_s$	$(M\{R(r_d) + w \mapsto R(r_s)\}, R, pc + 1)$

Fig. 3. Normal steps (assuming less memory protection)

incomplete: many states are "stuck", including those where $Dc(M_c(pc)) = illegal$.

– The relation $\rightarrow_a$ models attack steps. In such a step, an attacker may unconditionally and arbitrarily perturb data memory and non-distinguished registers. For example, the attacker may modify a part of memory to contain a bit pattern that appears elsewhere in memory. Thus, intuitively, the attacker can read all of memory.

An attack step is quite similar to the possible effect of a computation step in another execution thread (which our model does not represent). In particular, another thread can access all of memory, and can arbitrarily modify data memory. Moreover, registers are specific to a thread, and the values of the registers of one thread might be affected by another thread only if those values are read from memory (possibly after being "spilled" into memory). An attack step therefore corresponds to a computation step in another thread if the values of general registers may be read from memory but those of distinguished registers are not. On the other hand, for simplicity, an attack step need not be restricted to computable functions.

The relation $\rightarrow$, defined below, is the union of $\rightarrow_n$ and $\rightarrow_a$. Thus, this relation represents a computation step in general, either a normal state transition or one caused by an attacker.

$$\frac{S \rightarrow_n S'}{S \rightarrow S'} \qquad \frac{S \rightarrow_a S'}{S \rightarrow S'}$$

In security, it is important to identify assumptions, and to justify them to the extent possible, because an attacker that can invalidate assumptions can often circumvent security enforcement. Our definitions embody several assumptions, which we discuss next:

1. The definition of $\rightarrow_n$ implies NXD (that is, that data cannot be executed as code). Similarly, the definitions of $\rightarrow_n$ and $\rightarrow_a$ imply that code memory cannot be modified at runtime. We call this property NWC. As indicated in the introduction, NXD is often a reasonable assumption. NWC holds on most current systems (except at special times, such as during the initial loading of dynamic libraries).

2. The definition of $\rightarrow_a$ allows for the possibility that the attacker is in control of data memory. This aspect of the model of the attacker is conservative, but unfortunately close to reality. Buffer overflows and other vulnerabilities often allow an attacker to write to arbitrary locations in data memory even before subverting control flow [12].

3. The definition of $\rightarrow_a$ implies that the attacker cannot modify the distinguished registers r_0, r_1, and r_2. In practice, one may ensure this property by avoiding the use of r_0, r_1, and r_2 outside the CFI enforcement code and preventing those registers from "spilling" into memory. Our proofs require only a weaker assumption, namely that the attacker cannot modify r_0, r_1, and r_2 during the execution of CFI enforcement code.

4. The machine model and the definition of $\rightarrow_n$ exclude the possibility that a jump would land in the middle of an instruction. In practice, many architectures (RISC architectures, in particular) exclude this possibility, and our x86 CFI implementation prevents it. For simplicity, we do not address this feature in the formal analysis.

2.4   A More Permissive Semantics of Programs Under Attack

Assumptions NXD and NWC do not hold in some settings, for example on architectures without memory-protection facilities. We should therefore consider an alternative to the program semantics of Section 2.3. For brevity, and since there is no risk of ambiguity below, we reuse the symbols $\rightarrow_n$, $\rightarrow_a$, and $\rightarrow$.

The resulting, relaxed definition of normal execution steps is in Figure 3. These normal steps can arbitrarily violate NXD and NWC, possibly under the indirect influence of an attacker. On the other hand, the rules for attack steps and general steps remain those of Section 2.3. In particular, we still require that an attack step cannot directly alter code memory, the distinguished registers, or the program counter. We believe that these restrictions often hold in practice. Moreover, they are necessary: without them, an attacker could trivially create new code (outside the original CFG) and trigger its execution.

3   The CFG

Our instrumentation of a program relies on a CFG for the program, as specification of a CFI policy. Next we discuss this CFG.

The nodes of the CFG are words that represent program addresses. Given a graph G for M_c, and $w \in \text{dom}(M_c)$, we let $\text{succ}(w)$ be the set of words $w' \in \text{dom}(M_c)$ such that G has an edge from w to w'. We say that w' is a destination if there exists w such that $Dc(M_c(w))$ is a computed jump instruction $(jmp\ r_s)$ and $w' \in \text{succ}(w)$.

We need not constrain how the CFG is obtained, or how it matches the executions of the program before instrumentation. The CFG might be computed by analyses, static or dynamic. It might also be derived, at least in part, from a security policy, for example one expressed as a security automaton [5, 7]. (For our implementation, we derive the CFG by static analysis of binaries.) We do require:

1. If $Dc(M_c(w_0)) = label\ w$, or $add\ r_d, r_s, r_t$, or $addi\ r_d, r_s, w$, or $movi\ r_d, w$, or $ld\ r_d, r_s(w)$, or $st\ r_d(w), r_s$, then $\text{succ}(w_0) = \{w_0 + 1\} \cap \text{dom}(M_c)$.
2. If $Dc(M_c(w_0)) = bgt\ r_s, r_t, w$ then $\text{succ}(w_0) = \{w_0 + 1, w\} \cap \text{dom}(M_c)$.
3. If $Dc(M_c(w_0)) = jd\ w$ then $\text{succ}(w_0) = \{w\} \cap \text{dom}(M_c)$.
4. If $Dc(M_c(w_0)) = jmp\ r_s$ then $\text{succ}(w_0) \neq \emptyset$.
5. $Dc(M_c(w_0)) = illegal$ then $\text{succ}(w_0) = \emptyset$.
6. If $w_0, w_1 \in \text{dom}(M_c)$, then $\text{succ}(w_0) \cap \text{succ}(w_1) = \emptyset$ or $\text{succ}(w_0) = \text{succ}(w_1)$.

When these properties hold, we say that the graph in question is a CFG for M_c.

These properties hold by definition for many graphs that arise from code analysis. Only the last one (6) is non-trivial. Property 6 is not essential—we can avoid it at the cost of additional dynamic checks; on the other hand, it is convenient and often reasonable. Property 6 can be satisfied by adding edges to a graph; the additional edges result in a looser CFI policy. We believe that this approach is satisfactory in practice: when most addresses are not destinations, even a coarse CFG that allows control to flow from any jump instruction to any destination can thwart many attacks. Alternatively, property 6 can be satisfied by duplicating nodes where the condition is violated. In the extreme, unrealistic case where the condition is violated at all nodes, we may rely on the following construction: given a graph G, we define a new graph G' such that the nodes of G' are pairs of nodes of G, and there is an edge from (a_1, a_2) to (b_1, b_2) in G' when $b_1 = a_2$ and there is an edge from a_2 to b_2 in G. (We omit the straightforward proof that G' satisfies property 6.)

Because of property 6, we can put destinations into equivalence classes. We give each equivalence class an identifier, called an ID. We represent these IDs by words. For a jmp instruction at address w in M_c, we let $\text{dst}(w)$ be the ID of all successors of w. Thus, $\text{dst}(w)$ is the ID of any element of $\text{succ}(w)$.

We write $\text{succ}(M_c, G, w)$ and $\text{dst}(M_c, G, w)$, instead of $\text{succ}(w)$ and $\text{dst}(w)$ respectively, when we wish to be explicit on M_c and G.

4   CFI Enforcement (Without SMAC)

In this section we present and analyze our first technique for CFI enforcement.

4.1   CFI Enforcement by Instrumentation

CFI means that, during program execution, whenever a machine-code instruction transfers control, it targets a valid destination according to a given CFG.

For instructions that target a constant destination, this requirement can be discharged statically. On the other hand, for computed control-flow transfers (whose destination is determined at runtime), this requirement must be discharged with a dynamic check.

Machine-code rewriting offers an attractive, realistic strategy for implementing dynamic checks. Modern tools for binary instrumentation address the substantial technical difficulties of machine-code rewriting [15, 16].

Unfortunately, machine-code rewriting remains complex and tied to many implicit compiler-specific details. Therefore, for the sake of trustworthiness, CFI enforcement should preferably depend only on simple, final, static verification steps that check that the instrumentation has produced an acceptable result. These steps, but not the machine-code rewriting, will be part of the "trusted computing base".

For the present purposes, the verification steps consist in ensuring that a code memory M_c and a CFG G for M_c satisfy the following conditions:

1. If n is the length of $\mathrm{dom}(M_c)$, then the instruction at $n - 1$ is *illegal*. (In other words, the final instruction is *illegal*.)
2. If $w_0 \in \mathrm{dom}(M_c)$ is a destination, then the instruction at w_0 is *label w*, where w is w_0's ID. Conversely, if $w_0 \in \mathrm{dom}(M_c)$ holds a *label* instruction, then w_0 is a destination. (In other words, *label* instructions can be used only for inline tagging with IDs. This requirement applies to code memory, but not to data memory. In fact, the attacker may, at any time, write *label w* into any location in data memory.)
3. If $w_0 \in \mathrm{dom}(M_c)$ holds a *jmp* instruction, then this instruction is *jmp r_0* and it is preceded by a specific sequence of instructions, as follows:

$$addi\ r_0, r_s, 0$$
$$ld\ r_1, r_0(0)$$
$$movi\ r_2, IMM$$
$$bgt\ r_1, r_2, HALT$$
$$bgt\ r_2, r_1, HALT$$
$$jmp\ r_0$$

where r_s is some register, *HALT* is the address of the *illegal* instruction specified in condition (1), and *IMM* is the word w such that $Dc(w) = label\ dst(w_0)$. This code compares the dynamic target of a jump, which is initially in register r_s, to the *label* instruction that is expected to be the target statically. When the comparison succeeds, the jump proceeds. When it fails, the program halts.

4. If *bgt r_s, r_t, w* or *jd w* appear anywhere in M_c, then the target address w does not hold a *jmp* instruction or the occurrences of the instructions

$$ld\ r_1, r_0(0)$$
$$movi\ r_2, IMM$$
$$bgt\ r_1, r_2, HALT$$
$$bgt\ r_2, r_1, HALT$$

that precede a *jmp* instruction according to condition (3). The target address
may hold *addi* $r_0, r_s, 0$. (Note that (2) removes the possibility that a *jmp*
instruction can jump to another *jmp* instruction or to any of the preceding
instructions considered here.)

We let the predicate $I(M_c, G)$ mean that M_c and its CFG G satisfy the conjunction of the conditions above.

4.2   A Theorem About CFI

With these definitions, and under the semantics of Section 2.3, we can obtain
formal results about our instrumentation method.

Here we present a simple but fundamental result that expresses integrity
of control flow. The following theorem states that every execution step of an
instrumented program is either an attack step in which the program counter
does not change, or a normal step to a state with a valid successor program
counter. Thus, despite attack steps, the program counter always follows the
CFG.

Theorem 1. *Let S_0 be a state $(M_c|M_d, R, pc)$ such that $pc = 0$ and $I(M_c, G)$,
where G is a CFG for M_c, and let $S_1, \ldots, S_n$ be states such that $S_0 \to S_1 \to
\ldots \to S_n$. Then, for all $i \in 0..(n-1)$, either $S_i \to_a S_{i+1}$ and $S_{i+1}.pc = S_i.pc$, or
$S_{i+1}.pc \in \text{succ}(S_0.M_c, G, S_i.pc)$.*

The proof of this theorem consists in a fairly classical induction on executions,
with an invariant. In particular, the proof constrains the values of the distinguished registers within the instrumentation sequences, but puts no restrictions
on the use of these registers elsewhere in the program.

Although this theorem is fairly easy to state, it has strong consequences.
In particular, it implies that the attacker cannot cause the execution of code
that would appear unreachable according to the CFG. For example, if a certain
libc routine should not be reachable, then executing the code memory will
never result in running that routine. Thus, "jump-to-libc" attacks that target
dangerous routines (such as system in Unix and ShellExecute in Windows)
can be effectively thwarted.

As explained in the introduction, our first technique for CFI enforcement
depends on NXD. More specifically, the theorem depends on the formal version
of NXD, which says that, during execution, the targets of code transfers are
always in the domain of code memory. Without this property, the theorem would
fail, since data memory may well contain *label w* instructions that look like the
expected destinations of *jmp* instructions.

5   CFI Enforcement (with SMAC)

Our second technique for CFI enforcement builds on the first, eliminates the
need for NXD, and allows program execution steps to modify code memory.
While it may be viewed as a refinement of the first (perhaps via a simulation

relation), in this section we present it and study it on its own, as a complete and separate mechanism.

SMAC has a number of applications beyond the one described here. For instance, it can serve to protect a call stack in memory, and thereby serve to strengthen CFI by matching calls and returns dynamically [2]. For brevity, we do not formalize those applications in this paper.

5.1   CFI Enforcement by Instrumentation (with SMAC)

We assume that the minimum and maximum addresses of code and data memory are known at instrumentation time, and let $\min(M)$ and $\max(M)$ respectively return the minimum and maximum addresses in the domain of memory M.

The SMAC-based verification steps consist in ensuring that a code memory M_c and a CFG G for M_c satisfy the following conditions:

1. If n is the length of $\mathrm{dom}(M_c)$, then the instruction at $n-1$ is *illegal*.
2. If $w_0 \in \mathrm{dom}(M_c)$ is a destination, then the instruction at w_0 is *label w*, where w is w_0's ID. Conversely, if $w_0 \in \mathrm{dom}(M_c)$ holds a *label* instruction, then w_0 is a destination.
3. If $w_0 \in \mathrm{dom}(M_c)$ holds at a *st* instruction, then this instruction is *st* $r_0(0), r_s$ and it is preceded by a specific sequence of instructions, as follows:

$$addi\ r_0, r_d, w$$
$$movi\ r_1, \max(M_d)$$
$$movi\ r_2, \min(M_d)$$
$$bgt\ r_0, r_1, HALT$$
$$bgt\ r_2, r_0, HALT$$
$$st\ \ r_0(0), r_s$$

where r_d is some register, w is some offset (a word), and $HALT$ is the address of the *illegal* instruction specified in condition (1). This code constrains a store to memory, with address initially given by $R(r_d) + w$, to be between $\min(M_d)$ and $\max(M_d)$. This constraint is imposed by two dynamic comparisons. When these two comparisons succeed, the store proceeds; otherwise, the program halts.

4. If $w_0 \in \mathrm{dom}(M_c)$ holds a *jmp* instruction, then this instruction is *jmp* r_0 and it is preceded by a specific sequence of instructions, as follows:

$$addi\ r_0, r_s, 0$$
$$movi\ r_1, \max(M_c)$$
$$movi\ r_2, \min(M_c)$$
$$bgt\ r_0, r_1, HALT$$
$$bgt\ r_2, r_0, HALT$$
$$ld\ r_1, r_0(0)$$
$$movi\ r_2, IMM$$
$$bgt\ r_1, r_2, HALT$$
$$bgt\ r_2, r_1, HALT$$
$$jmp\ r_0$$

where r_s is some register, *HALT* is the address of the *illegal* instruction specified in condition (1), and *IMM* is the word w such that $Dc(w) = label$ dst(w_0). This code is a combination of the code for *jmp* described in Section 4 with an analogue of the code for *st* described above. As in the code for *st*, an address is constrained to be within a range; here the range is the domain of code memory, and the address is the dynamic target of a jump, held in r_s. Then, as in the code for *jmp* in Section 4, that dynamic target is compared with the *label* instruction expected statically. The program halts unless all checks succeed.

5. If *bgt* r_s, r_t, w or *jd* w appear anywhere in M_c, then the target address w is in code memory (that is, $w \in \mathrm{dom}(M_c)$), and w does not hold *st* instructions or any of the preceding instructions listed in (3), or *jmp* instructions or any of the preceding instructions listed in (4), except possibly the first of these instructions, namely *addi* r_0, r_d, w and *addi* $r_0, r_s, 0$, respectively.

We let the predicate $I_s(M_c, G)$ mean that M_c and its CFG G satisfy the conjunction of the conditions above.

5.2   A Theorem About CFI with SMAC

With the relaxed semantics of Section 2.4 and the instrumentation of Section 5, we obtain a direct analogue to Theorem 1.

Theorem 2. *Let S_0 be a state $(M_c|M_d, R, pc)$ such that $pc = 0$ and $I_s(M_c, G)$, where G is a CFG for M_c, and let $S_1, \ldots, S_n$ be states such that $S_0 \to S_1 \to \ldots \to S_n$. Then, for all $i \in 0..(n-1)$, either $S_i \to_a S_{i+1}$ and $S_{i+1}.pc = S_i.pc$, or $S_{i+1}.pc \in \mathrm{succ}(S_0.M_c, G, S_i.pc)$.*

The proof of this theorem is analogous to that of Theorem 1.

Because SMAC is implemented by inline checks, it could be circumvented by computed control-flow transfers into or around the code sequences that perform the checks. Therefore, SMAC is intimately tied to CFI, which prevents such subversive flows of control. Accordingly, our theorem is not about SMAC in isolation, but rather about the combination of SMAC and CFI.

6   Conclusion

In this paper we study techniques for the enforcement of Control-Flow Integrity (CFI). In a simple low-level language of the kind common in programming-language theory, we give definitions for program instrumentation and theorems about the executions of the instrumented programs. The rigorous clarification of assumptions and guarantees is helpful in the development and validation of software-security techniques, and more broadly beneficial for security. While our theorems do not directly say that nothing bad will ever happen—and indeed CFI does not prevent all security problems—they do imply fundamental properties that exclude a variety of attacks.

Many attacks make use of the fact that, at the lowest levels of systems, almost any behavior is considered valid—independently of whether the executing software is written in a structured fashion, e.g., as high-level functions in C or C++. For instance, even activity that is patently invalid for programs that originate in high-level, structured languages (such as jumping into the middle of a function body) is permitted at the hardware level. Similarly, even programs that use very limited system functionality (such as those that only draw on the screen but never use the file system or network) are typically allowed to invoke any operating system service or runtime library routine.

CFI can align low-level behavior with high-level intent, as specified in a CFG. In this respect, CFI is reminiscent of the use of typed low-level languages, such as TAL [9], and of efforts to bridge the gaps between high-level languages and actual behavior (e.g., [1]). Furthermore, the basic theory of CFI enforcement that we develop in this paper relies heavily on fundamental ideas and techniques of the modern literature on programming languages. We regard the viability of this theory as an important feature of CFI. More broadly, we believe that theories based on programming-language methods can enhance assurance and provide guidance for a wide range of approaches to software security.

Acknowledgments. Martín Abadi and Jay Ligatti participated in this work while at Microsoft Research, Silicon Valley. Discussions with Greg Morrisett and Ilya Mironov were helpful to this paper's development and improved its exposition. Milenko Drinic and Andrew Edwards of the Vulcan team were helpful to our implementation efforts.

References

1. M. Abadi. Protection in programming-language translations. In K.G. Larsen, S. Skyum, and G. Winskel, editors, *Proceedings of the 25th International Colloquium on Automata, Languages and Programming*, volume 1443 of *Lecture Notes in Computer Science*, pages 868–883. Springer-Verlag, 1998. Also Digital Equipment Corporation Systems Research Center report No. 154, April 1998.
2. M. Abadi, M. Budiu, Ú. Erlingsson, and J. Ligatti. Control-flow integrity: Principles, implementations, and applications. In *Proceedings of the ACM Conference on Computer and Communications Security*, 2005. A preliminary version appears as Microsoft Research Technical Report MSR-TR-05-18, February 2005.
3. M. Abadi, M. Budiu, Ú. Erlingsson, and J. Ligatti. Further formal material on CFI and SMAC. Manuscript, available at http://research.microsoft.com/research/sv/gleipnir, 2005.
4. C. Cowan, C. Pu, D. Maier, J. Walpole, P. Bakke, S. Beattie, A. Grier, P. Wagle, Q. Zhang, and H. Hinton. StackGuard: Automatic adaptive detection and prevention of buffer-overflow attacks. In *Proceedings of the Usenix Security Symposium*, pages 63–78, 1998.
5. Ú. Erlingsson and F.B. Schneider. SASI enforcement of security policies: A retrospective. In *Proceedings of the New Security Paradigms Workshop*, pages 87–95, 1999.

6. N. Hamid, Z. Shao, V. Trifonov, S. Monnier, and Z. Ni. A Syntactic Approach to Foundational Proof-Carrying Code. Technical Report YALEU/DCS/TR-1224, Dept. of Computer Science, Yale University, 2002.

7. J. Ligatti, L. Bauer, and D. Walker. Edit automata: Enforcement mechanisms for run-time security policies. *International Journal of Information Security*, 4(1–2):2–16, February 2005.

8. Microsoft Corporation. Changes to functionality in Microsoft Windows XP SP2: Memory protection technologies, 2004. `http://www.microsoft.com/technet/prodtechnol/winxppro/maintain/sp2mempr.mspx`.

9. G. Morrisett, D. Walker, K. Crary, and N. Glew. From System F to typed assembly language. *ACM Transactions on Programming Languages and Systems*, 21(3):527–568, 1999.

10. G. Necula. Proof-carrying code. In *Proceedings of the 24th ACM Symposium on Principles of Programming Languages*, pages 106–119, January 1997.

11. PaX Project. The PaX project, 2004. `http://pax.grsecurity.net/`.

12. J. Pincus and B. Baker. Beyond stack smashing: Recent advances in exploiting buffer overruns. *IEEE Security and Privacy*, 2(4):20–27, 2004.

13. O. Ruwase and M.S. Lam. A practical dynamic buffer overflow detector. In *Proceedings of Network and Distributed System Security Symposium*, pages 159–169, 2004.

14. H. Shacham, M. Page, B. Pfaff, E.-J. Goh, N. Modadugu, and D. Boneh. On the effectiveness of address-space randomization. In *Proceedings of the ACM Conference on Computer and Communications Security*, pages 298–307, 2004.

15. A. Srivastava, A. Edwards, and H. Vo. Vulcan: Binary transformation in a distributed environment. Technical Report MSR-TR-2001-50, Microsoft Research, 2001.

16. A. Srivastava and A. Eustace. ATOM: A system for building customized program analysis tools. Technical Report WRL Research Report 94/2, Digital Equipment Corporation, 1994.

17. G.E. Suh, J. W. Lee, D. Zhang, and S. Devadas. Secure program execution via dynamic information flow tracking. In *Proceedings of the International Conference on Architectural Support for Programming Languages and Operating Systems*, pages 85–96, 2004.

18. R. Wahbe, S. Lucco, T.E. Anderson, and S.L. Graham. Efficient software-based fault isolation. *ACM SIGOPS Operating Systems Review*, 27(5):203–216, 1993.

19. J. Wilander and M. Kamkar. A comparison of publicly available tools for dynamic buffer overflow prevention. In *Proceedings of the Network and Distributed System Security Symposium*, pages 149–162, 2003.

20. J. Xu, Z. Kalbarczyk, and R.K. Iyer. Transparent runtime randomization for security. In *Proceedings of the Symposium on Reliable and Distributed Systems*, pages 260–269, 2003.

Game Semantics Model for Security Protocols

Mourad Debbabi and Mohamed Saleh

Computer Security Laboratory,
Concordia Institute for Information Systems Engineering,
Concordia University
{debbabi, m_saleh}@ciise.concordia.ca

Abstract. Our aim is to present a game semantics model for the specification of security protocols. Game semantics has been used to give an operational flavor to denotational semantics, thereby combining the best of both worlds by having an elegant mathematical structure and at the same time describing steps of execution. Game semantics was successfully used to prove full abstraction of PCF and has since been used to describe the semantics of a variety of programming languages. It fits naturally in the framework of security protocols as the interactions between communicating parties can be described as moves in a game, where honest agents are the players and the intruder is the opponent. We propose a game-based calculus for the specification of security protocols. First, we define games that represent interactions in security protocols, these games are then used to ascribe denotational semantics to security protocols.

1 Introduction

Security protocols while communicating over an insecure network. Some objectives of a security protocol are [2]: Authentication of agents, confidentiality of transmitted data, integrity of transmitted messages, and non-repudiation of messages. To meet these goals, cryptographic functions are used (e.g. encryption, decryption, hashing, etc.). There remains however a number of very important issues such as what messages to encrypt and with which keys, etc. All of these issues are dealt with in the framework of security protocols, and they should be dealt with *correctly*. This is a difficult task, even for very simple protocols. Needham and Shroeder published the first cryptographic protocol in 1978 [17], which was discovered to be flawed after 17 years of service. In this paper we give a brief overview of the methods adopted for the specification and analysis of security protocols. We also, present a game semantics model for the same goal. The paper is organized in seven sections starting with the introduction. In Section 2, we present a brief survey of security protocols specification and verification methods. Section 3 deals with the syntax of a proposed security protocol calculus, while Section 4 gives a brief introduction about games. In Section 5 the game-based model for security protocols is described, it is then used in Section 6 to ascribe denotational semantics to security protocols. Finally, Section 7 concludes the paper.

K.-K. Lau and R. Banach (Eds.): ICFEM 2005, LNCS 3785, pp. 125–140, 2005.

2   Specification and Analysis of Security Protocols

Some specifications are informal narrations, written in what is called the "standard notation" of security protocols. As an example, the notation $A \rightarrow B : \{N_A\}_{k_{AB}}$ means that agent A sends to B a *nonce* encrypted by the private key shared between A and B. On the other hand, formal methods have been used in the specification and analysis of security protocols. The pioneering work was done by Dolev and Yao [9] and a survey is given in [16].

2.1   Formal Analysis of Security Protocols

Several methods are used for the verification of cryptographic protocols. Some of these methods are general methods which are not specifically developed for cryptographic protocols. For instance using CSP and the FDR model checker or tools for specification languages such as LOTOS, Z etc. Other methods have been specifically developed for cryptographic protocols. These include the inductive approach, the strand space approach, logic-based approaches and approaches based on process algebras. The inductive approach introduced by Paulson [18] models a protocol as a set of traces, which are sequences of actions. Security properties such as secrecy and authentication can be defined on the set of traces of the protocol and protocol rules are used to prove properties inductively. The strand space approach [19] is based on sequences of actions called strands. In contrast to the inductive approach, these are sequences of actions of an individual agent and not of a global protocol interaction. Security properties are defined and proved on the strand space that describes a protocol. Logic-based approaches model and verify cryptographic protocols using logics based on knowledge and belief. An example of this is the BAN logic [8]. Another approach is to develop formal models based on the specification of the security protocol using process algebra (e.g. the SPI calculus [3]). Novel approaches to the verification of cryptographic protocols are also developed. The use of type systems for the verification of security protocols is investigated in [1]. Game-theoretic approaches to the verification of fair exchange protocols are investigated in [12], [13], and [14].

2.2   Security Protocols and Game Semantics

The idea of using games in logic specifications dates back to Lorenzen [15] who viewed a logic proposition as a game between two players one trying to assert it (the proponent) and the other trying to attack it (the opponent). This idea was further developed by Andeas Blass [7], who used it to give semantics to linear logic. Abramsky [5] and Hyland [11] then, both independently, used game semantics to prove the full abstractness of PCF. The general idea behind game semantics is to model the *interaction* between the system and the environment by a game. A specific interaction is described by a strategy (sequence of moves) over the game. The use of game semantics for the description of security protocols is motivated by the the fact that game semantics can model the interaction between agents and the intruder in a natural way. It gives a dynamic view of how the protocol could proceed, especially when the execution of one step depends on all steps executed thus far. It is important to note that the use of games in security protocols was investigated in [13] where they followed a different approach than that of game semantics as taken by Abramsky and Hyland. Another effort in this regard is the Security Protocol Calculus (SPC) [6]. In this paper however we follow a different path defining various games and giving a denotational semantics to security protocols.

3   Syntax of Security Protocol

The proposed syntax of our GAme-based Security Protocol calculus (GASP) is demonstrated by the following BNF grammar:

$$
\begin{aligned}
Prot &::= Decl \,.\, Comm \mid \epsilon \\
Decl &::= \kappa_A \triangleright m \,.\, Decl \mid \nu_A \triangleright m \,.\, Decl \mid \epsilon \\
Comm &::= step\ i \triangleright A \rightarrow B : m \,.\, Comm \mid \epsilon \\
m &::= a \mid c \mid n \mid k \mid m, m \mid \{m\}_k \mid m\ op\ m
\end{aligned}
\tag{1}
$$

Here A and B are communicating agents, m is a certain message, $\kappa_A \triangleright m$ means m is part of the initial knowledge of A, and $\nu_A \triangleright m$ means m is fresh for A. The syntax above means that a protocol is just a number of declarations, followed by a number of communication steps. The last line is the syntax for messages. Here $op \in \{+, -, *, /\}$ and a ranges over agent names, c represents constant (text) messages, n represents natural numbers, and k represents cryptographic keys. The term m, m represents composed (concatenated) messages, and in some cases concatenation is written $m.m$ when it might be confused with elements in a set. The term $\{m\}_k$ denotes encrypted messages, where k is the encryption key.

3.1   Types of Messages

In our type system for messages, we have the following base types (sorts): Agent (agent names), Cryptkey (cryptographic keys), Natural (natural numbers), Text (constant messages, i.e., text), and Message (messages). A message is called *atomic* if its type is one of the first four types listed above, which are subtypes of Message. Typing rules for messages are given below:

$$a : \text{Agent} \qquad c : \text{Text} \qquad n : \text{Natural} \qquad k : \text{Cryptkey} \qquad m : \text{Message}$$

$$\frac{m_1 : \text{Message} \quad m_2 : \text{Message}}{m_1, m_2 : \text{Message}} \qquad \frac{k : \text{Cryptkey} \quad m : \text{Message}}{\{m\}_k : \text{Message}} \qquad \frac{m_1 : \text{Natural} \quad m_2 : \text{Natural}}{m_1\ op\ m_2 : \text{Natural}}$$

3.2   Messages and Knowledge

To express an agent's knowledge, we define the function Know : Agent $\rightarrow$ sets[Message], that maps a principal's name into the set $\mathcal{M}$ of messages known to this principal. Here we adopt the notation in [10] to express the fact that the function returns a set whose elements are of type Message. The set $\mathcal{M}$ satisfies the conditions:

$$
\begin{aligned}
(m \in \mathcal{M}) \wedge (m' \in \mathcal{M}) &\Rightarrow m \ op \ m' \in \mathcal{M} && \text{Arithmetic operation} \\
(m \ op \ m' \in \mathcal{M}) \wedge (m' \in \mathcal{M}) &\Rightarrow m \in \mathcal{M} && \text{Arithmetic operation} \\
(m \ op \ m' \in \mathcal{M}) \wedge (m \in \mathcal{M}) &\Rightarrow m' \in \mathcal{M} && \text{Arithmetic operation} \\
(m \in \mathcal{M}) \wedge (k \in \mathcal{M}) &\Rightarrow \{m\}_k \in \mathcal{M} && \text{Encryption} \\
(m \in \mathcal{M}) \wedge (m' \in \mathcal{M}) &\Rightarrow m.m' \in \mathcal{M} && \text{Concatenation} \\
(\{m\}_k \in \mathcal{M}) \wedge (k \in \mathcal{M}) &\Rightarrow m \in \mathcal{M} && \text{Decryption} \\
(\{m\}_k \in \mathcal{M}) \wedge (k' \in \mathcal{M}) \wedge (k' = k^{-1}) &\Rightarrow m \in \mathcal{M} && \text{Asymmetric decryption} \\
m.m' \in \mathcal{M} &\Rightarrow \{m, m'\} \subset \mathcal{M} && \text{Deconcatenation}
\end{aligned} \tag{2}
$$

4   Games

In game semantics, a game is a sequence of plays (moves) between two parties (*players*): A *proponent* P representing the system, and an *opponent* O representing the environment. Each move takes the form of a question Q or an answer A. For instance, the environment can ask for a value (question), and the system supplies this value (answer) directly, *or* asks the environment for more detail (question), and so on. We adopt the convention that the opponent always makes the first move then the game proceeds as alternating moves between player and opponent. Formally a game G is a structure (M_G, λ_G, P_G) where [4]:

$$
\begin{aligned}
M_G && \text{Set of game moves} \\
\lambda_G : M_G &\to \{P, O\} \times \{Q, A\} && \text{Labeling function signature} \\
\lambda_G &= \langle \lambda_G^{PO}, \lambda_G^{QA} \rangle && \text{Labeling function definition} \\
\lambda_G^{PO} : M_G &\to \{P, O\} && \text{Labeling proponent/opponent moves} \\
\lambda_G^{QA} : M_G &\to \{Q, A\} && \text{Labeling question/answer moves} \\
P_G &\subseteq^{nepref} M_G^{alt} && \text{Non-empty, prefix closed set of sequences}
\end{aligned} \tag{3}
$$

We write M_G^* for the set of finite sequences over M_G. A sequence $s = s_1.s_2 \ldots s_n$ has length $|s| = n$. Then, M_G^{alt} is a subset of M_G^* containing sequences s such that for even i, $\lambda_G^{PO}(s_i) = P$, and for odd i, $\lambda_G^{PO}(s_i) = O$. The domain P_G (the game tree) is a set of sequences, each of these sequences represents a path in the game tree. The domains P_G^{even} and P_G^{odd} are the sets of even- and odd- length sequences respectively. For any two sequences s and t, $\mathsf{pref}(st) = s$. For a set of sequences P_G, $\mathsf{Pref}(P_G) = \{\mathsf{pref}(s) \mid s \in P_G\}$. A set of sequences is prefix closed when $\mathsf{Pref}(P_G) = P_G$. A deterministic *strategy* σ on a game G is a subset $\sigma \subseteq P_G^{even}$ satisfying: $\epsilon \in \sigma$, $sab \in \sigma \Rightarrow s \in \sigma$, and $sab \wedge sac \in \sigma \Rightarrow b = c$. Here $s, t, u, \ldots$ represent sequences, and $a, b, c, \ldots$ represent single moves. Intuitively, a strategy is a path in the game tree that contains an even number of moves.

For any two sets X and Y, let the set $Z = X \uplus Y$ be their disjoint union. If the sequence $s \in Z^*$, then $s \restriction X \in X^*$, which means $s \restriction X$ is the sequence obtained by removing all the elements not in X from s. For any two games G and H, the tensor product $G \otimes H$ defines a game whose set of moves is $M_{G \otimes H} = M_G \uplus M_H$, the labeling function is then defined to be $\lambda_{G \otimes H} = [\lambda_G, \lambda_H]$. The game tree is: $P_{G \otimes H} = \{s \in M_{G \otimes H}^{alt} \mid (s \restriction M_G \in P_G) \wedge (s \restriction M_H \in P_H)\}$. As previously mentioned, all games start by O making a move. Here O can decide to make a move in G or H. The way the tensor product is defined makes that for any two consecutive moves s_i and s_{i+1} if s_{i+1} is a move of a subgame different than that of s_i, then $\lambda_{G \otimes H}^{PO}(s_i) = P$ and $\lambda_{G \otimes H}^{PO}(s_{i+1}) = O$. This is called the *switching* *condition* [4]. For any game G, its dual $G^{\perp}$ is obtained by interchanging the roles of the two players (P and O). The set of moves remains the same for both games, just the labeling function is changed, i.e., moves of O become those of P and vice versa. For any two games G and H, the game $G \multimap H$ is defined as $G^{\perp} \otimes H$. In this case, the first move (by O) will always be in H. The switching condition in $G \multimap H$ states that for any two consecutive moves s_i and s_{i+1} if s_{i+1} is a move of a subgame different than that of s_i, then $\lambda_{G \otimes H}^{PO}(s_i) = O$ and $\lambda_{G \otimes H}^{PO}(s_{i+1}) = P$ [4]. An *enabling* relation is defined over the set $M_G \cup \{\star\}$. The enabling relation means that a move cannot be played unless it was enabled (justified) by another move. The first move in the game is justified by $\star$. The enabling relation: $m \leadsto_G m'$ means that m' cannot be played unless m was played first. It is important to note that this relation is *not* transitive.

5 Definition of Games for Security Protocols

5.1 Atomic Messages

As explained earlier, atomic messages are messages that are of type Agent, Cryptkey, Natural, or Text. These types are represented by the games, Agt, Key, Nat, Txt respectively. In addition, we define the game Msg to represent the type Message. The idea is that games represent types, whereas strategies represent algorithms. An example is given below on how to represent constants and variables of the type Natural:

$$
\begin{array}{cc}
& \text{Nat} \multimap \text{Nat} \\
\begin{array}{cc}
\text{Nat} & \\
q & O \\
n & P \\
\end{array} &
\begin{array}{cc}
& q \quad O \\
q & \quad P \\
n' & \quad O \\
& n' \quad P \\
\end{array}
\end{array}
\qquad
\begin{array}{ccc}
\text{Emp} \overset{\sigma}{\multimap} \text{Nat} & \text{Nat} \overset{\tau}{\multimap} \text{Nat} \\
\end{array}
$$

The game to the left represents constants of natural numbers, a certain strategy over this game represents a particular constant, for instance the constant 3 is represented by the strategy $\sigma = q.3$. This means that the environment (O) asks for a constant and the system (P) replies with the number 3. The game in the middle represents variables of natural numbers, i.e., the lambda term $\lambda x : \text{Natural}.x$, which has type Natural $\rightarrow$ Natural (corresponding to the game Nat $\multimap$ Nat). Any strategy τ over this game represents a variable and has the form $\tau = q.q.n'.n'$, where n' is any natural number. If we apply the value 3 to the lambda term above we get $(\lambda x : \text{N}.x)3 = 3$, the equivalence of this operation in game semantics is interaction between strategies (parallel composition plus hiding). For any two strategies σ and τ, over the games $G \multimap H$ and $H \multimap I$ respectively, the composed strategy $\sigma; \tau$ is formally defined as:

$$
\begin{aligned}
\sigma; \tau &= (\sigma \| \tau)/H = \{s \upharpoonright G, I \mid s \in \sigma \| \tau\} \\
\sigma \| \tau &= \{s \in (M_G + M_H + M_I)^* \mid s \upharpoonright G, H \in \sigma \wedge s \upharpoonright H, I \in \tau\}
\end{aligned}
\tag{4}
$$

In order to conform with the definition of interaction between strategies, we redefine the game of constant naturals to be Emp $\multimap$ Nat, where Emp is the empty game (has no moves). We do this so that we can compose the two strategies $\sigma : \mathsf{Emp} \multimap \mathsf{Nat}$ ($\sigma = q.3$) and $\tau : \mathsf{Nat} \multimap \mathsf{Nat}$ ($\tau = q.q.n'.n'$). Now, hiding the common Nat game will leave us with a $\mathsf{Emp} \multimap \mathsf{Nat}$ game which represents the constant 3 as expected i.e., $\sigma; \tau = q.3$. Of course, *hiding* is done by removing whatever is included in the dashed rectangle (the last game to the right in the figure above). We notice here how the *copy cat* strategy between the two Nat games, where each player copies the other's moves (represented by the horizontal bar), served as a link between σ and τ. The copy cat strategy id_G over a game G and its dual is defined as:

$$id_G = \{s \in P_{G \multimap G}^{even} \mid \forall t \text{ even-length prefix of } \bullet \, s : t \upharpoonright G^1 = t \upharpoonright G^2\} \qquad (5)$$

Here the superscripts are just used to differentiate between the two copies of the game G. The same examples could be generalized to all types of atomic messages mentioned above.

5.2   Composed Messages

The composed messages that we define here result from the outcome of two operations: Concatenation, and encryption. The game used to express the operation of concatenation is the game $\mathsf{Msg} \multimap \mathsf{Msg} \multimap \mathsf{Msg}$ (representing type $\mathsf{Message} \rightarrow \mathsf{Message} \rightarrow \mathsf{Message}$). The game used to represent the encryption operation is the game $\mathsf{Msg} \multimap \mathsf{Key} \multimap \mathsf{Msg}$. The specific algorithms of concatenation and encryption are expressed by strategies over the respective games. For instance the concatenation operation is represented by the strategy $q.q.m_1.q.m_2.\mathsf{conc}(m_1, m_2)$. The encryption operation, on the other hand, is represented by the strategy $q.q.m.q.k.\mathsf{encr}(m, k)$. Here, the functions $\mathsf{conc} : \mathsf{Message} \rightarrow \mathsf{Message} \rightarrow \mathsf{Message}$ and $\mathsf{encr} : \mathsf{Message} \rightarrow \mathsf{Cryptkey} \rightarrow \mathsf{Message}$ represent the concatenation and encryption operations respectively.

5.3   Communication Part of the Protocol

Single Communication Step. As mentioned above, a certain message of type $\mathsf{Message}$ is considered as a play of the game Msg. The play in Msg proceeds as follows: The environment (the channel, intruder) asks a principal (proponent) for a message, and the principal, in turn, replies with a certain messages out of a possible number (probably infinite) of messages. This means that any strategy over Msg will have the form $q.m$, where m is a certain message. A communication step, on the other hand, is represented by a strategy over the game $\mathsf{Csg} = \mathsf{Msg} \multimap \mathsf{Msg}$. In this case, the succession of communication steps forming the protocol specification is represented by a strategy over the game $\mathsf{Csg} \otimes \mathsf{Csg} \ldots \otimes \mathsf{Csg}$. We need to define $\mathbb{M} : \mathsf{sets}[\mathsf{Message}]$ to be the set of all messages of type $\mathsf{Message}$ i.e. $\mathbb{M} = \{m | m : \mathsf{Message}\}$. The formal definition of the game is given hereafter:

$$\begin{aligned} M_{\mathsf{Msg}} &= \{q\} \cup \mathbb{M} \\ P_{\mathsf{Msg}} &= \{\epsilon\} \cup \{q\} \cup \{q.m \mid m \in \mathbb{M}\} \\ \lambda(q) &= OQ \\ \forall m \in \mathbb{M} \bullet \lambda(m) &= PA \end{aligned} \qquad (6)$$

We define the Communication Step Game Csg, where:

$$\begin{aligned} M_{\mathsf{Csg}} &= \{q^1\} \cup \{q^2\} \cup \{m^i \mid m \in \mathbb{M}, i \in \{1, 2\}\} \\ \lambda_{\mathsf{Csg}}(q^i) &= \begin{cases} PQ & i = 1 \\ OQ & i = 2 \end{cases} \quad \lambda_{\mathsf{Csg}}(m^i) = \begin{cases} OA \; \forall m \in \mathbb{M} \wedge i = 1 \\ PA \; \forall m \in \mathbb{M} \wedge i = 2 \end{cases} \end{aligned} \qquad (7)$$

The following enabling relation is defined over M_{Csg}:

$$\star \leadsto_{\mathsf{Csg}} q^2$$
$$q^2 \leadsto_{\mathsf{Csg}} q^1$$
$$q^1 \leadsto_{\mathsf{Csg}} m^1 \; \forall m \in \mathbb{M}$$
$$m^1 \leadsto_{\mathsf{Csg}} n^2 \; \forall m, n \in \mathbb{M} \tag{8}$$

The enabling relation affects the game tree:

$$P_{\mathsf{Csg}} = \{\epsilon\} \cup \{q^2, q^2.q^1\} \cup \{q^2.q^1.m^1\} \cup \{q^2.q^1.m^1.n^2\} \quad \forall m, n \in \mathbb{M}$$

We notice here that we used a superscript to differentiate between moves in each game, since the set of moves is the *disjoint* union of the sets of the individual games. We used the superscript 1 to denote moves of the game to the left of $\multimap$, and the superscript 2 for the other game. This is equivalent to denoting the games as $\mathsf{Msg}^1 \multimap \mathsf{Msg}^2$. The definition of the enabling relation in (8) makes sure that n^2 cannot be played unless m^1 is played first (any sequence in the game tree will be the prefix of a sequence in the form $q^2.q^1.m^1.m^2$). This results from the fact that we assumed that in any communication step (Csg game) an honest agent (the proponent) only sends a message in response to a message that they received from the intruder. We clarify these ideas by taking as example the first three steps of the Woo and Lam authentication protocol [20]: Step1. $A \rightarrow B : A$, Step2. $B \rightarrow A : N_b$, Step3. $A \rightarrow B : \{N_b\}_{K_{as}}$. Examining Step 1, we notice that A initiates the protocol. Since we assumed O (the channel) always plays first, we assume A gets a start message *"start"* from the channel and replies with his identity A. The *"start"* message serves as an action to begin the execution of the protocol. In Step 2 B receives the message A from the channel and replies with a nonce N_b, and other steps follow. We rewrite the first three steps as:

$$\begin{array}{lll} \text{Step1. } I \rightarrow A : start & \text{Step2. } I \rightarrow B : A & \text{Step3. } I \rightarrow A : N_b \\ \quad\quad A \rightarrow I : A & \quad\quad B \rightarrow I : N_b & \quad\quad A \rightarrow I : \{N_b\}_{K_{as}} \end{array} \tag{9}$$

The protocol description in (9) makes clear the role of the intruder I. Each communication step has the form: $I \rightarrow X : m_i$ followed by $X \rightarrow I : m_j$ where X is an honest agent. To respect the notation, a protocol will always end by an agent X sending a *terminate* message to the intruder. The *terminate* message marks the end of the protocol execution. Expressed this way, each communication step can be captured as a strategy σ over the game Csg. The execution of a number of steps in succession can be represented by a strategy over the tensor product of a number of Csg games. As an example, Step1 and Step2 are represented as a strategy over the game $(\mathsf{Msg}^{11} \multimap \mathsf{Msg}^{12}) \otimes (\mathsf{Msg}^{21} \multimap \mathsf{Msg}^{22})$. This strategy is the sequence $q^{12}.q^{11}.start^{11}.A^{12}.q^{22}.q^{21}.A^{21}.N_b^{22}$. Here, we note the use of superscripts to identify different copies of the Msg game. The tensor product, however, does not specify which game is played first (i.e., we can start by playing the game of Step 2). This is why we need the enabling relation to specify the order of moves.

Single Protocol Session (Functional View). The functional view of a security protocol describes how the protocol executes under the restriction that all agents behave honestly (i.e., the intruder only forwards messages between agents). For any protocol with $N-1$ communication steps, the Protocol Session Game $\mathsf{Psg}_{[N]}$ is defined by: $\mathsf{Psg}_{[N]} \overset{def}{=} !_N \mathsf{Csg}$ which is the tensor product of N copies of the Csg game under the condition that no play can take place in the ith copy unless a play was made in the $(i-1)^{th}$ copy. This insures that the protocol steps are done in order. The previous discussion is summarized by the following equations:

$$\mathsf{Psg}_{[N]} \stackrel{def}{=} \ !_N \mathsf{Csg}$$
$$!_N \mathsf{Csg} \stackrel{def}{=} \mathsf{Csg}^1 \otimes \mathsf{Csg}^2 \ldots \otimes \mathsf{Csg}^n \qquad \forall i' > i \, . \, \mathsf{Csg}^{i'} \text{ is started after } \mathsf{Csg}^i \qquad (10)$$
$$\stackrel{def}{=} (\mathsf{Msg}^{11} \multimap \mathsf{Msg}^{12}) \otimes (\mathsf{Msg}^{21} \multimap \mathsf{Msg}^{22}) \ldots \otimes (\mathsf{Msg}^{N1} \multimap \mathsf{Msg}^{N2})$$

The subscript [N] of the Psg game emphasizes the fact that this game is parameterized over the value of N. We notice that each copy of the Csg game is identified by a different superscript. Also, each Csg game contains two copies of the Msg game. For instance Csg^i is the game $\mathsf{Msg}^{i1} \multimap \mathsf{Msg}^{i2}$. Following the same notation, moves are identified according to which copy of the Msg game they belong, i.e., the move m^{ir} represents a message m played as a move in the copy ir of the Msg game. For instance the moves m^{12} and m^{21} represent the same message m played in different copies of the Msg game. We define $\mathsf{Psg}_{[N]}$ as:

$$M_{\mathsf{Psg}_{[N]}} = \{q^{i1}\} \cup \{q^{i2}\} \cup \{m^{i1}\} \cup \{m^{i2}\} \mid m \in \mathbb{M}, i \in \{1, 2, \ldots, N\}$$
$$\lambda_{\mathsf{Psg}_{[N]}}(q^{ir}) = \begin{cases} PQ \ r = 1 \\ OQ \ r = 2 \end{cases} \qquad \lambda_{\mathsf{Psg}_{[N]}}(m^{ir}) = \begin{cases} OA \ \forall m \in \mathbb{M} \wedge r = 1 \\ PA \ \forall m \in \mathbb{M} \wedge r = 2 \end{cases} \qquad (11)$$

The enabling relation is defined as follows:

$$\begin{aligned}
\star &\rightsquigarrow_{\mathsf{Psg}_{[N]}} q^{12} \\
m^{(i-1)2} &\rightsquigarrow_{\mathsf{Psg}_{[N]}} q^{i2} & m \in \mathbb{M} \quad \forall i \in \{2, \ldots N\} \\
q^{i2} &\rightsquigarrow_{\mathsf{Psg}_{[N]}} q^{i1} & \forall i \in \{1, \ldots N\} \\
q^{11} &\rightsquigarrow_{\mathsf{Psg}_{[N]}} start \\
m^{N1} &\rightsquigarrow_{\mathsf{Psg}_{[N]}} terminate \\
q^{i1} &\rightsquigarrow_{\mathsf{Psg}_{[N]}} m^{i1} & \forall i \in \{2, \ldots N\} \quad \forall m, n \in \mathbb{M} \, . \, n^{(i-1)2} \wedge m^{i1} \Rightarrow m = n \\
m^{i1} &\rightsquigarrow_{\mathsf{Psg}_{[N]}} n^{i2} & \forall m, n \in \mathbb{M} \, \forall i \in \{1, \ldots N - 1\}
\end{aligned}$$
$$(12)$$

The game tree $P_{\mathsf{Psg}_{[N]}}$ is the set of sequences, that is a subset of $M^{alt}_{\mathsf{Psg}_{[N]}}$, each sequence satisfies the switching condition, and the enabling relation. This definition of the game tree is also valid for all games defined in the rest of the paper. In the enabling relation, the first rule states that the game opens with a move by the opponent in Csg^1. Since Csg ends with a move by the proponent in Msg^2 (m^{i2}), the second rule results in that the Csg games are played one after the other (according to the order of the communication steps). The third rule implies the switching conditions between Msg^2 and Msg^1, while the fourth and fifth rules are special for the *start* and *terminate* messages respectively. The sixth rule states that questions enable answers in Msg^{i1} (in any step) and that these answers m^{i1} (by the intruder) equal the message received by the intruder in the previous communication step (i.e., the message $n^{(i-1)2}$). This is because in the functional description of the protocol, we assume an honest intruder that just forwards messages between different agents. The seventh rule states that n^{i2} cannot be played unless m^{i1} was played first (an agent does not send a message to the intruder unless it received a message from the intruder in return). The way the $\mathsf{Psg}_{[N]}$ game is defined makes that the play proceeds in Csg^1, followed by Csg^2 and so on till we reach Csg^N where the play ends with the terminating move. In this regard, a protocol with $N-1$ communication steps has a type expressed by the game $\mathsf{Psg}_{[N]}$, where $\mathsf{Psg}_{[N]} =!_N\mathsf{Csg}$. The protocol itself is a strategy $\sigma : \mathsf{Psg}_{[N]}$ from the set of possible strategies over $\mathsf{Psg}_{[N]}$. This strategy is obtained by replacing each move m^{ir} with the corresponding message from the protocol specification.

Multiple Protocol Sessions (Functional View). Running multiple sessions of the protocol can be represented by the game $!_M\mathsf{Psg}_{[N]}$ (assuming there are M sessions). In this case, a certain run of M sessions of a protocol $\mathcal{P}rot$ can be represented by a sequence of moves over the game $\mathsf{Prt}_{[M,N]}$, where $\mathsf{Prt}_{[M,N]}$ is defined as follows:

$$\mathsf{Prt}_{[M,N]} \stackrel{def}{=} !_M\mathsf{Psg}_{[N]}$$

$$!_M\mathsf{Psg}_{[N]} \stackrel{def}{=} \mathsf{Psg}_{[N]}^1 \otimes \mathsf{Psg}_{[N]}^2 \ldots \otimes \mathsf{Psg}_{[N]}^M \quad \forall j' > j \quad \mathsf{Psg}_{[N]}^{j'} \text{ is started after } \mathsf{Psg}_{[N]}^j$$

$$\stackrel{def}{=} \mathsf{Csg}^{1,1} \ldots \otimes \mathsf{Csg}^{1,N} \otimes \mathsf{Csg}^{2,1} \ldots \otimes \mathsf{Csg}^{2,N} \ldots \otimes \mathsf{Csg}^{M,1} \ldots \otimes \mathsf{Csg}^{M,N} \quad (13)$$

$$\stackrel{def}{=} \begin{array}{ll} (\mathsf{Msg}^{1,11} \multimap \mathsf{Msg}^{1,12}) \ldots & \otimes(\mathsf{Msg}^{1,N1} \multimap \mathsf{Msg}^{1,N2})\otimes \\ (\mathsf{Msg}^{2,11} \multimap \mathsf{Msg}^{2,12}) \ldots & \otimes(\mathsf{Msg}^{2,N1} \multimap \mathsf{Msg}^{2,N2})\otimes \\ \ldots & \otimes(\mathsf{Msg}^{M,N1} \multimap \mathsf{Msg}^{M,N2}) \end{array}$$

The symbols are read as follows: $\mathsf{Psg}_{[N]}^j$ is the jth copy of the $\mathsf{Psg}_{[N]}$ game (played in the jth session of the protocol), $\mathsf{Csg}^{j,i}$ is the game played in the ith communication step of the jth session, $\mathsf{Msg}^{j,ir}$ is the rth copy of Msg played in the ith communication step of the jth session, and finally $m_1^{j,ir}$ is a certain move m_1 played in $\mathsf{Msg}^{j,ir}$. For a certain protocol of $N-1$ communication steps, running M sessions of this protocol will result in the variables j, i, and r ranging over the values $\{1,\ldots M\}$, $\{1,\ldots N\}$, and $\{1,2\}$ respectively. This can be seen in (13).

$$M_{\mathsf{Prt}_{[M,N]}} = \{q^{j,i1}\} \cup \{q^{j,i2}\} \cup \{m^{j,i1}\} \cup \{m^{j,i2}\}$$
$$m \in \mathbb{M}, j \in \{1,\ldots,M\}, i \in \{1,\ldots,N\} \quad (14)$$
$$\lambda_{\mathsf{Prt}_{[M,N]}}(q^{j,ir}) = \begin{cases} PQ \ r=1 \\ OQ \ r=2 \end{cases} \quad \lambda_{\mathsf{Prt}_{[M,N]}}(m^{j,ir}) = \begin{cases} OA \ \forall m \in \mathbb{M} \wedge r = 1 \\ PA \ \forall m \in \mathbb{M} \wedge r = 2 \end{cases}$$

The enabling relation is defined as follows:

$$\begin{array}{lll} \star \rightsquigarrow_{\mathsf{Prt}_{[M,N]}} q^{1,12} \\ m^{j,(i-1)2} \rightsquigarrow_{\mathsf{Prt}_{[M,N]}} q^{j,i2} & m \in \mathbb{M} \\ q^{j,i2} \rightsquigarrow_{\mathsf{Prt}_{[M,N]}} q^{j,i1} & \forall j \in \{1,\ldots M\} \quad \forall i \in \{1,\ldots N\} \\ q^{j,11} \rightsquigarrow_{\mathsf{Prt}_{[M,N]}} start & \forall j \in \{1,\ldots M\} \\ m^{j,N1} \rightsquigarrow_{\mathsf{Prt}_{[M,N]}} terminate \ m \in \mathbb{M} \quad \forall j \in \{1,\ldots M\} & (15) \\ q^{j,i1} \rightsquigarrow_{\mathsf{Prt}_{[M,N]}} m^{j,i1} & \forall j \in \{1,\ldots M\} \quad \forall i \in \{2,\ldots N\} \\ & \forall m,n \in \mathbb{M} \cdot n^{j,(i-1)2} \wedge m^{j,i1} \Rightarrow m = n \\ m^{j,i1} \rightsquigarrow_{\mathsf{Prt}_{[M,N]}} n^{j,i2} & \forall m,n \in \mathbb{M} \quad \forall j \in \{1,\ldots M\} \quad \forall i \in \{1,\ldots N-1\} \\ m^{j-1,12} \rightsquigarrow_{\mathsf{Prt}_{[M,N]}} q^{j,12} & \forall j \in \{2,\ldots M\} \end{array}$$

In the enabling relation above, the first rule states that the initial move of the $\mathsf{Prt}_{[M,N]}$ game is by the opponent in Csg^1 (communication step 1) of session 1. The second to the seventh rules control moves within a certain protocol session j and were explained for the game $\mathsf{Psg}_{[N]}$. The eighth rule states that finishing the first communication step of a certain session enables the first communication step of the next session. The game tree $P_{\mathsf{Prt}_{[M,N]}}$ is defined as in the $\mathsf{Psg}_{[N]}$ game.

Single Protocol Session (Security View). In the security view of protocols, we consider different manipulations that can be done by the intruder to messages in order to execute an attack. To describe the security semantics of a protocol we redefine the $\mathsf{Psg}_{[N]}$ game to be the game $\mathsf{Ssg}_{[N]}$, which describes a single session of the protocol assuming intruder manipulations.

$$
\begin{aligned}
\mathsf{Ssg}_{[N]} &\overset{def}{=} \otimes_N \mathsf{Csg} \\
&\overset{def}{=} \mathsf{Csg}^1 \otimes \mathsf{Csg}^2 \ldots \otimes \mathsf{Csg}^N \\
&\overset{def}{=} (\mathsf{Msg}^{11} \multimap \mathsf{Msg}^{12}) \otimes (\mathsf{Msg}^{21} \multimap \mathsf{Msg}^{22}) \ldots \otimes (\mathsf{Msg}^{N1} \multimap \mathsf{Msg}^{N2})
\end{aligned} \tag{16}
$$

The difference between $\otimes_N \mathsf{Csg}$ and $!_N \mathsf{Csg}$ is that in the former we drop the condition that if $i > i'$ then play in Csg^i has to be started after $\mathsf{Csg}^{i'}$. The game $\mathsf{Ssg}_{[N]}$ is defined as the game Csg but with the following changed enabling relation:

$$
\begin{aligned}
\star &\leadsto_{\mathsf{Ssg}_{[N]}} q^{t2} & t \in \{1, \ldots N\} \\
q^{i2} &\leadsto_{\mathsf{Ssg}_{[N]}} q^{i1} & \forall i \in \{1, \ldots N\} \\
q^{11} &\leadsto_{\mathsf{Ssg}_{[N]}} start & \\
m^{N1} &\leadsto_{\mathsf{Ssg}_{[N]}} terminate & \\
q^{i1} &\leadsto_{\mathsf{Ssg}_{[N]}} m^{i1} & \forall m \in \mathbb{M} \quad \forall i \in \{2, \ldots N\} \\
m^{i1} &\leadsto_{\mathsf{Ssg}_{[N]}} q^{i'2} & \forall m \in \mathbb{M} \quad \forall i, i' \in \{1, \ldots N\}, i \neq i' \\
m^{i1} &\leadsto_{\mathsf{Ssg}_{[N]}} n^{i2} & \forall m, n \in \mathbb{M} \quad \forall i \in \{1, \ldots N-1\}
\end{aligned} \tag{17}
$$

In (17) above, the enabling relation is changed to reflect the fact that the game can start in any communication step (any Csg^i). Once intruder has sent a message in this step (m^{t2} above), he can start any other step. This modification to the enabling relation reflects in the game tree $P_{\mathsf{Ssg}_{[N]}}$. The first line of the enabling relation definition in (17) states this, to be consistent with the definition of $\otimes_N G$. Another major difference from the definition of the enabling relation of $\mathsf{Psg}_{[N]}$ is that we drop the condition that the intruder is restricted to forwarding messages between agents. This is reflected in the fifth rule in the enabling relation definition in (17). Here, we put no restrictions on answers by the intruder (m^{i1}). The only restriction will be that this answer (message) can be accepted by the honest agent at step i of the protocol. This is protocol-specific and should be determined by the semantic functions examining the protocol.

Multiple Protocol Sessions (Security View). In this case, the $\mathsf{Prt}_{[M,N]}$ game is redefined to be the game $\mathsf{Spr}_{[M,N]}$:

$$
\begin{aligned}
\mathsf{Spr}_{[M,N]} &\overset{def}{=} !_M \mathsf{Psg}_{[N]} \\
!_M \mathsf{Psg}_{[N]} &\overset{def}{=} \mathsf{Psg}^1_{[N]} \otimes \mathsf{Psg}^2_{[N]} \ldots \otimes \mathsf{Psg}^M_{[N]} \quad \forall j' > j \cdot \mathsf{Psg}^{j'}_{[N]} \text{ is started after } \mathsf{Psg}^j_{[N]} \\
&\overset{def}{=} \mathsf{Csg}^{1,1} \ldots \otimes \mathsf{Csg}^{1,N} \otimes \mathsf{Csg}^{2,1} \ldots \otimes \mathsf{Csg}^{2,N} \ldots \otimes \mathsf{Csg}^{M,1} \ldots \otimes \mathsf{Csg}^{M,N}
\end{aligned} \tag{18}
$$

Definitions of moves and labeling functions of $\mathsf{Spr}_{[M,N]}$ are the same as those of $\mathsf{Prt}_{[M,N]}$, but the enabling relation is changed to be:

$$
\begin{array}{lll}
\star \rightsquigarrow_{\mathsf{Spr}_{[M,N]}} q^{1,t2} & & t \in \{1,\dots N\} \\
m^{j-1,i1} \rightsquigarrow_{\mathsf{Spr}_{[M,N]}} q^{j,i'2} & & i,i' \in \{1,\dots N\} \quad \forall j \in \{2,\dots M\} \\
q^{j,11} \rightsquigarrow_{\mathsf{Spr}_{[M,N]}} start & & \\
m^{j,N1} \rightsquigarrow_{\mathsf{Spr}_{[M,N]}} terminate & & m \in \mathbb{M} \quad \forall j \in \{1,\dots M\} \\
q^{j,i2} \rightsquigarrow_{\mathsf{Spr}_{[M,N]}} q^{j,i1} & & \forall j \in \{1,\dots M\} \quad \forall i \in \{1,\dots N\} \\
q^{j,i1} \rightsquigarrow_{\mathsf{Spr}_{[M,N]}} m^{j,i1} & & \forall m \in \mathbb{M} \quad \forall j \in \{1,\dots M\} \quad \forall i \in \{2,\dots N\} \\
m^{j,i1} \rightsquigarrow_{\mathsf{Spr}_{[M,N]}} n^{j,i2} & & \forall m,n \in \mathbb{M} \quad \forall j \in \{1,\dots M\} \quad \forall i \in \{1,\dots N\} \\
m^{j,i1} \rightsquigarrow_{\mathsf{Spr}_{[M,N]}} q^{j,i'2} & & \forall m \in \mathbb{M} \quad \forall j \in \{1,\dots M\} \quad \forall i,i' \in \{1,\dots N\}, i \neq i'
\end{array}
\tag{19}
$$

The game tree $P_{\mathsf{Spr}_{[M,N]}}$ is affected by the enabling relation, where the first condition states that the play can begin in any step in Session 1. Notice that the first move of this step has to be a question by the opponent (i.e., $q^{1,t2}$). Once the game has started in any step in a certain session, *and* the intruder has sent a message in this step ($m^{j-1,i1}$), he can start the play in any step in the next session ($q^{j,i'2}$), this is stated by the second condition. The third condition is special for the start message, i.e., the start message is always enabled in communication step 1 in any session. The fourth condition states the condition for the termination of one session of the protocol (i.e., the reception of $m^{j,N1}$). The fifth, sixth and seventh rules put a condition on the sequence of moves in any communication step in a certain session. They simply state that in any communication step we cannot have a sequence $q^{j,i2}.m^{j,i2}$, this sequence means that an agent sends a message to the intruder without first getting a message form the intruder. This is to emphasize the rule that we established before that each communication step is an exchange between the intruder and an agent, where the intruder has to supply a message in order to get a message in return. The eighth rule is similar to the second rule but for the same session. It states that in any step in a certain session, once the intruder has sent a message in this step ($m^{j,i1}$), he can start the play in any step in the same session ($q^{j,i'2}$).

6 Semantics

6.1 Protocol Types

Any type τ of a certain protocol can be defined by the following BNF grammar: $\tau ::= \mathsf{Msg} \multimap \mathsf{Msg} \mid \tau \otimes \tau$. To assign a type to a protocol we use the typing rules below, where $\alpha, \beta, \dots$ represent single communication steps.

$$
\textbf{(Step)} \ \frac{\cdot}{\alpha : \mathsf{Msg} \multimap \mathsf{Msg}} \qquad \textbf{(Comm)} \ \frac{\alpha : \mathsf{Msg} \multimap \mathsf{Msg} \quad Comm : \tau}{\alpha.Comm : (\mathsf{Msg} \multimap \mathsf{Msg}) \otimes \tau}
$$

$$
\textbf{(Prot)} \ \frac{Decl : \tau \quad Comm : \tau'}{Decl.Comm : \tau'}
$$

From the rules above, a protocol type τ will have the form $(\mathsf{Msg} \multimap \mathsf{Msg}) \otimes (\mathsf{Msg} \multimap \mathsf{Msg}) \otimes \dots$ We define the function $\bar{\tau}$ over the algebra of types.

$$\overline{\mathsf{Msg}} = 0 \quad \overline{\mathsf{Msg} \multimap \mathsf{Msg}} = 1 \quad \overline{\tau' \otimes \tau'} = \overline{\tau'} + \overline{\tau'}$$

6.2   Semantics of Messages

If σ is a strategy over the game $\mathsf{Msg} \multimap \mathsf{Msg} \multimap \mathsf{Msg}$, we define the operator $\mathfrak{U}(\cdot)$ such that $\mathfrak{U}(\sigma)$ is the strategy over the game $\mathsf{Msg} \otimes \mathsf{Msg} \multimap \mathsf{Msg}$. This is similar to the operation of *un-currying* in functional programming. For any three Games G, H and F such that we have two strategies: The strategy $\sigma : G \multimap H$, and the strategy $\tau : G \multimap F$. We define the strategy $\langle \sigma, \tau \rangle$ as the strategy over the game $G \multimap (H \otimes F)$. The semantic function for messages is defined below. The function encr : Message $\rightarrow$ Cryptkey $\rightarrow$ Message is the encryption function and conc : Message $\rightarrow$ Message $\rightarrow$ Message is the concatenation function. The semantic function $\mathfrak{S}$ takes as arguments a certain message and returns a set of sequences over the game that represents the type of the message.

$$\mathfrak{S} : \mathsf{Message} \rightarrow \mathcal{S}_\tau$$
$$\mathfrak{S}[\![a]\!] = \{\sigma \mid \sigma : \mathsf{Emp} \multimap \mathsf{Agt}\} = \{\epsilon\} \cup \{q.a \mid a : \mathsf{Agent}\}$$
$$\mathfrak{S}[\![c]\!] = \{\sigma \mid \sigma : \mathsf{Emp} \multimap \mathsf{Txt}\} = \{\epsilon\} \cup \{q.c \mid c : \mathsf{Text}\}$$
$$\mathfrak{S}[\![k]\!] = \{\sigma \mid \sigma : \mathsf{Emp} \multimap \mathsf{Key}\} = \{\epsilon\} \cup \{q.K \mid K : \mathsf{Cryptkey}\}$$
$$\mathfrak{S}[\![n]\!] = \{\sigma \mid \sigma : \mathsf{Emp} \multimap \mathsf{Nat}\} = \{\epsilon\} \cup \{q.n \mid n : \mathsf{Natural}\}$$

The following is the concatenation algorithm, it is interpreted as a set of sequences (strategies) over the game $\mathsf{Msg} \multimap \mathsf{Msg} \multimap \mathsf{Msg}$. Each sequence in this set is a prefix of the sequence $q.q.m.q.m'.\mathsf{conc}(m, m')$ for all $m, m' \in \mathbb{M}$. The underlying semantic function is given below:

$$\mathfrak{S}[\![\_, \_]\!] = \{\sigma : \mathsf{Msg} \multimap \mathsf{Msg} \multimap \mathsf{Msg} \mid \forall m, m' : \mathsf{Message} \ . \ \sigma \in \Sigma_{conc}\}$$

Where $\Sigma_{conc} = \{\epsilon, q.q\} \cup \{q.q.m.q\} \cup \{q.q.m.q.m'.\mathsf{conc}(m, m')\}$. The following is the concatenation algorithm applied to messages m_1 and m_2. Function application is represented by interaction of strategies.

$$\mathfrak{S}[\![m_1, m_2]\!] = \{\sigma : \mathsf{Msg}\}, \ \sigma = \langle [\![m_1]\!], [\![m_2]\!] \rangle; \mathfrak{U}([\![\_, \_]\!])$$

The following is the semantics of the encryption function:

$$\mathfrak{S}[\![\{\_\}\_]\!] = \{\sigma : \mathsf{Msg} \multimap \mathsf{Key} \multimap \mathsf{Msg} \mid \forall m : \mathsf{Message}, k : \mathsf{Cryptkey} \ . \ \sigma \in \Sigma_{encr}\}$$

Where $\Sigma_{encr} = \{\epsilon, q.q\} \cup \{q.q.m.q\} \cup \{q.q.m.q.k.\mathsf{encr}(m, k)\}$. The following is the encryption algorithm applied to a message and a key:

$$\mathfrak{S}[\![\{m\}_k]\!] = \{\sigma : \mathsf{Msg}\}, \ \sigma = \langle [\![m]\!], [\![k]\!] \rangle; \mathfrak{U}([\![\{\_\}\_]\!])$$

6.3   Transmission of Messages

The honest agent, upon receiving a certain message, must check it against the message he expects to receive at this particular step of the protocol. If the message passes the check, the agent will accept it and continue the protocol, otherwise he will terminate execution. The message, if accepted, will be added to the agent's knowledge and used in further communication steps. To formalize this discussion, first we define the function knows : Know that given a principal's name will return the messages known to this principal as defined in (2). Then, we define the function check : Agent $\rightarrow$ Know $\rightarrow$ Message $\rightarrow$ Message $\rightarrow$ Message. This function given a principal's name A, a message m and another message m', will check m' against m. If there is no match, the function will return the *terminate* message signifying the termination of the protocol execution. If, on the other hand, m' passes the check, the function will return the message that will be added to the principal's knowledge as a result of accepting m'.

```
check(A, knows, m, m') =
if m is atomic then                                else if m = m₁.m₂ then
  if m ∉ knows(A) then                               let m'₁.m'₂ = m' in
    m'                                                 check(A, knows, m₁, m'₁) . check(A, knows, m₂, m'₂)
  else if m ∈ knows(A) ∧ m = m' then                end
    m'                                              else if m = m₁ op m₂ then
  else if m ∈ knows(A) ∧ m ≠ m' then                 if m₁ ∉ knows(A) ∧ m₂ ∉ knows(A) then
    terminate                                          m'
else if m = {m₁}_K then                              else if m₁ ∈ knows(A) ∧ m₂ ∉ knows(A) then
  if m₁ ∉ knows(A) ∧ K ∉ knows(A) then               let m₁ op m'₁ = m' in
    m'                                                 m₁ op m'₁
  else if m₁ ∈ knows(A) ∧ K ∉ knows(A) then          end
    m'                                              else if m₁ ∉ knows(A) ∧ m₂ ∈ knows(A) then
  else if m₁ ∉ knows(A) ∧ K ∈ knows(A) then          let m'₂ op m₂ = m' in
    let m'₁ = decrypt(m', K) in                       m'₂ op m₂
    {m'₁}_K                                           end
    end                                             else if m₁ ∈ knows(A) ∧ m₂ ∈ knows(A) then
  else if m ∈ knows(A) ∧ K ∈ knows(A) then           if m' = m₁ op m₂ then
    if m' = {m₁}_K then                                m'
      m'                                             else
    else                                               terminate
      terminate                                      end
    end                                            end
  end                                            end
end
```

6.4 Protocol Semantics (Functional View)

A protocol is *well-formed* if no message is sent unless: The message is part of the sender's initial knowledge, the message has been previously received by the sender, or the message can be deduced from initial knowledge and /or the set of received messages. Hereafter we define first the function Wf_Prot() that checks a protocol for well-formedness, then we define the semantic function of a well-formed protocol.

In the following let $\mathcal{P}$, $\mathcal{D}$ and $\mathcal{C}$ be a certain protocol, declaration and communication steps respectively. We also define the following:

knows : Know	Function that returns the set of messages known to an agent
fresh : Know	Function that returns the set of messages fresh to an agent

State $\overset{def}{=}$ Know $\times$ Know Definition of the type State

st : State	Variable of type State
Bool	Type of boolean values

We define the function $\mathfrak{D}$ that scans declarations and updates the agent's state accordingly:

$$\mathfrak{D} : \mathcal{D}ecl \rightarrow \text{State} \rightarrow \text{State}$$
$$\mathfrak{D}[\![\kappa_A \triangleright m.\mathcal{D}]\!](\text{knows}, \text{fresh}) = \mathfrak{D}[\![\mathcal{D}]\!](\text{knows} \dagger [A \mapsto \text{knows}(A) \cup \{m\}], \text{fresh})$$
$$\mathfrak{D}[\![\nu_A \triangleright m.\mathcal{D}]\!](\text{knows}, \text{fresh}) = \mathfrak{D}[\![\mathcal{D}]\!](\text{knows}, \text{fresh} \dagger [A \mapsto f(A) \cup \{m\}])$$
$$\mathfrak{D}[\![\epsilon]\!](\text{knows}, \text{fresh}) = (\text{knows}, \text{fresh})$$

Now, we can define the function Wf_Prot as:

$$\text{Wf\_Prot} : \mathcal{P}rot \rightarrow \text{Bool}$$
$$\text{Wf\_Prot}(\mathcal{P}) = \text{Wf\_Prot}(\mathcal{D}.\mathcal{C})$$
$$= \text{Wf\_Comm}(\mathcal{C})(\mathfrak{D}\llbracket\mathcal{D}\rrbracket([\,],[\,]))$$
$$\text{Wf\_Comm} : \mathcal{C}omm \rightarrow \text{State} \rightarrow \text{Bool}$$
$$\text{Wf\_Comm}(A \rightarrow B : m.\mathcal{C})(\text{knows}, \text{fresh}) =$$
$$m \in (\text{knows}(A) \cup \text{fresh}(A)) \;\wedge\; \text{Wf\_Comm}(\mathcal{C})(\text{knows}[B \rightarrow \text{knows}(B) \cup m], \text{fresh})$$

Functional Semantics

To define the semantic function $\mathfrak{P}$ of protocols we need the following defini-tions in addition to the ones made we defined with the function Wf_Prot:

Σ_G	Set of Strategies over the game G
s : Seq	Sequence of moves
end : $S \rightarrow M$	Function that returns the last move in the sequence

The semantic function $\mathfrak{P}$ will take as arguments a protocol and its type (the game representing the protocol) and will return a strategy over this game.

$$\mathfrak{P} : \mathcal{P}rot \rightarrow \prod \tau \in \mathcal{T} \,.\, \Sigma_{\text{Psg}_{[\overline{\tau}]}}$$
$$\mathfrak{P}\llbracket\mathcal{P}\rrbracket(\tau) = \mathfrak{P}\llbracket\mathcal{D}.\mathcal{C}\rrbracket(\tau)$$
$$= \mathfrak{C}\llbracket\mathcal{C}\rrbracket(\epsilon)(\mathfrak{D}\llbracket\mathcal{D}\rrbracket([\,],[\,]))$$

The function $\mathfrak{D}$ is defined above. The function $\mathfrak{C}$ returns a strategy over the game that represents the protocol type, assuming the intruder only forwards messages between agents. It is defined as:

$$\mathfrak{C} : \mathcal{C}omm \rightarrow \text{Seq} \rightarrow \text{State} \rightarrow \Sigma_{\text{Psg}_{[\overline{\tau}]}}$$
$$\mathfrak{C}\llbracket step\, i \triangleright A \rightarrow B : m.\mathcal{C}\rrbracket(s)(\text{knows}, \text{fresh}) =$$
$$\quad \text{if } s = \epsilon \text{ then}$$
$$\quad\quad \mathfrak{C}\llbracket\mathcal{C}\rrbracket(q.q.start.m)(\text{knows} \dagger [A \mapsto \text{knows}(A) \cup \{start\}, I \mapsto \text{knows}(I) \cup \{m\}], \text{fresh})$$
$$\quad \text{else}$$
$$\quad\quad \mathfrak{C}\llbracket\mathcal{C}\rrbracket(s.q.q.end(s).m)(\text{knows} \dagger [A \mapsto \text{knows}(A) \cup \{end(s)\}, I \mapsto \text{knows}(I) \cup \{m\}], \text{fresh})$$
$$\quad \text{end}$$
$$\mathfrak{C}\llbracket\epsilon\rrbracket(s)(\text{knows}, \text{fresh}) =$$
$$\quad \text{if } s = \epsilon \text{ then}$$
$$\quad\quad s$$
$$\quad \text{else}$$
$$\quad\quad s.q.q.end(s).terminate$$
$$\quad \text{end}$$

6.5   Protocol Semantics (Security View)

In security semantics, we investigate possible manoeuvres that can be performed by the intruder in order to break the protocol's security. For any protocol $\mathcal{P}$ that has type τ, if we assume that there are M running sessions, the semantic function in this case assigns to $\mathcal{P}$ a set of strategies over the game $\text{Spr}_{[M,\overline{\tau}]}$. First, we define the following:

sess : Session	Session : $\_ \rightarrow$ N sess is the session number.
P_G : GameTree	Game tree of the game G
P_G^{sub} : GameTree	$P_G^{sub} \subseteq P_G$ a subset of the game tree of the game G (subtree)

The semantic function $\mathfrak{P}$ accepts a protocol, the number of sessions to be generated, and a protocol type. It returns a subset of the game tree of the game Spr. This subset represent all possible sequences the game could proceed with.

$$\mathfrak{P} : \mathcal{P}rot \rightarrow \prod M \in \mathsf{Natural} \; . \; \prod \tau \in \mathcal{T} \; . \; P^{sub}_{\mathsf{Spr}_{[\overline{\tau},\mathsf{N}]}}$$
$$\mathfrak{P}[\![P]\!](M,\tau) = \mathfrak{P}[\![\mathcal{D}.\mathcal{C}]\!](M,\tau)$$
$$= \mathfrak{C}[\![\mathcal{C}]\!](\mathfrak{D}[\![\mathcal{D}]\!]([\,],[\,]))(\epsilon)(P_{\mathsf{Spr}_{[\overline{\tau},\mathsf{N}]}})$$

The function $\mathfrak{D}$ is the same as the one defined above. The function $\mathfrak{C}$ is defined differently however, it returns a subset of the game tree of the game that represents the protocol type. The way the function works is that it "cuts away" irrelevant sequences of the game tree by substituting strategies representing actual protocol messages in their respective places in the game tree. It calls the semantic function of messages $\mathfrak{S}[\![m]\!]$.

$\mathfrak{C} : \mathcal{C}omm \rightarrow \mathsf{State} \rightarrow \mathsf{Seq} \rightarrow \mathsf{GameTree} \rightarrow \mathsf{GameTree}$
$\quad \mathfrak{C}[\![step \, i \rhd A \rightarrow B : m_i.\mathcal{C}]\!](\mathsf{knows}, \mathsf{fresh})(s)(P_{\mathsf{Spr}_{[\overline{\tau},\mathsf{N}]}}) =$
$\qquad \mathbf{if} \; i = 1 \; \mathbf{then}$
$\qquad\quad \mathfrak{C}[\![\mathcal{C}]\!](\mathsf{knows} \dagger [\, A \mapsto \mathsf{knows}(A) \cup \{start\}, \; I \mapsto \mathsf{knows}(I) \cup \{m_i\}\,], \mathsf{fresh})$
$\qquad\quad (s.m_i)(P_\tau[\mathfrak{S}[\![start]\!]/P_{\mathsf{Spr}_{[\overline{\tau},\mathsf{N}]}} \upharpoonright \mathsf{Msg}^{\mathsf{sess},11}, \mathfrak{S}[\![m_i]\!]/P_{\mathsf{Spr}_{[\overline{\tau},\mathsf{N}]}} \upharpoonright \mathsf{Msg}^{\mathsf{sess},12}])$
$\qquad \mathbf{else}$
$\qquad\quad \mathbf{let} \; m \in (\mathsf{knows}(I) \cup \mathsf{fresh}(I))$
$\qquad\quad \mathbf{in}$
$\qquad\qquad \mathbf{let} \; m' = \mathsf{check}(A, \mathsf{knows}, \mathsf{end}(s), m)$
$\qquad\qquad\quad m'' = \mathsf{check}(A, \mathsf{knows}, m_i, m')$
$\qquad\qquad \mathbf{in}$
$\qquad\qquad\quad \mathfrak{C}[\![\mathcal{C}]\!](\mathsf{knows} \dagger [\, A \mapsto \mathsf{knows}(A) \cup \{m'\}, \; I \mapsto \mathsf{knows}(I) \cup \{m''\}\,], \mathsf{fresh})$
$\qquad\qquad\quad (s.m'')(P_{\mathsf{Spr}_{[\overline{\tau},\mathsf{N}]}}[\mathfrak{S}[\![m']\!]/P_\tau \upharpoonright \mathsf{Msg}^{\mathsf{sess},i1}, \mathfrak{S}[\![m'']\!]/P_{\mathsf{Spr}_{[\overline{\tau},\mathsf{N}]}} \upharpoonright \mathsf{Msg}^{\mathsf{sess},i2}])$
$\qquad\qquad \mathbf{end}$
$\qquad\quad \mathbf{end}$
$\qquad \mathbf{end}$
$\quad \mathfrak{C}[\![\epsilon]\!](\mathsf{knows}, \mathsf{fresh})(P_{\mathsf{Spr}_{[\overline{\tau},\mathsf{N}]}}) =$
$\qquad P_{\mathsf{Spr}_{[\overline{\tau},\mathsf{N}]}}$

7 Conclusion

In this paper, we presented a model of security protocols that expresses both communication and computation steps using a game semantics framework. This model was then used to ascribe functional and security semantics to security protocols. In order to specify the protocol, we presented a syntax that is an enhanced version of the currently used standard notation for security protocols. There remains issues to be investigated, for instance the elaboration of verification techniques based on the model presented. Moreover, the syntax can be extended to increase its expressiveness by adding the concept of time.

References

1. M. Abadi. Secrecy by typing in security protocols. *Theoretical Aspects of Computer Software, volume 1281 of LNCS*, pages 611–638, 1997.
2. M. Abadi. Security protocols and their properties. In F.L. Bauer and R. Steinbrueggen, editors, *Foundations of Secure Computation, 20th Int. Summer School, Marktoberdorf, Germany*, pages 39–60. IOS Press, 2000.
3. M. Abadi and A. B. Gordon. A calculus for cryptographic protocols: The SPI calculus. In *Proceedings of the 4th ACM Conference on Computer and Communications Security*, 1997.
4. S. Abramsky. Semantics of interaction: An introduction to game semantics. In *Proceedings of the 1996 CLiCS Summer School, Isaac Newton Institute, P. Dybjer and A. Pitts, eds. (Cambridge University Press)*, 1997.

5. S. Abramsky, P. Malacaria, and R. Jagadeesan. Full abstraction for PCF. In *Theoretical Aspects of Computer Software*, pages 1–15, 1994.
6. K. Adi. *Formal Specification and Analysis of Security Protocols*. PhD thesis, Universite Laval, 2002.
7. A. Blass. A game semantics for linear logic. *Annals of Pure and Applied Logic*, 56:183–220, 1992.
8. M. Burrows, M. Abadi, and R. Needham. A logic of authntication. Technical report, Digital Systems Research Center.
9. D. Dolev and A. Yao. On the security of public key protocols. *IEEE transactions on information theory*, 29(2):198–208, 1983.
10. W. M. Farmer. A basic extended simple type theory. Technical report, McMaster University, 2001.
11. J. M. E. Hyland and C.-H. L. Ong. On full abstraction for PCF: I, II, III. *Info. and Comp.*, 163:285–408, 2000.
12. D. Kahler, R. Kusters, and T. Wilke. Deciding properties of contract signing protocols. In *Proceedings of the 22nd Symposium on Theoretical Aspects of Computer Science (STACS'05)*, 2005.
13. S. Kremer and J. Raskin. A game approach to the verification of exchange protocols - application to non-repudiation protocols. In *Proceedings of the Workshop on Issues in the Theory of Security (WITS '00)*, 2000.
14. S. Kremer and J. Raskin. Game analysis of abuse-free contract signing. In *Proceedings of the 15th IEEE Computer Security Foundations Workshop (CSFW'02)*. IEEE Computer Society Press, 2002.
15. K. Lorenz. Basic objectives of dialogue logic in historical perspective. *Synthese (Elsevier)*, 127(1–2), April/May 2001.
16. C. Meadows. Formal methods for cryptographic protocol analysis: Emerging issues and trends. *IEEE Journal on Selected Areas in Communication*, 21(1):44–54, 2003.
17. R. Needham and M. Schroeder. Using encryption for authentication in large networks of computers. *Communications of the ACM*, 21(12), 1978.
18. L. C. Paulson. The inductive approach to verifying cryptographic protocols. *Journal of Computer Security*, (6):85–128, 1998.
19. J. Thayer, J. Herzog, and J. Guttman. Strand spaces: Proving security protocols correct. *Journal of Computer Security*, (7):191–230, 1999.
20. T.Y.C. Woo and S.S. Lam. A lesson on authentication protocol design. *Operating Systems Review*, pages 24–37, 1994.

Towards Dynamically Communicating Abstract Machines in the B Method

Nazareno Aguirre[1], Marcelo Arroyo[1], Juan Bicarregui[2], Lucio Guzmán[1], and Tom Maibaum[3]

[1] Departamento de Computación, FCEFQyN,
Universidad Nacional de Río Cuarto,
Ruta 36 Km. 601, Río Cuarto (5800), Córdoba, Argentina
{naguirre, marroyo, lucio}@dc.exa.unrc.edu.ar
[2] Rutherford Appleton Laboratory, Chilton, Didcot,
OXON, OX11 0QX, United Kingdom
J.C.Bicarregui@rl.ac.uk
[3] Department of Computing & Software, McMaster University,
1280 Main St. West, Hamilton, Ontario, Canada L8S 4K1
tom@maibaum.org

Abstract. In this paper we present an attempt to represent dynamic communication links between abstract machines in the B method. The approach complements a previously proposed extension to B, that supports dynamic creation and deletion of machine instances, providing a mechanism for dynamically connecting or disconnecting machine instances for communication. This mechanism is based on the concept of *connector*, in the software architectures sense.

We propose an extension to B's notation to support the definition of connectors. The extension has been defined with the intention of making it fully compatible with the standard B method, and allows one to enable communication, under certain restrictions, between abstract machines in a specification which presents dynamic creation and deletion of machine instances. We present the extension, its semantics and an example illustrating its use based on a producer-consumer specification. We also discuss possible ways of extending the proposed connector definitions to more general forms of communication.

Keywords: B method, structuring mechanisms, dynamic reconfiguration, object orientation.

1 Introduction

The B formal specification language is one of the most successful model based formalisms for software specification. It has an associated method, the B Method [1], and commercial tool support, including proof assistance [5][7]. As all formal methods, the B method provides a formal language in which one can describe systems, allowing for analysis and verification of certain system properties prior

K.-K. Lau and R. Banach (Eds.): ICFEM 2005, LNCS 3785, pp. 141–155, 2005.

to implementation. Moreover, the B method and its associated tools also cover refinement, implementation and code generation [5][7].

Various facilities for structuring specifications are provided in B, helping to make the specification and refinement activities scalable. However, the B method has an important restriction regarding structuring mechanisms, namely, it does not provide, as a structuring feature, the dynamic creation and deletion of modules or components. More precisely, all structuring mechanisms of B are *static*, in the sense that they allow one to define abstract machines whose architectural structure in terms of other components is fixed, i.e., it does not change at run time [8].

In this context of *static* configurations of abstract machines in the B method, communication between machines is achieved, essentially, in one of the following ways:

- either one of the machines is contained in the other (and therefore the second can access information from the first one respecting the visibility rules of the corresponding structuring mechanism employed), or
- a common substructure of these machines is "factored away" as a separate machine, and is shared in a "one writer-many readers" fashion [1]. Note that in this case the communication is in an *asynchronous* mode.

As we mentioned, B lacks dynamic management of abstract machines. Dynamic management of the population of components is a feature often associated with object oriented languages, since the replication of *objects* is intrinsic to these languages [12]. In fact, dynamic management of "objects" is currently accepted as a common software design practice, perhaps due to the success of object oriented methodologies and programming languages. In order to allow for dynamic management of components in B, it is not necessarily a good approach to extend B to support fully fledged object orientation, since this would imply a significant change to B's neat syntax and semantics, and would excessively complicate the tool support implementation (especially in relation to proof support). Nevertheless, we have been engaged in the development of extensions to the B method to support dynamic creation and deletion of machines [2][3], but we have done so trying to make the extensions fully compatible with the standard B method. Indeed, we have complemented B's structuring mechanisms with an extra clause, the AGGREGATES. A clause AGGREGATES M' within the definition of a machine M intuitively indicates that M counts on a dynamic set of *instances* of machines of type M', which can be created or deleted at run time [2]. Moreover, we have also shown how this clause can be treated at the refinement and implementation stages of the B method [3].

As we have advocated, having a structuring mechanism that allows for the dynamic creation/deletion of machine instances can favour the structuring of specifications, and therefore, contribute to the decomposability of proof obligations and the understandability of system specifications [2]. However, allowing for the dynamic creation and deletion of machine instances via the use of the AGGREGATES clause restricts the applicability of the above mentioned approaches for communicating machines. This is not surprising, since these were designed for static architectural configurations of abstract machines. In fact, when trying to achieve communication between dynamically generated machines (i.e., in "dynamic architecture scenarios"), one usually ends up building complex and unstructured specifications. The complexities associated with these specifications are related to the fact that the specifier has to manually construct the machinery for dynamic creation of "objects", for managing the communication, etc, usually all encapsulated in a single, *flat* abstract machine. Thus, we propose an alternative, based on an extension to B's notation to support the definition of *connectors* [4]. The extension is built on top of standard B, i.e., specifications written using the extension can be systematically translated into standard B specifications. The extension we propose here allows one to define synchronous communication between abstract machines in a specification with dynamic creation and deletion of machine instances. The mechanism we present is limited to some specific kinds of communications, but, as we will also show, more general forms of communication can also be characterised (although these need to be *asynchronous*). As for our previously proposed extensions, this extension has been defined with the intention of making it fully compatible with the standard B method. We present the extension, its semantics and an example illustrating its use based on a producer-consumer specification.

The remainder of this paper is organised as follows: In Section 2 we start by showing how machines are typically communicated (statically) in B. We argue about the unsuitability of these mechanisms when combined with dynamic aggregations of machines (Section 2.1). We then briefly describe the AGGRE-GATES structuring mechanism, its use and semantics. We show how a system with dynamic creation and deletion of components can be specified using aggregation, but these cannot be connected for communication using B's mechanisms (Section 2.2). In Section 3 we present the syntax we propose for connectors in B, and connectors' intuitive meaning. In Section 4 we are engaged with the description of the semantics of connectors, in terms of standard B constructs. We discuss the proof obligations associated with connector definitions (Section 4.2), and show how connectors are used by means of an example. We end Section 4 enumerating some of the limitations that our connectors have for defining communication between abstract machines, and discuss the characterisation of more general forms of communication. Finally, in Section 5 we present our conclusions, some comparison with related work and lines for future work.

2   Communicating Abstract Machines in the B Method

Let us introduce the problems that we attempt to solve (at least partially) in this paper by means of an example. This example is a simple variant of a component based specification given in [9] for the producer-consumer problem. Let us suppose that we need to specify a system consisting of a producer that sends "products" to a consumer. Assuming that the products are encoded as non-zero integer numbers, and choosing to specify the producer and the consumer as separate machines, one might define a basic machine *Channel* in order to

```
        MACHINE
            Channel
        VARIABLES
            var
        INVARIANT
            var ∈ INT
        INITIALISATION
            var := 0
        OPERATIONS
            set(i)  ≙   PRE i ∈ INT THEN var := i END;
            x ⟵ get  ≙   BEGIN x := var END
        END
```

Fig. 1. A simple abstract machine used for communication between a producer and a consumer

"implement" the communication, as in Fig. 1. Then, we can define the producer and the consumer as structured definitions on top of machine *Channel*, as shown in Figs. 2 and 3. Note that, for the sake of simplicity, we do not model the corresponding acknowledgement that the consumer should send after consuming a product (note that without the acknowledgement, a producer can overwrite a product before the consumer gets it). Such acknowledgements can be easily "implemented" in a structured way, by taking a renamed copy of *Channel*, say *Channel'*, and use it for "backward communication", i.e., the consumer writes on it (machine *Consumer* includes *Channel'*) and the producer reads it (machine *Producer* sees *Channel'*). Notice that machine *Producer* simultaneously includes *Channel* (for forward communication) and sees *Channel'* (for backward communication), and the converse is true for machine *Consumer*.

This corresponds to one of the alternatives that a specifier has for specifying the system, with producer and consumer as separate machines. Of course, one could also decide to specify the whole system as a sole, flat abstract machine; following this latter approach, although sound, does not favour the decomposition of the proofs of consistency (i.e., the proofs of the proof obligations) nor the understandability of the specification (more detail on this in Section 5).

```
        MACHINE
            Producer
        INCLUDES
            Channel
        VARIABLES
            p-var
        INVARIANT
            p-var ∈ INT
        INITIALISATION
            p-var := 0
        OPERATIONS
            prod(x)  ≙   PRE x ≠ 0 ∧ p-var = 0 THEN p-var := x END;
            send  ≙   PRE p-var ≠ 0 THEN p-var := 0 || set(p-var) END
        END
```

Fig. 2. A specification of *Producer* including a channel

```
MACHINE
    Consumer
SEES
    Channel
VARIABLES
    c-var
INVARIANT
    c-var ∈ INT
INITIALISATION
    c-var := 0
OPERATIONS
    obtain  ≙  PRE var ≠ 0 ∧ c-var = 0 THEN c-var := var END;
    cons    ≙  PRE c-var ≠ 0 THEN c-var := 0 END
END
```

Fig. 3. A specification of *Consumer* "seeing" a channel

2.1 Communication in the Presence of Aggregation

Let us now suppose that we need to specify a system with a varying number of producers and consumers, and with dynamism in the communication. For instance, suppose that, besides dynamically creating and deleting producers and consumers, we want to change dynamically the consumer a particular producer produces for. In order to specify such a system, we are unable to use the option of a common machine, such as *Channel*, for implementing the communication, since changing the consumer to which a producer is "connected" would not be possible to specify (it would require a dynamic change in the structural organisation of the system specification, not supported in B). So, we are left with a flat, unstructured machine as the only option for specifying this system, at least if we use standard B.

However, in this paper, we will show how we can specify the above described dynamic system of producers and consumers in a *structured* way, by using the AGGREGATES clause. As we previously described, this structuring mechanism intuitively allows one to manipulate a dynamic set of instances of the aggregated machine. Of course, we cannot enable the communication between these machines directly, so we first have to consider the uncommunicating versions of producer and consumer, as shown in Fig. 4. (We will "connect" these machines later.) Then, we can easily obtain a system with dynamic populations of (uncommunicating) producers and consumers, by aggregating these machines, as in Fig. 5. Note that, in this case, we are able to create and delete producers and consumers dynamically, but there is no interaction/communication between producer instances and consumer instances.

2.2 The AGGREGATES Clause

The aggregation of an abstract machine relies on the (systematic) generation of a population manager for the aggregated machine. A population manager of an abstract machine M puts together the relativisation of the operations of M (so they work for multiple instances) with operations that mimic the creation and deletion of machines instances. To illustrate the use of AGGREGATES, and its semantics in terms of a population manager, consider the simple machine

```
MACHINE                              MACHINE
      Producer                             Consumer
VARIABLES                            VARIABLES
      p-var                                c-var
INVARIANT                            INVARIANT
      p-var ∈ INT                          c-var ∈ INT
INITIALISATION                       INITIALISATION
      p-var := 0                           c-var := 0
OPERATIONS                           OPERATIONS
      prod(x)  ≘                           obtain(x)  ≘
         PRE    p-var = 0 ∧ x ∈ INT−{0}        PRE    c-var = 0 ∧ x ∈ INT−{0}
         THEN   p-var := x                     THEN   c-var := x
         END;                                  END;
      send()  ≘                           cons()  ≘
         PRE    p-var ≠ 0                     PRE    c-var ≠ 0
         THEN   p-var := 0                    THEN   c-var := 0
         END                                  END
END                                  END
```

Fig. 4. Abstract Machines *Producer* and *Consumer*

```
                MACHINE
                   SYSTEM
                AGGREGATES
                   PRODUCER, CONSUMER
                   ⋮
                END
```

Fig. 5. Fragment of a machine aggregating *Producer* and *Consumer*

Producer that we show in Fig. 4. The corresponding population manager for this abstract machine is shown in Figs. 6. Notice that, due to the automatic generation of the managers, some conjuncts in the invariants are redundant. For a detailed explanation of how these machines are synthesised see [2] .

The "AGGREGATES *Producer*" in the abstract machine *System* in Fig. 5 is simply interpreted as "EXTENDS *ProducerManager*". Within *System* we can manage the population of producers (resp. consumers) by invoking the implicitly defined *add_Producer* (resp. *add_Consumer*) and *del_Producer* (resp. *del_Consumer*). Furthermore, we can call *Producer* (resp. *Consumer*) operations, now operating on particular live instances. Consider, for instance, a *deliver* operation that enforces a live instance of *Consumer* to consume the product produced by a live *Producer p*.

```
deliver(p, c) ≘
      PRE
            p ∈ ProducerSet ∧ c ∈ ConsumerSet ∧ p.p-var ≠ 0 ∧ c.c-var = 0
      THEN
            p.send || c.obtain(p.p-var)
      END
```

Note that the AGGREGATES clause constitutes in effect a structuring mechanism: the consistency of machines aggregating other machines can be reduced to the consistency of the aggregate, and a number of further conditions on the aggregating machine. This is the case thanks to the fact that the population manager of a machine M is internally consistent *by construction*[1], provided that M is internally consistent. Then, the population manager of a basic machine M is *automatically constructed* and can be hidden from the specifier, who can use AGGREGATES as other conventional structuring mechanism of B [2]. Moreover, the population managers can be hidden from the developer even during refinement and implementation [3].

```
MACHINE
     Producer_Manager
VARIABLES
     p-var, ProducerSet
INVARIANT
     (∀n · n ∈ ProducerSet ⇒ p-var(n) ∈ INT) ∧
     (ProducerSet ⊆ NAME) ∧ (p-var ∈ ProducerSet → INT)
INITIALISATION
     p-var, ProducerSet := ∅, ∅
OPERATIONS
     prod(x, n)   ≙
          PRE    n ∈ ProducerSet ∧ x ∈ INT − {0} ∧ p-var(n) = 0
          THEN    p-var(n) := x
          END;
     send(n)   ≙
          PRE    n ∈ ProducerSet ∧ p-var(n) ≠ 0
          THEN    p-var(n) := 0
          END;
     add_Producer(n)   ≙
          PRE    n ∈ NAME − ProducerSet
          THEN
               ProducerSet := ProducerSet∪{n}||p-var := p-var∪{n, 0}
          END;
     del_Producer(n)   ≙
          PRE    n ∈ ProducerSet
          THEN
               p-var := {n} ⩤ p-var ||
               ProducerSet := ProducerSet − {n}
          END;
END
```

Fig. 6. *ProducerManager*: Population manager of abstract machine *Producer*

We adopt the "dot notation" to access variables and operations of the aggregated machines. For instance, the expression $m.y$ represents the value of variable y corresponding to instance m; analogously, the expression $m.op(x)$ represents a "call" to operation *op*, with argument x, corresponding to instance m (see the definition of operation *deliver*). The prefix of an expression employing the dot notation simply represents the "instance parameter" of the corresponding operation or variable (i.e., $m.y$ and $m.op(x)$ are convenient ways of writing $y(m)$ and $op(x,m)$, respectively).

---

[1] An abstract machine is *internally consistent* if it satisfies its *proof obligations*, i.e. if it satisfies the requirements imposed in the B method for considering a machine correct. Proof obligations for the correctness of an abstract machine include conditions such as nonemptiness of the state space determined by the machine, or the preservation of the machine's invariant by the machine's operations [1].

3   Communicating Dynamically Generated Machines

We now consider how to enable communication between dynamically generated machines. We propose to extend B's notation with the definition of *connectors* [4]. In software architectures [13], connectors represent communication "links" between components, and have the particularity of being external to the definition of the related components. This is precisely what we need, a mechanism for relating machine instances outside the definition of the interacting machines.

3.1   Connector Definitions in B

A connector consists of: *(i)* a name, *(ii)* a pair of participants (names of abstract machines), and *(iii)* a list of *connections*. The purpose of connections is to define how the operations of the participants are linked when two instances of the participants are connected. Consider, for instance, the connector definition in Fig. 7. This connector indicates that, whenever an instance p of *Producer* is connected to an instance c of *Consumer* via R, then the occurrence of $p.send()$ forces the occurrence of (or makes a call to) $c.obtain(p.p\text{-}var)$.

A connection can have one of the following forms:

$$op1 \rightarrow op2$$
$$op1 \leftarrow op2$$

where $op1$ is an operation of the first participant and $op2$ is an operation of the second one. The intended meaning of $op1 \rightarrow op2$ is that $op1$ "calls" $op2$; the connection in the other direction is interpreted in a similar way. Subsequently, given a connection c, we will denote by $src(c)$ the operation at the source of the arrow, and by $tgt(c)$ the operation at the target of the arrow.

For a connector R between two machines M_1 and M_2 to be well defined, we have a number of syntactic conditions:

- Machines M_1 and M_2 must be unrelated (i. e., M_1 cannot be defined in terms of M_2 and vice versa),
- if we have a connection $op1 \rightarrow op2$ (resp. $op1 \leftarrow op2$), then $op1$ must be an operation of M_1 and $op2$ an operation of M_2,
- if we have a connection c, then the formal parameters of $src(c)$ must be distinct variables different from the state variables of M_1 and M_2, and the parameters of $tgt(c)$ can only be linguistic elements of M_1 or M_2, or formal parameters of $src(c)$,
- a connector cannot contain two different connections $c1$ and $c2$ such that $src(c1) = src(c2)$.

We need to enforce these conditions to guarantee that we can build the machinery for representing connections in B, as we will show in the next section.

3.2   Intuitive Meaning of Connectors

Connectors allow us to intuitively define relations between instances of abstract machines. These relations also define an interaction between the related instances, described by the connections. In order to clarify how connectors can

```
                CONNECTOR
                    R
                PARTICIPANTS
                    Producer, Consumer
                CONNECTIONS
                    send() → obtain(p-var)
                END
```

Fig. 7. A connector for communicating producers and consumers

```
        MACHINE
            Prod_Cons
        AGGREGATES
            Producer, Consumer WITH R
        OPERATIONS
            feedback(c, p)  ≙
                PRE  c ∈ ConsumerSet ∧ p ∈ ProducerSet ∧ (p, c) ∈ RSet ∧
                p.p-var = 0 ∧ c.c-var ≠ 0
                THEN  c.cons() || p.prod(c.c-var)
                END
        END
```

Fig. 8. An example of a machine with aggregation and connectors

be used in practice, let us define an abstract machine *Prod_Cons* with dynamic sets of producers and consumers related by R, shown in Fig. 8. Within machine *Prod_Cons*, one can manage the population of producers and consumers as explained before; furthermore, one can dynamically connect and disconnect instances of producers and consumers by using two implicitly defined operations, *connect_R(x, y)* and *disconnect_R(x, y)*. As for the case of the AGGREGATES clause, connectors have an "instance set"; for our example, the instance set corresponding to connector R is denoted by *RSet* (see the definition of operation *feedback*).

Connector R then defines a relation between instances of producers and instances of consumers. Besides this relation, connector R has an important effect on the operations linked by R: whenever an instance p of *Producer* is related to an instance c of *Consumer*, a call to *p.send()* enforces a synchronous call to *c.obtain(p.p-var)*, as the connection of R indicates. If a producer p is not connected to a consumer c, then the effect of *p.send()* is not altered.

When a producer is connected to a consumer, we need to call the *obtain* operation on the corresponding consumer; therefore, we need to unequivocally determine which one is the consumer we have to call. So, we need to restrict the relation *RSet* to be *functional*. Conversely, when we have a connection on the other direction (e.g., from consumer to producer), we have to restrict the relation *RSet* to be *injective*. These restrictions will be clarified in the next section, regarding the semantics of connectors.

4   Semantics of Connectors

As we mentioned, it is our aim to extend the B method to support more sophisticated mechanisms for specification, but we want to do so in a way compatible with standard B. This would ensure that one could remain using the extensive work developed on B, as well as the traditional tool support. So, we have the same intention with our extension supporting connectors. Our connector definitions can be mapped into specifications in standard B. More precisely, we "implement" support for connectors as standard B specifications.

We build an abstract machine for the definition of a connector R relating two machine (types) M_1 and M_2. This machine, that we call $R\_Manager$, is structurally defined in terms of the managers for M_1 and M_2. Moreover, this machine contains the redefinition of those operations involved in connections. Then, a clause "AGGREGATES M_1, M_2 WITH R" within a machine M is simply interpreted as "EXTENDS $R\_Manager$." Note that $R\_Manager$ contains the population managers for M_1 and M_2.

4.1   Building the Connector Manager

Let M_1 and M_2 be two internally consistent abstract machines, and R a syntactically valid connector (see the syntactic conditions for valid connectors in the previous section) with M_1 and M_2 as participants. Let us assume that there are no name clashes between the definitions within M_1 and M_2 (note that name clashes can be avoided via renaming). We start by constructing the managers $M_1\_Manager$ and $M_2\_Manager$, for M_1 and M_2. Since machines M_1 and M_2 are internally consistent, we can ensure $M_1\_Manager$ and $M_2\_Manager$ are also consistent [2]. Then, we "prime" the operations in $M_1\_Manager$ and $M_2\_Manager$, and call the resulting machines $M_1\_Manager'$ and $M_2\_Manager'$, respectively. The priming is necessary, because we will need to redefine some of the operations (those involved in connections) of the related machines.

The general form of machine $R\_Manager$ is shown in Fig. 9. As it can be seen, this machine has a variable $RSet$, which represents the sets of active connectors. As is forced by the invariant, only instances of the corresponding participants can be connected. If the definition of R includes connections of the form $op1 \rightarrow op2$, then the invariant is complemented with $RSet \in M_1Set \leftrightarrow M_2Set$; if the definition of R includes connections of the form $op1 \leftarrow op2$, then the invariant is complemented with $RSet^{-1} \in M_1Set \leftrightarrow M_2Set$ (note that a given connector can have both types of connections).

The operation for disconnecting instances is easily defined. On the other hand, the operation for connecting machines depends on the types of connections. If a connection of type $op1 \rightarrow op2$ is present in the definition of R, then $R\_connect$ has to preserve the functionality of $RSet$; on the other hand, if a connection of type $op1 \leftarrow op2$ is present in the definition of R, then $R\_connect$ has to preserve the injectivity of $RSet$. This gives us four possible definitions for $R\_connect$, depending on the types of connections present. For instance, if we only have connections of type $op1 \rightarrow op2$, then $R\_connect$ is defined as follows:

$$R\_connect(x, y) \;\;\hat{=}$$
$$\text{PRE} \quad x \in M_1Set \wedge y \in M_2Set \quad \text{THEN} \quad RSet(x) := y \quad \text{END}$$

The other three possibilities are also easily defined, and are left as an exercise for the interested reader.

```
MACHINE
    R_Manager
EXTENDS
    M₁_Manager', M₂_Manager'
VARIABLES
    RSet
INVARIANT
    RSet ⊆ M₁Set × M₂Set ∧ ...
INITIALISATION
    RSet := ∅
OPERATIONS
    R_disconnect(x,y)   ≙
        PRE   (x,y) ∈ RSet   THEN   RSet := RSet − {(x,y)}   END
    R_connect(x,y)   ≙   ...
    op1(x)   ≙
        PRE   pre(op1'(x))   THEN
        (RSet[{x}] ≠ ∅ ⟹ op1'(x)||op2'(RSet(x))) [] (RSet[{x}] = ∅ ⟹ op1'(x))   END
    op3(x)   ≙   PRE   pre(op3'(x))   THEN   op3'(x)   END
        .
        .
        .
END
```

Fig. 9. The general form of a connector manager for machines M_1 and M_2

Notice the definition for operation $op1(x)$ in Fig. 9. This definition assumes that we have a connection $op1 \rightarrow op2$. It has as a precondition the precondition of the original $op1(x)$ operation (now primed). However, its effect, as shown in the THEN section of its definition, depends on whether x has a connected instance of M_2 or not. In the case it has a connected instance, the operation $op2'$ is called on the connected instance $R(x)$ (here it becomes clearer why we need to restrict $RSet$ to be functional/injective), in parallel with $op1'(x)$; in the case that x has no connected instance, we simply call $op1'(x)$.

The definition of $op3(x)$ in Fig. 9 assumes that $op3$ is not at the source of a connection of R, and therefore, it only needs to call $op3'(x)$.

4.2   Proof Obligations for Connector Definitions

The initialisation of the connector manager trivially respects the machine's invariant (since the empty relation is both injective and functional). Also, operations $R\_connect$ and $R\_disconnect$ are defined to make them comply with the machine's invariant (as we said, $R\_disconnect$ trivially preserves the invariant, whereas $R\_connect$ has four possible definitions, according to the types of connections present). However, some proof obligations which cannot be automatically discharged will be generated from the connector manager. These have to do with the way in which the original operations (the primed ones) are called. Whenever the connector contains a connection $op1 \rightarrow op2$, the definition of $op1$ in $R\_Manager$ invokes $op1'$ respecting its precondition; however, it is not guaranteed by construction that the call to $op2'$ within the definition of $op1$ respects the precondition of $op2'$, and therefore this will have to be proved.

Essentially, these proof obligations force us to prove that, whenever we have a connection $op1 \rightarrow op2$ (resp. $op1 \leftarrow op2$), we guarantee that the precondition of $op2$ (resp. $op1$) is *subsumed* by the precondition of $op1$ (resp. $op2$).

4.3   An Example

As an example, let us build the connector manager for our example of producers and consumers related by our previously defined R connector. The resulting machine is shown in Fig. 10. Note how operation *send*, which is involved in a connection, has changed its definition. Also, note how the *connect_R* operation and the invariant look like for this particular case. Operation *prod*, which was not involved in any connection, simply calls the original (now *prod'*) operation. Notice that, due to the automated generation of this specification, some (harmless) redundancies emerge (see the invariant of the connector manager, for instance).

```
MACHINE
      R_Manager
EXTENDS
      Producer_Manager', Consumer_Manager'
VARIABLES
      RSet
INVARIANT
      RSet ⊆ ProducerSet × ConsumerSet ∧ RSet ⊆ ProducerSet ↦ ConsumerSet
INITIALISATION
      RSet := ∅
OPERATIONS
      R_disconnect(x, y)  ≙
            PRE   (x, y) ∈ RSet    THEN    RSet := RSet − {(x, y)}    END
      R_connect(x, y)  ≙
            PRE    x ∈ ProducerSet ∧ y ∈ ConsumerSet
            THEN    RSet(x) := y
            END
      send(x)  ≙
            PRE    x ∈ ProducerSet ∧ x.p-var ≠ 0    THEN
            (RSet[{x}] ≠ ∅ ⟹ x.send'()||RSet(x).obtain'(x.p-var) []
            (RSet[{x}] = ∅ ⟹ x.send'())
            END
      prod(i, x)  ≙
            PRE    x ∈ ProducerSet ∧ (i ≠ 0) ∧ (x.p-var = 0)
            THEN    prod'(i, x)
            END
            ⋮
END
```

Fig. 10. The manager for connector R, relating machines *Producer* and *Consumer*

4.4   Current Limitations of Connector Definitions

According to our definition of connectors, there exist various limitations on how machine instances can be related.

First, connectors are just *binary*, i.e., they can involve only two participants. It is not difficult to think of more general n-ary connectors, although the functionality/injectivity restrictions on the corresponding relation will have to be generalised (restrictions of the kind of functional dependencies as in databases would be necessary for n-ary connectors).

Second, due to the functionality/injectivity restrictions, having a connector of type $op1 \rightarrow op2$ (resp. $op1 \leftarrow op2$) forbids having a one-to-many (resp. many-to-one) connector "topology". Clearly, the specifier cannot employ connectors, as we have defined them, for these kinds of communication. Nevertheless, in those cases where our extension is applicable, the specifier gets a structured definition of the dynamism, in which most of the proof obligations can be automatically discharged (except those related to preconditions of operations at the target of connections, as we explained). Furthermore, it is possible to generalise the mechanism to connectors of arbitrary multiplicities, but in the general case the communication needs to be done asynchronously, since it requires an iteration mechanism. Of course, iteration is not available at the specification stage in B, so it needs to be characterised as a transaction. Due to space restrictions, we are unable to show in full detail the generalised form of connectors. But, essentially, the mechanism is the following: Suppose that we have a connection $op1 \rightarrow op2$ in a connector R relating M_1 and M_2, and which requires a one-to-many multiplicity. Then, the characterisation of $n.op1$ within $R\_Manager$ consists of:

1. a set $remaining \subseteq M_2Set$, that keeps track of those instances waiting to be called,
2. a boolean variable $sending$ to indicate if the manager is engaged in a "sending" transaction,
3. an extra operation $send$, that:
    - if $remaining$ is nonempty and $sending$ is true, it nondeterministically chooses an element m from $remaining$, removes it from $remaining$ and calls $m.op2$,
    - if $remaining$ is empty and $sending$ is true, it finishes the sending transaction by setting $sending$ to false.
4. the assertion $sending = false$ is added as an extra precondition of all other operations (i.e., the other operations are *blocked* if the connector manager is involved in a sending transaction).

5   Conclusions and Future Work

We have defined an extension to the B method to support the definition of *connectors* [4], in the software architectures sense [13]. The extension allows one to relate dynamically generated instances of abstracts machines for communication. The approach complements a previously proposed extension to B to support dynamic creation and deletion of machine instances, using additional structuring mechanisms. The extension has been defined with the intention of making it fully compatible with the standard B method. Indeed, specifications written using our extensions are systematically mapped into standard B specifications.

The connector definitions that we propose allow us to enable the communication, under certain restrictions, between abstract machines in a specification which presents dynamic creation and deletion of machine instances. The way in which we provide semantics to the extension is based on the work in [6]. Although the allowed forms of communication are restricted, the use of connectors favours specification structuring (with its well known advantages for understandability and simplification of proofs), and allows one to specify systems with structural dynamism at a higher level of abstraction. The provided level of abstraction is based on ideas developed by the software architectures community, particularly, the view of component based systems as modules related by means of connectors, and the externalisation of component interaction. This higher level of abstraction might have a positive impact in the effort needed to complement the B method with modern system design methodologies, such as object orientation. In fact, currently there exist various approaches to the modelling of object oriented features in B, particularly the work of H. Treharne [15], K. Lano et al. [10] and C. Snook and M. Butler [14]. We believe that these approaches might benefit from our characterisation of dynamic creation/deletion of machine and connector instances, and their advantages in the decomposability of specifications. For example, in [15], classes and associations are translated into B as an *ad hoc* unstructured specification; in [10], a notion similar to that of class manager is the smallest unit of modularity (as opposed to our finer grained aggregation mechanism); in [14], entire class diagrams are translated into B as single abstract machines. Being able to exploit the modularisation of specifications not only benefits the specifier by alleviating the proof efforts (by decomposing proofs in smaller "lemmas") and making specifications easier to understand [5]; modularisation also greatly improves analysability. For example, a structured B specification of a system allows us to validate modules *independently*, via animation. It also allows fully automated verification mechanisms, such as those based on model checking [11], to scale up and be applicable to a wider range of system specifications, by contributing to cope with the well known combinatorial state explosion problem.

As work in progress, we are currently working on a better developed generalisation of connectors, that covers more cases of communication. We are also studying the treatment of our connector definitions at refinement and implementation stages. Notice that, since our extensions to the B language are *definitional*, the feasibility of refinement and implementation is guaranteed. Nevertheless, we are exploring ways of systematically producing correct implementations for connector definitions, supplementing what has been done in [3] for machine aggregation. Also, we are currently studying how our AGGREGATES structuring mechanism, together with the support for connectors, combines with other structuring mechanisms of B when the architectural organisation of a specification involves various layers of abstract machines.

References

1. J.-R. Abrial, *The B-Book, Assigning Programs to Meanings*, Cambridge University Press, 1996.
2. N. Aguirre, J. Bicarregui, T. Dimitrakos and T. Maibaum, *Towards Dynamic Population Management of Components in the B Method*, in Proceedings of the 3rd International Conference of B and Z Users ZB2003, Turku, Finland, LNCS, Springer-Verlag, 2003.

3. N. Aguirre, J. Bicarregui, L. Guzmán and T. Maibaum, *Implementing Dynamic Aggregations of Abstract Machines in the B Method*, in Proceedings of the International Conference on Formal Engineering Methods ICFEM 2004, Seattle, USA, LNCS, Springer-Verlag, 2004.
4. R. Allen and D. Garlan, *Formalizing architectural connection*, in Proceedings of the Sixteenth International Conference on Software Engineering ICSE '94, IEEE Computer Society Press, 1994.
5. *The B-Toolkit User Manual*, B-Core (UK) Limited, 1996.
6. J. Bicarregui, K. Lano and T. Maibaum, *Towards a Compositional Interpretation of Object Diagrams*, in Proceedings of IFIP TC 2 working conference on Algorithmic Languages and Calculi, Bird and Meertens (eds), Chapman and Hall, 1997.
7. Digilog, *Atelier B - Générateur d'Obligation de Preuve, Spécifications*, Technical Report, RATP SNCF INRETS, 1994.
8. T. Dimitrakos, J. Bicarregui, B. Matthews and T. Maibaum, *Compositional Structuring in the B-Method: A Logical Viewpoint of the Static Context*, in Proceedings of the International Conference of B and Z Users ZB2000, York, United Kingdom, LNCS, Springer-Verlag, 2000.
9. J.L. Fiadeiro and T. Maibaum, *Design Structures For Object-Based Systems*, in S. Goldsack and S. Kent (eds.), Formal Aspects of Object-Oriented Systems. Prentice Hall, 1994.
10. K. Lano, D. Clark and K. Androutsopoulos, *UML to B: Formal Verification of Object-Oriented Models*, in Proceedings of the International Conference on Integrated Formal Methods IFM 2004, Canterbury, United Kingdom, LNCS, Springer-Verlag, 2004.
11. M. Leuschel and M. Butler, *ProB: A Model Checker for B*, in Proceedings of FM 2003, Pisa, Italy, LNCS, Springer-Verlag, 2003.
12. B. Meyer, *Object-Oriented Software Construction*, Second Edition, Prentice-Hall International, 2000.
13. M. Shaw and D. Garlan, *Software Architecture: Perspectives on an Emerging Discipline*, Prentice-Hall, 1996.
14. C. Snook and M. Butler, *UML-B: Formal modelling and design aided by UML*, Technical Report, Electronics and Computer Science, University of Southampton, Southampton, United Kingdom, 2004.
15. H. Treharne, *Supplementing a UML Development Process with B*, in Proceedings of FME 2002: Formal Methods– Getting IT Right, Denmark, LNCS 2391, Springer, 2002.

Sweep-Line Analysis of TCP Connection Management

Guy Edward Gallasch, Bing Han, and Jonathan Billington

Computer Systems Engineering Centre,
School of Electrical and Information Engineering,
University of South Australia,
Mawson Lakes Campus, SA 5095, Australia
guy.gallasch@postgrads.unisa.edu.au
{bing.han, jonathan.billington}@unisa.edu.au

Abstract. Despite the widespread use of the Transmission Control Protocol (TCP) as the main transport protocol in the Internet, the procedures for connection establishment and release are still not fully understood. This paper extends the analysis of a Coloured Petri net model of TCP's Connection Management procedures by applying the state explosion alleviation technique known as the sweep-line method. The protocol is assumed to be operating over a reordering lossless channel. Termination and absence of deadlock properties are investigated for many scenarios, including client-server and simultaneous connection establishment, orderly release and abortion. The sweep-line method provides a reduction in memory usage of around a factor of 10 and allows investigation of many scenarios that were previously out of the reach of conventional methods.

Keywords: TCP Connection Management, State Space methods, Reachability analysis, Sweep-line analysis, Coloured Petri Nets, Verification.

1 Introduction

The Transmission Control Protocol (TCP), originally specified in [21] using informal narrative descriptions, a finite state machine and message sequence diagrams, provides a reliable data transfer service that ensures data is delivered without loss, duplication or reordering. It has since been modified and improved (e.g. see [1, 3, 8, 9, 14, 15, 16] although such complex protocols are notoriously difficult to understand without the aid of formal methods.

TCP Connection Management encompasses the procedures for establishing and terminating connections (TCP is a connection-oriented protocol). To facilitate greater understanding of the connection management procedures and detection of errors therein, a detailed Coloured Petri net (CPN) model of TCP Connection Management has been created and analysed in [12, 13]. This CPN model is parameterised with a set of user commands to be issued to each TCP entity and the maximum number of retransmissions of certain TCP segments.

K.-K. Lau and R. Banach (Eds.): ICFEM 2005, LNCS 3785, pp. 156–172, 2005.
© Springer-Verlag Berlin Heidelberg 2005

Many previous attempts have been made to verify the correctness of TCP Connection Management. A good survey of the literature in this area is given in [12]. In our own previous work [12, 13] termination properties, deadlocks and language analysis were investigated for various connection establishment, release and abortion scenarios and some problems were discovered and reported. However, the well-known *state explosion* problem [23] prevented analysis of scenarios with larger values of the maximum number of retransmission parameters.

In this paper we focus on the verification of termination properties and absence of deadlocks. We attempt to alleviate the state space explosion problem by applying the *sweep-line* state space exploration method [20] to the analysis of our TCP Connection Management CPN. To do so, we identify ways in which the CPN exhibits *progress* and then formalise them. This allows the sweep-line method to delete states on-the-fly based on the notion of progress, thus reducing peak memory usage and allowing larger state spaces to be investigated.

The contribution of this paper is threefold. Firstly, we believe this is the first application of the sweep-line method to a complex connection management protocol. We identify several sources of progress in the protocol, formalise them, and combine them to obtain an effective *progress mapping*. The development of effective progress mappings is still somewhat of an open question with the sweep-line method. Secondly, through application of this progress measure we have been able to extend our analysis of TCP Connection Management to configurations of retransmission counters that were previously out of reach. Thirdly we evaluate the effectiveness of the sweep-line method in this context.

The rest of this paper is organised as follows. Section 2 introduces our TCP Connection Management CPN. In Section 3 the sweep-line method is briefly introduced, multiple sources of progress are identified and a final combined *progress mapping* is identified. This combined mapping is then applied to the analysis of our CPN, the results of which are presented in Section 4. Conclusions are given in Section 5. We assume the reader to be familiar with basic CPN concepts and to have some basic knowledge of TCP procedures. For a thorough introduction to CPNs we refer the reader to [17, 19].

2   CPN Model of TCP Connection Management

TCP Connection Management consists of a number of procedures, including both normal (client-server) and simultaneous connection establishment and release, and abort procedures. Connection establishment is via a three way handshake [22] and connection release is an orderly release. Details of TCP Connection Management procedures can be found in e.g., [2, 12, 13]. A detailed Coloured Petri net (CPN) model of TCP Connection Management has been developed in [12, 13]. We introduce it briefly in the following subsections.

2.1   Modelling Scope and Assumptions

Since the scope of our model is confined to Connection Management, we do not consider any parameters or segment fields associated with data transfer. We only consider four of TCP's user commands: *active open, passive open, close* and *abort*. We consider that security and precedence are always met and we only consider a single connection between users. This allows us just to model the commands without their parameters. We only model the fields in the TCP segment header and the TCB that are related to TCP connection management, so in our model a segment only contains a sequence number, an acknowledgement number and the control bits: SYN, ACK, FIN and RST (reset). Apart from the ACK bit, there can only be one control bit set in a segment. Connection management procedures only consume a small portion of the sequence number space, thus we choose small values for the initial sequence numbers for each TCP entity to avoid the complications of modelling modulo arithmetic. We assume that the receive window is always big enough to accept incoming segments and we omit the window field in segments and any checks associated with window size. Finally we assume that segments can be lost, delayed, and re-ordered while traversing the network. For more details on these assumptions please refer to [12].

2.2   Model Structure

The aim of the following subsections is to give a feel for the structure of the model as we cannot go into details at anything other than a high level. For a complete description of this model, please see [12].

The Hierarchy page of this model is shown in Fig. 1. The CPN model contains a declarations page and 19 CPN pages. The 19 CPN pages are organised into a tree structure, which comprises 4 hierarchical levels.

The top-level page is the TCP_Overview page, which provides an abstract view of TCP and its environment. This page is described in more detail in Section 2.3. The second level contains the Event_Processing page modelling TCP's responses to user commands, segment arrivals and retransmission timeout via the third level pages User_Commands, Segment_Processing and Retransmissions respectively. The User_Commands page comprises three fourth level subpages: open, close and abort. The Segment_Processing page models the processing of segments for each of TCP's 11 states via 11 fourth level pages. The Retransmissions page models TCP retransmitting various segments, described in more detail in Section 2.4. There is one instance of each page from the second level downwards for each TCP entity, indicated by the inscriptions TCP'1 and TCP'2 on the arc from page TCP_Overview to page Event_Processing. The CPN model contains 7 places (8 in total when you consider the two instances of the Retransmissions page), 19 substitution transitions and 97 executable transitions.

2.3   TCP_Overview Page

As shown in Fig. 2, the TCP_Overview page comprises 6 places, 2 substitution transitions and 2 executable transitions. Places User_1 and User_2, typed by colour set COMMAND, each model a set of TCP user commands to be issued to the corresponding TCP entity by the corresponding user. Places TCB_1 and TCB_2, typed by colour set TCB, model the transmission control block for each TCP entity. Places H1_H2 and H2_H1, typed by SEG, model TCP buffers and

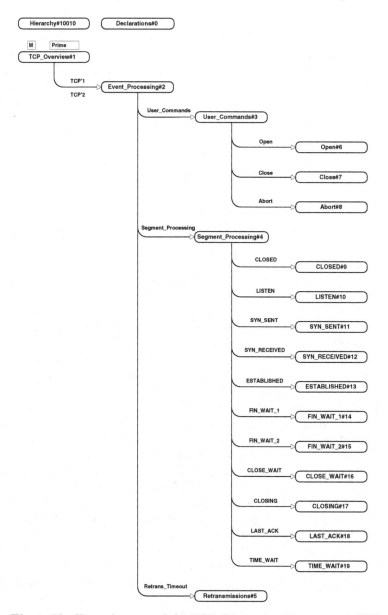

Fig. 1. The Hierarchy page of the TCP Connection Management CPN

all network storage (e.g., router buffers). H1_H2 models data flow from from host 1 to host 2 and vice versa for place H2_H1. Transitions Lossy_Channel1 and Lossy_Channel2 can be switched on and off by their guards to model lossy and non-lossy channels respectively. We analyse non-lossy channels in this paper.

The two TCP entities are modelled by the substitution transitions named TCP'1 and TCP'2, each corresponding to an instance of the Event_Processing

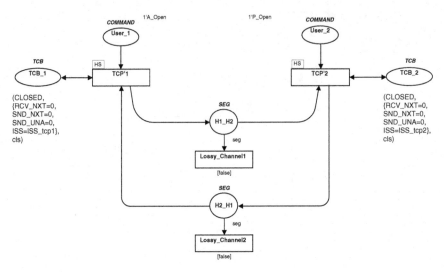

Fig. 2. Top level CPN page: TCP_Overview

page. Places connected to each substitution transition correspond to matching places on the Event_Processing subpage.

Fig. 3 shows the declarations associated with the TCP_Overview page. The declarations are divided into four groups: (1) user commands, (2) TCP segments, (3) Transmission Control Block, and (4) initial send sequence numbers. Comments are enclosed by (* and *).

The first group has one colour set, COMMAND (line 2), defining the set of user commands under consideration. The second group (lines 3 – 12) defines a TCP segment with the abstractions discussed in Section 2.1. CTLbit (line 4) defines the four control bits SYN, ACK, FIN and RST from the TCP segment header [21]. ACKflag (line 5) defines the status of the ACK bit. SEG_CTL (line 6) is the product of the two colour sets CTLbit and ACKflag. The colour set SEG represents TCP segments themselves. It is a record type that has three entries: SEQ, ACK and CTL, modelling the sequence number, the acknowledgement number and the control information in the TCP header, respectively. Finally, seg (line 12) is a variable of type SEG used in arc inscriptions in the CPN model.

The third group (lines 13 – 26) defines the Transmission Control Block. STATE (lines 14 – 16) is an enumeration of all the TCP entity states. SV (lines 17 – 21) defines the four sequence numbers that make up the TCP state variables: RCV_NXT (receive next sequence number); SND_NXT (send next sequence number); SND_UNA (send oldest unacknowledged); and ISS (initial send sequence number). LISTENstat (line 22) stores the history of the TCP state, that is, whether TCP entity has been in the LISTEN state previously (lis) or not (cls). This is used to determine the state a TCP entity enters upon receiving a RST segment in either the SYN_SENT or SYN_RCVD states. TCB (line 23) is a product of colour sets STATE, SV and LISTENstat and defines a TCB. The variables on lines 24 – 26 are used in inscriptions in the CPN model.

```
 1 (* User Commands *)
 2 color COMMAND = with A_Open | P_Open | Close | Abort;
 3 (* TCP Segments *)
 4 color CTLbit = with SYN | RST | ACK | FIN;
 5 color ACKflag = with on | off;
 6 color SEG_CTL = product CTLbit*ACKflag;
 7 color Int = int;
 8 color SEG = record
 9      SEQ: Int *
10      ACK: Int *
11      CTL: SEG_CTL;
12 var seg: SEG;
13 (* Transmission Control Block *)
14 color STATE = with CLOSED | LISTEN | SYN_SENT | SYN_RCVD | EST |
15                    CLOSE_WAIT | LAST_ACK | FIN_W1 | FIN_W2 |
16                    CLOSING | TIME_WAIT;
17 color SV = record
18      RCV_NXT: Int *
19      SND_NXT: Int *
20      SND_UNA: Int *
21      ISS:Int;
22 color LISTENstat = with lis | cls;
23 color TCB = product STATE*SV*LISTENstat;
24 var s : STATE;
25 var v : SV;
26 var i : LISTENstat;
27 (* Initial Sequence Numbers *)
28 val ISS_tcp1 = 10;
29 val ISS_tcp2 = 20;
```

Fig. 3. Colour sets for places on page TCP_Overview

Finally, the initial send sequence number for each TCP entity is represented by ISS_tcp1 (line 28) and ISS_tcp2 (line 29) respectively. We chose a small value of ISS for each TCP entity (i.e, 10 and 20), such that the sequence numbers will not need to wrap.

2.4   The Retransmissions Page

The retransmission mechanism is modelled on page Retransmissions in Fig. 1. A more detailed description of this page can be found in [12]. In brief, there is one instance of this page for each TCP entity. This page contains a single place called Retrans_Counter that stores what is essentially a 5-tuple recording the number of retransmissions that have occurred in each of the five states in the subset of states RS = {SYN_SENT, SYN_RCVD, FIN_WAIT_1, CLOSING, LAST_ACK} $\subset$ STATE. Each element in the tuple is a pair $\in$ RS $\times$ Int, with one element for each state $\in$ RC. All retransmission counters are initialised to 0 and increment by 1 each time a segment is retransmitted in one of the corresponding states.

Three types of segment can be retransmitted: SYN, SYNACK and FIN, with a distinction made between retransmitting a FIN in the FIN_WAIT_1 and/or CLOSING state and the LAST_ACK state. Each of these four types of retransmission has a maximum value specified as a parameter to the model, as will be seen in Section 4. The official TCP specification [21,3] is incomplete with respect to the retransmission mechanism, but Wright and Stevens [24] specify a value of two for the maximum retransmission counters for SYN and SYNACK. When the number of retransmissions of any of the segments reaches its maximum value the TCP entity aborts the connection, i.e., enters CLOSED and sends a RST to the peer entity. When the abort occurs, the number of retransmissions contained in the retransmission counter is reinitialised to 0.

3   Sweep-Line Analysis

3.1   The Sweep-Line Method

When conducting state space exploration, the primary reason for storing states in memory is for comparison with newly generated states to determine whether they have already been discovered. If the state space generation algorithm can identify states that can no longer be reached from any unexplored states, then these states can be safely deleted from memory while still guaranteeing full coverage of the reachability graph. This reduces memory usage and (potentially) saves time due to fewer comparisons being made between new states and states stored in memory. The cost is the additional overhead introduced by the mechanism that identifies states to be safely deleted.

The Sweep-line method allows identification of states that are guaranteed not to be reachable again [5] or are unlikely to be reached again [20] by allowing the user to define a *progress measure* $\mathcal{P} = (O, \sqsubseteq, \psi)$ which specifies a set of progress values O, an ordering $\sqsubseteq \subseteq O \times O$ on those values, and a *progress mapping* $\psi : \mathbb{M} \to O$ (where $\mathbb{M}$ represents all possible markings of the CPN [17]) from states of the model to progress values. If the mapping is defined sensibly then the ordering on the progress values can be used to determine on-the-fly whether or not states with a given progress value are reachable. Such progress mappings can be *monotonic*, i.e. the progress value of any given state must be no less than the progress values of all successor states, or *non-monotonic* if this condition does not hold.

When a state has a higher progress value than one of its immediate successors, then this edge in the reachability graph is called a *regress edge*. The sweep-line method deals with this by conducting multiple *sweeps* of the reachability graph. The result is that some parts of the reachability graph may be generated more than once, but the algorithm is guaranteed to both terminate and provide full coverage of the reachability graph. For technical details of the operation of the sweep-line method, please see [5,20].

In this paper, we use a vector of integers as the set of progress values ($O = \mathbb{N}^n$ for $n \geq 1$) and a lexicographical ordering on the elements of the integer vectors to give us $\sqsubseteq$. Our progress mapping thus becomes $\psi : \mathbb{M} \to \mathbb{N}^n$.

3.2   Sources of Progress

Before identifying sources of progress in our CPN, we define some notation and functions to be used in the formalisation of our progress mappings. Let M denote a marking of the CPN, where M_0 is the initial marking of the CPN and $M(p)$ denotes the marking of place p. We define four projection functions to extract state information from what is essentially a single 6-tuple (a token of type TCB) stored on each of TCB_1 and TCB_2. The marking of the TCB_1 and TCB_2 places is actually a singleton multiset, so we firstly define a function that converts this into its basis element:

Definition 1. *Let S_{MS_1} be the set of all singleton multisets over a basis set $S : S_{MS_1} = \{\{(s,1)\} \mid s \in S\}$. A function that converts a singleton multiset to its basis element is given by $f_c : S_{MS_1} \to S$, where $f_c(\{(s,1)\}) = s$.*

Definition 2. *The projection functions are given by*

- *State : STATE $\times$ Int^4 $\times$ LISTENstat $\to$ STATE,*
  where $State(s, (rcvnxt, sndnxt, snduna, iss), stat) = s$.
- *SndNxt : STATE $\times$ Int^4 $\times$ LISTENstat $\to$ Int,*
  where $SndNxt(s, (rcvnxt, sndnxt, snduna, iss), stat) = sndnxt$.
- *SndUna : STATE $\times$ Int^4 $\times$ LISTENstat $\to$ Int,*
  where $SndUna(s, (rcvnxt, sndnxt, snduna, iss), stat) = snduna$.
- *RcvNxt : STATE $\times$ Int^4 $\times$ LISTENstat $\to$ Int,*
  where $RcvNxt(s, (rcvnxt, sndnxt, snduna, iss), stat) = rcvnxt$.

We also define five projection functions to extract the values of the retransmission counters from the 5-tuple on the Retrans_Counter place.

Definition 3. *Let $f_c(M(\text{Retrans\_Counter})) = ((SYN\_SENT, a), (SYN\_RCVD, b), (LAST\_ACK, c), (FIN\_W1, d), (CLOSING, e))$. The projection functions are given by*

- *RetSynSent : $(RS \times Int)^5 \to Int$,*
  where $RetSynSent(f_c(M(\text{Retrans\_Counter}))) = a$
- *RetSynRcvd : $(RS \times Int)^5 \to Int$,*
  where $RetSynRcvd(f_c(M(\text{Retrans\_Counter}))) = b$
- *RetLastAck : $(RS \times Int)^5 \to Int$,*
  where $RetLastAck(f_c(M(\text{Retrans\_Counter}))) = c$
- *RetFinW1 : $(RS \times Int)^5 \to Int$,*
  where $RetFinW1(f_c(M(\text{Retrans\_Counter}))) = d$
- *RetClosing : $(RS \times Int)^5 \to Int$,*
  where $RetClosing(f_c(M(\text{Retrans\_Counter}))) = e$

TCP Major State Both TCP entities in the CPN model progress through the *major states* defined by colour set STATE. We define an ordering on the major states that preserves as closely as possible the order in which TCP entities progress through these states. Table 1 defines this ordering and a function

$MajorState$: STATE $\to$ $\mathbb{N}$ to map from states to integers. To help reduce the amount of re-exploration we introduce a new major state, CLOSED_F, to differentiate between the initial CLOSED state and the final CLOSED state. This does not invalidate the model as we only model one connection instance. We now define the progress mapping $\psi^1_{major\_state}$: $\mathbb{M} \to \mathbb{N}$ for TCP entity 1:

$$\psi^1_{major\_state}(M) = MajorState(State(f_c(M(\mathsf{TCB\_1}))))$$

The progress mapping $\psi^2_{major\_state}$ is defined analogously for TCP entity 2.

State Variables. The state variables stored within the singleton TCB tokens on places TCB_1 and TCB_2 increase as the protocol progresses through connection establishment and release, although there are instances where they reset to 0, i.e. when a TCP entity enters CLOSED_F or when a TCP server returns to LISTEN. Given our modelling assumptions about the non-wrapping of sequence numbers (described in Section 2.3) we can simply add the state variables together to create the progress mapping $\psi^1_{state\_vars}$: $\mathbb{M} \to \mathbb{N}$ for TCP entity 1 (given below) and a corresponding progress mapping $\psi^2_{state\_vars}$ for TCP entity 2 (not shown).

$$\psi^1_{state\_vars}(M) = SndNxt(f_c(M(\mathsf{TCB\_1}))) + SndUna(f_c(M(\mathsf{TCB\_1}))) + RcvNxt(f_c(M(\mathsf{TCB\_1})))$$

User Commands. As model execution progresses the number of commands to issue to each TCP entity (i.e. the number of tokens on the User_1 and User_2 places) decreases until there are no commands left to issue. This represents progress and is captured by the mapping ψ_{user_comm} : $M \to \mathbb{N}$ given below.

$$\psi_{user\_comm}(M) = 4 - |M(\mathsf{User\_1})| - |M(\mathsf{User\_2})|$$

We do not analyse any sets of user commands greater than size 2 on either User_1 or User_2, hence the '4' in the equation.

Table 1. An ordering and corresponding mapping for TCP major states

state $\in$ STATE	$MajorState$(state)
CLOSED	1
LISTEN	2
SYN_SENT	3
SYN_RCVD	4
EST	5
FIN_W1	6
FIN_W2	7
CLOSE_WAIT	8
CLOSING	9
LAST_ACK	10
TIME_WAIT	11
CLOSED_F	12

Retransmission Counters. The action of retransmitting a segment can be considered as progress of a sort, as we are hopefully closer to our goal after retransmitting a segment than before retransmitting it. We capture this in $\psi_{retrans} : \mathbb{M} \to \mathbb{N}^5$ shown below. Implicitly we define $\psi_{retrans}^1$ and $\psi_{retrans}^2$ for instance 1 and 2 of Retrans_Counter.

$$\psi_{retrans}(M) = (RetClosing(f_c(M(\textsf{Retrans\_Counter}))),$$
$$RetLastAck(f_c(M(\textsf{Retrans\_Counter}))), RetFinW1(f_c(M(\textsf{Retrans\_Counter}))),$$
$$RetSynRcvd(f_c(M(\textsf{Retrans\_Counter}))), RetSynSent(f_c(M(\textsf{Retrans\_Counter}))))$$

We have weighted the retransmission counters to give greater weight to retransmissions occurring in states encountered later in the connection management procedures, to reflect the mapping given by *MajorState* in Table 1.

(Decreasing) Channel Content. Once both TCP entities enter their final states there may be many segments left in the channels. These are received and processed by each TCP entity with little or no change to the marking of the model apart from the marking of the channel places. We attempt to capture some progress related to the change in both the number and type of the segments in channel H1_H2 by mapping $\psi_{ch\_content}^1 : \mathbb{M} \to \mathbb{N}$.

$$\psi_{ch\_content}^1(M) = 10^4 - 10^3 * synsInH1\_H2(M) - 10^2 * finsInH1\_H2(M)$$
$$- 10^1 * acksInH1\_H2(M) - 10^0 * resetsInH1\_H2(M)$$

The progress mapping $\psi_{ch\_content}^2$ is defined analogously. We weight the types of segment according to how soon we expect to see that type of segment in the channel, e.g. the presence of SYN segments in the channel results in lower progress values than the presence of ACK segments. We use a base of 10 to construct our weighting as there will never be more than 10 segments of a given type in the channel at any one time. We check the validity of this assumption on-the-fly during reachability graph generation. The function $synsInH1\_H2$ takes the multiset of segments on place H1_H2 and returns the number of SYN segments in that multiset, and analogously for FIN, ACK and RST segments. Due to length considerations we do not formally define these functions here.

3.3 Combining Sources of Progress

Based on intuition and experimental results for small configurations of the model, the sources of progress and derived mappings are combined into the mapping $\psi_{combined} : \mathbb{M} \to \mathbb{N}^{16}$ which will be used to analyse our CPN model:

$$\psi_{combined}(M) = (\psi_{retrans}^1(M), \psi_{retrans}^2(M), \psi_{major\_state}^1(M), \psi_{major\_state}^2(M),$$
$$\psi_{state\_vars}^1(M), \psi_{state\_vars}^2(M), \psi_{user\_comm}(M),$$
$$\psi_{ch\_content}^1(M) + \psi_{ch\_content}^2(M))$$

A formal comparison of the performance of the sweep-line method with different orderings of progress mappings within $\psi_{combined}$ is beyond the scope of this paper, however there are some interesting points worth highlighting.

The first is that we combine both $\psi^1_{ch\_content}$ and $\psi^2_{ch\_content}$ into one mapping by adding them together. Interestingly, combining them in this way gave much better performance than if one channel was given a greater significance than the other. The second is that we give $\psi^1_{retrans}$ and $\psi^2_{retrans}$ greater significance than everything else. While naive intuition would suggest that the TCP major state progress should be given greatest significance, doing so resulted in significantly worse performance. The third is that the mapping ψ_{user_comm} actually has no effect on the performance of the sweep-line method, regardless of its position in the vector $\psi_{combined}$, as the action of a TCP entity receiving a user command always corresponds to another action in the system that also represents progress.

3.4 Comparison with Previous Construction of Progress Mappings

In [11] an early incarnation of the sweep-line method was used to analyse the Wireless Transaction Protocol (WTP), a part of the Wireless Application Protocol (WAP). The WTP consists of two protocol entities (an initiator and a responder) communicating over a bidirectional channel and is similar to TCP in many ways, at least superficially. This early version of the sweep-line method required a monotonic progress mapping [5] and the existing software support restricted the set of progress values to the set of integers. Sources of progress identified for WTP included the internal state of the two interacting protocol entities, the retransmission counters in each of the protocol entities and a progress mapping that captured the decreasing number of messages in the channel in both directions, but only when both initiator and responder were in their final states. This work did not take into account the progress related to shrinking sets of user commands.

A more recent investigation using the sweep-line method [10] involved the analysis of the Internet Open Trading Protocol (IOTP) [4]. IOTP is a transaction protocol involving four *trading roles* interacting via a set of *document exchanges*. Here, progress was identified in the sequence numbers and retransmission counters of each trading role, in the progression of each trading role through its internal states and the particular combination of document exchanges being undertaken by the four trading roles at any point in time. The IOTP investigation did not take into account the number or type of messages in the channels as we do in $\psi^1_{ch\_content}$ and $\psi^2_{ch\_content}$, nor was there any concept of a set of user commands in the IOTP model analysed in [10].

Both the WAP and IOTP investigations uncovered very similar sources of progress to those identified in this paper and gave us ideas as to what to examine in the TCP Connection Management model to identify progress. These common themes may contribute to a general methodology for the application of sweep-line to communication and transaction protocols, although this is beyond the scope of this paper.

4   Experimental Results

The TCP Connection Management CPN from Section 2 was analysed with the sweep-line method using $\psi_{combined}$ over a lossless reordering channel. Tables 2 and 3 show the 11 configuration classes (labelled A - K) that were investigated. Table 2 describes the initial marking (M_0) of places User_1 and User_2 while Table 3 shows the initial marking of TCB_1 and TCB_2. Places H1_H2 and H2_H1 are always initially empty and both instances of the Retrans_Counter place always contain retransmission counters initialised to 0 for each of the five states in RS. These places are therefore omitted from Tables 2 and 3. Configuration classes A and B are used to analyse the client-server and simultaneous open procedures. Configuration classes C-E examine the connection release procedures. The remaining classes investigate connection management procedures involving aborts. For more details on these configuration classes, please see [12]. All experiments were conducted on a Pentium 2.6 GHz PC with 1Gb RAM.

Each of the configurations A - K were investigated for different values of the maximum number of retransmission parameters. Table 4 shows the results obtained, where the first column gives the configuration being analysed and the 4-tuple gives the maximum number of retransmissions for each of the SYN and SYNACK segments, and both cases of the FIN segment as described in Section 2.4. A dash for any element in the 4-tuple signifies that the corresponding maximum retransmission counter is not relevant for that particular configuration. For a more detailed explanation, please see [12]. A dash is interpreted as a 0 with

Table 2. Initial markings of User_1 and User_2

Configuration Class	Initial Markings	
	$M_0(User\_1)$	$M_0(User\_2)$
A	$1'A\_Open$	$1'P\_Open$
B	$1'A\_Open$	$1'A\_Open$
C	$1'Close$	$1'Close$
D	$1'A\_Open + +1'Close$	$1'P\_Open + +1'Close$
E	$1'A\_Open + +1'Close$	$1'A\_Open + +1'Close$
F	$1'A\_Open + +1'Abort$	$1'P\_Open + +1'Abort$
G	$1'A\_Open + +1'Abort$	$1'A\_Open + +1'Abort$
H	$1'Close + +1'Abort$	$1'Close + +1'Abort$
I	$1'A\_Open + +1'Close$	$1'P\_Open + +1'Abort$
J	$1'A\_Open + +1'Abort$	$1'P\_Open + +1'Close$
K	$1'A\_Open + +1'Close$	$1'A\_Open + +1'Abort$

Table 3. Initial markings of TCB_1 and TCB_2

Configuration Class	Initial Markings	
	$M_0(TCB\_1)$	$M_0(TCB\_2)$
A - B	$1'(CLOSED, (0,0,0,10), cls)$	$1'(CLOSED, (0,0,0,20), cls)$
C	$1'(EST, (21,11,11,10), cls)$	$1'(EST, (11,21,21,20), cls)$
D - G	$1'(CLOSED, (0,0,0,10), cls)$	$1'(CLOSED, (0,0,0,20), cls)$
H	$1'(EST, (21,11,11,10), cls)$	$1'(EST, (11,21,21,20), cls)$
I - K	$1'(CLOSED, (0,0,0,10), cls)$	$1'(CLOSED, (0,0,0,20), cls)$

Table 4. Selected Sweep-line Results for Configurations A - K

Config.	Conventional		Sweep-line			% space	% time	terminal markings	deadlocks
	nodes	time	total nodes	peak nodes	time				
A-(2,2,-,-)	2880	00:00:03	3118	1073	00:00:03	37.3	100.0	24	0
B-(2,1,-,-)	247977	03:40:24	268558	62643	00:15:14	25.3	6.9	63	0
B-(2,2,-,-)	-	-	1015905	153466	01:54:21	-	-	126	0
C-(-,-,2,2)	87291	00:09:25	93213	10228	00:02:04	11.7	21.9	50	0
D-(1,0,1,1)	126098	00:48:35	135680	20179	00:05:23	16.0	11.1	32	0
D-(1,1,0,1)	65381	00:05:07	67921	17237	00:03:14			24	4
D-(1,1,1,0)	-	-	523790	61594	00:43:01	-	-	52	0
D-(1,1,1,1)	-	-	825101	109919	01:34:42	-	-	68	0
E-(0,0,1,1)	-	-	235342	39226	00:16:56	-	-	16	0
E-(0,1,0,1)	328023	09:10:37	341323	70104	00:42:57	21.4	7.8	29	8
E-(0,1,1,0)	-	-	1603626	166639	03:16:23	-	-	51	0
E-(0,1,1,1)	-	-	3209068	407333	16:14:37	-	-	67	0
E-(1,0,0,1)	-	-	713661	175539	04:24:55	-	-	32	8
F-(2,2,-,-)	14563	00:00:23	17444	3480	00:00:20	23.9	87.0	30	0
G-(1,1,-,-)	103670	00:10:59	110609	16669	00:03:35	16.1	32.6	60	0
G-(1,2,-,-)	-	-	492913	48165	00:26:53	-	-	128	0
G-(2,1,-,-)	-	-	945299	125745	01:30:58	-	-	135	0
G-(2,2,-,-)	-	-	4123514	376227	15:33:26	-	-	288	0
H-(-,-,2,2)	229587	03:36:12	239384	22528	00:07:02	9.8	3.3	215	0
I-(2,2,1,-)	193990	02:02:58	226500	28449	00:11:43	14.7	9.5	42	0
I-(2,2,2,-)	-	-	431465	46054	00:32:25	-	-	54	0
J-(2,2,1,-)	167525	00:46:06	182246	31480	00:08:43	18.8	18.9	48	0
J-(2,2,2,-)	-	-	362458	53278	00:25:04	-	-	66	0
K-(0,2,1,-)	-	-	435917	55654	00:36:17	-	-	44	0
K-(0,2,2,-)	-	-	881372	94966	01:48:13	-	-	56	0
K-(1,0,2,-)	-	-	300509	59825	00:35:21	-	-	32	0
K-(1,1,0,-)	264144	04:45:25	268862	25193	00:12:45	9.5	4.5	56	0
K-(1,1,1,-)	-	-	1791167	242801	08:18:18	-	-	84	0
K-(1,1,2,-)	-	-	3632349	411259	28:42:11	-	-	108	0
K-(1,2,0,-)	-	-	1503260	92610	03:12:25	-	-	112	0
K-(2,0,0,-)	-	-	202276	30628	00:12:37	-	-	36	0
K-(2,0,1,-)	-	-	1524996	266338	11:48:00	-	-	54	0
K-(2,1,0,-)	-	-	2654613	187710	09:22:22	-	-	126	0

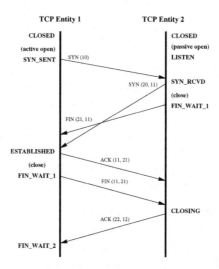

Fig. 4. Connection Release Failure in Configuration D

respect to the initial marking of the model. Except for configurations D and E where each maximum number of retransmissions is limited to 1, we investigate maximum numbers of retransmissions up to 2.

The second and third columns show the total number of nodes and the total generation time for the full reachability graph, as reported in [12, 13]. Columns 4, 5 and 6 show the total number of states explored, the peak state storage and the time taken for sweep-line exploration. The space and time used by the sweep-line method relative to conventional generation is shown in columns 7 and 8. Column 9 shows the number of terminal markings detected and column 10 shows the number of terminal markings that are undesirable, which we discuss below. Rows containing '-' indicate configurations which were not able to be generated with the conventional reachability algorithm of Design/CPN due to memory constraints. We have omitted arc-related statistics from the table due to size constraints.

To reduce unnecessary duplication of the results presented in [12, 13] we include only the largest scenario that could be analysed using conventional generation for each configuration (plus another scenario for illustration purposes in Configuration D). All other scenarios analysed are new results that could not be obtained using conventional generation.

The sweep-line method has given us a reduction in peak state storage of up to a factor of 10 and a reduction in time of up to a factor of 30, for large configurations of the CPN model. This is quite reasonable when compared to previous applications of the sweep-line method [10, 11] where a reduction of a factor of around 6 was achieved for larger configurations.

All scenarios satisfied the termination properties defined in [12, 13] and all but configurations D and E were free from deadlocks. Detailed analysis of the deadlocks in configurations D and E has been carried out in [12, 13] and so will not be duplicated here. In brief, the deadlock occurs because the connection fails to release correctly. Figure 4 illustrates one such scenario for configuration D (client-server establishment). This figure shows that the SYN sent by the TCP server upon entering SYN_RCVD is overtaken by the FIN sent when the server receives a close command from its user. This FIN is then ignored by the client as specified in RFC793 [21]. When the client receives a close command from its user it sends a FIN which the server interprets as a simultaneous release request. The server sends back an ACK and enters the CLOSING state. When the client receives this ACK it enters the FIN_WAIT_2 state. The system is now deadlocked, with the client waiting for a FIN from the server to complete the graceful release and the server waiting for an acknowledgement of its first FIN which will never come.

Retransmission of the FIN when the TCP server is in the CLOSING state prevents the deadlocks from occurring. As can be seen in Table 4, whenever the maximum number of retransmissions is greater than 0 for a FIN when in the FIN_WAIT_1 or CLOSING state (the third element in the 4-tuple in column 1) we can see that the deadlocks in configurations D and E no longer exist. For a more detailed discussion please refer to [12, 13].

5   Conclusions and Future Work

TCP is a very complex protocol that is still not fully understood due to its complexity. This is borne out by the fact that some 60 pages of errors were reported in TCP implementations in [7]. A thorough understanding is very important, particularly given that TCP is so widespread and is being used as the basis for the development of new Internet protocols like the Datagram Congestion Control Protocol (DCCP) [18] and the Stream Control Transmission Protocol (SCTP) [6]. To aid in the understanding of TCP connection management a detailed CPN model has been developed with a view to verifying its correctness. Because the official TCP specification [21,3] is incomplete in terms of specifying the retransmission mechanism our detailed CPN model is parameterised by the maximum number of retransmissions of segments in four situations. Unfortunately, the well known state explosion problem has prevented analysis of some of the larger configurations of this model.

In this paper we have applied the sweep-line state space exploration method to the analysis of the TCP Connection Management CPN operating over a lossless but reordering medium, in an attempt to alleviate the state explosion problem. We have successfully analysed the TCP Connection Management CPN for many configurations that were previously not possible using conventional reachability graph methods, thus extending the analysis results reported in [12,13]. We confirm the results that TCP terminates correctly for client-server and simultaneous connection establishment, orderly release after connection establishment, and aborting of connections. We also confirm that TCP can deadlock under some circumstances when the user initiates connection release before a connection is fully established and that this deadlock can be avoided by allowing the retransmission of FIN segments.

Applying the sweep-line method successfully to another non-trivial problem is also significant in that we begin to see many common themes emerging in the development of progress mappings for the analysis of communication protocols. Looking to the future, there are three topics we would like to pursue. The first is an evaluation and comparison of different combinations and orderings of component progress mappings within the combined mapping $\psi_{combined}$. The second is application of the sweep-line method to the analysis of TCP Connection Management procedures operating over lossy and reordering media. The third is the formalisation of generic guidelines for the successful application of the sweep-line method to the verification of communication and transaction protocols, based on our experience with TCP in this paper coupled with previous experience in [11, 10].

References

1. M. Allman, V. Paxson, and W. Stevens. TCP Congestion Control. RFC 2581, April 1999.
2. J. Billington, G. E. Gallasch, and B. Han. A Coloured Petri Net Approach to Protocol Verification. In *Lectures on Concurrency and Petri Nets, Advances in Petri Nets*, volume 3098 of *Lecture Notes in Computer Science*, pages 210–290. Springer-Verlag, 2004.
3. R. Braden. Requirements for Internet Host – Communication Layers. RFC 1122, October 1989.
4. D. Burdett. Internet Open Trading Protocol - IOTP Version 1.0. RFC 2801, IETF, April 2000.
5. S. Christensen, L.M. Kristensen, and T. Mailund. A Sweep-Line Method for State Space Exploration. In *Proceedings of TACAS 2001*, volume 2031 of *Lecture Notes in Computer Science*, pages 450–464. Springer-Verlag, 2001.
6. R. Stewart et al. Stream Control Transmission Protocol. RFC 2960, October 2000.
7. V. Paxson et al. Known TCP Implementation Problems. RFC 2525, March 1999.
8. S. Floyd. HighSpeed TCP for Large Congestion Windows. RFC 3649, December 2003.
9. S. Floyd and T. Henderson. The NewReno Modification to TCP's Fast Recovery Algorithm. RFC 2582, April 1999.
10. G.E. Gallasch, C. Ouyang, J. Billington, and L.M. Kristensen. Experimenting with Progress Mappings for the Application of the Sweep-Line Analysis fo the Internet Open Trading Protocol. In *Fifth Workshop and Tutorial on Practical Use of Coloured Petri Nets and the CPN Tools*. Department of Computer Science, University of Aarhus, 2004. Available via http://www.daimi.au.dk/CPnets/workshop04/cpn/papers/.
11. S. Gordon, L.M. Kristensen, and J. Billington. Verification of a Revised WAP Wireless Transaction Protocol. In *Proceedings of ICATPN'02*, volume 2360 of *Lecture Notes in Computer Science*, pages 182–202. Springer-Verlag, 2002.
12. B. Han. *Formal Specification of the TCP Service and Verification of TCP Connection Management*. PhD thesis, Computer Systems Engineering Centre, School of Electrical and Information Engineering, University of South Australia, Adelaide, Australia, December 2004.

13. B. Han and J. Billington. Termination Properties of TCP's Connection Management Procedures. In *Proceedings of ICATPN'05*, Lecture Notes in Computer Science. Springer-Verlag, 2005 (to appear).
14. V. Jacobson and R. Braden. TCP Extensions for Long Delay Paths. RFC 1072, October 1988.
15. V. Jacobson, R. Braden, and D. Borman. TCP Extensions for High Performance. RFC 1323, May 1992.
16. V. Jacobson, R. Braden, and L. Zhang. TCP Extension for High-Speed Paths. RFC 1185, October 1990.
17. K. Jensen. *Coloured Petri Nets: Basic Concepts, Analysis Methods and Practical Use. Vol. 1, Basic Concepts*. Springer-Verlag, 2nd edition, 1997.
18. E. Kohler, M. Handley, and S. Floyd. Datagram Congestion Control Protocol. draft-ietf-dccp-spec-11, March 2005.
19. L.M. Kristensen, S. Christensen, and K. Jensen. The Practitioner's Guide to Coloured Petri Nets. *International Journal on Software Tools for Technology Transfer*, 2(2):98–132, 1998.
20. L.M. Kristensen and T. Mailund. A Generalised Sweep-Line Method for Safety Properties. In *Proceedings of FME'02*, volume 2391 of *Lecture Notes in Computer Science*, pages 549–567. Springer-Verlag, 2002.
21. J. Postel. Transmission Control Protocol. RFC 793, September 1981.
22. C.A. Sunshine and Y. K. Dalal. Connection Management in Transport Protocols. *Computer Networks*, pages 2(6):346–350, December 1978.
23. A. Valmari. The State Explosion Problem. In *Lectures on Petri Nets I: Basic Models*, volume 1491 of *Lecture Notes in Computer Science*, pages 429–528. Springer-Verlag, 1998.
24. G. R. Wright and W. R. Stevens. *TCP/IP Illustrated, Vol. 2 : The Implementation*. Addison-Wesley, 1995.

2/3 Alternating Simulation Between Interface Automata*

Yanjun Wen, Ji Wang, and Zhichang Qi

National Laboratory for Parallel and Distributed Processing,
Changsha, P.R. China
{y.j.wen, ji.wang}@263.net

Abstract. Interface automata is a light-weight formalism to be used for describing the temporal interface behaviors of software components. This paper investigates the refinement of interface automata and shows its application to serve as a semantic foundation for software architectural description languages. Firstly, inspired by 2/3 simulation, the 2/3 *alternating simulation* between interface automata is presented, and the corresponding refinement relation is also derived between interface automata. The distinguished feature is that it can preserve *deadlock-freedom*. Then, a concise formal semantics is provided for the architectural description language WRIGHT, based on interface automata, where the checking of compatibility and deadlock-freedom becomes simpler.

1 Introduction

Interface automata [1] is a light-weight formalism that captures the *temporal* aspects of software component interfaces. Automatic compatibility checking and refinement checking can be made to support component based software development. It has been applied in several cases as a method for modelling the interface behavior of software [2–5].

A remarkable feature of interface automata is its capability to model explicitly the assumptions of a component to environments. The virtue is due to the special semantics of action synchronization when several automata are composed in parallel. Concretely, on the one hand, an interface automaton can refuse some actions at a state. On the other hand, if an interface automaton sends out some action at a state, then there must exist another automaton which can accept the action at that moment. In another words, all output actions must be accepted right now, while it is not required that all input actions be accepted at all states. If an output action can not be accepted by any automaton, then a failure takes place. If all failures can be avoided, then the system is compatible. Thus both the static interfaces of actions and the dynamic behaviors determine

---

* Supported by National Natural Science Foundation of China under the grants 60233020 and 60303013, National Hi-Tech Programme (863) of China under the grant 2005AA113130, and Program for New Century Excellent Talents in University.

K.-K. Lau and R. Banach (Eds.): ICFEM 2005, LNCS 3785, pp. 173–187, 2005.

the compatibility of two interface automata. So, the component specification in interface automata expresses not only its behavior, but also the assumptions to environments.

With the new mechanism defined for action synchronization, the refinement between interface automata is also defined differently. Roughly, an interface automaton refines another if it can provide more services (that is, accept more actions) and send out fewer requests (that is, output fewer actions). This *contravariant* requirement on input actions and output actions is described by a new simulation relation: *alternating simulation* [3]. The corresponding refinement can preserve compatibility. That is to say, if an interface automaton is compatible with the environment, then after replacing the automaton with a more refined version, the new system is still compatible. This capability is described by the theorem 4 of [1].

Although being able to preserve compatibility, the refinement between interface automata can not preserve deadlock-freedom: if the abstract automaton is compatible with the environment and their composition is deadlock-free, then after replacing the abstract automaton with a more refined version the new system may be deadlocked, yet compatible. Consider three interface automata P, P' and E such that P refines P', and P' is compatible with E. As mentioned above, roughly, P refines P' if P can accept more actions and send out less actions. However, if both P and E do not send out actions, the system may get into deadlock. At the same time, P' and E may be able to avoid deadlock because P' may send out some actions which can be accepted by E.

The main contributions of this paper is to present a new refinement between interface automata, which can preserve deadlock-freedom. Technically, as a basis of the new refinement, we present a new simulation, 2/3 *alternating simulation*, which is an improvement to alternating simulation. The core idea comes from the 2/3 simulation [6, 7] in CCS [8].

After the revisions to refinements, we explore the application by employing interface automata as a formal basis for WRIGHT [9–11], a famous architectural description language (ADL). Although the research on ADLs has been paid lots of attentions for several years, some improvement is still needed. For example, it is pointed out in [12] that in order to ease the acceptance of ADLs by developers, a simple formal semantics is needed. WRIGHT adopts CSP [13] as its formal basis, and supports the automatic verification of software architectures. However, the testing rules of WRIGHT are still somewhat complex and difficult to understand. As shown in this paper, interface automata has some specific advantages in acting as the formal basis of WRIGHT. For example, the testing rule which is used to check the compatibility between ports and roles will become much simpler, if using interface automata as the semantic model. Additionally, simpler tests are needed to ensure the deadlock-freedom property of the whole system after attaching ports to the roles of a connector.

By the way, we also present an alternative fix solution to an existent defect in [1], which is known and fixed in [14]. The difference is that instead of restricting interface automata to be *input-deterministic*, we propose a conservative definition of parallel composition between interface automata, avoiding to influence the flexibility of modelling.

The rest of the paper is organized as follows. After Section 2 gives some concepts of interface automata, Section 3 presents a conservative definition of parallel composition between interface automata. Then, Section 4 presents 2/3 alternating simulation, and redefines the refinement between interface automata. Section 5 provides a formal semantics for architectural connection which is described in WRIGHT. The conclusion is summarized finally.

2   Preliminary

Interface automata have been presented as a light-weight formalism for modelling the interface behavior of software components.

Definition 1 (Interface Automata). *An* interface automaton *is a structure*

$$P = < V_P, V_P^{init}, A_P^I, A_P^O, A_P^H, \Delta_P >$$

where

- V_P *is a set of* states.
- $V_P^{init} \subseteq V_P$. *It is a set of* initial states *and contains at most one state. If* $V_P^{init} = \emptyset$, *then* P *is called* empty.
- A_P^I, A_P^O, *and* A_P^H *are mutually disjoint sets of* input, output, *and* internal *actions. We denote by* $A_P = A_P^I \cup A_P^O \cup A_P^H$ *the set of all actions,* $A_P^L = A_P^O \cup A_P^H$ *the set of all* locally-controlled *actions, and* $A_P^X = A_P^I \cup A_P^O$ *the set of all* external *actions.*
- $\Delta_P \subseteq V_P \times A_P \times V_P$. *It is a set of transitions.*

The interface automaton P is *closed* if $A_P^X = \emptyset$; otherwise it is *open*. An action $a \in A_P$ is *enabled* at a state $v \in V_P$ if there exists a state $v' \in V_P$ such that $(v, a, v') \in \Delta_P$. The set of input (output and internal, respectively) actions which are enabled at the state v is denoted as $A_P^I(v)$ ($A_P^O(v)$ and $A_P^H(v)$, respectively).

For an interface automaton P, two states $s_1, s_2 \in V_P$, an action $a \in A_P$, and a finite action sequence $\alpha = a_1 a_2 \cdots a_n \in (A_P)^n$, we define several relations as follows.

- $s_1 \xrightarrow{a}_P s_2$ iff $(s_1, a, s_2) \in \Delta_P$.
- $s_1 \xrightarrow{\tau}_P s_2$ iff $s_1 \xrightarrow{b}_P s_2$ for some $b \in A_P^H$.
- $s_1 \xrightarrow{\alpha}_P s_2$ iff $s_1 \xrightarrow{a_1}_P \xrightarrow{a_2}_P \cdots \xrightarrow{a_n}_P s_2$. Especially, $s_1 \xrightarrow{\varepsilon}_P s_1$.

where juxtaposition is a composition of relations.

Two interface automata are composable [1] if their actions are disjoint, except that an input action of one may be an output action of the other.

Definition 2 (Composable). *Two interface automata P and Q are compos-able if*

$$A_P^H \cap A_Q = A_Q^H \cap A_P = A_P^I \cap A_Q^I = A_P^O \cap A_Q^O = \emptyset.$$

We let $shared(P, Q) = A_P \cap A_Q$.

The product [1] of interface automata is similar to the composition of I/O automata [15], except that the shared actions are hidden.

Definition 3 (Product). *If P and Q are composable interface automata, their product $P \otimes Q$ is the interface automaton defined by*

$$
\begin{aligned}
V_{P \otimes Q} &= V_P \times V_Q \\
V_{P \otimes Q}^{init} &= V_P^{init} \times V_Q^{init} \\
A_{P \otimes Q}^I &= (A_P^I \cup A_Q^I) \setminus shared(P, Q) \\
A_{P \otimes Q}^O &= (A_P^O \cup A_Q^O) \setminus shared(P, Q) \\
A_{P \otimes Q}^H &= A_P^H \cup A_Q^H \cup shared(P, Q)
\end{aligned}
$$

$$
\begin{aligned}
\Delta_{P \otimes Q} = &\{((u, v), a, (u', v)) \mid (u, a, u') \in \Delta_P \wedge a \notin shared(P, Q) \wedge v \in V_Q\} \\
\cup &\{((u, v), a, (u, v')) \mid (v, a, v') \in \Delta_Q \wedge a \notin shared(P, Q) \wedge u \in V_P\} \\
\cup &\{((u, v), a, (u', v')) \mid (u, a, u') \in \Delta_P \wedge (v, a, v') \in \Delta_Q \wedge a \in shared(P, Q)\}.
\end{aligned}
$$

Definition 4 (Illegal States [1]). *Given two composable interface automata P and Q, the set $Illegal(P, Q) \subseteq V_P \times V_Q$ of illegal states of $P \otimes Q$ is the following set:*

$$
\left\{ (u, v) \in V_P \times V_Q \mid \exists a \in shared(P, Q). \begin{pmatrix} a \in A_P^O(u) \wedge a \notin A_Q^I(v) \\ \vee \\ a \in A_Q^O(v) \wedge a \notin A_P^I(u) \end{pmatrix} \right\}.
$$

In the product of two interface automata, the compatible states are those from which the environment can prevent all illegal states from being entered in one or more steps.

Definition 5 (Compatible States). *Consider two composable interface automata P and Q. A pair $(u, v) \in V_{P \otimes Q}$ of states is compatible if the following condition holds.*

$$\nexists(u', v') \in Illegal(P, Q). \beta \in (A_{P \otimes Q}^L)^*. (u, v) \xrightarrow{\beta}_{P \otimes Q} (u', v')$$

We write $Cmp(P, Q)$ for the set of compatible states of $P \otimes Q$.

It is worth noting that this definition coincides with the original definition [1] of compatible states.

Definition 6 (Compatible Interface Automata). *Two interface automata P and Q are compatible if they are nonempty, composable, and their initial states are compatible.*

3   Parallel Composition of Interface Automata

The theorem 4 of [1] states two important properties of refinements between interface automata. The first property is the preservation of compatibility. The second one is compositionality: in order to check $P \parallel Q \preceq P' \parallel Q'$, it is sufficient to check both $P \preceq P'$ and $Q \preceq Q'$. The two properties give support to component-based design and compositional refinement checking.

However, the theorem does not hold in some cases because in the original framework of interface automata there exist some minor defects, which are known to the authors of [1]. They provide a patch in [14]. In their solution, interface automata are limited to be *input-deterministic*, because the problems may arise only when interface automata are nondeterministic on input actions. The limitation weakens the flexibility in modelling interface behaviors. In this section, we present an alternative solution, in which the limitation is not necessary.

Technically, we provide a conservative definition to the parallel composition of interface automata. The idea is that instead of deleting incompatible states we delete dangerous transitions.

In the paper, the notions defined in [1] are followed. For example, $ExtEn_P^I(u)$ denotes the set of externally enabled input actions of P at the state u, and $\varepsilon\text{-}closure_P(u)$ is the ε-closure of the state u in interface automaton P.

Definition 7 (Dangerous Transitions). *Given two composable interface automata P and Q, a transition $t = (s, a, s') \in \Delta_{P\otimes Q}^I$ is a* dangerous transition *of $P \otimes Q$ if the following condition is satisfied. The set of all dangerous transitions of $P \otimes Q$ is denoted as $\Delta_{P\otimes Q}^{dgr}$.*

$$s \in Cmp(P, Q) \wedge \exists s'' \in (V_{P\otimes Q} \backslash Cmp(P, Q)).\ (s, a, s'') \in \Delta_{P\otimes Q}$$

According to the definition, all the transitions from compatible states to incompatible states are dangerous; moreover, if a transition has the same source state and action with a dangerous transition, then it is also dangerous. That is to say, if (s, a, s') is a dangerous transition, then all the transitions of the type $(s, a, *)$ are all dangerous, where '$*$' can be any state. The reason is that since (s, a, s') is a dangerous transition, the environment should not be allowed to output the action a while $P \otimes Q$ stays at the state s, and thus all transitions of the type $(s, a, *)$ are impossible to be triggered.

Definition 8 (Parallel Composition). *Consider two composable interface automata P and Q. The* parallel composition *$P \parallel Q$ is defined as follows.*

$$<V_{P\otimes Q}, V_{P\otimes Q}^{init} \cap Cmp(P, Q), A_{P\otimes Q}^I, A_{P\otimes Q}^O, A_{P\otimes Q}^H, \Delta_{P\otimes Q} \backslash \Delta_{P\otimes Q}^{dgr}>$$

In the original definition of parallel composition, the incompatible states are deleted from the product. Correspondingly, all the transitions from compatible states to incompatible states are deleted at the same time. However, these transitions compose only part of the dangerous transitions. Thus according to the new definition, more transitions are excluded from parallel composition. After redefining the parallel composition of interface automata, the theorem 4 of [1] holds. In the next section, we will restate it according to the new definition.

4   2/3 Alternating Simulation

The refinement of interface automata is based on alternating simulation. Although being able to preserve compatibility, it can not preserve deadlock-freedom. We illustrate this by the three interface automata shown in Figure 1.

Example 1. Interface automata *In* and *Out* describe respectively the behaviors of a data-input interface and a data-output interface. At the state 0, *In* can accept the message *data* and then enter the state 1, or accept the message *close* and then terminate successfully at the state √. At state 1, *In* sends out a message *next* to request for the next data. The behavior of the interface automaton *Out* is just contravariant to *In*. Obviously, *In* and *Out* can work together nicely. That is, they are compatible and deadlock-free.

Now consider the interface automaton *Out'*. At the state 0, *Out'* can accept the message *next* and then terminates successfully at the state √. But it can not output any message at the state 0. Obviously, *Out'* refines *Out*. Since *In* and *Out* are compatible, it can be inferred that *Out'* and *In* are also compatible. However, if replacing *Out* with *Out'*, the new system (*Out'* ∥ *In*) will be deadlocked: at the state (0,0), neither *Out'* nor *In* can send out any message, and thus the whole system is deadlocked. By the example, it can be seen that the refinement between interface automata can not preserve deadlock-freedom.

In this section, in order to endow the refinements between interface automata with the important capability of preserving deadlock-freedom, we present a new simulation relation: 2/3 alternating simulation, and redefine the refinements between interface automata based on this new simulation.

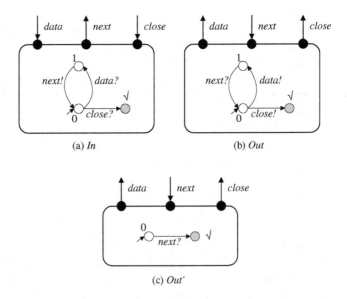

(a) *In*   (b) *Out*

(c) *Out'*

Fig. 1. Interface automata *In*, *Out* and *Out'*

In the following, we assume that every interface automaton P has a special state $s_P^\vee$ such that $A_P(s_P^\vee) = \emptyset$, which means the successful termination of P. Furthermore, for any two composable interface automata P and Q, both $s_{P\|Q}^\vee$ and $s_{P\otimes Q}^\vee$ are defined to be the state $(s_P^\vee, s_Q^\vee)$.

The idea of 2/3 alternating simulation comes from the 2/3 simulation [6, 7] in CCS [8]. The necessary adjustments are made to conform with the context of interface automata.

Definition 9 (2/3 Alternating Simulations). *Consider two interface automata P and Q. A binary relation $\preceq \subseteq V_P \times V_Q$ is a 2/3 alternating simulation from P to Q if for all state-pairs $(u, v) \in \preceq$, the following conditions hold:*

1. *$ExtEn_P^I(u) \supseteq ExtEn_Q^I(v)$ and $ExtEn_P^O(u) \subseteq ExtEn_Q^O(v)$.*
2. *For all actions $a \in ExtEn_Q^I(v) \cup ExtEn_P^O(u)$ and all states $u' \in ExtDest_P$ (u, a), there is a state $v' \in ExtDest_Q(v, a)$ such that $u' \preceq v'$.*
3. *If there is a state $u'' \in \varepsilon-closure_P(u)$ such that $u'' \neq s_P^\vee$ and $A_P(u'') \subseteq A_P^I$, then there is also a state $v'' \in \varepsilon-closure_Q(v)$ such that $v'' \neq s_Q^\vee$ and $A_Q(v'') \subseteq A_Q^I$.*
4. *If $s_P^\vee \in \varepsilon-closure_P(u)$, then there is a state $v'' \in \varepsilon-closure_Q(v)$ such that $A_Q(v'') \subseteq A_Q^I$.*

It can be seen that the difference between alternating simulation and 2/3 alternating simulation lies in the third and fourth conditions, whose intuitive meaning is that: in any compatible environment, if the more refined interface automaton P can get into a deadlock state then the more abstract interface automaton Q can also.

Based on 2/3 alternating simulation, we can define the refinements between interface automata.

Definition 10 (Refinements). *Consider two nonempty interface automata P and Q. P refines Q, written $P \preceq Q$, if the following conditions hold:*

1. *$A_P^I = A_Q^I$ and $A_P^O = A_Q^O$.*
2. *There is a 2/3 alterating simulation $\preceq$ from P to Q such that for all states $u \in V_P^{init}$, there exists a state $v \in V_Q^{init}$ satisfying $u \preceq v$.*

It is worth noting that the original definition [1] of refinements requires that $A_P^I \supseteq A_Q^I$ and $A_P^O \subseteq A_Q^O$. However, as we have pointed out in [16], by a special 'hiding' operator the input actions in $A_P^I \setminus A_Q^I$ can be deleted safely without affecting the refinement relation between P and Q. Similarly, the output actions in $A_Q^O \setminus A_P^O$ can also be added to the action set of P safely without affecting their refinement relation. Thus in the definition below, we require that $A_P^I = A_Q^I$ and $A_P^O = A_Q^O$.

Theorem 1. $\preceq$ *is a preorder.*

The next theorem restates the theorem 4 of [1]. It shows that refinements between interface automata can preserve compatibility. That is, if an interface automaton P' can work nicely (be compatible) in an environment Q, then after substituting P' with a more refined version P the new system can work nicely too. Due to the space limitation, we omit the proof of the theorem.

Theorem 2. *Consider three interface automata P, P' and Q such that P and Q are composable. If P' and Q are compatible and $P \preceq P'$, then P and Q are also compatible and $P \parallel Q \preceq P' \parallel Q$.*

Definition 11 (Unique Internal-Action Condition). *A set of interface automata P_1, P_2, $\ldots$, P_n satisfies the* unique internal-action condition *if the following proposition holds:*

$$\forall i, j \in \{1 \ldots n\}. \; i \neq j \rightarrow A_{P_i}^H \cap A_{P_j} = \emptyset.$$

Corollary 1. *Consider a set of interface automata P, P', Q and Q' that satisfies the unique internal-action condition. If P' and Q' are compatible, $P \preceq P'$, and $Q \preceq Q'$, then P and Q are also compatible and $P \parallel Q \preceq P' \parallel Q'$.*

Proof. By $P \preceq P'$, it can be known that $A_P^I = A_{P'}^I$ and $A_P^O = A_{P'}^O$. Similarly, $A_Q^I = A_{Q'}^I$ and $A_Q^O = A_{Q'}^O$. Because P' and Q' are compatible, they are composable of course. Since the set of interface automata P, P', Q and Q' satisfies the unique internal-action condition, it can be inferred that P and Q', and P and Q are both composable.

Because P' and Q' are compatible, and $P \preceq P'$, by Theorem 2 we know that P and Q' are also compatible, and $P \parallel Q' \preceq P' \parallel Q'$. Moreover, because P and Q' are compatible, and $Q \preceq Q'$, by Theorem 2 we know that P and Q are also compatible, and $P \parallel Q \preceq P \parallel Q'$. Since $\preceq$ is transitive, $P \parallel Q \preceq P' \parallel Q'$ follows. $\qquad\square$

The corollary can be extended further.

Corollary 2. *Consider a set of interface automata P_1, P_2, $\ldots$, P_n, Q_1, Q_2, $\ldots$, and Q_n that satisfies the unique internal-action condition. If $Q_1, Q_2, \ldots, Q_n$ are compatible, and for all $i \in \{1 \ldots n\}$ it holds that $P_i \preceq Q_i$, then $P_1, P_2, \ldots, P_n$ are also compatible and $\prod_{i=1}^n P_i \preceq \prod_{i=1}^n Q_i$.*

4.1   Deadlock-Freedom

In this subsection, it is shown that refinements between interface automata can preserve deadlock-freedom.

Definition 12 (Deadlock). *Consider a nonempty and closed interface automaton P. Let $V_P^{init} = \{q_P\}$. a state $s_P \in V_P$ is deadlocked if $s_P \neq s_P^{\checkmark}$ and $A_P(s_P) = \emptyset$. The set of all deadlock states of P is written $Deadlock(P)$. P is deadlocked if there is a state $s_P \in (Deadlock(P) \cap \varepsilon\text{--}closure_P(q_P))$. Otherwise, P is deadlock-free.*

The next theorem shows that refinements between closed interface automata can preserve deadlock-freedom.

Theorem 3. *Consider two interface automata P and Q such that $P \preceq Q$. If P is deadlocked, then Q is also deadlocked.*

Proof. By $P \preceq Q$, it follows that P and Q are both nonempty, $A_P^I = A_Q^I$ and $A_P^O = A_Q^O$. Additionally, there is a 2/3 alternating simulation $\preceq$ from P to Q such that the following proposition holds:

$$\forall u \in V_P^{init}. \ \exists v \in V_Q^{init}. \ u \preceq v.$$

Let $V_P^{init} = \{q_P\}$ and $V_Q^{init} = \{q_Q\}$. Then $q_P \preceq q_Q$ follows. Suppose that P is deadlocked. Then P and Q are both closed, and there is a state $s_P \in Deadlock(P) \cap \varepsilon\text{-}closure_P(q_P)$. Since $s_P \in Deadlock(P)$, it follows that $s_P \neq s_P^{\vee}$ and $A_P(s_P) = \emptyset$. Thus $A_P(s_P) \subseteq A_P^I$. Because $q_P \preceq q_Q$ and $s_P \in \varepsilon\text{-}closure_P(q_P)$, there is a state $s_Q \in \varepsilon\text{-}closure_Q(q_Q)$ such that $s_Q \neq s_Q^{\vee}$ and $A_Q(s_Q) \subseteq A_Q^I$. However $A_Q^I = \emptyset$. Thus $A_Q(s_Q) = \emptyset$ and $s_Q \in Deadlock(Q)$. So Q is also deadlocked. $\qquad\square$

The next theorem shows that refinements between open interface automata can preserve deadlock-freedom. That is, if an interface automaton P' can work nicely (be compatible and deadlock-free) in an environment Q, then after substituting P' with a more refined version P the new system can work nicely too.

Theorem 4. *Consider a set of interface automata P, P' and Q such that (1) P' and Q are compatible, (2) $P \preceq P'$, and (3) the unique internal-action condition is satisfied by them. If $P \parallel Q$ is deadlocked, then $P' \parallel Q$ is also deadlocked.*

Proof. Because P' and Q are compatible, and $P \preceq P'$, by Corollary 2 it follows that P and Q are compatible, and $P \parallel Q \preceq P' \parallel Q$. If $P \parallel Q$ is deadlocked, then by Theorem 3 we know that $P' \parallel Q$ is also deadlocked. $\qquad\square$

Reconsider the example 1. There is an alternating simulation $\preceq = \{(0,0)\}$ from Out' to Out. However, $\preceq$ is not a 2/3 alternating simulation from Out' to Out because $A_{Out}(0) \not\subseteq A_{Out}^I$ while $A_{Out'}(0) \subseteq A_{Out'}^I$. Since there exists no 2/3 alternating simulation from Out' to Out, $Out' \preceq Out$ does not hold according to the new definition of refinements. From this example, it can be confirmed that the refinements based on 2/3 alternating simulation can preserve deadlock-freedom.

5   Refinement of Wright Based on Interface Automata

WRIGHT [9–11] is a famous architectural description language, which uses a subset of CSP as its formal basis. In this section, we try to explore the possibility of using interface automata as a new formal basis for WRIGHT.

5.1   Introduction to Wright

WRIGHT introduces a group of notations, such as components, connectors, ports, roles and glues, to describe software architectures. We take a simple procedure-call system as an example to illustrate the basic notations of WRIGHT. Figure 2 describes the system in WRIGHT.

System ProcedureCall
    component Definer =
        port provide *[provide protocol]*
        spec *[Definer protocol]*
    component Caller =
        port request *[request protocol]*
        spec *[Caller protocol]*
    connector D-C-connector =
        role definer *[definer protocol]*
        role caller *[caller protocol]*
        glue *[glue protocol]*
Instances
    d: Definer
    c: Caller
    dc: D-C-connector
Attachments
    d.provide **as** dc.definer;
    c.request **as** dc.caller
end ProcedureCall.

Fig. 2. A Procedure-Call System

The description can be divided into three parts. The first part describes *component* and *connector* types. A component can have a set of *ports* and a *component-spec* which specifies its implementation. Each port describes the behavior of the component at a logical point of interaction. A connector can have a set of *roles* and a *glue* specification. Each role describes the expected behavior of an interacting object, and the glue specification defines the behavior of the connector, which interacts with each role. The roles of a connector can not interact with each other directly. In the simple procedure-call system, there are two components and one connector. Each component has only one port in this specific example.

The second part is a set of component and connector *instances*. Each instance specifies an actual entity that will appear at the configuration. In the third part, the entities are combined together by attaching the ports to the roles. Each port can be attached to at most one role, and vice versa.

Detailed introductions can be found in [10] and [11].

5.2 Formal Semantics

In WRIGHT, the protocols of ports, roles and glues are all described in a subset of CSP. In this paper, we describe the protocols in interface automata, and define the semantics of connectors using interface automata as the formal basis, similar to the use of CSP in [11] in WRIGHT.

In order to endow irrelevant actions with different names, a relabelling operation is needed.

Definition 13 (Relabelling). *The* relabelling *of an interface automaton P on a name L is the interface automaton Q defined as follows, written* L:P.

- $V_Q = V_P$ *and* $V_Q^{init} = V_P^{init}$.
- $A_Q^I = \{L.a \mid a \in A_P^I\}$, $A_Q^O = \{L.a \mid a \in A_P^O\}$ *and* $A_Q^H = \{L.a \mid a \in A_P^H\}$.
- $\Delta_Q = \{(s, L.a, s') \mid (s, a, s') \in \Delta_P\}$.
- $s_Q^{\vee} = s_P^{\vee}$.

It can be seen that after relabelling, a prefix (L) is attached to each action name. In an action name, each part that is separated by a dot is called a *field* of the name. For the sake of simplicity, we assume that every internal-action name of every constructor (such as port, role and glue) contains (before relabelling) only one field and is globally unique. That is to say, there exists no constructor of which an internal-action has the same name with an (internal or external) action of another constructor. Since internal-action names can be renamed without influencing the behavior of a constructor, the assumption above is appropriate.

Definition 14. *The* meaning *of a connector description with roles* R_1, R_2, ..., R_n, *and glue Glue is the interface automaton:*

$$Glue \parallel (R_1 {:} R_1 \parallel R_2 {:} R_2 \parallel \ldots \parallel R_n {:} R_n)$$

where R_i *is the name of role* R_i.

We assume that the role names of a connector are distinct with each other. After relabelling, any two roles of a connector do not have the same action names, and thus can not interact directly.

Definition 15. *The* meaning *of attaching ports* $P_1 \ldots P_n$ *as roles* $R_1 \ldots R_n$ *of a connector with glue Glue is the interface automaton:*

$$Glue \parallel (R_1 {:} P_1 \parallel R_2 {:} P_2 \parallel \ldots \parallel R_n {:} P_n).$$

The next theorem states that if the connector is deadlock-free and each port refines the corresponding role, then after substituting the roles with the ports, the whole system will still be deadlock-free.

Theorem 5. *Consider a connector* $C = Glue \parallel (R_1 {:} R_1 \parallel R_2 {:} R_2 \parallel \ldots \parallel R_n {:} R_n)$ *and ports* $P_1 \ldots P_n$. *If* C *is deadlock-free and for all* $i \in \{1 \ldots n\}$ *it holds that* $P_i \preceq R_i$, *then* $C' = Glue \parallel (R_1 {:} P_1 \parallel R_2 {:} P_2 \parallel \ldots \parallel R_n {:} P_n)$ *is also deadlock-free.*

Proof. For C is deadlock-free, C must be closed. Thus $A_{Glue}^I = \bigcup_{i=1}^n A_{R_i:R_i}^O$ and $A_{Glue}^O = \bigcup_{i=1}^n A_{R_i:R_i}^I$. Considering the fact that each internal-action name of every constructor has only one field and is globally unique, it can be proved that the unique internal-action condition is satisfied by the set of interface automata $Glue$, $R_1 {:} R_1$, ..., $R_n {:} R_n$, $R_1 {:} P_1$, ..., and $R_n {:} P_n$.

Because for all $i \in \{1 \ldots n\}$, $P_i \preceq R_i$, it is obvious that $Glue \preceq Glue$, and for $i \in \{1 \ldots n\}$, $R_i {:} P_i \preceq R_i {:} R_i$. Since C is deadlock-free, $Glue$, $R_1 {:} R_1$, ..., $R_n {:} R_n$ are compatible. Moreover, we have known that the unique internal-action condition is satisfied by the set of interface automata $Glue$, $R_1 {:} R_1$, ..., $R_n {:} R_n$, $R_1 {:} P_1$, ..., and $R_n {:} P_n$. Thus by Corollary 2, it follows that $C' \preceq C$. Since C is deadlock-free, by Theorem 3 we have that C' is also deadlock-free. $\qquad\square$

As mentioned above, WRIGHT adopts CSP as its semantic model. Comparing with CSP, the checking of compatibility and deadlock-freedom becomes simpler when employing interface automata as the formal basis of WRIGHT:

1. In WRIGHT, in order to check the compatibility between ports and roles, the following testing rule[1] is checked:

   A port P is compatible with a role R if
   $$R_{+(\alpha P \backslash \alpha R)} \sqsubseteq (P_{+(\alpha R \backslash \alpha P)} \parallel det(R)).$$

   However, when based on interface automata, it is enough to check that $P \preceq R$. The simplicity is due to the capability of interface automata to express explicitly the assumptions to environments. As a contrast, in WRIGHT one has to calculate the assumptions $(det(R))$ separately. Thus using interface automata as the semantic model, we can avoid the calculation of the deterministic process $det(R)$, which is complex.

2. In WRIGHT, in order to ensure a system deadlock-free, three conditions[2] should be satisfied: (1) the connectors should be *conservative*; (2) the connectors should be deadlock-free; (3) Ports should be compatible with the corresponding ports. However, when based on interface automata, only the last two conditions are necessary.

5.3   Case Study

Reconsider the simple procedure-call system shown in Figure 2. The protocols of the connector **D-C-connector** are displayed in Figure 3, including the protocols of roles **caller** and **definer**, and the glue. In all figures, the transitions with the same source and sink states are merged. It can be seen that the role **definer** can accept a procedure-call request **call** at the initial state 0. It can also accept an action **close**, which notifies the role to stop the procedure-call service. After accepting the **call** request, **definer** can return signals **return** or **fail** to the client, which mean respectively the result after executing successfully the procedure, and the failure of execution.

The behavior of the ports **request** and **provide** is also described in interface automata, as shown in Figure 4.

It can be seen that $C = Glue \parallel (\text{caller}:caller \parallel \text{definer}:definer)$ is deadlock-free. Furthermore, $request \preceq caller$ and $provide \preceq definer$. Thus substituting **caller** and **definer** with **request** and **provide** respectively, the new system $C' = Glue \parallel (\text{caller}:request \parallel \text{definer}:provide)$ is also deadlock-free.

However, if the protocol of the port **provide** looks like the interface automaton $provide'$ shown in Figure 5, then after substitution, the new system $C' = Glue \parallel (\text{caller}:request \parallel \text{definer}:provide')$ will be deadlocked. The reason lies in the fact that $provide'$ does not refine $definer$. It is worth mentioning that according to the original definition of refinements between interface automata, which is based on alternating refinements, $provide'$ refines $definer$ indeed. There

---

[1] See the definition 4 of [11].

[2] See the theorem 1 of [11].

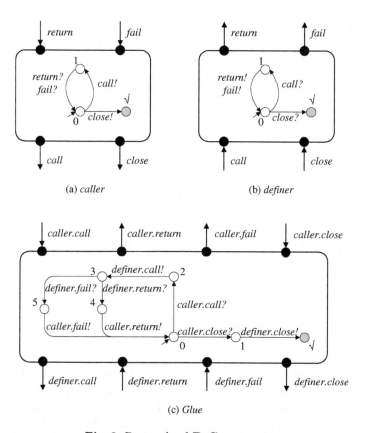

(a) caller

(b) definer

(c) Glue

Fig. 3. Protocols of **D-C-connector**

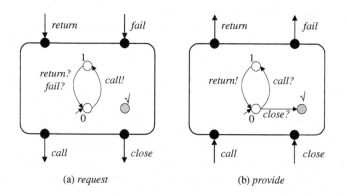

(a) request

(b) provide

Fig. 4. Protocols of **Caller** and **Definer**

is an alternating simulation $\preceq = \{(0,0),(1,1),(\sqrt{},\sqrt{})\}$ from $provide'$ to $definer$. However, $\preceq$ is not a 2/3 alternating simulation from $provide'$ to $definer$ because $A_{definer}(1) \nsubseteq A_{definer}^I$ while $A_{provide'}(1) \subseteq A_{provide'}^I$. From this case, it can be

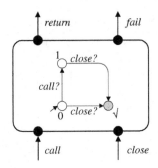

Fig. 5. Interface automaton *provide'*

seen that if connectors are deadlock-free and ports refine their corresponding roles, then after substitution the new system is still deadlock-free.

6   Conclusion

This paper attempts to improve the theory of interface automata from two aspects: parallel composition and refinement. The parallel composition is redefined to provide an alternative fix solution to an existent defect. The solution can avoid weakening the flexibility in modelling interface behaviors. The refinement is presented to achieve the capability of preserving deadlock-freedom. Technically, a new simulation, 2/3 alternating simulation, is presented, whose core idea comes from the 2/3 simulation in CCS. After these revision, we explore the application by employing interface automata as the formal basis of WRIGHT. The result shows that interface automata can provide a simple and convenient semantic foundation for component based development.

Our future work will attempt to analyze typical software architectures in the framework of WRIGHT and interface automata.

References

1. de Alfaro, L., Henzinger, T.A.: Interface automata. In: 9th Symposium on Foundations of Software Engineering, ACM Press (2001)
2. Chakrabarti, A., de Alfaro, L., Henzinger, T.A., Jurdzinski, M., Mang, F.Y.C.: Interface compatibility checking for software modules. In: Proceedings of the 14th International Conference on Computer-Aided Verification. Volume 2404 of LNCS., Springer-Verlag (2002)
3. de Alfaro, L., Henzinger, T.A.: Interface theories for component-based design. In: Proceedings of the First International Workshop on Embedded Software (EMSOFT). Volume 2211 of LNCS., Springer-Verlag (2001) 148–165
4. Jin, Y., Esser, R., Lakos, C., Janneck, J.W.: Modular analysis of dataflow process networks. In Pezzè, M., ed.: FASE. Volume 2621 of Lecture Notes in Computer Science., Springer (2003) 184–199

5. Lee, E.A., Xiong, Y.: Behavioral types for component-based design. In: Memorandum UCB/ERL M02/29. University of California, Berkeley, CA 94720, USA (2002)
6. Jifeng, H., Hoare, T.: Equating bisimulation with refinement. Technical Report 282, UNU-IIST, P.O.Box 3058, Macau (2003)
7. Larsen, K.G., Skou, A.: Bisimulation through probabilistic testing. Inf. Comput. **94** (1991) 1–28
8. Milner, R.: Communication and Concurrency. Prentice-Hall, Inc. (1989)
9. Allen, R., Garlan, D.: Formalizing architectural connection. In: Proceedings of the Sixteenth International Conference on Software Engineering, Sorrento, Italy (1994) 71–80
10. Allen, R., Garlan, D.: The Wright architectural specification language. Technical report, Draft Report CMU-CS-96-TBD, Carnegie Melon University, School of Computer Science, Pittsburgh PA (1996)
11. Allen, R., Garlan, D.: A formal basis for architectural connection. ACM Transactions on Software Engineering and Methodology **6** (1997) 213–249
12. Clarke, L.A.: Improving architectural description languages to support analysis better. In: Proceedings of the International Workshop on the Role of Software Architecture in Testing and Analysis (ROSATEA 1998), Marsala, Sicily, Italy (1998) 78–80
13. Brookes, S.D., Hoare, C.A.R., Roscoe, A.W.: A theory of communicating sequential processes. Journal of the ACM (JACM) **31** (1984) 560–599
14. de Alfaro, L., Henzinger, T.: Interface-based design. In: Engineering Theories of Software Intensive Systems, proceedings of the Marktoberdorf Summer School, Kluwer (2004)
15. Lynch, N., Tuttle, M.: An introduction to input/output automata. CWI Quarterly **2** (1989) 219–246
16. Wen, Y., Wang, J., Qi, Z.C.: Bridging refinement of interface automata to forward simulation of I/O automata. In Davies, J., Schulte, W., Barnett, M., eds.: ICFEM. Volume 3308 of Lecture Notes in Computer Science., Springer (2004) 259–273

Formal Model-Driven Development of Communicating Systems

Linas Laibinis[1], Elena Troubitsyna[1], Sari Leppänen[2], Johan Lilius[1], and Qaisar Malik[1]

[1] Åbo Akademi, Department of Computer Science,
Lemminkäisenkatu 14 A, FIN-20520 Turku, Finland
{Linas.Laibinis, Elena.Troubitsyna,
Johan.Lilius, Qaisar.Malik}@abo.fi
[2] Nokia Research Center, Computing Architectures Laboratory,
P.O. Box 407, 00045, Helsinki, Finland
Sari.Leppanen@nokia.com

Abstract. Telecommunicating systems should have a high degree of availability, i.e., high probability of correct and timely provision of requested services. To achieve this, correctness of software for such systems should be ensured. Application of formal methods helps us to gain confidence in building correct software. However, to be used in practice, the formal methods should be well integrated into existing development process. In this paper we propose a formal model-driven approach to development of communicating systems. Essentially our approach formalizes Lyra – a top-down service-oriented method for development of communicating systems. Lyra is based on transformation and decomposition of models expressed in UML2. We formalize Lyra in the B Method by proposing a set of formal specification and refinement patterns reflecting the essential models and transformations of Lyra. The proposed approach is illustrated by a case study.

1 Introduction

Modern telecommunicating systems are usually distributed software-intensive systems providing a large variety of services to their users. Development of software for such systems is inherently complex and error prone. However, software failures might lead to unavailability or incorrect provision of system services, which in turn could incur significant financial losses. Hence it is important to guarantee correctness of software for telecommunicating systems.

Formal methods have been traditionally used for reasoning about software correctness. However they are yet insufficiently well integrated into current development practice. Unlike formal methods, Unified Modelling Language (UML) [10] has a lower degree of rigor for reasoning about software correctness but is widely accepted in industry. UML is a general purpose modelling language and, to be used effectively, should be tailored to the specific application domain.

Nokia Research Center has developed the design method *Lyra* [8] – a UML-based service-oriented method specific to the domain of communicating systems and communication protocols. The design flow of Lyra is based on concepts of decomposition

K.-K. Lau and R. Banach (Eds.): ICFEM 2005, LNCS 3785, pp. 188–203, 2005.

and preservation of the externally observable behaviour. The system behaviour is modularised and organized into hierarchical layers according to the external communication and related interfaces. It allows the designers to derive the distributed network architecture from the functional system requirements via a number of model transformations.

From the beginning Lyra has been developed in such a way that it would be possible to bring formal methods (such as program refinement, model checking, model-based testing etc.) into more extensive industrial use. A formalisation of the Lyra development would allow us to ensure correctness of system design via automatic and formally verified construction. The achievement of such a formalisation would be considered as significant added value for industry.

In this paper we propose a set of formal specification and refinement patterns reflecting the essential models and transformations of Lyra. Our approach is based on stepwise refinement of a formal system model in the B Method [1,13] – a formal framework with automatic tool support. While developing a system by refinement, we start from an abstract specification and gradually incorporate implementation details into it until executable code is obtained. While formalizing Lyra, we single out a generic concept of a communicating service component and propose patterns for specifying and refining it. In the refinement process the service component is decomposed into a set of service components of smaller granularity specified according to the proposed pattern. Moreover, we demonstrate that the process of distributing service components between different network elements can also be captured by the notion of refinement. The proposed formal specification and development patterns establish a background for automatic generation of formal specifications from UML models and expressing model transformations as refinement steps. Via automation of the UML-based Lyra design flow we aim at smooth incorporation of formal methods into existing development practice. The proposed approach is illustrated by a case study – development of a 3GPP positioning system [15,16].

2   Lyra: Service-Based Development of Communicating Systems

Overview of Lyra. Lyra [8] is a model-driven and component-based design method for the development of communicating systems and communication protocols. It has been developed in the Nokia Research Center by integrating the best practices and design patterns established in the area of communicating systems. The method covers all industrial specification and design phases from prestandardisation to final implementation. It has been successfully applied in large-scale UML2-based industrial software development, e.g., for specification of architecture for several network components, standardisation of 3GPP protocols, implementation of several network protocols etc.

Lyra has four main phases: Service Specification, Service Decomposition, Service Distribution and Service Implementation. The *Service Specification* phase focuses on defining services provided by the system and their users. The goal of this phase is to define the externally observable behaviour of the system level services via deriving logical user interfaces. In the *Service Decomposition* phase the abstract model produced at the previous stage is decomposed in a stepwise and top-down fashion into a set of service components and logical interfaces between them. The result of this phase is the logical architecture of the service implementations. In the *Service Distribution* phase, the logical architecture of services is distributed over a given platform architecture. Finally, in the *Service Implementation* phase, the structural elements are adjusted and integrated into the target environment, low-level implementation details are added and platform-specific code is generated. Next we discuss Lyra in more detail with an example.

Lyra by Example. We model part of a Third Generation Partnership Project (3GPP) positioning system [15,16]. The positioning system provides positioning services to calculate the physical location of a given item of user equipment (UE) in a mobile network. We focus on Position Calculation Application Part (PCAP) – a part of the positioning system allowing communication in a 3GPP network. PCAP manages the communication between the Radio Network Controller (RNC) and the Stand-alone Assisted Global Positioning System Serving Mobile Location Centre (SAS) network elements. The functional requirements for the RNC-SAS communication have been specified in [15,16].

The Service Specification phase starts from creating a domain model of the system. It describes the system with the included system-level services and different types of external users. Each association connecting an external user and a system level service corresponds to a logical interface. For the system and the system level services we define active classes, while for each type of an external user we define the corresponding external class. The relationships between the system level services and their users become candidates for *PSAPs – Provided Service Access Points* of the system level services. The logical interfaces are attached to the classes with ports. The domain model for the *Positioning* system and its service *PositionCalculation* is shown in Fig.1a and PSAP of the Positioning system – *I_User PSAP* is shown in Fig.1b. The UML2 interfaces *I_ToPositioning* and *I_FromPostioning* define the signals and signal parameters of *I_user PSAP*.

A valid execution order of signals on PSAP can be specified by the corresponding use case and sequence diagrams. For the *Positioning* system, the use case diagram would merely depict splitting the *PositionCalculation* use case into two main use cases: successful and unsuccessful. The sequence diagrams would draft the communication in each use case. (We omit presentation of these diagrams for brevity). Finally, we formally describe the communication between a system level service and its user(s) in the *PSAPCommunication* state machine as illustrated in Fig.1c. The positioning request *pc_req* received from the user is always replied: with the signal *pc_cnf* in case of success, and with the signal *pc_fail_cnf* otherwise.

To implement its own services, the system usually uses external entities. For instance, to provide the *PositionCalculation* service, the positioning system should first request Radio Network Database *(DB)* for an approximate position of User Equipment *(UE)*. The information obtained from *DB* is used to contact *UE* and request it to emit a radio signal. At the same time, the Reference Local Measurement Unit *(ReferenceLMU)* is requested to emit a radio signal. The strengths of radio signals obtained from *UE* and *ReferenceLMU* are used to calculate the exact position of *UE*. The calculation is done by the Algorithm service provider *(Algorithm),* which provides the user with the final estimation of the UE location. Let us observe that services provided by the external entities partition execution of the *PositionCalculation* service into the corresponding stages. In the next phase of the Lyra development – *Service Decomposition* – we focus on specifying service execution according to the identified stages.

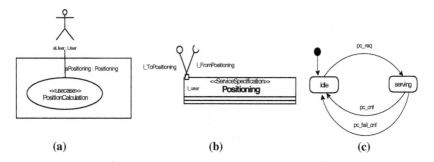

Fig. 1. (a) Domain model. (b) PSAP of Positioning. (c) State diagram.

In the Service Decomposition phase, we introduce the external service providers into the domain model constructed previously, as shown in Fig 2a. The model includes the external service providers *DB, UE, ReferenceLMU* and *Algorithm,* which are then defined as external classes. For each association between a system level service and the corresponding external class we define a logical interface. The logical interfaces are attached to the corresponding classes via ports called *USAPs – Used Sevice Access Points,* as presented in Fig.2b.

To specify the required stages of service implementation, we decompose the behaviour of the main use cases accordingly. For instance, the successful calculation of a UE position can be decomposed as shown in Fig.2c. The sequence diagrams (omitted here) are created to model signalling scenarios for each stage of service implementation. Observe that the behaviour is modularised according to the related service access points – PSAPs and USAPs. Moreover, the functional architecture is defined in terms of service components, which encapsulate the functionalities related to a single execution stage or other logical piece of functionality.

In Fig.2d we present the architecture diagram of the *Positioning* system. Here *ServiceDirector* plays two roles: it manages the execution control in the system and handles the communication on the PSAP. The behaviour of *ServiceDirector* is presented in Fig.2e. The top-most state machine specifies the communication on PSAP, while the state submachine *Serving* specifies a valid execution flow of the position calculation. The substates of *Serving* encapsulate the stage-specific behaviour and can be represented as the corresponding submachines. In their turns, these machines (omitted here) include specifications of the specific PSAP-USAP communications.

The modular system model produced at the Service Decomposition phase allows us to analyse various distribution models. In the next phase – Service Distribution – the service components are distributed over a given network architecture. The signalling network protocols are used for communication between the service components in distant network elements.

In Fig.3a we illustrate the physical structure of the distributed positioning system. Here *Positioning_RND* and *Positioning_SAS* represent network elements in a UMTS network. The Protocol Data Unit (PDU) interface *Iupc* is used in communication

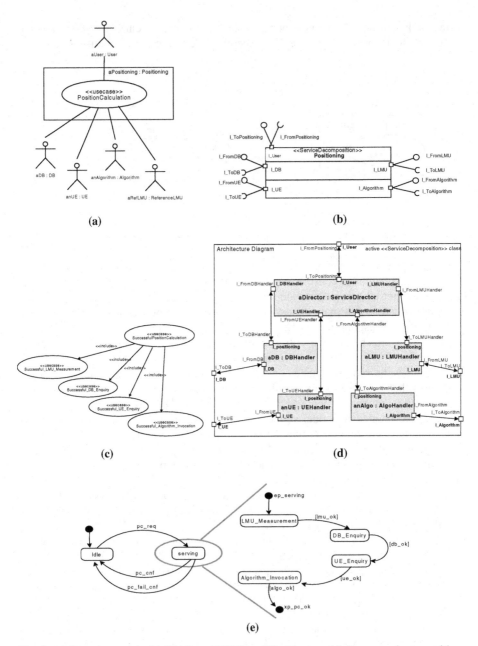

Fig. 2. (a) Domain model. (b) PSAP and USAPs of Positioning. (c) Use case decomposition. (d) PositionCalculation functional architecture. (e) ServiceDirector: PSAP communication and execution control.

between the network elements. We map the functional architecture to the given physical structure by including the service components into the network elements. The functional architecture of the SAS network element is illustrated in Fig 3b. The functionality of *ServiceDirector* specified at the Service Decomposition phase is now decomposed and distributed over the given network. *ServiceDirector_SAS* handles the PDU interface towards the RNC network element and controls the execution flow of the positioning calculation process in the SAS network element.

Finally, at the *Service Implementation* phase we specify how the virtual PDU communication between entities in different network nodes is realized using the underlying transport services. We also implement data encoding and decoding, routing of messages and dynamic process management. The detailed discussion of this stage can be found elsewhere [8, 15, 16].

In the next section we give a brief introduction into our formal framework – the B Method, which we will use to formalize the development flow described above.

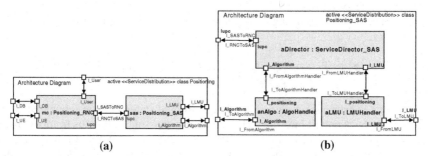

Fig. 3. (a) Architecture of service. (b) Architecture of Positioning_SAS.

3   Modelling in the B Method

The B Method: Background. The B Method [1] (further referred to as B) is an approach for the industrial development of highly dependable software. The method has been successfully used in the development of several complex real-life applications [4,9]. The tool support available for B provides us with the assistance for the entire development process. For instance, Atelier B [13], one of the tools supporting the B Method, has facilities for automatic verification and code generation as well as documentation, project management and prototyping. The high degree of automation in verifying correctness improves scalability of B, speeds up development and, also, requires less mathematical training from the users.

The development methodology adopted by B is based on stepwise refinement [1]. While developing a system by refinement, we start from an abstract formal specification and transform it into an implementable program by a number of correctness preserving steps, called *refinements*. A formal specification is a mathematical model of the required behaviour of a system, or a part of a system.

The B method provides us with mechanisms for structuring the system architecture by modularisation. A module is represented as an *abstract machine*. An abstract machine encapsulates state (a set of program variables) and operations of the specification. The abstract machines can be composed by means of several mechanisms providing different forms of encapsulation. For instance, if the machine C INCLUDES the machine D then all variables and operations of D are visible in C. However, to guarantee internal consistency (and hence independent verification and reuse) of D, the machine C can change the variables of D only via the operations of D.

Each abstract machine is uniquely identified by its name. The state variables of the machine are declared in the VARIABLES clause and initialised in the INITIALISATION clause. The variables in B are strongly typed by constraining predicates of the INVARIANT clause. All types in B are represented by non-empty sets.

The operations of the machine are defined in the OPERATIONS clause. The operations in B can be described as guarded statements of the form SELECT cond THEN body END. Here cond is a state predicate, and body is a B statement. If cond is satisfied, the behaviour of the guarded operations corresponds to the execution of their bodies. However, if cond is false, then execution of the corresponding operation is suspended, i.e., the operation is in waiting mode until cond becomes true. Such B operations are suitable for specifying system reactions on events, i.e., for modelling common reactive systems.

B statements that we are using to describe a state change in operations have the following syntax:

$$S \quad == \quad x := e \quad | \quad \text{IF cond THEN S1 ELSE S2 END} \quad | S1 \text{ ; } S2 \quad | \quad x :: T \quad |$$
$$S1 \parallel S2 \quad | \quad \text{ANY } z \text{ WHERE cond THEN S END}$$

The first three constructs – assignment, the conditional statement and sequential composition have the standard meaning. The remaining constructs allow us to model non-deterministic or parallel behaviour in a specification. For example, $x :: T$ denotes a nondeterministic assignment where any value from set T can be assigned to variable x. Usually such statements are not implementable so they have to be refined (replaced) with executable constructs at some point of program development. The detailed description of the B statements can be found elsewhere [1].

To illustrate basic principles of modelling in B, next we present our approach to formal specification of a service component.

Modelling a Service Component in B. Above we have described a service component as a coherent piece of functionality that provides its services to a service consumer via PSAP(s). We used this term to refer to external service providers introduced at the Service Decomposition phase. However, the notion of a service component can be generalized to represent service providers at the different levels of abstraction. Indeed, even the entire *Positioning* system can be seen as the service component providing the *Position Calculation* service. On the other hand, peer proxies introduced at the lowest level of abstraction can also be seen as the service components providing the physical data transfer services. Therefore, the notion of a service component is central to the entire Lyra development process.

A service component has two essential parts: functional and communicational. The functional part is a "mission" of a service component, i.e., the service(s) which it is capable of executing. The communicational part is an interface via which the service component receives requests to execute the service(s) and sends the results of service execution.

Usually execution of a service involves certain computations. We call the B representation of this part of service component an *Abstract CAlculating Machine (ACAM)*. The communicational part is correspondingly called *Abstract Communicating Machine (ACM)*, while the entire B model of a service component is called *Ab-*

stract Communicating Component (ACC). The abstract machine ACC below presents the proposed pattern for specifying a service component in B.

In our specification we abstract away from the details of computations required to execute a service. Our specification of *ACAM* is merely a statement non-deterministically generating results of the service execution in case of success or failure. The communication with a service component is conducted via two channels – inp_chan and out_chan – shared between the service component and the service consumer. While specifying a service component, we adopt a systemic approach, i.e., model the service component together with the relevant part of its environment, the service consumer. Namely, we model how the service consumer places requests to execute a service in the operation env_req and reads the results of the service execution in the operation env_resp.

The operations read and write are internal to the service component. The service component reads the requests to execute a service from inp_chan as defined in the operation read. As a result of the execution of read, the request is stored into the internal data buffer input, so it can be used by *ACAM* while performing the required computing. Symmetrically the operation write models placing the results of computations performed by *ACAM* into the output channel, so it can be read by the service consumer. We reserve the abstract constants INPUT_NIL and OUT_NIL to model the absence of data, i.e., the empty channel . The operations discussed above model the communicational *(ACM)* part of *ACC*.

```
MACHINE  ACC

VARIABLES  inp_chan, input, out_chan, output

INVARIANT

 inp_chan : INPUT_DATA & input : INPUT_DATA &
 out_chan : OUT_DATA &   output : OUT_DATA

INITIALISATION
 inp_chan, input := INPUT_NIL, INPUT_NIL ||
 out_chan, output := OUT_NIL, OUT_NIL

OPERATIONS
```

```
ACAM

 calculate =
  SELECT not(input = INPUT_NIL) &
         (output = OUT_NIL)
  THEN
   CHOICE
    output ::
       OUT_DATA - {OUT_NIL,OUT_FAIL}
   OR
    output := OUT_FAIL
   END ||
   input := INPUT_NIL
  END;

 END
```

```
ACM
 env_req =
  SELECT inp_chan = INPUT_NIL THEN
   inp_chan :: INPUT_DATA - {INPUT_NIL}
  END;

 read =
  SELECT not(inp_chan = INPUT_NIL) &
         (input = INPUT_NIL) THEN
   input,inp_chan := inp_chan,INPUT_NIL
  END;

 write =
  SELECT not(output = OUT_NIL) &
         (out_chan = OUT_NIL) THEN
   out_chan,output := output,OUT_NIL
  END;

 env_read =
  SELECT not(out_chan = OUT_NIL)
  THEN
   out_chan := OUT_NIL
  END
```

We argue that the machine ACC can be seen as a specification pattern which can be instantiated by supplying the details specific to a service component under construction. For instance, the *ACM* part of *ACC* models data transfer to and from the service component very abstractly. While developing a realistic service component, this part can be instantiated with real data structures and the corresponding protocols for transferring them.

In the next section we demonstrate how Lyra development flow can be formalized as refinement and decomposition of an abstract communicating component (ACC).

4   Formal Service-Oriented Development

As described in Section 2, usually a service component is represented as an active class with the PSAP(s) attached to it via the port(s). The state diagram depicts the signalling scenario on PSAP including the signals from and to the external class modelling the service consumer. Essentially these diagrams suffice to specify the service component according to the *ACC* pattern proposed in Section 3. The general principle of translation is shown in Fig.4.

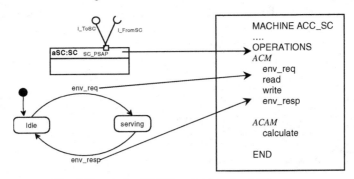

Fig. 4. Translating UML2 model into the ACC pattern

The UML2 description of PSAP of the service component *SC* is translated into the communicational (*ACM*) part of the machine ACC_SC specifying *SC* according to the *ACC* pattern. The functional (*ACAM*) part of ACC_SC instantiates the non-deterministic assignment of ACC by the data types specific to the modelled service component. These translations formalize the *Service Specification* phase of Lyra.

In the next phase of Lyra development – *Service Decomposition* – we decompose the service provided by the service component into a number of stages (subservices). The service component can execute certain subservices itself as well as request the external service components to do it. At the *Service Decomposition* phase two major transformations are performed:

1. the service execution is decomposed into a number of stages (or subservices).
2. communication with the external entities executing these subservices is introduced via USAPs.

Each transformation corresponds to a separate refinement step in our approach.

According to Lyra, the flow of the service execution is orchestrated by *Service Director* (often called a Mediator). It implements the behaviour of PSAP of the service component as specified earlier, as well as co-ordinates the execution by enquiring the required subservices from the external entities according to the execution flow.

Assume that the service component *SC* specified by the machine ACC_SC at the Service Specification phase is providing the service *S* which is decomposed into the subservices *S1, S2,* and *S3*. Moreover, let assume that the state machine of *Service Director* defines the desired order of execution: first *S1*, then *S2* and finally *S3*. The UML2 representation of this is given in Fig.5, in which we also demonstrate that such decomposition can be represented as a refinement of our abstract pattern *ACC* instantiated to model *SC*.

This decomposition step focuses on refinement of the functional *(ACAM)* part of *ACC*. As in *ACAM*, in the refinement of it - *ACAM'*- the operation calculate puts the results of service execution on the output channel. However, calculate is now preceded by the operation director, which models *Service Director* orchestrating the stages of execution. We introduce the variables S1_data, S2_data and S3_data to model the results of execution of the corresponding stages. The operation director specifies the desired execution flow by assigning corresponding values to the variable curr_service. In general, execution of any stage of service can fail. In its turn, this might lead to failure of the entire service provision. In this paper, due to the lack of space, we omit the presentation of failures of service provision and error recovery while specifying *Service Director*. The detailed description of this can be found in the accompanying technical report [5].

To derive the pattern for translating UML2 diagrams modelling the functional architecture and the platform-distributed service architecture at these two phases, we should consider two general cases:

1. The service director of *SC* is "centralized", i.e., it resides on a single network element.
2. The service director of *SC* is "distributed", i.e., different parts of the execution flow are orchestrated by distinct service directors residing on different network elements. The service directors communicate with each other while passing the control over the corresponding parts of the flow.

In both cases the model of the initial service component SC looks as shown in Fig.6. The service distribution architecture diagram for the first case is given in Fig.7.

It is easy to observe that the service component *SC* plays a role of the service consumer for the service components *SC1, SC2* and *SC3*. We specify the service components *SC1, SC2* and *SC3* as the separate machines ACC_SC1, ACC_SC2, ACC_SC3 according to the proposed pattern *ACC,* as depicted in Fig.8. The process of translating their UML2 models into B is similar to specifying *SC* at the *Service Specification* phase. The communicational *(ACM)* parts of the included machines specify their PSAPs. To ensure the match between the corresponding USAPs of *SC* and PSAPs of the external service components, we derive USAPs of *SC* from PSAPs of *SC1, SC2* and *SC3*.

Besides defining separate machines to model the external service components, in this refinement step we also define the mechanisms for communicating with them. We refine the operation director to specify the communication on USAPs. Namely, we replace the nondeterministic assignments modelling stages of the service execution by the corresponding signalling scenario: at the proper point of the execution flow, director requests a desired service by writing into the input channel of the corresponding included machine, e.g., SC1_write_ichan, and later reads the produced

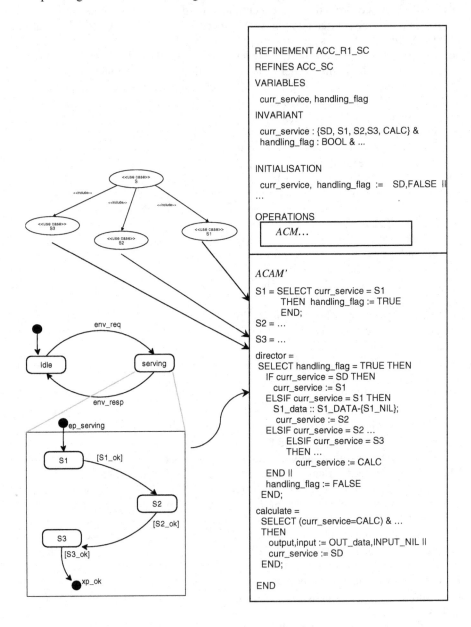

Fig. 5. Service decomposition and refinement

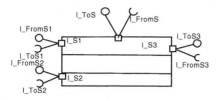

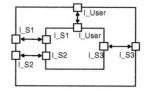

Fig. 6. Service component with USAPs   **Fig. 7.** Architecture diagram (case 1)

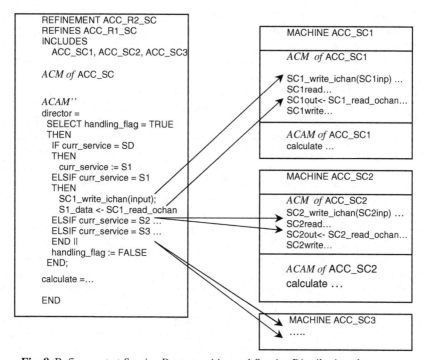

Fig. 8. Refinement at *Service Decomposition* and *Service Distribution* phases

results from the output channel of this machine, e.g., SC1_read_ochan. Graphically this arrangement is depicted in Fig.9.

Modelling case (2) of the distributed service director is more complex. Let assume that the execution flow of the service component *SC* is orchestrated by two service directors: the *ServiceDirector1*, which handles the communication on PSAP of *SC* and communicates with *SC1*, and *ServiceDirector2*, which orchestrates the execution of the *SC2* and *SC3* services. The architecture diagram depicting the overall arrangement is shown in Fig.10.

The service execution proceeds according to the following scenario: via PSAP of *SC ServiceDirector1* receives the request to provide the service *S*. Upon this, via USAP of *SC*, it requests the component *SC1* to provide the service *S1*. After the result

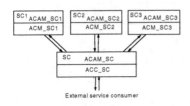
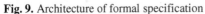

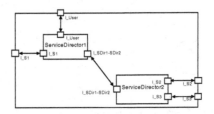

Fig. 9. Architecture of formal specification   **Fig. 10.** Architecture diagram (case 2)

of *S1* is obtained, *ServiceDirector1* requests *Service Director2* to execute the rest of the service and return the result back. In its turn, *ServiceDirector2* at first requests *SC2* to provide the service S2 and then *SC3* to provide service *S3*. Upon receiving the result from *S3*, it forwards it to *ServiceDirector1*. Finally, *Service Director1* returns to the service consumer the result of the entire service *S* via PSAP of *SC*.

This complex behaviour can be captured in a number of refinement steps. At first, we observe that *ServiceDirector2*, co-ordinating execution of *S2* and *S3*, can be modelled as a "large" service component *SC2-SC3* which provides the services *S2* and *S3*. Let us note that the execution flow in *SC2-SC3* is orchestrated by the "centralized" service director *ServiceDirector2*. We use this observation in our next refinement step. Namely we refine the B machine modelling *SC* by including into it the machines modelling the service components *SC1* and *SC2-SC3* and introducing the required communicating mechanisms. In our consequent refinement step we focus on decomposition of *SC2-SC3*. The decomposition is performed according to the proposed scheme: we introduce the specification of *ServiceDirector2* and decompose the functional (*ACAM*) part of *SC2-SC3*. Finally, we single out separate service components *SC2* and *SC3* as before and refine *ServiceDirector2* to model communication with them. The final architecture of formal specification is shown in Fig.11. We omit the presentation of the detailed formal specifications – they are again obtained by the recursive application of the proposed specification and refinement patterns.

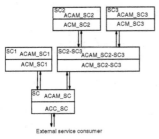

Fig. 11. Architecture (case 2)

At the consequent refinement steps we focus on particular service components and refine them (in the way described above) until the desired level of granularity is obtained. Once all external service components are in place, we can further decompose their specifications by separating their *ACM* and *ACAM* parts. Such decomposition will allow us to concentrate on the communicational parts of the components and further refine them by introducing details of the required concrete communication protocols.

Discussion. In the proposed approach we have used our B formalisation of Lyra to verify correctness of the Lyra decomposition and distribution phases. We have done this by introducing generic patterns for communicating service components and then associating the Lyra development steps with the corresponding B refinements on these patterns. In development of real systems we merely have to establish by proof that the corresponding components in a specific functional or network architecture are valid instantiations of these patterns. All together this constitutes a basis for automating industrial design flow of communicating systems.

The decomposition model that we have used for testing our approach is still relatively simple. As a result, all refinement steps were automatically proved by AtelierB –a tool supporting B. While describing the formalisation of Lyra in B, we considered only the sequential model of service execution. However, parallel execution of services is also a valid interpretation of the considered UML2 models. Currently we are working on extending our B models to include parallel execution of services. Furthermore, we will incorporate more sophisticated fault tolerance mechanisms (e.g., different types of fault recovery procedures) into our models. We foresee that such extensions will make automatic proof of model refinements more difficult. However, by developing generic proof strategies, we will try to achieve high degree of automation in formal verification of our models.

5 Conclusions

In this paper we proposed a formal approach to development of communicating distributed systems. Our approach formalizes Lyra [8] – the UML2-based design methodology adopted in Nokia. The formalization is done within the B Method [1,13] – a formal framework supporting system development by stepwise refinement. We derived the B specification and refinement patterns reflecting models and model transformations used in the development flow of Lyra. The proposed approach establishes a basis for automatic translation of UML2-based development of communicating systems into the specification and refinement process in B. Such automation would enable a smooth integration of formal methods into existing development practice. Since UML is widely accepted in industry, we believe that our approach has a potential for wide industrial uptake.

Lyra adopts the service-oriented style for development of communicating systems. We presented the guidelines for deriving B specifications from corresponding UML2 models at each development stage of Lyra and validated the development by the corresponding B refinements. The major model transformations aim at service decomposition and distribution over the given platform. The proposed formal model of communication between the distributed service components is generic and can be instantiated by virtually any concrete communication protocol.

The initial formalization of Lyra has been undertaken using model checking techniques [8]. However, since telecommunicating systems tend to be large and data intensive, this formalization was prone to the state explosion problem. Our approach helps to overcome this limitation.

Development of distributed communicating systems has been a topic of ongoing research over several decades. Our review of related work is confined to the consideration of the recent research conducted within the B Method.

Treharne et al. [14] investigated verification of safety and liveness properties of communicating components by combining the B Method and the process algebra CSP. However, they do not consider service decomposition and distribution aspects of communicating system development.

Boström and Walden [2] proposed a formal methodology (based on the B Method) for developing distributed grid systems. In their approach the B language is extended with grid-specific features. In their work, the system development is governed by B refinement. In our approach the system development is guided by the existing development practice, so that the refinement process is hidden behind the facade of UML.

There is active research going on translating UML to B [3,6,7,11,12]. Among these, the most notable is research conducted by Snook and Butler [11] on designing the method and the U2B tool to support the automatic translation. In our future work we are planning to integrate our efforts with the U2B developers to achieve the automatic translation of Lyra into B. While doing this, we will focus specifically on translating models and model transformations used in Lyra to automate formalisation of the entire UML-based development process in the domain of the communicating distributed systems. We are already working on creating the Lyra UML2 metamodel, which will assist us in achieving this goal. Furthermore, we are planning to further enhance the proposed approach to address issues of fault tolerance, concurrency and integration of process algebraic approaches to verify the dynamic properties of communication protocols between network elements.

Acknowlegements. This work is supported by EU funded research project IST 511599 RODIN (Rigorous Open Development Environment for Complex Systems). We are also grateful to anonymous reviewers for their very helpful comments.

References

1. J.-R. Abrial. *The B-Book*. Cambridge University Press, 1996.
2. P.Boström and M.Waldén. *An Extension of Event B for Developing Grid Systems*, in H. Treharne et al (Eds.), Formal Specification and Development in Z and B:,UK, 2005.
3. P.Facon, et al. *Combining UML with the B formal method for the specification of database applications*. Research report, CEDRIC laboratory, Paris, 1999.
4. P.Behm, et al. *METEOR: A successful application of B in a large project*. In Wing et all (editors), Proc. of the World Congress on Formal Methods. LNCS 1709, Springer, 1999.
5. L.Laibinis, E.Troubitsyna, S.Leppänen, J.Lilius, and Q.Malik. *Formal Model-Driven Development of Communicating Systems*. TUCS Technical Report No. 691. Finland, 2005.
6. K.Lano, D.Clark, and K.Adroutsopoulos. *UML to B: Formal Verification of Object-Oriented Models*. In E.A.Boiten et al (Eds.): Integrated Formal Methods,. Springer, LNCS 2999.
7. H.LeDang and J.Souquieres. *Integrating UML and B specification techniques*. In Proc. of the Workshop on Integrating Diagrammatic and Formal Specification Techniques, 2001.
8. S.Leppänen, M.Turunen, and I.Oliver. *Application Driven Methodology for Development of Communicating Systems*.Forum on Specification and Design Languages. France, 2004.
9. MATISSE Handbook for Correct Systems Construction. 2003. http://www.esil.univ-mrs.fr/~spc/matisse/Handbook/.
10. J.Rumbaugh, I.Jacobson, and G.Booch. *The Unified Modelling Language* Reference Manual. Addison-Wesley, 1998.
11. C.Snook and M.Butler. *U2B - A tool for translating UML-B models into B*, in Mermet, J., Eds. UML-B Specification for Proven Embedded Systems Design. Springer, 2004.
12. C.Snook and M.Waldén. *Use of U2B for Specifying B Action Systems*. In Proc. of Workshop on Refinement of Critical Systems: Methods, Tools and Experience, France, 2002.

13. Steria, Aix-en-Provence, France. Atelier B, User and Reference Manuals, 2001. Available at http://www.atelierb.societe.com/index uk.html
14. H.Treharne et al. *Composing Specifications Using Communication*, in D. Bert et al (Eds.), Proc. of Formal Specification and Development in Z and B, Finland. Springer, 2003.
15. 3GPP. Technical specification 25.305: Stage 2 functional specification of UE positioning in UTRAN. See http://www.3gpp.org/ftp/Specs/html-info/25305.htm
16. 3GPP. Technical specification 25.453: UTRAN Iupc interface positioning calculation application part (pcap) signalling. See http://www.3gpp.org/ftp/Specs/html-info/25453.htm

JAHUEL: A Formal Framework for Software Synthesis*

I. Assayad[1], V. Bertin[2], F.-X. Defaut[1], Ph. Gerner[1], O. Quévreux[1], and S. Yovine[1]

[1] VERIMAG, Centre Equation, 2 Ave. Vignate, 38610 Gières, France
[2] STMicroelectronics, 850 rue Jean Monnet, 38921 Crolles, France

Abstract. We present a theoretically sound and automated model-based design, analysis, and implementation framework for synthesizing correct-by-construction code. Special emphasis is put on multi-threaded software and multi-processor architectures. The framework consists in (1) a formal language which provides platform-independent constructs to specify the behavior of an application using an abstract execution model, and (2) a compilation chain for refining the application abstract model into its concrete implementation on a target platform. The prototype JAHUEL is currently being used for developing experimental industrial applications.

1 Introduction

In current industrial engineering practices for developing embedded real-time systems, application requirements and design constraints are spread out and do not easily integrate and propagate through the development process. Moreover, the increasing complexity of applications tends to enlarge the abstraction gap between application description and hardware. Consequently, ensuring non-functional requirements (e.g., timing properties, resource management, ...) is costly and error-prone.

During the development cycle, two models of execution are distinguished. The first one is the abstract model inherent to the specification of an application, which typically corresponds to logically concurrent activites, with data and control dependencies. The second one is the concrete execution model provided by a particular platform (run-time system and hardware architecture). The problem consists in exploiting platform capabilities (e.g., multithreading, pipelinening, dedicated devices, multiprocessors, ...) to implement the abstract model, or eventually restricting the latter because of constraints imposed by the concrete model (e.g., synchronous communication, shared memory, single processor, bus contention, ...). In any case, the programmer must handle both types of execution models during the development cycle. Therefore, there is a need for (1) appropriate mechanisms for expressing these models, and (2) tools for formally relating them, in order to produce executable code which (a) is correct with respect to application's logic, and (b) ensures non-functional requirements are met on the concrete execution platform.

In this paper we are specially interested in two issues: concurrency and timing constraints. Current practices to handle them could be summarized as follows.

---

* Contact: Sergio.Yovine@imag.fr. Partially supported by MEDEA+ Project NEVA.

K.-K. Lau and R. Banach (Eds.): ICFEM 2005, LNCS 3785, pp. 204–218, 2005.

Run-Time Libraries and Compiler Directives. A very common practice consists in using a language with no support for concurreny or time (e.g., C), together with specific libraries or system calls (e.g., POSIX threads or MPI [10]) provided by the underlying runtime system or using compiler directives (e.g., OpenMP [18]).[1] This approach has several inconveniences. First, there is no way to distinguish between abstract and concrete execution models at program level, and therefore, the reason that motivated the programmer's choice (i.e., application design or platform capability) is irrecoverable from program code. This gives rise to a messy development cycle, where application design and system deployment are not handled separately, and application code is too early customized for a specific target, therefore impeding reusability and portability. Second, correctness verification is almost impossible due to system calls.

Domain-Specific Programming Languages. Another practice consists in using a language with a (more or less formal) abstract execution model where time and concurrency are syntactic and semantic concepts (e.g., Lustre [11], Ada [5].) It is entirely the role of the compiler to implement the abstract execution model on the target platform. This approach enhances formal analysis. Nevertheless, these languages provide no constructs for dealing with cross-cutting non-functional issues, and rely on a fully automatic implementation phase that makes retargetting, platform exploration, and optimization hard to achieve. For instance, a typical industrial practice for exploiting multiprocessor architectures for synchronous programs consists in manually cutting the code into pieces, and adding hand-written wrappers. This practice breaks down formal analysis and suffers from the same inconveniences of the library/directives approach. Although there is ongoing work to solve this problem for specific execution platforms (e.g., [6]), there is no attempt neither to provide language support nor to develop a general framework.

Modelling Frameworks and Architecture Description Languages. To some extent, some of the abovementioned problems could be avoided using (domain-specific) architecture description languages that provide means to integrate software and hardware models (e.g., [4].) Still, in all ADL-based approaches we are aware of, description of the application execution model is tied up to a platform-dependent execution model, which is, consequently, implemented using platform primitives by direct translation of the application code. Model-integrated development [14] also handles requirements composed horizontally at the same level of abstraction. However, it does not seem to be well adapted to reason about cross-cutting non-functional requirements that need vertical propagation and composition through different abstraction layers. Platform-based design [20] is a methodology that supports vertical integration, but it is mainly focused on composing functionality while abstracting away non-functional properties. PTOLEMY II [19] is a design framework that supports composition of heterogeneous models of concurrent computation, but it is oriented towards modeling and simulation rather than to application-code synthesis.

Aspect-Oriented Software Development. Aspects could help in bridging the gap between application's specification and the actual platform-specific implementation. However, to

---

[1] Java provides some mechanisms, but they are (typically) implemented using platform libraries.

our knowledge, current AOP-based approaches require an important programming effort, do not handle timing constraints, and are not specifically focused on code synthesis for different platforms, but are typically used for monitoring and optimization [15].

To overcome the aforementioned problems, we think compilation tools and their associated technologies (analysis, optimization, ...) must play the central role of mapping platform independent software into target execution platforms (operating system and hardware), while ensuring at compile time that non-functional requirements provided by system's engineers will be met at runtime.

Integrating in the same toolset (1) a compiler, and (2) model-based formal analysis and synthesis techniques for handling non-functional constraints and heterogeneous architectures, is an innovative way to provide correct by construction code. This enables code generation for specific platforms (including software-to-processor mapping and scheduling), and platform-independent functional analysis, to be linked together in the same tool-chain without semantic gap.

Such a framework will considerably increase the overall quality of industrial systems designed with these tools, guaranteeing the correctness of the resulting solution. This approach enhances the applicability of formal verification and analysis techniques in industrial design flows, leading to a significant reduction in overall system's validation time.

Nevertheless, building representative models that adequately relate functional and non-functional behavior, of both application software and execution platforms, is challenging [23]. Multi-threaded software and processors, and multi-processor architectures bring in additional complexity.

To circumvent this complexity, we propose a framework consisting of a formal language and its associated compilation chain. The purpose of the language is threefold. First, it provides simple and platform-independent constructs to specify the behavior of the application using an abstract execution model. Second, it provides semantic and syntactic support for correctly refining the abstract execution model into the concrete one. Third, the language and the compilation chain are extensible to easily support new concrete execution models, without semantic break-downs. Besides, the language can be used by the programmer to express program structure, functionality, requirements and constraints, as well as by the compiler as a representation to be directly manipulated to perform program analyses and program transformations to generate executable code which achieves application requirements and complies to platform constraints.

In this paper, we present the basic language and its semantics, and the compilation chain. The current prototype compilation-chain, called JAHUEL, is implemented using an XML intermediate representation format, and Java for the algorithmic transformations. JAHUEL is connected with STMicroelectronics FlexCC2 compilation-suite [3]. We briefly illustrate the application of the framework on an industrial case study: an MPEG-4 video encoder [1].

2   Informal Presentation of the Language

The underlying basic idea of our language, called FXML, is that computation units are concurrent by default, while explicit precedences can be expressed to limit concurrency.

The granularity of computation units is not fixed, the smaller grain is the assignment or legacy code. Data dependencies are implicit, but can be explicitely added to express data dependencies in legacy code.

FXML provides a `forall` primitive to declare several concurrent iterations of the same block. This construct is similar to FORTRAN 95 with the difference that we do allow dependencies between iterations. FXML also has "parallel" and "sequential" composition, similar to CSP [13]. However, a major difference with CSP is that our "parallel" composition does not entail parallel execution at runtime, but it is only a mechanism to specify logically concurrent activities.

An important difference with other languages is that basic FXML does not provide any specific synchronization or communication primitives (like channels or rendezvous). Instead, the basic language can be extended with non-functional information about the concrete execution model (e.g., execution times, synchronization mechanisms, number of processors), and the target platform (e.g., OpenMP, Pthreads, MPI).

2.1   A Simple Producer/Consumer

Let us start with a simple producer-consumer system to informally introduce FXML. Fig. 1 (left) shows the C program of this system. Pragmas are the actual syntax used by FlexCC2. The abstract syntax of FXML will be given later in this section. The concrete syntax of FXML is defined as an XML schema, which is not presented here.

The pragma `parallel writer user` declares that the C functions `writer()` ▮ and `user()` invoked by `main()` are logically concurrent. The abstract syntax symbol

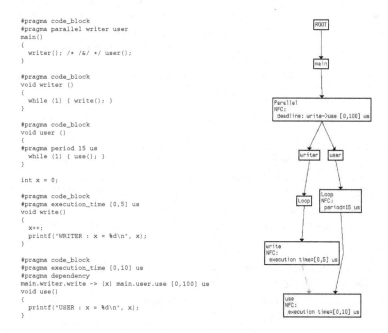

Fig. 1. Simple producer/consumer

for `parallel` is `/&/`. Functions `writer()` and `user()` are non-terminating executions, `user()` has a period of $15\mu s$ (pragma `period`). `writer()` calls `write()` which has an execution time less or equal than $5\mu s$. `user()` calls `use()` which completes in at most $10\mu s$. `dependency` expresses that there is a data dependency between `write()` and `use()` on x, with a *freshness* interval $[0, 100]$, that is, `use()` can only take place if the time elapsed since the last `write()` is less than $100\mu s$.

FlexCC2 analyzes the program (pragmas and C code) and extracts a description of it in the concrete XML syntax of FXML. Fig. 1 (right) shows a graphical representation of the program in (the XML representation of) FXML. The dotted arrow depicts the dependency. The graph is also generated by FlexCC2. Functions `write()` and `use()`, and variable x are considered as legacy C-code in FXML. The compilation chain must preserve the data dependency, as well as the atomicity of the read and write operations on variable x. This is done by adding the appropriate mutual exclusion and synchronization mechanisms.

3   Formal Definition and Semantics of FXML

3.1   Syntax

The *body* of an FXML specification is composed of blocks called *pnodes*. The term *pnode* stands for "presentation node". This notion comes from model theory: a *pnode* "presents" an abstract execution. Fig. 2 shows the abstract syntax for *pnodes*. The concrete syntax in XML is defined by an XML schema (not presented here).

Basic pnodes. `nil` denotes an empty set of executions. Let X be the set of variables. Variables store values from a set V. An *assignment* α has the form $x_0 = \zeta(x_1, \ldots, x_n)$, where $x_i \in X, i \in [0, n]$, and $\zeta : V^n \to V$ is a computable function. We write α_i for x_i. A block of *legacy* code (`legacy`) and a function *call* (`eval`) are *basic pnodes*.

Conditional pnodes are of the form `if` $\zeta(x_1, \ldots, x_n)$ `then` p `else` q, where p and q are *pnodes*, and $\zeta : V^n \to V$ is a boolean function.

Sequential composition of p and q is the *pnode* p `;` q.

Iterations. The *pnodes* `for(`$i = init(x_1, \ldots, x_n)$`;` $i = inc(i)$`;` $test(i)$`)[per=P]` p, and `while(`$test(x_1, \ldots, x_n)$`)[per=P]` p, express iterations: i is the iteration variable, $init : V^n \to \mathbb{N}$ is a computable function that gives the initial value of i, $inc : \mathbb{N} \to \mathbb{N}$ is the increment function, and $test : \mathbb{N} \to V$ is a boolean function that defines the looping condition. i is assumed not to be modified in p. The optional declaration `[per=P]` gives the period of the loop, that is, the time distance between two successive iterations of p.

Parallel Composition. FXML has two operators for expressing parallelism. The *pnode* p `/&/` q specifies that p and q are concurrent. Several parallel executions of p are specified by the *pnode* `forall(`$i = init(x_1, \ldots, x_n)$`;` $i = inc(i)$`;` $test(i)$`)` p where i, *init*, *inc* and *test* are as for `for`-loops.

Labeling. Pnodes can be labeled. `L:` p is a *pnode*.

Dependencies. Let p be a (composite) *pnode*, with two descendants p_i, $i = 1, 2$, labeled L1 and L2, respectively. $p\{L1 [d] \rightarrow L2\}$ specifies a *dependency* between p_1 and p_2. Intuitively, this means that p_2 can only occur *after* p_1. The optional [d] expresses a *data dependency*. [2] Fig. 1 shows a data dependency on variable x from write to use.

Let q_i be iteration *pnodes* which are descendants of p, and p_i be descendants of q_i, labeled Li, $i = 1, 2$. We write $p \{L1(k) [d] \rightarrow L2(f(k))\}$ to express that there is a (data) dependency between the occurrence p_1^k in the k-th iteration of q_1, and the occurrence $p_2^{f(k)}$ in the $f(k)$-th iteration of q_2. Examples of indexed dependencies will be given in Sec. 5.

Timing Constraints. Besides periods attached to iterations, all *pnodes* can be annotated with timing constraints. Let p be a *pnode* and, for simplicity, let $a, b \in \mathbb{N}^3$. $p[a,b]$ means that the execution time of p is in the interval $[a, b]$. Intervals can also be associated with all dependencies. Let p_i be descendants of p labeled Li, $i = 1, 2$. $p\{L1 \rightarrow [a,b]L2\}$ means that the time difference between the end of p_1 and the start of p_2 belongs to the interval $[a, b]$. Temporal data dependencies are useful for specifying freshness constraints: the written value cannot be read (e.g., appear in the right-hand side of an assignment) if the time distance between the write and read operations is outside the specified interval. Fig. 1 shows a freshness constraint of $100\mu s$ on variable x from write to use.

3.2   Executions

The semantics of an FXML specification is a set of *executions*. Intuitively, an execution is a partial order of evaluated assignments. Before giving semantics to FXML specifications, we need to introduce some definitions.

Indexed assignments. An index is a list I of natural numbers and labels. $\langle \ell_1, \ldots \rangle$ denotes the list consisting of elements $\ell_1, \ldots$, and $\circ$ denotes concatenation of lists. An *indexed* assignment is denoted α^I. A set of indexed assignments is denoted $\mathcal{A}$.

Timing. Time is modeled with a timing function $\tau : \mathcal{A} \rightarrow \mathbb{R}^+ \times \mathbb{R}^+$. We write, $\tau^b(\alpha^I) = \pi_1(\tau(\alpha^I))$, and $\tau^e(\alpha^I) = \pi_2(\tau(\alpha^I))$, which denote respectively the beginning and ending times of assignment α^I. τ satisfies the set of indexed assignments $\mathcal{A}$, denoted $\tau \models \mathcal{A}$, iff for each $\alpha^I \in \mathcal{A}$, $\tau^b(\alpha^I) \leq \tau^e(\alpha^I)$.

Dependencies Let $Out = \{x \in X \mid \exists \alpha^I \in \mathcal{A} : x = \alpha_0\}$ be the set of variables assigned in $\mathcal{A}$. The relation $\xrightarrow{d} \subseteq \mathcal{A} \times \mathcal{A}$ models data dependencies: for all $\beta^J \in \mathcal{A}$, for all β_j, if $\beta_j \in Out$, then there exists a *unique* $\alpha^I \in \mathcal{A}$ s.t. $\alpha_0 = \beta_j$ and $\alpha^I \xrightarrow{d} \beta^J$. We write $\alpha^I \xrightarrow{\beta_j} \beta^J$ as a shorthand for $\alpha^I \xrightarrow{d} \beta^J \land \alpha_0 = \beta_j$. τ satisfies the data dependency relation $\xrightarrow{d}$, denoted $\tau \models \xrightarrow{d}$, iff for any $\alpha^I, \beta^J \in \mathcal{A}$, $\alpha^I \xrightarrow{d} \beta^J \implies \tau^e(\alpha^I) \leq \tau^b(\beta^J)$. The relation $\xrightarrow{i} \subseteq \mathcal{A} \times \mathcal{A}$ gives an order between

---

[2] This is not strictly necessary from a semantical point of view. Indeed, it is needed to be able to express data dependencies hidden in legacy code. In this case, the data dependency declaration is automatically inserted by the compiler during the data dependency analysis phase.

[3] The actual syntax allows for more complex expressions.

indexed assignments in $\mathcal{A}$, thus modeling sequential dependencies. τ satisfies $\overset{\cdot}{\longrightarrow}$, denoted $\tau \models \overset{\cdot}{\longrightarrow}$, iff for any $\alpha^I, \beta^J \in \mathcal{A}$, $\alpha^I \overset{\cdot}{\longrightarrow} \beta^J \implies \tau^e(\alpha^I) \leq \tau^b(\beta^J)$. We define $\longrightarrow = \overset{d}{\longrightarrow} \cup \overset{\cdot}{\longrightarrow}$. τ satisfies $\longrightarrow$, denoted $\tau \models \longrightarrow$, iff $\tau \models \overset{d}{\longrightarrow}$ and $\tau \models \overset{\cdot}{\longrightarrow}$.

Valuations. $\mathcal{A}$ can be seen as a family $({}^n\mathcal{A} \mid n \in \mathbb{N})$ of sets of indexed assignments, where ${}^n\mathcal{A}$ contains only indexed assignments $\alpha^I \in \mathcal{A}$, where α is of the form $x_0 = \zeta(x_1, \ldots, x_n)$. Let $\nu = ({}^n\nu \mid n \in \mathbb{N})$ be a family of $\mathbb{N}$-indexed valuation functions, with ${}^n\nu : {}^n\mathcal{A} \to V^{n+1}$. ${}^n\nu$ gives the value of variables for indexed assignments of $\mathcal{A}$: ${}^n\nu(\alpha^I) = (v_0, v_1, v_2, \ldots, v_n)$, with $v_0 = \zeta(v_1, v_2, \ldots, v_n)$. ν satisfies $\overset{d}{\longrightarrow}$, denoted $\nu \models \overset{d}{\longrightarrow}$, iff for any $\alpha^I \in {}^n\mathcal{A}$, $\beta^J \in {}^m\mathcal{A}$, with ${}^n\nu(\alpha^I) = (v_0, v_1, v_2, \ldots, v_n)$ and ${}^m\nu(\beta^J) = (w_0, w_1, w_2, \ldots, w_m)$, we have that $\alpha^I \overset{\beta_j}{\longrightarrow} \beta^J \implies w_j = v_0$.

Executions. An execution e is $(X, \mathcal{A}, V, \overset{d}{\longrightarrow}, \overset{\cdot}{\longrightarrow}, \tau, \nu)$, s.t. $\tau \models \mathcal{A}$, $\tau \models \longrightarrow$, $\nu \models \overset{d}{\longrightarrow}$.

Timing constraints. $\tau^b(e) = \min_{\alpha^I \in A_e} \tau^b(\alpha^I)$, and $\tau^e(e) = \max_{\alpha^I \in A_e} \tau^e(\alpha^I)$, are the starting and ending time of e, respectively.

Subexecutions. f is a subexecution of e, $f \subseteq e$, iff $\mathcal{A}_f \subseteq \mathcal{A}_e$, and $\overset{d}{\longrightarrow}_f = \overset{d}{\longrightarrow}_e \lceil_{\mathcal{A}_f \times \mathcal{A}_f}$, $\overset{\cdot}{\longrightarrow}_f = \overset{\cdot}{\longrightarrow}_e \lceil_{\mathcal{A}_f \times \mathcal{A}_f}$, $\tau_f = \tau_e \lceil_{\mathcal{A}_f}$, ${}^n\nu_f = {}^n\nu_e \lceil_{n\mathcal{A}_f}$, where $\lceil$ means "restricted to".

Partitions. A partition of e is a collection of n, $n > 1$, subexecutions $e_1, e_2, \ldots, e_n$, of e, s.t. $e_1, e_2, \ldots, e_n$ are non-trivial, disjoint $(\mathcal{A}_i \cap \mathcal{A}_j = \emptyset$ for $i \neq j)$, and $\bigcup_{i=1,\ldots,n} \mathcal{A}_i = \mathcal{A}$. We write $e = e_1 \& e_2 \& \ldots \& e_n$.

Sequential partition. A partition is sequential, denoted $e = e_1 ; e_2 ; \ldots ; e_n$, if $\forall \alpha^I \in \mathcal{A}_i, \beta^J \in \mathcal{A}_j : i < j \implies \alpha^I \overset{\cdot}{\longrightarrow}_e \beta^J$.

Sequence dependency. For $h, f, g \subseteq e$, we write $f \overset{\cdot}{\longrightarrow}_e g$ if $h = f; g$.

Indexed executions. The indexing of e with K is the execution e^K where $\mathcal{A}_{e^K}$ is defined s.t. for all $\alpha^I \in \mathcal{A}_e$, $\alpha^{K \circ I} \in \mathcal{A}_{e^K}$.

3.3 Semantics

We use an algebraic definition of the semantics [8]. If p is a *pnode* and e is an execution, $e \models p$ means that e is an execution for p. The semantics of p is $[\![p]\!] = \{e \mid e \models p\}$.

Nil. The semantics of `nil` is the empty execution $(\emptyset, \emptyset, \emptyset, \emptyset, \emptyset, \emptyset, \emptyset)$.

Assignments. $e \models \alpha$ iff $A_e = \{\alpha^I\}$ for some index I.

Conditional Statements. $e \models$ `if` $\zeta(x_1, \ldots, x_n)$ `then` p `else` q iff $e = e_1; e_2$ with e_1 and e_2 s.t. $e_1 \models \zeta(x_1, \ldots, x_n)$, with $A_{e_1} = \{\alpha^I\}$, and $e_2 \models p$ if ${}^n\nu_{e_1}(\alpha^I) = true$, otherwise $e_2 \models q$.

Sequential Composition. $e \models p_1; p_2$ iff $e = e_1 ; e_2$, s.t. $e_i \models p_i$, $i = 1, 2$.

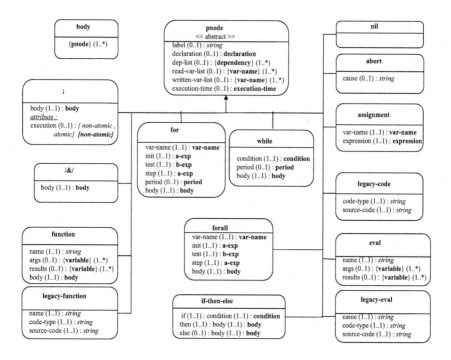

Fig. 2. Syntax of an FXML body

Iterations. Let $S = \{k_1, \ldots, k_N\}$ be the indexed set of the values taken by the iteration variable i. S is defined by *inc*, which is increasing: $i < j \implies k_i \leq k_j$. $e \models$ for(...) p iff $e = f_1^{\langle 1 \rangle}; \ldots; f_N^{\langle N \rangle}$, where $f_j \models p$, $j \in [1, N]$, and for every $\alpha^I \in {}^m\mathcal{A}_{f_j}$ (for any $m \in \mathbb{N}$) with ${}^m\nu_{f_j}(\alpha^I) = (v_0, v_1, v_2, \ldots, v_m)$: $\alpha_l = $ i $\implies v_l = k_j$. That is, the value of the iteration variable i is equal to k_j in f_j.

The semantics of while-loops is similar. Assignments are indexed using a hidden variable, whose values are $1, \ldots, N$, when the loop stops after the N-th iteration. [4] $e \models$ while($test(x_1, \ldots, x_n)$) p iff $e = c_1; f_1^{\langle 1 \rangle}; \ldots; c_N; f_N^{\langle N \rangle}; c_{N+1}$, where $c_j \models test(x_1, \ldots, x_n)$, $j \in [1, N+1]$, $f_j \models p$, $j \in [1, N]$, and the conditions evaluate to *true* in c_j, $j \in [1, N]$, and to *false* in c_{N+1}.

Parallel Composition. $e \models p_1 /\&/ p_2$ iff $e = e_1 \& e_2$, $e_i \models p_i$, $i = 1, 2$. Composition is commutative and associative. The semantics of forall-loops is as follows. Let $S = \{k_1, \ldots, k_N\}$ be the set of indices defined by *inc*. $e \models$ forall(...) p iff $e = f_1^{\langle 1 \rangle} \& \ldots \& f_N^{\langle N \rangle}$, where $f_j \models p$, $j \in [1, N]$, and for every $\alpha^I \in {}^m\mathcal{A}_{f_j}$ (for any $m \in \mathbb{N}$) with ${}^m\nu_{f_j}(\alpha^I) = (v_0, v_1, v_2, \ldots, v_m)$: $\alpha_l = $ i $\implies v_l = k_j$.

Dependencies. Let p be a composite *pnode*, with two descendants p_i, labeled Li, $i = 1, 2$. $e \models p\{$L1 $\rightarrow$ L2$\}$ iff $e \models p$, and for each $e_2 \subseteq e$, s.t. $e_2 \models p_2$, there exists

---

[4] The semantics of a non-terminating loop is an infinite execution.

$e_1 \subseteq e$, $e_1 \models p_1$, s.t. $e_1 \xrightarrow{\cdot}_e e_2$. That is, every occurrence of p_2 in an execution of p should be preceded by an occurrence of p_1 in the same execution. Notice that there might be more than one occurrence of p_2 in the execution (e.g., due to iterations), but only one of p_1 is required to exist. The semantics for data dependencies ($\rightarrow$d) is similar, except that e_1, e_2 are s.t. $e_1 \xrightarrow{d}_e e_2$.

An execution e models the iteration dependency $p \{\texttt{L1(k)} \rightarrow \texttt{L2(f(k))}\}$ iff $e \models p$, and for all $k \in [1, N]$, if $e_1^{\langle k \rangle} \subseteq e$ is a model of the k-th iteration of p_1, i.e., $e_1^{\langle k \rangle} \models p_1$, and $e_2^{\langle f(k) \rangle} \subseteq e$ is a model of the $f(k)$-th iteration of p_2, i.e., $e_2^{\langle f(k) \rangle} \models p_2$, then there is a sequential dependency between $e_1^{\langle k \rangle}$ and $e_2^{\langle f(k) \rangle}$, i.e., $e_1^{\langle k \rangle} \xrightarrow{\cdot}_e e_2^{\langle f(k) \rangle}$. Similarly for iteration data dependencies.

Timing Constraints. $e \models p[a,b]$ iff $e \models p$ and $\tau^e(e) - \tau^b(e) \in [a,b]$. For dependencies: $e \models p\{\texttt{L1}\rightarrow\texttt{[a,b]}\texttt{L2}\}$ iff $e \models p[a,b]$, and for all $e_i \subseteq e$, $e_i \models p_i$, $i = 1, 2$, $e_1 \xrightarrow{\cdot}_e e_2 \implies \tau^b(e_2) - \tau^e(e_1) \in [a,b]$. Similarly for temporal data dependencies. For periods: $e \models \texttt{for(...)}\ \texttt{[per=P]}\ p$ iff $e \models \texttt{for(...)}\ p$, where $e = f_1^{\langle 1 \rangle}; \ldots; f_N^{\langle N \rangle}$, s.t., for all $i \in [1, N]$, $[\tau^b(f_i^{\langle i \rangle}), \tau^e(f_i^{\langle i \rangle})] \subseteq [(i-1)P, iP[$. Similarly for `while`-loops. [5]

4   The Compilation Chain

4.1   Transformations

Compiling an FXML specification consists in transforming it until actual executable code for a specific platform could be generated. Let $\mathcal{L}$ denote a language. Concretely, $\mathcal{L}$ is given by an XML schema, where each element definition has an associated type. Thus, the compilation chain looks like a sequence $\mathcal{L}_0 \mapsto^* \mathcal{L}_0 \mapsto \mathcal{L}_1 \mapsto^* \ldots \mathcal{L}_n$, where $\mathcal{L}_i \mapsto^* \mathcal{L}_i$ is a sequence of *refinements* without changing the language (e.g., by adding new sequential dependencies), and $\mathcal{L}_i \mapsto \mathcal{L}_{i+1}$ is a transformation that adds information not expressible in $\mathcal{L}_i$ (e.g., the number of processors in the architecture, the communication and synchronization mechanisms, ...).

For simplicity, we define a transformation from $\mathcal{L}$ to $\mathcal{L}'$ to be an injective map $\phi : \mathcal{L} \rightarrow \mathcal{L}'$, that is, every element of the XML schema $\mathcal{L}$ is in the set of elements $\mathcal{L}'$. For transformations more complex than injective maps see, e.g., [9]. Let $E_\mathcal{L}$ be the set of executions "of type $\mathcal{L}$", and $F_\phi : E_{\mathcal{L}'} \rightarrow E_\mathcal{L}$ be the "forgetting" function that forgets all information that is specific to executions "of type $\mathcal{L}'$". $\phi : \mathcal{L} \rightarrow \mathcal{L}'$ is *correct* iff for all executions $e' \models_{\mathcal{L}'} \phi(p)$ it follows that $F_\phi(e') \models_\mathcal{L} p$.

4.2   JAHUEL

JAHUEL is an FXML-based prototype compilation chain. The tool smoothly handles different kinds of interacting non-functional issues as a mix of language features, analyses, and transformations: (a) timing requirements of the application (such as deadlines, periods and freshness), are part of the program and used for scheduling; (b) timing assumptions about execution times can be either added by the programmer and passed

---

[5] The principle is the same for non-terminating loops.

to the back-end compiler as constraints, or synthesized by program analysis; and (c) code optimization and scheduling are uniformly treated as transformations. JAHUEL is constructed to be easily extended to cope with new execution models, by extending the basic FXML schema and by adding transformations. JAHUEL provides some general transformations that can be customized for different execution platforms.

4.3   Using JAHUEL: The Producer/Consumer Example

The starting point is the FXML specification extracted by FlexCC2 from the annotated C program. Fig. 1(right) shows the graphical structure of the actual specification. Boxes are *pnodes*. A composite *pnode* is connected by a plain arrow to its components. The temporal data dependency on variable x from write to use is attached to the *pnode* /&/ (labeled "parallel" in the figure). The dotted arrow only serves for visualisation purposes (it is automatically added by FlexCC2 to the graphical representation).

JAHUEL performs a first transformation to put the input description into a canonical form. Second, it applies a transformation where all dependencies are replaced by a generic synchronization mechanism. This transformation, denoted $\mathcal{G}$, generates an extension of FXML, denoted FXML^g, with primitives mutex X (denoting a mutual exclusive access on a set of variables X), signal L (for signaling the termination of the execution of the pnode labeled L), and wait *cond* (for waiting until condition *cond* is satisfied). Fig. 3 shows the transformation rules for a timed data dependency. C1 is a continuous variable whose value evolves with time. The semantics is that the value of C1 is the time elapsed since the termination of pnode L1. The test a $\leq$ C1 $\leq$ b corresponds to the requirement $\tau^e(e) - \tau^b(e) \in [a,b]$, in the semantics of timed dependencies defined before. It is not difficult to define the semantics of FXML^g as an extension of the semantics of FXML given in Sec. 3.

$$\frac{L1:p_1}{\text{mutex}\{x\}\mathcal{G}(p_1);\text{C1}:=0;\text{signal L1}} \qquad \frac{L2:p_2}{\text{wait L1} \wedge \text{ a}\leq\text{C1}\leq\text{b};\text{mutex}\{x\}\mathcal{G}(p_2)}$$

Fig. 3. Transformation $\mathcal{G}$ for a timed data dependency L1 d$\rightarrow$[a,b] L2 on x

The generic synchronization structure is used to generate code for more concrete mechanisms. Indeed, FXML^g allows factoring the processing of dependencies which is a common step to all platform-dependent implementations guaranteeing the dependency. FXML^g specifications can be transformed by JAHUEL to enable code-generation for widely used mechanisms provided by real-time operating systems APIs (e.g., POSIX) and programming languages (e.g., Java): lock, unlock, wait, and notify. We denote $\mathcal{S}$ the transformation and FXML^s the extension of FXML^g with these constructs. For simplicity, we only give here the transformation rule for a timed data dependency (Fig. 4), but JAHUEL handles all dependencies.

After having processed the dependencies, and generated the specification of the producer/consumer in FXML^s, JAHUEL applies a generic transformation whose role is to structure the representation for generating code for thread-based runtime platforms. This gives a specification in FXMLth. The basic idea is simple: *pnodes* writer and user composed with the parallel composition operator /&/ become *threads*. In the

$$\frac{L1:p_1}{\texttt{lock(Lx);}\mathcal{S}(p_1)\texttt{;unlock(Lx);lock(L1);} \quad \texttt{C1:=0; L1.b:=true; notify(L1); unlock(L1)}}$$

$$\frac{L2:p_2}{\texttt{lock(L1); while(!(L1.b} \wedge \texttt{a} \leq \texttt{C1} \leq \texttt{b))wait(L1); unlock(L1)lock(Lx);}\mathcal{S}(p_2)\texttt{;unlock(Lx)}}$$

Fig. 4. Transformation $\mathcal{S}$ for a timed data dependency

main *pnode*, the calls to legacy C-functions `writer()` and `user()` are wrapped-up by an FXMLth-construct `start` whose (intuitive) meaning is launching a thread. The semantics of FXMLth can be formally defined along the same lines of FXML.

From FXMLth, different transformations for specific thread interfaces (e.g., Pthreads, SystemC, ...) can be directly applied (e.g., using XSLT). Fig. 5 shows part of the C+Pthreads and SystemC implementations generated by JAHUEL for the example.

JAHUEL also implements a transformation into discrete-time stop-watch automata to enable scheduler synthesis using the tool described in [17,16].

```
void User()                                    SC_MODULE(User)
{                                              {
X_lock_simply(&thUser,&initialization);        sc_inout<int> Synchro;
X_unlock_simply(&thUser,&initialization);
                                               void User_function()
X_clock User_LCLOCK;                           {
X_clock_init(&User_LCLOCK);
                                               while (true)
while (true)                                    {
{                                              while (Synchro == -1)
X_lock(&thUser,-1,&write_happened);             {
                                                   wait();
while (((write_happened_CONTROL) == (-1)) ||    }
(X_clock_get(&thUser,-1,&write_GCLOCK,"us") > 100))
{                                              Synchro = -1;

    X_wait(&thUser,-1,-1,&write_happened);     wait(SC_ZERO_TIME);
}
                                               } // end User_function
X_unlock(&thUser,-1,&write_happened);// end CTOR User
                                               SC_CTOR(User)
X_lock(&thUser,-1,&x_shared);                  {
                                                   SC_THREAD(User_function);
X_clock use_task_LCLOCK;                            sensitive << Synchro;
X_task_b(&thUser,-1,"use",&use_task_LCLOCK,0,10,"us");
use();                                         } // end CTOR User
X_task_e(&thUser,-1,"use",&use_task_LCLOCK,0,10,"us"); }; // end MODULE User

X_unlock(&thUser,-1,&x_shared);

X_wait_for_period(&thUser,-1,&User_LCLOCK,15,"us");
}
}
```

Fig. 5. Producer/consumer's C+Pthreads (left) and SystemC (right) code

5   Case Study: An MPEG-4 Video Encoder

We have used the language and the tool for generating parallel implementations of an MPEG-4 video encoder under development at STMicroelectronics. We have produced code for different run-time platforms, such as Pthreads, OpenMP and MPI, and hardware architectures. For the sake of simplicity, we present here only a part of the FXML representation (and not the actual C code with pragmas) and the code synthesis phases for a grid running MPI. More details about the full application can be obtained in [1].

Our FXML model describes the existing concurrency in the compression standard originally hidden in the block diagram model [2]. The specification is composed of forall *pnodes* and legacy C functions, together with dependencies in the MPEG encoding algorithm. A *frame* is a $W \times H$ matrix of *macroblocks*, which contain picture data. The standard specifies computations on macroblocks, such as, motion estimation (ME), motion vector prediction (MVP), ..., and functional dependencies between computations. The main `encode` procedure is depicted in Fig. 6. For lack of space, and to enhance readability, we do not present here the actual FXML specification, but only a graphical representation of (part of) it. `forall(x,y)` is a shorthand for: `forall(x=0; x++; 0<=x<W){forall(y=0; y++; 0<=y<H)}`. All dependencies shown in Fig. 6 are iteration dependencies between instances of nested `forall`s. For example, the standard specifies that the Choice computation on a macroblock must be done after the motion estimation on it. This property is expressed in FXML as the dependency `ME(x,y)→Choice(x,y)` which specifies that the (x,y)-instance of the ME *pnode* (which encapsulates the legacy C function of the motion estimation algorithm) must finish before starting the (x,y)-instance of the Choice *pnode*.

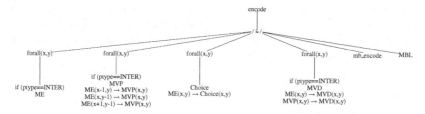

Fig. 6. MPEG-4 encode function with macroblock dependencies

```
forall(x=0; x++; 0 <= x < W)
   forall(y=0; y++; 0 <= y < H)
      QiQ(x,y)=F[QiQ(x-1,y),QiQ(x-1,y-1),QiQ(x,y-1)]
```

Fig. 7. QiQ algorithm

Pnode mb_encode is the parallel composition of several *pnodes*. One of these, namely QiQ, is shown in Fig. 7. [6] The dependencies associated to (x,y)-instances of QiQ are graphically represented by the matrix in Fig. 8 (left). Each bullet at position (x,y) corresponds to the execution of `QiQ(x,y)`. The arrows illustrate the dependencies: `QiQ(x-1,y-1)`, `QiQ(x-1,y)`, and `QiQ(x,y-1)` must be computed before `QiQ(x,y)`. Indeed, these dependencies can be eliminated applying automatic parallelization techniques (e.g., [7]) (Fig. 8 (right)) to obtain dependency-free `forall`s which can be implemented without communication overhead. The transformed QiQ specification is obtained by replacing the `forall` *pnode* by the sequential composition of three *pnodes* as shown in Fig. 9. Clearly, the new specification is a *refinement* of the previous one.

At this point, we can take care of implementation constraints imposed by the runtime platform. Let us first handle code-partitioning for functions f other than QiQ

---

[6] QiQ computes the quantization and the inverse quantization functions specified in the standard.

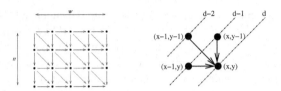

Fig. 8. QiQ dependencies

(which needs no further refinement). Let p the number of processors. We decide to divide each dependency-free `forall` into n tasks, where $n > \lceil \frac{H}{p} \rceil$. We choose n to be the number of rows H. *Pnodes* of the form `forall(0<=x<W,0<=y<H) f(x,y)` get transformed as `forall(0<=y<H) for(0<=x<W) f(x,y)`, that is, a sequential execution of `f` on a *row* of macroblocks on one processor. This syntactic transformation is a refinement.

Let us now consider the task-to-processor mapping. The mapping consists in first transforming the parallel composition (`/&/`) (Fig. 6) into a sequential one `;`. This syntactic transformation is a refinement and does not need adding new constructs. We now assign to each `forall` *pnode* the whole set of processors. This is done by extending the language to be able to attach a number of processors to *pnodes*.

```
for(0 <= d <= min(H,W)-1)
  forall(0 <= y <= d)
    QiQ(d-y,y)=F[QiQ(d-y,y),QiQ(d-y-1,y-1),QiQ(d-y,y-1)] ;
for(min(H,W) <= d <= max(H,W)-1)
  forall(0 <= y <= min(H,W)-1)
    QiQ(d-y,y)=F[QiQ(d-y,y),QiQ(d-y-1,y-1),QiQ(d-y,y-1)] ;
for(max(H,W) <= d <= H+W-1)
  forall(d-max(H,W)+1 <= y <= min(H,W)-1)
    QiQ(d-y,y)=F[QiQ(d-y,y),QiQ(d-y-1,y-1),QiQ(d-y,y-1)] ;
```

Fig. 9. Transformed QiQ

The last transformation produces the platform-dependent implementation of the MPEG-4 encoder. In this case, we decided to generate code for MPI using a master/slave organization and a dynamic scheduling strategy. Indeed, this phase requires adding new constructs to account for platform characteristics (e.g., dynamic scheduling, code distribution, ...). These constructs are not meant to be used by the programmer who only needs to specify the appropriate compilation option. The tool will automatically apply the corresponding model transformation, followed by the code generation phase for the actual platform.

To evaluate the parallel encoder performances we measured the relative gain in compression time $\mathcal{G}(p) = \frac{T_1 - T_p}{T_1}$, where T_p is the execution time for p processors, compared with the execution time T_1 of the sequential implementation. Performance results (detailed in [1]) show that even if the speedup is sub-linear, since some encoding phases cannot be parallelized, the addition of new processing units to the architecture has a positive impact in encoding time: the parallel compression time is smaller than the sequential time by nearly 15% for two processors and reaches nearly 70% for sixteen processors. [7]

6 Conclusions and Future Work

We have presented the FXML language for specifying concurrent real-time applications. FXML has a simple abstract execution model based on the notion of atomic assignment and dependencies. FXML can be incrementally extended with information related to refinements of the abstract model into more concrete ones. A compiler is a sequence of transformations going from a language (or model) to another (more concrete one). Based on this idea, we have developed the compilation chain JAHUEL that provides several translation phases which can be easily customized for different runtime platforms.

Our framework is grounded on well established notions such as program analysis and transformation, refinement and scheduler synthesis. The main contribution of our work is to have shown that these techniques could be put together into a pre-industrial, extensible, and customizable compilation chain for generating code without semantic break-downs along the way.

We are currently working on (1) applying our framework in other industrial applications, (2) strengthening the integration into FlexCC2, and (3) generating code for other platforms. Special effort is being put on generating SystemC/TLM code. The main motivation for this is early prototyping, verification and testing of embedded applications on simulated hardware platforms. Automated generation of both executable and simulation code from the same formal model ensures simulation results are trustworthy.

Acknowledgements. We thank the anonymous reviewers for the helpful remarks.

References

1. I. Assayad, Ph. Gerner, S. Yovine, and V. Bertin. Modelling, analysis and implementation of an on-line video encoder. In *DFMA'05*. IEEE Computer Society, 2005
2. *Inf. tech - Coding of audio-visual objects - P. 2: Visual.* Prentice Hall, ISO/IEC 14496-2:2001.
3. V. Bertin, J.M. Daveau, P. Guillaume, T. Lepley, D. Pilat, C. Richard, M. Santana, T. Thery. FlexCC2: An optimizing retargetable C compiler for DSP proc. *EMSOFT'02*, LNCS 2491.
4. P. Binns and S. Vestal. Formalizing software architectures for embedded systems. In *EMSOFT'01*. LNCS 2211, 2001.
5. A. Burns and A. Wellings. Concurrency in Ada. Cambridge University Press, 1998.
6. P. Caspi, A. Curic, A. Maignan, C. Sofronis, S. Tripakis, P. Niebert. From Simulink to SCADE/Lustre to TTA: a layered approach for distrib. embedded applications. *LCTES'03*.
7. A. Darte, Y. Robert, and F. Vivien. *Scheduling and Automatic Parallelization*. Birkhäuser, Boston, 2000.
8. J. Goguen and G. Malcolm. Algebraic Semantics of Imperative Programs. MIT Press, 1996.

---

[7] Other implementations are currently under evaluation on different embedded platforms.

9. J. Goguen, G. Wang, Young-Kwang Nam, and Kai Lin. Abstract schema morphisms and schema matching generation. Tech. Rep. DCSE, UCSD, 2004.
10. W. Groppa, E. Lusk, and A. Skjellum. *Using MPI*. Scientific and Engineering Computation. MIT Press, 2nd edition, November 1999.
11. N. Halbwachs, P. Caspi, P. Raymond, and D. Pilaud. The synchronous dataflow programming language Lustre. *Proc. IEEE*, 79(9), Sept. 1991.
12. L.Hammond, B.A. Nayfeh, K.Olukotun. A single-chip multiprocessor. *Comp.*, 30(9), 1997.
13. C.A.R. Hoare. Communicating Sequential Processes. Prentice Hall, 1985.
14. G. Karsai, J. Sztipanovits, A. Ledeczi, and T. Bapty. Model-integrated development of embedded software. In *Proc. IEEE*, 91(1), 2003.
15. M. Kersten. Comparison of the leading AOP tools. In *Aspect-Oriented Software Development, AOSD'05*. Industry track. Invited talk.
16. C. Kloukinas, C. Nakhli, and S. Yovine, A Methodology and Tool Support for Generating Scheduled Native Code for Real-Time Java Applications, In *EMSOFT'03*, LNCS 2855. 2003.
17. C. Kloukinas and S. Yovine, Synthesis of Safe, QoS Extendible, Application Specific Schedulers for Heterogeneous Real-Time Systems, In *ECRTS'03*, 2003.
18. www.openmp.org
19. http://ptolemy.eecs.berkeley.edu/ptolemyII
20. A. Sangiovanni-Vincentelli. Defining platform-based design. EEDesign, February 5, 2002.
21. M. Schlett. Trends in embedded-microprocessor design. *IEEE Computer*, 31(8), 1998.
22. J. Sifakis. Modeling real-time systems - challenges and work directions. In *EMSOFT'01*. LNCS 2211, 2001.
23. J. Sifakis, S. Tripakis, and S. Yovine. Building models of real-time systems from application software. *Proceedings of the IEEE*, 91(1):100–111, January 2003.

Modelling and Refinement of an On-Chip Communication Architecture

Juha Plosila, Pasi Liljeberg, and Jouni Isoaho

Dept. of Information Technology,
University of Turku, Finland
{juha.plosila, pasi.liljeberg, jouni.isoaho}@utu.fi

Abstract. In this paper, we present a formal modeling and refinement approach for on-chip communication architecture development, based on the Action Systems formalism. Stepwise refinement from an abstract high-level initial model to an implementable parallel switch based model is discussed. The focus is on gradually decomposing the initial specification into a composition of concurrently operating subsystems. Data transactions are modelled with atomic message passing events via interface procedures, for which a new notation is introduced. The concept is demonstrated by a network-like pipelined bus platform.

1 Introduction

Advances in VLSI technology over recent years have considerably increased both physical and functional complexity of single-chip systems, i.e., *systems-on-chip* (SoC) [3,4]. One of the most important challenges in such systems is to manage interaction within and between components. Hence, efficient ways to model, develop, and verify on-chip communication media are needed. Formal methods of concurrent programming can be used to abstractly specify the behavior of an on-chip communication platform and to systematically refine the specification towards an implementable more detailed model. The *Action Systems* [1] is one of such methods. It provides a mathematical framework for design specification, reasoning about concurrency, and correctness-preserving refinement of systems.

In this paper, the Action Systems formalism is used to stepwise decompose the initial abstract model of a generic communication platform into a more concrete hierarchical model composed of concurrently operating dedicated subsystems. Distinct action system components exchange information via remote procedure calls, i.e., communication is based on atomic message-passing events, where no shared (global) variables are used. A new notation for procedure based communication is presented. As a case study, the method is applied to a network-like pipelined bus [6] communication architecture.

2 Hierarchical Action Systems

Action Systems [1,2] is a state based formalism for concurrent system specification and correctness-preserving development. It has its roots in an extended version of the guarded command language of Dijkstra [5]. The basic building blocks

K.-K. Lau and R. Banach (Eds.): ICFEM 2005, LNCS 3785, pp. 219–234, 2005.

of the formalism are called *actions*, which include, for example: *skip* (empty statement), $x := e$ ((multiple) assignment), $x := x'.P$ (non-deterministic assignment), $P \rightarrow B$ (guarded action), $A_1; \ldots; A_m$ (sequential composition), and $A_1 \, [\!] \ldots [\!] \, A_m$ (non-deterministic choice). Here x is a variable or a list of variables, x' symbolizes new values assigned to the variables x, e is an expression or a list of expressions, P is a predicate i.e. boolean expression, and A_j, $j=1, \ldots, m$ as well as B are actions.

An action is considered *atomic*. This means that only its state before and after the execution can be observed, and when selected for execution, it is completed without interference from other actions. Formal semantics of actions is defined using Dijkstra's *weakest preconditions*. The weakest precondition for an action A to establish a postcondition Q is denoted by $\text{wp}(A, Q)$. We have for example: $\text{wp}(skip, Q) \,\hat{=}\, Q$, $\text{wp}(x := x'.P, Q) \,\hat{=}\, (\forall x'.P \Rightarrow Q[x'/x])$, $\text{wp}(P \rightarrow B, Q) \,\hat{=}\, P \Rightarrow \text{wp}(B, Q)$. The *guard* gA of an action A is defined by $gA \,\hat{=}\, \neg\text{wp}(A, false)$. Considering a guarded action $A \,\hat{=}\, P \rightarrow B$ we have that $gA = P \wedge gB$. An action A is said to be *enabled* in some state, if its guard is *true* in that state. Otherwise A is *disabled*.

Non-atomic action compositions enable efficient modeling of complex system behavior. In this paper, we will use the *non-atomic sequential composition* in certain system models. Non-atomicity means that an action outside the composition can execute between two component actions of the construct, which is not possible in the *atomic* sequential composition. We will use the bold semicolon (**;**) as the operator symbol for non-atomic sequences. It can be defined in terms of the non-deterministic choice ($[\!]$) and an auxiliary local *program counter* variable p (initialized to 1) as follows: $(A_1 \; ; \; A_2) \,\hat{=}\, (p = 1 \rightarrow A_1; p := 2 \; [\!] \; p = 2 \rightarrow A_2; p := 1)$.

Action System. A hierarchical action system $\mathcal{A}$ (with a procedure interface) has the form:

> **sys** $\mathcal{A}$ (**exp** *exported procedures*; **imp** *imported procedures*) [*generic parameters*] ::
> |[**var** *local variables*;
>   **proc** *procedure (local and exported) definitions*;
>   **subsys** *subsystem instances*;
>   **actions** *list of actions*;
>   **init** *variable initialization*;
>   **exec**
>   **do** *action composition* **od** || *subsystem composition*
>]|

The *exported procedures* are defined in the **proc**-clause of the system $\mathcal{A}$, but are called by other systems. The *imported procedures* are defined in and exported by some other systems and called by the system $\mathcal{A}$. The exported and imported procedures are jointly refered to as *interface procedures* with which atomic message passing events between systems can be modeled. The local, exported, and imported procedures must be distinct. Each procedure may have a set of value (**val**), result (**res**), and update (**upd**) parameters. Formal parameters are replaced with actual ones at each procedure call, and the operation carried out by a procedure (procedure body) is considered a part of the calling atomic action. Hence, procedures are treated as parametrizable subactions.

The *local variables* declared in the **var**-clause are exclusively used by the system $\mathcal{A}$. Their initial values are specified in the **init**-clause. The *generic parameters* typically deal with ranges of some variables, sizes of arrays, and other static information needed by the system. The **actions**-clause lists the uniquely named actions of the system. They may access the local variables of $\mathcal{A}$ and contain calls to the local and imported procedures. In the **subsys**-clause, the *subsystem instances* are defined, replacing the formal interface lists of the subsystems with the actual ones and giving a unique name for each instance. The subsystems themselves, the components, are defined separately from the main system $\mathcal{A}$ and may contain subsystems of their own.

The execution part, the **exec**-clause, contains an iteration (**do-od**-loop) of the actions defined in the **actions**-clause. In this paper, the *action composition* within the loop is either a non-deterministic choice ($[\![$) or a combination of choices and non-atomic sequences (;). The loop is composed in parallel ($\|$) with the *subsystem composition*, i.e., the parallel composition of the subsystem instances defined in the **subsys**-clause. In general, the parallel composition of the main system's loop and a subsystem instance S is interpreted as the loop **do** A_M $[\![$ $S.A_S$ **od**, where A_M and A_S represent the action compositions in the main system and subsystem, respectively. The notation $S.A_S$ indicates that each local identifier (action name, local variable, etc.) in the subsystem is provided with the prefix "$S.$", where S is the unique name of the subsystem instance given in the **subsys**-clause of the main system. The prefixed identifiers are then implicitly considered local distinct identifiers of the main system.

An action system operates as follows. First, the state variables are initialized in the **init**-clause. Then the system's **do-od**-loop, including also the actions of the subsystems as explained above, starts to execute enabled actions one at a time. Parallel execution is modeled by simultaneously enabled independent actions which can be executed in any order (interleaved) without affecting the result of computation. If all the actions of the system become disabled, the loop temporarily stops and resumes execution when some other system enables at least one of the actions via the interface procedures.

Composing Action Systems. Consider two hierarchical action systems $\mathcal{A}$ and $\mathcal{B}$ with distinct local variables, exported and local procedures, subsystem instances, and actions. The *parallel composition* of such systems $\mathcal{A}$ and $\mathcal{B}$ is denoted by $\mathcal{A} \parallel \mathcal{B}$. It is defined to be another action system whose global and local identifiers (procedures, variables, subsystem instances, actions) consist of the identifiers of the component systems and whose **exec**-clause has the form: **do** A $[\![$ B **od** $\parallel$ S_A $\parallel$ S_B. Here A and B denote the action compositions, and S_A and S_B the subsystem compositions in $\mathcal{A}$ and $\mathcal{B}$, respectively. The constituent systems communicate via their shared interface procedures. The definition of the parallel composition is used inversely in system derivation to *decompose* a system description into a composition of smaller separate systems or internal subsystems.

Quantified Constructs. Any action-level composition operator $\bullet \in \{ [\![, ; \text{(atomic)},$; (non-atomic) $\}$, and the system-level parallel composition operator $\parallel$ can be quantified using the notation defined as follows: $[\bullet \, 1 \leq i \leq n : A(i) \,] \mathrel{\widehat{=}} A(1) \bullet$ $\ldots \bullet A(n)$, and $[\, \| \, 1 \leq i \leq n : \mathcal{A}(i) \,] \mathrel{\widehat{=}} \mathcal{A}(1) \, \| \ldots \| \, \mathcal{A}(n)$.

Procedure Based Communication. In this paper, we use remote procedures to model communication channels between action systems. For this, a new notation is introduced. Consider the parallel composition $\mathcal{S}nd \, \| \, \mathcal{R}ec$ of the generic sender and receiver systems given as

sys $\mathcal{S}nd$ (**imp** p) ::
$\|[$ **var** v_S;
   actions
    $S \; : \; (S_1; \; p(v_S); \; S_2)$;
   exec do S **od**
$]\|$

sys $\mathcal{R}ec$ (**exp** p) ::
$\|[$ **var** v_R;
   proc $p(\textbf{val } x) : P$;
   actions
    $R \; : \; (R_1; \; \textbf{await } p; \; R_2)$;
   exec do R **od**
$]\|$

where v_S and v_R are distinct variables accessed by the atomic actions S and R, respectively. $S_{1,2}$ and $R_{1,2}$ denote arbitrary subactions of S and R. The interface procedure p is defined in and exported by the receiver, and imported and called by the sender with the variables v_S as actual value parameters. The body P of p can be any atomic action writing onto the variables v_R. According to the definition of the parallel composition of action systems, the **exec**-clause of the composed system $\mathcal{S}nd \, \| \, \mathcal{R}ec$ has the form: **do** $S \, \| \, R$ **od**. The construct $S \, \|$ R, where S calls p and R awaits such a call (**await** command), is regarded as a single atomic action SR, defined by: $SR \mathrel{\widehat{=}} (S_1; \; R_1; \; P[v_S/x]; \; R_2; \; S_2)$. Hence, communication is based on sharing an action, in which data is atomically passed from $\mathcal{S}nd$ to $\mathcal{R}ec$ by executing the body P of the procedure p.

Refinement. Refinement means stepwise development of an abstract formal specification into a concrete implementable form in such a way that the logical properties of the original description are preserved throughout the derivation process. Comprehensive studies on refinement can be found for example in [2].

We say that an abstract action A on is (correctly) *refined* by a concrete action C, denoted $A \leq C$, if the following condition holds for all possible postconditions Q: $I \wedge \mathrm{wp}(A, Q) \Rightarrow \mathrm{wp}\,(C, I \wedge Q)$, where I represents the invariant that must be preserved by the refinement. Similarly, refinement of an abstract action system $\mathcal{A}$ by a concrete action system $\mathcal{C}$ is denoted by $\mathcal{A} \leq \mathcal{C}$. Such a system-level refinement can be proven in terms of action-level refinements and some auxiliary conditions dealing with validity of the invariant, enabledness of actions, termination of auxiliary internal computation introduced in the refinement, and possible fairness issues.

3   Generic Platform Model

In this section, we present an Action Systems model $\mathcal{S}$ for a generic single-chip system composed of n concurrently operating processing elements and a communication platform providing a medium for data exchange between the processors. The processing elements, hosts, are modeled by n distinct instances *Master*(i) (with $0 \leq i \leq n{-}1$) of an abstract tranceiver module $\mathcal{M}$ whose task is to continuously send and receive data without actually processing it. The communication platform, in turn, is modeled by a single instance *Platform* of a module $\mathcal{P}$ which directs data from its n input ports to n output ports according to the destination addresses specified by the attached sending hosts. Communication channels between the system components are modeled by shared interface procedures. The overall abstract system model $\mathcal{S}$, regarded here as a closed system for simplicity, is given as:

$$
\begin{aligned}
&\textbf{sys } \mathcal{S}() :: \\
&|[\textbf{ const } n : natural; \\
&\quad \textbf{type } datagram : \textbf{record } (src, dst : 0..n-1; \ d : data); \\
&\quad \textbf{proc } M2P[0..n{-}1]\,(\textbf{val } datagram), \ P2M[0..n{-}1]\,(\textbf{val } datagram); \\
&\quad \textbf{subsys} \\
&\qquad Platform \quad : \mathcal{P}\,(M2P[0..n{-}1], P2M[0..n{-}1])[n]; \\
&\qquad Master(i) : \mathcal{M}\,(M2P[i], P2M[i])[i, n]; \\
&\quad \textbf{exec} \quad Platform \parallel [\parallel\ 0 \leq i \leq n\text{-}1 \colon Master(i)] \\
&]|
\end{aligned}
$$

where the subsystem modules $\mathcal{M}$ and $\mathcal{P}$, with the host indentification number i and host count n as generic parameters, are defined by:

$$
\begin{aligned}
&\textbf{sys } \mathcal{M}(\textbf{exp } P2M, \textbf{imp } M2P)[i, n : natural] :: \\
&|[\textbf{ var } dg : datagram; \ mem : \textbf{set of } datagram; \\
&\quad \textbf{proc } P2M(\textbf{val } a : datagram) : \\
&\qquad\qquad (mem := mem \cup \{a\}); \\
&\quad \textbf{actions} \\
&\quad\ Snd : (dg.src := i; \\
&\qquad\qquad dg.dst := x.((0 \leq x < n) \wedge (x \neq i)); \\
&\qquad\qquad dg.d := y.(y \in data); \ M2P(dg)); \\
&\quad\ Rec : \textbf{await } P2M; \\
&\quad \textbf{exec do } Snd \parallel Rec \textbf{ od} \\
&]|
\end{aligned}
$$

$$
\begin{aligned}
&\textbf{sys } \mathcal{P} \ (\textbf{exp } M2P[0..n\text{-}1], \textbf{imp } P2M[0..n\text{-}1]) \\
&\qquad [n : natural] :: \\
&|[\textbf{ proc } M2P[i](\textbf{val } a : datagram) : \\
&\qquad\qquad (P2M[a.dst](a)); \\
&\quad \textbf{actions} \\
&\quad\ Trf(i) : \textbf{await } M2P[i]; \\
&\quad\ \textbf{exec do } [\parallel 0 \leq i \leq n\text{-}1 \colon \ Trf(i)] \textbf{ od} \\
&]|
\end{aligned}
$$

Each host $Master(i)$ is connected to $Platform$ via two interface procedures $M2P[i]$ and $P2M[i]$. The former is used to transfer data from the host to the platform, while the latter is used to transfer data from the platform to the host's local variable mem. Data (dg), prepared by the send action Snd of the host, is of the type $datagram$, a 3-field record composed of the source and destination addresses $(dg.src, dg.dst)$ and the actual payload $(dg.d)$. It is communicated via the value parameters of the two interface procedures. The procedure $M2P[i]$ is exported by $Platform$, imported by $Master(i)$, and called by the send action Snd of $Master(i)$. The procedure $P2M[i]$, which constitutes the receive action Rec of $Master(i)$, is exported by $Master(i)$, imported by $Platform$, and can be called by any transfer action $Trf(j)$, i.e., procedure $M2P[j]$ in $Platform$, where $j \neq i$. The restriction $j \neq i$ comes from the fact that the above host module $\mathcal{M}$ is specified not to send data to itself in the action Snd.

Hence, transfering a datagram dg from a source host $dg.src$ to a destination host $dg.dst$ is an atomic message-passing event, where $Master(dg.src)$ calls the procedure $M2P[dg.src]$ in $Platform$ which then further calls the procedure $P2M[dg.dst]$ in $Master(dg.dst)$. Atomicity means here that when a transfer has been selected for execution, it will be completed without interruption. Furthermore, transfers with different destination addresses are independent of each other and can therefore be considered parallel when enabled simultaneously. Those simultaneously enabled transfers that have a same destination address, i.e., are not independent, are considered sequential, selected for execution in a nondeterministic (arbitrary) order.

The module $\mathcal{P}$ can be thought to represent, at a very abstract level, a variety of actual network-like communication platforms. In fact, it can be even viewed as a shared bus model, if we consider $\mathcal{P}$ a completely sequential system, also when executing independent simultaneously enabled actions. The module $\mathcal{P}$ inherently guarantees, by atomicity of transactions, that every initiated transfer is completed, and that datagrams arrive to a host in the same order they were sent from another host. Parallelism is still quite limited, as transfers with a same destination address cannot be initiated simultaneously.

4   Increasing Parallelism by Pipelining

The initial specification $\mathcal{P}$ of the communication platform is first refined into a more parallel and concrete model, in which receive events via a procedure $M2P[0..n-1]$ can take place concurrently with send events via the procedures $P2M[0..n-1]$, as separate independent actions. This is obtained by pipelining the execution of the procedure $M2P[i]$, which constitutes the transfer action $Trf(i)$ of $\mathcal{P}$, into three separate phases: receive, move, and send, where receive and send operations are independent and can thereby be considered parallel. The transformation is platform independent in the sense that the resulting model does not yet specify how a datagram is in practice propagated from a source to a destination and can therefore be thought to represent still a number of actual on-chip transmission media. The environment model of the communication platform, composed of the n hosts, is kept intact from now on.

As the first substep, the exported procedure $M2P[i]$ of $\mathcal{P}$ is transformed into an atomic sequence of three actions, i.e., we refine: $M2P[i](a) \leq (ibuf[i] := a;$ $Mov(i); Snd(ibuf[i].dst))$, with

$$Mov(i) \; \hat{=} \; \neg full[ibuf[i].dst] \to obuf[ibuf[i].dst] := ibuf[i]; full[ibuf[i].dst] := true$$
$$Snd(j) \; \hat{=} \; full[j] \to P2M[j](obuf[j]); \; full[j] := false$$

Here $ibuf[0..n-1]$ (input buffer) and $obuf[0..n-1]$ (output buffer) are new local array variables of the type $datagram$ introduced to allow separation of the input events from the output events. The idea is that data received from the host i is first stored to the input buffer $ibuf[i]$, then transfered (moved) by the action $Mov(i)$ to the destination output buffer $obuf[j]$ $(j = ibuf[i].dst)$, and finally sent to the destination host j by the action $Snd(j)$ which calls the interface procedure $P2M[j]$. The enabledness of the actions $Mov(i)$ and $Snd(j)$ is controlled by the element j of another new local variable, the boolean flag array $full[0..n-1]$ used to inform whether the destination output buffer $obuf[j]$ is occupied $(full[j] = true)$ or vacant $(full[j] = false)$.

Notice that the above local refinement of the procedure $M2P(i)$ does not yet change the operation of the system in any way, because atomicity is still completely preserved. To take advantage of the introduced input and output buffers, i.e., to enable parallel execution of the receive action $ibuf[i] := a$ and the send action $Snd(j)$, we need to split the procedure into three separate atomic entities. This is accomplished in practice by moving the actions $Mov(i)$ and

$Snd(j)$ from the procedure body to the **do-od** loop of the system, so that only the receive event $ibuf[i] := a$ is left in the procedure $M2P[i]$. Hence, considering first a single sender host i and all possible receiver hosts j, $0 \leq j \leq n - 1$, we refine (simplified notation):

    proc $M2P[i](a) : (ibuf[i] := a;\ Mov(i);\ Snd(ibuf[i].dst));$ **do** $Trf(i)$ **od**
    $\leq$
    proc $M2P[i](a) : (ibuf[i] := a);$ **do** $(Rec(i)\ ;\ Mov(i)) \parallel [\ \parallel 0 \leq j \leq n - 1\ :\ Snd(j)]$ **od**

where $Trf(i), Rec(i) \mathrel{\widehat{=}}$ **await** $M2P[i]$. Observe that the correct order of the receive and move actions $Rec(i)$ and $Mov(i)$ is enforced by the non-atomic sequential composition, while the ordering of $Mov(i)$ and any subsequent send action $Snd(j)$ is based on the state of the flag $full[j]$. $Snd(j)$ becomes enabled when the corresponding move action has been executed ($full[j] = true$), and the next occurrence of $Mov(i)$ for the same destination j is postponed until $Snd(j)$ has been completed ($full[j] = false$).

The refined configuration thus preserves the order of the related receive, move, and send events. However, as now $Rec(i)$ and $Snd(j)$ are independent separate actions in the **do-od** loop accessing distinct variables $ibuf[i]$ and $obuf[j]$, their execution is considered parallel whenever they are simultaneously enabled. In other words, a new datagram can be received to $ibuf[i]$ simultaneously with sending the previous datagram from $obuf[j]$, which was the main goal of this refinement step. Furthermore, a send action $Snd(j)$ can be considered concurrent with any other send action $Snd(j')$ and the corresponding move action, where the destination j' differs from j ($j' \neq j$). This actually indicates that the above refinement is valid only if we assume that the selection between simultaneously enabled send actions is *weakly fair*, i.e., that every continuously enabled action will eventually be selected for execution. Such a fairness property means here that each initiated transfer is guaranteed to be eventually completed, as is inherently the case in the initial platform model $\mathcal{P}$ with atomic transfers.

Including now all possible sender hosts i, $0 \leq i \leq n - 1$, we finally obtain the refined communication platform model $\mathcal{P}^1$ given below. In $\mathcal{P}^1$, all the n receive actions $Rec(i)$ are independent of each other and can therefore be considered parallel. Also those move actions $Mov(i)$ that access different destinations are potentially concurrent. However, in order to have a valid refinement $\mathcal{P} \leq \mathcal{P}^1$, we have to consider the selection between simultaneously enabled move actions in $\mathcal{P}^1$ *strongly fair*, in addition to considering the selection between send actions weakly fair as explained above. This is because if the move actions $Mov(i)$ and $Mov(i')$, where $i \neq i'$, simultaneously try to access the same destination j, the one selected for execution disables the other by setting $full[j]$ to *true*. The disabled move action is eventually re-enabled by the send action $Snd(j)$, but can again become temporarily disabled by another simultaneously enabled move action with the same destination. By assuming strong fairness, i.e., that any action which becomes enabled infinitely often will eventually be selected for execution, we can conclude that each move action will be executed and that each initiated transfer will eventually be completed. Then the behavior of the new model $\mathcal{P}^1$ conforms to the initial model $\mathcal{P}$, and the refinement $\mathcal{P} \leq \mathcal{P}^1$ is valid.

sys $\mathcal{P}^1$ (**exp** $M2P[0..n-1]$, **imp** $P2M[0..n-1]$) $[n:natural]$ ::
$|[$ **var** $ibuf[0..n-1], obuf[0..n-1] : datagram; full[0..n-1] : boolean;$
   proc $M2P[i](\textbf{val}\ a:datagram):(ibuf[i]:=a);$
   actions
      $Rec(i)$: **await** $M2P[i];$
      $Mov(i)$: $\neg full[ibuf[i].dst] \rightarrow obuf[ibuf[i].dst] := ibuf[i];\ full[ibuf[i].dst] := true;$
      $Snd(i)$: $full[i] \rightarrow P2M[i](obuf[i]);\ full[i] := false;$
   init $full := false;$
   exec **do** $[\ \|\ 0 \leq i \leq n\text{-}1:\ (Rec(i)\ ;\ Mov(i))\ \|\ Snd(i)]$ **od**
$]|$

5   Implementing Data Transfers

In this section, we show how the move action $Mov(i)$ of the still generic platform model $\mathcal{P}^1$ is further refined into a set of pipelined actions conforming to a specific communication platform, a *pipelined bus*, which can be regarded as an extreme simplification of a switching network and which will be used as the example platform. Below, the pipelined bus architecture is briefly presented in Section 5.1, and refinement of the platform model $\mathcal{P}^1$ is then discussed in Section 5.2.

5.1   Case Study: Pipelined Bus

The pipelined bus [6], illustrated in Figure 1, is a distributed organization based on self-timed communication both between switches and between a switch and its host element. The pipelined bus can be simultaneously accessed by all the attached processing elements. This is because the control is evenly distributed among the asynchronously operating switches which buffer the data flow dividing the transfer medium into segments which can transfer data simultaneously. Furthermore, a segment between adjacent switches is capable to concurrent transactions to both directions. Hence, the whole system acts as a self-timed bidirectional pipeline providing a platform for modular construction of high-performance systems.

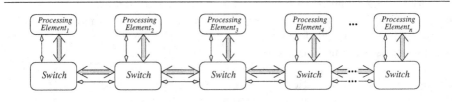

Fig. 1. Pipelined bus architecture

5.2   Introducing Shift Actions

To refine the platform model $\mathcal{P}^1$ of Section 4 towards a pipelined bus platform model, two local array variables of the type *datagram* are first introduced: $rbuf[0..n-1]$ (right buffer) and $lbuf[0..n-1]$ (left buffer). They are used to shift data respectively to the right and to the left from a source host i to a destination host j. A data item stored in the input buffer position $ibuf[i]$ by the source host i is first copied to the right buffer position $rbuf[i]$, if $j > i$, or to the left buffer position $lbuf[i]$, if $j < i$. Then it is shifted step by step towards its destination until the position $rbuf[j]$ or $lbuf[j]$ is reached. Finally, the shifted data item is copied to the output buffer position $obuf[j]$ from which it is further passed to the destination host j completing the transfer. A right shift event copies the contents of a buffer position $rbuf[k]$ to the position $rbuf[k+1]$ ($i \leq k \leq j-1$), while a left shift event copies the contents of $lbuf[k]$ to $lbuf[k-1]$ ($i \geq k \geq j+1$).

The first step is to refine the action $Mov(i)$ of the model $\mathcal{P}^1$ into $Mov'(i)$, an atomic sequence of an insert action $Ins(i)$, a number of right shift actions $RShift(k)$ and left shift actions $LShift(k)$, and a remove action $Rem(j)$ where $j = ibuf[i].dst$: $Mov(i) \leq Mov'(i)$, where

$$Mov'(i) \cong (Ins(i); (\; [; \; i \leq k \leq j-1: RShift(k)] \; [\!] \; [; \; i \geq k \geq j+1: LShift(k)]); Rem(j))$$

Then, to enable parallel execution of the subactions of $Mov'(i)$ in a pipelined manner, the atomicity of $Mov'(i)$ is broken, and the subactions are placed as separate atomic entities into the system's **do-od**-loop. The resulting refined platform model $\mathcal{P}^2$ is as follows:

```
sys P² (exp M2P [0..n-1], imp P2M [0..n-1]) [n : natural] ::
|[ var rbuf [0..n − 1], lbuf [0..n − 1], ibuf [0..n − 1], obuf [0..n − 1] : datagram;
     fr [0..n − 1], fl [0..n − 1] : boolean;
   proc M2P [i](val a : datagram) : (ibuf [i] := a);
   actions
     Rec (i) : await M2P [i];
     Ins (i) : (ibuf [i].dst > i ∧ ¬fr [i] → rbuf [i], fr [i] := ibuf [i], true
             [] ibuf [i].dst < i ∧ ¬fl [i] → lbuf [i], fl [i] := ibuf [i], true);
     RShift (i) : fr [i] ∧ ¬fr [i+1] ∧ rbuf [i].dst ≠ i →
                 rbuf [i+1], fr [i], fr [i+1] := rbuf [i], false, true;
     LShift (i) : fl [i] ∧ ¬fl [i−1] ∧ lbuf [i].dst ≠ i →
                 lbuf [i−1], fl [i], fl [i−1] := lbuf [i], false, true;
     Rem (i) : (rbuf [i].dst = i ∧ fr [i] → obuf [i], fr [i] := rbuf [i], false
             [] lbuf [i].dst = i ∧ fl [i] → obuf [i], fl [i] := lbuf [i], false);
     Snd (i) : P2M [i](obuf [i]);
   init fr, fl := false;
   exec  do [ [] 0 ≤ i ≤ n-1: (Rec (i) ; Ins (i)) [] (Rem (i) ; Snd (i))]
           [] [ [] 0 ≤ i ≤ n-2 : RShift (i)] [ [] 1 ≤ i ≤ n-1 : LShift (i)] od
]|
```

The action $Ins(i)$ copies the data item stored in the input buffer to either the left or right shift buffer depending on the destination address. The shifting from a source i to a destination j is carried out by either the actions $RShift(k)$, where $i \leq k \leq j-1$, or $LShift(k)$, where $i \geq k \geq j+1$. The action $Rem(j)$ removes the shifted data from the pipeline copying it from the shift buffer to the output buffer. The new local boolean arrays $fr[0..n-1]$ and $fl[0..n-1]$, initialized to *false*, act as flags indicating whether a position k in the right or left buffer is empty ($fr[k], fl[k] = false$) or full ($fr[k], fl[k] = true$). Their role is to sequence the execution of the right and left shift actions in an appropriate way.

Notice that the old flag $full[i]$ in the previous model $\mathcal{P}^1$, indicating the status of the output buffer position i, has been replaced in $\mathcal{P}^2$ with a non-atomic sequential composition between the actions $Rem(i)$ and $Snd(i)$. This simplification is possible, because in $\mathcal{P}^2$ a send operation can be enabled by the corresponding unique remove operation only.

The right shift actions are indexed from 0 upto $n-2$ and the left shift actions from $n-1$ downto 1. This is because at the right end of the pipeline (position $n-1$) a right shift is not possible, and correspondingly at the left end (position 0) a left shift cannot be carried out. By analyzing $\mathcal{P}^2$ the following conclusions on potential concurrency (independency) of the new actions can be drawn:

- $Ins\,(i)$ can be parallel with $RShift\,(j)$, where $0 \leq i \leq n-1$ and $0 \leq j \leq n-2$, except when $i = 0 \wedge j = 0$. Correspondingly, $Ins\,(i)$ can be parallel with $LShift\,(j)$, where $0 \leq i \leq n-1$ and $1 \leq j \leq n-1$, except when $i = n-1 \wedge j = n-1$.
- $RShift\,(i)$ can be parallel with $LShift\,(j)$, where $0 \leq i \leq n-2$ and $1 \leq j \leq n-1$.
- $RShift\,(i)$ can be parallel with $RShift\,(j)$, where $0 \leq i \leq n-2$ and $0 \leq j \leq i-2$ or $i+2 \leq j \leq n-2$. Correspondingly, $LShift\,(i)$ can be parallel with $LShift\,(j)$, where $1 \leq i \leq n-1$ and $1 \leq j \leq i-2$ or $i+2 \leq j \leq n-1$.
- $Rem\,(i)$ can be parallel with $RShift\,(j)$, where $0 \leq i \leq n-1$ and $0 \leq j \leq n-2$, except when $i = n-1 \wedge j = n-2$. Correspondingly, $Rem\,(i)$ can be parallel with $LShift\,(j)$, where $0 \leq i \leq n-1$ and $1 \leq j \leq n-1$, except when $i = 0 \wedge j = 1$.
- $Rem\,(i)$ can be parallel with $Ins\,(j)$, where $0 \leq i, j \leq n-1$.
- $Rem\,(i)\,(Ins\,(i))$ can be parallel with $Rem\,(j)\,(Ins\,(j))$, where $i \neq j$.

Hence, several datagrams can concurrently propagate in $\mathcal{P}^2$ from different sources towards different destinations in a pipelined fashion. To be able to conclude that the refinement $\mathcal{P}^1 \leq \mathcal{P}^2$ is valid, a number of fairness assumptions needs to be made, just like in the previous refinement presented in Section 4:

- Selection between simultaneously enabled right and left shift actions $RShift\,(i)$ and $LShift\,(j)$, for all possible i and j, is considered weakly fair.
- Selection between simultaneously enabled remove actions $Rem\,(i)$ and $Rem\,(j)$, for $i \neq j$, is considered weakly fair.
- Selection between an insert action $Ins\,(i)$ and the right (left) shift action $RShift\,(i-1)$ $(LShift\,(i+1))$, which can be simultaneously enabled and can temporarily disable each other, is considered strongly fair.
- Selection between the two components of a remove action $Rem\,(i)$ is considered strongly fair when they are simultaneously enabled, i.e., when both $rbuf\,[i]$ and $lbuf\,[i]$ contain data heading towards the host i.

These fairness assumptions guarantee that every initiated non-atomic move operation in the refined platform model $\mathcal{P}^2$ will eventually be completed.

6   Extracting Switches

The next step is to develop the platform model $\mathcal{P}^2$ into a parallel composition of n subsystem instances modeling the *switches* or *transfer stages* of the pipelined bus (see Figures 1 and 2). Each stage will be connected to one of the n hosts. This decomposition operation includes introduction of new local procedures for inter-stage communication and dividing the global and local identifiers (procedures, variables, actions) into groups from which the subsystem instances are created. Only spatial decomposition is carried out — the functionality of the system is not enhanced by the refinement, i.e., the degree of atomicity and thereby the degree of parallelism remains actually the same as before.

6.1   Generic Decomposition Step

Let us first study a decomposition step considering a simple generic system module $\mathcal{M}$ of the form

$$\begin{aligned}
&\textbf{sys } \mathcal{M} \ (E_A, E_B) :: \\
&|[\ \textbf{var } v_A, v_B; \\
&\quad \textbf{actions} \\
&\quad\quad AB \ : \ (A_1; \ B; \ A_2); \\
&\quad\quad O_A; \ O_B; \\
&\quad\quad \textbf{init } v_A, v_B := v_A0, v_B0; \\
&\quad\quad \textbf{exec do } AB \ [\!] \ O_A \ [\!] \ O_B \ \textbf{od} \\
&\ ]|
\end{aligned}$$

where the action AB consists of the subactions $A_{1,2}$ and B such that the subactions $A_{1,2}$ access only the variables v_A, while the subaction B reads the variables v_A but writes onto the variables v_B. The variables v_A and v_B are distinct: $v_A \cap v_B = \emptyset$. The symbolic procedures E_A and E_B model the interface to the environment accessing the variables v_A and v_B, respectively. O_A and O_B denote those actions of $\mathcal{M}$ that exclusively access the variables v_A and v_B, respectively.

Decomposition of $\mathcal{M}$ is based on procedurizing the subaction B of AB. This new local procedure, which will act as a communication channel between the eventual subsystems, is here called $A2B$. As the result, we obtain the system $\mathcal{M}'$ given below. The refinement $\mathcal{M} \le \mathcal{M}'$ is quite straightforward containing the simple action-level transformation $AB \le (A \ [\!] \ W)$. Atomicity is preserved, and other actions are kept intact.

Notice that the actions in the **exec**-clause of $\mathcal{M}'$ are grouped to reflect the division between two subsystem instances that will be created as the next transformation step. Hence, by first renaming the identifiers $a \in \{v_A, A, O_A\}$ to $I_A.a$ and the identifiers $b \in \{v_B, W, O_B\}$ to $I_B.b$, and then using the definition of the parallel composition of subsystems (Section 2), we refine $\mathcal{M}' \le \mathcal{M}''$, where the new system $\mathcal{M}''$ and its components $\mathcal{A}$ and $\mathcal{B}$ are given below.

$$\begin{aligned}
&\textbf{sys } \mathcal{M}' \ (E_A, E_B) :: \\
&|[\ \textbf{var } v_A, v_B; \\
&\quad \textbf{proc } A2B(\textbf{val } x : data) : (B[x/v_A]); \\
&\quad \textbf{actions} \\
&\quad\quad A \ : \ (A_1; \ A2B(v_A); \ A_2); \\
&\quad\quad W \ : \ \textbf{await } A2B; \\
&\quad\quad O_A \ ; \ O_B; \\
&\quad\quad \textbf{init } v_A, v_B := v_A0, v_B0; \\
&\quad\quad \textbf{exec do } (A \ [\!] \ O_A) \ [\!] \ (W \ [\!] \ O_B) \ \textbf{od} \\
&\ ]|
\end{aligned}$$

$$\begin{aligned}
&\textbf{sys } \mathcal{M}'' \ (E_A, E_B) :: \\
&|[\ \textbf{proc } A2B(\textbf{val } data); \\
&\quad \textbf{subsys} \\
&\quad\quad I_A \ : \ \mathcal{A}(E_A, A2B); \\
&\quad\quad I_B \ : \ \mathcal{B}(E_B, A2B); \\
&\quad\quad \textbf{exec } \ I_A \ \| \ I_B \\
&\ ]|
\end{aligned}$$

$$\begin{aligned}
&\textbf{sys } \mathcal{A} \ (E_A^f; \ \textbf{imp } A2B^f) :: \\
&|[\ \textbf{var } v_A; \\
&\quad \textbf{actions} \\
&\quad\quad A \ : \ (A_1; \ A2B^f(v_A); \ A_2); \\
&\quad\quad O_A[E_A^f/E_A]; \\
&\quad\quad \textbf{init } v_A := v_A0; \\
&\quad\quad \textbf{exec do } A \ [\!] \ O_A \ \textbf{od} \\
&\ ]|
\end{aligned}$$

$$\begin{aligned}
&\textbf{sys } \mathcal{B} \ (E_B^f; \ \textbf{exp } A2B^f) :: \\
&|[\ \textbf{var } v_B; \\
&\quad \textbf{proc } A2B^f(\textbf{val } x : data) : (B[x/v_A]); \\
&\quad \textbf{actions} \\
&\quad\quad W \ : \ \textbf{await } A2B^f; \\
&\quad\quad O_B[E_B^f/E_B]; \\
&\quad\quad \textbf{init } v_B := v_B0; \\
&\quad\quad \textbf{exec do } W \ [\!] \ O_B \ \textbf{od} \\
&\ ]|
\end{aligned}$$

The subsystem instances I_A (component $\mathcal{A}$) and I_B (component $\mathcal{B}$) communicate atomically via the procedure $A2B$ which transfers data from I_A to I_B. To exemplify instantiation of subsystems, formal names, indicated by a superscript 'f', are used for the interface procedures of the above component systems $\mathcal{A}$ and

$\mathcal{B}$. These formal names are then replaced with the actual names in the **subsys**-clause of $\mathcal{M}''$. For the instance I_A we have the mapping $[E_A, A2B / E_A^f, A2B^f]$, and for the instance I_B we have the mapping $[E_B, A2B / E_B^f, A2B^f]$.

6.2 Decomposition of the Platform Model

The decomposition operation discussed above is now applied to the platform model $\mathcal{P}^2$ of Section 5.2. First, the shift operations performed by the actions $RShift(i)$ and $LShift(i)$ are procedurized by refining: $RShift(i) \leq (RFwd(i) \,\|\, RRec(i+1))$ and $LShift(i) \leq (LFwd(i) \,\|\, LRec(i-1))$, where

$$RFwd(i) \triangleq rbuf[i].dst \neq i \wedge fr[i] \rightarrow R[i+1](rbuf[i]); fr[i] := false$$
$$LFwd(i) \triangleq lbuf[i].dst \neq i \wedge fl[i] \rightarrow L[i-1](lbuf[i]); fl[i] := false$$
$$RRec(i+1) \triangleq \textbf{await } R[i+1] \quad , \quad LRec(i-1) \triangleq \textbf{await } L[i-1]$$

The new local procedures $R[i]$, where $1 \leq i \leq n-1$, and $L[i]$, where $0 \leq i \leq n-2$, are used to forward data right and left on the buffer arrays $rbuf$ and $lbuf$, respectively. By calling $R[i]$ ($L[i]$) the contents of $rbuf[i-1]$ ($lbuf[i+1]$) is copied to $rbuf[i]$ ($lbuf[i]$). The procedures $R[i]$ and $L[i]$ will act as communication channels between the platform's switches and are defined by

$$\textbf{proc } R[i](\textbf{val } a : datagram) : (\neg fr[i] \rightarrow rbuf[i], fr[i] := a, true);$$
$$\textbf{proc } L[i](\textbf{val } a : datagram) : (\neg fl[i] \rightarrow lbuf[i], fl[i] := a, true);$$

By introducing the above procedures, the flat platform model $\mathcal{P}^2$ can be transformed into a hierarchical model $\mathcal{P}^3$ (see Figure 2) by refining $\mathcal{P}^2 \leq \mathcal{P}^3$.

```
sys P³ (exp M2P[0..n-1], imp P2M[0..n-1]) [n : natural] ::
|[ proc R[1..n-1] (val datagram), L[0..n-2] (val datagram);
    subsys
        Stage(0) : Tl (M2P[0], L[0], P2M[0], R[1]);
        Stage(i) : T (M2P[i], R[i], L[i], P2M[i], R[i+1], L[i-1])[i];
        Stage(n-1) : Tr (M2P[n-1], R[n-1], P2M[n-1], L[n-2]);
        exec  Stage(0) ‖ [‖ 1 ≤ i ≤ n-2: Stage(i)] ‖ Stage(n-1)
    ]|
```

Here the component $\mathcal{T}$, the switch model for $1 \leq i \leq n-1$, is defined by

```
sys T (exp M2P, RR, LR; imp P2M, RS, LS) [i : natural] ::
|[ var rbuf, lbuf, obuf, ibuf : datagram;  fr, fl : boolean;
    proc
        M2P(val a : datagram) : (ibuf := a);
        RR (val a : datagram) : (¬fr → rbuf, fr := a, true);
        LR (val a : datagram) : (¬fl → lbuf, fl := a, true);
    actions
        Rec  : await M2P;  RRec : await RR;  LRec : await LR;
        Ins  : (ibuf.dst > i ∧ ¬fr → rbuf, fr := ibuf, true
                ‖ ibuf.dst < i ∧ ¬fl →  lbuf, fl := ibuf, true);
        RFwd : rbuf.dst ≠ i ∧ fr → RS(rbuf); fr := false;
        LFwd : lbuf.dst ≠ i ∧ fl → LS(lbuf); fl := false;
        Rem : (rbuf.dst = i ∧ fr → obuf, fr := rbuf, false
                ‖ lbuf.dst = i ∧ fl → obuf, fl := lbuf, false);
        Snd  : P2M(obuf);
    init fr, fl := false;
    exec do (Rec ; Ins) ‖ RRec ‖ LRec ‖ RFwd ‖ LFwd ‖ (Rem ; Snd) od
    ]|
```

In $\mathcal{T}$, the formal interface procedures RR (receives right-moving data) and LS (sends left-moving data) correspond to the actual interface procedures $R[i]$ and $L[i-1]$ of the switch instance $Stage(i)$ in $\mathcal{P}^3$, modeling the interface to the left-hand-side neighboring switch instance $Stage(i-1)$. The formal interface procedures LR (receives left-moving data) and RS (sends right-moving data), in turn, correspond to the actual interface procedures $L[i]$ and $R[i+1]$ of $Stage(i)$, modeling the interface to the right-hand-side neighboring switch $Stage(i+1)$. Observe that the identification number or address of the stage, i, is specified as a generic parameter of the component $\mathcal{T}$.

For $i = 0$ and $i = n-1$ the transfer stage models are simpler than the above general model $\mathcal{T}$ for $1 \leq i \leq n-2$. This is because in the left-end stage $(i = 0)$ there is no left-hand-side interface, and, correspondingly, in the right-end stage $(i = n-1)$ there is no right-hand-side interface. The left-end stage model $\mathcal{T}l$ is obtained from $\mathcal{T}$ by removing the actions $RRec$ and $LFwd$ and the corresponding interface procedures RR and LS. Similarly, the right-end stage model $\mathcal{T}r$ is obtained from $\mathcal{T}$ by removing the actions $LRec$ and $RFwd$ and the interface procedures LR and RS.

Notice that the local array variables $v[i]$ of the previous platform model $\mathcal{P}^2$, where $v \in \{ibuf, obuf, rbuf, lbuf, fr, fl\}$ and $0 \leq i \leq n-1$, are replaced in $\mathcal{P}^3$ with the unique instance-specific variables $Stage(i).v$, where v are now local variables of each subsystem component $\mathcal{T}$, $\mathcal{T}l$, or $\mathcal{T}r$. The same applies to any indexed action name $A(i)$: it is renamed to $Stage(i).A$ in the new platform model $\mathcal{P}^3$.

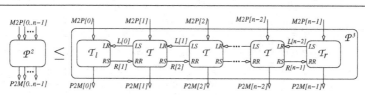

Fig. 2. Refining $\mathcal{P}^2$ into $\mathcal{P}^3$

7   Refinement of the Switches

The decomposition process is completed by developing the switch (transfer stage) model $\mathcal{T}$ into a parallel composition of three distinct subsystems (see Figure 3). One of them acts as the stage's *interface module* being responsible of data exchange with the attached host module via the interface procedures $M2P$ and $P2M$. The two others, the *right* and *left repeaters*, take care of forwarding data to the neighboring stages in the opposite directions and, by communicating with the interface module, receiving and removing data to and from the pipelined communication platform. The refinement does not increase parallelism of the system but focuses only on increasing modularity by spatial decomposition.

The transformation is started by procedurizing the buffer update operations carried out by the insert action Ins (updates $rbuf$ and $lbuf$) and remove action Rem (updates $obuf$) of the transfer stage model $\mathcal{T}$. The following action-level refinements are performed:

$$(Rec \; ; \; Ins) \; \leq \; ((Rec \; ; \; Ins') \; \| \; IRRec \; \| \; ILRec)$$
$$(Rem \; ; \; Snd) \; \leq \; (RRem \; \| \; LRem \; \| \; (ORec \; ; \; Snd))$$

where

$$
\begin{array}{ll}
Ins' & \cong (ibuf.dst > i \rightarrow IPR\,(ibuf) \;[\!]\; ibuf.dst < i \rightarrow IPL\,(ibuf)) \\
IRRec, ILRec & \cong \textbf{await } IPR\,, \textbf{await } IPL \\
RRem & \cong rbuf.dst = i \wedge fr \rightarrow OPR\,(rbuf); \; fr := false \\
LRem & \cong lbuf.dst = i \wedge fl \rightarrow OPL\,(lbuf); \; fl := false \\
ORec & \cong (\textbf{await } OPR \;[\!]\; \textbf{await } OPL)
\end{array}
$$

where the introduced local procedures IPR ("input to right"), IPL ("input to left"), OPR ("output from right"), and OPL, ("output from left") which will be used as communication channels between the interface module and the two repeaters, are specified as

$$
\begin{array}{l}
\textbf{proc } IPR\,(\textbf{val } a : datagram) : (\neg fr \rightarrow rbuf, fr := a, true) \\
\textbf{proc } IPL\,(\textbf{val } a : datagram) : (\neg fl \rightarrow lbuf, fl := a, true) \\
\textbf{proc } OPR\,(\textbf{val } a : datagram) : (obuf := a) \\
\textbf{proc } OPL\,(\textbf{val } a : datagram) : (obuf := a)
\end{array}
$$

By analyzing the created new actions and the unchanged actions of $\mathcal{T}$, we can conclude that the boolean flags fr and fl can be replaced with non-atomic sequential compositions by further refining:

$$
(RRec \;[\!]\; IRRec \;[\!]\; RFwd \;[\!]\; RRem) \le ((RRec' \;[\!]\; IRRec')\,;\,(RFwd' \;[\!]\; RRem'))
$$
$$
(LRec \;[\!]\; ILRec \;[\!]\; LFwd \;[\!]\; LRem) \le ((LRec' \;[\!]\; ILRec')\,;\,(LFwd' \;[\!]\; LRem'))
$$

where the primed actions are obtained by straightforwardly removing the boolean variables fr and fl from the corresponding unprimed actions or from the procedures referenced by the unprimed actions. For example:

$$
\begin{array}{l}
RRem' \cong rbuf.dst = i \rightarrow OPR\,(rbuf) \\
IRRec' \cong \textbf{await } IPR'\,, \; \text{where: } \textbf{proc } IPR'(\textbf{val } a) : (rbuf := a)
\end{array}
$$

After the above preparatory refinements, we can decompose the switch model into a composition of an interface unit and two independent instances of a single repeater component. To summarize, we have the overall refinement $\mathcal{T} \le \mathcal{T}^1$, where the decomposed switch model $\mathcal{T}^1$, as shown in Figure 3, is defined by

```
sys T¹ (exp M2P, RR, LR;  imp P2M, RS, LS)[i : natural] ::
|[ proc IPR (val datagram), IPL (val datagram),
        OPR (val datagram), OPL (val datagram);
     subsys
        RepeaterR : R(RR, IPR, RS, OPR)[i];
        RepeaterL : R(LR, IPL, LS, OPL)[i];
        Interface  : I(M2P, OPR, OPL, P2M, IPR, IPL)[i];
     exec  RepeaterR || RepeaterL || Interface
  ]|
```

where the interface module $\mathcal{I}$ and the repeater module $\mathcal{R}$ are given as

```
sys I (exp M2P, OPR, OPL ;
       imp P2M, IPR, IPL) [i : natural] ::
var obuf, ibuf : datagram;
|[ proc
     M2P (val a : datagram) : (ibuf := a);
     OPR (val a : datagram) : (obuf := a);
     OPL (val a : datagram) : (obuf := a);
   actions
     Rec  : await M2P;
     Ins  : (ibuf.dst > i → IPR (ibuf)
             [] ibuf.dst < i → IPL (ibuf));
     ORec : (await OPR [] await OPL);
     Snd  : P2M (obuf);
     exec do (Rec ; Ins) [] (ORec ; Snd) od
  ]|
```

```
sys R (exp PRV, IP ;  imp NXT, OP)
       [i : natural] ::
|[ var buf : datagram;
   proc
     PRV (val  a : datagram) : (buf := a);
     IP (val  a : datagram) : (buf := a);
   actions
     Rec : await PRV ;  IRec : await IP;
     Fwd : buf.dst ≠ i → NXT (buf);
     Rem : buf.dst = i → OP (buf);
     exec do (Rec [] IRec) ; (Fwd [] Rem) od
  ]|
```

In the repeater component $\mathcal{R}$, the formal interface procedures PRV ("previous") and NXT ("next") represent the interfaces to the corresponding repeaters in the two neighboring transfer stages, and the procedures IP ("input") and OP ("output") model the communication channels between the repeater and the stage's own interface module. In the right repeater instance $RepeaterR$, the procedures PRV, NXT, IP, and OP correspond to, respectively, the procedures RR, RS, IPR, and OPR of the transfer stage model $\mathcal{T}^1$. In the left repeater instance $RepeaterL$, they correspond to, respectively, the procedures LR, LS, IPL, and OPL of $\mathcal{T}^1$. Furthermore, the actions Rec, $IRec$, Fwd, and Rem of $\mathcal{R}$ correspond to, respectively, the above mentioned actions $RRec'$, $IRRec'$, $RFwd'$ and $RRem'$ in the case of the right repeater, and $LRec'$, $ILRec'$, $LFwd'$ and $LRem'$ in the case of the left repeater. The local variable buf of $\mathcal{R}$, in turn, corresponds to the variable $rbuf$ or $lbuf$ of the original transfer stage model $\mathcal{T}$.

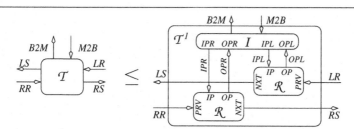

Fig. 3. Refinement of $\mathcal{T}$ into $\mathcal{T}^1$

8   Conclusion

A formal approach, based on the Action Systems formalism, to model and refine an on-chip communication platform was presented. The considered transformation steps included pipelining of data transfers and spatial decomposition of system models. Communication between components was modelled by remote procedure calls, for which a novel notation was introduced. We will continue the work by focusing on refinement of procedure based communication channels into concrete variable based channels and transformation of refined Action Systems models into signal transition graph (STG) models which can be automatically synthesized into gate-level circuit netlists.

References

1. R. Back and K. Sere. "From Action Systems to Modular Systems." *Software — Concepts and Tools*, 17, p. 26-39, Springer-Verlag, 1996.
2. R. Back and J. von Wright. Refinement Calculus: A Systematic Introduction. Springer-Verlag. April 1998.
3. H. Bakoglu. *Circuits, Interconnections, and Packaging for VLSI*. Addison-Wesley, 1990.

4. W. Dally and J. Poulton. *Digital System Engineering*. Cambridge University Press, 1998.
5. E. Dijkstra. *A Discipline of Programming*. Prentice Hall Series in Automatic Computation, Prentice Hall, 1976.
6. P. Liljeberg, J. Plosila and J. Isoaho. "Self-Timed communication platform for implementing high-performance system-on-chip" in *VLSI Journal of Integration*, Elsevier, Volume 38, Issue 1, pages 43-67, October 2004.

Finding Bugs in Network Protocols Using Simulation Code and Protocol-Specific Heuristics

Ahmed Sobeih, Mahesh Viswanathan, Darko Marinov, and Jennifer C. Hou

Department of Computer Science,
University of Illinois at Urbana-Champaign, Urbana, IL 61801, USA
{sobeih, vmahesh, marinov, jhou}@uiuc.edu

Abstract. Traditional network simulators perform well in evaluating the performance of network protocols but lack the capability of verifying the correctness of protocols. To address this problem, we have extended the J-Sim network simulator with a model checking capability that explores the state space of a network protocol to find an execution that violates a safety invariant. In this paper, we demonstrate the usefulness of this integrated tool for verification and performance evaluation by analyzing two widely used and important network protocols: AODV and directed diffusion. Our analysis discovered a previously unknown bug in the J-Sim implementation of AODV. More importantly, we also discovered a serious deficiency in directed diffusion. To enable the analysis of these fairly complex protocols, we needed to develop protocol-specific search heuristics that guide state-space exploration. We report our findings on discovering *good* search heuristics to analyze network protocols similar to AODV and directed diffusion.

1 Introduction

Network simulators have been used for decades to provide an environment for a protocol designer to build a prototype of a network protocol and evaluate its performance. One major deficiency of traditional network simulators, however, is that they only evaluate the performance of network protocols in scenarios provided by the designer but can *not* exhaustively analyze possible scenarios for correctness. For example, a network simulator can evaluate the performance of a routing protocol but cannot check whether this protocol may suffer from routing loops. If the error cases do not appear (and hence cannot be investigated) in the scenarios studied, subtle errors in the protocol specification/implementation may not be identified in the simulation. These errors may then eventually manifest themselves after the protocol has been implemented and deployed. In the light of recent research [1] that creates a physical implementation of a protocol from the existing simulation code, without modification, this seems to be highly likely. Therefore, building an integrated tool that allows a network protocol designer to *both* verify a prototype *and* evaluate its performance is an important task.

K.-K. Lau and R. Banach (Eds.): ICFEM 2005, LNCS 3785, pp. 235–250, 2005.

Design of special-purpose model checkers for network simulator code enjoys several benefits over using general-purpose verification tools. First, it saves the protocol designer the task of building a special-purpose model of the protocol for verification and a separate model for performance analysis. Since building a formal model of a protocol is an onerous, time-consuming and error-prone task, by designing special-purpose model checkers for network simulator code, we not only ensure that verifying a protocol is easier for the designer but also ensure that the model being verified is consistent with the implementation. Second, using a model checker for C or Java (like [2,3,4,5,6,7]) to verify the protocol code *along* with the simulator code might likely be intractable due to the complexity of the general-purpose simulator code.

We have built a tool that extends J-Sim [8]—a component-based network simulator written entirely in Java—with the model checking [9] capability to explore the state space created by a network protocol up to a (configurable) maximum depth in order to find violations of a safety property (e.g., the absence of routing loops). We previously provided a proof-of-concept case study [10] in which we used our tool to model-check an automatic repeat request (ARQ) protocol. In this paper, we demonstrate the usefulness and effectiveness of our tool in analyzing much more complicated protocol code. We examine two widely used and fairly complex network protocols: the Ad-Hoc On-Demand Distance Vector (AODV) routing protocol [11,12] for wireless ad hoc networks and the directed diffusion protocol [13] for wireless sensor networks. These are reasonably complex protocols whose J-Sim implementations (not including the J-Sim library) have about 1200 and 1400 lines of code, respectively. Our choice of AODV and directed diffusion was motivated by their potential to become representative routing and data dissemination protocols, respectively, in ad hoc networks and sensor networks. We investigate whether these protocols satisfy the *loop-free* safety property, i.e., data packets are not routed through loops.

Our surprising discoveries illustrate the practical importance of our tool. First, we find a previously unknown bug in the J-Sim implementation of AODV. This shows that even if the protocol specification [12] is correct, the simulator code could have bugs that may eventually find their way to the deployed implementation. Second, we identify a serious deficiency in the directed diffusion protocol [13] not only in its J-Sim implementation. Specifically, our tool produces scenarios leading to corruption of data caches due to timeouts and/or node reboots in a sensor network. This deficiency would result in data packets being routed in a loop.

To analyze such large protocol implementations, we have developed search heuristics that better guide the model checker to discover bugs. Specifically, we develop best-first search (BeFS) strategies that exploit *properties inherent to the network protocol and the safety property being checked*. An interesting and important research question is how to determine a suitable BeFS strategy for a specific network protocol. In this paper, we make an attempt towards answering this question by studying the performance of several BeFS strategies for both AODV and directed diffusion. Unlike [3,14,15,16], we found that the strategies need to explicitly make use of *both* protocol-specific characteristics *and* the property being verified in order to be successful. The results show that using good protocol-specific heuristics outperforms standard breadth-first search (BFS) and depth-first search (DFS) strategies.

In this paper, we make the following contributions. First, we demonstrate the ability of our tool to find bugs in complex network protocols with large simulation code. Second, we discover a previously unknown deficiency in directed diffusion. Third, we report our findings on discovering *good* protocol-specific heuristics to analyze network protocols similar to AODV and directed diffusion.

The rest of the paper is organized as follows. In Section 2, we give an overview of the model checking framework in J-Sim, and in Section 3, we present our performance results. In Section 4, we discuss related work. Finally, we conclude the paper in Section 5 with a list of future research work.

2   The Model Checking Framework

The model checker, that we incorporated into J-Sim, is an explicit-state model checker [9] that checks a network protocol by executing the J-Sim simulation code of that network protocol *directly* and exploring the state space on-the-fly until either a counterexample disproving a safety property is found or the state space is explored up to a maximum depth (MAX_DEPTH). In order to explore the state space created by a network protocol, the notion of the "state" has to be adequately defined. To this end, the model checker makes use of the *GlobalState* class. A state is an instance of *GlobalState*. The model checking procedure modelCheck, shown in Figure 1, keeps track of three instances of *GlobalState*; namely, *initialState* (the initial state of the network protocol), *currentState* (the current state being explored) and *nextState* (one of the possible successors of the current state). As shown in Figure 1, the two major data structures are *NonVisitedStates* (which stores the states that have not yet been visited) and *AlreadyVisitedStates* (which stores the states that have already been visited). Figure 1 presents a stateful search that avoids visiting a state if another equivalent state has already been visited before (i.e., a state that already exists in *AlreadyVisitedStates*). *AlreadyVisitedStates* stores concrete states, and two states s_1 and s_2 are considered equivalent if $s_1.equals(s_2)$ returns true.

In each state in the state space, some transitions (i.e., events) may or may not be enabled, and an enabled transition may generate multiple successor states. For instance, a packet arrival event may generate multiple successor states. This is because if the network contains two packets m_1 and m_2 whose destination is node n, two successor states can be generated depending on whether node n receives m_1 first and then m_2 or receives m_2 first and then m_1. In modelCheck, the enabling function (Figure 1, line 9) returns the number of possible successor states (zero if the event is disabled). For each state being explored (*currentState*), modelCheck generates all the possible successor states (*nextState*) by executing the event handlers of the events that are enabled in *currentState*. However, since an event handler is only invoked from modelCheck but actually executed inside

```
procedure modelCheck()
 1. AlreadyVisitedStates = { } ;
 2. NonVisitedStates = { initialState } ;
 3. while ( | NonVisitedStates | > 0 ) {
 4.    currentState = NonVisitedStates.remove() ;
 5.    if ( currentState does not exist in AlreadyVisitedStates ) {
 6.        AlreadyVisitedStates = AlreadyVisitedStates ∪ { currentState } ;
 7.        for ( all protocol entities p ) { /* for all protocol entities */
 8.            for ( all possible events e ) { /* for all events */
 9.                NumberOfNextStates = e.EnablingFunction(p) ;
10.                for ( int i = 0 ; i < NumberOfNextStates ; i++ ) {
11.                    CopyFromModelToEntities(currentState) ;
12.                    nextState = currentState ;   /* Start with nextState equal to currentState */
13.                    nextState.depth += 1 ;   /* Increment the depth of nextState */
14.                    e.EventHandler(p) ;   /* Invoke e's event handler */
15.                    CopyFromEntitiesToModel(nextState) ;
16.                    if (nextState does not exist in AlreadyVisitedStates) {
17.                        if ( nextState.verifySafety() == false ) {
18.                            printPath(nextState) ; exit ;
                            } /* end if safety property is violated at nextState */
19.                        else if ( nextState.depth < MAX_DEPTH )
20.                            NonVisitedStates = NonVisitedStates ∪ { nextState } ; } } } } } }
```

Fig. 1. Stateful model checking procedure

the protocol entities (i.e., the classes that implement the network protocol being model-checked) themselves, modelCheck must first restore the state of the protocol entities to the state reflected in *currentState* before the execution of the event handler. This is achieved by the *CopyFromModelToEntities()* function call (line 11). After the execution of the event handler (line 14), the *CopyFromEntitiesToModel()* function is called (line 15) to extract the new state information from the protocol entities and copy them to *nextState*. If *nextState* has not been visited before (line 16), modelCheck then checks whether *nextState* violates a safety property (line 17). (The network protocol designer specifies the safety property that needs to be checked as a Java method whose output is true/false.) If so, a counterexample is printed by calling the *printPath()* function (line 18); otherwise, *nextState* is added to *NonVisitedStates* (line 20) in order to be explored later if its depth is strictly less than MAX_DEPTH. Adding a state to *NonVisitedStates* (line 20) or *AlreadyVisitedStates* (line 6) needs a function that creates a copy of a state (e.g., *clone()*).

It should be mentioned that the model checking process is not fully automated. To model-check a network protocol, the protocol designer needs to do the following:

1. Provide an implementation of *GlobalState* (including writing the safety property as a Java method, the function *equals*, and a function that creates a copy of a state), and specify how to construct the initial state. To reduce the protocol designer's burden, we provide an implementation of a class, called *SystemState*, that includes the protocol-independent information (e.g., the depth of a state, which event generated the state). *GlobalState*, which can be implemented as a sub-class of *SystemState*, includes the protocol-specific information.

2. Specify (a) the set of events that exist in the network protocol, (b) when each event is enabled, and (c) how each event is handled (i.e., an event handler

that makes a transition from one state to another). Note that the protocol designer has to write the event handlers anyway in order to have a working prototype of the network protocol in J-Sim, even if he/she does not intend to model-check the protocol.

3. Provide implementations for *CopyFromModelToEntities()* and *CopyFromEntitiesToModel()*. To facilitate programming, we make use of *ports* (a feature provided by J-Sim) to provide a seamless interface between components; in this case, between the model checker and the protocol entities [17].

4. (Required only in the case of using a BeFS strategy) Write a Java method that assigns to each state a metric that represents how "good" this state is. The model checking procedure will explore the "best" state first.

3   Evaluation and Results

We applied the model checking framework to the J-Sim implementations of the AODV (Section 3.1) and directed diffusion (Section 3.2) protocols. For each protocol, we give an overview of the key functionality, describe the protocol actions and property being checked, present several BeFS heuristics, discuss detected errors, and show performance results for model checking. We ran all experiments on a Pentium 4 1.6 GHz machine with Microsoft Windows XP 2002 SP2 with 1 GB memory. We used Sun's Java 2 SDK 1.4.2 JVM with 512 MB allocated memory.

3.1   AODV Routing in Multihop Wireless Ad Hoc Networks

Overview of AODV. The implementation of AODV [11] in J-Sim is based on the AODV Draft (version 11) [12]. In AODV, each node n in the ad hoc network maintains a routing table. A routing table entry (RTE), at node n, to a destination node d contains, among other fields: $nexthop_{n,d}$ (the address of the node to which n forwards packets destined for d), $hops_{n,d}$ (the number of hops needed to reach d from n) and $seqno_{n,d}$ (a measure of the freshness of the route information). Each RTE is associated with a lifetime. Periodically, a route timeout event is triggered invalidating (but not deleting) all the RTEs that have not been used (e.g., to send or forward packets to the destination) for a time interval that is greater than the lifetime. Invalidating a RTE involves incrementing $seqno_{n,d}$ and setting $hops_{n,d}$ to ∞.

When a node n requires a route to a destination d, it *broadcasts* a route request (RREQ) packet. When a node receives the RREQ, if it has a fresh enough route to d (or it is d itself), it satisfies the RREQ by *unicasting* a route reply (RREP) packet back to n; otherwise, it rebroadcasts the RREQ. The unicast RREP travels back to n. Each intermediate node along the path of RREP sets up a forward pointer to the node from which the RREP came, thus establishing a forward route to d, and forwards the RREP packet to the next hop towards n. If node m offers node n a new route to d, n compares $seqno_{m,d}$ of the offered route to $seqno_{n,d}$, and accepts the route with the greater sequence number. If the sequence numbers are equal, the offered route is accepted only if $hops_{n,d} > hops_{m,d}$.

Each node maintains two monotonically increasing counters: $seqno_n$ and bid_n. When node n broadcasts a RREQ packet, it includes the current value of bid_n in the RREQ packet and then increments bid_n. Therefore, the pair $< n, bid_n >$ uniquely identifies a RREQ packet. Each node, receiving the RREQ packet from node n, keeps the pair $< n, bid_n >$ in a broadcast ID cache so that it can later check if it has already received a RREQ with the same source address and broadcast ID. Each entry in this cache has a lifetime. Periodically, a broadcast ID timeout event is triggered causing the deletion of entries in the cache that have expired.

Model Checking AODV. We next present the steps that we follow to model-check AODV. These steps constitute a generic methodology for model-checking a network protocol in J-Sim.

(1) Definitions of the global state, the initial state, state equality and safety property: We define *GlobalState* as a tuple that has two components; namely, the protocol state and the network cloud. The protocol state of a node n includes n's routing table, broadcast ID cache, $seqno_n$ and bid_n. The network cloud models the network as an unbounded set that contains AODV packets, and also maintains the neighborhood information. A broadcast AODV packet whose source is node s is modeled as a set of packets, each of which is destined for one of the neighbors (i.e., the nodes that are within the transmission range) of s.

In the initial global state, the network does not contain any packets and the AODV process at each node is initialized as specified by the constructor of the AODV class in J-Sim. Specifically, the AODV process starts with an empty routing table, empty broadcast ID cache, $seqno_n = 2$ and $bid_n = 1$.

Two states, s_1 and s_2, are considered equal if they have the same (unordered) set of AODV packets, the same neighborhood information, and for each node n, s_1 and s_2 have equal corresponding values for $seqno_n$, bid_n, and node n's routing table and broadcast ID cache (each viewed as an unordered set of entries).

An important safety property in a routing protocol such as AODV is the *loop-free* property. Consider two nodes n and m such that m is the next hop of n to some destination d; i.e., $nexthop_{n,d} = m$. The loop-free property can be expressed as follows [18,3]:

$$((seqno_{n,d} < seqno_{m,d}) \vee (seqno_{n,d} == seqno_{m,d} \wedge hops_{n,d} > hops_{m,d}))$$

(2) Events: Next, we specify the set of events, when each event is enabled, and how each event is handled. The events can be listed as follows:

T_0 Initiation of a route request to a destination d: This event is enabled if the node does not have a valid RTE to the destination d. The event is handled by broadcasting a RREQ.

T_1 Delivering an AODV packet to node n: This event is enabled if the network contains at least one AODV packet such that n is the destination (or the next hop towards the destination) of the packet and n is one of the neighbors of the source of the packet. The event is handled by removing this packet from the network and forwarding it to node n.

T_2 Restart of the AODV process at node n: This event may take place because of a node reboot. The event is always enabled and is handled by reinitializing the state of the AODV process at node n.

T_3 Loss of an AODV packet destined for node n: This event is enabled if the network contains at least one AODV packet that is destined for node n. The event is handled by removing this packet from the network.

T_4 Broadcast ID timeout at node n: This event is enabled if there is at least one entry in the broadcast ID cache of node n. The event is handled by deleting this entry.

T_5 Timeout of the route to destination d at node n: This event is enabled if n has a valid RTE to d. The event is handled by invalidating this RTE.

(3) Use of protocol-specific properties to facilitate a BeFS strategy: A suitable BeFS strategy for exploring the state space of AODV can be obtained by inspecting the loop-free property. A node, which does not have a valid RTE to the destination d, does not affect the truth value of the loop-free property. Therefore, a suitable BeFS strategy (which we call AODV-BeFS-1) is to consider a state s_1 better than a state s_2 if the number of *valid* RTEs to any node in s_1 is greater than that in s_2. Another BeFS strategy (which we call AODV-BeFS-2) can also be obtained by inspecting the loop-free property, which can be rewritten as follows:

$$(((seqno_{n,d} - seqno_{m,d}) < 0) \vee (seqno_{n,d} == seqno_{m,d} \wedge ((hops_{m,d} - hops_{n,d}) < 0)))$$

Therefore, the greater $(seqno_{n,d} - seqno_{m,d})$ and/or $(hops_{m,d} - hops_{n,d})$ in a state s, the more likely s is close to an error. Hence, AODV-BeFS-2 considers a state s_1 better than a state s_2 if the following summation

$$S = \sum_{n \neq d}((seqno_{n,d} - seqno_{m,d}) + (hops_{m,d} - hops_{n,d}))$$

in s_1 is greater than that in s_2, where $nexthop_{n,d} = m$. The summation S includes only the nodes n and m that have valid RTEs to the destination d. If none of the nodes have a valid RTE to d, S is set to $-\infty$. In addition to AODV-BeFS-1 and AODV-BeFS-2, we also study the performance of the following BeFS strategies:

1. AODV-BeFS-3: This strategy considers a state s_1 better than a state s_2 if the number of valid RTEs *to the destination d* in s_1 is greater than that in s_2. However, if s_1 and s_2 are equally good, s_1 is considered better than s_2 if the number of valid RTEs *to any node* in s_1 is greater than that in s_2.

2. AODV-BeFS-4: Since a valid RTE is established upon receiving a RREP packet, AODV-BeFS-4 considers a state s_1 better than a state s_2 if the number of RREP packets in s_1 is greater than that in s_2.

3. AODV-BeFS-5: AODV-BeFS-5 is the same as AODV-BeFS-4, except that if s_1 and s_2 are equally good under the condition specified in AODV-BeFS-4, s_1 is considered better than s_2 if the number of valid RTEs to any node in s_1 is greater than that in s_2.

Errors Discovered. We consider an initial state of an ad hoc network consisting of 3 nodes: n_0, n_1 and n_2 (the only destination node) arranged in a chain topology where each node is a neighbor of both the node to its left and the node to its right (if any exists). Although this initial state is simple, it ensures that n_0 requires a multihop route to reach n_2; i.e., AODV multihop routing is needed. We will study larger network topologies later in this section. In the course of model checking, we have discovered an error (which we call Counterexample 1) in the J-Sim implementation of AODV caused by not following part of the AODV specification. Conceptually, if $nexthop_{0,2} = 1$ and the AODV process at n_1 restarts, the net effect is that all the RTEs stored at n_1 will be deleted. As a result, n_1 may later accept a route that was offered by n_2 with a lower sequence number than that of n_0 (i.e., $seqno_{0,2} > seqno_{1,2}$), hence violating the loop-free property. We also manually injected two errors (which we call Counterexamples 2 and 3 respectively): in Counterexample 2, $seqno_{n,d}$ is not incremented when a RTE is invalidated and in Counterexample 3, a RTE is deleted (instead of invalidated) when its lifetime expires. The model checking framework was able to find these two errors too.[1] A routing loop may occur due to either of these two errors because if $nexthop_{0,2} = 1$ and a route timeout event takes place at n_1, in either Counterexample 2 or 3, if n_1 is later offered a route to n_2 by n_0, this route will be accepted (because in Counterexample 2, $hops_{1,2} = \infty$; hence, $hops_{1,2} > hops_{0,2}$; whereas in Counterexample 3, $seqno_{0,2} > seqno_{1,2}$). The interested reader is referred to [17] for a detailed account (along with the traces) of the three counterexamples.

Performance of the Search Strategies. Table 1 gives the performance evaluation criteria: (i) time, (ii) space, and (iii) number of transitions explored for finding the three counterexamples using several search strategies, including breadth-first (BFS) and depth-first (DFS). As shown in Table 1, AODV-BeFS-1 achieves an order of magnitude reduction with respect to the performance criteria when compared to BFS. Also, the choice of the BeFS strategy has an impact on the performance. For instance, as shown in Table 1, AODV-BeFS-2 performs worse than AODV-BeFS-1 for the three counterexamples. This is because AODV-BeFS-2 requires a node (and its next hop towards the destination) to have valid RTEs to the destination. This may not be true in the first few stages (i.e., lower depths) of the search space. Therefore, in the first few stages of the search, the nonvisited states may look equally good and thus, AODV-BeFS-2 may not be able to explore the states that are most likely to lead to the error first. AODV-BeFS-3 tackles this problem by further differentiating equally good states by using a two-level best-first search approach. As shown in Table 1, AODV-BeFS-1 and AODV-BeFS-3 outperform the other BeFS strategies because they are more able to guide the BeFS towards the error even at the lower depths of the search space.

Next, we study the effect of the size of the network on the performance of the model checking framework in J-Sim. As shown in Table 2, the model checking

---

[1] For Counterexamples 2 and 3, we require that the counterexample contain at least one state that is generated due to the route timeout event, T_5.

Table 1. AODV case study: Time (in seconds) and space (in number of states explored) requirements and the number of transitions explored for finding the three counterexamples in a 3-node chain ad-hoc network using different search strategies. MAX_DEPTH = 10.

	Counterexample 1			Counterexample 2			Counterexample 3		
	Time	Space	Transitions	Time	Space	Transitions	Time	Space	Transitions
BFS	4262.039	19886	40445	4231.124	20072	40781	4094.928	19056	39489
DFS	940.672	1844	21135	962.935	1833	20979	893.896	1817	20814
AODV-BeFS-1	139.310	1156	7493	137.168	1151	7440	127.053	1150	7431
AODV-BeFS-2	833.719	1753	19617	810.035	1750	19581	775.766	1739	19468
AODV-BeFS-3	14.882	535	2118	14.120	535	2079	14.400	534	2070
AODV-BeFS-4	367.038	1626	14151	3905.015	4901	44851	365.215	1617	14051
AODV-BeFS-5	347.529	1923	13577	3076.274	4649	38853	323.515	1889	13101

Table 2. AODV case study: Time (in seconds) and space (in number of states explored) requirements and the number of transitions explored for finding Counterexample 3 in a N-node chain ad-hoc network using AODV-BeFS-1

N	MAX_DEPTH	Time	Space	Transitions
3	15	0.200	93	134
4	20	12.609	575	1971
5	25	944.769	3256	19803
6	30	1393.955	2640	25052
7	35	3784.462	3339	46532

framework was able to find a counterexample in larger network topologies within reasonable time and space requirements.

3.2   Directed Diffusion in Wireless Sensor Networks (WSNs)

Overview of Directed Diffusion. Directed diffusion [13] is a *data-centric* information dissemination paradigm for wireless sensor networks (WSNs). In directed diffusion, a *sink node* periodically broadcasts an INTEREST packet, containing the description of a sensing task that it is interested in (e.g., detecting a chemical weapon in a specific area). INTEREST packets are diffused throughout the network (e.g., via flooding), and are used to set up *exploratory gradients*. A gradient is the direction state created in each node that receives an INTEREST, where the gradient direction is set toward the neighboring node from which the INTEREST is received. Each node maintains an interest cache. Each interest entry in this cache corresponds to a distinct interest and stores information about the gradients that a node has (up to one gradient per neighbor) for that interest. Each gradient in an interest entry has a lifetime that is determined by the sink node. When a gradient expires, it is removed from its interest entry. When all gradients in an interest entry have expired, the interest entry itself is removed from the interest cache.

When an INTEREST packet arrives at a *sensor node* that senses data which matches the interest (this sensor node is called a *source node*), the source node prepares DATA packets (each of which describes the sensed data) and sends them to neighbors for whom it has a gradient once every *exploratory interval*. Each node also maintains a data cache that keeps track of recently seen DATA packets. When a node receives a DATA packet, if the DATA packet has a matching data cache entry, the DATA packet is discarded; otherwise, the node adds the received DATA packet to the data cache and forwards the DATA packet to each neighbor for whom it has a gradient. As a result, DATA packets are forwarded toward the sink node(s) along (possibly) multiple gradient paths.

Upon receipt of a DATA packet, a sink node *reinforces* its preferred neighbor that is determined based on a data-driven local rule. For instance, the sink node may reinforce any neighbor from which it received previously unseen data (i.e., the neighbor from which it first received the latest data matching the interest). The data cache is used to determine that preferred neighbor. In order to reinforce a neighbor, the sink node sends a *positive reinforcement* packet to that neighbor to inform it of sending data at a smaller interval (i.e., higher rate) than the exploratory interval, thereby establishing a *reinforced gradient* (also called *data gradient*) towards the sink node. The reinforced neighbor will in turn reinforce its preferred neighbor. This process repeats all the way back to the data source, resulting in a reinforced path (i.e., a chain of reinforced gradients) between the source and the sink nodes.

Model Checking Directed Diffusion. In order to illustrate the applicability of the model checking framework, we follow the same steps given in Section 3.1.

(1) Definitions of the global state, the initial state, state equality and safety property: To model-check directed diffusion, we use the same definitions of *GlobalState* and network cloud that were introduced in Section 3.1. On the other hand, since the protocol state is protocol-specific, the protocol state in directed diffusion includes each node's interest cache and data cache. In the initial global state, the network does not contain any packets and the directed diffusion process at each node starts with an empty interest cache and an empty data cache.

Two states, s_1 and s_2, are considered equal if they have the same (unordered) set of packets, the same neighborhood information, and for each node n, s_1 and s_2 have correspondingly equal node n's interest cache and data cache (each viewed as an unordered set of entries).

An important safety property in the directed diffusion protocol is the *loop-free* property of the reinforced path. Consider two nodes n and m where $RPath(n, m)$ is true if and only if there is a reinforced path from n to m. The loop-free property can be expressed as follows:

$$\neg\ (\ RPath(n, m)\ \wedge\ RPath(m, n)\ )$$

(2) Events: The events can be listed as follows:

T_0 Initiation of a sensing task by node n: This event is enabled if n is a sink node. The event is handled by broadcasting an INTEREST packet.

T_1 Delivering a packet to node n: This event is enabled if the network contains at least one packet that is destined for node n such that node n is one of the neighbors of the source of the packet. The event is handled by removing this packet from the network and forwarding it to node n.

T_2 Restart of the directed diffusion process at node n: This event may take place because of a node reboot. The event is always enabled and is handled by reinitializing the state of the directed diffusion process at node n.

T_3 Loss of a packet destined for node n: This event is enabled if the network contains at least one packet that is destined for node n. The event is handled by removing this packet from the network.

T_4 Gradient timeout at node n: This event is enabled if the interest cache of node n contains at least one interest entry that has at least one gradient. The event is handled by deleting this gradient.

T_5 Data cache timeout[2] at node n: This event is enabled if there is at least one entry in the data cache of node n. The event is handled by deleting this entry.

(3) Use of protocol-specific properties to facilitate a BeFS strategy: In the course of model-checking AODV, AODV-BeFS-1 and AODV-BeFS-3 provided comparatively good performance results. We use these two BeFS strategies to devise two corresponding BeFS strategies for directed diffusion. In particular, as the loop-free property involves only valid RTEs to a destination d in AODV; by analogy, the loop-free property involves only reinforced gradients in directed diffusion. Similarly, forwarding of data packets in AODV is based on the next hop information stored in the valid RTEs; by analogy, forwarding of data packets in directed diffusion is based on the gradients established at the nodes. Therefore, two good BeFS strategies for exploring the state space of directed diffusion are:

1. DD-BeFS-1: This strategy considers a state s_1 better than a state s_2 if the total number of *both exploratory and reinforced gradients* in s_1 is greater than that in s_2.
2. DD-BeFS-2: This strategy considers a state s_1 better than a state s_2 if the number of *reinforced* gradients in s_1 is greater than that in s_2. However, if s_1 and s_2 are equally good, s_1 is considered better than s_2 if the total number of *both exploratory and reinforced* gradients in s_1 is greater than that in s_2.

Along a similar line of arguments, we also devise the following BeFS strategies:

1. DD-BeFS-3: Since a reinforced gradient is established upon receiving a positive reinforcement packet, DD-BeFS-3 considers a state s_1 better than a state s_2 if the number of positive reinforcement packets in s_1 is greater than that in s_2.
2. DD-BeFS-4: DD-BeFS-4 is the same as DD-BeFS-3, except that if s_1 and s_2 are equally good under the condition specified in DD-BeFS-3, s_1 is considered better than s_2 if the total number of *both exploratory and reinforced* gradients in s_1 is greater than that in s_2.

---

[2] For practical reasons, previously received DATA packets can not be kept in the data cache for an indefinitely long time; otherwise, the size of the data cache can increase arbitrarily. In the implementation of directed diffusion in J-Sim, each DATA packet in the data cache is associated with a lifetime. Periodically, a data cache timeout event is triggered causing the deletion of entries in the cache that have expired.

3. DD-BeFS-5: This strategy considers a state s_1 better than a state s_2 if the total number of data cache entries at all nodes in s_1 is greater than that in s_2.

4. DD-BeFS-6: DD-BeFS-6 is the same as DD-BeFS-5, except that if s_1 and s_2 are equally good under the condition specified in DD-BeFS-5, s_1 is considered better than s_2 if the total number of *both exploratory and reinforced* gradients in s_1 is greater than that in s_2.

Errors Discovered. Next, we give two previously unknown errors that the model checking framework in J-Sim was able to discover in directed diffusion (which we call Counterexamples 1 and 2 respectively). We consider an initial state that consists of a chain topology of 4 nodes: n_0 (the only sink node), n_1, n_2 and n_3 (the only source node). The errors take place because in directed diffusion, the interest and gradient setup mechanisms themselves do *not* guarantee loop-free reinforced paths between the source and the sink nodes. In order to prevent loops from taking place, the data cache is used to suppress previously seen DATA packets. However, we discover that, in case of (a) a node reboot (which effectively deletes all the entries in the data and interest caches) and/or (b) the deletion of a DATA packet from the data cache, a loop may be created. For instance, in the 4-node chain topology, if n_1 accepts a DATA packet sent by n_2, n_2 becomes n_1's preferred neighbor. Now, if n_2 deletes the DATA packet from its data cache due to a data cache timeout (Counterexample 1) or a node reboot (Counterexample 2), it may later accept the DATA packet sent by n_1 (because it will be previously unseen data) causing n_1 to become n_2's preferred neighbor. Therefore, n_1 and n_2 may positively reinforce each other causing a loop in the reinforced path. In fact, positive reinforcement packets may not eventually reach the source node causing a disruption in the reinforced path (i.e., the reinforced path may include a loop that does not include the source node).[3] The interested reader is referred to [19] for a detailed account, and traces, of the two counterexamples.

Performance of the Search Strategies. Table 3 gives the performance of the various search strategies in finding the two counterexamples. As shown in Table 3, DD-BeFS-1 provides comparatively good results in terms of time and space requirements and the number of transitions explored for finding a violation of a safety property. Furthermore, DD-BeFS-4 outperforms DD-BeFS-3, and DD-BeFS-6 outperforms DD-BeFS-5. This is because both DD-BeFS-4 and DD-BeFS-6 are two-level BeFS strategies that use DD-BeFS-1 if the non-visited states are equally good and are thus more able to guide the BeFS in the lower depths of the search space than DD-BeFS-3 and DD-BeFS-5 respectively.

Table 4 gives the time and space requirements and the number of transitions explored for finding Counterexample 1 in a chain topology consisting of N nodes using DD-BeFS-4. For sensor networks consisting of more than four nodes, both BFS and DFS failed to find counterexamples.

---

[3] For Counterexample 2, we require that the counterexample contain at least one state that is generated due to a node reboot event, T_2. Furthermore, in order to show that the error may still take place even if the data cache timeout event, T_5, does not happen (i.e., the data cache size is infinite), we disabled T_5.

Table 3. Directed diffusion case study: Time (in seconds) and space (in number of states explored) requirements and the number of transitions explored for finding the two counterexamples in a 4-node chain sensor network using different search strategies. N/A indicates that the model checker was not able to find a counterexample in 8 hours.

	Counterexample 1, $MAX\_DEPTH = 15$			Counterexample 2, $MAX\_DEPTH = 20$		
	Time	Space	Transitions	Time	Space	Transitions
BFS	22287.938	21224	84530	N/A	N/A	N/A
DFS	23876.914	4736	95706	N/A	N/A	N/A
DD-BeFS-1	3.475	200	1051	3900.118	6026	41132
DD-BeFS-2	4.026	200	1168	12189.227	6640	57124
DD-BeFS-3	19536.362	4630	93924	N/A	N/A	N/A
DD-BeFS-4	0.981	124	469	726.024	1870	17656
DD-BeFS-5	N/A	N/A	N/A	N/A	N/A	N/A
DD-BeFS-6	24743.349	12920	72911	N/A	N/A	N/A

Table 4. Directed diffusion case study: Time (in seconds) and space (in number of states explored) requirements and the number of transitions explored for finding Counterexample 1 in a N-node chain sensor network using DD-BeFS-4

N	MAX_DEPTH	Time	Space	Transitions
4	15	0.981	124	469
5	20	335.833	925	11816
6	25	857.303	1346	19245
7	30	1538.152	1985	27640
8	35	7244.277	3679	59093

3.3 Lessons Learned

In this subsection, we summarize the lessons that we learned. First, the ability of the model checking framework to model-check large and complex network protocols such as AODV and directed diffusion demonstrates that the model checking framework is general enough and not tied to a particular network protocol. Specifically, for model-checking another network protocol, one needs to follow the steps that we followed in sections 3.1 and 3.2.

Second, we demonstrate that the use of BeFS strategies (that leverage *protocol-specific* properties) reduces the time and space requirements by several orders of magnitude. Based on the results obtained for the BeFS strategies that we studied, we recommend deriving the BeFS strategy from properties inherent to the network protocol and the safety property being checked. This is justified by the fact that AODV-BeFS-1 (and DD-BeFS-1) provided good performance results in terms of time and space requirements and number of transitions explored for finding a violation of a safety property. Furthermore, using a two-level BeFS strategy, in which a BeFS strategy such as AODV-BeFS-1 (or DD-BeFS-1) is used if the nonvisited states are equally good, also improved the performance. This is justified by the fact that AODV-BeFS-5 outperforms AODV-BeFS-4, DD-BeFS-4 outperforms DD-BeFS-3, and DD-BeFS-6 outperforms DD-BeFS-5.

4 Related Work

Our work is inspired by previous work on model-checking the implementation code directly for C and C++ (e.g., CMC [3, 14] and VeriSoft [20]). Although

CMC has been applied to model-check Linux implementations of networking code (e.g., AODV and TCP), the major distinction between our approach and CMC is that CMC uses *protocol-independent* properties in guiding the best-first search. It does so by attempting to focus on states that are the most different from previously explored states. However, our approach uses *protocol-dependent* properties, which exploit properties inherent to the network protocol and the safety property being checked, to guide the best-first search strategy. Likewise, VeriSoft uses *protocol-independent* techniques, namely partial-order reduction (POR) using the persistent/sleep sets [20]. Traditional POR was static, but recent work shows how to perform dynamic POR [21]. POR can be combined with BeFS strategies; while POR determines what transitions to explore, BeFS determines the order in which to explore them [22].

In contrast to model-checking the implementation code directly, conventional model checkers (e.g., SPIN [23], SMV [24], Murphi [25]) require that the system be first specified using a high-level modeling language. This may not be desirable, as the process of describing the system in a high-level modeling language is time-consuming, painstaking, and error-prone. To deal with this problem, there has been recent work (e.g., [26,2,27,7]) on translating programming languages (e.g., Java) into the input modeling languages of several conventional model checkers. However, this may not be always feasible because some features of C or Java (e.g., bit operations) do not have corresponding ones in the destination modeling language. Therefore, our approach of model-checking the simulation code, which has to be written by a network protocol designer anyway for the purpose of performance evaluation, directly reduces the network protocol designer's effort and avoids the limitations of the input languages of conventional model checkers. This also provides an important advantage when compared to previous work on testing and verification of network protocols (e.g., [28, 29]), which requires building *another* model for verification purposes.

Java PathFinder [30] performs model checking at the bytecode level. This involved building a new Java Virtual Machine that is called from the model checker to interpret Java bytecode. In contrast, our approach does not require any modifications to the Java Virtual Machine. Our approach, however, requires the user to provide the code for state manipulation (Section 2). Java PathFinder provides automatic manipulation of the *entire* Java states (including stack and heap); to use Java PathFinder for a tractable checking of protocol simulation code in J-Sim, the user would still need to manually provide the code that manipulates state by abstracting the stack and parts of the heap.

The idea of using best-first search strategies and/or heuristics to expedite the model checking process has been explored in previous work (e.g., [15, 22, 31, 32, 33]). However, what distinguishes our work is that we study the use of protocol-specific heuristics in model-checking the simulation code directly and we focus on a specific domain; namely, routing protocols for wireless ad hoc and sensor networks, and attempt to discover effective protocol-specific heuristics that enable a best-first search strategy to find counterexamples with less time and space requirements than classic breadth-first and depth-first search strategies.

5   Conclusions and Future Work

This paper presents our research on extending the J-Sim network simulator with the capability of verifying network protocols using on-the-fly model checking. We demonstrate the effectiveness of the model checker to model-check two widely used and fairly complex network protocols: AODV and directed diffusion. To the best of our knowledge, the deficiency identified in directed diffusion has not been discovered before. Experimental results show that the model checker is able to find violations of a safety property within acceptable time and space requirements. Furthermore, we study several best-first search strategies for both AODV and directed diffusion, and provide recommendations based on our results.

We have identified several research avenues for future work. First, we intend to extend the model checker to check general temporal properties. Second, the experiments reported in this paper require considerable manual effort; in future research, we will consider how to reduce such manual effort. An important research question is how to (semi-)automatically derive the heuristics from the simulation code and the safety property. Another interesting research avenue lies in studying to what extent symbolic model checking can expedite model-checking the simulation code.

References

1. A. K. Saha, K. To, S. PalChaudhuri, S. Du, and D. B. Johnson, "Physical implementation of ad hoc network routing protocols using unmodified ns-2 models," ACM MobiCom'04, Poster.
2. K. Havelund, "Java Pathfinder, a translator from Java to Promela," in *Proc. of SPIN'99*.
3. M. Musuvathi, D. Y.W. Park, A. Chou, D. R. Engler, and D. L. Dill, "CMC: A pragmatic approach to model checking real code," in *Proc. of OSDI'02*.
4. T. Ball, and S. K. Rajamani, "The SLAM Toolkit," in *Proc. of CAV'01*.
5. S. Chaki, E. Clarke, A. Groce, S. Jha, and H. Veith, "Modular Verification of Software Components in C," in *Proc. of ICSE'03*.
6. T. A. Henzinger, R. Jhala, R. Majumdar, and G. Sutre, "Lazy Abstraction," in *Proc. of POPL'02*.
7. A. Farzan, F. Chen, J. Meseguer, and G. Rosu, "Formal analysis of Java programs in JavaFAN," in *Proc. of CAV'04*.
8. J-Sim, "http://www.j-sim.org/"
9. E. M. Clarke, O. Grumberg, and D. Peled, *Model Checking*, MIT Press, 1999.
10. A. Sobeih, M. Viswanathan, and J. C. Hou, "Check and Simulate: A case for incorporating model checking in network simulation," in *Proc. of ACM-IEEE MEMOCODE'04*.
11. C. E. Perkins and E. M. Royer, "Ad-hoc on-demand distance vector routing," in *Proc. of IEEE WMCSA'99*.
12. C. E. Perkins, E. M. Royer, and S. Das, "Ad hoc on demand distance vector (aodv) routing," IETF Draft, January 2002.
13. C. Intanagonwiwat, R. Govindan, and D. Estrin, "Directed diffusion: A scalable and robust communication paradigm for sensor networks," in *Proc. of ACM MobiCom'00*.

14. M. Musuvathi and D. R. Engler, "Model checking large network protocol implementations," in *Proc. of NSDI'04*.

15. S. Edelkamp, S. Leue and A. Lluch-Lafuente, "Directed Explicit-State Model Checking in the Validation of Communication Protocols," *International Journal on Software Tools for Technology Transfer (STTT)*, vol. 5, no. 2-3, pp. 247–267, March 2004.

16. P. E. Hart, N. J. Nilsson, and B. Raphael, "A formal basis for heuristic determination of minimum path cost," *IEEE Transactions on Systems Science and Cybernetics*, vol. 4, pp. 100–107, 1968.

17. A. Sobeih, M. Viswanathan and J. C. Hou, "Incorporating Bounded Model Checking in Network Simulation: Theory, Implementation and Evaluation," Tech. Rep. UIUCDCS-R-2004-2466, Department of Computer Science, University of Illinois at Urbana-Champaign, July 2004.

18. K. Bhargavan, D. Obradovic, and C. A. Gunter, "Formal verification of standards for distance vector routing protocols," *Journal of the ACM*, vol. 49, no. 4, pp. 538–576, July 2002.

19. A. Sobeih, M. Viswanathan and J. C. Hou, "Bounded Model Checking of Network Protocols in Network Simulators by Exploiting Protocol-Specific Heuristics," Tech. Rep. UIUCDCS-R-2005-2547, Department of Computer Science, University of Illinois at Urbana-Champaign, April 2005.

20. P. Godefroid, "Model checking for programming languages using VeriSoft," in *Proc. of ACM POPL'97*.

21. C. Flanagan and P. Godefroid. Dynamic partial-order reduction for model checking software. In *Proc. of ACM POPL'05*.

22. P. Godefroid and S. Khurshid. Exploring very large state spaces using genetic algorithms. In *Proc. of TACAS'02*.

23. G. J. Holzmann, "The model checker SPIN," *IEEE Trans. on Software Engineering*, vol. 23, no. 5, pp. 279–295, May 1997.

24. K. McMillan, *Symbolic Model Checking*, Kluwer Academic Publishers, 1993.

25. D. L. Dill, A. J. Drexler, A. J. Hu, and C. H. Yang, "Protocol verification as a hardware design aid," in *Proc. of IEEE ICCD'92*.

26. D. Y. Park, U. Stern, J. U. Skakkebæk, and D. L. Dill. Java model checking. In *Proc. of IEEE ASE'00*.

27. J. Corbett, M. Dwyer, J. Hatcliff, C. Păsăreanu, Robby, S. Laubach, and H. Zheng. Bandera: Extracting finite state models from Java source code. In *Proc. of ICSE'00*.

28. D. Lee, D. Chen, R. Hao, R. E. Miller, J. Wu, and X. Yin, "A formal approach for passive testing of protocol data portions," in *Proc. of IEEE ICNP'02*.

29. G. N. Naumovich, L. A. Clarke, and L. J. Osterweil, "Verification of communication protocols using data flow analysis," in *Proc. of ACM SIGSOFT'96*.

30. W. Visser, K. Havelund, G. Brat, and S.Park, "Model checking programs," in *Proc. of IEEE ASE'00*.

31. J. Tan, G. S. Avrunin, L. A. Clarke, S. Zilberstein, and S. Leue. Heuristic-guided counterexample search in FLAVERS. In *Proc. of ACM SIGSOFT'04/FSE-12*.

32. C. H. Yang and D. L. Dill. Validation with guided search of the state space. In *Proc. of ACM/IEE DAC'98*.

33. A. Groce and W. Visser "Heuristics for Model Checking Java Programs," *International Journal on Software Tools for Technology Transfer (STTT)*, vol. 6, no. 4, pp. 260–276, August 2004.

Adaptive Random Testing by Bisection with Restriction

Johannes Mayer

University of Ulm,
Dept. of Applied Information Processing,
89069 Ulm, Germany
johannes.mayer@uni-ulm.de

Abstract. Random Testing is a strategy to select test cases based on pure randomness. Adaptive Random Testing (ART), a family of algorithms, improves pure Random Testing by taking common failure pattern into account. The best—in terms of the number of test cases necessary to detect the first failure—ART algorithms, however, are too runtime inefficient. Therefore, a modification of a fast, but not so good ART algorithm, namely ART by Bisection, is presented. This modification requires much less test cases than the original method while retaining its computational efficiency.

1 Introduction

An important part of software quality assurance is software testing, i. e. the execution of a program with the intention to detect failures [1]. It is, however, quite time-consuming to generate a large number of test cases. Furthermore, reliability estimates are not possible for arbitrary strategies for test case generation. Therefore, Random Testing [2–6], i. e. the random generation of test cases, has been proposed. It allows to make reliability predictions [4, 7, 8]. Being compared to partition testing [9–13], i. e. the partitioning of the input (or output) domain and the generation of test cases from each element of the partition, it has proven to be inferior under certain circumstances [9, 11]. Furthermore, Myers [1] criticized that Random Testing does not use information about the program under test. Therefore, Adaptive Random Testing (ART) [12] has been proposed that performes better than pure Random Testing for common failure patterns in terms of test cases necessary to detect the first failure. This aim is achieved through wide spread test cases. The best ART algorithms (D-ART [12] and RRT [14–16]), however, require a huge amount of distance computations. Recently, ART algorithms inspired by partition testing have been published [17]. These algorithms require much less runtime. Their performance measures in terms of the number of test cases necessary to detect the first failure are better than that of pure Random Testing, but not nearly as good as the best ART algorithms. Therefore, a combination of ART by Bisection [17] with the notion of restriction [14] is presented. The result is an ART algorithm that does not require any distance computation at all, but performs (in terms of the test cases necessary to detect

K.-K. Lau and R. Banach (Eds.): ICFEM 2005, LNCS 3785, pp. 251–263, 2005.

the first failure) better than the fast ART algorithms [17] and for some failure patterns even better than all common ART algorithms. The performance of the presented algorithm is at least much better than that of the original method [17] for other failure patterns, while still being as fast as the original method [17].

The following section presents preliminaries regarding the notation and common failure patterns. The novel algorithm is described in Section 3. An empirical evaluation of the proposed algorithm is described and discussed in Section 4, followed by a conclusion.

2   Preliminaries

2.1   Notation

The input domain is assumed to be bounded. The failure rate, i. e. the percentage of failure-causing inputs, is denoted θ. For a finite input domain of size d with m failure-causing inputs, $\theta = m/d$.

The *F-measure* is the number of test cases necessary to detect the first failure. This is a very natural measure for the performance of a testing strategy, since often testing is stopped when the first failure is detected. The F-measure has been used in all publications on ART. It is therefore ideal for comparison purposes.

For Random Testing with uniform usage profile and replacement, the theoretical mean F-measure is equal to $1/\theta$. For example, for a failure rate of $\theta = 0.01$, the theoretical mean F-measure of random testing with replacement is 100.

2.2   Failure Patterns

Chan et al. [10] describe three typical patterns failure-causing inputs form within the input domain (cf. Figure 1). The block pattern (cf. Figure 1a) describes the situation where the failure-causing inputs are located next to each other within a small region of the input domain. The strip pattern (cf. Figure 1b) is achieved if the failure-causing inputs form a narrow strip within the input domain. Finally, the situation when there are many wide spread failure-causing inputs or small

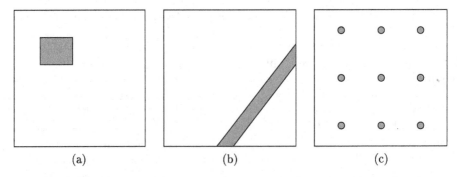

| (a)   (b)   (c) |

Fig. 1. Block, strip, and point patterns in a two-dimensional input domain

clusters is described by the point pattern (cf. Figure 1c). According to Chan et al. [10], the block and the strip failure pattern are the most common. These patterns support the intuition of ART that wide spread test cases have a higher probability of earlier detecting failures.

3   The Algorithm

ART by Bisection [17] is an ART algorithm that iteratively divides the input domain into equally sized sub-domains and randomly selects a test case from each of these sub-domains in random order. This algorithm is very efficient regarding runtime. However, it has a significant higher F-measure than D-ART and RRT, since nearby test cases cannot be avoided sufficiently (cf. Figure 2). Using the

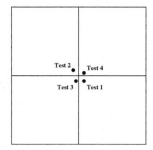

Fig. 2. Nearby test cases possible with ART by Bisection

idea of restriction, the following algorithm proceeds as ART by Bisection, but it selects the test cases from restricted sub-domains. This restriction can easily be achieved and has the effect that the inputs have a (decreasing) minimum distance. Through this minimum distance, nearby test cases can partially be prohibited other than with ART by Bisection [17].

It is assumed that the two-dimensional input domain is rectangular with lower left corner $(x_{\min}, y_{\min})$ and upper right corner $(x_{\max}, y_{\max})$.[1] Therefore, the inputs are two-dimensional vectors (x, y) of real values with $x_{\min} \leq x \leq x_{\max}$ and $y_{\min} \leq y \leq y_{\max}$. It can trivially be adapted to a bounded region of integers or higher dimensional input domains. The exclusion factor f must be chosen from $[0, 0.5)$.

Algorithm 1: Adaptive Random Testing by Bisection with Restriction

1. Initialize the list of untested regions L_{untested} with $\{\{(x_{\min}, y_{\min})(x_{\max}, y_{\max})\}\}$. Initialize the list of tested regions L_{tested} with the empty list.
2. While L_{untested} is not empty:
   (a) Randomly select a test region $T = \{(x_0, y_0)(x_1, y_1)\}$ from L_{untested} and remove it.

---

[1] Such rectangles are denoted $\{(x_{\min}, y_{\min})(x_{\max}, y_{\max})\}$ in the following.

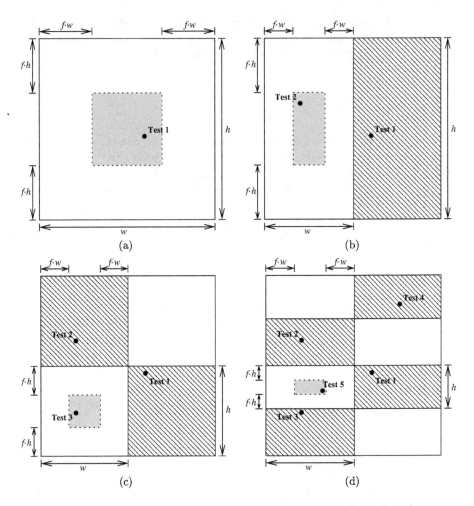

Fig. 3. ART by Bisection with Restriction: Some steps of the algorithm

(b) Randomly select a point (x, y) from within the restricted test region
$T' := \{(x_0 + fw, y_0 + fh)(x_1 - fw, y_1 - fh)\}$.

(c) If the point (x, y) is a failure-causing input, report failure and terminate.

(d) Otherwise append $(T, (x, y))$ to L_{tested}.

3. Initialize L_{temp} with the empty list.

4. For each element $(\{(x_0, y_0)(x_1, y_1)\}, (x, y))$ from L_{tested}:

(a) Let $T := \{(x_0, y_0)(x_1, y_1)\}$. Furthermore, let $w := x_1 - x_0$ be the width of T and $h := y_1 - y_0$ be the height of T.

(b) If $w \geq h$, divide T into the two regions $T_1 := \{(x_0, y_0)(x_0 + w/2, y_1)\}$ and $T_2 := \{(x_0 + w/2, y_0)(x_1, y_1)\}$. Otherwise divide T into the two regions $T_1 := \{(x_0, y_0)(x_1, y_0 + h/2)\}$ and $T_2 := \{(x_0, y_0 + h/2)(x_1, y_1)\}$.

(c) If $(x, y) \in T_2$, exchange T_1 and T_2.

(d) Add $(T_1, (x, y))$ to L_{temp} and T_2 to L_{untested}.

5. Copy L_{temp} into L_{tested} and proceed with step 2.

The algorithm starts with the whole input domain as the initial sub-domain (cf. Figure 3a). Within each sub-domain that does not contain a previously executed test case a test case is selected randomly within a restriction of the respective sub-domain, in each pass. The sub-domains are processed in a random order. If all sub-domains contain a previously executed test case, they are bisected and the next pass starts as long as no failure is detected.

Figure 3 illustrates several steps of the algorithm. The initial sub-domain is the input domain. The algorithm selects the first test case from the restricted input domain (cf. Figure 3a). Thereafter, all sub-domains—at the moment, there is only one—are bisected (cf. Figure 3b). The right sub-domain contains the previously executed test case. For this reason, another test case is chosen from the restricted left sub-domain. Then, both sub-domains are bisected again (cf. Figure 3c). There are four sub-domains now, and the upper-left and the lower-right sub-domain contain already executed test cases. One test case is, thus, chosen in the restricted lower-left sub-domain and the other is chosen in the restricted upper-right sub-domain. After further bisection (cf. Figure 3d) there are eigth sub-domains, and four of them contain previously executed test cases. An "empty" (i. e. without previously executed test cases) sub-domain is chosen and Test Case 5 is generated within this restricted domain.

4   Simulation Study

The mean F-measure has to be determined to measure the performance of the presented algorithm. However, this seems not to be straightforward—at least theoretically. Therefore, the Monte Carlo method is applied to determine this characteristic through simulation.

4.1   Preliminaries

Let $X_1, \ldots, X_n$ be independent and identically distributed random variables. $\overline{X_n} := \frac{1}{n} \sum_1^n X_i$ is the sample mean of the X_i. According to the central limit theorem [18],

$$\frac{\overline{X_n} - \mu}{\sigma / \sqrt{n}}$$

is standard Gaussian distributed as n approaches infinity. It is also a good approximation for $n \geq 30$ (a common rule of thumb). μ denotes the true mean and σ^2 the true variance of the X_i. Since usually μ and σ are unknown, they are replaced by the sample mean $\overline{X_n}$ and the square root of the sample variance

$$S_n^2 := \frac{1}{n-1} \sum_{i=1}^{n} (X_i - \overline{X_n})^2$$

as an approximation, respectively.

It follows that

$$|\overline{X_n} - \mu| \leq \frac{\sigma}{\sqrt{n}} \cdot \Phi^{-1}\left(\frac{2-\alpha}{2}\right)$$

on confidence level $1 - \alpha$ and for $n \geq 30$, where $\Phi^{-1}(\cdot)$ denotes the inverse standard Gaussian distribution function. Furthermore, σ can be approximated by S_n. Therefore, it is possible to determine the accuracy of an estimation $\overline{X_n}$ on confidence level $1 - \alpha$.

4.2   The Simulation Design

For the simulations, the sample size n was chosen 50000, i.e. the algorithm was run with 50000 randomly chosen failure patterns. The confidence level $1 - \alpha$ was chosen 0.99. In a table for the Gaussian distribution one can look up $\Phi^{-1}(0.995) \approx 2.58$. Therefore,

$$|\overline{X_n} - \mu| \leq \frac{S_n}{\sqrt{50000}} \cdot 2.58 \approx 0.01154 \cdot S_n.$$

The failure pattern was randomly generated. The area θA of the failure pattern was determined by the failure rate θ and the area A of the input domain. For the block pattern, a square was chosen randomly, totally within the input domain. For the strip pattern, two adjacent sides and two points on these sides were chosen randomly. The strip was then constructed centered on the line connecting these points and its width was computed so that the strip had the desired area θA. Points near the corners were rejected to avoid overly wide strips. For the point pattern, 50 non-overlapping discs with equal radius lying totally within the input domain where randomly generated to achieve the total area θA.

The first part of the simulations were to investigate the performance of the presented ART algorithm and to find suitable values for the factor f. These simulations were done for the following

- failure rates: $0.01, 0.005, 0.002, 0.001, 0.0005$
- failure patterns: block, strip, and point
- factors f: $0.0, 0.05, 0.1, 0.15, 0.2, \ldots, 0.45$.

The second part of the simulations was performed in order to compare the novel ART algorithm with related ART algorithms. The parameters of the various ART methods were chosen as suggested in the respective publications: RRT ($R = 1.5$), D-ART ($k = 10$), ART by Random Partitioning with Localization and RRT ($R = 0.4$) resp. D-ART ($k = 3$), and ART by Bisection with Restriction ($f = 0.3$). (The last parameter has been determined by the first part of the simulations.) In this case, the above failure rates and patterns were also used complemented by the point pattern with 10 discs.

4.3   Results and Discussion

Tables 1–3 show the results of the first part of the simulations. Each table contains the relative[2] empirical mean F-measure for one particular failure pattern and all factors f and all failure rates θ. The accuracy of the mean is also given

Table 1. The mean F-measure of ART by Bisection with Restriction related to the theoretical mean F-measure of Random Testing for the block failure pattern

	$\theta = 0.01$	$\theta = 0.005$	$\theta = 0.002$	$\theta = 0.001$	$\theta = 0.0005$
$f = 0$	0.745 (± 0.007)	0.741 (± 0.007)	0.737 (± 0.007)	0.741 (± 0.007)	0.736 (± 0.007)
$f = 0.05$	0.713 (± 0.007)	0.711 (± 0.007)	0.709 (± 0.007)	0.714 (± 0.007)	0.708 (± 0.007)
$f = 0.1$	0.689 (± 0.007)	0.691 (± 0.007)	0.689 (± 0.007)	0.697 (± 0.007)	0.698 (± 0.007)
$f = 0.15$	0.679 (± 0.007)	0.672 (± 0.007)	0.689 (± 0.006)	0.688 (± 0.007)	0.693 (± 0.006)
$f = 0.2$	0.668 (± 0.007)	0.670 (± 0.006)	0.678 (± 0.006)	0.678 (± 0.007)	0.685 (± 0.006)
$f = 0.25$	**0.660** (± 0.007)	0.662 (± 0.006)	**0.674** (± 0.006)	0.674 (± 0.006)	0.686 (± 0.006)
$f = 0.3$	0.661 (± 0.007)	**0.662** (± 0.006)	0.681 (± 0.006)	**0.674** (± 0.006)	**0.684** (± 0.007)
$f = 0.35$	0.662 (± 0.007)	0.669 (± 0.007)	0.689 (± 0.007)	0.687 (± 0.007)	0.694 (± 0.007)
$f = 0.4$	0.683 (± 0.007)	0.686 (± 0.007)	0.705 (± 0.007)	0.693 (± 0.007)	0.716 (± 0.007)
$f = 0.45$	0.715 (± 0.007)	0.711 (± 0.007)	0.727 (± 0.007)	0.709 (± 0.007)	0.738 (± 0.007)

on confidence level 99% below the mean. The minimum of each column is in bold face.

The optimal factor f is between 0.25 and 0.3 for the block failure pattern, between 0.3 and 0.4 for the strip failure pattern, and is not obvious for the point failure pattern.

To determine the best choice for the factor f, a relative squared distance criterion has been used as follows: For each failure pattern p, failure rate θ, and factor f, the relative empirical mean F-measure is denoted $F_{p,\theta,f}$. For fixed p and θ, let $F_{p,\theta}^{min} := \min_f \{F_{p,\theta,f}\}$. Then, the relative squared difference is

$$d_{f,p} := \sum_{\theta} \left(\frac{F_{p,\theta,f} - F_{p,\theta}}{F_{p,\theta}} \right)^2$$

for one single failure pattern, and

$$d_f := \sum_{p} d_{f,p}$$

---

[2] To the theoretical mean F-measure of pure Random Testing (with replacement).

Table 2. The mean F-measure of ART by Bisection with Restriction related to the theoretical mean F-measure of Random Testing for the strip failure pattern

	$\theta = 0.01$	$\theta = 0.005$	$\theta = 0.002$	$\theta = 0.001$	$\theta = 0.0005$
$f = 0$	0.922 (±0.010)	0.945 (±0.011)	0.963 (±0.011)	0.972 (±0.011)	0.984 (±0.011)
$f = 0.05$	0.915 (±0.010)	0.932 (±0.010)	0.958 (±0.011)	0.967 (±0.011)	0.982 (±0.011)
$f = 0.1$	0.905 (±0.010)	0.928 (±0.010)	0.955 (±0.011)	0.962 (±0.011)	0.975 (±0.011)
$f = 0.15$	0.901 (±0.010)	0.918 (±0.010)	0.953 (±0.011)	0.964 (±0.011)	0.975 (±0.011)
$f = 0.2$	0.889 (±0.010)	0.915 (±0.010)	0.944 (±0.011)	0.958 (±0.011)	0.977 (±0.011)
$f = 0.25$	0.894 (±0.010)	0.915 (±0.010)	0.945 (±0.011)	0.958 (±0.011)	0.968 (±0.011)
$f = 0.3$	0.889 (±0.010)	**0.905** (±0.010)	0.942 (±0.011)	0.955 (±0.011)	0.970 (±0.011)
$f = 0.35$	0.889 (±0.010)	0.908 (±0.010)	**0.936** (±0.010)	0.957 (±0.011)	**0.968** (±0.011)
$f = 0.4$	0.887 (±0.009)	0.909 (±0.010)	0.953 (±0.011)	**0.951** (±0.011)	0.968 (±0.011)
$f = 0.45$	**0.885** (±0.010)	0.914 (±0.010)	0.948 (±0.011)	0.953 (±0.011)	0.972 (±0.011)

Table 3. The mean F-measure of ART by Bisection with Restriction related to the theoretical mean F-measure of Random Testing for the point failure pattern with 50 discs

	$\theta = 0.01$	$\theta = 0.005$	$\theta = 0.002$	$\theta = 0.001$	$\theta = 0.0005$
$f = 0$	0.987 (±0.011)	0.990 (±0.011)	0.987 (±0.011)	0.985 (±0.011)	0.980 (±0.011)
$f = 0.05$	0.961 (±0.011)	0.960 (±0.011)	0.971 (±0.011)	0.981 (±0.011)	0.985 (±0.011)
$f = 0.1$	0.956 (±0.011)	0.957 (±0.011)	0.971 (±0.011)	0.975 (±0.011)	**0.968** (±0.011)
$f = 0.15$	0.956 (±0.011)	0.959 (±0.011)	0.969 (±0.011)	0.970 (±0.011)	0.974 (±0.011)
$f = 0.2$	0.954 (±0.011)	0.963 (±0.011)	**0.963** (±0.011)	0.971 (±0.011)	0.975 (±0.011)
$f = 0.25$	**0.947** (±0.011)	0.966 (±0.011)	0.974 (±0.011)	0.980 (±0.011)	0.972 (±0.011)
$f = 0.3$	0.949 (±0.011)	**0.956** (±0.011)	0.970 (±0.011)	0.972 (±0.011)	0.975 (±0.011)
$f = 0.35$	0.953 (±0.011)	0.959 (±0.011)	0.969 (±0.011)	0.973 (±0.011)	0.975 (±0.011)
$f = 0.4$	0.949 (±0.011)	0.963 (±0.011)	0.968 (±0.011)	0.971 (±0.011)	0.973 (±0.011)
$f = 0.45$	0.950 (±0.011)	0.961 (±0.011)	0.966 (±0.011)	**0.965** (±0.011)	0.971 (±0.011)

Table 4. Determination of the optimal factor f for ART by Bisection with Restriction through the relative squared difference

	block	strip	point	sum
$f = 0$	0.05520	0.00532	0.00433	0.06485
$f = 0.05$	0.01924	0.00300	0.00089	0.02314
$f = 0.1$	0.00594	0.00175	0.00029	0.00798
$f = 0.15$	0.00214	0.00105	0.00019	0.00339
$f = 0.2$	0.00035	0.00035	0.00019	0.00089
$f = 0.25$	**0.00001**	0.00039	0.00051	0.00092
$f = 0.3$	0.00009	**0.00008**	0.00018	**0.00036**
$f = 0.35$	0.00121	0.00008	0.00022	0.00152
$f = 0.4$	0.00744	0.00035	0.00017	0.00797
$f = 0.45$	0.02742	0.00026	**0.00007**	0.02775

Table 5. The mean F-measure of the respective ART method related to the theoretical mean F-measure of Random Testing for the block failure pattern

	$\theta = 0.01$	$\theta = 0.005$	$\theta = 0.002$	$\theta = 0.001$	$\theta = 0.0005$
RRT	**0.648** ($\pm$0.005)	**0.633** ($\pm$0.005)	**0.612** ($\pm$0.005)	**0.603** ($\pm$0.005)	**0.595** ($\pm$0.005)
D-ART	0.673 ($\pm$0.006)	0.659 ($\pm$0.006)	0.650 ($\pm$0.006)	0.639 ($\pm$0.006)	0.635 ($\pm$0.006)
ART-RP	0.768 ($\pm$0.008)	0.777 ($\pm$0.008)	0.791 ($\pm$0.008)	0.795 ($\pm$0.008)	0.794 ($\pm$0.008)
ART-Bi.	0.735 ($\pm$0.007)	0.738 ($\pm$0.007)	0.734 ($\pm$0.007)	0.740 ($\pm$0.007)	0.734 ($\pm$0.007)
ART-RP Loc. RRT	0.681 ($\pm$0.006)	0.686 ($\pm$0.006)	0.690 ($\pm$0.007)	0.697 ($\pm$0.007)	0.698 ($\pm$0.007)
ART-RP Loc. D-ART	0.707 ($\pm$0.007)	0.713 ($\pm$0.007)	0.721 ($\pm$0.007)	0.725 ($\pm$0.007)	0.731 ($\pm$0.007)
ART-Bi. Res.	0.658 ($\pm$0.007)	0.663 ($\pm$0.006)	0.674 ($\pm$0.006)	0.679 ($\pm$0.007)	0.686 ($\pm$0.006)

for all failure patterns. The values of $F_{p,\theta,f}$ are given in Tables 1–3. The values of $d_{f,p}$ are given in the first three columns of Table 4. The fourth column contains the values of d_f. The factor $f = 0.3$ has minimal squared difference d_f. Therefore, this choice for f is optimal for ART by Bisection with Restriction.

For the optimal factor $f = 0.3$ the F-measure is between 0.661 and 0.684 for the block failure pattern, between 0.889 and 0.97 for the strip failure pattern, and between 0.949 and 0.975 for the point pattern (with 50 discs).

Tables 5–8 show the results of the second part of the simulation study— the comparison of ART by Bisection with Restriction with other common ART methods.

For the block failure pattern the relative mean F-measure is between 0.658 and 0.686 for the new ART method. This is close to the results for RRT and D-ART if the failure rate is high. And otherwise the difference between the relative

Table 6. The mean F-measure of the respective ART method related to the theoretical mean F-measure of Random Testing for the strip failure pattern

	$\theta = 0.01$	$\theta = 0.005$	$\theta = 0.002$	$\theta = 0.001$	$\theta = 0.0005$
RRT	**0.866** (±0.010)	0.910 (±0.010)	**0.932** (±0.011)	**0.943** (±0.011)	0.962 (±0.011)
D-ART	0.869 (±0.010)	**0.903** (±0.010)	0.934 (±0.011)	0.958 (±0.011)	**0.958** (±0.011)
ART-RP	0.950 (±0.010)	0.967 (±0.011)	0.968 (±0.011)	0.983 (±0.011)	0.992 (±0.011)
ART-Bi.	0.916 (±0.010)	0.943 (±0.011)	0.957 (±0.011)	0.969 (±0.011)	0.990 (±0.011)
ART-RP Loc. RRT	0.927 (±0.010)	0.937 (±0.010)	0.958 (±0.011)	0.969 (±0.011)	0.978 (±0.011)
ART-RP Loc. D-ART	0.922 (±0.010)	0.948 (±0.010)	0.967 (±0.011)	0.973 (±0.011)	0.979 (±0.011)
ART-Bi. Res.	0.885 (±0.009)	0.907 (±0.010)	0.937 (±0.010)	0.956 (±0.011)	0.965 (±0.011)

Table 7. The mean F-measure of the respective ART method related to the theoretical mean F-measure of Random Testing for the point failure pattern with 10 discs

	$\theta = 0.01$	$\theta = 0.005$	$\theta = 0.002$	$\theta = 0.001$	$\theta = 0.0005$
RRT	0.975 (±0.010)	0.958 (±0.010)	0.942 (±0.010)	0.936 (±0.010)	0.924 (±0.010)
D-ART	0.960 (±0.010)	0.946 (±0.010)	0.929 (±0.010)	0.919 (±0.010)	0.926 (±0.010)
ART-RP	0.945 (±0.011)	0.948 (±0.011)	0.949 (±0.011)	0.953 (±0.011)	0.952 (±0.011)
ART-Bi.	0.934 (±0.010)	0.933 (±0.010)	0.931 (±0.010)	0.930 (±0.010)	0.932 (±0.010)
ART-RP Loc. RRT	0.926 (±0.010)	0.927 (±0.010)	0.926 (±0.010)	0.921 (±0.010)	0.929 (±0.010)
ART-RP Loc. D-ART	0.930 (±0.010)	0.929 (±0.010)	0.932 (±0.010)	0.936 (±0.010)	0.936 (±0.010)
ART-Bi. Res.	**0.871** (±0.009)	**0.881** (±0.010)	**0.899** (±0.010)	**0.900** (±0.010)	**0.903** (±0.010)

mean F-measure of ART by Bisection and Restriction and RRT is at most 0.09. However, for the fast ART methods (ART with Random Partitioning, short ART-RP, ART by Bisection, short ART-Bi., ART with Random Partitioning and Localization with RRT/D-ART), ART by Bisection and Restriction is optimal—even better than ART with Random Partitioning and Localization with RRT, that requires significantly more runtime.

The relative mean F-measure is between 0.885 and 0.965 for the presented ART algorithm and the strip failure pattern. These values are quite close to those of the RRT and D-ART methods. They are only worse by at most 0.02, which is close to the accuracy (the sum of both accuracies). As for the block failure pattern, ART by Bisection with Restriction is optimal among the fast

Table 8. The mean F-measure of the respective ART method related to the theoretical mean F-measure of Random Testing for the point failure pattern with 50 discs

	$\theta = 0.01$	$\theta = 0.005$	$\theta = 0.002$	$\theta = 0.001$	$\theta = 0.0005$
RRT	1.022 (± 0.011)	1.003 (± 0.011)	1.000 (± 0.011)	0.995 (± 0.011)	0.986 (± 0.011)
D-ART	1.002 (± 0.011)	1.006 (± 0.011)	0.989 (± 0.011)	0.986 (± 0.011)	0.985 (± 0.011)
ART-RP	0.979 (± 0.011)	0.980 (± 0.011)	0.982 (± 0.011)	0.986 (± 0.011)	0.992 (± 0.011)
ART-Bi.	0.986 (± 0.011)	0.986 (± 0.011)	0.977 (± 0.011)	0.977 (± 0.011)	0.975 (± 0.011)
ART-RP Loc. RRT	0.967 (± 0.011)	0.972 (± 0.011)	0.981 (± 0.011)	0.987 (± 0.011)	0.987 (± 0.011)
ART-RP Loc. D-ART	0.984 (± 0.011)	0.983 (± 0.011)	0.985 (± 0.011)	0.984 (± 0.011)	0.989 (± 0.011)
ART-Bi. Res.	**0.948** (± 0.011)	**0.948** (± 0.011)	**0.968** (± 0.011)	**0.964** (± 0.011)	**0.970** (± 0.011)

ART methods. The relative mean F-measure is by between 0.013 and 0.031 better than those for the other "fast" methods.

The results for the point pattern with 10 discs and with 50 discs are surprising: The proposed ART algorithm achieves the best relative mean F-measure for both point patterns and all failure rates. For 10 discs, the relative mean F-measure is between 0.871 and 0.903, which is an improvement of at least between 0.019 and 0.055 over the values for all the other ART methods. For 50 discs, the relative mean F-measure is between 0.948 and 0.97, which is an improvement of at least between 0.005 and 0.019 over the values for all the other ART methods.

The proposed ART method, thus, performs best (among all ART methods) for the point pattern, and best (among all "fast" ART methods) for the block and the strip pattern. Due to its computational efficiency, ART by Bisection with Restriction is the best choice among the "fast" ART methods and altogether a very good choice. The F-measure of RRT and D-ART is significantly better than that of the proposed method in case of the block failure pattern. However, the runtime of RRT and D-ART is at least quadratic in the number of test cases generated, whereas it is linear for the presented algorithm. Therefore, the proposed method is in each case a very good choice.

As the original method ART by Bisection, ART by Bisection with Restriction retains important properties: It has properties of the Equal-Size-Equal-Number and the Proportional Sampling strategies. Each sub-domain is of the same size, and the same number of test cases is chosen from each sub-domain. Therefore, ART by Bisection with Restriction has also at least the same probability of detecting at least one failure, in addition to the smaller number of test cases necessary to detect the first failure.

As with all Adaptive Random Testing methods, the proposed algorithm only solves the generation of the test cases from bounded rectangular two-dimensional input domains. This can, however easily be adapted to higher dimension. More complex inputs need special treatment.

As with all Random Testing methods, the proposed algorithm only shows a method to generate test inputs. However, a test oracle, i. e. a program that evaluates the outputs and decides "pass" or "no pass", is also required for efficient test execution. This is the key problem in software testing and not covered by the present paper.

5 Conclusion

Based on ART by Bisection, which iteratively bisects the input domain and randomly selects test cases from all "empty" sub-domains, a novel ART method, namely ART by Bisection with Restriction, has been presented. This algorithm selects the test cases from restricted sub-domains. One of the advantages of the new algorithm is its computational efficiency, besides its simplicity. A simulation study has been performed to compute the mean F-measure, the mean number of test cases necessary to detect the first failure. For the simulation study, all common failure patterns (block, strip, and point) and a set of failure rates have been used. In the first part of the simulation study, the optimal factor used for the restriction has been determined. It turned out that it is optimal to have a restriction by two times 30% of the width resp. the height of the sub-domains. The second part of the simulation study compared the novel ART algorithm with common ART methods. Surprisingly, the new method is best (among all ART methods) for the point failure pattern, and best (among all "fast" ART methods) for the block and the strip failure pattern. Taking the runtimes into account, the proposed method is also a good alternative to RRT and D-ART for the block failure pattern, since RRT and D-ART have at least quadratic runtime, whereas the presented algorithm has linear runtime.

The comparison of the proposed method with other ART algorithms was done with a simulation study using artificially simulated failure patterns. A comparison using real programs with randomly seeded bugs would be desirable to gain a more reliable and more practical performance comparison.

Acknowledgement

The author is grateful to T.Y. Chen for discussions and help regarding the simulation of failure patterns.

References

1. Myers, G.J.: The Art of Software Testing. Wiley, New York (1979)
2. Agrawal, V.D.: When to use random testing. IEEE Transactions on Computers **27** (1978) 1054–1055
3. Duran, J.W., Ntafos, S.C.: An evaluation of random testing. IEEE Transactions on Software Engineering **10** (1984) 438–444
4. Hamlet, R.: Random testing. In: Encyclopedia of Software Engineering. Wiley (1994) 970–978

5. Loo, P.S., Tsai, W.K.: Random testing revisited. Information and Software Technology **30** (1988) 402–417
6. Schneck, P.B.: Comment on "when to use random testing". IEEE Transactions on Computers **28** (1979) 580–581
7. Frankl, P.G., Hamlet, R.G., Littlewood, B., Strigini, L.: Evaluating testing methods by delivered reliability. IEEE Transactions on Software Engineering **24** (1998) 586–601
8. Frankl, P.G., Hamlet, R.G., Littlewood, B., Strigini, L.: Correction to: Evaluating testing methods by delivered reliability. IEEE Transactions on Software Engineering **25** (1999) 286
9. Weyuker, E.J., Jeng, B.: Analysing partition testing strategies. IEEE Transactions on Software Engineering **17** (1991) 703–711
10. Chan, F.T., Chen, T.Y., Mak, I.K., Yu, Y.T.: Proportional sampling strategy: Guidelines for software testing practitioners. Information and Software Technology **38** (1996) 775–782
11. Chen, T.Y., Yu, Y.T.: On the relationship between partition and random testing. IEEE Transactions on Software Engineering **20** (1994) 977–980
12. Chen, T.Y., Tse, T.H., Yu, Y.T.: Proportional sampling strategy: A compendium and some insights. The Journal of Systems and Software **58** (2001) 65–81
13. Hamlet, R.G., Taylor, R.: Partition testing does not inspire confidence. IEEE Transactions on Software Engineering **16** (1990) 1402–1411
14. Chan, K.P., Chen, T.Y., Towey, D.: Restricted random testing. In Kontio, J., Conradi, R., eds.: Proceedings of the 7th European Conference on Software Quality (ECSQ 2002). Volume 2349 of Lecture Notes in Computer Science., Springer (2002) 321–330
15. Chan, K.P., Chen, T.Y., Towey, D.: Normalized restricted random testing. In: Proceedings of the 18th Ada-Europe International Conference on Reliable Software Technologies. Volume 2655 of Lecture Notes in Computer Science., Springer (2003) 368–381
16. Chan, K.P., Chen, T.Y., Kuo, F.C., Towey, D.: A revisit of adaptive random testing by restriction. In: Proceedings of the 28th International Computer Software and Applications Conference (COMPSAC 2004), IEEE Computer Society (2004) 78–85
17. Chen, T.Y., Eddy, G., Merkel, R., Wong, P.K.: Adaptive random testing through dynamic partitioning. In: Proceedings of the 4th International Conference on Quality Software (QSIC 2004), IEEE Computer Society (2004) 79–86
18. Casella, G., Berger, R.L.: Statistical Inference. Wadsworth Group, Duxbury, CA, USA (2002)

Testing Real-Time Multi Input-Output Systems

Laura Brandán Briones and Ed Brinksma

Faculty of Computer Science, University of Twente,
P.O.Box 217, 7500AE Enschede, The Netherlands
{brandanl, brinksma}@cs.utwente.nl

Abstract. In formal testing, the assumption of *input enabling* is typically made. This assumption requires all inputs to be enabled anytime. In addition, the useful concept of *quiescence* is sometimes applied. Briefly, a system is in a *quiescent* state when it cannot produce outputs.

In this paper, we relax the *input enabling* assumption, and allow some input sets to be enabled while others remain disabled. Moreover, we also relax the general bound M used in timed systems to detect *quiescence*, and allow different bounds for different sets of outputs.

By considering the **tioco**$_M$ theory, an enriched theory for timed testing with repetitive *quiescence*, and allowing the partition of input sets and output sets, we introduce the **mtioco**$_\mathcal{M}$ relation. A test derivation procedure which is nondeterministic and parameterized is further developed, and shown to be sound and complete wrt **mtioco**$_\mathcal{M}$.

1 Introduction

Testing is the dominating validation activity in industry today. The necessity to improve it is urgent. The formal approach to testing and test generation, which aims to automatically generate test cases from models of the system under test (SUT), provides a structured way to improve and control the quality of testing.

Formal testing theory was introduced by De Nicola and Hennessy in their seminal paper [17], further elaborated in [16,9]. The first attempts to use De Nicola-Hennessy testing theory for finding algorithms to derive tests automatically from formal specifications were made by Brinksma in [3,4]. Tretmans [19] studied test generation for I/O transition systems. Building on this work, Heerink [8] extended the theory to deal with multiple channels, providing a more realistic scenario. These two approaches, depicted on Figure 1 (left) do not consider time in their models (i.e. are *untimed*). Recently, Tretmans' theory was extended to the timed setting by the authors [5], as shown in Figure 1 (top right).

It seems natural to ask whether a timed testing theory can also be extended to deal with multiple channels, thus completing Figure 1 (bottom right). In this paper we answer this question affirmatively, and we extend our theory [5] to account for multiple channels.

In black box, or functional, testing the model specifies the intended communication between the system and its environment, typically in terms of inputs (or *stimuli*) and outputs (or *responses*). In addition, the assumption of *input enabling* is commonly required. This assumption requests all inputs to a SUT

K.-K. Lau and R. Banach (Eds.): ICFEM 2005, LNCS 3785, pp. 264–279, 2005.

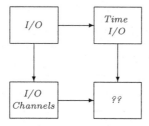

Fig. 1. Relation between test generation approaches

to be allowed at any time. A test case, then, provides inputs to the SUT and observes outputs from it. When it is not possible to recognize differences in the observable behaviour of two systems, it is concluded the systems are equal, i.e. a system is defined by its observable behaviour. In other words, the richer the observable behaviour is, the richer the distinguishing power of the test is. One way to improve this observable behaviour is by using the concept of *quiescence*. Briefly, a system is in a *quiescent* state when it cannot produce outputs without further inputs.

In [5] a real-time testing theory is formulated for *quiescent* time systems, which is parameterized by a bound M that is the explicit representation of the time a system should idle until *quiescence* can be concluded. Treating *quiescence* as a special sort of system output provides us with information to differentiate systems that have intuitively different deadlocking properties (cf. [5,12,19]).

In this paper we introduce the model of *timed multi input-output transition systems TMIOTS*. They model timed systems that communicate with the environment via multiple input and output channels. This allows us to consider *input enabling* and *quiescence* properties not only for an entire system but also on a per channel basis, thus relaxing global system assumptions.

Formally, channels are represented as a partitioning of the sets of input and output actions, each partition class defining the inputs (outputs) belonging to an individual input (output) channel. Following the ideas of Heerink [8] for the untimed case, we replace *input enabledness* by the requirement that for each input channel either all inputs are allowed, or they are all blocked. Often, this requirement is quite natural: a cash machine with a PIN card inserted would not accept the insertion of another card in the same slot.

In a similar way, we relax the treatment of *quiescence* by replacing the global bound M of **tioco**$_M$, by a vector of bounds $\mathcal{M} = \langle M_1, \cdots, M_n \rangle$ for the different output channels. In **tioco**$_M$ the global bound M is a parameter which inform for how long a system should wait before conclude *quiescent*. Relaxing the global bound M for a vector of bounds means that we will not have to wait for the slowest response time to conclude the *quiescence* of a faster channel.

The combination of these ideas is formalized as the **mtioco**$_{\mathcal{M}}$ conformance relation. We develop a test derivation procedure for **mtioco**$_{\mathcal{M}}$, which is shown to be sound and complete. Therefore, our work can be seen as a real-time extension of Heerink's **mioco** theory, which introduced the channel-based treatment of *input enabling/blocking* and *quiescence* in the untimed setting.

Organization of the Paper. The paper consists of two main parts: Models and Relations (Section 2) and Test Generation Framework (Section 3). In the first part, starting from a simple model and a simple conformance relation we build in three steps (Subsections: 2.1, 2.2 and 2.3) an extended model and its conformance relation **mtioco**$_\mathcal{M}$. In the second part, we develop a parameterized nondeterministic test derivation procedure and prove that the set of test are sound and complete with respect to the **mtioco**$_\mathcal{M}$ relation. Finally, Section 4 presents the conclusions of the paper. To save space we omitted the proof of lemmas and theorems in this paper, but they can be found in the extended version of this paper [6].

2   Models and Relations

This section presents three related models, and a conformance relation is formulated for each of them. First, we introduce timed transition systems and the **tmior** relation. Later on, the timed transition relation is extended with *quiescence* and *refusals* and a parameterized relation is defined: **mtiorf** relation. Finally, the concept of *observed outputs set* is introduced and the **mtioco**$_\mathcal{M}$ relation is given. Throughout, a model of a cash machine is used as a running example.

2.1   A Basic Model and Relation

Basically, a *timed labelled transition system* is a *labelled transition system* extended with time delay transitions. This leads to three types of actions: *time-passage actions*, *visible actions* and the special *internal action* τ. All except the time-passage actions are thought of as occurring instantaneously, i.e. without consuming time. To specify time, a continuous dense time domain is used.

Definition 1. *A Timed Labelled Transition System (TLTS) is a 4-tuple* $\langle S, s_0, L_{\tau T}, \rightarrow \rangle$, *where*

- *S is a non-empty set of states. With $s_0 \in S$ as the initial state.*
- *$L_{\tau T} \triangleq L \cup \{\tau\} \cup T$ are the actions L including the internal action τ and time-passage actions. Where $\tau \notin L$ and $T \triangleq \{d \mid d \in \mathbb{R}^{\geq 0}\}$ with $L \cup \{\tau\} \cup T = \emptyset$*
- *$\rightarrow \subseteq (S \times L_{\tau T} \times S)$ is the timed transition relation with the following consistency constraints: $\forall d, d_1, d_2 \in T; \forall s, s', s'' \in S$*
  - **Time Determinism** *whenever $s \xrightarrow{d} s'$ and $s \xrightarrow{d} s''$ then $s' = s''$*
  - **Time Additivity** *($\exists s' : s \xrightarrow{d_1} s' \xrightarrow{d_2} s''$) if and only if $s \xrightarrow{d_1 + d_2} s''$*
  - **Null Delay** *$s \xrightarrow{0} s'$ if and only if $s = s'$.*

The labels in L_T ($L_T \triangleq L \cup T$) represent the observable actions of a system, i.e. labelled actions and passage of time. The τ label represents an unobservable internal action. A transition $(s, \mu, s') \in \rightarrow$ is denoted as $s \xrightarrow{\mu} s'$. A *computation* is a finite or infinite sequence of transitions:

$$s_0 \xrightarrow{\mu_1} s_1 \xrightarrow{\mu_2} s_2 \xrightarrow{\mu_3} \cdots \xrightarrow{\mu_{n-1}} s_{n-1} \xrightarrow{\mu_n} s_n (\rightarrow \dots)$$

When a *timed labelled transition system* has the set of actions partitioned into input and output actions is called a *timed input-output transition system*, denoted as $TIOTS(L_I, L_U)$ where L_I represents the set of inputs and L_U the set of outputs.

Our framework is based on *timed transitions systems* even though all examples we present are given as timed automata. In comparison, a timed automata have less expressiveness than a *timed transition systems* but they have a more compact representation. The relation between a timed automata and its corresponding semantics in terms of *timed transition system* can be found in [18].

Example 1. Our example is an adapted version of the cash machine in [8]. Figure 2 is the representation of a cash machine where a card can be inserted and for a limited period of time a PIN can be typed in. After the machine has decided if the PIN was correct, an amount of money can be requested. In case the machine has sufficient money, it will return the card and then give the requested money. If there is not enough money it will produce an error and return the card. In case the PIN or the amount of money are to late the machine return the card.

Throughout the paper we denote an input as a label followed with a ?-symbol and an output with a !- symbol. The example shows a system where there are inputs, outputs and real-time constraints. In terms of Definition 1 the cash machine is specified as a $TIOTS(L_I, L_U)$ where $\langle S, s_0, L_{\tau T}, \rightarrow \rangle$, with $S = \{q_0, \cdots, q_{11}\}$, $s_0 = q_0$, $L_I = \{card?, PIN?, amount?\}$ and $L_U = \{card!, amount!, Ok!, Err-P!, Err-a!\}$.

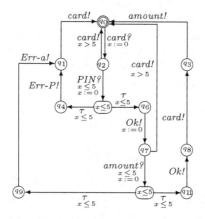

Fig. 2. A cash machine, a modified version of [8]

To explicitly encode the inability for a state to perform any action in a set A or any internal action τ, we extend the *timed transition relation* with self-loop transitions: $s \xrightarrow{A} s$, in case A is a *refusal* of s

$$s \xrightarrow{A} s' \triangleq \forall \mu \in (A \cup \{\tau\}) : s \xnrightarrow{\mu} \wedge s = s'.$$

We use the well-known notation: $p \xRightarrow{\sigma}$ to denote that there exists a reachable state q from p by performing σ while abstracting from the internal actions. In the rest of the paper, we do not always distinguish between p a *TLTS* and its initial state s_0, e.g. we write $p \xRightarrow{\sigma}$ instead of $s_0 \xRightarrow{\sigma}$.

Definition 2. *Let p be an $TLTS(L)$, with P a set of states in p, then*

f-ttraces$(p) = \{\sigma \in (\mathcal{P}(L) \cup L_T)^* \mid p \overset{\sigma}{\Rightarrow}\}$, $\mathcal{P}(L)$ *denotes the power set of L*

ttraces$(p) = $ f-ttraces$(p) \cap L_T^*$

init$(p) = \{\mu \in L_{\tau T} \mid \exists\, p' : p \overset{\mu}{\rightarrow} p'\}$

der$(p) = \{p' \mid \exists\, \sigma \in L_T^* : p \overset{\sigma}{\Rightarrow} p'\}$

P **after** $\sigma = \{p' \mid \exists\, p \in P : p \overset{\sigma}{\Rightarrow} p'\}$

p *is deterministic if and only if* $\forall\, \sigma \in L_T^* : |\{p\}$ **after** $\sigma| \leq 1$.

As expected, a *timed trace* (ttrace) is a standard trace extended with time. A *failure ttrace* (f-ttrace) is a *ttrace* extended with sets of actions that can not be performed, in other words actions that are *refused*. The *init* is the set of all possible actions from a given state, the *der* is the set of all reachable states from a given state, and the **after** is the set of all states reachable after a given *ttrace*. We call a system *deterministic* if for all *ttrace*'s it has at most one reachable state.

In Figure 2 we can observe that the $init(q_0) = \{card?\}$, the $der(q_0)$ is the set of all states $\{q_1, \cdots, q_{11}\}$ and $(\{q_{11}, q_9\}$ **after** Ok!$) = \{q_8\}$. Moreover, we can recognize the cash machine is not *deterministic*.

As we already anticipated in the introduction, the novelty of this paper is to consider *real-time transition systems* where the input set and output set are partitioned into subsets, called channels. More precisely, a $TIOTS(\mathcal{L}_I, \mathcal{L}_U)$ is a *timed input-output transition system* $TIOTS(L_I, L_U)$ where the set of inputs and outputs are partitioned into channels $\mathcal{L}_I = \{L_I^1, \cdots, L_I^n\}$ and $\mathcal{L}_U = \{L_U^1, \cdots, L_U^m\}$.

The partition in channels gives us the possibility to introduce the first relation : **tmior** (Definition 3). This relation refers to the inclusion of *f-ttraces* where the *refusals* can only be full channels.

Definition 3. *Let p and q be $TIOTS(\mathcal{L}_I, \mathcal{L}_U)$, then*

$q \sqsubseteq_{\textbf{tmior}} p \overset{\triangle}{=}$ f-ttraces$(q) \cap (L_T \cup \mathcal{L}_I \cup \mathcal{L}_U)^* \subseteq$ f-ttraces(p).

2.2   An Extended Model and Relation

The **tmior** relation, from Section 2.1 induced us to define an extension of $TIOTS$ where the input and output sets are subdivides in channels. Then, a *timed multi input-output transition system* ($TMIOTS(\mathcal{L}_I, \mathcal{L}_U)$) is a $TIOTS(L_I, L_U)$ where, in each reachable state each input channel is either blocked or all inputs of that channel are accepted (*input enabling* for particular channels). More formally:

Definition 4. *For $\mathcal{L}_I = \{L_I^1, \cdots, L_I^n\}$ and $\mathcal{L}_U = \{L_U^1, \cdots, L_U^m\}$ a Timed Multi Input-Output Transition System p $TMIOTS(\mathcal{L}_I, \mathcal{L}_U)$ is a $TIOTS$ with $L_I = \underset{1 \leq i \leq n}{\cup} L_I^i$ and $L_U = \underset{1 \leq j \leq m}{\cup} L_U^j$, where*

$$\forall\, s \in der(p) : (\forall\, \mu \in L_I^i : s \overset{\mu}{\nrightarrow}) \vee (\forall\, \mu \in L_I^i : s \overset{\mu}{\rightarrow})$$

Moreover, whenever a channel L_I^i is blocked in state s, it is denoted $\gamma^i(s)$.

Example 2. It is possible to see the cash machine of Figure 2 as a *TMIOTS* $(\mathcal{L}_I, \mathcal{L}_U)$ $\langle S, s_0, L_{\tau T}, \rightarrow \rangle$, where $S = \{q_0, \cdots, q_{11}\}$, $s_0 = q_0$, $\mathcal{L}_I = \{L_I^1, L_I^2\}$ and

$\mathcal{L}_U = \{L_U^1, L_U^2, L_U^3\}$ with $L_I^1 = \{card?\}$, $L_I^2 = \{PIN?, amount?\}$ and $L_U^1 = \{card!\}$, $L_U^2 = \{amount!\}$, $L_U^3 = \{Ok!, Err\text{-}P!, Err\text{-}a!\}$. With the corresponding saturation for each channel (i.e. every state with an outgoing transition labeled by input from a channel, is assumed, to have the rest of the inputs from that channel as self-loop transitions. Even when this might not be explicit).

Since the definition of $\mathrm{TMIOTS}(\mathcal{L}_I, \mathcal{L}_U)$ implies *input enabling* or no input at all for each channel, we use it only when the *input enabling* property is necessary. Otherwise, we use the more general notation $\mathrm{TIOTS}(\mathcal{L}_I, \mathcal{L}_U)$, implying TIOTS with the input and output sets partitioned in channels.

The notion of *quiescence* is crucial, since some systems can only be distinguished by their *quiescent* states. Intuitively, the underlying idea is that the environment may observe not only output actions, but also the *absence* of output actions (i.e. in a given state, the system does not emit any output for the environment to observe).

There are two possible ways to deal with *quiescence*. First, we may consider the situation in which the environment can only observe one channel. In this case, it is not relevant for the notion of *quiescence* whether the remaining channels stay silent or not. Second, we may consider the environment to be able to observe all possible channels. In this case, to conclude *quiescence* in one particular channel L_U^j must imply that the remaining channels stay silent for at least the period of time L_U^j stayed silent. We adopt the latter direction, assuming an environment which can observe simultaneously all channels. This choice fits well with the testing framework of [5], where tests synchronize on all output actions. Partial observations of system output can be dealt with by considering modified SUTs where the unobservable channels have become internal actions to the system.

Definition 5. *Let p be a $TIOTS(\mathcal{L}_I, \mathcal{L}_U)$ with s an state of p is called L_U^j-quiescent, denoted $\delta^j(s)$, if and only if $\forall \mu \in L_U^j : \forall d \in \mathbb{R}^+ : s \overset{\mu(d)}{\not\Rightarrow}$. Where $s \overset{d}{\Rightarrow}$ is used as the syntactic sugar for $\exists s' : s \overset{d}{\Rightarrow} s' \overset{\mu}{\Rightarrow}$, and $s \overset{\mu(d)}{\not\Rightarrow}$ its corresponding negation.*

We would like to point out that in the non-timed framework, the *quiescence* definition uses a single arrow notation $\rightarrow$, namely without abstracting from τ transitions. In the timed case this is not possible. For example, take the definition above with a single arrow, and the following system, with $o! \in L_U^j : s \overset{d}{\rightarrow} s' \overset{\tau}{\rightarrow} s'' \overset{d'}{\rightarrow} s''' \overset{o!}{\rightarrow}$. Then, with the new definition the state s is *quiescent* because is not possible to reach from s'' from s with a single arrow. Consequently, in *timed systems* it is essential that the definition of *quiescent* have double arrow.

With the definition of L_U^j-*quiescence*, we extend the *timed transition relation* to include self-loop transitions for *refusals* and *quiescence*. Therefore, $s \overset{\gamma^i}{\rightarrow} s$ if and only if s refuses L_I^i, and $s \overset{\delta^j}{\rightarrow} s$ if and only if s is L_U^j-*quiescent*. We denote p a $TIOTS(\mathcal{L}_I, \mathcal{L}_U)$ with the extended timed transition relation for *refusals* and *quiescence* as $\Delta(p)$. A consequence of this extension is: f-ttraces$(p) \cap (L_\mathcal{T} \cup \mathcal{L}_I \cup$

$\mathcal{L}_U)^* = $ ttraces$(\Delta(p))$. Therefore, using this notation we can re-write the **tmior** relation as: $q \sqsubseteq_{\mathbf{tmior}} p$ if and only if: $\textit{ttraces}(\Delta(q)) \subseteq \textit{ttraces}(\Delta(p))$.

Example 3. Figure 3 illustrates the cash machine with the extended timed transition relation with *refusals*(γ^i) and *quiescence*(δ^j). To avoid too much detail, it is assumed that in each state without a self-loop for *refusal* of an input channel, all the absent inputs of that channel have self-loop transitions in that state.

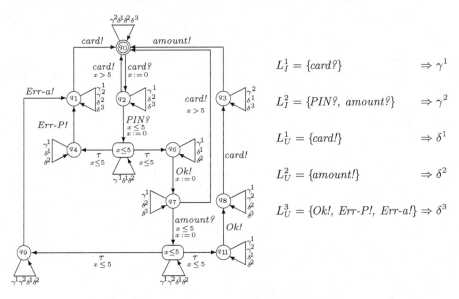

Fig. 3. A cash machine, a modified version of [8]

An immediate problem, in black box testing, is how to detect *quiescence* in implementations. Given that a *quiescent* state in an implementation is only recognizable after a period of time where there was no output observations, it is necessary to fix for how long a test should be waiting before concluding *quiescence*. Therefore, we define three properties. First, we define what it means for a state to be *quiescent* with respect to a channel and a particular time bound. Intuitively, for a state to be *quiescent* on a channel wrt a particular bound means that all reachable states after delaying by the given bound are *quiescent* on that particular channel. More precisely, a state of a system is M_j-*quiescent*, for an output channel j, if and only if all reachable states from that state after M_j are *quiescent*. Second, the definition is extended to all state in the system. Third, the definition is extended to include all output channels.

Definition 6. *Let p be a $TIOTS(\mathcal{L}_I, \mathcal{L}_U)$ with S as its states, $s \in S$ and $\mathcal{M}$ an ordered set of bounds $\mathcal{M} = \langle M_1, \cdots, M_m \rangle : \forall\, 1 \leq j \leq m : M_j \in \mathbb{R}^{\geq 0}$, then*

- s *is $\mathcal{M}_j$-quiescent if and only if* $\forall\, s' \in (s \text{ after } M_j) : s' \in L_U^j$-quiescent
- p *is $\mathcal{M}_j$-quiescent if and only if* $\forall\, s \in S : \mathcal{M}_j$-quiescent$(s)$
- p *is $\mathcal{M}$-quiescent if and only if* $\forall\, 1 \leq j \leq m : \mathcal{M}_j$-quiescent$(q)$.

An interpretation of this definition is that for a tester to check for *quiescence* in channel j, it is enough with wait a period of time equal to M_j, without observing outputs. There are two important principles involved in this definition. We are spending different times for detecting *quiescence* for different channels. Moreover, we assume that after delaying by the corresponding bound of a channel there will not be any spontaneous output on that channel.

Lemma 1. *If a system $p \in TIOTS(\mathcal{L}_I, \mathcal{L}_U)$ is M_j-quiescent with S as its states and $s \in S$, then:* $\delta^j(s) \triangleq \forall \mu \in L_U^j : \forall d \in \mathbb{R}^{\geq 0} : d \leq M_j : s \overset{\mu(d)}{\nrightarrow}$.

Corollary 1. *Let $p \in TIOTS(\mathcal{L}_I, \mathcal{L}_U)$ be M-quiescent with S as its states, $s \in S$, and $M = \langle M_1, \cdots, M_m \rangle$, then*

$$\forall j = 1, \cdots, m : (\delta^j(s) \Leftrightarrow (\forall \mu \in L_U^j : \forall d \in \mathbb{R}^{\geq 0} : d \leq M_j : s \overset{\mu(d)}{\nrightarrow})).$$

Considering the cash machine in Figure 3 for $M = \langle M_1, M_2, M_3 \rangle$ with $M_1 = 6$, $M_2 = 6$ and $M_3 = 6$ we can recognize that state q_0 is M_1-*quiescent*.

Since in an implementation we can detect *quiescence* only with the observation of absence of outputs for a period of time, and using the property of M-*quiescence* for a system, we define the **mtiorf** relation, parameteraized by M. In the *traces* considered in **mtiorf** a δ^j can only occur after M_j timed units.

Definition 7. *Let p be a $TIOTS(\mathcal{L}_I, \mathcal{L}_U)$ and q be a M-quiescent TMIOTS $(\mathcal{L}_I, \mathcal{L}_U)$, then*

$$q \sqsubseteq_{\mathbf{mtiorf}}^{M} p \quad \textit{if and only if} \quad \Delta_M(q) \subseteq \Delta_M(p)$$

where for $r \in TIOTS(\mathcal{L}_I, \mathcal{L}_U)$, with ϵ as the empty word:
$$\Delta_M(r) \triangleq ttraces(\Delta(r)) \cap \bigcup_i \bigcup_j (((\mathcal{T} \cup \{\epsilon\}) \cdot (L \cup \gamma^i)) \cup M_j \cdot \delta^j)^*.$$

2.3   The Relation: *mtioco_M*

Up to now, we considered relations built up from information based on knowledge of the behaviour of both specifications and implementations. A relation that uses information from the behaviour of only the specification is more desirable in the context of black box testing, which is our main goal in the present paper. To this end, we now define the *observed output set*, which condenses the whole information as perceived by the environment, and a more practical notation in the form of *nttraces*.

Similarly to the definition of *nttraces* for **tioco_M** theory in [5], we present the *normalized ttraces* for *TMIOTS*.

Definition 8. *Let p be M-quiescent and σ be a ttraces in $\Delta(p)$, then*

- *σ is a normalized ttrace if and only if $\sigma \in \bigcup_i \bigcup_j (\mathcal{T} \cdot (L \cup \gamma^i \cup \delta^j))^*$*

- *nttraces$(p) = \{\sigma \in \bigcup_i \bigcup_j (\mathcal{T} \cdot (L \cup \gamma^i \cup \delta^j))^* \mid p \overset{\sigma}{\Rightarrow}\}$*

- *for nttraces $\sigma = d_0 \delta^1 d_1 \gamma^1 d_2 a!$ we also write $\hat{\sigma} = \delta^1(d_0) \gamma^1(d_1) a!(d_2)$.*

Moreover, the definition of *nttraces* already assumes that $TIOTS(\mathcal{L}_I, \mathcal{L}_U)$ systems have the *timed transition relation* extended, implying

$$nttraces(\Delta(r)) = nttraces(r).$$

An example of an *nttrace* in the cash machine is:

$$card?(3)PIN?(2)Err-P!(5)\gamma^1(6)card!(0).$$

For consistency, we need to prove that with this new notation we are not losing expressiveness, as it is crucial to have that the inclusion of *nttraces* for two systems is equal to the inclusion of *ttraces* for the corresponding extended systems. This result is given in the following lemma.

Lemma 2. *Let* $p_1, p_2 \in TIOTS(\mathcal{L}_I, \mathcal{L}_U)$, *then*
   $ttraces(\Delta(p_1)) \subseteq ttraces(\Delta(p_2))$ *if and only if* $nttraces(p_1) \subseteq nttraces(p_2)$.

The *observed output set* of a given set of states P, denoted $obsOut_{\mathcal{M}}(P)$, is defined as the union of two sets: the set of output actions enriched with *quiescent*, denoted $obsOut^o_{\mathcal{M}}$, and the set of *refusals*, denoted $obsOut^r_{\mathcal{M}}$. Hence, $obsOut^o_{\mathcal{M}}$ is the set of outputs that could happen after a period of time plus the special symbol $\delta^j(M_j)$ expressing *quiescence* on output channel j in case a reachable state after M_j is *quiescent* on channel j. And, the set $obsOut^r_{\mathcal{M}}$ is the set of *refusals* $\gamma^i(d)$ for each input channel i that is refused after d timed units.

Definition 9. *Let* P *be a set of states of a* $TIOTS(\mathcal{L}_I, \mathcal{L}_U)$ *with timed transition relation extended, then:*
$obsOut_{\mathcal{M}}(P) = \bigcup_{p \in P} obsOut^o_{\mathcal{M}}(p) \ \bigcup \ \bigcup_{p \in P} obsOut^r_{\mathcal{M}}(p)$

where: $obsOut^o_{\mathcal{M}}(p) = \{\mu(d) \mid \mu \in L_U \wedge p \overset{\mu(d)}{\Rightarrow} \} \cup \bigcup_j \{\delta^j(M_j) \mid p \overset{\delta^j(M_j)}{\Rightarrow} \}$

$obsOut^r_{\mathcal{M}}(p) = \bigcup_i \{\gamma^i(d) \mid \forall \mu \in L^i_I : p \overset{\mu(d)}{\not\Rightarrow} \}$

A immediate and useful consequence of this definition is that a system has an *nttrace* if and only if the *observed output set*, $obsOut_{\mathcal{M}}$, of the system after that *nttrace* is not empty.

Lemma 3. *Let* $p \in TIOTS(\mathcal{L}_I, \mathcal{L}_U)$ *and* $\sigma \in nttraces$, *then*
   $obsOut_{\mathcal{M}}(p \textbf{ after } \sigma) = \emptyset$ *if and only if* $\sigma \notin nttraces(p)$.

We also prove that the parameterized **mtiorf** relation is equal to checking the inclusion of *observed output set* for all *nttraces* that only have δ^j after M_j timed units.

Lemma 4. *Let* p *be* $TIOTS(\mathcal{L}_I, \mathcal{L}_U)$ *and* q *be* $\mathcal{M}$-*quiescent* $TMIOTS(\mathcal{L}_I, \mathcal{L}_U)$, *then* $q \sqsubseteq^{\mathcal{M}}_{\textbf{tmiorf}} p$ *if and only if* $\forall \sigma \in \Delta_{\mathcal{M}}$:

$$obsOut_{\mathcal{M}}(q \textbf{ after } \sigma) \subseteq obsOut_{\mathcal{M}}(p \textbf{ after } \sigma).$$

Finally, we are in position to define the **mtioco**$_{\mathcal{M}}$ relation, based solely on information from the *observed output set* and the specification. Particularly, without any internal knowledge of the implementation, which complies with the requirement of black box testing.

For p a specification in $TIOTS(\mathcal{L}_I, \mathcal{L}_U)$ and q an implementation in $TMIOTS$ $(\mathcal{L}_I, \mathcal{L}_U)$: q will be **mtioco**$_\mathcal{M}$ to p if and only if the *observed output set* of q, after every *nttrace* of p is a subset of the *observed output set* of p after the same *nttrace*.

Definition 10. *Let p be a $TIOTS(\mathcal{L}_I, \mathcal{L}_U)$ and q be $\mathcal{M}$-quiescent $TMIOTS$ $(\mathcal{L}_I, \mathcal{L}_U)$, then:*
$$q \textbf{ mtioco}_\mathcal{M} p \triangleq \forall \sigma \in \Delta_\mathcal{M}(p) : obsOut_\mathcal{M}(q \textbf{ after } \sigma) \subseteq obsOut_\mathcal{M}(p \textbf{ after } \sigma).$$

The **mtioco**$_\mathcal{M}$ relation is a parameterized timed relation that consider *quiescent* for each particular channel. Moreover, in the next section, we use this relation to build our test derivation framework over $TMIOTS(\mathcal{L}_I, \mathcal{L}_U)$.

.3   Test Generation Framework

In this section we define the concept of real-time test cases, the nature of their execution, and the evaluation of their success or failure. Later, a test generation procedure is presented for **mtioco**$_\mathcal{M}$ relation. Moreover, it is shown that this procedure is sound and complete.

A *test case* **t** is a $TIOTS(\mathcal{L}_I, \mathcal{L}_U)\langle S, s_0, L_\mathcal{T} \cup \{\delta\}, \rightarrow\rangle$ such that is deterministic and has *bounded behaviour*, in the sense that all computations have finitely many action occurrences and its accumulative time is bounded. The set of states also contains the terminal states **pass** and **fail** without outgoing transitions. For any state different from **pass** and **fail** there exists a bounded time to observe *quiescence* or to be able to make an input action. Moreover, tests under consideration are deterministic and therefore τ-transitions are not allowed. The class of test cases over $\mathcal{L}_I$ and $\mathcal{L}_U$ is denoted as $TTEST(\mathcal{L}_I, \mathcal{L}_U)$. A *test suite* **T** is a set of test cases: $\textbf{T} \subseteq TTEST(\mathcal{L}_I, \mathcal{L}_U)$. Again, to simplify notation we represent tests as timed automata.

A *test run* of an implementation with a test case is modelled by the synchronous parallel execution of the test case together with the implementation under test. This run continues until no more interactions are possible, i.e. until a deadlock occurs.

Definition 11. *Let **t** be a test in $TTEST(\mathcal{L}_I, \mathcal{L}_U)$ and imp be a $\mathcal{M}$-quiescent implementation in $TMIOTS(\mathcal{L}_I, \mathcal{L}_U)$, then*

- *Running a test case **t** with an implementation imp is modelled by the parallel operator $\| : TTEST(\mathcal{L}_I, \mathcal{L}_U) \times TMIOTS(\mathcal{L}_I, \mathcal{L}_U) \rightarrow TIOTS(\mathcal{L}_I, \mathcal{L}_U)$ which is defined by the following inference rules:*

$$imp \xrightarrow{\tau} imp' \qquad\qquad\qquad \vdash\ \textbf{t}\|imp \xrightarrow{\tau} \textbf{t}\|imp'$$

$$\textbf{t} \xrightarrow{\delta^j} \textbf{t}' \qquad\qquad\qquad\qquad \vdash\ \textbf{t}\|imp \xrightarrow{\delta^j} \textbf{t}'\|imp$$

$$\textbf{t} \xrightarrow{\gamma^i} \textbf{t}', imp \xrightarrow{\mu}\!\!\!\!\!\!/\ imp', \mu \in L_I^i \quad \vdash\ \textbf{t}\|imp \xrightarrow{\gamma^i} \textbf{t}'\|imp$$

$$\textbf{t} \xrightarrow{\mu} \textbf{t}', imp \xrightarrow{\mu} imp', \mu \in L \quad \vdash\ \textbf{t}\|imp \xrightarrow{\mu} \textbf{t}'\|imp'$$

$$\textbf{t} \xrightarrow{d} \textbf{t}', imp \xrightarrow{d} imp', d \in \mathbb{R}^{\geq 0} \vdash\ \textbf{t}\|imp \xrightarrow{d} \textbf{t}'\|imp'$$

- *A test run of* **t** *with an implementation imp, is a* σ *in* $\Delta_M(\mathbf{t}\|imp)$ *leading to a terminal state of* **t**. *Then, an implementation imp* **passes** *test case* **t**, *if all their test runs lead to the* **pass** *state of* **t**. *Moreover, an implementation imp* **passes** *a test suite* **T**, *if it* **passes** *all test cases in* **T**. *And finally, if imp does not* **pass** *the test suite, it* **fails**.

$$
\begin{aligned}
\text{test run of } \mathbf{t} \text{ and } imp \ &\triangleq\ \exists\, imp' : (\mathbf{t}\|imp \overset{\sigma}{\Rightarrow} \mathbf{pass}\|imp')\ or\\
&\qquad\qquad (\mathbf{t}\|imp \overset{\sigma}{\Rightarrow} \mathbf{fail}\|imp')\\
imp \ \mathbf{passes}\ \mathbf{t}\ &\triangleq\ \forall\, \sigma \in \Delta_M : \forall\, imp' : \mathbf{t}\|imp \overset{\sigma}{\not\Rightarrow} \mathbf{fail}\|imp'\\
imp \ \mathbf{passes}\ \mathbf{T}\ &\triangleq\ \forall\, \mathbf{t} \in \mathbf{T} : imp \ \mathbf{passes}\ \mathbf{t}\\
imp \ \mathbf{fails}\ \mathbf{T}\ &\triangleq\ \exists\, \mathbf{t} \in \mathbf{T} : imp \ \mathbf{passes}\ \mathbf{t}.
\end{aligned}
$$

If an implementation can behave nondeterministically, then different test runs of the same test case may lead to different terminal states with different verdicts. This implies that an implementation **passes** a test case if an only if all possible test runs lead to the verdict **pass**.

For the description of test cases we use a process algebraic behavioural notation with a syntax inspired by LOTOS [10]:
$$ B\ \triangleq\ a; B \mid B + B \mid \Sigma\, \mathcal{B} $$
where $a \in L_{\mathcal{T}\gamma\delta}$ $(L_{\mathcal{T}\gamma\delta} \triangleq L_{\mathcal{T}} \cup \{\gamma^i \mid 1 \le i \le n\} \cup \{\delta^j \mid 1 \le j \le m\})$, $\mathcal{B}$ is a countable set of behaviour expressions, and axioms plus inference rules are:

$$
\begin{array}{ll}
a \in L & \vdash\ a; B \overset{a}{\to} B'\\[4pt]
a = d, d' < d & \vdash\ d; B \overset{d'}{\longrightarrow} d - d'; B\\[4pt]
a = d & \vdash\ B \overset{d}{\longrightarrow} B'\\[4pt]
B_1 \overset{\mu}{\to} B_1',\ \mu \in L_{\mathcal{T}\gamma\delta} & \vdash\ B_1 + B_2 \overset{\mu}{\to} B_1'\\[4pt]
B_2 \overset{\mu}{\to} B_2',\ \mu \in L_{\mathcal{T}\gamma\delta} & \vdash\ B_1 + B_2 \overset{\mu}{\to} B_2'\\[4pt]
B \overset{\mu}{\to} B', B \in \mathcal{B}, \mu \in L_{\mathcal{T}\gamma\delta} & \vdash\ \Sigma\, \mathcal{B} \overset{\mu}{\to} B'
\end{array}
$$

Here, we use $\mu(d)$ as syntactic sugar for $d; \mu$, following Definition 8.

3.1   Test Case Generation Procedure

We define a procedure to generate test cases from a given specification in *TIOTS* $(\mathcal{L}_I, \mathcal{L}_U)$. Similar to [19,5] test cases result from the nondeterministic, recursive application of three test generation steps: (1) *termination*, (2) *inputs* (including *refusals*), and (3) *waiting for outputs* (including *quiescence*).

The construction steps involve negations of predicates of the form: $o(d) \in obsOut_{\mathcal{M}}(S)$ or $\gamma^i(d) \in obsOut_{\mathcal{M}}(S)$; which on the general level of *TMIOTS* are undecidable. Then, the procedure given here, should be seen as a meta-algorithm that can be used to generate tests effectively for subclasses of *TMIOTS* for which these predicates are decidable, such as timed automata [11,13] with sub partitioning of the input and output sets.

1. *termination*

    pass

2. *inputs*

choose $k \in [0, Max\{M_1, \cdots, M_m\})$

and $\mu \in L_I$

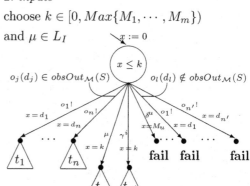

3. *waiting for outputs*

choose j

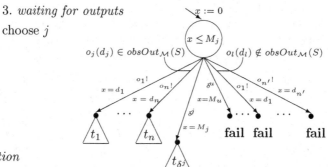

1. *termination*

    $t := \textbf{pass}$

It is possible to stop the recursion at any time using this step.

2. *inputs*

$$
\begin{aligned}
t := \quad & \Sigma\{o_j(d_j); t_j \mid o_j \in L_U \wedge d_j < k \wedge o_j(d_j) \in obsOut_\mathcal{M}(S)\} \\
& + \{\mu(k); t_\mu \mid \mu \in L_I^i \wedge \exists\, s \in S : \gamma^i(k) \notin obsOut_\mathcal{M}(s)\} \\
& + \{\mu(k); \textbf{fail} \mid \mu \in L_I^i \wedge \forall\, s \in S : \gamma^i(k) \in obsOut_\mathcal{M}(s)\} \\
& + \{\gamma^i(k); \textbf{fail} \mid \mu \in L_I^i \wedge \gamma^i(k) \notin obsOut_\mathcal{M}(S)\} \\
& + \{\gamma^i(k); t_{\gamma^i} \mid \mu \in L_I^i \wedge \gamma^i(k) \in obsOut_\mathcal{M}(S)\} \\
& + \Sigma\{\delta^u(M_u); \textbf{fail} \mid M_u \in \mathcal{M} \wedge M_u < k \wedge \delta^u(M_u) \notin obsOut_\mathcal{M}(S)\} \\
& + \Sigma\{o_l(d_l); \textbf{fail} \mid o_l \in L_U \wedge o_l(d_l) \notin obsOut_\mathcal{M}(S)\}
\end{aligned}
$$

where x is a clock, k is a timed variable and t_j, t_μ and t_{γ^i} are obtained by recursively applying the algorithm to $(S \textbf{ after } o_j(d_j))$, $(S \textbf{ after } \mu(k))$ and $(S \textbf{ after } \gamma^i(k))$, respectively.

3. *waiting for outputs*

$$
\begin{aligned}
t := \quad & \Sigma\{o_j(d_j); t_j \mid o_j \in L_U \wedge o_j(d_j) \in obsOut_\mathcal{M}(S)\} \\
& + \Sigma\{\delta^j(M_j); t_{\delta^j} \mid \delta^j \in obsOut_\mathcal{M}(S \textbf{ after } M_j)\} \\
& + \Sigma\{\delta^j(M_j); \textbf{fail} \mid \delta^j \notin obsOut_\mathcal{M}(S \textbf{ after } M_j)\} \\
& + \Sigma\{\delta^u(M_u); \textbf{fail} \mid M_u \in \mathcal{M} \wedge M_U < M_j \wedge \delta^u(M_u) \notin obsOut_\mathcal{M}(S)\} \\
& + \Sigma\{o_l(d_l); \textbf{fail} \mid o_l \in L_U \wedge o_l(d_l) \notin obsOut_\mathcal{M}(S)\}
\end{aligned}
$$

where x is a clock and t_j and t_{δ_j} are obtained by recursively applying the algorithm for $(S$ **after** $o_j(d_j))$ and $(S$ **after** $\delta^j(M_j))$, respectively.

Note 1. Case 2: *inputs* and case 3: *waiting for outputs* are overlapping. If in a derivation of the *input* case test there exists an arrow for a δ^u, then it is clear that the test will never succeed to make the input or check for γ^i. This knowledge could be used, once it is known that an arrow for δ^u exists for the *inputs* case, the test could be forced to choose the *waiting for outputs* case with $j = u$. On the other hand, this overlapping can improve the speed of an error detection.

Note 2. In case 2: *inputs*, to check γ^i seams to mean that we should check that for all μ in L_I^i the impossibility to do μ at a precise time. However, this is not feasible in practice, at least in one step. It is possible to try with any input in that channel, thanks to the *input enabling* assumption.

Example 4. Figure 4 shows a test for the cash machine. The test checks that it is not possible to ask for money before a card is authenticated. Then a card and a PIN are inserted and if the PIN was correct it is possible to ask for money.

For simplicity, in the figure the outputs are represented as follows: *card!* as *c!*, *amount!* as *a!*, *Ok!* as *o!*, $Err-P!$ as *eP!* and $Err-a!$ as *ea!*.

Soundness. The test generation procedure presented is sound with respect to **mtioco**$_\mathcal{M}$ relation. This very important property is shown in the following theorem.

Theorem 1. *Let spec be a specification in* $TIOTS(\mathcal{L}_I, \mathcal{L}_U)$*, then for all* $\mathcal{M}$*-quiescent implementations imp in* $TMIOTS(\mathcal{L}_I, \mathcal{L}_U)$ *and all test cases* **t** *obtained from spec by the above procedure:*

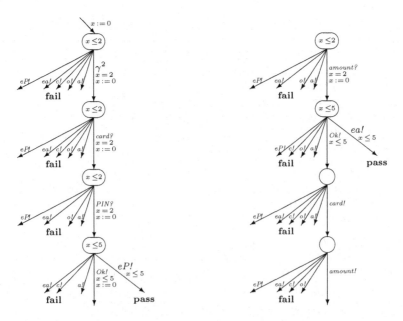

Fig. 4. A test case for the cash machine

$$imp \; \textbf{mtioco}_\mathcal{M} \; spec \Rightarrow imp \; \textbf{passes} \; \textbf{t}.$$

The proof of this theorem as well as that of the following on completeness build on the notion of *saturation* of *nttraces*. Its definition can be found, together with the proofs, in [6].

Completeness. The test generation procedure is also exhaustive in the sense that for each non-conforming implementation a test case can be generated that detects the non-conformance.

Theorem 2. *Let spec be a specification in* $TIOTS(\mathcal{L}_I, \mathcal{L}_U)$, *then for all M-quiescent implementation imp in* $TMIOTS(\mathcal{L}_I, \mathcal{L}_U)$ *with: imp* $\textbf{mtioco}_\mathcal{M} spec$, *there exists a test case* **t** *generated from spec by the above procedure such that:*
$$imp \; \textbf{passes} \; \textbf{t}.$$

The exhaustiveness of our test generation procedure, similar to the one in [5], is less useful than the corresponding result in the untimed case. There, the repeated execution of the test generation algorithm in a fair, nondeterministic manner, will generate for every error a test exposing it in finite time. This is not feasible for the real-time case, as the number of potential test cases is uncountable because of the underlying continuous time domain. It is possible to recover such *limit-completeness* by considering suitable equivalent classes of errors (i.e. an implementation has either all or no errors of a given class), such that a repeated test generation procedure will automatically expose an error in every equivalence class. This is ongoing work.

4   Conclusions

To the best of our knowledge, we propose the first attempt to generate test cases from multi input-output real-time specifications. More specifically, our contributions are:

- We show how the concept of *multi input-output transition systems* can be applied to the modelling of real-time systems.
- We develop a new parameterized conformance relation using the enriched *real-time multi input-output transition systems*.
- The relevance of the model and its theory for test generation is illustrated by modification of a small but realistic example of a cash machine due to Heerink [8].

Related Work. Heerink's work in [8] is an extension of Tretmans' **ioco** theory [19]. Its testing theory is based on singular observers: only one output channel is observed at the time. In [15] a similar theory is presented with an alternative type of observers: all-observer, which can observe all the output channels simultaneously. Both approaches are concerned with untimed systems. In [5] a test generation framework for real-time systems with repetitive *quiescence* is presented, extending the Tretmans' **ioco** theory [19] for real-time systems. This framework is the basis for the approach taken in this paper.

Of the wealth of literature on test generation for real-time systems we mention the related work that can be found in [11,14], but these authors consider neither *quiescence* nor multiple channels. A related approach involving symbolic data can be found in [7].

Future Work. We are continuing our work along three lines. First, we are studying the *limit-completeness* over our approach as explained above. Second, we are working on a more detailed comparison of the present approach and the tioco$_M$ theory [5]. Finally, we are working on the implementation of the multiple input-output theory as an extension of the TorX tool [1,2].

References

1. A. Belinfante, J. Feenstra, R. deVries, J. Tretmans, N. Goga, L. Feijs, S. Mauw, and L. Heerink. Formal test automation: A simple experiment. In G. Csopaki, S. Dibuz, and K. Tarnay, editors, *Int. Workshop on Testing of Communicating Systems 12*, pages 179–196. Kluwer, 1999.
2. H. Bohnenkamp and A. Belinfante. Timed testing with torx. In J. Fitzgerald, I.J. Hayes, and A. Tarlecki, editors, *FM 2005: Formal Methods*, pages 173–188. Springer, 2005.
3. E. Brinksma. On the existence of canonical testers. In *Memorandum INF-87-5*. University of Twente, Enschede, The Netherlands, 1987.
4. E. Brinksma. A theory for the derivation of tests. In *Protocol Specification, Testing, and Verification VIII, North-Holland*, page 6374. S. Aggarwal and K. Sabnani, 1988.
5. L. Brandán Briones and E. Brinksma. A test generation framework for quiescent real-time systems. In *Formal Approaches to Software Testing: 4th International Workshop, FATES*, volume 3395/2005. Springer-Verlag GmbH. Extended Version http://fmt.cs.utwente.nl/research/testing/files/BBB04.ps.gz, 2004.
6. L. Brandán Briones and E. Brinksma. Testing real-time multi input-output systems. Extended Version. Number TR-CTIT-05-40. http://fmt.cs.utwente.nl/re-search/testing/files/BBB05.ps.gz, 2005.
7. L. Frantzen, J. Tretmans, and T.A.C. Willemse. Test generation based on symbolic specifications. In *FATES 2004*. Springer-Verlag, 2005.
8. L. Heerink. Ins and outs in refusal testing. In *PhD thesis*, 1998.
9. M. Hennessy. Algebraic theory of processes. In *Foundations of Computing. Series. The MIT Press*, 1988.
10. ISO8807. *A formal description technique based on the temporal ordering of observational behaviour*. Int. Organization for Standardization, 1989.
11. M. Krichen and S. Tripakis. Black-box conformance testing for real-time systems. In *SPIN 2004*, pages 109–126. Springer-Verlag Heidelberg, 2004.
12. R. Langerak. A testing theory for lotos using deadlock detection. In *Proceedings of the IFIP WG 6.1 Ninth int. Symp. on Protocol Spec., Testing, and Verification*, pages 87–98. IFIP, 1990.
13. K. Larsen, M. Mikucionis, and B. Nielsen. Real-time system testing on-the-fly. In K Sere, M Walden, and A Karlsson, editors, *The 15th Nordic Workshop on Programming Theory (NWPT)*, Åbo Akademi University, Turku, Finland, oct 2003. Extended abstract.
14. K. Larsen, M. Mikucionis, and B. Nielsen. Online testing of real-time system using uppaal. In *Formal Approaches to Software Testing*, Linz, Austria, 2004.

15. Z. Li, J. Wu, and X. Yin. Testing multi input/output transition system with all-observer. In *TestCom*, pages 95–111, 2004.
16. R. De Nicola. Extensional equivalences for transition systems. In *Acta Informatica*, page 24:211237, 1987.
17. R. De Nicola and M.C.B. Hennessy. Testing equivalences for processes. In *Theoretical Computer Science*, page 34:83133, 1984.
18. J. Springintveld, F. Vaandrager, and P. D'Argenio. Testing timed automata. *Theoretical Computer Science*, 254(1–2):225–257, 2001.
19. J. Tretmans. Test generation with inputs, outputs and repetitive quiescence. In *Software-Concepts and Tools, 17(3)*, pages 103–120. Also: Technical Report N0. 96-26, Center for Telematics and Information Technology, University of Twente, The Netherlands, 1996.

Formal Verification of a Memory Model
for *C*-Like Imperative Languages

Sandrine Blazy and Xavier Leroy

INRIA Rocquencourt,
78 153 Le Chesnay cedex, France
{Sandrine.Blazy, Xavier.Leroy}@inria.fr

Abstract. This paper presents a formal verification with the *Coq* proof
assistant of a memory model for *C*-like imperative languages. This model
defines the memory layout and the operations that manage the memory. The model has been specified at two levels of abstraction and implemented as part of an ongoing certification in *Coq* of a moderately-
optimising *C* compiler. Many properties of the memory have been verified in the specification. They facilitate the definition of precise formal
semantics of *C* pointers. A certified *OCaml* code implementing the memory model has been automatically extracted from the specifications.

1 Introduction

Formal verification of computer programs – be it by model checking, program
proof, static analysis, or any other means – obviously requires that the semantics
of the programming language in which the program is written be formalized in
a way that is exploitable by the verification tools used. In the case of program
proofs, these formal semantics are often presented as operational semantics or
specialized logics such as Hoare logic. The need for formal semantics is even
higher when the program being verified itself operates over programs: compilers,
program analyzers, etc. In the case of a compiler, for instance, no less than
three formal semantics are required: one for the implementation language of the
compiler, one for the source language, and one for the target language. More
generally speaking, formal semantics "on machine" (that is, presented in a form
that can be exploited by verification tools) are an important aspect of formal
methods.

Formal semantics are relatively straightforward in the case of declarative programming languages such as pure functional or logic languages. Many programs
that require formal verification are written in imperative languages, however.
These languages feature assignments to variables and in-place modification of
data structures. Giving semantics to these imperative constructs requires the
development of an adequate *memory model*, that is, a formal description of the
memory layout and the operations over it. The memory model is often one of the
most delicate parts of a formal semantics for an imperative programming language: an excessively concrete memory model (*e.g.* representing the memory as a

K.-K. Lau and R. Banach (Eds.): ICFEM 2005, LNCS 3785, pp. 280–299, 2005.

single array of bytes) can fail to validate algebraic laws over loads and stores that are actually valid in the programming language and thus make program proofs more difficult; an excessively abstract memory model can fail to account for *e.g.* aliasing or partial overlap between memory areas, thus causing the semantics to be incorrect.

This paper reports on the design, formalization and verification, using the *Coq* proof assistant, of a memory model for *C*-like imperative languages. In addition to being widely used for programming safety-critical software, *C* and related languages are challenging from the standpoint of the memory model, because they feature both pointers and pointer arithmetic, on the one hand, and isolation and freshness guarantees on the other. For instance, pointer arithmetic can result in aliasing or partial overlap between the memory areas referenced by two pointers; yet, it is guaranteed that the memory areas corresponding to two distinct variables or two successive calls to `malloc` are disjoint. This stands in contrast with both higher-level imperative languages such as *Java*, where two distinct references always refer to disjoint data, and lower-level languages such as machine code, where unrestricted address arithmetic invalidates all isolation guarantees.

The memory model presented here is used in the formal verification of a moderately-optimising compiler that translates a large subset of the *C* programming language down to *PowerPC* assembly code [13]. The memory model is used by the formal semantics of all languages manipulated by the compiler: the source language (large subset of *C*), the target language (subset of *PowerPC* assembly), and 5 intermediate languages that bridge the semantic gap between source and target. Certain passes of the compiler perform non-trivial transformations on memory allocations and accesses: for instance, the `auto` variables of a *C* function, initially mapped to individually-allocated memory blocks, are at some point mapped to sub-blocks of a single stack-allocated activation record, which at a later point is extended to make room for storing spilled temporaries. Proving the correctness (semantic preservation) of these transformations require extensive reasoning over the memory model, using the properties of this model given further in the paper.

The remainder of this paper is organized as follows. Section 2 presents how we have formally verified a compiler with the *Coq* proof assistant. Section 3 describes the formal verification of our memory model. Section 4 explains how *OCaml* code has been automatically generated from this verification. Section 5 discusses related work. Finally, section 6 concludes.

2   Certification of a *C*-Like Compiler

The formal verification of a compiler is the formal proof of the following equivalence result: any source program that terminates on some final memory state is compiled into a program that also terminates and produces the same memory state. Usually, such an equivalence result relies on a more general notion of equivalence between memory states. But, our memory model aims at facilitating this correctness proof and it is designed in such a way that the memory states are the same at the end of the execution of source and compiled programs. The correctness result is not proved directly but in several steps. Each step corresponds to a transformation (that is, either a translation or an optimisation) achieved by the compiler. Each correctness proof of a transformation proceeds by induction on the execution of the original program using a simulation lemma: if the original program executes one statement, the transformed program executes zero, one or several statements.

Our compiler treats a large subset of C. It compiles any C program in which jump statements (*i.e.* goto, setjmp and longjmp) are not allowed, and functions have a fixed number of arguments. The expression evaluation order is defined in the compiler: expressions are evaluated from left to right, thus leaving less freedom to the compiler. Furthermore, as dynamic allocation of variables is done explicitly in C by calling the library functions malloc and free, the semantics of these functions is not defined in our formal semantics and there is no garbage collector in the compiler. The proof that these functions ensure lack of dangling pointers is thus out of the scope of this paper.

The formal verification of the memory model belongs to an ongoing formal verification with the *Coq* proof assistant of this compiler, and it consists of:

- a formal specification at several levels of abstraction a memory model,
- a formal proof about many properties of this memory model,
- the automatic generation from the specification of a certified code that verifies the same properties as the formal specification.

The *Coq* proof assistant [1,4] consists mainly of a language called *Gallina* for writing formal specifications and a language for developing mathematical proofs to verify some properties on the formal specifications. *Gallina* relies on the *Calculus of Inductive Constructions*, a higher-order typed λ−calculus with dependent types and capabilities for inductive definitions. Proving a simple property consists in writing interactively proof commands that are called tactics. Tactics may also consist of user-defined tactics, thus making it possible to decompose a property into simpler reasoning steps and to reuse proof scripts.

Coq provides a way to structure specifications in large units called modules. The *Coq* module system [7] reuses the main features of the *OCaml* module system. A module is a collection of definitions of types, values and modules. It consists of two parts: a signature and an implementation. The signature of a module is an abstract specification of the components that must occur in all possible implementations of that module. The type of a module is its signature. Modules can be parametrised by modules. Parametrised modules are called functors (*i.e.* functions from modules to modules). One way to build modules is to apply a functor. The other way is to build it definition by definition. A module may be associated with a signature to verify that the definitions of the module are compatible with the signature. Properties may be defined in modules. When a property is defined in the signature of a module, it must be proved in any implementation of this module. The property is thus called an axiom (resp. theorem) in the signature (resp. implementation) of the module.

Coq provides also an automated mechanism for extracting functional programs from specifications [14]. The extraction from a *Coq* function or proof removes all logical statements (*i.e.* predicates) and translates the remaining content to a program written in *OCaml*. As the extracted program verifies the same properties as the *Coq* specification, the extracted code is called the certified code. The *Coq* extraction mechanism handles the module system: *Coq* modules are extracted to *OCaml* modules, *Coq* signatures are extracted to *OCaml* signatures, and *Coq* functors are extracted to *OCaml* functors.

3   Formal Specification

This section describes the formal verification in *Coq* of our memory model. It specifies the memory layout and the operations that manage the memory. This formal specification is written at two levels of abstraction:

- The abstract specification is suitable for most of imperative languages. It defines a general memory model, parametrised by some characteristics of the language it applies to (*e.g.* the values of the language), and properties that need to be verified by a more concrete specification.
- The concrete specification is devoted to *C*-like languages with pointer arithmetic. It implements the operations defined in the abstract specification, and proves that they satisfy the abstract specification. The properties that have been stated in the abstract specification are proved in the concrete specification. Other properties are also stated (and proved) in the concrete specification.

This section presents two concrete specifications. The first one is devoted to an infinite memory model of a *C* compiler. The second one defines a finite memory model that corresponds to the first concrete specification. In this paper, we will use familiar mathematical notation to present our development in *Coq*. For instance, inductive definitions will be presented in BNF format and *Coq* arrows will be replaced by either conjunctions or implications.

3.1   Abstract Specification

The abstract specification defines the memory layout in terms of records and maps. Several types are left unspecified. The operations that manage the memory are only defined by their types. Some axioms are also defined in the abstract specification.

Memory Layout. Figure 1 describes the types that specify the memory layout. The memory is separated into four areas that do not overlap:

- the free memory called mem_{free} that can be allocated during the execution of a program,
- the null memory called mem_{null} that is not accessible during the execution of a program,

- the memory called mem_{data} that stores data,
- the memory called mem_{code} that stores code, *i.e.* the procedures of a program. [1]

The type of memory is called *Tmem*. It is a record whose four fields represent the four areas. Each area is represented by a map (that is, a partial finite function) of type $Tmem_i$ from blocks identifiers *Tblock* to blocks $Tblock_i$, where i denotes a memory area. *Tblock* is an ordered type and $\leq$ denotes an order relation on *Tblock*. A block consists of a low bound, a high bound and a map from offsets *Tofs* (*i.e.* cells identifiers) to memory cells $Tcell_i$. $Tcell_i$ is equipped with a comparison relation that we write $=$. The high and low bounds of a block are block identifiers. The contents of the cells in a block depend on the area the block belongs to. Usually, each cell of the data area stores a value on a given number of bytes. Each cell of the code area stores a procedure (*i.e.* a C function). Each cell of the null area stores either a deallocated cell or a null cell that has never been deallocated.

The types that are left unspecified in the abstract specification are related to the way blocks and cells are addressed (*cf. Tblock* and *Tofs*) and to the contents of memory cells (*cf. $Tcell_i$*, $\forall i \in \{data, free, null\}$ and *Tprocedure*). The four areas of the memory are handled in a similar way. For space reasons, this paper focuses on the memory area that stores data.

MEMORY LAYOUT:

$Tmem$ $\quad ::= \{mem_{data} := Tmem_{data}$
$\quad ; mem_{free} := Tmem_{free}$
$\quad ; mem_{null} := Tmem_{null}$
$\quad ; mem_{code} := Tmem_{code} \}$

MEMORY AREAS:

$\forall i \in \{data, free, null, code\},\ Tmem_i\ ::= \mathsf{Map}\,(Tblock, Tblock_i)$

MEMORY BLOCKS:

$\forall i \in \{data, free, null\},\ Tblock_i ::= \{high := Tblock$
$\quad ; low := Tblock$
$\quad ; contents := \mathsf{Map}\,(Tofs, Tcell_i)\ \}$

$Tblock_{code} \qquad\qquad ::= Tprocedure$

Fig. 1. Abstract specification of the memory layout: type definitions

Figure 2 defines some relations between blocks and memory and some of their properties. The relation called valid_data_block states that a block b is valid with respect to a memory m if it has been allocated in the area of m that stores data

---

[1] In the sequel of this paper, we use the word *procedure* to denote a C function. The word *function* is reserved to *Coq* mathematical functions that are defined in the specification.

(*i.e.* it belongs to the domain of the map *m.memdata.*). This relation is often used as a precondition in the operations that manage the memory (see for instance the definition of load in figure 5). The axiom called valid_not_valid_diff states that any block is either valid or not.

The relation called block_agree is an agreement relation between blocks. Two blocks belonging to two memories agree between two bounds called *lo* and *hi* if they share a same identifier *b* and if each of their cells that is between the bounds *lo* and *hi*, stores the same value. This relation is an equivalence relation: it verifies the three axioms called block_agree_refl, block_agree_sym and block_agree_trans.

The relation called extends states that a memory *m2* extends another memory *m1* if each valid block *b* of *m1* is also a block of *m2*. More precisely, if *b* identifies a valid block $(m1.memdata)(b)$ of *m1*, then it identifies also a bigger block $(m2.memdata)(b)$ of *m2* (*i.e.* a block such that its cells are included in the cells of $(m2.memdata)(b)$) and both blocks agree between the bounds of the smallest block $m1(b)$. The picture of figure 2 shows an example of two such blocks. The compilation process relies on a run-time stack of memory blocks called stack frames. At the beginning of the compilation process of a program, a stack frame is allocated for each instance of a called procedure. Information that are computed in further steps of the compilation process are stored in stack frames and reused in further steps of the process. The relation called extends is useful to specify the extension of stack frames during the compilation process.

Memory Management. The main operations that manage the memory are alloc, free, load and store. They are specified in the figure 3, where alloc, load and store are related to the memory area that stores data. Similar operations related to the memory area that stores code have also been specified. Each operation that manage the memory may fail (*e.g.* alloc may fail if there are no free cells left). Thus, its results is of type $\text{option}(\tau)$. The values of such a type are either None (when the operation fails) or Some(v) where v is of type τ.

load and store operations are parametrised by memory chunks. A memory chunk indicates the size and the type of accessed data. Its type is called *Tchunk* and is left unspecified in the abstract specification. Memory chunks ensure that each load operation follows a store operation that supplied the value retrieved by the load. For instance, when an operation such as (store *chunk1* *m1* *b* *ofs1* = Some *m2*) is followed by an operation such as (load *chunk2* *m* *b* *ofs2*) then the load does not fail only if *chunk1*, *chunk2*, *ofs1* and *ofs2* are compatible.

The functionalities of the memory management operations are the following:

- alloc is the function that allocates a block with given bounds. If it does not fail, this function yields a newly allocated block and the modified memory.
- free is the function that deallocates a given block of data.
- load is the function that given a memory chunk fetches the value stored in a given block of data.
- store is the function that given a memory chunk stores a value in a given block of data. The load (resp. store) function fails if the value to load (resp. store) is not compatible with the memory chunk and the offset (*e.g.* if the

Definition valid_data_block (m: $Tmem$) (b: $Tblock$) := $b \in$ domain($m.memdata$).

Axiom valid_not_valid_diff:
$\forall$ (m: $Tmem$) (b b': $Tblock$),
valid_data_block m b $\wedge$ $\neg$(valid_data_block m b') $\Rightarrow$ $b \neq b'$.

Definition block_agree (b: $Tblock$) (lo hi: $Tblock$) ($m1$ $m2$: $Tmem$) :=
$\forall$ $ofs \in [lo,hi]$,
$((m1.memdata)(b).contents)(ofs) = ((m2.memdata)(b).contents)(ofs)$.

Axiom block_agree_refl:
$\forall$ (m: $Tmem$) (b: $Tblock$) (lo hi: $Tblock$),
    block_agree b lo hi m m.

Axiom block_agree_sym:
$\forall$ ($m1$ $m2$: $Tmem$) (b: $Tblock$) (lo hi: $Tblock$),
block_agree b lo hi $m1$ $m2$ $\Rightarrow$
    block_agree b lo hi $m2$ $m1$.

Axiom block_agree_trans:
$\forall$ ($m1$ $m2$ $m3$: $Tmem$) (b: $Tblock$) (lo hi: $Tblock$),
block_agree b lo hi $m1$ $m2$ $\wedge$ block_agree b lo hi $m2$ $m3$ $\Rightarrow$
    block_agree b lo hi $m1$ $m3$.

Definition extends ($m1$ $m2$: $Tmem$) :=
$\forall$ (b: $Tblock$),
    valid_data_block $m1$ b $\Rightarrow$
        $(m2.memdata)(b).low \leq (m1.memdata)(b).low$ $\wedge$
        $(m1.memdata)(b).high \leq (m2.memdata)(b).high$ $\wedge$
        block_agree b $(m1.memdata)(b).low$ $(m1.memdata)(b).high$ $m1$ $m2$

Fig. 2. Abstract specification of the memory layout: properties

memory chunk is to large). As these functions are left unspecified at the abstract level, this property consists of axioms such as loaded_block_is_valid and loaded_block_is_in_bounds that will be proved once the functions will be defined.

The axiom called loaded_block_is_in_bounds uses a property called in_bounds that defines when a value may be loaded from or stored in the two bounds of a block. in_bounds is used as a precondition that triggers loads and stores in memory. As block identifiers and offsets are left unspecified in the abstract specification, in_bounds is also left unspecified. It is a relation, *i.e.* a function

---

MEMORY MANAGEMENT OPERATIONS:

alloc : $Tmem \rightarrow Tblock \rightarrow Tblock \rightarrow$ option ($Tmem * Tblock$)
free : $Tmem \rightarrow Tblock \rightarrow$ option ($Tmem$)
load : $Tchunk \rightarrow Tmem \rightarrow Tblock \rightarrow Tofs \rightarrow$ option ($Tvalue$)
store : $Tchunk \rightarrow Tmem \rightarrow Tblock \rightarrow Tofs \rightarrow Tvalue \rightarrow$ option ($Tmem$)

RELATION BETWEEN BLOCKS AND MEMORY CHUNKS:

in_bounds : $Tchunk \rightarrow Tofs \rightarrow Tblock \rightarrow Tblock \rightarrow$ Prop

SOME PROPERTIES OF MEMORY MANAGEMENT OPERATIONS:

Axiom loaded_block_is_valid:
  $\forall$ ($chunk$: $Tchunk$) (m: $Tmem$) (b: $Tblock$) (ofs: $Tofs$) (v: $Tvalue$),
  load $chunk$ m b ofs = Some v $\Rightarrow$
    valid_data_block m b.

Axiom loaded_block_is_in_bounds:
  $\forall$ ($chunk$: $Tchunk$) (m: $Tmem$) (b: $Tblock$) (ofs: $Tofs$) (v: $Tvalue$),
  load $chunk$ m b ofs = Some v $\Rightarrow$
    in_bounds $chunk$ ofs ($m.memdata$)(b).low ($m.memdata$)(b).$high$.

Axiom valid_block_store:
  $\forall$ ($chunk$: $Tchunk$) ($m1$ $m2$: $Tmem$) (b b': $Tblock$) (ofs: $Tofs$) (v: $Tvalue$),
  store $chunk$ $m1$ b' ofs v = Some $m2$ $\wedge$
  valid_data_block $m1$ b $\Rightarrow$
    valid_data_block $m2$ b.

Axiom store_agree:
  $\forall$ ($chunk$: $Tchunk$) ($m1$ $m2$ $m1$' $m2$': $Tmem$) (b b': $Tblock$)
    (lo hi: $Tblock$) (ofs: $Tofs$) (v: $Tvalue$),
  block_agree b lo hi $m1$ $m2$ $\wedge$
  store $chunk$ $m1$ b' ofs v = Some $m1$' $\wedge$
  store $chunk$ $m2$ b' ofs v = Some $m2$' $\Rightarrow$
    block_agree b lo hi $m1$' $m2$'.

Axiom load_extends:
  $\forall$ ($chunk$: $Tchunk$) ($m1$ $m2$: $Tmem$) (b: $Tblock$) (ofs: $Tofs$) (v: $Tvalue$),
  extends $m1$ $m2$ $\wedge$
  load $chunk$ $m1$ b ofs = Some v $\Rightarrow$
    load $chunk$ $m2$ b ofs = Some v.

Fig. 3. Abstract specification of the memory management

that yields values of a type called Prop. This *Coq* type is used to define logical propositions.

Other properties of the operations that manage the memory express that the relations between blocks are preserved by the memory management operations. For instance, the axiom called valid_block_store expresses that the load operation does not invalidate valid blocks. More precisely, it states that if a value v is stored in a memory $m1.memdata$, any block b that was valid before the operation remains valid after. The axiom called store_agree states that the store operation preserves the agreement relation. The axiom load_extends states that the load operation preserves the extension relation. Figure 3 shows only some axioms of the specification. Similar axioms have been defined for all memory management operations.

3.2   Implementation of an Infinite Memory

This section presents an implementation of our memory model that is devoted to a C-like compiler. The implementation of values and addresses is adapted to C pointer arithmetic and the implementation of memory chunks follows the C arithmetic types. In this implementation, the memory is unlimited and thus the allocation never fails. New properties of the memory management are added in this implementation.

For each language manipulated by our compiler, we have encoded in *Coq* operational semantics rules that detail how the memory is accessed and modified during the execution of a program. For instance, the evaluation of a procedure respects the following judgements of the source and target languages of the compiler (called respectively C and PPC):

$G_c \vdash p_c, lv, m \Rightarrow v, m'$ states that in the global environment G_c and the memory m, the evaluation in C of the procedure p_c called with the list of values lv of its arguments computes a value v. The memory at the end of the evaluation in C is m'.

$G_{ppc} \vdash r, m \dashrightarrow r', m'$ states that in the global environment G_{ppc}, the evaluation in PPC of the current function updates the set of registers r into r' and the memory m into m'.

These semantics rely on the memory management operations. For instance, in the dynamic semantics of PPC, references to variables correspond to explicit loads and stores. There are 13 load instructions and 10 store instructions in PPC. In the dynamic semantics of C:

- A block of memory is allocated for each declared variable. The cells of the block that stores an array consist of the elements of the array.
- Such a block is deallocated at the end of the scope of the variable.
- The evaluation of a left value loads a value from memory.
- The execution of any assignment statement is based on the load and store operations.

Memory Layout. Figure 4 defines the types that were left unspecified in the abstract specification in figure 1. The blocks and the offsets of a block are identified by integers. The sizes of stored values are one, two, four and eight bytes. Values are either undefined values, or integers or floats or non null pointer values. The undefined value Vundef is a junk value that represents the value of uninitialised variables. A value of type pointer is either the integer 0 (that represents the NULL pointer) or a pair of a block identifier (that is, the address of the first cell of the block) and an offset between the block and the cell the pointer points to. This representation of pointers is adapted to C pointer arithmetic. For instance, the expression (Vptr b ofs) + (Vint i) evaluates to the pointer value (Vptr b Vint (ofs + i)) if this evaluation does not fail. In other words, the only integers i that can be added to a pointer value are those such that (ofs + i) is in the bounds of the block b. Another example is the comparison between pointers: two pointers that are not NULL may be compared only if they point to a same block.

ADDRESSES:

$Tblock$	$::= \mathbb{Z}$	
$Tofs$	$::= \mathbb{Z}$	

VALUES:

$Tcell_{data}$	$::= Tsize * Tvalue$	a data cell is a pair of a size and a value
$Tsize$	$::= \{1, 2, 4, 8\}$	number of bytes of a cell
$Tvalue$	$::= \text{Vint } Tinteger$	integer
	$\mid \text{Vfloat } Tfloat$	float
	$\mid \text{Vptr } Tblock\ Tofs$	pointer (a block and an offset)
	$\mid \text{Vundef}$	undefined value

Fig. 4. An implementation of the memory layout

Usually, properties of memory layouts are classified into separation, adjacency and containment properties [26]. This is also the kind of properties of our memory model. Separation and adjacency of memory blocks are valid in our model by construction. By construction, each memory block belongs to only one memory area. Two different blocks are also separated by construction since a cell of a block can not be accessed from another block. The containment property we use is the extends relation.

Memory Management. The memory chunks that were left unspecified in figure 3 are implemented in figure 5 in the following way: integers are stored on either one, two or four bytes, and floats are stored on either four or eight bytes. Integers that are stored on one or two bytes are either signed or unsigned. Pointer values are implemented by integers stored on four bytes.

The alloc and free functions never fail. The allocation method is linear. load *chunk m b ofs* fails when b does not identify a block of the data area of m and when the property in_bounds *chunk ofs b* is not true. The load function calls the load_result function in order to load each cell that needs to be loaded in the block b from the offset *ofs*. The load_result function fetches a value in memory and casts this value to a value of a type defined by a memory chunk, when the memory chunk is compatible with the value. Memory chunks determine also if a block needs to be filled with digits. For instance, when an integer that is stored on one or two bytes is loaded, it is automatically extended to four bytes (by the function called load_result), either by adding zeroes if the integer is unsigned, or by replicating the sign bit if the integer is signed (see the function cast1signed called by load_result). The load_result function fails if the memory chunk is not compatible with the value, for instance if it attempts to load a float value when the memory chunk corresponds to an integer. For space reasons, the definition of this function is not fully detailed in figure 5.

MEMORY CHUNKS:

$Tchunk$ ::= `Mint1signed`   signed integer stored on one byte
| `Mint1unsigned` unsigned integer stored on one byte
| `Mint2signed`   signed integer stored one on two bytes
| `Mint2unsigned` unsigned integer stored on two bytes
| `Mint4`   integer stored on four bytes
| `Mfloat4`   float stored on four bytes
| `Mfloat8`   float stored on eight bytes

MEMORY MANAGEMENT OPERATIONS:

Definition size_chunk ($chunk$: $Tchunk$) := ...
  (* number of bytes corresponding to chunk, $e.g.$ 4 for `Mint4` *)

Definition in_bounds ($chunk$: $Tchunk$) (ofs: $Tofs$) (lo hi: $Tblock$) :=
  $lo \le ofs \land ofs + $ size_chunk $chunk \le hi$.

Definition load_result ($chunk$: $Tchunk$) (v: $Tvalue$) :=
  match $chunk$, v with
  | Mint1signed, Vint n : Some (Vint (cast1signed n))
    (* values are casted in order to fit the memory chunks *)
  | ...
  | Mint4, Vptr b ofs : Some (Vptr b ofs)
  | Mfloat4, Vfloat f : Some (Vfloat (singleoffloat f))
  | ...
  | _, _ : None
    (* erroneous cases, $e.g.$ an integer chunk such as `Mint4` and a float value *)
end.

Definition load ($chunk$: $Tchunk$) (m: $Tmem$) (b: $Tblock$) (ofs: $Tofs$) :
  if valid_data_block m b $\land$ in_bounds $chunk$ ofs $m(b).low$ $m(b).high$
  then load_result $chunk$ ...
    (* the second parameter is the value that is found in cell b at offset ofs *)
  else None.

Fig. 5. An implementation of the memory management

Some new properties of the operations that manage the memory are defined in the implementation. They have not been defined in the abstract specification because they rely on the implementation of the memory management operations. These properties express that the memory blocks remember correctly the stored values. More precisely:

1. If an operation updates a block of a memory area by storing a value in it, then the content of this block becomes this value,

2. and the other blocks of memory are not modified.
3. A block which is modified by an operation belongs to the memory that results from the modification.

These properties are often called the good variable properties [25]. Our certification uses them in order to prove analogous properties on stack frames built by the compiler. As these properties are related to memory blocks consisting of memory cells, their proof relies on analogous properties for memory cells.

Figure 6 specifies some of the good variable properties. In the two theorems called load_store_same and load_store_other, a value v is stored in a memory $m1$ at the offset $ofs1$ of a block $b1$, given a memory chunk called $chunk$. The resulting memory is called $m2$. The first theorem called load_store_same states that v is also the value that is loaded in $m2$ at the address where it has been stored. The second theorem called load_store_other states that the store operation of v (in a block $b1$ at the offset $ofs1$) does not change any other value of the memory, *i.e.* any other value that is fetched either in another block $b2$ or in the same block $b1$ but at another valid offset $ofs2$. An offset is valid in a block if there are enough remaining cells in the block in order to store a value form this offset.

Theorem load_store_same:
  $\forall$ (*chunk*: *Tchunk*) (*m1 m2*: *Tmem*) (*b1*: *Tblock*) (*ofs1*: *Tofs*) (*v*: *Tvalue*),
  store *chunk m1 b1 ofs1 v* = Some *m2* $\Rightarrow$
    load *chunk m2 b1 ofs1* = Some (load_result *chunk v*).

Theorem load_store_other:
  $\forall$ (*chunk1 chunk2*: *Tchunk*) (*m1 m2*: *Tmem*) (*b1 b2*: *Tblock*)
    (*ofs1 ofs2*: *Tofs*) (*v*: *Tvalue*),
  store *chunk1 m1 b1 ofs1 v* = Some *m2* $\wedge$
  (*b1* $\neq$ *b2* $\vee$ *ofs2* + size_chunk *chunk2* $\leq$ *ofs1* $\vee$ *ofs1* + size_chunk *chunk1* $\leq$ *ofs2*)
    $\Rightarrow$ load *chunk2 m2 b2 ofs2* = load *chunk2 m1 b2 ofs2*.

Fig. 6. Some good-variable properties

Other properties are related to the high and low bounds of memory blocks. They express the compatibility between the bounds of a block and the offset from where a value is stored or loaded in that block. For instance, the theorem low_bound_store of figure 7 states that if a value v is stored in a memory $m1$, then the resulting memory $m2$ has the same low bound as $m1$. Finally, a few other relations between the memory management operations. For instance, the theorem called store_alloc states that a value may be stored from a given offset in a newly allocated block if the memory chunk and the offset are compatible with the bounds of this block.

3.3   Implementation of a Finite Memory

The execution of a source program may exceed the memory of the target machine. Thus, we have implemented another memory model where the size of

---

Theorem low_bound_store:
  ∀ (*chunk*: *Tchunk*) (*m1 m2*: *Tmem*) (*b b'*: *Tblock*) (*ofs*: *Tofs*) (*v*: *Tvalue*),
  store *chunk m1 b ofs v* = Some *m2* ⇒
      (*m2.memdata*)(*b'*).*low* = (*m1.memdata*)(*b'*).*low*.

Theorem store_alloc:
  ∀ (*chunk*: *Tchunk*) (*m1 m2*: *Tmem*) (*b lo hi*: *Tblock*) (*ofs*: *Tofs*) (*v*: *Tvalue*),
  alloc *m1 lo hi* = Some (*m2, b*) ∧
  in_bounds *chunk ofs lo hi* ⇒
      ∃ *m3*| store *chunk m2 b ofs v* = Some *m3*.

Fig. 7. Other properties of memory management operations

memory cells and the number of blocks in each memory area are finite. The only difference with the previous model relies in the implementation of the alloc operation: the allocation of a block fails if there is no free cell left. Thus, the theorems such as store_alloc that are defined in the first implementation still hold in this second implementation. When the allocation does not fail, it behaves as the allocation of the infinite memory. This is shown in figure 8. The theorem alloc_finite_to_infinite results from the definition of both allocation operations.

ABSTRACT SPECIFICATION:

alloc : *Tmem* → *Tofs* → *Tofs* → option (*Tmem* ∗ *Tblock*)

TWO IMPLEMENTATIONS:

Definition alloc1 (*m*: *Tmem*) (*lo hi*: *Tblock*) :=
    Some ...   (* never fails *)

Definition alloc2 (*m*: *Tmem*) (*lo hi*: *Tblock*) :=
    if (* no free cell left *) then None
    else alloc1 *m lo hi*.

Theorem alloc_finite_to_infinite:
  ∀ (*m1 m2*: *Tmem*) (*b lo hi*: *Tblock*),
  alloc2 *m1 lo hi* = Some (*m2, b*) ⇒ alloc1 *m1 lo hi* = Some (*m2, b*).

Fig. 8. Reuse of the allocation operation

The compilation of a program fails as soon as an allocation fails. As each step of the compilation process allocates memory blocks, there are many opportunities for the compiler to fail. In the memory that stores data, the evolution of block allocation during the compilation process is the following. For each instance of a called procedure:

- The dynamic semantics of C allocates a block for each declared variable.
- The translation from C to the first intermediate language L_1 of the compiler allocates a single block for all the local variables of the procedure that

are either of array type or whose addresses are taken. Thus the number of allocated blocks decreases but the size of each block increases.

In the case of the translation from C to L_1, the size of all allocated blocks in the data area is the same in the semantics of C and L_1. In other translations from one intermediate language L_i to another intermediate language L_j, the number of allocated blocks increases slightly. The translation allocates indeed the blocks that correspond to the blocks of L_i but also other blocks that are built by the translation of long expressions made up of several variables and function calls.

Concerning the memory area that stores code, each translation of the compilation process computes information that need to be stored in memory. At the end of the process, all the information have been computed and the target code may be emitted. If for instance a translation from one intermediate language L_i to another intermediate language L_j occurs, the semantics of L_i allocates as many blocks as the dynamic semantics of L_j. However, the blocks allocated by the dynamic semantics of L_j are becoming bigger. For instance, the return address of a called procedure is only known (and stored) at the end of the compilation process. As the translations do not preserve the contents of memory blocks, they may fail because they translate blocks into bigger blocks. Thus:

- During the compilation process, any translation fails when it translates a block into a bigger block.
- The execution of a translated program may fail, although the execution of the program does not fail.

With such a finite memory model, we prove the following correctness result for each translation: if the translation of a program does not fail, if that program terminates on some final memory state, and if the translated program also terminates, then it terminates on the same memory state. This property is weaker than the property we prove for an infinite memory model.

Instead of defining a more precise memory model, we intend to perform a static analysis that will track the amount of allocated memory for a given compilable program and compute an approximation of this amount if the control flow graph of the program is acyclic. We will then have to prove an equivalence result between the execution of the program and its execution in a stack discipline language where only one block is allocated. This will require the definition of such a language and the proof of semantic equivalence between this language and the corresponding language of the compiler.

4   From Formal Specifications to Code

This section gives an overview of the architecture of the *Coq* development. Figures 9 and 10 show the *Coq* modules that have been built in order to formally verify the memory model. *OCaml* modules have been automatically generated from them. The generated modules have the same architecture as the *Coq* modules. The *Coq* extraction mechanism removes the axioms and theorems, and more generally the terms of type `Prop`.

The abstract specification consists of the three signature modules of figure 9. They are declared with the keyword **Module Type**. The module called *MEM_PARAMS* collects the parameters of the memory model. These are *Coq* variables of type **Set** that *Coq* uses to type abstract specifications. They define the contents and the addressing of memory cells and are left abstract in the signature modules. The module called *MEM_LAYOUT* specifies the memory layout. It defines the functions and axioms that are detailed in figures 1 and 2. These definitions refer to unspecified types (*e.g. Tblock*) that are declared in a module called *MemP* of type *MEM_PARAMS*. The module called *MEM_OPS* specifies the memory management operations. It defines the functions and axioms that are detailed in figure 3.

Module Type *MEM_PARAMS*.
  Parameters *Tchunk, Tofs, Tcell, Tvalue*: **Set**.
  . . .
End *MEM_PARAMS*.

Module Type *MEM_LAYOUT*.
  Declare Module *MemP* : *MEM_PARAMS*.

  Record *Tblockdata* := {*high*: *Tblock* ; *low*: *Tblock* ; *contents*: **Map** (*Tblock*, *Tcell*)}.
  . . .
  Record *Tmem* := {*memdata*: **Map** (*Tblock*, *Tblockdata*); . . . }.

  Definition valid_data_block (*m*:*Tmem*)(*b*:*Tblock*) := ∃ *v*, *m.memdata*(*b*) = **Some** *v*.

  Axiom valid_not_valid_diff:
    ∀ *m b b'*, valid_data_block *m b* ∧ ¬(valid_data_block *m b'*) ⇒ *b* ≠ *b'*.
End *MEM_LAYOUT*.

Module Type *MEM_OPS*.
  Declare Module *MemP*: *MEM_PARAMS*.
  Declare Module *MemL*: *MEM_LAYOUT*.

  Parameter load: *Tchunk* → *Tmem* → *Tblock* → *Tofs* → option *Tvalue*.
  . . .

  Axiom loaded_block_is_valid:
    ∀ *chunk m b ofs v*, load *chunk m b ofs* = **Some** *v* ⇒ valid_data_block *m b*.
  . . .

End *MEM_OPS*.

Fig. 9. Architecture of the specification (signature modules)

The figure 10 shows the modules that implement the signature modules. For instance, the module *MEM_PARAMS_IMPL* implements the module *MEM_PARAMS* (see figures 4 and 5). The module called *MAKE_MEM_LAYOUT* is the functor that builds a module of type *MEM_LAYOUT* from a module of type *MEM_PARAMS*. All axioms that have been defined in the signature modules are proved in the implementation modules (thus becoming theorems). For instance, figure 10 shows the proof script of the theorem called valid_not_valid_diff. This is a very simple proof script that consists of a few *Coq* tactics. In this example, the proof script unfolds the definitions and prove by contradiction that b can not be equal to b'. More generally, these tactics can be user defined and correspond to the steps that would be used in a hand proof. They are reused to prove interactively the theorems.

Module *MAKE_MEM_LAYOUT* (*P*: *MEM_PARAMS*)
    $<$: *MEM_LAYOUT* with Module *MemP* := *P*.
    . . .

    Theorem valid_not_valid_diff:
        $\forall$ m b b ', valid_data_block m b $\land$ $\neg$(valid_data_block m b') $\Rightarrow$ $b \neq b$'.
    Proof. *intros*; *red*; *intros*; *subst b*; *contradiction*. **Qed.**
End *MAKE_MEM_LAYOUT*.

Module *MEM_PARAMS_IMPL* $<$: *MEM_PARAMS*.
    Definition *Tblock*:= $\mathbb{Z}$.
    Inductive *Tchunk* := *Mint1signed* | *Mint1unsigned* | . . .
    . . .
End *MEM_PARAMS_IMPL*.

Module *MEM_LAYOUT_IMPL* $<$: *MEM_LAYOUT* :=
    MAKE_MEM_LAYOUT MEM_PARAMS_IMPL.

Module *MEM_OPS_IMPL* $<$: *MEM_OPS*.
    Module *MemP* := *MEM_PARAMS_IMPL*.
    Module *MemL* := *MEM_LAYOUT_IMPL*.

    Definition load (*chunk*: *Tchunk*) (*m*: *Tmem*) (*b*:*Tblock*) (*ofs*: *Tofs*) : option *Tvalue*
        := . . .

    Theorem loaded_block_is_valid: $\forall$ *chunk m b ofs v*,
        load *chunk m b ofs* = Some v $\Rightarrow$ valid_data_block m b.
    Proof. . . . **Qed.**

    Theorem load_store_same: $\forall$ *chunk m1 m2 b1 ofs1 v*,
        store *chunk m1 b1 ofs1 v* = Some *m2* $\Rightarrow$
            load *chunk m2 b1 ofs1* = Some (load_result *chunk v*).
    Proof. . . . **Qed.**
End *MEM_OPS_IMPL*.

Fig. 10. Architecture of the specification (implementation modules)

Our memory model consists of several thousands lines of *Coq* specifications and proofs. The compilable *OCaml* modules that have been automatically extracted from the *Coq* specifications implement the operations that manage the memory.

5   Related Work

Several low-level memory models (often called architecture-centric models) have been defined. They are dedicated to hardware architectures and study the impact of features such as write buffers or caches, especially in multiprocessor systems. For instance, [22] uses a term rewriting system to define a memory model that decomposes load and store operations into finer-grain operations. This model formalises the notions of data replication and instruction reordering. It aims as defining the legal behaviours of a distributed shared-memory system that relies on execution trace of memory accesses. These memory models are lower-level than ours (thus relying on a very different representation of memory) and are not dedicated to C-like languages.

Other research has concentrated on the formalisation of properties of programs that manipulate recursive data structures defined by pointers. New logics that capture common storage invariants have also been defined in order to facilitate and automate the proof of properties about pointers. These logics are based on separation logic [5], an extension of Hoare logic where assertions may refer to pointer expressions in a more concise and meaningful way. Two operators facilitate the expression of memory properties in separation logic: a separative conjunction allows one to express the separation of one piece of memory with respect to another, a separating implication allows one to introduce hypotheses about the memory layout. The definition of a refinement calculus for the separation logic is currently investigated [16]. In the near future, separation logic should be implemented, as is Hoare logic in tools dedicated to the B method.

Some ideas of separation logic have been formalised in *Isabelle/HOL* in order to verify the correctness of *Java* programs with pointers [15]. [9] presents a tool for formally proving that a *C* program is free of null pointer dereferencing and out-of-bounds array access. Some of our properties of memory management operations are also stated in [15] and [9].

Another way to prove properties about programs involving pointers is to define type systems that enable compilers to detect errors in programs. Some type systems are dedicated to a specific part of a compiler (*e.g.* assembly code [8]). Type systems for memory management have been applied for low-level memory management [24]. For instance, typed region systems where each memory location has an intended type and an actual type, have been defined to verify garbage collectors.

Much work has been done on verifying the complete correctness of a compiler. [11] and [3] use refinement as a compilation model. In the former, a refinement calculus is defined to support the compilation of programs written in an idealised high-level language into the .NET assembler. The aim of this work is to refine the whole compilation process and this approach is not automated by tools. The latter uses a term rewriting system to reduce programs into normal forms representing target programs.

The translation validation approach [18,19,10,20,21] aims at validating every run of the compiler, producing a formal proof that the produced target code is a correct implementation of the source code. This approach is based on program checking and on static analysis. It has been applied a lot for validating a variety of compiler optimizations, with a recent focus on loop transformations [27]. In the proof carrying code approach [17,2,12], the compiler is rewritten in a certifying compiler that produces both a compiled code and a proof term of some properties (called safety rules) to verify, that have been added in the source program. Safety rules are written in first-order predicate logic extended with predicates for type safety and low-level memory safety. Many specialised type systems have been used in this approach tat has been extensively applied to *Java* bytecode certification.

Our work belongs to a project that investigates the feasibility of formally verifying the correctness of a *C*-like compiler itself. The goal is to write the compiler directly in the *Coq* specification language. Other projects that develop machine-checked proofs of compiler correctness focus on data flow analyses and other compiler transformations [6,23]. They do not require a memory model as precise as ours.

6   Conclusion

This paper has presented a formalisation and a verification in *Coq* of a memory model for *C*-like languages. Thanks to the use of *Coq* modules, this formalisation has been specified at two levels of abstraction. Two concrete specifications have been implemented from an abstract specification. They describe an infinite memory and a finite memory. Both memory models have a similar behaviour except in the case of failure of the allocation of memory blocks. A significant part of the specifications and correctness proofs have been factored out through the use of modules. The memory model has been implemented as part of an ongoing certification of a moderately-optimising *C* compiler. This compiler relies on 7 different languages whose formal semantics refer to the memory model, and on transformations that require extensive reasoning over the memory model. Many properties have been proved and certified programs have been synthesised from the formalisation.

A limitation of our compiler is that the correctness proofs of the transformations use simulation lemmas that apply only when every statement of the source code is mapped to zero, one or several statements of the transformed code. This is not sufficient to prove the correctness of more sophisticated optimisations such as code motion, lifting of loop-invariant computations or instruction scheduling, where computations occur in a different order in the source and transformed code. Because of this limitation, we envision to define a notion of equivalence between memory states and to perform these optimisations on a higher-level intermediate language, whose big-step semantics make it easier to reorder computations without worrying about intermediate computational states that are not equivalent.

Another current focus is the formalisation of non-terminating programs. The languages of our compiler are defined by big-step semantics that hide non-termination of programs. Our correctness proof states that any source program that terminates on some final memory state is compiled into a program that also terminates, produces the same memory state and calls the same functions in the same contexts. Previous experiments in the writing of small-step semantics showed us that they are not adapted for proving on machine properties such as semantic equivalence between languages. We intend to define semantics that collect more information than big-step semantics but that are not as concrete as small-step semantics.

Acknowledgements

We would like to thank C.Dubois and P.Letouzey for fruitful discussions about this work.

References

1. The Coq proof assistant. http://coq.inria.fr.
2. A.W. Appel. Foundational proof-carrying code. In *IEEE Symp. on Logic in Computer Science (LICS)*, page 247, Washington, DC, USA, June 2001.
3. A.Sampaio. *An algebraic approach to compiler design*, volume 4 of *AMAST series in computing*. World Scientific, 1997.
4. Y. Bertot and P. Castéran. *Interactive Theorem Proving and Program Development Coq'Art: The Calculus of Inductive Constructions*. Springer Verlag, 2004.
5. R. Bornat. Proving pointer programs in Hoare logic. In *5th Conf. on Mathematics of Program Construction*, pages 102–126. Springer-Verlag, 2000.
6. D. Cachera, T. Jensen, D. Pichardie, and V. Rusu. Extracting a Data Flow Analyser in Constructive Logic. In *Proc. of Europ. Symp. on Programming (ESOP'04)*, number 2986 in Lecture Notes in Computer Science, pages 385–400. 2004.
7. J. Chrząszcz. *Modules in Type Theory with Generative Definitions*. PhD thesis, Warsaw Univerity and University of Paris-Sud, January 2004.
8. D.Yu and Z. Shao. Verification of safety properties for concurrent assembly code. In *Int. Conf. on Functional Programming (ICFP)*, pages 175–188, Snowbird, USA, September 2004.
9. J.-C. Filliâtre and C. Marché. Multi-Prover Verification of C Programs. In *6th Int. Conf. on Formal Engineering Methods (ICFEM)*, volume 3308 of *Lecture Notes in Computer Science*, pages 15–29, Seattle, November 2004. Springer-Verlag.
10. G. Goos and W. Zimmermann. Verification of compilers. In *Correct System Design, Recent Insight and Advances,* , pages 201–230, London, UK, 1999. Springer-Verlag.
11. G.Watson. Compilation of refinement for a practical language. In *5th Int. Conf. on Formal Engineering Methods (ICFEM)*, volume 2885 of *Lecture Notes in Computer Science*, Singapore, November 2003. Springer-Verlag.
12. N. Hamid, Z. Shao, V. Trifonov, S. Monnier, and Z. Ni. A syntactic approach to foundational proof-carrying code. *Journal of Automated Reasoning*, 31(3-4):191–229, September 2003.
13. X. Leroy. Formal certification of a compiler back-end, or: programming a compiler with a proof assistant. 2005. draft, submitted for publication.
14. P. Letouzey. *Programmation fonctionnelle certifiée – L'extraction de programmes dans l'assistant Coq*. PhD thesis, Université Paris-Sud, July 2004.

15. F. Mehta and T. Nipkow. Proving pointer programs in higher-order logic. In *Automated Deduction (CADE-19)*, volume 2741 of *Lecture Notes in Computer Science*, pages 121–135. Springer-Verlag, 2003.

16. I. Mijajlovic and N. Torp-Smith. Refinement in separation context. In *Second workshop on semantics, program anlysis and computing analysis for memory management (SPACE)*, Venice, Italy, January 2004.

17. G. Necula. Proof carrying code. In *Proc. of Principles Of Progamming Languages Conf. (POPL)*, January 1997.

18. G. Necula. Translation validation for an optimizing compiler. In *ACM SIGPLAN Conf. on Programming Language Design and Implementation (PLDI)*, pages 83–95, 2000.

19. A. Pnueli, M. Siegel, and E. Singerman. Translation validation. In *Proc. of the 4th Int. Conf. on Tools and Algorithms for Construction and Analysis of Systems (TACAS)*, pages 151–166, London, UK, 1998. Springer-Verlag.

20. M. Rinard and D. Marinov. Credible compilation with pointers. In *Workshop on Run-Time Result Verification (RTRV)*, Trento, Italy, July 1999.

21. X. Rival. Symbolic transfer function-based approaches to certified compilation. In *Principles Of Progamming Languages Conf. (POPL)*, pages 1–13. 2004.

22. X. Shen, Arvind, and L. Rudolph. Commit-reconcile & fences (CRF): a new memory model for architects and compiler writers. In *ISCA '99: 26th symposium on Computer architecture*, pages 150–161, Washington, DC, USA, 1999.

23. S.Lerner, T.Millstein, E.Rice, and C.Chambers. Automated soundness proofs for dataflow analyses and transformations. In *Principles Of Progamming Languages Conf. (POPL)*, Long Beach, USA, 2005.

24. S.Monnier. Typed regions. In *workshop on semantics, program anlysis and computing analysis for memory management (SPACE)*, Venice, Italy, January 2004.

25. R.D. Tennent and D.R. Ghica and. Abstract models of storage. *Higher-Order and Symbolic Computation*, 13(1/2):119–129, 2000.

26. D. Walker. Stacks, heaps and regions: one logic to bind them. In *Second workshop on semantics, program anlysis and computing analysis for memory management (SPACE)*, Venice, Italy, January 2004. invited talk.

27. Y.Hu, C.Barrett, B.Goldberg, and A. Pnueli. Validating more loop optimizations. In *Workshop on Compiler Optimization Meets Compiler Verification (COCV)*, Edinburgh, UK, 2005.

Symbolic Verification of Distributed Real-Time Systems with Complex Synchronizations*

Farn Wang

Dept. of Electrical Engineering, National Taiwan University,
1, Sec. 4, Roosevelt Rd., Taipei, Taiwan 106, ROC
+886-2-33663602; FAX:+886-2-23671909
farn@cc.ee.ntu.edu.tw
http://cc.ee.ntu.edu.tw/~farn
http://cc.ee.ntu.edu.tw/~val

Abstract. CSP-style synchronizations have been used extensively in the construction of mathematical models for the verification of embedded systems. Although they allow for the modeling of complex cooperation among many processes in a natural environment, not many tools have been developed to support the modeling capability in this regard. In this paper, we first give examples to argue that special algorithms are needed for the efficient verification of systems with complex synchronizations. We then define our models of distributed real-time systems with synchronized cooperation among many processes. We present algorithms for the construction of BDD-like data-structures for the characterization of complex synchronizations among many processes. We present weakest precondition algorithms that take advantage of the just-mentioned BDD-like data-structures for the efficient verification of complex real-time systems. Finally, we report experiments and argue that the techniques could be useful in practice.

Keywords: distributed, real-time, model-checking, verification, synchronization.

1 Introduction

In the verification of distributed real-time systems, the appropriate abstraction of the system behaviors is crucial to the balance between the precision of the models and the efficiency of verification. For instance, if we model how a missile is directed to hit a jet-fighter at the granularity of sub-atomic particle interaction, then of course we have an extremely precise model. However, such cumbersome models can also involve too many details irrelevant to the verification of the system and likely incur infeasible and unnecessary computing resource requirement. One commonly used abstraction technique is to model several events as

---

* The work is partially supported by NSC, Taiwan, ROC under grants NSC 92-2213-E-002-103, NSC 92-2213-E-002-104, and by the System Verification Technology Project of Industrial Technology Research Institute, Taiwan, ROC (2004).

K.-K. Lau and R. Banach (Eds.): ICFEM 2005, LNCS 3785, pp. 300–314, 2005.

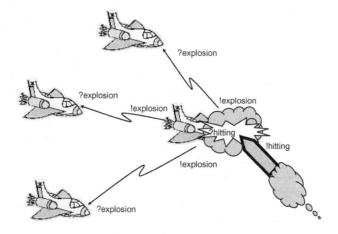

Fig. 1. A system with one missile and 4 jet-fighters

a simultaneous happening. For example, in figure 1, we have a system of an anti-aircraft missile and multiple hostile jet-fighters. There are two events: the 'hitting' of the missile on a jet-fighter and the observations of the 'explosion' of the hapless jet-fighter by other jet-fighters. On one hand, the hitting event is an interaction between the missile and the hapless jet-fighter. On the other hand, right after the hitting event, the explosion event is broadcasted to all the remaining enemy jet-fighters and may affect their actions afterwards. In most verification tasks, what happen in the split-second between the hitting event and the explosion event does not matter. To the missile launcher, what matters is when it can start tracking the next target. To the remaining jet-fighters, what matters is their reaction after the observation. Thus, it is only natural to model the hitting event and the explosion event as a simultaneous happening. Modeling them as two separate events only unnecessarily adds to the verification complexity and does not help engineers in analyzing the behavior of the system.

One language device designed to model simultaneous actions in two processes is the *channel* concept for binary synchronization in Hoare's *CSP (Communicating Sequential Processes)* [9]. Conceptually, the device glues two process transitions[1] from two different processes to model a *global transition*.[2] Such a device can greatly help to improve the modularity of model descriptions. In the above-mentioned anti-aircraft missile example, the action that a missile hits a jet-fighter can be modeled with a channel named hitting between the missile and the hapless jet-fighter. The language device !hitting represents the sending (or output) event by the missile through the channel while ?hitting represents the receiving (or input) event by the hapless jet-fighter through the same chan-

---

[1] A *process transition* models the observation of a global state-change from a process in a concurrent system.

[2] A *global transition* models a global state-change and could be the simultaneous interaction of several process transitions.

nel. Two process transitions labeled respectively with the sending event and receiving event through the same channel must happen at the same instant to make a global transition. Modeling such a global transition as two synchronized process transitions can greatly enhance the modularity in model construction.

Although the CSP-style channels are good for binary synchronizations between two parties, we can use them to construct complex global transitions out of many simultaneous process transitions. For example, in figure 1, the event that the missile hits one jet-fighter can cause an explosion observed by the other three jet-fighters. By constructing the following 5 process transitions,

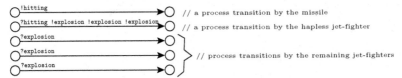

we can glue the five process transitions to make a global transition that models the simultaneity of the `hitting` event and the observations of the `explosion` event. The above-mentioned idea of using binary synchronizations to construct complex interactions among many processes, although plausible, has not been supported by many verification tools [4,16]. In this paper, we investigate the various issues involved in implementing the idea for the model-checking of communicating timed automata [10]. There are two issues involved in the implementation. First, *"how do we generate the set of global transitions ?"* Intuitively, we can first record, for each event type σ, the process transitions with $?\sigma$ and those with $!\sigma$. Then we use this recording and some heuristics to enumerate the set of global transitions. However, this enumeration can be expensive because in practice the number of elements in this enumeration can be of exponential complexity to the input size. The reason is that a particular synchronization label (say $!\sigma$), can be labeled on many process transitions of the same process. For example, suppose that when an `explosion` happens, a jet-fighter can observe the event in one of two modes: `cruise` and `evasive maneuver` with different triggering conditions. Thus, we need to construct two process transitions respectively from these two modes to receive the `explosion` event for each jet-fighter process. In other words, a surviving jet-fighter can execute either of these two process transitions, one from the `cruise` mode and the other from the `evasive maneuver` mode, to receive an `explosion` event. If there are n such surviving jet-fighters, there are 2^n such synchronization combinations. Thus, even just to enumerate all the synchronization combinations may have become infeasible when large numbers of jet-fighters are involved. One contribution of the paper is the presentation of an algorithm that takes advantage of the data-sharing capability of BDD-like data-structures to calculate the symbolic characterizations of global transitions.

The second issue in the implementation is *"how do we efficiently evaluate the weakest precondition of global transitions when the number of such global transitions is exponential to the input size ?"* Another contribution of this paper is the presentation of an algorithm that uses the data-sharing capability of BDD-like data-structures [3,5,12] to effectively avoid the explicit enumeration of all global transitions in the evaluation of weakest preconditions of discrete transitions. Please note that the two issues are not specific to distributed real-time systems. Our techniques can also apply whenever we need to analyze the synchronization combinations in a set of (untimed or timed) processes.

We have endeavored to implement the ideas and carried out experiments to see how our ideas work in practice. What we have found is that for global transitions with simple synchronizations, weakest precondition calculation with direct enumeration of such global transitions can be more efficient. However, for global transitions with complex synchronizations involving many processes, calculation that takes advantage of data-sharing capability of BDD-like data-structures results in higher efficiency. In this article, we also propose a hybrid scheme that uses a threshold for the number of processes involved in a global transition to decide which way we should use for the weakest precondition calculation through the global transition. The experiment shows that the techniques could really be useful in the verification of real-world projects. The tool and benchmarks can be downloaded for free at http://cc.ee.ntu.edu.tw/~val.

2 Safety Analysis Problem of Communicating Timed Automata

We use the widely accepted model of *communicating timed automata (CTA)* [2, 10, 15] to describe the transitions in dense-time state-spaces. A CTA is a set of *process timed automata (PTA)* that communicate with one another through CSP-style synchronization channels. Each PTA is a finite-state automaton equipped with a finite set of clocks which can hold nonnegative real-values. At any moment, the PTA can stay in only one *mode* (or *control location*). Each mode is labeled with an invariance condition on clocks. In its operation, a group of the process transitions can be triggered when the corresponding synchronization requirement is met and the corresponding triggering conditions are satisfied. Upon being triggered, the PTAs instantaneously transit from their source modes to their respective destination modes and reset some clocks to zero. In between transitions, all clocks increase their readings at a uniform rate.

For convenience, given a set P of atomic propositions and a set X of clocks, we use $B(P, X)$ as the set of all Boolean combinations of atoms of the forms p and $x \sim c$, where $p \in P$, $x \in X \cup \{0\}$, '$\sim$' is one of $\leq, <, =, >, \geq$, and c is an integer constant.

Definition 1. process timed automata (PTA) A PTA is given as a tuple $\langle \Sigma, X, Q, I, \mu, E, \gamma, \lambda, \tau, \pi \rangle$ with the following restrictions. Σ is a finite set of event names. X is a finite set of clocks. Q is a finite set of modes. $I \in B(Q, X)$ is the initial condition. $\mu : Q \mapsto B(\emptyset, X)$ defines the conjunctive invariance condition of each mode. E is the finite set of process transitions. $\gamma : E \mapsto (Q \times Q)$ defines the source and destination modes of each process transition. $\lambda : (E \times \Sigma) \mapsto \mathcal{Z}$ defines the number of instances of an event type that happen on each process transition. For $e \in E$ and $\sigma \in \Sigma$,

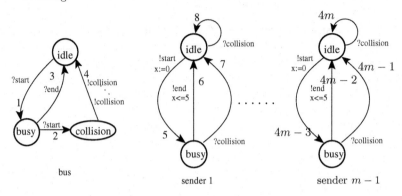

Fig. 2. the model of bus-contending systems

- if $\lambda(e,\sigma) < 0$, it intuitively means that $|\lambda(e,\sigma)|$ messages of type σ must be received by the process executing process transition e;
- if $\lambda(e,\sigma) = 0$, it intuitively means that the execution of process transition e does not involve the reception or transmission of messages of type σ; and
- if $\lambda(e,\sigma) > 0$, it intuitively means that $|\lambda(e,\sigma)|$ messages of type σ must be transmitted by the process executing process transition e.

Such a general scheme allows for the modeling of broadcasting and multicasting of many generic transmission events. $\tau : E \mapsto B(\emptyset, X)$ and $\pi : E \mapsto 2^X$ respectively defines the conjunctive triggering condition and the clock set to reset of each process transition. ∎

Definition 2. Communicating timed automata (CTA) A CTA is a tuple $\langle \Sigma, A_1, \ldots, A_m \rangle$ where for each $1 \leq p \leq m$, A_p is a PTA like $\langle \Sigma, X_p, Q_p, I_p, \mu_p, E_p, \gamma_p, \lambda_p, \tau_p, \pi_p \rangle$. The *concurrency* (or number of processes) of the CTA is m. For each $1 \leq p \leq m$, A_p is also called *process p*.

For convenience of presentation, we assume that for all $1 \leq p < p' \leq m$, $X_p \cap X_{p'} = \emptyset$, $Q_p \cap Q_{p'} = \emptyset$, and $E_p \cap E_{p'} = \emptyset$. Given an $x \in X_p$, $q \in Q_p$, and $e \in E_p$, we let $\text{proc}(x) = p$, $\text{proc}(q) = p$, and $\text{proc}(e) = p$ represent the process indices of x, q, e respectively. ∎

In figure 2, we have a bus-contending system with one bus PTA and m sender PTAs. The circles represent modes while the arcs represent process transitions, which may be marked with synchronization labels (e.g., !start, ?end, !collision, ...), triggering conditions (e.g., $x \leq 5$), and assignments (e.g., $x := 0;$). For convenience, we have labeled the process transitions with numbers. In the system, a sender process may synchronize through channel start with the bus to start sending messages on the bus. While one sender is using the bus, another may also synchronize through channel start to start placing messages on the bus and corrupt the bus contents. When this happen, the bus then send m bus collision signals to all the senders through transition 4.

Definition 3. states Suppose we have a CTA $M = \langle \Sigma, A_1, \ldots, A_m \rangle$ where for each $1 \leq p \leq m$, $A_p = \langle \Sigma, X_p, Q_p, I_p, \mu_p, E_p, \gamma_p, \lambda_p, \tau_p, \pi_p \rangle$. A state of M is a valuation from $\{1, \ldots, m\} \cup \bigcup_{1 \leq p \leq m} X_p$ such that

- for each $1 \leq p \leq m$, $\nu(p) \in Q_p$ defines the mode of process p in state ν;
- for each $x \in \bigcup_{1 \leq p \leq m} X_p$, $\nu(x) \in \mathcal{R}^+$ defines the reading of clock x in state ν. ($\mathcal{R}^+$ is the set of non-negative reals.)

Given $\delta \in \mathcal{R}^+$, $\nu + \delta$ is a new state that agrees with ν except that for all $x \in \bigcup_{1 \leq p \leq m} X_p$, $(\nu + \delta)(x) = \nu(x) + \delta$. Given an $X \subseteq \bigcup_{1 \leq p \leq m} X_p$, νX is a new state that agrees with ν except that for every $x \in X$, $\nu \bar{X}(x) = 0$. Given a $Q \subseteq \bigcup_{1 \leq p \leq m} Q_p$ of process modes such that $\forall 1 \leq p \leq m (|\{q \mid q \in Q \cap Q_p\}| \leq 1)$, νQ is the new state that agrees with ν except that $\forall q \in Q \wedge Q_p, (\nu Q)(p) = q$. $\blacksquare$

We say a state ν satisfies a state predicate $\eta \in B(\bigcup_{1 \leq p \leq m} Q_p, \bigcup_{1 \leq p \leq m} X_p)$ iff the following inductive conditions are satisfied.

- $\nu \models q$ iff $\nu(\mathtt{proc}(q)) = q$;
- $\nu \models x \sim c$ iff $\nu(x) \sim c$;
- $\nu \models \eta_1 \vee \eta_2$ iff $\nu \models \eta_1$ or $\nu \models \eta_2$;
- $\nu \models \neg \eta_1$ iff it is not the case that $\nu \models \eta_1$.

A PTA cannot execute its process transitions by its own. According to CSP's semantics [9], a process transition can be executed if and only if all its received messages have been sent out by some processes at the same time and all its transmitted messages have also been received by some processes at the same time. Thus, several process transitions may have to be grouped together for simultaneous execution. Now we have to define what a legitimate synchronization combination is in order not to violate the widely accepted interleaving semantics. A *transition plan* is a set $T \subseteq \bigcup_{1 \leq p \leq m} E_p$ such that there is at most one element in T from each E_p, i.e., $\forall 1 \leq p \leq m, |E_p \cap T| \leq 1$. If $E_p \cap T = \emptyset$, it means that process p does not participate in transition plan T.

A transition plan is *consistent* iff each output event from a process is received by exactly one unique corresponding process with a unique matching input event. Formally speaking, in a consistent transition plan T, for each channel σ, the number of output events must match that of input events. Or in arithmetic, $\forall \sigma \in \Sigma (\sum_{e \in T} \lambda(e, \sigma) = 0)$.

However, that a transition plan is consistent does not mean it is atomic in the sense of interleaving semantics. For example, we may have four processes that respectively may execute transitions e_1, e_2, e_3, e_4. Suppose these four transitions are respectively labeled with synchronization labels '!a,' '!a,' '?a,' and '?a.' Then plans $\{e_1, e_3\}$, $\{e_1, e_4\}$, $\{e_2, e_3\}$, and $\{e_2, e_4\}$ are all consistent. Moreover, $\{e_1, e_2, e_3, e_4\}$ is also consistent but not quite compatible with the interleaving semantics since it is not minimal. Here *minimality* means the transition plan cannot be broken down to two smaller non-empty and consistent transition plans. Thus, we would like also to require all our transition plans to be both consistent and minimal. A consistent and minimal transition plan is called a *(legitimate) global transition*. For example, in figure 2, for any $k \geq 1$, process transitions 1 and $4k + 1$ can combine to be a global transition. Also process transitions $4, 7, \ldots, 4m + 3$ can make a global transition since m '!collision' on process transition 4 matches m '?collision' respectively labeled on process transitions $7, \ldots, 4m + 3$.

Note that the empty set is a valid global transition since it is consistent and minimal. Intuitively, it represents the global transition of 'no action.'

Given two states ν, ν' of a CTA M and a global transition T, we say ν transits to ν' through T, in symbols $\nu \xrightarrow{T} \nu'$, iff ν is identical to ν' except that

- for all $e \in T \cap E_p$, $\gamma(e) = (\nu(\mathtt{proc}(e)), \nu'(\mathtt{proc}(e)))$; and
- $\nu \models \bigwedge_{e \in T} \tau_{\mathtt{proc}(e)}(e)$; and
- $\left(\nu \bigcup_{e \in T} \pi_{\mathtt{proc}(e)}(e)\right) \bigcup_{e \in T} \{\nu'(\mathtt{proc}(e))\} = \nu'$.

Definition 4. <u>runs</u> Suppose we are given a CTA $M = \langle \Sigma, A_1, A_2, \ldots, A_m \rangle$ such that for each $1 \leq p \leq m$, $A_p = \langle \Sigma, X_p, Q_p, I_p, \mu_p, E_p, \gamma_p, \lambda_p, \tau_p, \pi_p \rangle$. A *run* of M is an infinite sequence of state-time pairs $(\nu_1, t_1)(\nu_2, t_2) \ldots (\nu_k, t_k) \ldots \ldots$ such that $t_1 t_2 \ldots t_k \ldots \ldots$ is a monotonically increasing real-number (time) divergent sequence and for all $k \geq 1$,

- for all $t \in [0, t_{k+1} - t_k]$, $\nu_k + t \models \bigwedge_{1 \leq p \leq m} \mu_p(\nu_k(p))$; and

- there is a global transition T such that $\nu_k + t_{k+1} - t_k \xrightarrow{T} \nu_{k+1}$.   ∎

For convenience of discussion, we adopt *safety analysis* as our verification framework. Given a safety predicate $\eta \in B(\bigcup_{1 \leq p \leq m} Q_p, \bigcup_{1 \leq p \leq m} X_p)$ and a run $(\nu_1, t_1)(\nu_2, t_2) \ldots (\nu_k, t_k) \ldots \ldots$ of a CTA, we say the run satisfies η iff for every $k \geq 1$ and every $t \in [0, t_{k+1} - t_k]$, $\nu_k + t \models \eta$. A CTA is *safe* with respect to η iff for every run $(\nu_1, t_1) \ldots \ldots$ of the CTA such that $\nu_1 \models \bigwedge_{1 \leq p \leq m} I_p$, the run satisfies η. Our *safety analysis problem* asks whether a given CTA is safe with respect to a given safety predicate.

3   Symbolic Characterization of Global Transitions

To implement a model-checker with general and flexible global transitions, we need to know what the global transitions in a CTA are. A straightforward way to do this is to try out every subset T of $\bigcup_{1 \leq p \leq m} E_p$ with $\forall 1 \leq p \leq m (|T \cap E_p| \leq 1)$ and check if T is both consistent and minimal. But this could be infeasible in practice. For example, in figure 2, as the number of senders increases to an arbitrary natural number m, since signal 'collision' emulates a broadcasting, process transition 4 will then be labeled with m '!collision.' Thus the number of global transitions for collision will be 2^m which is of exponential complexity. Moreover, in a well-designed programming language, all the senders may very likely share the same procedure template. Thus, the program input size is roughly the size of one sender procedure template plus the size of one bus procedure template. This makes the exponential blow-up even more unbearable.

In the following, we first prove an equivalence condition for the minimality and consistency of transition plans. The condition helps us understand the interactions among the synchronizers in a global transition. Based on this condition, we then present an algorithm, which may very well avoid the exponential blow-up in enumerating the global transitions in the average cases, for the construction of a symbolic characterization of global transitions. In short, the symbolic characterization is a BDD-like data-structure, which allows us to take advantage of the data-sharing capability of BDD-like data-structures for efficient manipulation.

For convenience of presentation, we use positive integers to index the process transitions. For each process p, we introduce variable T_p, which records the transition to be executed by process p in a global transition. Specifically, $\mathsf{T}_p = \perp$ if process p does not participate in the global transition. For the system in figure 2, the characterization is in figure 3. In the characterization, the label on a node

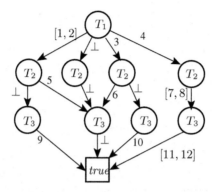

Fig. 3. The symbolic characterization of global transitions for the CTA in figure 2

together with the label on an outgoing arc specifies the participation of a process in a global transition. For example, the arc labeled with 3 from the root means that $T_1 = 3$, i.e., process 1 executing process transition 3 in a global transition. A root-to-sink path specifies global transitions. For example, in figure 3, the following path $(T_1) \xrightarrow{[1,2]} (T_2) \xrightarrow{\perp} (T_3) \xrightarrow{9} \boxed{true}$ represents global transitions $\{1,9\}$ and $\{2,9\}$. The set of all root-to-sink paths in such a characterization represents the set of all global transitions.

Given a transition plan T, a *synchronization plan* Ψ_T for T represents how the output events of each process are to be received by the corresponding input events of peer processes. Formally speaking, Ψ_T is a mapping from $T \times \Sigma \times T$ to $\mathcal{Z}$ such that

- if $\Psi_T(e, \sigma, e') \geq 0$, it represents the number of event σ sent form process transition e (by process $\mathrm{proc}(e)$) to be received by process transition e' (by process $\mathrm{proc}(e')$) in T.
- if $\Psi_T(e, \sigma, e') \leq 0$, its absolute value represents the number of event σ received by process transition e (by process $\mathrm{proc}(e)$) to be sent from process transition e' (by process $\mathrm{proc}(e')$) in T.

Thus $\Psi_T(e, \sigma, e') = -\Psi_T(e', \sigma, e)$. A synchronization plan Ψ_T is *consistent* iff for all $e \in T$, the total number of inputs and outputs for each $\sigma \in \Sigma$ is consistent with $\lambda_{\mathrm{proc}(e)}(e, \sigma)$. Formally speaking, this means that $\sum_{e' \in T} \Psi_T(e, \sigma, e') = \lambda_{\mathrm{proc}(e)}(e, \sigma)$. From now on, we shall assume that all our synchronization plans are consistent.

A sequence $e_1 \dots e_k$ of process transitions in a synchronization plan Ψ_T is called a *connecting sequence* between e_1 and e_k in Ψ_T iff for each $1 \leq i < k$, there is a $\sigma_i \in \Sigma$ such that $\Psi_T(e_i, \sigma_i, e_{i+1}) \neq 0$. We have the following lemma, which helps laying the keel of our algorithm for the construction of the symbolic characterization of global transitions.

Lemma 1. *A consistent transition plan T is* minimal *iff for all synchronization plans Ψ_T, we cannot partition T into non-empty consistent transition plans $\dot{T}, \ddot{T}$ such that for each two transitions $\dot{e} \in \dot{T}, \ddot{e} \in \ddot{T}$, there is no connecting sequence between $\dot{e}$ and $\ddot{e}$ in Ψ_T.* ∎

The proof of the lemma is omitted due to page-limit. Lemma 1 implies that we can use connecting sequences to construct the symbolic characterization of global transitions. Intuitively, a global transition T is a maximal set of process transitions such that there is a synchronization plan Ψ_T and between any two elements in T, there must be a connecting sequence in Ψ_T. For each $e \in T$, the connecting sequences from e compose a spanning tree in T. We use the following recursive procedure to construct the characterization of global transitions. Conceptually, we start a nondeterministic process to traverse the connecting sequences from each process transition at statement (a). In each recursive invocation, we make a nondeterministic choice of the value of $\Psi_T(e, \sigma, e')$ for some e, σ, e' at statement (c). Also we need a mapping $H : \Sigma \mapsto \mathcal{Z}$ to record the numbers of standing receiving and sending requests for the signals in Σ. Given $\sigma \in \Sigma$ and $z \in \mathcal{Z}$, notationally, $H[\sigma \leftarrow z]$ is a mapping identical to H except that $H(\sigma) = z$.

```
global-transitions(M) /* M is a CTA M = ⟨Σ, A₁, A₂, ..., Aₘ⟩ such that
```
for each $1 \le p \le m$, $A_p = \langle \Sigma, X_p, Q_p, I_p, \mu_p, E_p, \gamma_p, \lambda_p, \tau_p, \pi_p \rangle$. */ {

    $\Phi := \emptyset$; $\phi := \mathit{false}$;

    for each $e \in \bigcup_{1 \le p \le m} E_p$, do { .... (a)

        $H := \emptyset$; for $\sigma \in \Sigma$, $H := [\sigma \leftarrow \lambda_{\mathrm{proc}(e)}(e, \sigma)]$;

        $\phi := \phi \vee (T_{\mathrm{proc}(e)} = e \wedge \textbf{rec-global-transitions}(H, \{\mathrm{proc}(e)\}))$;

    }

    return ϕ;

}

```
rec-global-transitions(H, K) {
```
    if $\exists \phi((H, K, \phi) \in \Phi)$, return ϕ; .... (b)

    if $\forall \sigma \in \Sigma(H(\sigma) = 0)$,

        { $\phi := \bigwedge_{1 \le p \le m; p \notin K} T_p = \bot$; $\Phi := \Phi \cup \{(H, K, \phi)\}$; return ϕ; } .... (c)

    $\phi := \mathit{false}$;

    get one $\sigma \in \Sigma$ such that $H(\sigma) \ne 0$;

    for each $1 \le p \le m$ such that $p \notin K$, do {

        for each $e \in E_p$ such that $H(\sigma) \cdot \lambda_{\mathrm{proc}(e)}(e, \sigma) < 0$, do {

            $H' := H$; for $\sigma' \in \Sigma$, $H' := H'[\sigma' \leftarrow H(\sigma') + \lambda_{\mathrm{proc}(e)}(e, \sigma')]$; .... (d)

            $\phi := \phi \vee (T_{\mathrm{proc}(e)} = e \wedge \textbf{rec-global-transitions}(H', K \cup \{\mathrm{proc}(e)\}))$;

    } }

    $\Phi := \Phi \cup \{(H, K, \phi)\}$; return ϕ; .... (e)

}

The procedure basically traverses through all trees composed of the connecting sequences. What makes it efficient is that we use the set variable Φ to record the argument pairs that have already been processed. Suppose we have recursively invoked `rec-global-transitions()` by picking $e_1, \ldots, e_k$ at statement (d) when we enter a particular instance of `rec-global-transitions()` to execute statement (b). At this moment, the record for the current invocation is a triple like (H, K, ϕ). Here H is the accumulation of the standing transmission and receiving events along $e_1, \ldots, e_k$, i.e., for each $\sigma \in \Sigma$, $H(\sigma) = \sum_{1 \leq i \leq k} \lambda(e_i, \sigma)$. K shows which processes have already participated in the global transition, i.e., $K = \{\text{proc}(e_i) \mid 1 \leq i \leq k\}$. ϕ is the result BDD-like data-structure for argument pair H and K. In statement (b), every time when we find out that the argument pair has been processed before, we simply return the recorded result and save the computation resources. If the argument pair has not been processed before, we calculate and record the result in either statement (c) or (e). Statement (c) takes care of the case that a minimal transition plan has been generated. Statement (e) is executed when further traversing is still needed by invoking `rec-global-transitions()` to explore further along the connecting sequences.

The set of global transitions for CTA M can be enumerated as the set of root-to-sink paths in `global-transitions`(M). For convenience of presentation, we let $\Gamma_M =$ `global-transitions`(M).

4   Weakest Precondition Calculation for Backward Reachability Analysis

To calculate a representation of the backwardly reachable state-space, we need two basic procedures, one for the computation of weakest preconditions of all global transitions and the other for those of backward time-progressions. We call the former `xplans_bck()` and the latter `time_bck()`. Specifically, `xplans_bck`(η) returns the weakest precondition of states in description η through any global transitions. `time_bck`(η) returns the weakest precondition of state description η through backward time-progress. Details about `time_bck()` can be found in [8,11,14]. In subsections 4.1 and 4.2, we discuss two algorithms of `xplans_bck()`. The two ways both involve double-loops. The former is traditional in that it enumerates all paths (i.e. global transitions) in Γ_M to calculate a weakest precondition. The latter is our innovation and takes advantage of the BDD-like data-structure Γ_M to calculate the weakest precondition of all global transitions as a whole.

With these two basic procedures, the backward reachability procedure, denoted `reachable_bck`(η_1, η_2), which characterizes the state-space for $\exists \eta_1 \mathcal{U} \eta_2$ [8,11,12,14], can be implemented as the least fixpoint of equation:

$$Y = \eta_2 \vee (\eta_1 \wedge \text{time\_bck}(\eta_1 \wedge \text{xplans\_bck}(Y)))$$

i.e., $\texttt{reachable\_bck}(\eta_1, \eta_2) \equiv \texttt{lfp} Y. (\eta_2 \vee (\eta_1 \wedge \texttt{time\_bck}(\eta_1 \wedge \texttt{xplans\_bck}(Y))))$.
The monotonicity of F in fixpoint equation $Y = F(Y)$ and finite structures of
CTA state-space [1] together ensure the computability of the least fixpoint.

We can answer the safety of a CTA with respect to a safety predicate η by
calculating $\bigwedge_{1 \leq p \leq m} I_p \wedge \texttt{reachable\_bck}(true, \neg\eta)$. If the cacluation results in
false, the system is safe. Otherwise it is unsafe.

Note that all the symbolic state-space characterizations can be represented as
either sets of pairs of modes and DBMs [6] or BDD-like data-structures [11, 12].
Our algorithms are independent of the representation scheme of η.

4.1   Algorithm I for xplans_bck()

We use for each $1 \leq p \leq m$, a variable $\texttt{mode}_p$ that records the current mode of
process p. We need a procedure, $\texttt{FM\_elim}(\eta, W)$, that implements the Fourier-
Motzkin elimination [7] of variables in W from predicate η. There could be
clock variables and mode variables in W. Geometrically, $\texttt{FM\_elim}(\eta, W)$ is the
projection of η on the space without dimensions W. Algebraically, given $W = \{w_1, \ldots, w_h\}$, $\texttt{FM\_elim}(\eta, W) = \exists w_1 \exists w_2 \ldots \exists w_h(\eta)$. The implementation of
$\texttt{FM\_elim}()$ with BDD-like data-structures for dense-time spaces has been dis-
cussed in [12]. The first implementation of $\texttt{xplans\_bck}(\eta)$ is as follows.

$\texttt{xplans\_bck}(\eta)$ /* with context CTA M */ {
    Let $\psi := false$;
    for each T in the set of global transitions in Γ_M, do { .... (f)
        $\phi := \eta \wedge \bigwedge_{e \in T; x \in \pi_{\texttt{proc}(e)}} x = 0 \wedge \bigwedge_{e \in T; \gamma(e) = (q, q')} \texttt{mode}_{\texttt{proc}(e)} = q'$; .... (g)
        $\phi := \texttt{FM\_elim}\left(\phi, \bigcup_{e \in T}(\pi(e) \cup \{\texttt{mode}_{\texttt{proc}(e)}\})\right)$; .... (h)
        $\psi := \psi \vee \left(\phi \wedge \bigwedge_{e \in T; \gamma(e) = (q, q')} \left(\tau(e) \wedge \texttt{mode}_{\texttt{proc}(e)} = q\right)\right)$; .... (i)
    }
    return ψ;
}

Algorithm I is realized as a double-loop. It first enumerates all paths (i.e.
global transitions) in Γ_M in the outer-loop (at statement (f)) and then enumerates the process transitions (at statement (g)) in the current global transition
in the inner-loop to calculate a weakest precondition. Statement (g) calculates
the postcondition right after a global transition. Statement (h) calculates the
precondition right before the assignments (or clock-resets) of the global transition. Statement (i) calculates the preconditions right at the satisfaction of the
triggering conditions of all the participating process transitions.

Algorithm I may perform badly when there are too many global transitions.
This could be the case when there are synchronization plans involving all processes and each process can participate in such plans with many process transitions. Suppose G is the number of global transitions. In the worst case, G
can be exponential to the input sizes in bits. But when there is no such huge
synchronization plan, this algorithm can be efficient in that it extracts the state-
predicate into G small chunks to calculate weakest preconditions.

4.2   Algorithm II for xplans_bck()

Algorithm II works on $\eta \wedge \Gamma_M$ in the following way.

```
xplans_bck(η) /* with context CTA M */ {
    Let η := η ∧ ΓM;
    for each 1 ≤ p ≤ m, do { ................................................ (j)
        ψ := η ∧ (Tp =⊥);
        for each e ∈ Ep with γ(e) = (q, q'), { .................................. (k)
            φ := η ∧ (Tp = e) ∧ (⋀x∈πp(e) x = 0) ∧ (modep = q'); .................... (l)
            ψ := ψ ∨ FM_elim (φ, π(e) ∪ {modep}); ............................... (m)
        }
        η := ψ;
    }
    η = η ∧ ⋀1≤p≤m(Tp =⊥ ∨ ⋁e∈Ep;γ(e)=(q,q')(Tp = e ∧ modeproc(e) = q ∧ τp(e)); .. (n)
    return FM_elim(η, {T1, ..., Tm}); ............................................. (o)
}
```

Algorithm II is also a double-loop (at statements (j) and (k)). Suppose after the $(p-1)$'st iteration of the outer loop, the value of ψ is ψ_{p-1}. In the p'th iteration of the outer loop, it partitions ψ_{p-1} into $|E_p| + 1$ chunks. For the chunk for $T_p = e$, statement (l) calculates the postcondition through the assignments (or clock-resets) of process transition e. Then, statement (m) calculates the precondition before the assignments (or clock-resets) of process transition e. After the preconditions of the assignments (or clock-resets) of all process transitions have been considered, statement (n) then takes into consideration the triggering conditions of all process transitions. Variables $T_1, \ldots, T_m$ can then be removed with the Fourier-Motzkin elimination with statement (o).

The number of iterations of the inner loop of algorithm II is always $\sum_{1 \leq p \leq m} |E_p|$. Thus, it does not suffer from the possible combinatorial explosion of global transition count as algorithm I does. But in iteration p of the outer loop, it partitions η into $|E_p| + 1$ chunks to calculate weakest preconditions. Since $|E_p| + 1$ is independent of the concurrency size, when the concurrency is high, such chunks can be large BDD-like data-structures with complexities exponential to the input sizes in bits. Usually the performance of BDD operations may degrade as the sizes of the BDDs increase.

4.3   A Hybrid Scheme to Combine Algorithms I and II

As mentioned in the last two subsections, algorithm I may show its drawbacks when the number of global transitions is large. And algorithm II could show its drawbacks when the number is small. We have designed a hybrid of algorithms I and II so that global transitions of smaller sizes can be handled with algorithm I while those of larger sizes can be ‚with algorithm II. Specifically, we have a run-time threshold parameter β so that global transitions of sizes $\leq \beta$ will be evaluated with algorithm I and those of sizes $> \beta$ will be evaluated with algorithm II. In our experiment, we have observed that usually smaller values of β, like 2, 3, or 4, engender good verification performance.

5   Implementation and Experiments

We have implemented the ideas in our model-checker/simulator, **RED** version 6.0 with the new BDD-like data-structure, *CRD* (Clock-Restriction Diagram) [12,13,15]. Due to page-limit, we only report experiment with the following four benchmarks that use global transitions involving all processes.

- *CSMA/CD* [16]: This is the Ethernet bus arbitration protocol with the idea of collision-and-retry. There can be one bus process and m sender processes. Global transitions involving all processes happen when the bus process sends out collision signals to all senders at the same time. We want to verify that at any moment, at most one process is in the transmission mode for ≥ 52 time units.
- *SAM, Missile against hostile jet-fighters*: This is the system illustrated in figure 1. There can be a missile process and m jet-fighter processes. It is assumed that for a system with m jet-fighters, the missile updates its status $2m+1$ times more frequently than the jet-fighters. Global transitions involving all processes happen when a hapless jet-fighter is hit and the explosion is observed by all the other jet-fighters. The properties we want to verify is that no jet-fighter can stay close to the target for more than $2m$ time units.
- *FIFO channel*: There can be a user process, a queue manager process, and m queue slot processes. We use a local variable **number** of each slot process to record the position of the slot in the queue. Global transitions involving all processes happen when the queue head slot is dequeued and the other occupied slot processes must decrement their **numbers**. We want to verify that the values of variables **number** correctly record the queue formation.
- *ARP, Ethernet address resolution protocol*: This protocol is used by a sender to get the Ethernet address (48 bits long) of the receiver in Ethernet. Initially, the sender onlys know the IP address of the receiver. There are one sender process and m receiver processes. Global transitions involving all processes happen when the sender broadcasts the IP address of the receiver along the Ethernet. We want to verify that when the sender starts sending the messages, it knows the correct Ethernet address of the receiver.

The four benchmarks are all parameterized, i.e., the concurrency sizes are adjustable through the parameter m. We use parameterized benchmarks so that we can observe how our techniques scale with respect to concurrency sizes, which are a major factor for combinatorial explosion in verification complexity.

In table 1, please find the performance data. For each benchmark, we collected data with $\beta = 0$ (corresponding to running Algorithm II alone), a medium value for β (corresponding to running the hybrid scheme), and the maximum value for β, i.e., the number of processes (corresponding to running Algorithm I alone). The medium values for β were chosen through trials and errors. We found that the medium values equal to the sizes of small global transitions usually engender the best verification performance.

Table 1. Performance data of scalability with respect to number of processes

spec.	m	$\beta = 0$	medium β values	$\beta =\#$ procs
CSMA/CD	2	0.01s/47k	0.00s/28k	0.00s/21k
	3	0.05s/86k	0.03s/54k	0.06s/43k
medium β	4	0.20s/134k	0.11s/89k	0.26s/93k
values = 2	5	0.42s/192k	0.40s/138k	1.73s/208k
	6	0.84s/304k	0.78s/299k	12.9s/499k
	7	1.70s/681k	1.76s/674k	132s/1262k
	8	3.37s/1551k	3.79s/1546k	2572s/3316k
	9	7.56s/3548k	7.76s/3541k	
	10	18.4s/8075k	18.5s/8072k	
	11	54.2s/18272k	51.5s/18274k	N/A
	12	144s/41105k	146s/41083k	
	13	385s/91826k	397s/91873k	
SAM	2	0.18s/92k	0.17s/45k	0.10s/45k
	3	1.29s/188k	0.75s/132k	0.80s/130k
medium β	4	6.01s/387k	4.03s/352k	4.60s/400k
values = 2	5	26.5s/899k	17.3s/752k	23.6s/931k
	6	99.4s/1763k	61.5s/1344k	144s/1959k
	7	284s/3195k	185s/2205k	750s/5703k
	8	734s/5204k	537s/3384k	N/A
FIFO	2	0.04s/72k	0.02s/51k	0.02s/51k
	3	0.22s/172k	0.15s/103k	0.17s/152k
medium β	4	0.59s/346k	0.31s/231k	0.79s/428k
values = 4	5	1.46s/620k	1.27s/471k	4.97s/1230k
	6	5.07s/1023k	4.32s/872k	84.9s/3728k
	7	24.0s/1665k	18.2s/1540k	938s/11734k
	8	90.0s/3853k	76.7s/3372k	N/A
	9	304s/9035k	290s/9894k	
ARP	2	0.55s/186k	0.40s/149k	0.40s/141k
	3	5.59s/526k	3.21s/460k	3.92s/615k
medium β	4	72.0s/1578k	33.0s/1105k	58.7s/2709k
values = 2	5	872s/7318k	435s/5837k	703s/13494k
	6	8575s/84086k	4194s/84087k	N/A

data collected on a Pentium 4 Mobile 1.6GHz with 256MB memory running LINUX;
s: seconds; k: kilobytes of memory in data-structure; N/A: not available;

As can be seen from the data, the techniques proposed in this work really help in enhancing the verification performance of our model-checker. Invariably, when the number of global transitions is big, running Algorithm I alone always ends up with the worst performance.

Against three out of the four benchmarks, the hybrid scheme performs better than Algorithm II. But even when the hybrid scheme performs worse (against CSMA/CD), the difference in performance is still very small. The experiment data seems to suggest that the hybrid scheme could be a safe choice. More experiments could be carried out to check this conjecture in the future.

Note that we did not compare our implementation with famous tools like Kronos [16] and UPPALL [4] since they do not support complex behaviors constructed out of binary synchronizations. Thus it could be difficult for them to run the high-level behavior models used in our experiment.

6   Conclusion

Successful verification of complex systems demands both an appropriate abstraction level and efficient verification techniques for such systems. Toward this end, we have made the following contributions: (1) A flexible synchronization scheme to model complex high-level behaviors in distributed real-time systems. (2) A BDD-based algorithm to calculate the characterizations of complex synchronizations among process transitions. (3) A BDD-baase algorithm for the weakest preconditions of all transition synchronizations calculated in a bulk. (4) A hybrid scheme to tune the performance our techniques.

References

1. R. Alur, C. Courcoubetis, D.L. Dill. Model Checking for Real-Time Systems, IEEE LICS, 1990.
2. R. Alur, D.L. Dill. Automata for modelling real-time systems. ICALP' 1990, LNCS 443, Springer-Verlag, pp.322-335.
3. J.R. Burch, E.M. Clarke, K.L. McMillan, D.L.Dill, L.J. Hwang. Symbolic Model Checking: 10^{20} States and Beyond, IEEE LICS, 1990.
4. J. Bengtsson, K. Larsen, F. Larsson, P. Pettersson, Wang Yi. UPPAAL - a Tool Suite for Automatic Verification of Real-Time Systems. Hybrid Control System Symposium, 1996, LNCS, Springer-Verlag.
5. R.E. Bryant. Graph-based Algorithms for Boolean Function Manipulation, IEEE Trans. Comput., C-35(8), 1986.
6. D.L. Dill. Timing Assumptions and Verification of Finite-state Concurrent Systems. CAV'89, LNCS 407, Springer-Verlag.
7. J.B. Fourier. (reported in:) Analyse des travaux de l'Académie Royale des Sciences pendant l'année 1824, Partie Mathématique, 1827.
8. T.A. Henzinger, X. Nicollin, J. Sifakis, S. Yovine. Symbolic Model Checking for Real-Time Systems, IEEE LICS 1992.
9. C.A.R. Hoare. Communicating Sequential Processes, Prentice Hall, 1985.
10. A. Shaw. Communicating Real-Time State Machines. IEEE Transactions on Software Engineering 18(9), September, 1992.
11. F. Wang. Efficient Data-Structure for Fully Symbolic Verification of Real-Time Software Systems. TACAS'2000, LNCS 1785, Springer-Verlag.
12. F. Wang. Efficient Verification of Timed Automata with BDD-like Data-Structures, STTT (Software Tools for Technology Transfer), Vol. 6, Nr. 1, June 2004, Springer-Verlag; special issue for the 4th VMCAI, Jan. 2003, LNCS 2575, Springer-Verlag.
13. F. Wang. Model-Checking Distributed Real-Time Systems with States, Events, and Multiple Fairness Assumptions. AMAST'2004, LNCS 3116, Springer-Verlag.
14. F. Wang, P.-A. Hsiung. Efficient and User-Friendly Verification. IEEE Transactions on Computers, Jan. 2002.
15. F. Wang, G.-D. Huang, F. Yu. Symbolic Simulation of Real-Time Concurrent Systems. 9th RTCSA, Feb. 2003, LNCS 2968, Springer-Verlag.
16. S. Yovine. Kronos: A Verification Tool for Real-Time Systems. International Journal of Software Tools for Technology Transfer, Vol. 1, Nr. 1/2, October 1997.

An Improved Rule for While Loops in Deductive Program Verification

Bernhard Beckert[1], Steffen Schlager[2], and Peter H. Schmitt[2]

[1] University of Koblenz-Landau, Institute for Computer Science,
D-56072 Koblenz, Germany
beckert@uni-koblenz.de
[2] Universität Karlsruhe, Institute for Theoretical Computer Science,
D-76128 Karlsruhe, Germany
{schlager, pschmitt}@ira.uka.de

Abstract. Performance and usability of deductive program verification systems can be enhanced if specifications not only consist of pre-/post-condition pairs and invariants but also include information on which memory locations are modified by the program. This allows to separate the aspects of (a) which locations change and (b) how they change, state the change information in a compact way, and make the proof process more efficient. In this paper, we extend this idea from *method specifications* to *loop invariants*; and we define a proof rule for while loops that makes use of the change information associated with the loop body. It has been implemented and is successfully used in the KeY software verification system.

1 Introduction

The Idea of Specifying Change Information and a Motivating Example. Deductive program verification systems are mostly based on program logics, such as dynamic logic [11,13,12] and Hoare logic [3]. Their performance and usability can be greatly enhanced if specifications of programs not only consist of the usual pre-/post-condition pairs and invariants but also include additional information, such as knowledge about which memory locations are changed by a program. More precisely, we associate with a program p a set Mod_p of expressions, called the modifier set (for p), with the understanding that Mod_p is part of the specification of p. Its semantics is that those parts of a program state that are *not* referenced by an expression in Mod_p will never be changed by executing p.

As a motivating example, consider the following program $p_{\min}$ that computes the minimum of an array a of integers:

$$m := a[0];\ i := 1;$$
```
while (i < length(a)) do
    if (a[i] < m) then m := a[i]; fi
    i := i + 1;
od
```

K.-K. Lau and R. Banach (Eds.): ICFEM 2005, LNCS 3785, pp. 315–329, 2005.
© Springer-Verlag Berlin Heidelberg 2005

A correct (though incomplete) post-condition for this program is

$$\phi_{\min} = (\forall x)(0 \le x < length(a) \rightarrow a[x] \le m)$$

stating that, after running $p_{\min}$, the variable m indeed contains the minimum of a. However, a specification that just consists of $\phi_{\min}$ is rather weak. The problem is that $\phi_{\min}$ can also be established using, for example, a program that sets m as well as all elements of a to 0, which of course is not the *intended* behaviour. To exclude such programs, the specification must also state what the program does modify (the variables i and m) and does not modify (the array a and its elements). One way of doing this is to extend the post-condition with an additional part

$$\phi_{inv} = (\forall x)(0 \le x < length(a) \rightarrow a[x] = a'[x])$$

where a' is a new array variable (not allowed to occur in the program) that contains the "old" values of the array elements. To make sure a' has the same elements as a, the formula ϕ_{inv} must also be used as a pre-condition and, thus, be turned into an invariant. In Dynamic Logic, this specification of $p_{\min}$ is written as $\phi_{inv} \rightarrow [p_{\min}](\phi_{\min} \land \phi_{inv})$.

But, then, ϕ_{inv} also has to be made part to the loop invariant

$$\phi_{loopinv} = \phi_{inv} \land 0 \le i \le length(a) \land (\forall x)(0 \le x < i \rightarrow a[x] \le m)$$

that is used during the proof that $p_{\min}$ indeed satisfies its specification, making that proof more complex and proof construction more difficult and less efficient.

In general, loop invariants are "polluted" by formulas stating what the loop does *not* do. All relevant properties of the pre-state that need to be preserved have to be encoded into the invariant, even if they are in no way affected by the loop. Thus, two aspects are intermingled:

- Information about what intended effects the loop *does* have.
- Information about what non-intended effects the loop *does not* have.

This problem can be avoided by encoding the second aspect (i.e., the change information) with a modifier set instead of adding it to the invariant. The two aspects then get separated both in the specification and in the correctness proof, as the (sub-)proofs that a program (a) satisfies its post-condition and (b) satisfies its modifier set are also separated as well.

For our program $p_{\min}$, an appropriate modifier set is

$$Mod_{\min} = \{i, m\} .$$

It states in a very compact and simple way that $p_{\min}$ only changes i and m and, in particular, does *not* change the array a.

Besides the separation of the two different aspects, modifier sets have the advantage that they encode what is changed, while invariants must encode all locations that are *not* changed, which for non-trivial programs are many more.

Extension to Loops. Modifier sets that are part of method or function specifications have been investigated before (see the section on related work). Now, in this paper, we extend the idea of modifier sets from *method specifications* to *loop invariants*. Here, as well, modifier sets allow

- to separate the aspects of which locations change and how they change,
- state the change information in a compact way
- make the proof process more efficient.

To achieve the latter point, we define a new Dynamic Logic proof rule for while loops that makes use of the information contained in a modifier set for the loop *body* (as is also described in the following, the rule can easily be adapted to other program logics, such as Hoare logic).

Loops in general can—and in practice often will—change a finite but *unknown* number of memory locations (though in our simple motivating example p_{min} the number of changed locations is known to be 2). A loop may, for example, change all elements in a list whose length is not known at proof time but only at run time. Therefore, to handle loops, we use an extended version of modifier sets that can describe location sets of unknown size (the modifier sets for methods described in [6] cannot do that).

Related Work. The Java Modeling Language (JML) [14,15] allows to express change information for Java methods via what in JML jargon is called *assignable clauses*.

The ESC/Java tool (Extended Static Checker for Java) [9] uses a subset of JML as assertion language; an extension of ESC/Java for checking JML *assignable clauses* is described in [8]. Despite the undisputed usefulness of this tool its results are still very preliminary: failing assertions of a rather simple kind go undetected and failures are reported, where in reality the assertion is correct. In [22], a static analysis algorithm is proposed that checks assignable clauses for a simple object-oriented in vitro language. Correctness is proved via abstract interpretation over a trace semantics.

Daikon [18,10] is a heuristic approach to automatic detection of likely invariants by analysing program runs with concrete input values.

In [6], we have defined a precise semantics for method modifier sets and defined a transformation on first-order formulas based on modifier sets such that $\Gamma \to \phi_{Mod}$ implies validity of $\Gamma \to [p]\phi$, where ϕ_{Mod} is the transformation of ϕ using the modifier set Mod that is part of the specification of method p. This transformation can be used to employ modifier sets for proving the correctness of methods. However, it is restricted to modifier sets describing sets of memory location of fixed size, and it cannot easily be adapted to loop invariants—though the basic idea is similar to the new loop rule we present here.

Further related work is the Hoare calculus for a variant of C that is developed within the Verisoft project [21]. It allows to add simple modifier sets to procedure specifications. In [7], a method is presented that does not use explicit modifier sets but assumes that only what is mentioned in the pre- and post-condition may be changed.

Implementation in the KeY System. The work reported in this paper has been carried out as part of the KeY project [1,2]. The goal of this project is to develop a tool supporting formal specification and verification of JAVA CARD programs within a commercial platform for UML based software development.

Both the modifier set technique for methods from [6] and the rule for handling rules presented in this paper have been implemented in KeY. Experiments show that the performance of the prover is greatly enhanced using these extensions. KeY also contains functionality for verifying correctness of modifier sets [20].

Plan of This Paper. After reviewing the necessary pre-requisites in Section 2, we define our extended version of modifier sets in Section 3, which allows to describe location sets of unknown size. In Section 4, we introduce the notion of *quantified updates*. These updates, that are used in our verification rules, can be seen as a form of generalised substitutions. The new loop rule that makes use of modifier sets for loop bodies is introduced in Section 5. The implementation of the rule is described in Section 6. In Section 7, we give an extended example for its application. And, finally, in Section 8 we draw some conclusions.

2   Program Logic

To keep things simple in the paper, we consider as a programming language a simple deterministic while-language with assignments, if-then-else, while-loops, and arrays (due to lack of space we refrain from a formal definition of syntax and semantics). However, our approach applies to all deterministic programming languages whose semantics can be described by Kripke structures in terms of Def. 1. In the KeY tool we have implemented the invariant rule for the real object-oriented language JAVA CARD taking all the difficulties likes aliasing and abrupt termination into account (see Sect. 6).

The program logic we consider in this paper is an instance of Dynamic Logic (DL) which is a multi-modal logic with a modality $[p]$ for every program p of the considered programming language. The formula $[p]\phi$ expresses that, if the program p terminates in a state s, then ϕ holds in s. A formula $\psi \to [p]\phi$ expresses that, for every state s_1 satisfying pre-condition ψ, if a run of the program p starting in s_1 terminates in s_2, then the post-condition ϕ holds in s_2. For deterministic programs, there is exactly one such world s_2 (if p terminates) or there is no such world (if p does not terminate). The formula $\psi \to [p]\phi$ is thus equivalent to the Hoare triple $\{\psi\}p\{\phi\}$. In contrast to Hoare logic, the set of formulas of DL is closed under the usual logical operators.

The semantic domains used to interpret DL formulas are Kripke structures $\mathcal{K} = (S, \rho)$, where S is the set of states for $\mathcal{K}$ and ρ is the transition relation interpreting programs. Since we consider deterministic programs, ρ is a (partial) function, i.e., for every program p, $\rho(p) : S \to S$. The states $s \in S$ are typed first-order structures s, for some fixed signature Σ. We restrict attention to purely functional signatures Σ and we work under the constant domain assumption, i.e., for any two states $s_1, s_2 \in S$ the universes of s_1 and s_2 are the same set U.

We sometimes refer to U as *the* universe of $\mathcal{K}$. Furthermore we assume that the set of states S of any Kripke structure $\mathcal{K}$ consists of *all* first-order structures with signature Σ over some fixed universe. Some symbols of the signature are declared *rigid* and have a fixed interpretation for all $s \in S$. E.g., addition $+$ on integers cannot be changed by executing a program and will therefore be declared *rigid*. In contrast, the interpretation of *non-rigid* function symbols may differ from state to state. E.g., program variables occur as non-rigid 0-ary function symbols (constants) in Σ, and n-dimensional arrays are represented by non-rigid n-ary function symbols (i.e., $a[i_1, ..., i_n]$ is the same as $a(i_1, ..., i_n)$) (similarly, object attributes in an object-oriented language can be represented by unary function symbols). The interpretation of a function symbol f in a state s is denoted by f^s. Logical variables, which are different from program variables, never occur in programs. They are rigid in the sense that if a value is assigned to a logical variable, it is the same for all states.

Once the signature Σ and the universe U are fixed, the set S of states is also fixed and our Kripke structures will only differ in the state transition function ρ interpreting programs. When a programming language is chosen (in this case a while-language), the possible choices for ρ have to be restricted as well, such that the constructs of the programming language are interpreted in the right way.

From now on, we assume that a fixed set $\mathbf{K}_\Sigma$ of Kripke structures $\mathcal{K} = (S, \rho)$ is given that, as described above, depends (only) on the signature Σ, the universe U, and the restrictions on ρ, i.e., the semantics of our while-language with arrays. The set S of states is the same for all elements of $\mathbf{K}_\Sigma$.

Definition 1. *Let S be the set of all first-order structures over signature Σ with some fixed universe U. Then, the semantics of the programming language is given by a set $\mathbf{K}_\Sigma$ of Kripke structures that all share S as their set of states.*

Definition 2. *A Σ-formula ϕ is called* valid *if*

$$s, \beta \models \phi$$

for every state $s \in S$ of every Kripke structure $(S, \rho) \in \mathbf{K}_\Sigma$ and every variable assignment β (mapping logical variables to elements of the universe U).

3   Modifier Sets

A *modifier set* Mod_p for a program p is a set of ground terms denoting locations (i.e., the terms must not contain logical variables but they can contain program variables, which are constants in the logic). In contrast to [6] where modifier sets are written as lists of ground terms of fixed length, we consider in this paper modifier sets describing location sets of unknown size, since while loops in general may modify an unknown number of locations that depends on the state in which the loop is started. Of course, such modifier sets can no longer be represented as simple enumerations of ground terms. Rather, we use formulas to define the set of ground terms that may change.

Definition 3. *Let χ^j be a Dynamic Logic formula over Σ, $f^j \in \Sigma$ a non-rigid function symbol, and $t_1^j, \ldots, t_{n_j}^j$ terms $(j \geq 1)$. Then, the set*

$$\{ \langle \chi^1, f^1(t_1^1 \ldots, t_{n_1}^1) \rangle, \ldots, \langle \chi^k, f^k(t_1^k \ldots, t_{n_k}^k) \rangle \}$$

of pairs is a modifier set.

Intuitively, a location $f(s_1, \ldots, s_n)$ may be changed by a program p when started in a state s if the modifier set for p contains an element $\langle \chi, f(t_1, \ldots, t_n) \rangle$ and there is variable assignment β such that the following conditions hold:

1. $s, \beta \models t_i \doteq s_i$ for $1 \leq i \leq n$, i.e. β assigns the free logical variables occurring in t_i values such that t_i coincides with s_i.
2. $s, \beta \models \chi$, i.e. the characteristic formula χ holds for the variable assignment β.

A modifier set *Mod* is said to be correct for a program p if p at most changes the value of locations mentioned in *Mod*.

Definition 4. *Let Mod be a modifier set and let S be the set of states.*
A pair $(s_1, s_2) \in S \times S$ satisfies Mod, denoted by

$$(s_1, s_2) \models Mod \ ,$$

iff, for

(a) all n-ary function symbols $f \in \Sigma$ $(n \geq 0)$,
(b) all n-tuples $o_1, \ldots, o_n$ from the universe U,

the following condition holds:

$$f^{s_1}(o_1, \ldots, o_n) \neq f^{s_2}(o_1, \ldots, o_n)$$

implies that there is a pair $\langle \chi, f(t_1, \ldots, t_n) \rangle \in Mod$ and a variable assignment β such that

$$o_i = t_i^{s_1, \beta} \ (1 \leq i \leq n) \ and \ s_1, \beta \models \chi \ .$$

The modifier set Mod is correct *for a program p, if*

$$(s_1, s_2) \models Mod$$

for all state pairs $(s_1, s_2) \in \rho(p)$.

Example 1. Consider the following program, where a is a one-dimensional array of integers.

$$i := 0; \ j := 0; \ \texttt{while} \ (i < length(a)) \ \texttt{do} \ a[i] := a[i] * 2; \ i := i + 1; \ \texttt{od}$$

We assume that the size $s = length(a)$ of the array is not fixed in advance but unknown. Thus, for giving a correct modifier set, it is not possible to enumerate the locations $a[0], a[1], \ldots, a[s]$ as s is not known.

However, a correct modifier set for the above program can be written as

$$\{\langle 0 \leq x < length(a) \rangle, a[x]\rangle, \langle true, i \rangle, \langle true, j \rangle\} \ .$$

illustrating that modifier sets are not necessarily minimal (j is not modified).

The modifier set $\{\langle 0 \leq x < length(a) \rangle, a[x]\rangle\}$ is not correct for the above program, since i is actually changed by the program.

4   Quantified Updates

The rules in calculi for deductive program verification (such as Hoare logic or Dynamic Logic) in a certain sense symbolically execute the program to be verified. And, usually, a state update, i.e., an assignment like $x := t$, is done by applying a substitution that replaces occurrences of x by t. This straightforward method works fine for simple programming languages but causes problems for more complex languages like JAVA CARD. In JAVA CARD (as in all other object-oriented programming languages) the same object may be referenced by several different reference variables (*aliasing*). We face the aliasing problem already for our simple while-language, because it contains arrays. An assignment $a[i] := 5$ changes the value of $a[j]$ if $i \doteq j$, i.e., $a[i]$ and $a[j]$ reference the same same array element. As a consequence, every array assignment causes a case distinction making verification infeasible. This is even more true for object-oriented languages where every assignment to an object attribute causes case distinctions. The solution to this problem proposed in [4] and implemented in the KeY System are so-called *updates*. The idea is to not immediately perform substitutions for assignments. Rather assignments are collected as state updates and not applied before the program has been completely symbolically executed. The advantage of this method is that assignments often cancel out previous ones rendering case distinctions for alias analysis unnecessary.

Definition 5 (Syntax of updates). *The set of Dynamic Logic formulas is extended as follows. For all non-rigid ground terms t, and all terms v, if ϕ is a formula, then $\{t := v\}\phi$ is a formula as well. The expressions $\{t := v\}$ are called updates.*

The formula $\{t := v\}\phi$ has the same semantics as $[t := v;]\phi$. Thus, one might ask why updates are introduced as a separate syntactic category instead of using assignments. Indeed, the goal of postponing the symbolic execution of state changes can be achieved without updates. However, there are some immediate extensions to updates that cannot be mimicked with assignments. E.g., one can introduce *quantified updates* that use a logical formula to describe the state change. This is a useful extension in the current context and is introduced below.

Anyway, it is important to note that updates are introduced for efficiency reasons but do not make the logic more expressive. A formula ϕ containing updates can always be transformed (in a uniform way) into an formula ϕ' without updates such that ϕ is valid iff ϕ' is valid. Therefore, the idea of modifier sets for loop bodies and the rule we introduce in the following section work just as well in calculi without updates.

The transformation for removing an update basically works by performing the symbolic execution that the state update represents (i.e., it does what updates try to avoid). It introduces new variables for preserving the old values of the changed variables (the value before the update is applied). However, due to aliasing the set of variables (or locations) that is affected by an update cannot be determined syntactically. Rather, all references (of compatible types) have to be checked for whether they point to the location that is updated or not.

Example 2. We consider the DL formula

$$(a[i] \doteq 0 \land a[j] \doteq 0) \rightarrow \{a[i] := a[i] + 1\}a[j] \doteq 0$$

which holds iff $i \neq j$. The transformed formula without updates is

$$
\begin{aligned}
(a'[i] \doteq 0 \land a'[j] \doteq 0) \;\rightarrow\; (\; &a[i] \doteq a'[i] + 1 \;\land \\
&(i \neq j \rightarrow a[j] \doteq a'[j]) \;\land \\
&(i \doteq j \rightarrow a[j] \doteq a'[i] + 1) \;) \;\rightarrow\; a[j] \doteq 0 \; .
\end{aligned}
$$

We now extend the idea of updates to *quantified updates*, a generalised form of updates proposed in [19] that allows to update arbitrary sets of locations described by a characteristic formula.

Definition 6 (Syntax of quantified updates). *The set of Dynamic Logic formulas is extended as follows. For all DL formulas χ, terms $f(t_1, \ldots, t_n)$ with a non-rigid function symbol f, and (arbitrary) terms v, if ϕ is a DL formula, then $\{\chi \; ? \; f(t_1, \ldots, t_n) := v\}\phi$ is a DL formula as well. The expressions $\{\chi \; ? \; f(t_1, \ldots, t_n) := v\}$ are called* quantified updates.

Example 3. The quantified update $\{0 \leq i < \mathit{length}(a) \; ? \; a[i] := 0\}\phi$ assigns 0 to all elements of the array a.

Quantified updates—in contrast to "simple" updates (Def. 5)—may contain clashes. For example, the update $\{0 \leq i \leq 1 \; ? \; c := i\}$ tries to assign to the non-rigid constant c both the values 0 and 1. We define that, in case of a clash, an arbitrary (unknown) but fixed element is used. However, the updates we consider in this paper cannot contain clashes by construction. And without clashes, the semantics of the formula $\{\chi \; ? \; t := v\}\phi$ is the same as that of the transformed formula $(\forall_{Cl})((\chi \rightarrow \{t := v\}\phi) \land (\neg\chi \rightarrow \phi))$. Thus, as with simple updates, a formula containing quantified updates can always be transformed into an equivalent formula without them.

Definition 7 (Semantics of quantified updates). *Let s be a state, and let*

$$\mathcal{U} = \{\chi \; ? \; f(t_1, \ldots, t_n) := v\}$$

be a quantified update.

  The state $\mathcal{U}(s)$ is defined as follows: $\mathcal{U}(s)$ coincides with s except for the interpretation of the function symbol f, which is defined by

$$
\begin{aligned}
V(o_1, \ldots, o_n) = \{&\mathit{val}_{s,\beta}(v) \mid \mathit{val}_{s,\beta}(\chi) = \mathit{tt} \text{ and } \mathit{val}_{s,\beta}(t_i) = o_i \; (1 \leq i \leq n), \\
&\text{where } \beta \text{ is a variable assignment}\}
\end{aligned}
$$

$$
f^{\mathcal{U}(s)}(o_1, \ldots, o_n) = \begin{cases}
w & \text{if } V(o_1, \ldots, o_n) = \{w\} \\
f^s(o_1, \ldots, o_n) & \text{if } V(o_1, \ldots, o_n) = \emptyset \\
w \in V(o_1, \ldots, o_n) \text{ arbitrarily} & \text{otherwise}
\end{cases}
$$

for all elements $o_1, \ldots, o_n$ of the universe.

  The semantics of the application $\mathcal{U}\phi$ of a quantified update $\mathcal{U}$ to a formula ϕ is defined by

$$s \models \mathcal{U}\phi \qquad \text{iff} \qquad \mathcal{U}(s) \models \phi \; .$$

5   Invariant Rule Using Change Information

5.1   Motivation

Before we present our invariant rule that uses modifier sets and the change information they encode, we recall what the invariant rule in Dynamic Logic (with updates) looks like:

$$\frac{\Gamma \vdash \mathcal{U}Inv, \ \Delta \qquad Inv, \ \epsilon \vdash [\alpha]Inv \qquad Inv, \ \neg\epsilon \vdash \phi}{\Gamma \vdash \mathcal{U}[\texttt{while } \epsilon \texttt{ do } \alpha \texttt{ od}]\phi, \ \Delta} \tag{1}$$

Intuitively the above rule states that, if one can find an invariant Inv such that the three premisses hold, which state that (a) Inv holds in the beginning, (b) Inv is indeed an invariant, and (c) the conclusion ϕ follows from Inv and the negated loop condition ϵ, then ϕ holds after executing the loop (provided it terminates).

As a motivation for why using change information is useful, consider the following example program p defined as

$$q; \ i := 0; \ \texttt{while } (i < length(a)) \texttt{ do } a[i] := 0; \ i := i + 1; \texttt{ od} \ ,$$

where q is a (sub-)program. In order to prove some post-condition ϕ under the pre-condition ψ for p we have to show the validity of the DL formula $\psi \to [p]\phi$. Using our DL sequent calculus, symbolic execution of q results in a sequence $\mathcal{U}$ of updates describing the program state after execution of q. Then, considering that the while loop simply assigns all the elements of array a the value 0, an obvious invariant for the loop might be $i \leq length(a) \land (\forall x)(0 \leq x < i \to a[x] \doteq 0)$. In fact, this is an invariant for the loop (i.e., it holds at the beginning of the loop and holds after each iteration of the loop body) but it is not strong enough to entail the post-condition ϕ in general, i.e. the third premiss of the loop rule does not hold. The reason is that the second and the third premiss of the invariant rule omit the formulas Γ, Δ and the sequence $\mathcal{U}$ of updates, i.e., all information about the state reached before running the while loop is lost though it may be unrelated to the array a (one can construct similar examples where the second premiss does not hold). The only way to keep this information—as long as no modifier sets are used—is to add it to the invariant which, as already explained in the introduction, has several disadvantages.

The invariant rule proposed in this paper allows to keep as much context information as possible without explicitly encoding the context in the invariant. This is achieved by only throwing away those parts of Γ, Δ and $\mathcal{U}$ (i.e., of the descriptions of the initial state) that may be changed by the loop. Anything that remains unchanged is kept and can be used to establish the invariant (second premiss) and the post-condition (third premiss).

Our new rule is still available if, for some reason, no modifier sets is known for the loop body. In that case, it assumes that the loop potentially changes everything, and it then coincides with the traditional invariant rule. However, programmers usually know what is changed by a piece of code and can (or even *should*) annotate the code with the appropriate information.

An important advantage of using modifier sets is that usually a loop only changes few locations and only these locations must be put in a modifier set. On the other hand, using the traditional rule, all locations that do *not* change and whose value is of importance have to be included in the invariant and, typically, the number of locations that are not changed by the loop is much bigger than the number of locations that are actually changed. Of course, in general not everything that remains unchanged is needed to establish the post-condition in the third premiss. But when applying the invariant rule it is often not obvious what information must be preserved, in particular if the loop is followed by a non-trivial program. That can lead to repeated failed attempts to find the right invariant that allows to complete the proof. Whereas, to figure out the locations that are possibly changed by the loop, it is usually enough to look at the small piece of code in the loop body.

5.2   The New Invariant Rule for Dynamic Logic

Let *Mod* be a modifier set that is correct for the loop body α. The basic idea of the new version of the loop rule we define in this section is that the context $\Gamma, \Delta, \mathcal{U}$ is *not* removed from the second and third premiss. Then, however, information on locations appearing in the context $\Gamma, \Delta, \mathcal{U}$ that are mentioned in *Mod* must not be used. It must be removed. To meet this requirement, we introduce so-called *anonymous updates* which assign an arbitrary unknown value (represented by a Skolem symbol) to the locations mentioned in the modifier set and, thus, since nothing is known about the new unknown values, destroy the information on these (and only these) locations.

Definition 8 (Anonymous Update). *Let*

$$Mod_p = \{\langle \chi_1, f_1(t_1, \ldots, t_{n_1}) \rangle, \ldots, \langle \chi_m, f_m(t_1, \ldots, t_{n_m}) \rangle\}$$

be a correct modifier set for a program p. For every f_i, let f_i^{sk} be a fresh rigid function symbol with the same arity as f_i. Then, the sequence $\mathcal{V} = \mathcal{V}_1 \cdots \mathcal{V}_m$ of quantified updates where

$$\mathcal{V}_i = \{\chi_i ? f_i(t_1, \ldots, t_{n_i}) := f_i^{sk}(t_1, \ldots, t_{n_i})\}$$

is called an anonymous update *with respect to Mod_p. By abuse of terminology we call the new function symbols f_i^{sk} Skolem functions.*

Now, we can proceed to define the new invariant rule for while loops using change information:

$$\frac{\Gamma \vdash \mathcal{U} Inv, \Delta \quad \Gamma, \mathcal{U}\mathcal{V}(Inv \wedge \epsilon) \vdash \mathcal{U}\mathcal{V}[\alpha] Inv, \Delta \quad \Gamma, \mathcal{U}\mathcal{V}(Inv \wedge \neg\epsilon) \vdash \mathcal{U}\mathcal{V}\phi, \Delta}{\Gamma \vdash \mathcal{U}[\texttt{while } \epsilon \texttt{ do } \alpha \texttt{ od}]\phi, \Delta} (2)$$

where $\mathcal{V}$ is an anonymous update (Def. 8) w.r.t. the modifier set *Mod*, which is correct for the loop body α (Def. 4).

Depending on the particular proof goal, the context encoded in $\Gamma, \Delta, \mathcal{U}$ may only be needed in either the second or the third premiss of the rule and not in both of them. In that case, the premiss where the context is not needed can be simplified and replaced by the corresponding premiss from the classical Rule (1). If both premisses are simplified, Rules (2) and (1) become identical.

Theorem 1 (Soundness). *Let Inv be an arbitrary formula and $\mathcal{V}$ an anonymous update w.r.t. a correct modifier set Mod_α for the loop body α.*

If all premisses of Rule (2) are valid in all states, then its conclusion is valid in all states.

Proof. See [5].

Even the main focus in this paper is on Dynamic Logic, the approach is not restricted to this particular logic. A version of the improved invariant rule for Hoare logic can be found in [5].

6   Implementation

We have implemented the invariant rule that uses change information in the KeY system for the programming language JAVA CARD. Advanced features like

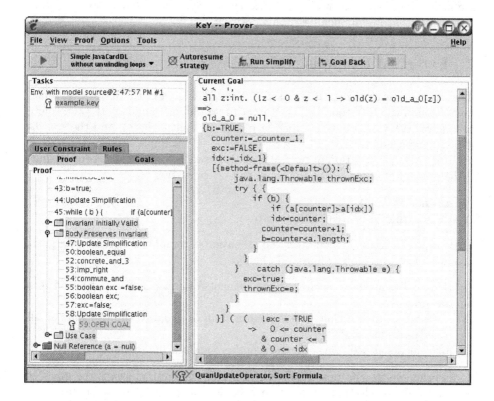

Fig. 1. KeY prover window with the example from Sect. 7 after applying the invariant rule

abrupt termination, exceptions, side-effects of expressions, break- and continue-statements of a real object-oriented language like JAVA CARD make the implemented rule more involved than the one presented above. For example, in case of side-effects the invariant rule cannot be applied directly. Beforehand, the following rule has to be applied that performs a program transformation and ensures that the loop condition does not have side-effects

$$\frac{\Gamma \vdash \mathcal{U}[\text{boolean } b = expr; \ \text{while } (b) \ \{\alpha'; b = expr; \}]\phi, \ \Delta}{\Gamma \vdash \mathcal{U}[\text{while } (expr) \ \{\alpha\}]\phi, \ \Delta}$$

where b is a new Boolean variable and α' is the result of inserting the statement $b = expr$; in front of every continue-statement in the loop body α.

Fig. 1 shows the KeY prover window with the example from Sect. 7. The lower left pane displays the proof tree with three open branches corresponding to the three premisses of the invariant rule. For better user interaction, the goals are labelled with "Invariant Initially Valid", "Body Preserves Invariant", and "Use Case". The right pane shows the sequent that is currently under consideration. Rules can be applied automatically by pressing the button in the upper left corner or interactively using the mouse: pointing at a certain term or formula highlights the respective item and pressing the left mouse button offers (only) those rules that are applicable at this position.

7   Extended Example

The example in this section is based on the calculus and the loop rule implementation in the KeY tool, i.e., the target programming language is JAVA (more precisely JAVA CARD but the difference does not matter here), and the specification language is UML/OCL [17,16] or—as in the example—JML [15].

The JML specification of the JAVA method swapMax (see Fig. 2) states that, if the pre-condition (*requires* clause, lines 1–2) consisting of

a. a is not *null* and
b. the length of a is greater than zero

holds in the beginning, then after the execution of swapMax the following post-condition (*ensures* clause, lines 3–7) holds:

a. there exists an index such that the elements of a at position index and zero are swapped,
b. the element at position zero is greater than or equal to the elements at all other positions, and
c. all elements at positions different from zero and the index remain unchanged.

In other words, the post-condition says that the method swaps the greatest element and the element at position zero and all other elements remain unchanged. In JML post-conditions, one can use \old(expr) to refer to the value of *expr* at the beginning of the method.

```
   /*@ requires
2  @ a!=null && a.length > 0;
   @ ensures
4  @ (\ exists int idx;  0 <= idx && idx<\old(a).length;
   @ a[idx]==\old(a)[0] && a[0]==\old(a)[idx] &&
6  @ (\ forall int i; 0 <= i && i<\old(a).length;
   @ a[0] >= a[i] && (i!=0 && i!=idx ==> a[i]==\old(a)[i])));
8  @*/
   void swapMax(int[] a) {
10    int counter = 0, int index = 0;
      /*@ loop_invariant
12    @ 0<=counter && counter<=a.length &&
      @ 0<=index && index<a.length &&
14    @ (\ forall int x; x>=0 && x<counter; a[index]>=a[x]);
      @ assignable index, counter;                             .
16    @*/
      while (counter<a.length) {
18      if (a[counter] > a[index])
          index = counter;
20      counter = counter+1;
      }
22    int tmp = a[index];
      a[index] = a[0];
24    a[0] = tmp;
   }
```

Fig. 2. JML specification and JAVA implementation of method swapMax

The body of swapMax is divided into two parts. In the first part (lines 17–21), we iterate through the elements of array a and store the index of the greatest element in variable *index*. In the second part (lines 22–24), the elements at position *index* and zero are swapped.

Using JML, it is possible to annotate loops with loop invariants. The invariant in our example states that

a. *counter* and *index* stay in the correct range (lines 12–13), and
b. the element at position *index* is greater than or equal to all elements at positions zero to *counter* − 1 (line 14).

The only locations that are modified in the loop body are *index* and *counter*. To make this information explicit we use the *assignable* clause of JML (line 15).[1]

The KeY tool is able to use the invariant given as annotation in the code when applying an invariant rule. Our example can be proved almost fully automatically using the above invariant. The only user interaction required is the

---

[1] Following the JML standard [15] assignable clauses, which are the JML-equivalent of modifier sets, are restricted to methods. Recent discussions on the JML mailing list suggest that the assignable clause will also be applicable to loops in the future.

simple instantiation of the existential quantifier in the post-condition with the term *index* at the end of the proof.

Using the traditional invariant rule, the above invariant is not strong enough. Fig. 3 shows the additional conjuncts that have to be added to the invariant in order to prove the post-condition using the classical loop rule.

```
/*@ (\ forall  int  x; x>=0 && x<counter; a[x]==\old(a)[x]) &&
2    @ a.length==\old(a.length) && a.length>0 && a==\old(a) && a!=null
     @*/
```

Fig. 3. Additional conjuncts for the invariant preserving the context information

Line 1 expresses that the elements in array *a* are the same before and after execution of the loop body. Line 2 states that the length of the array does not change and is greater than zero and that the array reference *a* is an invariant of the loop and is different from *null*.

As one can see, the invariant for the traditional rule is more complicated and has to contain information not directly related to the while loop (there is an indirect relationship, however, since the additional conjuncts express what the loop does *not* do).

8   Conclusion

We have extended the idea of modifier sets from to method specification to loops, and have defined a DL loop invariant rule that makes use of such change information. Our new definition of *quantified* modifier sets overcomes the restrictions from [6], where modifier sets could only describe location sets of fixed length. The new loop rule has been implemented in the KeY System and in experiments has proved to be a great improvement over rules not using change information.

References

1. W. Ahrendt, T. Baar, B. Beckert, R. Bubel, M. Giese, R. Hähnle, W. Menzel, W. Mostowski, A. Roth, S. Schlager, and P. H. Schmitt. The KeY tool. *Software and System Modeling*, 4:32–54, 2005.
2. W. Ahrendt, T. Baar, B. Beckert, M. Giese, E. Habermalz, R. Hähnle, W. Menzel, and P. H. Schmitt. The KeY approach: Integrating object oriented design and formal verification. In M. Ojeda-Aciego, I. P. de Guzman, G. Brewka, and L. M. Pereira, editors, *Proceedings, Logics in Artificial Intelligence (JELIA), Malaga, Spain*, LNCS 1919. Springer, 2000.
3. K. R. Apt. Ten years of Hoare logic: A survey – part I. *ACM Transactions on Programming Languages and Systems*, 1981.
4. B. Beckert. A dynamic logic for the formal verification of Java Card programs. In I. Attali and T. Jensen, editors, *Java on Smart Cards: Programming and Security. Revised Papers, Java Card 2000, International Workshop, Cannes, France*, LNCS 2041, pages 6–24. Springer, 2001.

5. B. Beckert, S. Schlager, and P. H. Schmitt. An Improved Rule for While Loops in Deductive Program Verification. Technical Report in Computing Science 2005-26, Fakultät für Informatik, Universität Karlsruhe, Germany, September 2005. Available at http://i12www.ira.uka.de/~schlager/publications/TRInvRule.ps.gz.
6. B. Beckert and P. H. Schmitt. Program verification using change information. In *Proceedings, Software Engineering and Formal Methods (SEFM), Brisbane, Australia*, pages 91–99. IEEE Press, 2003.
7. A. Borgida, J. Mylopoulos, and R. Reiter. On the frame problem in procedure specifications. *IEEE Transactions on Software Engineering*, 21(10):785–798, 1995.
8. N. Cataño and M. Huisman. Chase: A static checker for JML's assignable clause. In *Proceedings, Verification, Model Checking and Abstract Interpretation (VMCAI)*, LNCS 2575, pages 26–40. Springer, 2003.
9. D. L. Detlefs, K. R. M. Leino, G. Nelson, and J. B. Saxe. Extended static checking. Research Report 159, Compaq Systems Research Center, 1998.
10. M. D. Ernst. *Dynamically Discovering Likely Program Invariants*. PhD thesis, University of Washington, Seattle, August 2000.
11. D. Harel. Dynamic Logic. In D. Gabbay and F. Guenthner, editors, *Handbook of Philosophical Logic, Volume II: Extensions of Classical Logic*. Reidel, 1984.
12. D. Harel, D. Kozen, and J. Tiuryn. *Dynamic Logic*. The MIT Press, 2000.
13. D. Kozen and J. Tiuryn. Logic of programs. In J. van Leeuwen, editor, *Handbook of Theoretical Computer Science*, chapter 14, pages 89–133. Elsevier, 1990.
14. G. T. Leavens, A. L. Baker, and C. Ruby. JML: A notation for detailed design. In Haim Kilov, Bernhard Rumpe, and Ian Simmonds, editors, *Behavioral Specifications of Businesses and Systems*, chapter 12, pages 175–188. Kluwer Academic Publisher, 1999.
15. G. T. Leavens, A. L. Baker, and C. Ruby. Preliminary design of JML: A behavioral interface specification language for Java. Technical Report 98-06z, Iowa State University, Department of Computer Science, December 2004.
16. Object Modeling Group. *UML 2.0 OCL Specification*, October 2003.
17. Object Modeling Group. *UML 2.0 Superstructure Specification*, October 2004.
18. J. H. Perkins and M. D. Ernst. Efficient incremental algorithms for dynamic detection of likely invariants. In *Proceedings of the ACM SIGSOFT 12th Symposium on the Foundations of Software Engineering (FSE 2004)*, pages 23–32, Newport Beach, CA, USA, November 2–4, 2004.
19. P. Rümmer. A Language for Sequential, Parallel and Quantified Updates of First-order Structures, 2005. Forthcoming.
20. R. Sasse. Proof obligations for correctness of modifies clauses. Studienarbeit, Fakultät für Informatik, Universität Karlsruhe, 2004. Available at http://i12www.ira.uka.de/~key/doc/2004/sasse2004.pdf.
21. N. Schirmer. A verification environment for sequential imperative programs in Isabelle/HOL. In F. Baader and A. Voronkov, editors, *Proceedings, Logic for Programming, Artificial Intelligence, and Reasoning(LPAR)*, LNAI 3452, pages 398–414. Springer, 2004.
22. F. Spoto and E. Poll. Static analysis for JML's assignable clauses. In *Proceedings, Foundations of Object-Oriented Languages (FOOL10)*, 2003.

Using Stålmarck's Algorithm to Prove Inequalities

Byron Cook and Georges Gonthier

Microsoft Research

Abstract. Stålmarck's 1-saturation algorithm is an incomplete but fast method for computing partial equivalence relations over propositional formulae. Aside from anecdotal evidence, until now little has been known about what it can prove. In this paper we characterize a set of formulae with bitvector-inequalities for which 1-saturation is sufficient to prove unsatisfiability. This result has application to fast predicate abstraction for software with fixed-width bit-vectors.

1 Introduction

Stålmarck's n-saturation algorithm [7,12] is a method for automatically finding consequences of propositional logic formulae. The complexity of n-saturation is $O(g^{2n+1})$, where g is the number of nodes in the graph representing the formula. In practice, when $n \leq 2$, Stålmarck's algorithm is fast but incomplete. The limited forms of saturation (where $n \leq 2$) can be used in situations when completeness is not required. Alternatively, if completeness is required, it can be used as a method of pruning the search space traversed with complete techniques—as was done in [1]. The advantage to this approach is the fact that Stålmarck's algorithm can infer many consequences simultaneously. The disadvantage, given that the limited forms of saturation are not complete, is that little is known about the category of formulae for which they are sufficient to prove unsatisfiability.

The goal of this paper is to address the question of what 1-saturation can prove with respect to an important class of formulae that often arise during model checking: transitive arguments using arithmetic relations such as $\leq$, $<$ and $=$ over Boolean vectors. Informally stated, we show that Stålmarck's algorithm can prove the unsatisfiability of unsatisfiable formulae containing inequalities on vectors of Boolean variables, such as $\ldots w \leq x \wedge \ldots \wedge x \leq y \wedge \ldots \wedge y \leq z \wedge \ldots \wedge \neg(w \leq z) \wedge \ldots$, or $\ldots w = x \wedge \ldots \wedge x < y \wedge \ldots \wedge y \leq z \wedge \ldots \wedge z \leq w \wedge \ldots$, etc. The aspect that makes proving this difficult is the fact that the outcome of saturation greatly depends on how $\leq$, $<$, and $=$ are represented in the propostional formulae.

1.1 Application

The motivation for this paper is rooted in our search for fast proof methods for propositional reasoning within the SLAM software model checker for C pro-

K.-K. Lau and R. Banach (Eds.): ICFEM 2005, LNCS 3785, pp. 330–344, 2005.

grams[1]. We would like to find fast approximative methods that are guaranteed to be able to prove at least a certain limited class of properties.

SLAM currently treats program variables as unbounded integers, and treats bitwise operations as uninterpreted functions. In reality C programs are primarily written over fixed-width types, and often use bitwise operators in non-trivial ways. In order to switch SLAM's semantics from arbitrary-length to the more accurate fixed-width types we must adapt our methods used to improve the performance of SLAM's implementation of predicate abstraction [6,10].

The key step behind predicate abstraction is the computation of *coverings*. A covering C of a formula f is a set of monomials drawn from a set of predicates P such that for all $m \in C$, $m \Rightarrow f$. In principle the covering can be computed by enumerating over candidate monomials and calling an automatic theorem prover (such as COGENT [4] or ZAPATO [3]) with arithmetic support to determine which monomials imply f.

The strongest covering can be computed using enumeration over all $3^{|P|}$ possible monomials. However, as described in [9,10], a faster approach is to use incomplete *symbolic decision procedures* that quickly compute an approximation of the needed coverings. Later, if the approximation is not strong enough, we use a technique described in [2] to lazily refine the quality of the abstraction.

Stålmarck's algorithm is a candidate method for computing these appoximative coverings when a bit-level semantics is used (see [4] for more information on the encoding of C expressions into propositional logic). But how good will the approximative coverings be if 1-saturation is used? Since the vast majority of the formulae involved in this application involve $\leq$, $<$, and $=$, it is important that our initial incomplete abstraction method at least finds the connections between these relations even if it is incomplete over others. This is the question that we are addressing in this paper.

2   Stålmarck's Algorithm

In this section we provide a formal definition for Stålmarck's n-saturation algorithm and a sound but incomplete validity procedure based on 1-saturation. We also prove a number of basic properties about the algorithm.

Finite Boolean vectors are sequences whose elements can be $\top$ (`true`), $\bot$ (`false`), propositional variables, and negated propositional variables. Fig. 1 defines the set of all finite Boolean vectors, S. We use subscripts to indicate indexing into vectors. For example, if x is a Boolean vector, then x_5 represents the element at the 5th position of x. Vectors are addressed starting at 1. We use superscripts to differentiate between vectors. For example, x^1 and x^2 should be considered different vectors. They could, of course, have equivalent values.

A partial equivalence relation (PER) over a set S is a relation that is transitive and symmetric. A PER may not necessarily be defined for all arguments in S, but it is reflexive for those in which it is. A finite PER (or FPER) is defined only for a finite subset of S.

---

[1] SLAM is the basis of Microsoft's Static Driver Verifier product [11].

$$
\begin{aligned}
\mathcal{B} &::= \top \mid \bot \\
\mathcal{V} &::= \ldots \mid p \mid q \mid r \mid \ldots \\
\mathcal{E} &::= \mathcal{B} \mid \mathcal{V} \mid \neg \mathcal{V} \\
\mathcal{S} &::= \langle \mathcal{E}_1, \ldots, \mathcal{E}_n \rangle
\end{aligned}
$$

Fig. 1. Grammar defining Finite Boolean vectors

Stålmarck's algorithm is defined in terms of finite PERs over the type $\mathcal{E}$ (from Fig. 1). For simplicity we will fix the set of variables for which PERs that we consider are defined. We define $=$, $<$ and $\leq$ on finite PERs in the standard way using when the PER is treated as a set of pairs. We say that a PER R is unsatisfiable iff $R(\top, \bot)$:

$$\textsc{Unsatisfiable}(R) \triangleq R(\top, \bot)$$

We assume that redundant $\neg$ symbols in arguments to equivalence relations are removed. For example, $\neg\top$ is treated as an alternative notation for $\bot$ and $\neg(\neg x)$ is considered the same as x.

Let R be a PER. As in [12], we use the notation $R(x \equiv y)$ to represent a *union* operation over the equivalence classes in the PER. This operation constructs a new relation based on R where x and y's equivalence classes have been merged. This can be (naively) implemented as:

$$
R(x \equiv y) \triangleq \begin{cases} \mathcal{E}^2 & \text{if } \textsc{Unsatisfiable}(Q) \\ Q & \text{if } \neg\textsc{Unsatisfiable}(Q) \end{cases}
$$
$$\textbf{where } Q \triangleq (R \cup \{(x,y),(y,x),(\neg x, \neg y),(\neg y, \neg x)\})^*$$

P^* is the transitive closure of the relation P. We assume the existence of a base finite PER called Base that is defined for $\top$ and $\bot$:

$$\textsc{Base} = \{(\top, \top),(\bot, \bot)\}$$

We assume that all finite PERs are constructed from Base and a series of $\equiv$ operations. Quantification over finite PERs will be limited to this set.

A meet operation over finite PERs is defined as: $\textsc{Meet}(Q, R) \triangleq Q \cap R$.

Lemma 1. $\forall A, B, C.\ A \leq B \wedge A \leq C \Rightarrow A \leq \textsc{Meet}(B, C)$

Lemma 2. $\forall R, x, y.\ R \leq R(x \equiv y)$

Lemma 3. $\forall x, y, R.\ R(x \equiv y)(x, y)$

Fig. 2 defines a function called Initial which constructs a finite identity PER. The type FPER is used to represent finite PERs. The polymorphic type constructor FSet is used to represent finite sets. We assume that a foreach statement over a finite set (as found in Fig. 2) always terminates so long as the loop's body terminates. Therefore (given that the $\equiv$ operation terminates) Initial terminates.

```
FPER INITIAL (FSet<Formulae> S)
{
        FPER R := BASE;
        foreach x ∈ S { R := R(x≡x); }
        return R;
}
```

Fig. 2. INITIAL – Constructs a finite identity PER

2.1 Triples

The first step in Stålmarck's algorithm is to break the input propositional logic formula into an equisatisfiable directed acyclic graph represented as a set of *triples*. A triple is defined by the grammar $\mathcal{T} ::= \mathcal{E} \Leftrightarrow (\mathcal{E} \Rightarrow \mathcal{E}) \mid \mathcal{E} \Leftrightarrow (\mathcal{E} \Leftrightarrow \mathcal{E})$. We assume the existence of a function, called TRIPLES, which returns the representative directed acyclic graph together with a variable representing the original input. As an example, let $\leq_n$, $<_n$, and $=_n$ be defined as:

$$x \leq_n y \triangleq \begin{cases} \top & \text{if } n = 0 \\ (\neg x_n \vee y_n) \wedge ((\neg x_n \Leftrightarrow y_n) \vee (x \leq_{n-1} y)) & \text{if } n > 0 \end{cases}$$

$$x <_n y \triangleq \begin{cases} \bot & \text{if } n = 0 \\ (\neg x_n \vee y_n) \wedge ((\neg x_n \Leftrightarrow y_n) \vee (x <_{n-1} y)) & \text{if } n > 0 \end{cases}$$

$$x =_n y \triangleq \bigwedge_{i \in \{1...n\}} x_i \Leftrightarrow y_i$$

Let x and y be 1-length Boolean vectors. In this case we assume that TRIPLES will produce the following output:

$$\begin{aligned} \text{TRIPLES}(x \leq_1 y) = (\beta_1 \\ , \quad & (\rho_1^1 \Leftrightarrow (\neg x_1 \Leftrightarrow y_1)) \wedge (\rho_2^1 \Leftrightarrow (x_1 \Rightarrow y_1)) \\ & \wedge (\rho_3^1 \Leftrightarrow (\neg \rho_1^1 \Rightarrow \beta_2)) \wedge (\neg \beta_1 \Leftrightarrow (\rho_2^1 \Rightarrow \neg \rho_3^1)) \\ & \wedge (\beta_2 \Leftrightarrow \top) \\ ) \end{aligned}$$

The variable β_1 is equisatisfiable with $x \leq_1 y$ when constrained by these triples. The variables ρ_1^1, ρ_2^1, ρ_3^1 and β_1 are assumed to be previously unused. In the case where the vectors are of length 2, TRIPLES would return:

$$\begin{aligned} \text{TRIPLES}(x \leq_2 y) = (\beta_1 \\ , \quad & (\rho_1^2 \Leftrightarrow (\neg x_2 \Leftrightarrow y_2)) \wedge (\rho_2^2 \Leftrightarrow (x_2 \Rightarrow y_2)) \\ & \wedge (\rho_3^2 \Leftrightarrow (\neg \rho_1^2 \Rightarrow \beta_3)) \wedge (\neg \beta_2 \Leftrightarrow (\rho_2^2 \Rightarrow \neg \rho_3^1)) \\ & \wedge (\rho_1^1 \Leftrightarrow (\neg x_1 \Leftrightarrow y_1)) \wedge (\rho_2^1 \Leftrightarrow (x_1 \Rightarrow y_1)) \\ & \wedge (\rho_3^1 \Leftrightarrow (\neg \rho_1^1 \Rightarrow \beta_2)) \wedge (\neg \beta_1 \Leftrightarrow (\rho_2^1 \Rightarrow \neg \rho_3^1)) \\ & \wedge (\beta_3 \Leftrightarrow \top) \\ ) \end{aligned}$$

The relation LTE is defined in Fig. 3. This relation takes three inputs (i, p, and q) and produces an output o. The t is used as a source of intermediate variables. We can use this relation to characterize the translation of triples over $\leq_n$:

$$\text{TRIPLES}(x \leq_n y) = (\beta_1, \wedge_{i \in \{1...n\}} \{\text{LTE}(\beta_i, \beta_{i+1}, x_i, y_i, \rho^i)\} \wedge \beta_{n+1} \Leftrightarrow \top)$$

where β and ρ are families of fresh variables. Think of LTE as a basic cell (or circuit building-block). The β variables are used to establish communication between other cells. $\text{TRIPLES}(x \leq_n y)$ has a similar definition:

$$\text{TRIPLES}(x <_n y) = (\beta_1, \wedge_{i \in \{1...n\}} \{\text{LTE}(\beta_i, \beta_{i+1}, x_i, y_i, \rho^i)\} \wedge \beta_{n+1} \Leftrightarrow \bot)$$

$$
\begin{aligned}
\text{LTE}(o, i, p, q, t) &\triangleq (t_1 \Leftrightarrow (\neg p \Leftrightarrow q)) \\
&\wedge (t_2 \Leftrightarrow (p \Rightarrow q)) \\
&\wedge (t_3 \Leftrightarrow (\neg t_1 \Rightarrow i)) \\
&\wedge (\neg o \Leftrightarrow (t_2 \Rightarrow \neg t_3))
\end{aligned}
\qquad
\begin{aligned}
\text{GT}(o, i, p, q, t) &\triangleq (t_1 \Leftrightarrow (p \Leftrightarrow q)) \\
&\wedge (\neg t_2 \Leftrightarrow (p \Rightarrow q)) \\
&\wedge (\neg t_3 \Leftrightarrow (t_1 \Rightarrow \neg i)) \\
&\wedge (o \Leftrightarrow (\neg t_2 \Rightarrow t_3))
\end{aligned}
$$

$$\text{EQ}(o, i, p, q, t) \triangleq (t_1 \Leftrightarrow (p \Leftrightarrow q)) \wedge (\neg o \Leftrightarrow (t_1 \Rightarrow \neg i))$$

Fig. 3. The relations LTE, GT, and EQ

We can negate LTE to produce GT, also defined in Fig. 3. We can use GT to characterize the translation of triples over the negation of $\leq_n$:

$$\text{TRIPLES}(\neg(x \leq_n y)) = (\beta_1, \wedge_{i \in \{1...n\}} \{\text{GT}(\beta_i, \beta_{i+1}, x_i, y_i, \rho^i)\} \wedge \beta_{n+1} \Leftrightarrow \bot)$$

To characterize the $=_n$ relation we can use EQ (Fig. 3):

$$\text{TRIPLES}(x =_n y) = (\beta_1, \wedge_{i \in \{1...n\}} \{\text{EQ}(\beta_i, \beta_{i+1}, x_i, y_i, \rho^i)\} \wedge \beta_{n+1} \Leftrightarrow \top)$$

2.2   0-Saturation

The function in Fig. 4, called ZEROSATURATE, implements a version of 0-saturation. Essentially ZEROSATURATE iteratively applies the 0-saturation step function ZEROSATURATESTEP from Fig. 9 until a fixpoint is reached. Note that Fig. 9 appears later in the paper so that the proofs in Section 3.1 are easier to follow.

Lemma 4. ZEROSATURATESTEP *terminates.*

Proof. By the structure of ZEROSATURATESTEP's control-flow graph and the termination assumption about `foreach` statements over finite sets. $\square$

```
            FPER ZeroSaturate(FPER Q,FSet<Formulae> F)
            {
                FPER newQ := ZeroSaturateStep (Q,F);
                if (newQ ≠ Q) {
                  return ZeroSaturate(newQ,F);
                } else {
                  return Q;
                }
            }
```

Fig. 4. ZeroSaturate: 0-saturation algorithm

Lemma 5. $\forall R, F.\ R \leq$ ZeroSaturateStep(R, F)

Proof. All paths through ZeroSaturateStep lead to an update of R with $\equiv$ or R itself. Therefore, by Lemma 2, $R \leq$ ZeroSaturateStep(R, F). □

Lemma 6. ZeroSaturate *computes a fixpoint.*

Proof. The powerset of finite PERs over a fixed set of variables is a finite set. By Lemma 5, ZeroSaturateStep is order-preserving. Therefore, by the Knaster-Tarski fixpoint theorem ([5], p.93), ZeroSaturate computes a fixpoint. □

Lemma 7. $\forall R, F.\ R \leq$ ZeroSaturate(R, F)

Proof. By induction on the structure of ZeroSaturate. Due to Lemma 6 we know that the result of ZeroSaturate is a finite composition of applications of ZeroSaturateStep. By Lemma 5 and the transitivity of $\leq$, $R \leq$ ZeroSaturate(R, F). □

2.3 General n-Saturation

Stålmarck's n-saturation procedure is defined in Fig 5. Based on this procedure, we also define a validity procedure, called StålmarckValidity, in Fig. 6. The function Vars, when applied to a finite PER, returns the variables for which the PER is defined.

Lemma 8. $\forall R, F, n.\ R \leq$ Saturate(n, R, F)

Proof. By induction on n with Lemma 7 in the base case and an argument based on Lemma 2 and Lemma 1 in the inductive case. □

Lemma 9. Saturate *computes a fixpoint.*

Proof. The powerset of finite PERs over a fixed set of variables is a finite set. By Lemma 8, Saturate is order-preserving. Therefore, by the Knaster-Tarski fixpoint theorem, Saturate computes a fixpoint. □

Lemma 10. $\forall R, F, v, n \geq 0.$ ZeroSaturate$(R, F) \leq$ SaturateStep(n, v, R, F)

Proof. By induction on n, the definition of Saturate, and Lemma 1. □

We use the following two properties to structure the proof in Section 3.

```
1     FPER SATURATE(int n,FPER R,FSet<Formulae> F)
2     {
3         if (n<1) { return ZEROSATURATE(R,F); }
4         FPER prevR;
5         do {
6             prevR := R;
7             foreach v ∈ VARS(F) {
8                 R := SATURATESTEP(n,v,R,F);
9             }
10        } while (R ≠ prevR);
11        return R;
12    }
13
14    FPER SATURATESTEP(int n,Formulae v,FPER R,FSet<Formulae> F)
15    {
16        assume(n>0);
17        FPER R1 := SATURATE(n-1,R(v≡⊥),F)
18        FPER R2 := SATURATE(n-1,R(v≡⊤),F)
19        return MEET(R1,R2);
20    }
```

Fig. 5. Stålmarck's SATURATE algorithm

```
bool STÅLMARCKVALIDITY(Formulae f)
{
    Formulae root;
    FSet<Formulae> F;
    (root,F) := TRIPLES(¬f);
    FPER S := INITIAL(VARS(F));
    FPER Q := SATURATE(1,S(root≡⊤),F);
    return UNSATISFIABLE(Q);
}
```

Fig. 6. STÅLMARCKVALIDITY: a validity procedure based on 1-saturation

3   What Can 1-Saturation Prove?

Now that we have defined Stålmarck's algorithm we are prepared to reason about what it can prove. Due to Lemma 9 we know that SATURATE does terminate and that there is a finite PER that is a fixpoint of SATURATE. We use the symbol $\Leftrightarrow$ to denote this relation. The reasoning in this section is about the equivalences contained in $\Leftrightarrow$.

In this paper we consider formulae of the following form: $\bigwedge E \Rightarrow \bigvee F$, where $\{\mathcal{R}^1(x^1,x^2),\ldots,\mathcal{R}^{k-1}(x^{k-1},x^k)\} \subseteq E$ and $\mathcal{R}^k(x^1,x^k) \in F$. The idea is that the $\mathcal{R}^i$s are instances of $\leq$, $<$, etc. We assume that $x^1 \ldots x^k$ are Boolean vectors of length n. The proof could be easily generalized to cases where the vectors are of different size—we limit ourselves to n-length vectors to simplify the notation. We assume that there exists a family of relations (or cells), $\mathcal{C}$, such that for all $j \in \{1, \ldots, k-1\}$,

$$\text{TRIPLES}(\mathcal{R}^j(x,y)) = (\beta_1^j, e \wedge_{i \in \{1 \ldots n\}} \{\mathcal{C}^{j,i}(\beta_i^j, \beta_{i+1}^j, x_i, y_i, \rho^{j,i})\} \wedge \beta_{n+1}^j \Leftrightarrow \top)$$

We assume that $\text{TRIPLES}(\neg(\bigwedge E \Rightarrow \bigvee F))$ is equivalent to $\text{TRIPLES}(\bigwedge(E \cup \neg F))$. If we push the $\neg$ through F (which is in disjunctive form) the result is another conjuction. Therefore, for our purposes, it is sufficient to consider the following conjunction

$$\bigwedge \{\mathcal{R}^1(x^1, x^2), \ldots, \mathcal{R}^{k-1}(x^{k-1}, x^k), \neg \mathcal{R}^k(x^1, x^k)\}$$

and then assume that

$$\text{TRIPLES}(\neg \mathcal{R}^k(x,y)) = (\beta_1^k, \wedge_{i \in \{1 \ldots n\}} \{\mathcal{C}^{k,i}(\beta_i^k, \beta_{i+1}^k, x_i, y_i, \rho^{k,i})\} \wedge \beta_{n+1}^k \Leftrightarrow \bot)$$

Fig. 7 displays an instance of this configuration where $n = 3$ and $k = 4$.

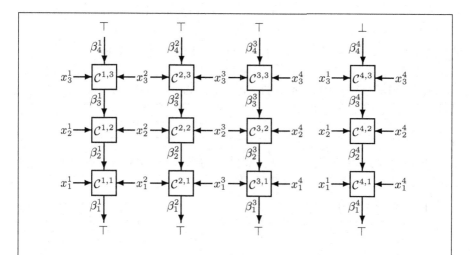

Fig. 7. An example configuration of triples where $n = 3$ and $k = 4$. $\mathcal{C}^{1,1}$ to $\mathcal{C}^{4,3}$ represent cells (see Fig. 3 for examples of cells).

We will prove that, when several properties hold of $\{\mathcal{R}^1(x^1, x^2), \ldots, \mathcal{R}^{k-1}(x^{k-1}, x^k), \neg \mathcal{R}^k(x^1, x^k)\}$ that $\text{STÅLMARCKVALIDITY}(\bigwedge E \Rightarrow \bigvee F) = \top$. We assume (based on Lemma 10) that the first iteration of saturation in Fig. 5 will find $\beta_1^i \Leftrightarrow \top$ for each $i \in \{1, \ldots, k\}$.

Assumption 1. $\forall i \in \{1, \ldots, k\}.\ \beta_1^i \Leftrightarrow \top$.

This is a key assumption: it allows us to ignore the exact structure of the original formula and relations that are passed to SATURATE. In the case of $\bigwedge E \Rightarrow \bigvee F$, this will be found by 0-saturation. There may be many additional triples and equivalences, and they may have incrementally been added or discovered—but all we need to know is that each component in the transitive argument has been asserted to $\top$.

We structure the proof of STÅLMARCKVALIDITY$(\bigwedge E \Rightarrow \bigvee F) = \top$ as follows:

- We define four predicates (POSRGTRIPPLE, POSLFTRIPPLE, NEGRGTRIPPLE, NEGLFTRIPPLE) over the signature of the cells ($\mathcal{C}^{i,j}$) used in each $\mathcal{R}^i$ and then constrain the cells using three of these predicates—the fourth predicate is not strictly required due to an uninteresting technicality.
- We inductively find a set of equivalences in $\Leftrightarrow$.
- We then use the equivalences in $\Leftrightarrow$ to demonstrate UNSATISFIABLE($\Leftrightarrow$).

The predicates are defined in Fig. 8. In a later section we prove that they hold for LTE, GT, EQ, etc.

These predicates are used to represent relationships between the β variables and x variables. For example, POSRGTRIPPLE$(0, C)$ holds when (by using 0-saturation over C) we can prove that if both the output β-variable and left-hand input-variable are true, then the input β-variable and right-hand input-variable must be true.

Assumption 2. $\forall i \in \{1 \ldots k - 1\}, j \in \{1 \ldots n\}$. POSRGTRIPPLE$(0, \mathcal{C}^{i,j})$

In Fig. 7 this corresponds to asserting that the cells in the first three columns are constrained by POSRGTRIPPLE. The next assumption corresponds to asserting that the cells in the fourth column are constrained by NEGRGTRIPPLE.

$$\text{RIPPLE}(n, T, a, b, c, d, v) \triangleq \forall Q. \ [Q(a, \top) \wedge Q(c, v)] \Rightarrow [R(b, \top) \wedge R(d, v)]$$
$$\textbf{where } R = \text{SATURATE}(n, Q, T)$$

$$\text{POSRGTRIPPLE}(n, C) \quad \triangleq \forall T, a, b, x, y, w.$$
$$C(a, b, x, y, w) \subseteq T \Rightarrow \text{RIPPLE}(n, T, a, b, x, y, \top)$$

$$\text{POSLFTRIPPLE}(n, C) \quad \triangleq \forall T, a, b, x, y, w.$$
$$C(a, b, x, y, w) \subseteq T \Rightarrow \text{RIPPLE}(n, T, a, b, y, x, \top)$$

$$\text{NEGRGTRIPPLE}(n, C) \quad \triangleq \forall T, a, b, x, y, w.$$
$$C(a, b, x, y, w) \subseteq T \Rightarrow \text{RIPPLE}(n, T, a, b, x, y, \bot)$$

$$\text{NEGLFTRIPPLE}(n, C) \quad \triangleq \forall T, a, b, x, y, w.$$
$$C(a, b, x, y, w) \subseteq T \Rightarrow \text{RIPPLE}(n, T, a, b, y, x, \bot)$$

Fig. 8. The relation RIPPLE, and several specialized versions of it

Assumption 3. $\forall j \in \{1 \ldots n\}.$ NEGRGTRIPPLE$(0, \mathcal{C}^{k,j})$

Assumption 4. $\forall i \in \{1 \ldots k-1\}, j \in \{1 \ldots n\}.$ NEGLFTRIPPLE$(0, \mathcal{C}^{i,j})$

Lemma 11.

$\forall i \in \{1 \ldots k\}, m \in \{0 \ldots n\}.$ $(\beta^i_{m+1} \Leftrightarrow \top) \wedge (\forall j \in \{1 \ldots k\}.\ m > 0 \Rightarrow x^i_m \Leftrightarrow x^j_m)$

Proof. By induction on m.

Base case $(m = 0)$: $(\forall j \in \{1 \ldots k\}.\ m > 0 \Rightarrow x^i_m \Leftrightarrow x^j_m)$ is trivially true. By Assumption 1, $\beta^i_{m+1} \Leftrightarrow \top$. ✓

Inductive case $(m > 0)$: Assume that we are splitting on the variable x^1_m (in Fig. 5). We prove this lemma by cases.

  Case $x^1_m \equiv \bot$ **(line 17 of Fig. 5):** By Lemma 7 and Lemma 3, R1$(x^1_m, \bot)$. By the inductive hypothesis, $\forall i \in \{1 \ldots k\}.$ R1$(\beta^i_m, \top)$. By Assumption 3, NEGRGTRIPPLE$(0, \mathcal{C}^{k,m})$. Therefore, because $\mathcal{C}^{k,m}(\beta^k_m, \beta^k_{m+1}, x^1_m, x^k_m, \rho^k)$, we know that R1$(x^k_m, \bot)$. By Assumption 4, NEGLFTRIPPLE$(0, \mathcal{C}^{i,m})$ for $i \in \{1 \ldots k-1\}$. By induction on i and Assumption 4, $\forall i \in \{1, \ldots, k\}.$ R1$(x^i_m, \bot)$ and $\forall i \in \{1 \ldots k\}.$ R1$(\beta^i_{m+1}, \top)$. By the transitivity of PERs, we know that $\forall i, j.$ R1(x^i_1, x^j_1). ✓

  Case $x^1_m \equiv \top$ **(line 18 of Fig. 5):** By Lemma 7 and Lemma 3, R2$(x^1_m, \top)$. By the inductive hypothesis, $\forall i \in \{1 \ldots k\}.$ R2$(\beta^i_m, \top)$. By Assumption 2, POSRGTRIPPLE$(0, \mathcal{C}^{i,m})$ for $i \in \{1 \ldots k-1\}$. Therefore, by induction on i and Assumption 2, $\forall i \in \{1, \ldots, k\}.$ R2$(x^i_m, \top)$ and $\forall i \in \{1 \ldots k\}.$ R2$(\beta^i_{m+1}, \top)$.. By the transitivity of PERs, $\forall i, j.$ R2(x^i_m, x^j_m). ✓

Because R1(x^i_m, x^j_m) and R2(x^i_m, x^j_m), by Lemma 1, $x^i_m \Leftrightarrow x^j_m$. Similarily, because R1$(\beta^i_{m+1}, \top)$ and R2$(\beta^i_{m+1}, \top)$, $\beta^i_{m+1} \Leftrightarrow \top$. ✓

□

Theorem 1. UNSATISFIABLE$(\Leftrightarrow)$

Proof. As a consequence of Lemma 11, $\beta^k_{n+1} \Leftrightarrow \top$. However, by definition, TRIPLES$(\neg \mathcal{R}^k(x^1, x^k))$ is

$$\wedge_{i \in \{1 \ldots n\}} \{ \mathcal{C}^{k,i}(\beta^k_i, \beta^k_{i+1}, x^1_i, x^k_i, \rho^{k,i}) \} \wedge \beta^k_{n+1} \Leftrightarrow \bot$$

Therefore, $\beta^k_{n+1} \Leftrightarrow \bot$. By the transitivity of $\Leftrightarrow$, $\top \Leftrightarrow \bot$. And therefore, UNSATISFIABLE$(\Leftrightarrow)$. □

3.1 Proving Conditions About LTE, GT and EQ

We now use Theorem 1 to show that STÅLMARCKVALIDITY can reliably prove transitive arguments using $=_n$, $<_n$, and $\leq_n$ from Section 2.1. By Theorem 1, if we prove the relations POSRGTRIPPLE, POSLFTRIPPLE, etc for LTE, GT, and EQ then we know that STÅLMARCKVALIDITY can prove transitive arguments of the form $\bigwedge E \Rightarrow \bigvee F$, where E and F contain terms with $\leq_n$, $<_n$, and $=_n$ applied to vectors of Boolean variables.

During the following proofs we are implicitly using Lemmas 6 and 7. That is, we assume throughout these proofs that $Q \leq R$.

```
FPER ZeroSaturateStep (FPER R,FSet<Formulae> T) {
 foreach t ∈ T {
  switch(t) {
   pattern (X ⇔ (Y ⇒ Z)):
/*Z01*/ if (R(X,⊥) && ¬ R(Y,⊤)) { return R(Y ≡ ⊤); }
/*Z02*/ if (R(X,⊥) && ¬ R(Z,⊥)) { return R(Z ≡ ⊥); }
/*Z03*/ if (R(Z,⊤) && ¬ R(X,⊤)) { return R(X ≡ ⊤); }
/*Z04*/ if (R(Y,⊥) && ¬ R(X,⊤)) { return R(X ≡ ⊤); }
/*Z05*/ if (R(X,Y) && ¬ R(X,⊤)) { return R(X ≡ ⊤); }
/*Z06*/ if (R(X,¬Z) && ¬ R(X,⊤)) { return R(X ≡ ⊤); }
/*Z07*/ if (R(Y,Z) && ¬ R(X,⊤)) { return R(X ≡ ⊤); }
/*Z08*/ if (R(Y,¬Z) && ¬ R(X,Z)) { return R(X ≡ Z); }
/*Z09*/ if (R(Y,⊤) && ¬ R(X,Z)) { return R(X ≡ Z); }
/*Z10*/ if (R(Z,⊥) && ¬ R(X,¬Y)) { return R(X ≡ ¬Y); }
     break;
   pattern (X ⇔ (Y ⇔ Z)):
/*Z11*/ if (R(X,Y) && ¬ R(Z,⊤)) { return R(Z ≡ ⊤); }
/*Z12*/ if (R(Y,Z) && ¬ R(X,⊤)) { return R(X ≡ ⊤); }
/*Z13*/ if (R(X,Z) && ¬ R(Y,⊤)) { return R(Y ≡ ⊤); }
/*Z14*/ if (R(X,¬Y) && ¬ R(Z,⊥)) { return R(Z ≡ ⊥); }
/*Z15*/ if (R(Y,¬Z) && ¬ R(X,⊥)) { return R(X ≡ ⊥); }
/*Z16*/ if (R(X,¬Z) && ¬ R(Y,⊥)) { return R(Y ≡ ⊥); }
/*Z17*/ if (R(X,⊤) && ¬ R(Y,Z)) { return R(Y ≡ Z); }
/*Z18*/ if (R(X,⊥) && ¬ R(Y,¬Z)) { return R(Y ≡ ¬Z); }
/*Z19*/ if (R(Y,⊤) && ¬ R(X,Z)) { return R(X ≡ Z); }
/*Z20*/ if (R(Y,⊥) && ¬ R(X,¬Z)) { return R(X ≡ ¬Z); }
/*Z21*/ if (R(Z,⊤) && ¬ R(X,Y)) { return R(X ≡ Y); }
/*Z22*/ if (R(Z,⊥) && ¬ R(X,¬Y)) { return R(X ≡ ¬Y); }
     break;
  }
 }
 return R;
}
```

Fig. 9. ZeroSaturateStep – Function used in ZeroSaturate

Lemma 12. PosRgtRipple$(0, \text{LTE})$ *and* NegLftRipple$(0, \text{LTE})$

Proof. Recall the definition of LTE from Fig. 3:

$$\text{LTE}(o, i, p, q, t) \triangleq (t_1 \Leftrightarrow (\neg p \Leftrightarrow q))$$
$$\wedge (t_2 \Leftrightarrow (p \Rightarrow q))$$
$$\wedge (t_3 \Leftrightarrow (\neg t_1 \Rightarrow i))$$
$$\wedge (\neg o \Leftrightarrow (t_2 \Rightarrow \neg t_3))$$

We can assume $Q(o, \top) \wedge R = \text{ZeroSaturate}(Q, T) \wedge \text{LTE}(o, i, p, q, t) \subseteq T$ and we must prove the following three conditions $Q(p, \top) \Rightarrow R(q, \top)$, $Q(q, \bot) \Rightarrow$

$R(p, \bot)$, and $R(p, q) \Rightarrow R(i, \top)$. By $R(o, \top)$, $R(\neg o, \bot)$. By Case Z01 in Fig. 9, $R(t_2, \top)$. By Case Z02 in Fig. 9, $R(\neg t_3, \bot)$, hence $R(t_3, \top)$.

- Assume $Q(p, \top)$. By Case Z09 in Fig. 9, $R(t_2, q)$. Because $R(t_2, \top)$, by transitivity, $R(q, \top)$. ✓
- Assume $Q(q, \bot)$. By Case Z10 in Fig. 9, $R(p, \neg t_2)$. Therefore, $R(\neg p, t_2)$. Because $R(t_2, \top)$, $R(\neg p, \top)$. Hence, $R(p, \bot)$. ✓
- Assume $R(p, q)$. by Case Z15 in Fig. 9, $R(t_1, \bot)$. Therefore, by Case Z09 in Fig. 9, $R(t_3, i)$. Because $R(t_3, \top)$, by transitivity of PERs, $R(i, \top)$. ✓

□

Lemma 13. POSLFTRIPPLE$(0, GT)$ *and* NEGRGTRIPPLE$(0, GT)$

Proof. Recall the definition of GT from Fig. 3:

$$\begin{aligned}
GT(o, i, p, q, t) \triangleq\ & (t_1 \Leftrightarrow (p \Leftrightarrow q)) \\
& \wedge (\neg t_2 \Leftrightarrow (p \Rightarrow q)) \\
& \wedge (\neg t_3 \Leftrightarrow (t_1 \Rightarrow \neg i)) \\
& \wedge (o \Leftrightarrow (\neg t_2 \Rightarrow t_3))
\end{aligned}$$

We can assume $Q(o, \top) \wedge R = $ ZEROSATURATE$(Q, T) \wedge GT(o, i, p, q, t) \subseteq T$ and we must prove that $Q(q, \top) \Rightarrow R(p, \top)$, $Q(p, \bot) \Rightarrow R(q, \bot)$, and $R(p, q) \Rightarrow R(i, \top)$.

- Assume $Q(q, \top)$. By Case Z03 in Fig. 9, $R(\neg t_2, \top)$. Therefore, by Case Z09 in Fig. 9 $R(o, t_3)$. Because $Q(o, \top)$, by transitivity of PERs, $R(t_3, \top)$. Hence, $R(\neg t_3, \bot)$. By Case Z01 in Fig. 9, $R(t_1, \top)$. By Case Z17 in Fig. 9, $R(p, q)$. Because $R(q, \top)$, $Q(p, \top)$. ✓
- Assume $Q(p, \bot)$. By Case Z04 in Fig. 9, $R(\neg t_2, \top)$. Using the same argument as above, $R(p, q)$. Because $R(p, \bot)$, by transitivity, $R(q, \bot)$,
- Assume $R(p, q)$. By Case Z07 in Fig. 9, $R(\neg t_2, \top)$. Therefore, by Case Z09 in Fig. 9, $R(o, t_3)$. By transitivity, $R(t_3, \top)$. That is, $R(\neg t_3, \bot)$. By Case Z02 in Fig. 9, $R(\neg i, \bot)$. Therefore, $R(i, \top)$. ✓

□

Lemma 14. POSRGTRIPPLE$(0, EQ)$, POSLFTRIPPLE$(0, EQ)$, NEGRGTRIPPLE $(0, EQ)$, *and* NEGLFTRIPPLE$(0, EQ)$.

Proof. Recall the definition of EQ from Fig. 3.

$$EQ(o, i, p, q, t) \triangleq (t_1 \Leftrightarrow (p \Leftrightarrow q)) \wedge (\neg o \Leftrightarrow (t_1 \Rightarrow \neg i))$$

We can assume $Q(o, \top) \wedge R = $ ZEROSATURATE$(Q, T) \wedge EQ(o, i, p, q, t) \subseteq T$ and we must prove that $Q(p, \top) \Rightarrow R(q, \top)$, $Q(q, \bot) \Rightarrow R(p, \bot)$, $Q(p, \bot) \Rightarrow R(q, \bot)$, $Q(q, \top) \Rightarrow R(p, \top)$, and $R(p, q) \Rightarrow R(i, \top)$. By $R(o, \top)$, $R(\neg o, \bot)$. By Case Z01 in Fig. 9, $R(t_1, \top)$. By Case Z17 in Fig. 9, $R(p, q)$. The first 4 cases are true by transitivity of PERs. The 5th case is true by Case Z02 in Fig. 9. □

Alternative Implementations. There are many other ways to implement $\leq$, $<$, and $=$. For example, we could define $\leq$ in terms of $<$ and $=$:

$$x \leq_n y \triangleq x <_n y \vee x =_n y$$

In this case, we can find a LTE$'$—displayed in Fig. 10—such that

$$(\beta_3^1, \wedge_{i \in \{1...n\}} \{\text{LTE}'(\beta^i, \beta^{i+1}, x_i, y_i, \rho^i)\} \wedge \beta_{n+1} \Leftrightarrow \langle \bot, \top \rangle \wedge \beta_3^1 \Leftrightarrow (\beta_1^1 \vee \beta_2^1))$$

We have proven the same result as Theorem 1 for this implementation. Unfortunately we had to modify the proof and RIPPLE predicate sufficiently that we are not able to include this proof here.

$$\text{LTE}'(o, i, p, q, t) \triangleq \text{LTE}(o_1, i_i, p, q, t') \wedge \text{EQ}(o_2, i_2, p, q, t'')$$

Fig. 10. LTE$'$: an alternative to LTE. Assume that t' and t'' are vectors with fresh variables. Note that the $\wedge$ is only asserting the triples in LT and EQ and not asserting that the answer is $<$ and $=$. LTE$'$'s first and second parameters are Boolean vectors of size 2.

Another possibility is displayed in Fig. 11. This is based on an implementation where the unneccesary $\Leftrightarrow$ has been removed:

$$x \leq_n y \triangleq \begin{cases} \top & \text{if } n = 0 \\ (\neg x_n \vee y_n) \wedge ((\neg x_n \wedge y_n) \vee (x \leq_{n-1} y)) & \text{if } n > 0 \end{cases}$$

$$\begin{aligned}\text{LTE}''(o, i, p, q, t) \triangleq & (t_1 \Leftrightarrow (q \Rightarrow p)) \\ \wedge & (t_2 \Leftrightarrow (p \Rightarrow q)) \\ \wedge & (t_3 \Leftrightarrow (t_1 \Rightarrow i)) \\ \wedge & (\neg o \Leftrightarrow (t_2 \Rightarrow \neg t_3))\end{aligned}$$

Fig. 11. LTE$''$: an alternative to LTE Assume that t' and t'' are vectors with fresh variables.

Lemma 15. POSRGTRIPPLE$(0, \text{LTE}'')$ *and* NEGLFTRIPPLE$(0, \text{LTE}'')$

Proof. We can assume $Q(o, \top) \wedge R = \text{ZEROSATURATE}(Q, T) \wedge \text{LTE}''(o, i, p, q, t) \subseteq T$ and we must prove the following three conditions $Q(p, \top) \Rightarrow R(q, \top)$, $Q(q, \bot) \Rightarrow R(p, \bot)$, and $R(p, q) \Rightarrow R(i, \top)$ (assuming that either $R(p, \top)$ or $R(q, \bot)$). By $Q(o, \top)$, $Q(\neg o, \bot)$. By Case Z01 in Fig. 9, $R(t_2, \top)$. By Case Z02 in Fig. 9, $R(t_3, \top)$. The first two conditions are proved by the same argument used in Lemma 12. As for the final condition: if $R(p, \top)$ then, by Case Z03 in Fig. 9, $R(t_1, \top)$. If $R(q, \bot)$ then, by Case Z04 in Fig. 9, $R(t_1, \top)$. Since (in either case) $R(t_1, \top)$, by Case Z09 in Fig. 9, $R(t_3, i)$. Because $R(t_3, \top)$, by transitivity of PERs, $R(i, \top)$. □

4   Conclusion

Stålmarck's 1-saturation is a fast but incomplete method of computing finite partial equivalence relations over propositional logic formulae. It can be used in situations when completeness is not required or as a method of pruning the search space traversed by more complete techniques such as backtracking.

We have proved that, under several implementations of inequalities for finite vectors, 1-saturation can be used to compute transitive arguments. This provides some intuition as to what Stålmarck's algorithm can prove. Notably, we now know that a limited form of 2-saturation can be used to compute a useful approximation of transitive closure over relations such as $\leq$ that is representable by equivalences in the triples. This is precisely what SLAM needs.

This paper could be a starting point for future efforts of the same kind. There are other incomplete SAT-based techniques—such as *recursive learning* [8]— that play a role that is similar to Stålmarck's algorithm. We would also like to prove more results about Stålmarck's algorithm (or a similar procedure), such that we could get a complete characterization of its relative completeness over propositional logic extended with linear arithmetic and uninterpreted functions. As these proofs are quite tedious (especially the proofs about the relations POSRGTRIPPLE, etc)—we would like to automate them in a mechanical theorem prover.

Acknowledgements. Koen Classen, John Harrison, and Mary Sheeran have made helpful comments regarding this work.

References

1. G. Andersson, P. Bjesse, B. Cook, and Z. Hanna. A proof engine approach to solving combinational design automation problems. In *2002 Design Automation Conference*, 2002.
2. T. Ball, B. Cook, S. Das, and S. K. Rajamani. Refining approximations in software predicate abstraction. In *TACAS 04: Tools and Algorithms for Construction and Analysis of Systems*. Springer-Verlag, 2004.
3. T. Ball, B. Cook, S. K. Lahiri, and L. Zhang. Zapato: Automatic theorem proving for predicate abstraction refinement. In *CAV 04: International Conference on Computer-Aided Verification*, 2004.
4. B. Cook, D. Kroening, and N. Sharygina. Cogent: Accurate theorem proving for program verification. In *To appear at CAV 05: Conference on Computer Aided Verification*, 2005.
5. B. A. Davey and H. Priestley. *Introduction to Lattices and Order*. Cambridge University Press, Cambridge, 1990.
6. S. Graf and H. Saïdi. Construction of abstract state graphs with PVS. In *CAV 97: Conference on Computer Aided Verification*, 1997.
7. J. Harrison. Stålmarck's method as a HOL derived rule. In *TPHOLs 96: International Conference on Theorem Proving in Higher Order Logics*, 1996.
8. W. Kunz and P. K. K. Recursive learning: An attractive alternative to the decision tree for test generation in digital circuits. In *ITC'92: International Test Conference*, 1992.

9. S. K. Lahiri, T. Ball, and B. Cook. Predicate abstraction via symbolic decision procedures. In *To appear at CAV 05: Conference on Computer Aided Verification*, 2005.

10. S. K. Lahiri, R. E. Bryant, and B. Cook. A symbolic approach to predicate abstraction. In *CAV 03: International Conference on Computer-Aided Verification*, pages 141–153, 2003.

11. Microsoft Corporation. Static Driver Verifier. Available at www.microsoft.com/whdc/devtools/tools/SDV.mspx.

12. M. Sheeran and G. Stålmarck. A tutorial on Stålmarck's proof procedure for propositional logic. *Formal Methods in System Design*, 16(1), January 2000.

Automatic Refinement Checking for B

Michael Leuschel[1,2] and Michael Butler[1]

[1] School of Electronics and Computer Science,
University of Southampton,
Highfield, Southampton, SO17 1BJ, UK
{mjb, mal}@ecs.soton.ac.uk
[2] Institut für Informatik, Heinrich-Heine Universität Düsseldorf,
Universitätsstr. 1, D-40225 Düsseldorf
leuschel@cs.uni-duesseldorf.de

Abstract. Refinement is a key concept in the B-Method. While refinement is at the heart of the B Method, so far no automatic refinement checker has been developed for it. In this paper we present a refinement checking algorithm and implementation for B. It is based on using an operational semantics of B, obtained in practice by the PROB animator. The refinement checker has been integrated into PROB toolset and we present various case studies and empirical results in the paper, showing the algorithm to be surprisingly effective. The algorithm checks that a refinement preserves the trace properties of a specification. We also compare our tool against the refinement checker FDR for CSP and discuss an extension for singleton failure refinement.

Keywords: B-Method, Tool Support, Refinement Checking, Model Checking, Animation, Logic Programming, Constraints.[1]

1 Introduction

The B-method is a well-established theory and methodology for the rigorous development of computer systems and programs. B was originally devised by Abrial [1] and has been applied to a wide range of safety-critical applications.

B is based on the notion of *abstract machine*. The variables of an abstract machine are typed using set theoretic constructs such as sets, relations and functions. Each machine has a certain number of operations that can update the variables of the machine, as well as an invariant specified using predicate logic.

Refinement is a key concept in the B-Method. It allows one to start from a high-level specification and then gradually refine it into an implementation, which can then be automatically translated into executable code. While there is tool support for proving refinement via semi-automatic proof (within Atelier-B [24], the B-Toolkit [19], and now also Click'n Prove[3]), there has been up to now

---

[1] This research is being carried out as part of the EU funded projects: IST 511599 RODIN (Rigorous Open Development Environment for Complex Systems) and IST-2001-38059 ASAP (Advanced Specialization and Analysis for Pervasive Systems).

K.-K. Lau and R. Banach (Eds.): ICFEM 2005, LNCS 3785, pp. 345–359, 2005.

no automatic refinement checker in the style of FDR [12] for CSP [15,21]. The proof-based approach to refinement checking requires that a gluing invariant be provided. In contrast, with our automatic approach no gluing invariant needs to be provided. The proof based approach to refinement is a labour intensive activity. Indeed, when a refinement does not hold it may take a while for a B user to realise that the proof obligations cannot be proven, resulting in a lot of wasted effort. In this paper we wish to speed up B development time by providing an automatic refinement checker that can be used to locate errors before any formal refinement proof is attempted. In some cases the refinement checker can actually be used as an alternative to the prover,[2] but in general the method presented in this paper is complementary to the traditional B tools.

In this paper we formalise the notion of refinement checking and present an algorithm which is at the heart of an automatic refinement checker. This new refinement checker has been implemented and integrated within the PROB validation tool for the B method [16]. At the heart of PROB is a fully automatic animator implemented mainly in SICStus Prolog. The undecidability of animating B is overcome in PROB by restricting animation to finite sets and integer ranges, while efficiency is achieved by delaying the enumeration of variables as long as possible. PROB comprises various visualization facilities [18] to display the state space in a user-friendly way. PROB also contains a model checker [9] which tries to find a sequence of operations that, starting from an initial state, leads to a state which violates the invariant (or exhibits some other error, such as deadlocking, assertion violations, or abort conditions). To compute the set of reachable states of a B machine the model checker makes use of the same underlying interpreter as the animator. In fact, the PROB interpreter can be viewed as providing the operational semantics of a B machine. In this paper we will re-use the same PROB interpreter as the foundation of the refinement checker. In the case where a refinement is violated, the refinement checker displays a sequence of operations that can be performed by the "refinement" machine but not by the specification.

2   Scheduler Example

In this section we present a small example of a specification and its refinement in B to help motivate the work. Later we will be more precise about the meaning of refinement and refinement checking. Familiarity with B notation is assumed in the remainder of the paper.

Figure 1 presents a B specification (*Scheduler0*) of a system for scheduling processes on a single resource. In this model, each process has a state which is either *idle*, *ready* to become active or *active* whereby it controls the resource. The current set of processes is modelled by the variable *proc* and the *pst* variable maps each current process to a state. There is a further invariant stating that there should be no more than one active process ($pst^{-1}[\{active\}]$, the image

---

[2] Namely when all sets and integer ranges are already finite to start with and do not have to be reduced to make animation by PROB feasible.

of $\{active\}$ under the inverse of pst, represents the set of active processes). $Scheduler0$ contains events for creating new processes, making a process ready, allowing a process to take control of the resource ($enter$) and allowing a process to relinquish control ($leave$). Each of these events is appropriately guarded by a WHEN clause[3]. In particular, the $enter$ event is enabled for a process p when p is ready and no other process is active.

```
MACHINE  Scheduler0
SETS
    PROC;
    STATE = {idle, ready, active}
VARIABLES  proc, pst
INVARIANT
    proc ∈ ℙ(PROC) ∧
    pst ∈ proc → STATE ∧
    card(pst⁻¹[{active}]) ≤ 1

INITIALISATION  proc, pst := {}, {}

OPERATIONS
new(p : PROC) ≙
    WHEN
        p ∈ PROC \ proc
    THEN
        pst(p) := idle ||
        proc := proc ∪ {p}
    END;
```

```
ready(p : PROC) ≙
    WHEN
        pst(p) = idle
    THEN
        pst(p) := ready
    END;

enter(p : PROC) ≙
    WHEN
        pst(p) = ready ∧
        pst⁻¹[{active}] = {}
    THEN
        pst(p) := active
    END;

leave(p : PROC) ≙
    WHEN
        pst(p) = active
    THEN
        pst(p) := idle
    END
```

Fig. 1. Scheduler specification

Figure 2 presents a B refinement of $Scheduler0$. In this refinement, instead of mapping each current process to a state, we have a pool of idle processes $idleset$ and a queue of ready processes $readyq$. We also have a flag indicating whether or not there is a process currently active ($activef$). When $activef$ is true, the identity of the currently active process is stored in $activep$. The queue of ready processes means that processes will become active in the order in which they became ready[4]. Now the $enter$ event is enabled for process p when p is the first element in the queue and there is no active process.

We expect that $Scheduler1$ is a valid refinement of $Scheduler0$ since any sequence of operations in $Scheduler0$ should also be possible in $Scheduler1$. Refinement checking of $Scheduler0$ against $Scheduler1$ with our tool for a maximum of three processes ($PROC = \{p1, p2, p3\}$) finds no counterexamples. If we were to weaken the guard of the refined $enter$ event, removing the clause $activef = FALSE$, this weaker refinement would allow more than one process

---

[3] WHEN is the the Event B syntax for the SELECT clause of classical B.

[4] In the $ready$ event, $readyq \leftarrow p$ represents appending of p to the end of $readyq$.

MACHINE *Scheduler1*
REFINES *Scheduler0*
VARIABLES
   proc, idleset, readyq, activep, activef
INVARIANT
   idleset $\in \mathbb{P}(PROC) \wedge$
   readyq $\in seq(PROC) \wedge$
   activep $\in PROC \wedge$
   activef $\in BOOL$

INITIALISATION
   proc := {} $||$ *readyq* := [ ] $||$
   activep :$\in PROC$ $||$
   activef := $FALSE$ $||$
   idleset := {}

OPERATIONS

$new(p : PROC) \; \hat{=}$
   WHEN
     $p \in PROC \setminus proc$
   THEN
     idleset := *idleset* $\cup \{p\}$ $||$
     proc := *proc* $\cup \{p\}$
   END;

$ready(p : PROC) \; \hat{=}$
   WHEN
     $p \in idleset$
   THEN
     readyq := *readyq* $\leftarrow p$ $||$
     idleset := *idleset* $\setminus \{p\}$
   END;

$enter(p : PROC) \; \hat{=}$
   WHEN
     readyq $\neq$ [ ] $\wedge$
     $p = first(readyq) \wedge$
     activef $= FALSE$
   THEN
     activep := p $||$
     readyq := $tail(readyq)$ $||$
     activef := $TRUE$
   END;

$leave(p : PROC) \; \hat{=}$
   WHEN
     activef $= TRUE \wedge$
     $p = activep$
   THEN
     idleset := *idleset* $\cup \{p\}$ $||$
     activef := $FALSE$
   END

Fig. 2. Refinement of the scheduler

to take control of the single resource. In terms of operation sequences, it would allow sequences in the refinement in which, for example, *enter*(p1) is followed by *enter*(p2) without *leave*(p1) occurring in between. It would thus be an incorrect refinement. The following counterexample is generated by PROB for the incorrect refinement: *new*(p1), *new*(p2), *ready*(p1), *ready*(p2), *enter*(p1), *enter*(p2). This counterexample discovered by PROB is a trace allowed by the incorrect refinement that is not a trace of the specification *Scheduler0*.

3   Refinement Checking for B

In this section we outline the B notion of refinement. We also outline the trace behaviour of B machines and trace refinement for B machines and relate it to standard B refinement.

    Classical B distinguishes between an enabling condition (guard) and a precondition. PROB supports guards but not preconditions[5]. If we ignore precon-

---

[5] The B syntax supported by PROB allows preconditions, but they are treated as guards. The more recent Event B approach [4] supports guards but not preconditions.

ditions but allow for guards, then all B operations have a normal form defined by a predicate P relating before state v and after state v' as follows [1, Chapter 6]: ANY v' WHERE $P(v, v')$ THEN $v := v'$ END.

Classical B refinement is expressed in terms of a gluing invariant which links concrete states to abstract states. The meaning of operations in B is defined in terms of weakest precondition formulae as are the refinement proof obligations for B. In this paper we will find it more convenient to take a standard relational view of operations and gluing invariants. This view is easily reconciled with the generalised substitution notation by treating the predicate P in the normal form for operations above as characterising a relation between before and after states.

The proof obligations for B correspond to the standard relational definition of forward simulation.[6] Let R be the gluing relation, AI and CI be the abstract and concrete initial states respectively and AOP and COP stand for corresponding abstract and concrete operations. The usual relational definition of forward simulation is as follows [14]:

- Every initial concrete state must be related to some initial abstract state:
  $c \in CI \implies \exists a \in AI \cdot c \, R \, a$
- If states are linked and the concrete one enables an operation, then the abstract state should enable the corresponding abstract operation and both operations should result in states that are linked: $c \, R \, a \, \wedge \, c \, COP \, c' \implies \exists a' \cdot a \, AOP \, a' \wedge c' \, R \, a'$

The proof obligations for refinement are automatically generated from the gluing invariant and the definitions of the abstract and concrete operations by, e.g., AtelierB or the BToolkit. The user can then try to prove these using the semi-automatic provers of those systems. If the proof obligations are all proven, every execution sequence performed by the refinement machine can be matched by the abstract machine [8]. Automatic refinement checkers work directly on the execution sequences and try to *disprove* refinement by finding traces that can be performed by the refinement machine but not by the specification. For this we need to formalise the notions of execution sequences (traces) for B.

Traces. The use of event traces to model system behaviour is well-known from process algebra, especially CSP [15]. Although event traces are not part of the standard semantic definitions in B, many authors have made the link between B machines and event traces including [8,10,23].

For a B operation of the form $X \longleftarrow op(Y) \hat{=} S$, we regard execution of operation op with input value a resulting in output value b as corresponding to the occurrence of event $op.a.b$. An event trace is a sequence of such events and the behaviour of a system may be defined by a set of event traces. For example, the following is a possible trace of the scheduler specification of Figure 1: $\langle$ *new.p1, new.p2, ready.p1, ready.p2, enter.p1, leave.p1* $\rangle$.

The state space of a machine is defined as the cartesian product of the types of each of the machine variables. We represent the machine variables by a vector

---

[6] This is easy to demonstrate by using the normal form for operations characterised by a before-after predicate and the weakest precondition rules for B.

v. The normal form for a B operation operating on v with inputs x and outputs y is characterised by a predicate $P(x, v, v', y)$. Characterising a B operation of the form $X \longleftarrow op(Y)$ as a predicate in this way gives rise to a labelled transition relation on states: state s is related to state s' by event $op.a.b$, denoted by $s \to^M_{op.a.b} s'$, when $P(a, s, s', b)$ holds. This transition relation $\to^M_e$ is lifted to traces using relational composition: $\to^M_{\langle \rangle} = ID$ and $\to^M_{\langle e \rangle t} = \to^M_e ; \to^M_t$. Now t is a possible trace of machine M if $\to^M_t$ relates some initial state to some state reachable through trace t: $t \in traces(M) = \exists c, c' \cdot c \in CI \wedge c \to^M_t c'$.

Trace Refinement Checking. A machine M is a trace refinement of a machine N if any trace of N is a trace of M, that is, any trace that is possible in the concrete system is also possible in the abstract system. It is straightforward to show by induction over traces that if we can exhibit a forward simulation between M and N with some gluing relation, then M is trace refined by N. It is known that forward simulation is not complete, i.e., there are systems related by trace refinement for which it not possible to find a forward simulation. The related technique of backward simulation together with forward simulation make simulation complete [14]. A backward simulation is defined as follows:

$$c \in CI \wedge c \, R \, a \implies a \in AI$$
$$c \, COP \, c' \wedge c' \, R \, a' \implies \exists a \cdot c \, R \, a \wedge a \, AOP \, a'$$

The B tools produce proof obligations for forward simulation only. There are cases of refinement where, although the trace behaviour of the concrete system is more deterministic, an individual concrete operation is less deterministic than its corresponding abstract operation. Backwards refinement is required in such cases. Typical developments B involve the reduction of nondeterminism in operations so that forward simulation is sufficient in most cases.

A single complete form of simulation can be defined by enriching the gluing structure. Gardiner and Morgan [13] have developed a single complete simulation rule by using a predicate transformer for the gluing structure. Such a predicate transformer characterises a function from *sets* of abstract states to *sets* of concrete states. Refinement checking in PROB works by constructing a gluing structure between the concrete and abstract states as it traverses the state spaces of both systems. So that we have a complete method of refinement checking, the PROB checking algorithm constructs a gluing structure that relates concrete states with sets of abstract states: $R \in C \leftrightarrow \mathbb{P}(A)$. On successful completion of an exhaustive refinement checking run the constructed gluing structure R will relate each individual concrete initial state to the set of abstract initial states and for each pair of corresponding concrete and abstract states, the following simulation condition will be satisfied: $c \, R \, as \wedge c \, COP \, c' \implies \exists as' \cdot as \, AOP \, as' \wedge c' \, R \, as'$. Here as and as' represent sets of abstract states and $as \, AOP \, as'$ is defined as $AOP[as] = as'$. It can be shown by induction over traces that this entails trace refinement, i.e., a successful outcome of the algorithm guarantees trace refinement. Because PROB works on finite state systems, the algorithm always terminates. Completeness of the algorithm is proven by demonstrating that whenever the outcome is failure, then there is a violation of trace refinement.

4   The Algorithm

We now present an algorithm to perform refinement checking. The gluing structure discussed in the previous Section is stored in *Table*, and for every entry (c, A) the algorithm checks whether all operations of the concrete state c can be matched by some abstract state in A; if not, a counter example has been found, otherwise all concrete successor states are computed and put into relation with the corresponding abstract successor states. To ensure termination of the algorithm it is crucial to recognise when the same configuration is re-examined. This is done by the check "(ConcNode,AbsNodes) $\in$ Table". If that check succeeds we know that we can safely stop looking for a counter example. Indeed, if one counter example exists we know that we can find a shorter version starting from the configuration that is already in the Table.

In the previous section we have introduced the relation $\rightarrow^M$, where $s \rightarrow^M_{op.a.b}$ s' signifies that the operation op can be performed with inputs a and outputs b in state s, resulting in a new state s' of the machine M. For the algorithm below it is convenient to also model the initialisations by adding a special state *root*, and extending $\rightarrow^M$ such that $root \rightarrow^M_{initialise\_machine} s$ holds for all valid initial states s of the machine M.

Algorithm 4.1[*Refinement Checking*]

    Input: An abstract machine M_A and a refinement machine M_R
    Table := {} ;   Res := refineCheck(root,{root});
    if Res = $\langle\rangle$ **then println** 'Refinement OK'
    else println('Counter Example:',Res)
    end if

    function refineCheck(ConcNode,AbsNodes)
    if (ConcNode,AbsNodes) $\in$ Table **then**
      return $\langle\rangle$
    else
      Table := Table $\cup$ {(ConcNode,AbsNodes)};
      for all CSucc,Op **such that** $ConcNode \rightarrow^{M_R}_{Op} CSucc$ **do**
        TraceS := concat(Trace,[(Op,CSucc)]);
        ASuccs := $\{as \mid \exists an \in AbsNodes \land an \rightarrow^{M_A}_{Op} as\}$;
        if ASuccs = $\varnothing$ **then**
          return TraceS
        else
          Res := refineCheck(CSucc,ASucss,TraceS);
          if Res $\neq \langle\rangle$ **then return** Res; **end if**
        end if
      end for
    end if
    end function

Implementation. We have actually performed two implementations of the above algorithm. The first one is implemented inside the PROB toolset, i.e., using SICStus Prolog. The tabling is done by maintaining a Prolog fact database which is updated using `assert/1`. The second implementation has been done in XSB Prolog. The code of the XSB refinement checker is almost identical, but instead of using a Prolog fact database it uses XSB's efficient tabling mechanism [22]. As we will see later, this implementation is faster than the SICStus Prolog one, but the overhead of starting up a new XSB Prolog process and loading the states space is only worth the effort for larger state spaces with no or difficult to find counter examples. From a pragmatic point of view, this approach also requires the PROB user to separately install XSB Prolog.

For both implementations the abstract state space currently has to be computed beforehand (using PROB). To ensure completeness of the refinement checking, it should be fully computed. However, our refinement checker also allows the abstract state space to be only partially computed. In that case, the refinement checker will detect whether enough of the state space has been computed to decide the refinement (and warn the user if not).

For the SICStus Prolog implementation the state space of the implementation can, but does not have to be computed beforehand. In other words, the implementation state space will be expanded *on-the-fly*, depending on how the refinement checking algorithm proceeds. This is of course most useful when counter examples are found quickly, as in those cases only a fraction of the state space will have to be computed. In future work we plan to enable this on-the-fly expansion also for the abstract state space. For the XSB implementation, running separately from PROB, this interaction is currently not possible, and hence both the abstract and implementation state space have to be computed beforehand.

5   Experiments

To test our refinement checker we have conducted a series of experiments with various models. As well as using the scheduler example from Section 2, we have experimented with a much larger development of a mechanical by press by Abrial [2]. The development of the mechanical press started from a very abstract model and went through several refinements. The final model contained "about 20 sensors, 3 actuators, 5 clocks, 7 buttons, 3 operating devices, 5 operating modes, 7 emergency situations, etc." [2]. We were able to apply our new refinement checker to successfully validate various refinement relations. Furthermore, as no abstraction was required for PROB (i.e., all sets were already finite to start with), the refinement checker can actually be used in place of the traditional B refinement provers. In other words, were thus able to automatically prove refinement using our new tool. To check the ability of our tool to find errors we have also applied it to an erroneous refinement (m2_err.ref), and PROB was able to locate the problem in a few seconds. We have also experimented with a simple example of a server allowing clients to log in. Precise timings and results for these and other experiments are presented in the next subsections.

Consistency Checking. In a first phase we have performed classical consistency and deadlock checking on our examples using PROB's model checker. The results can be found in Table 1, and give an indication of the size of the state space and how expensive it is to compute the operational semantics. The experiments were all run on a PowerPC G5 Dual 2.5 GHz, running Mac OS X 10.3.9, SICStus Prolog 3.12.1 and ProB version 1.1.5. Note, while the machine had 4.5 Gigabyte of RAM, only 256 Megabyte are available in SICStus Prolog 3.12 for dynamic data (such as the state space of B machines). scheduler0.mch and scheduler1.ref are the machines presented above in Section 2 for 3 processes, while scheduler0_6.mch and scheduler1_6.ref are the same machines but for 6 processes. The machines m0.mch, m1.ref, m2.ref, m2_err.ref, and m3.ref are from the mechanical Press example discussed above. Server.mch is a simple B machine describing the server example, while ServerR.ref is a refinement thereof.

Refinement Checking. Table 2 are the results of performing various refinement checks on these machines. Entries marked with an asterisk mean that no previous consistency checking was performed, i.e., the operational semantics of the implementation machine was computed on-the-fly, as driven by the refinement checker. For entries without an asterisk the experiment was run straight after the consistency checking of Table 1, i.e., the operational semantics was already computed and the time is thus of the refinement checking proper. The figures show that our checker was very effective, especially if counter examples existed.

In Table 3 we have conducted some of the experiments where the refinement checker is run as a separate process using XSB Prolog [22], rather than inside PROB under SICStus Prolog. Our experiments confirm that XSB's tabling mechanism leads to a more efficient refinement checking (cf. the third column). However the time to start up XSB and load the state space is not negligible, meaning that the XSB approach does not always pay off. This can be seen in the fourth column which contains the total time for loading and checking: e.g., the approach pays off for the m2.ref check against m1.ref (overall gain of 30 seconds) but not for the smaller examples nor when a counter example is found quickly.

Comparison with FDR. We have compared our new refinement checker against the most widely known refinement checker, namely FDR [12]. FDR is a commercial tool for the validation of CSP specifications [15]. While B machines cannot easily be translated into CSP, the state space explored by PROB can easily be translated into a CSP specification using just choice and process definitions. While this automatically generated CSP is not a typical CSP specification, it is still useful for two purposes. First, it allows us to evaluate our refinement Algorithm 4.1 against the counterpart in FDR. Second, we can determine whether it would make sense, from an implementation point of view, to outsource the refinement checks to FDR, rather than using our own algorithm. The experiments were conducted as follows. After consistency checking (Table 1) the state space was saved as a simple CSP file using an export facility added to PROB. Basically, every state was encoded as a separate CSP Process and defined

Table 1. PROB consistency checking and size of state space

Machine	Time	States	Transitions
Server.mch	0.013 s	5	9
ServerR.ref	0.05 s	14	39
scheduler0.mch	46 s	55	190
scheduler1.ref	0.93 s	145	447
scheduler0_6.mch	41.37 s	2,188	14,581
scheduler1_6.ref	501.61 s	37,009	145,926
m0.mch	3.19 s	65	9,924
m1.ref	20.38 s	293	47,574
m2.ref	44.29 s	393	59,588
m2_err.ref	31.51 s	405	61,360
m3.ref	364.90 s	2,693	385,496

Table 2. PROB refinement checking and size of refinement relation

Refinement	Specification	Time	Size of table
Successful refinements:			
ServerR.ref	Server.mch*	0.05 s	14
”	Server.mch	0.00 s	”
scheduler1.ref	scheduler0.mch*	0.73 s	145
”	scheduler0.mch	0.00 s	”
scheduler1_6.ref	scheduler0_6.mch	3.80 s	37,009
m1.ref	m0.mch*	25.4 s	585
”	m0.mch	6.28 s	”
m2.ref	m0.mch	8.10 s	785
m2_err.ref	m0.mch	8.13 s	809
m2.ref	m1.ref	70.57 s	3,804
m3.ref	m0.mch	51.96 s	5,345
m3.ref	m1.ref	429.37 s	24,039
m3.ref	m2.ref	333.85 s	21,205
Counter examples found:			
scheduler1err.ref	scheduler0.mch*	0.12 s	19
scheduler1err_6.ref	scheduler0_6.mch*	1.80 s	121
m1.ref	m2.ref	0.01 s	13
m2_err.ref	m1.ref*	4.22 s	92
”	m1.ref	0.03 s	”

by an external choice of all the outgoing transitions. Every transition was represented by a CSP prefix operation, were the right-hand side is the CSP Process corresponding to the destination state of the transition. To obtain the left-hand side, operation arguments were flattened out, e.g., the operation $new(p1)$ got translated into a new CSP channel new_p1.[7] As an illustration, here are the first few lines for m0.mch:

---

[7] This had no impact for the mechanical press examples written in Event B style, as there are no operation arguments in any of the machines anyway.

Table 3. PROB refinement checking using XSB Prolog

Refinement	Specification	Checking Time	Total Time
Successful refinements:			
ServerR.ref	Server.mch	0.00 s	0.06 s
scheduler1.ref	scheduler0.mch	0.00 s	0.11 s
m1.ref	m0.mch	2.85 s	13.76 s
m2.ref	m1.ref	26.66 s	40.24 s
m3.ref	m2.ref	136.12 s	219.03 s
Counter examples found:			
m1.ref	m2.ref	0.00 s	22.68 s
m2_err.ref	m1.ref	0.01 s	12.79 s

```
Nroot = initialise_machine->N3448 [] initialise_machine->N3449 []
        initialise_machine->N3450 [] initialise_machine->N3451
N3448 = demarrer_presse->N3452 [] presse_descend->N3450 [] ...
```

FDR 2.8.1 was then run on the same hardware as for the earlier experiments to check CSP trace refinement and the results can be found in Table 4. Timings do not include the time needed to load the CSP file, but include the compilation, normalization and checking time of FDR. Due to a small bug in the TclTk interface of FDR timings were not displayed for ServerR.ref and scheduler1.ref; but the response was very quick. For scheduler1_6.ref FDR ran approximatively 3 hours (but again precise timings were not displayed). For the other examples FDR spent most of the time on compilation and normalization of the CSP model. This means subsequent refinement checks of the same combination of machines would have been substantially faster. In practice, however, there is only one refinement check that one is interested in for any two machines (namely that the "refinement" machine is a refinement of the specification machine).

We have also modelled the scheduler and its refinement in CSP by hand using what we believe is a natural CSP style using CSP constructs such as parallelism and synchronization wherever possible. These are named scheduler1.csp and scheduler0.csp and for 3 processes and scheduler1_6.csp and scheduler0_6.csp for 6 processes. We had to manually limit the size of the communication queue for FDR to terminate (this was not necessary in the B model), but after that refinement checking worked fine. After feedback from Michael Goldsmith from Formal Systems, we have also tested versions that were better suited for FDR, named Gscheduler1_6.csp and Gscheduler0_6.csp for 6 processes.

For checking m1.ref against m0.mch it can be noted that our algorithm is about 16 times faster than FDR (one has to compare the 101 s against 6.28 s as the computation of the operational semantics has in both cases been done beforehand by ProB; arguably FDR is at a disadvantage as the state space is in CSP form rather than stored as facts in a Prolog database). For the scheduler1_6.ref check against scheduler0_6.ref our implementation is even roughly 2800 times faster than using FDR. Our relatively simple refinement checking algorithm thus proves surprisingly effective in practice. When counter examples exist the differ-

Table 4. Refinement checking on the already expanded state space with FDR

Refinement	Specification	Time	States	Transitions
Successful refinements:				
ServerR.ref	Server.mch	< 1s	5	9
scheduler1.ref	scheduler0.mch	< 1s	69	205
scheduler1_6.ref	scheduler0_6.mch	+/- 3 hours	10,529	41,281
scheduler1.csp	scheduler0.csp	< 1 s	68	204
scheduler1_6.csp	scheduler0_6.csp	+/− 100s	10,528	41,280
Gscheduler1_6.csp	Gscheduler0_6.csp	+/− 2s	130,768	630,720
m1.ref	m0.mch	101 s	447	71,910
m2.ref	m1.ref	152 s	3,239	492,401
Counter examples found:				
m1.ref	m2.ref	120 s	2	8
m2_err.ref	m1.ref	150 s	464	71,107

ence is even more pronounced, as FDR spends a lot of effort on compiling and normalising the CSP specification before (quickly) finding the counter example. One explanation is that FDR's compilation is not well adapted to large, monolithic processes. Another point is that our algorithm normalises the abstract state space on the fly rather than beforehand. Indeed, Algorithm 4.1 can also be viewed as linking concrete states with sets of abstract states, by exploring in parallel all possible alternatives of the abstract machine. This corresponds to normalisation in FDR [12], but done *on-the-fly rather* than beforehand. Thus, when a counter example is found (quickly) only a fraction of the abstract space will have been normalised. Furthermore, even when no counter example is found, only that part of the abstract system is normalised which is in common with the implementation. As the implementation often has more restricted behaviour, this can result in big reductions and allows our tool to handle bigger examples. FDR's approach would only pay off if one did many refinement checks of the same abstract system, covering a large part of its state space, and if one has enough memory to normalise the entire abstract system. In our particular case studies, this was not the case. Note that for the well designed Gscheduler1_6.csp CSP specification, FDR was able to exploit properties of CSP to achieve very good performance (2 s compared to 100s for the unoptimised CSP and 3.8 s for PROB). We plan to undertake a more thorough comparison of PROB and FDR by comparing more examples modelled naturally in CSP and naturally in B. Still, as a preliminary conclusion, we can state that our algorithm compares favourably with FDR and that FDR is for the moment not very well suited for checking CSP models which directly encode fully expanded transition systems.

6   Extensions

Singleton Failures. We have extended our refinement checking algorithm to also check singleton failure refinement (see, e.g., [6]). A *singleton failure trace* is a pair consisting of a trace t as defined earlier and either the empty set or singleton

Table 5. PROB refinement checking using singleton failures

Refinement	Specification	Time	Size of table
Successful refinements:			
ServerR.ref	Server.mch*	0.07 s	14
Counter examples found:			
scheduler1.ref	scheduler0.mch*	0.06 s	9
m1.ref	m0.mch*	0.05 s	2
m2.ref	m1.ref *	0.07 s	2
m3.ref	m2.ref *	0.08 s	2

set containing a single operation F (with arguments). The intuitive meaning of $(t, \{F\})$ is that the machine can perform all the operations in the trace t and then be in a state where the operation F is not enabled, i.e., can be refused. The meaning of $(t, \varnothing)$ is that the machine can perform all the operations in t and then all operations are enabled for all possible arguments. A machine m_1 is said to be a *singleton failure refinement* of m_0 iff all singleton failure traces of m_1 are also singleton failure traces of m_0. Singleton Failures refinement can be situated in between trace refinement and CSP's failure refinement as implemented in FDR (in the latter, rather than talking about an single operation that can be refused one talks about sets of possible combinations of operations that can be refused).

To implement singleton failure refinement checking, Algorithm 4.1 has been extended to check for an additional condition when a counter example is found. More precisely, the function *refineCheck(ConcNode, AbsNodes)* also looks for operation calls that are possible in all states in *AbsNodes* but not in *ConcNode*.

As B does not have the distinction between internal and external choice, singleton failure refinement is mainly useful for refinements that should not decrease the choices offered by the machine, e.g., data refinement or when moving non-deterministic choices later. Note, however, when treating parameters of B operations, a choice of input values could be treated as an external choice, while a choice of output values could be treated as internal. In future, we plan to make this distinction. (It is not necessary to make this distinction for trace refinement, since the traces model does not distinguish internal and external choice.)

Some empirical results can be found in Table 5. All experiments were run on-the-fly, i.e., the implementation transition was not computed beforehand. As one can see, several refinement checks that were successful using trace refinement now yield a counter example. For example, for the m1.ref vs m0.mch check the algorithm finds the counter example $(\langle initialise\_machine \rangle, demarrer\_presse)$, meaning that there is an initial state of m1.ref where *demarrer_presse* is not enabled, but in all initial states of $m0.mch$ this operation is enabled.

Application to B and CSP. In recent work [7] we have shown how to combine B and CSP for specification purposes (a specification is partly written in B and partly in CSP) or for property checking of B machines (the CSP is used as a temporal property that a B machine must satisfy). Our new refinement checker is language independent, in the sense that any interpreter plugged into the PROB toolset can be used. In practice this means that we can check whether a B machine is a refinement of a CSP machine, or the other way around. For example, the mutual exclusion property of the scheduler of Section 2 can be specified as the following CSP process: $LOCK = enter?p \rightarrow leave.p \rightarrow LOCK$. We can check that both B schedulers (Figures 1 and 2) are trace refinements of the $LOCK$ CSP process. We can also check whether a combined B/CSP specification is a refinement of another combined specification. One can even use other formalisms, such as Object Petri nets as implemented in [11]. All this opens up new possibilities for validation.

7   Related and Future Work, and Conclusion

The idea of using (tabled) logic programming for verification is not new. The inspiration for the current refinement checker came from the earlier developed CTL model checker presented in [17]. Another related work is [5], which presents a bisimulation checker written in XSB Prolog.

In future, we plan to extend the refinement checker to also allow on-the-fly expansion of the abstract state space. We also wish to move away from the pure depth first strategy that it currently employs; using a similar mixed breadth-first depth-first strategy as the PROB model checker. This should allow the refinement checker to be applied when the abstract and implementation state spaces are big or even infinite. In our approach, no gluing invariant needs to be provided by the user. Another extension to our approach would be to check whether a gluing invariant provided by the user can be satisfied. This is the approach taken by Robinson for Z refinement using the Possum animation tool [20]. To improve the scalability we are also looking at symbolic state space reduction techniques.

We have presented the first automatic refinement checker for B. The checker is implemented within PROB and has been applied to various case studies. Our experiments have shown that, at least for the case studies under consideration, the algorithm is very effective and surprisingly competitive. Its ability to normalise the abstract machine on-the-fly seemed to be a key ingredient of its success.

Acknowledgements: We would like to thank Michael Goldsmith and anonymous referees of ICFEM for their useful feedback. We are also grateful to Letu Yang for his help in the B to CSP translator.

References

1. J.-R. Abrial. *The B-Book*. Cambridge University Press, 1996.
2. J.-R. Abrial. Case study of a complete reactive system in Event-B: A mechanical press controller. In *Tutorial at ZB'2005*, 2005. Available at http://www.zb2005.org/.
3. J.-R. Abrial and D. Cansell. Click'n prove: Interactive proofs within set theory. In D. A. Basin and B. Wolff, editors, *Proceedings TPHOLs 2003*, LNCS 2758, pages 1–24. Springer, 2003.
4. J.-R. Abrial and L. Mussat. Introducing dynamic constraints in B. In D. Bert, editor, *Second International B Conference*, April 1998.

5. S. Basu, M. Mukund, C. R. Ramakrishnan, I. V. Ramakrishnan, and R. M. Verma. Local and symbolic bisimulation using tabled constraint logic programming. In *Proceedings ICLP'01*, LNCS 2237, pages 166–180, November 2001. Springer.
6. C. Bolton and J. Davies. A comparison of refinement orderings and their associated simulation rules. *Electr. Notes Theor. Comput. Sci.*, 70(3):440 –453, 2002.
7. M. Butler and M. Leuschel. Combining CSP and B for specification and property verification. In J. Fitzgearld, I. Hayes, and A. Tarlecki, editors, *Proceedings FM'2005*, LNCS 3582, pages 221–236. Springer, 2005.
8. M. J. Butler. An approach to the design of distributed systems with B AMN. In J. P. Bowen, M. G. Hinchey, and D. Till, editors, *Proceedings ZUM '97*, LNCS 1212, pages 223–241. Springer, 1997.
9. E. M. Clarke, O. Grumberg, and D. Peled. *Model Checking*. MIT Press, 1999.
10. S. Dunne and S. Conroy. Process refinement in B. In H. Treharne, S. King, M. C. Henson, and S. Schneider, editors, *Proceedings ZB 2005*, LNCS 3455, pages 45–64. Springer, 2005.
11. B. Farwer and M. Leuschel. Model checking object Petri nets in Prolog. In *Proceedings PPDP '04*, pages 20–31, 2004. ACM Press.
12. Formal Systems (Europe) Ltd. *Failures-Divergence Refinement — FDR2 User Manual*.
13. P. H. B. Gardiner and C. Morgan. A single complete rule for data refinement. *Formal Asp. Comput.*, 5(4):367–382, 1993.
14. J. He, C. A. R. Hoare, and J. W. Sanders. Data refinement refined. In B. Robinet and R. Wilhelm, editors, *ESOP 86*, LNCS 213, pages 187–196. Springer, 1986.
15. C. A. R. Hoare. *Communicating Sequential Processes*. Prentice–Hall, 1985.
16. M. Leuschel and M. Butler. ProB: A Model Checker for B. In K. Araki, S. Gnesi, and D. Mandrioli, editors, *Proceedings FME 2003, Pisa, Italy*, LNCS 2805, pages 855–874. Springer, 2003.
17. M. Leuschel and T. Massart. Infinite state model checking by abstract interpretation and program specialisation. In A. Bossi, editor, *Proceedings of LOPSTR'99*, LNCS 1817, pages 63–82, 2000.
18. M. Leuschel and E. Turner. Visualizing larger states spaces in ProB. In H. Treharne, S. King, M. Henson, and S. Schneider, editors, *Proceedings ZB'2005*, LNCS 3455, pages 6–23. Springer-Verlag, April 2005.
19. B-Core. B-toolkit manuals. 1999.
20. N. J. Robinson. Checking z data refinements using an animation tool. In D. Bert, J. P. Bowen, M. C. Henson, and K. Robinson, editors, *Proceedings ZB 2002*, LNCS 2272, pages 62–81. Springer, 2002.
21. A. Roscoe. *The Theory and Practice of Concurrency*. Prentice–Hall, 1998.
22. K. Sagonas, T. Swift, and D. S. Warren. XSB as an efficient deductive database engine. In *Proceedings SIGMOD'94*, pages 442–453, Minneapolis, May 1994. ACM.
23. S. Schneider and H. Treharne. Communicating B machines. In D. Bert, J. P. Bowen, M. C. Henson, and K. Robinson, editors, *Proceedings ZB 2002*, LNCS 2272, pages 416–435. Springer, 2002.
24. Steria. Atelier B, user and reference manuals. 1997.

Slicing an Integrated Formal Method for Verification*

Ingo Brückner[1] and Heike Wehrheim[2]

[1] Universität Oldenburg, Department Informatik, 26111 Oldenburg, Germany
`ingo.brueckner@informatik.uni-oldenburg.de`
[2] Universität Paderborn, Institut für Informatik 33098 Paderborn, Germany
`wehrheim@uni-paderborn.de`

Abstract. Model checking specifications with complex data and behaviour descriptions often fails due to the large state space to be processed. In this paper we propose a technique for *reducing* such specifications (with respect to certain properties under interest) before verification. The method is an adaption of the *slicing technique* from program analysis to the area of integrated formal notations and temporal logic properties. It solely operates on the syntactic structure of the specification which is usually significantly smaller than its state space. We show how to build a reduced specification via the construction of a so called program dependence graph, and prove correctness of the technique with respect to a projection relationship between full and reduced specification. The reduction thus preserves all properties formulated in temporal logics which are invariant under stuttering, as for instance LTL_{-X}.

1 Introduction

Modelling complex systems usually involves the description of different views. In the UML this is facilitated by providing designers with a large number of different diagram types for modelling various aspects of systems. In the area of formal modelling notations *integrated formal methods* allow for a convenient specification of different views. Integrated formalisms combine different existing notations while still giving a semantics to the combination and thus preserving the formal rigour in a design. Models of complex systems in integrated specification formalisms usually contain views describing state-based aspects plus views describing the dynamic behaviour. A number of such integrations have been proposed in recent years [5,21,18,12,16,6,11]. They often combine state-based notations like Z or B with process algebras like CCS or CSP.

In this paper, we will be concerned with *verifying* specifications written in an integrated notation. Applications of model checking techniques often fail for such specifications due to the large amount of data (coming from the state-based side)

---

* This work was partly supported by the German Research Council (DFG) as part of the Transregional Collaborative Research Center "Automatic Verification and Analysis of Complex Systems" (SFB/TR 14 AVACS, `www.avacs.org`).

K.-K. Lau and R. Banach (Eds.): ICFEM 2005, LNCS 3785, pp. 360–374, 2005.

combined with the large number of interleavings of parallel components (coming from the process algebra side). Consequently, the development of techniques for avoiding the state explosion problem is even more compelling for integrated formalisms. Here, we propose a method for reducing the specification (and as a consequence its state space) by removing all those parts which are irrelevant for the validity of a particular property under interest. The technique for determining relevant (or irrelevant) parts is an adaption of the *slicing* technique from program analysis to formal specifications. Slicing has originally been introduced by Weiser [20] (for an overview see [17]) to reduce programs for debugging. It basically involves the construction of a *program dependence graph* which precisely reflects the dependencies in a program. On this graph it is possible to determine the parts of a program which might affect the value of a variable at a certain program point. The irrelevant parts can then be sliced away. A similar principle is applied in hardware verification under the name *cone of influence reduction* [4]. In software verification slicing has for instance been applied to Java [7], PROMELA [13], and SAL [19]. Being a static analysis technique slicing just operates on the *syntactic* level of the program, and a reduction of this can substantially facilitate the following model checking.

This work builds on previous ideas for slicing Object-Z specifications [2]. Here, we present a slicing technique for an *integrated* specification language. The formalism, called CSP-OZ [5], is a combination of the process algebra CSP [8] with the state-based formalism Object-Z [15]. For this notation we show how to construct graphs reflecting the mutual dependencies in a specification, in particular between the Object-Z and the CSP part. The slicing criteria are temporal logic formulae over atomic propositions (speaking about the state of the Object-Z part) *and* events (speaking about occurrence of operations of the CSP part). Instead of looking at one particular logic, we take a more general approach. We show that our reduction preserves properties formulated in any (linear-time) logic which is invariant under *stuttering*, i.e. which cannot distinguish between runs of a system which are equivalent up to some stuttering steps (defined by a set of irrelevant atomic propositions and events). This is obtained by proving that the runs of the reduced specification are *projections* of the runs of the full specification, projection being a particular form of stuttering. A logic fulfilling the requirements is for instance LTL_{-X} (linear time temporal logic without Next operator) or the state/event based interval logic proposed in [2].

The paper is structured as follows. The next section introduces CSP-OZ by means of a small example and moreover defines a Kripke structure semantics for CSP-OZ. In section 3 we present the dependence graph construction and the slicing algorithm. The slicing algorithm will be proven correct with respect to a projection relationship in section 4. The last section concludes.

2   CSP-OZ Specifications: An Example

For illustrating our approach we use a CSP-OZ specification of an air condition system. Initially the air condition is off. When it is switched on (*workswitch*), it starts to run. While running, the air condition either heats or cools the room and simultaneously allows the user to switch the mode (*modeswitch*), refill fuel (*refill*) or switch it off again. Cooling or heating is modelled by a consumption of one unit of fuel (*consume*) and an emission of hot or cold air (*dtemp*). For the specification we first define the mode of operating and a type for the fuel.

$$Mode ::= heat \mid cool \qquad Fuel == 0..100$$

___AC_____

chan *workswitch, consume, off*   **chan** *modeswitch* : $[m? : Mode]$
chan *refill* : $[f? : Fuel]$ **chan** *dtemp* : $[t! : Mode]$
chan *level* : $[f! : Fuel]$

main $=$ *workswitch* $\rightarrow$ *On*   *Operate* $=$ *modeswitch* $\rightarrow$ *Operate*
On $=$ $($*Operate* $\mid\mid\mid$ *Work*$)$ $\mathbin{\raise0.5ex\hbox{$\scriptscriptstyle\bullet$}}$ *main* $\Box$ *refill* $\rightarrow$ *Operate*
Work $=$ *consume* $\rightarrow$ *dtemp* $\rightarrow$ *level* $\rightarrow$ *Work* $\Box$ *workswitch* $\rightarrow$ *SKIP*
        $\Box$ *off* $\rightarrow$ *SKIP*

work : $\mathbb{B}$ *mode* : *Mode*; *fuel* : *Fuel*	__Init_____ $\neg$*work* *mode* $=$ *heat*

___effect_workswitch___   ___enable_consume_____   ___effect_consume_____
$\Delta(work)$ $\Delta(fuel)$
_____   *work* $\wedge$ *fuel* > 5 _____
$work' = \neg work$ $fuel' = fuel - 1$

___effect_modeswitch___   ___effect_dtemp_____   ___effect_level_____
$\Delta(mode)$; $m? : Mode$ $t! : Mode$ $f! : Fuel$
_____   _____   _____
$mode' = m?$ $t! = mode$ $f! = fuel$

___enable_off_____   ___enable_refill_____   ___effect_refill_____
_____   _____ $\Delta(fuel)$; $f? : Fuel$
$\neg work$ $fuel < 100$ _____
                                      $fuel' = min(fuel + f?, 100)$

_____

The first part of the class defines its interface towards the environment. The next part specifies its dynamic behaviour, i.e. the allowed ordering of method execution. It is defined via a set of CSP process equations. The operators appearing here are prefixing $\rightarrow$ (sequencing), sequential composition $\mathbin{\raise0.5ex\hbox{$\scriptscriptstyle\bullet$}}$, interleaving $\mid\mid\mid$ (parallel composition with no synchronisation) and external choice $\Box$. The third part of a CSP-OZ class describes the attributes of the class and the methods. For every method we might have an *enabling* schema fixing a guard for the method execution (enabling schemas equivalent to *true* are left out) and an effect schema describing the effect of a method upon execution. For instance, for method *consume* the enabling schema tells us that the air condition has to be on and a minimal amount of fuel is necessary for *consume* to take place, and that upon execution one unit of fuel is consumed. The method *level* on the other hand is always enabled, it just displays the current level of fuel.

The semantics of such specifications is defined in terms of labelled Kripke structures. In contrast to ordinary Kripke structures, transitions are labelled with events. This allows us to also use temporal logics for property specification which talk about execution of events.

Definition 1. *Let AP be a non-empty set of atomic propositions, E an alphabet of events (consisting of method names plus values of parameters).*

An (event-)labelled Kripke structure $K = (S, S_0, \rightarrow, L)$ over AP and E consists of a finite set of states S, a set of initial states $S_0 \subseteq S$, a transition relation $\rightarrow \subseteq S \times E \times S$ and a labelling function $L : S \rightarrow 2^{AP}$.

For our example atomic propositions might for instance be *mode = cool* or *fuel > 5*. The Kripke structure for a CSP-OZ class is derived in two steps: first, we separately compute the semantics of the CSP and the Object-Z part. In a second step, we combine the Kripke structure of the components by parallel composition. In the following we assume a global set of atomic propositions AP and events E which are built over method names $m \in M$, i.e. an event e has the form $m.i.o$ where m is the name of a method and i and o are (potential) values for input and output parameters. The transition relation for the CSP part is computed via the operational semantics of CSP [14].

Definition 2. *The Kripke structure semantics of the CSP part* **main** *of a CSP-OZ class is the labelled Kripke structure $K^{CSP} = (\mathcal{L}^{CSP}, \{\mathtt{main}\}, \rightarrow^{CSP}, L^{CSP})$ with $\mathcal{L}^{CSP}$ being the set of all CSP terms, $\rightarrow^{CSP}$ the transition relation derived via the operational semantics of CSP and $L^{CSP}(P) = AP$ for all $P \in \mathcal{L}^{CSP}$.*

In the states of the Kripke structure for the CSP part all atomic propositions hold since the CSP part makes no restrictions on values of attributes of the class.

Definition 3. *The Kripke structure semantics of the Object-Z part $C = (State, Init, (\mathtt{enable\_m})_{m \in M}, (\mathtt{effect\_m})_{m \in M})$ of a CSP-OZ class is the labelled Kripke structure $K^{OZ} = (State, Init, \rightarrow^{OZ}, L^{OZ})$ with the transition relation $\rightarrow^{OZ} = \{(s, m.i.o, s') \mid \mathtt{enable\_m}(s, i) \wedge \mathtt{effect\_m}(s, i, o, s')\}$, and the labelling function $L^{OZ}(s) = \{p \in AP \mid s \models p\}$.*

The states of the Kripke structure are simply the set of bindings of the state schema. These two Kripke structures are then combined via parallel composition. In the following we assume the alphabet of the CSP part and the set of methods in the Object-Z part to be equal, thus synchronisation takes places on all methods. Only one event remains which is executed by the CSP part alone, the invisible event τ which might arise out of internal choices in CSP processes.

Definition 4. *The parallel composition of two labelled Kripke structures[1] $K_i = (S_i, S_{0,i}, \rightarrow_i, L_i)$, $i \in \{1, 2\}$ over the same sets of atomic propositions AP and events E, $K_1 \parallel K_2$, is the Kripke structure $K = (S, S_0, \rightarrow, L)$ with*

---

[1] Note that our definition is symmetric, while for the parallel composition of CSP and Object-Z Kripke structures we assume only the CSP side to have τ transitions.

$-\ S = S_1 \times S_2,\ S_0 = S_{0,1} \times S_{0,2},$

$$-\ \rightarrow\ =\left\{((s_1,s_2),e,(s_1',s_2'))\ \middle|\ \begin{matrix} (s_1 \xrightarrow{e}_1 s_1' \wedge s_2 \xrightarrow{e}_2 s_2') \\ \vee\ (s_1 \xrightarrow{\tau}_1 s_1' \wedge s_2' = s_2) \vee (s_2 \xrightarrow{\tau}_2 s_2' \wedge s_1' = s_1) \end{matrix}\right\}$$

$-\ L(s) = L(s_1) \cap L(s_2),\ \text{where } s = (s_1, s_2).$

For describing properties of CSP-OZ classes we can now use any temporal logic which can be interpreted on labelled Kripke structures. For the purpose of this paper we assume the logic to be a *linear-time* logic, i.e. which is interpreted on the *paths* without considering the branching structure. We furthermore only consider paths which are fair [4] with respect to a set of events.

Definition 5. *Let $K = (S, S_0, \rightarrow, L)$ be a Kripke structure. An infinite sequence of events and states $s_0 e_1 s_2 e_3 s_4 \ldots$ is a* path *of the Kripke structure iff $s_0 \in S_0$ and $(s_i, e_{i+1}, s_{i+2}) \in\ \rightarrow$ holds for all $i \geq 0, i$ even.*

A path is fair *with respect to a set of events $E' \subseteq E$ (or E'-fair) iff $inf(\pi) \cap E' \neq \varnothing$ where $inf(\pi) = \{e \in E \mid \exists\ infinitely\ many\ i \in \mathbb{N} : e_i = e\}$.*

Here, we will not introduce one particular logic, but instead only assume that our logic is invariant under projection, i.e. that it cannot distinguish paths where one is a projection of the other onto some set of atomic propositions and events of interest. A precise definition of projection is given in section 4. A temporal logic fulfilling this requirement is for instance the next-less part of LTL or the state-event interval logic presented in [2]. For our example we use the former logic. One property of interest for our air condition specification could for instance be whether the amount of fuel is always greater than 5 when the air condition is on (which in fact is not true): $\varphi := \square(work \Rightarrow fuel > 5)$.

The main purpose of the technique proposed in this paper is to determine now which part of the specification actually has to be considered when checking for the property, i.e. whether it is possible to check the property on a reduced specification S^{red} such that the following holds (where $S \models \varphi$ stands for "the formula φ holds on the Kripke structure of the specification S"):

$$S \models \varphi \text{ iff } S^{red} \models \varphi$$

As we will see it is possible to omit both some of the attributes and some of the methods of the air condition for checking our property.

3   Slicing

Slicing means reducing a program or specification such that the reduced program/specification only contains those parts of the full specification which can influence a certain property under interest called the slicing criterion.

In order to determine these influences, slicing needs precise information about dependencies between different parts of a program/specification. Such dependencies are represented in a *program (or system) dependence graph*[2]. This section explains the construction of program dependence graphs for CSP-OZ classes and their slicing with respect to some temporal logic formula φ.

---

[2] We stick to the word program, although we treat specifications.

Control flow graph. In preparation for the construction of the program dependence graph we first construct the specification's control flow graph (CFG) which represents the execution order of the specification's schemas according to the specification's CSP processes. Starting with the *start.main* node, its nodes $(n \in N)$ and edges $(\longrightarrow \subseteq N \times N)$ are derived from the syntactical elements of the specification's CSP part, based on an inductive definition for each CSP operator. Nodes either correspond to schemas of the Object-Z part (like `enable_m`) or to operators in the CSP part (like nodes *interleave* and *uninterleave* for operator ||| or nodes *extchoice* and *unextchoice* for operator □). We refrain from giving a precise definition here. The result of this inductive definition for the first two process definitions in our AC example specification can be seen in fig. 1.

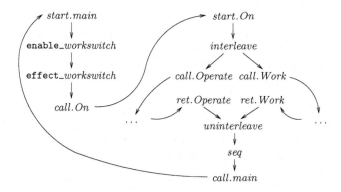

Fig. 1. Part of the control flow graph for the AC specification

Note, that we assume each syntactical CSP element and each associated CFG node to have a unique name. This can, for example, be achieved by extending their names by an index that represents the position of their textual occurrence inside the specification. For sake of clarity we omit these indices here.

Program dependence graph. The program dependence graph (PDG) represents data and control dependencies between nodes of the CFG. Thus both graphs have the same set of nodes $(n \in N)$, but not the same set of edges. An edge connects two nodes in the PDG if control or data dependencies exist between these nodes according to the definitions given below. Before we continue with the construction of the PDG we first introduce some abbreviations. When reasoning about paths inside the CFG, we let $path_{CFG}(n, n')$ denote the set of sequences of CFG nodes that are visited when walking along CFG edges from node n to node n'. When we refer to the sets of variables appearing inside schemas associated to PDG nodes, we let $mod(n)$ denote the set of variables appearing in primed form (those modified by the method of the node), $ref(n)$ denote the set of variables appearing in unprimed form (those referenced by the method of the node), and $vars(n) = mod(n) \cup ref(n)$ denote the set of all variables inside the schema.

The further construction of the PDG starts with the introduction of *control dependence edges* ($\rightarrowtail \; \subseteq N \times N$). The idea behind these edges is to represent the fact that an edge's source node controls whether the target node will be executed. In particular, a node cannot be control dependent on itself. We distinguish the following types of control dependence edges:

- Control dependence due to *nontrivial precondition* exists between an `enable` node and its `effect` node iff the `enable` schema is non-empty (i.e. not equivalent to true).
- Control dependence due to *external (resp. internal) choice* exists between an *extch* (resp. *intch*) node and its immediate CFG successors.

Additionally, some further control dependence edges are introduced in order to achieve a well-formed graph:

- *Call* and *termination* edges exist between a *call* (resp. *term*) node and its associated *start* (resp. *ret*) node.
- *Start* and *return* edges exist between a *start* (resp. *ret*) node and its immediate CFG successor.

Finally, all previously defined (direct) control dependence edges are extended to CFG successor nodes as long as they do not bypass existing control dependence edges. The idea of this definition is to integrate indirectly dependent nodes (that would otherwise be isolated) into the PDG.

- *Indirect control dependence* edges exist between two nodes n and n' iff
  $$\exists \pi \in path_{CFG}(n, n'): \forall m, m' \in \operatorname{ran} \pi : m \rightarrowtail m' \Rightarrow m = n$$

The idea of *data dependence edges* ($\rightsquigarrow \; \subseteq N \times N$) is to represent the influence that one node might have on a different node by modifying some variable that the second node references. Therefore, the source node always represents an `effect` schema, while the target node may also represent an `enable` schema. We distinguish the following types of data dependence edges:

- *Direct data dependence* exists between two nodes n and n' iff there is a CFG path between both nodes without any further modification of the relevant variable: $\exists v \in (mod(n) \cap ref(n')), \exists \pi \in path_{CFG}(n, n')$:

  $$\forall m \in \operatorname{ran} \pi : v \in mod(m) \Rightarrow (m = n \lor m = n')$$

- *Interference data dependence* exists between two nodes n and n' iff both nodes are located in different CFG branches attached to the same interleaving operator: $mod(n) \cap ref(n') \neq \varnothing \land \exists m = interleave$:

  $$\exists \pi \in path_{CFG}(m, n) \land \exists \pi' \in path_{CFG}(m, n'): \operatorname{ran} \pi \cap \operatorname{ran} \pi' = \{m\}$$

The resulting program dependence graph for the AC specification is depicted in fig. 2. Note, that two aspects of the PDG have been slightly modified in order to achieve a more concise graphical representation without changing the outcome of the slicing algorithm for the given example.

1. The separate nodes for `enable` and `effect` schemas have been combined into one single node for each event.
2. Instead of explicitly drawing all control dependence edges originating from one node to different target nodes, this set of edges is represented by a single edge between the first node and a box around the set of target nodes.

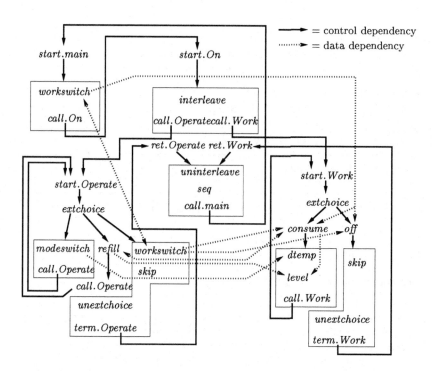

Fig. 2. Program dependence graph for the AC specification

Backward slice. For our purpose, slicing is used to determine that part of the specification that is directly or indirectly relevant for the property to be verified. Computation of this slice starts from the set of events E_φ and the set of variables V_φ that appear directly in the given formula φ. Based on this slicing criterion (E_φ, V_φ) we can determine the set of PDG nodes with direct influence on the property under interest:

$$N_\varphi = \{n \mid mod(n) \cap V_\varphi \neq \varnothing\} \cup \{n \mid \exists e \in E_\varphi : n = \texttt{enable\_}e\}$$

From this initial set of nodes we compute the backward slice by a reachability analysis of the PDG. The resulting set contains all nodes that lead via an arbitrary number of control or data dependence edges to one of the nodes that already are in N_φ. Additional to all nodes from N_φ, the backward slice contains therefore also all PDG nodes with indirect influence on the given property, i.e. it is the set of all relevant nodes for the specification slice:

$$N' = \{n' \in N \mid \exists n \in N_\varphi \colon n' \ (\mapsto \cup \rightsquigarrow)^* \ n\}$$

Thus relevant events are those associated to nodes from N'

$$E' = \{e \mid \exists n \in N' \colon n = \texttt{enable\_}e_i \vee n = \texttt{effect\_}e_i\}$$

and relevant variables are those associated to nodes from N': $V' = \bigcup\limits_{n \in N'} vars(n)$.

Reduced specification. Having determined the sets E' and V' which might influence the property (formula) under interest the slice of a specification can next be determined. In contrast to the original specification it contains

- only channels from E',
- only CSP process definitions that are projections (as defined in sect. 4, def. 8) of CSP process definitions from the original specification onto E',
- inside the state schema only variables from V',
- inside the Init schema only predicates restricting variables from V', and
- only Object-Z schemas associated with events from E'.

When slicing the class AC with respect to the formula $\varphi := \Box(work \Rightarrow fuel > 5)$, i.e. $N_\varphi = \{\mid workswitch, consume, refill \mid\}^3$, the result is:

$$N' = N \setminus \{\texttt{effect\_modeswitch}, \texttt{effect\_dtemp}, \texttt{effect\_level}\}$$
$$E' = E \setminus \{\mid modeswitch, dtemp, level \mid\}, \quad V' = V \setminus \{mode\}$$

This leads to the following specification slice:

__AC__

chan *workswitch, consume, off*   **chan** *refill* : [*f?* : *Fuel*]

main $=$ *workswitch* $\rightarrow$ *On*   *Operate* $=$ *Operate*
On $\quad=$ (*Operate* ||| *Work*) $\,\S\,$ *main* $\Box$ *refill* $\rightarrow$ *Operate*
Work $=$ *consume* $\rightarrow$ *Work* $\Box$ *workswitch* $\rightarrow$ SKIP
$\qquad\quad \Box$ *off* $\rightarrow$ SKIP

---

work : $\mathbb{B}$; *fuel* : *Fuel*   __Init__ $\neg work$

__effect_workswitch__   __enable_consume__   __effect_consume__
$\Delta(work)$ *work* $\wedge$ *fuel* > 5 $\Delta(fuel)$
work' $= \neg work$ *fuel'* $=$ *fuel* $- 1$

__enable_off__   __enable_refill__   __effect_refill__
$\neg work$ *fuel* < 100 $\Delta(fuel)$; *f?* : *Fuel*
                    fuel' $= min(fuel + f?, 100)$

---

^{3} Let $\{\mid M \mid\}$ denote the set of events over the set of methods M.

The reductions achieved by applying our slicing algorithm to this example are:

1. Event *modeswitch* has been removed together with variable *mode*, which is sensible, since the air condition's mode (heating or cooling) does not have any influence on the slicing criterion (property $\Box(work \Rightarrow fuel > 5)$).
2. Events *dtemp* and *level* have been removed, which is also sensible, since neither modelling the effect on the environment (*dtemp*) nor communicating the current amount of fuel (*level*) influences the given property.

To summarise, the specification's state space has not only been reduced with respect to its control flow space (events *dtemp*, *modeswitch* and *level*) but also with respect to its data state space (variable *mode*).

Note, that neither original nor sliced AC specification satisfies the given property, so the verification result will be negative in both cases. Nevertheless, this is exactly what we wanted to achieve: A specification slice must satisfy a slicing criterion if and only if the original specification does so.

In the next section we will show that our slicing algorithm guarantees this outcome for any specification and any slicing criterion (formulated in a linear-time stuttering invariant logic).

4   Correctness

In this section we show correctness of the slicing algorithm, i.e. we show that the Kripke structure of the reduced specification is a projection of that of the full specification. As a consequence, the property (and slicing criterion) φ (if formulated in a projection-invariant logic) then holds on the full specification if and only if it holds on the reduced specification.

We start with the definition of the notion of projection that is used in the actual correctness proof. The projection relation is first defined on paths and then lifted to Kripke structures. Intuitively, when computing the projection of a given path onto a set of atomic propositions and a set of events, one divides the path into blocks such that all states inside a block are projection-equivalent (i.e. they coincide on the given set of atomic propositions) and all events inside a block are irrelevant events (i.e. events not from the given set of events) except for the last event which is a relevant event (i.e. an event from the given set of events). The projection of the original path contains then any path such that for each of the blocks of the original path all states and irrelevant events are mapped onto one single state of the new path, while the relevant event remains in the new path as illustrated in the following sketch of a projection of a path:

	Block 0	Block 1	Block 2	Block 3
$\pi \ =$	$s_0 \ e_0 \ s_1 \ e_1$	$s_2 \ e_2$	$s_3 \ e_3 \ s_4 \ e_4$	$\ldots$
$Pr(\pi) \ \ni$	$r_0 \ e_1$	$r_1 \ e_2$	$r_2 \ e_4$	$\ldots$

Definition 6. *Let* $\pi = s_0 e_0 s_1 e_1 s_2 e_2 s_3 \ldots$ *be an* E'*-fair path over a set of atomic propositions* AP *and a set of events* $E \supseteq E'$. *The projection of* π *onto a set of atomic propositions* AP' *and a set of events* E' $(Pr_{AP',E'}(\pi))$ *contains any* E'*-fair path* $\rho = r_0 f_0 r_1 f_1 r_2 f_2 r_3 \ldots$ *such that there is a sequence of indices* $0 = i_0 < i_1 < i_2 < \ldots$ *(that divides* π *into blocks) and the following holds:*

- $\forall k \geq 0: L(s_{i_k}) \cap AP' = L(s_{i_k+1}) \cap AP' = \cdots = L(s_{i_{k+1}-1}) \cap AP' = L(r_k) \cap AP'$
  (relevant atomic propositions do not change within a block and are the same in the correspondent state of ρ),
- $\forall l \in \mathbb{N}, \forall k : i_l \leq k < i_{l+1} - 1 : e_k \notin E'$ *(no relevant events inside a block),*
- $\forall l \geq 1 : e_{i_l-1} = f_{l-1} \in E'$ *(transitions between blocks are labelled with the same relevant event as the correspondent transition of* ρ).

For comparing the Kripke structures we restrict the definition to fair paths since we are only considering satisfaction of formulae on fair paths.

Definition 7. *Let* $K_i = (S_i, S_{0,i}, \rightarrow_i, L_i)$, $i \in \{1, 2\}$, *be labelled Kripke structures over a set of atomic propositions* AP *and a set of events* E, $AP' \subseteq AP$ *a subset of the atomic propositions and* $E' \subseteq E$ *a subset of the events.* K_2 *is in the projection of* K_1 *onto* AP' *and* E' $(K_2 \in Pr_{AP',E'}(K_1))$ *iff the following holds:*

1. *For each* E'*-fair path* π *in* K_1 *there exists an* E'*-fair path* π' *in* K_2 *such that* $\pi' \in Pr_{AP',E'}(\pi)$,
2. *and vice versa, for each* E'*-fair path* π' *in* K_2 *there exists an* E'*-fair path* π *in* K_1 *such that* $\pi' \in Pr_{AP',E'}(\pi)$.

Given a temporal logic which is interpreted on paths (i.e. a linear time logic) and which is invariant under projections, such a projection relationship between two Kripke structures then guarantees that formulae which only mention propositions from AP' and events from E' hold for either both or none of the Kripke structures. Note that projection is a particular form of stuttering.

In the following we will show how such a projection relationship can be proven between full and sliced specification. For this we now first have to give a precise definition of the residual CSP processes which remain after slicing with respect to some set of events E'.

Definition 8. *Let* P *be the right side of a process definition from the CSP part of a specification and* E *be the set of events that appear in the specification. The projection of* P *w.r.t. a set of events* $E' \subseteq E$ *is inductively defined:*

1. $skip|_{E'} := skip$ *and* $stop|_{E'} := stop$
2. $(e \rightarrow P)|_{E'} := \begin{cases} P|_{E'} & \text{if } e \notin E' \\ e \rightarrow P|_{E'} & \text{else} \end{cases}$
3. $(P \circ Q)|_{E'} := P|_{E'} \circ Q|_{E'}$ *with* $\circ \in \{; , \|\|, \sqcap, \square\}$

The projection of the complete CSP part w.r.t. a set of events $E' \subseteq E$ is defined by applying the above definition to each process definition.

Next, we start the actual correctness proof with several lemmas showing the relationships between CSP processes and events and variables which remain in the specification. Due to space restrictions we only present the main ideas of the proofs. The complete proofs can be found in [1].

Our first lemma states that the projection of each residual CSP process associated to a state inside a projection block as defined in definition 6 can mimic the behaviour of the residual CSP process associated to the last state of the projection block, i.e. the relevant event at the end of the block is enabled at any previous step inside the block when computing the CSP projection.

Lemma 1 (Transitions of CSP process projections). *Let* $P_j, \ldots, P_{j+k+1}$ *be CSP processes,* E' *a set of relevant events,* $e_{j+1}, \ldots, e_{j+k-2}$ *irrelevant events* $(\notin E')$, *and* e_{j+k} *a relevant event* $(\in E')$, *such that*

$$P_j \xrightarrow{e_{j+1}} P_{j+2} \xrightarrow{e_{j+3}} \ldots \xrightarrow{e_{j+k-2}} P_{j+k-1} \xrightarrow{e_{j+k}} P_{j+k+1}$$

is a valid transition sequence. Then the following holds[4]:

$$P \xrightarrow{e_{j+k}} P_{j+k+1}|_{E'} \text{ with } P \in \{P_j|_{E'}, \ldots, P_{j+k-1}|_{E'}\}$$

Proof: The proof builds up on another lemma considering the case of a single CSP transition: Either this transition is labelled with a relevant event $e \in E'$ or with an irrelevant event $e \notin E'$. In the former case it is easy to see that the associated projection also can perform this event e, while in the latter case some further considerations lead to the conclusion that the associated projection will finally perform the same relevant event as the original process. Both cases are shown by induction over the structure of the respective CSP processes. For the proof of the present lemma we then only need to combine these two cases in an induction over the length of the projection block and come to the desired result.

Next, we bridge the gap between transition sequences that we can observe for CSP processes and paths that are present in the associated control flow graph.

Lemma 2 (CSP transition sequences and control flow graph paths). *Let* C *be a class specification,* CFG *the control flow graph of* C, K^{CSP} *the Kripke structure associated to the CSP part of* C, *and* $P \xrightarrow{e} Q \xrightarrow{f} R$ *a transition sequence of* K^{CSP}. *Then the two nodes* enable_e *and* enable_f *of* CFG *are related in either one of the following ways:*

1. *There exists a path in* CFG *which leads from* enable_e *to* enable_f.
2. *There exists a node interleave[i] in* CFG *which has* enable_e *and* enable_f *as successors in different branches.*

Proof: The proof consists of two layers of induction over the structure of P and Q such that each possible combination of CSP constructs is considered and shown to fall into one of the two cases mentioned in the lemma.

Our last lemma states that the set of irrelevant events appearing inside a projection block does not have any influence on the relevant variables (resp. atomic propositions) associated to the states inside the block.

---

[4] Note, that $P_j|_{E'} = \ldots = P_{j+k-1}|_{E'}$ does not necessarily hold.

Lemma 3 (No influence of irrelevant events on relevant variables). *Let C be a class specification with an associated Kripke structure K, let*

$$(s_j, P_j) \xrightarrow{e_{j+1}} (s_{j+2}, P_{j+2}) \xrightarrow{e_{j+3}} \ldots \xrightarrow{e_{j+k-2}} (s_{j+k-1}, P_{j+k-1}) \xrightarrow{e_{j+k}} (s_{j+k+1}, P_{j+k+1})$$

be a transition sequence that is part of a path of K. Let furthermore E' be the set of relevant events computed by the slicing algorithm with respect to some formula φ (with an associated set of variables V_φ), and $e_{j+1}, \ldots, e_{j+k-2} \notin E'$, and $e_{j+k} \in E'$. Then the following holds:

$$s_j|_{\overline{V}} = \ldots = s_{j+k-1}|_{\overline{V}} \quad with \ \overline{V} = V_\varphi \cup \bigcup_{e \in \{e_i \in E' | i \geq j\}} ref(e)$$

Proof: We show this by contradiction: Supposed, the equality does not hold, we show that this implies the existence of a data dependence between an event inside the block and the relevant event. In consequence, this leads to the event inside the block being a member of the set of relevant events.

Now we come to our main theorem that states the existence of a projection relationship between the Kripke structures associated to the original and to the sliced specification.

Theorem 1. *Let C^{full} be a class specification and C^{red} the class obtained when slicing C^{full} wrt. a formula φ, associated with sets of events E_φ, variables V_φ and atomic propositions AP_φ over V_φ. Let E' and AP' be the set of events and atomic propositions, respectively, which the slicing algorithm delivers as those of interest (in particular $E_\varphi \subseteq E'$ and $V_\varphi \subseteq V'$). Let furthermore K^{full} (resp. K^{red}) be the corresponding Kripke structures. Then the following holds:*

$$K^{red} \in Pr_{AP_\varphi, E'}(K^{full})$$

Proof: According to the definition of the projection relation we need to consider two cases: (1) We have to show that for any E'-fair path of K^{full} we can construct an E'-fair path of K^{red} and (2) vice versa. For both directions we define a set of variables $\overline{V}_i$ that contains all variables associated to the slicing criterion and for each position i of the respective path all variables that are referenced by relevant events $e_i \in E'$ at position i or beyond:

$$\overline{V}_i = V_\varphi \cup \bigcup_{e \in \{e_j \in E' | j \geq i\}} ref(e)$$

1. Let $\pi = s_0 e_1 s_2 e_3 \ldots$ be an E'-fair path of K^{full} with $s_i = (s_i^{OZ}, P_i)$. We construct a sequence $\rho' = t_0 f_1 t_2 f_3 \ldots$ with $t_i = (t_i^{OZ}, Q_i)$ and

$$t_i^{OZ} : s_i^{OZ}|_{\overline{V}_i}, \qquad Q_i : P_i|_{E'} \qquad f_i : \begin{cases} e_i & \text{if } e_i \in E' \\ nop & \text{else} \end{cases}$$

Out of ρ' we construct a sequence ρ by eliminating all subsequences of the form $nop\ t_i$. We have to show that ρ is an E'-fair path of K^{red}. To this end we use induction over the length of ρ where we apply lemma 3 and lemma 1 when showing that we can remove some intermediate sequences from the original path such that all schemas and all process definitions from the reduced specifications are satisfied.

2. Let $\rho = t_0 f_1 t_2 f_3 \ldots$ be an E'-fair path of K^{red} with $t_i = (t_i^{OZ}, Q_i)$. We inductively construct a path of K^{full}

$$\pi = s_0 e_0^1 s_0^1 e_0^3 \ldots s_0^{n_0} e_1 s_2 e_2^1 s_2^2 e_2^3 \ldots s_2^{n_2} e_3 s_4 e_4^1 s_4^2 \ldots$$

with s_i of the form (s_i^{OZ}, P_i) and s_i^j of the form $(s_i^{OZ,j}, P_i^j)$ such that $s_i^{OZ,j}|_{\overline{V}_i} = s_i^{OZ}|_{\overline{V}_i} = t_i^{OZ}|_{\overline{V}_i}$ and the P_i^j are intermediate processes towards P_i^{j,n_i} which projected onto E' gives Q_i, and $e_i = f_i \in E'$ and $e_i^j \notin E'$.

In the induction we apply lemma 3 to show that we can safely insert the necessary additional steps in the Object-Z part of ρ such that the associated schemas of the full specification are satisfied. Furthermore, we apply lemma 2 to show that these additional steps are possible according to the process definitions from the full specification such that π is indeed a path of K^{full}.

5   Conclusion

In this paper we have proposed a slicing algorithm for an integrated formal method covering state-based as well as behaviour-oriented aspects. We have shown correctness of the algorithm with respect to a projection relationship between the paths of the full and the reduced specification (starting from some set of relevant variables and events). Thus the reduction preserves formulae (speaking about these relevant variables and events) of any linear-time temporal logic which is invariant under projection. Slicing can thus help to reduce the specification before verification. Since the program dependence graph is in size linear in the syntactic representation of the specification (and thus usually much smaller than the state space), slicing can also be carried out in cases when model checking is too complex. Furthermore, the program dependence graph only has to be constructed once for every specification, only backward reachability has to be computed for every formula. Our slicing technique acts as a preparatory step in the verification of CSP-OZ specifications; the following model checking step is carried out by a constraint-based abstraction refinement model checker as recently proposed by Hoenicke and Maier [9].

In the future we plan to extend this technique to a third modelling dimension, namely timing requirements as covered by the formalism CSP-OZ-DC [10] (an extension of CSP-OZ with Duration Calculus). Furthermore, in order to complete the process of slicing and model checking, a non-trivial problem still remains to be solved: How can we relate a counterexample obtained for a reduced specification to a corresponding one for the original specification?

Related work. There are two strands of research which touch upon our work. The first is on slicing of formal specifications, which has mainly been done for Z specifications [3,22]. These works, however, do not consider verification, i.e. slicing is not carried out with respect to temporal logic properties of the specification. The second area of related work concerns slicing used for reducing programs before verification, as for instance done in [7] for Java (preserving LTL$_{-X}$ properties) and in [19] for SAL programs (preserving CTL$^*_{-X}$ properties). Slicing for integrated specification techniques has so far not been considered.

References

1. I. Brückner and H. Wehrheim. Slicing CSP-OZ Specifications for Verification. Technical Report 7, SFB/TR 14 AVACS, http://www.avacs.org/, 2005.
2. I. Brückner and H. Wehrheim. Slicing Object-Z Specifications for Verification. In *ZB 2005*, volume 3455 of LNCS, pages 414–433. Springer-Verlag, 2005.
3. D. Chang and D. Richardson. Static and Dynamic Specification Slicing. In *ACM SIGSOFT ISSTA*, pages 138–153. ACM, 1994.
4. E. Clarke, O. Grumberg, and D. Peled. *Model Checking*. MIT Press, 1999.
5. C. Fischer. CSP-OZ: A Combination of Object-Z and CSP. In *FMOODS '97*, volume 2, pages 423–438. Chapman & Hall, 1997.
6. W. Grieskamp, M. Heisel, and H. Dörr. Specifying Embedded Systems with Statecharts and Z: An Agenda for Cyclic Software Components. In Egidio Astesiano, editor, *FASE '98*, volume 1382 of *LNCS*, pages 88–106. Springer, 1998.
7. J. Hatcliff, M. Dwyer, and H. Zheng. Slicing Software for Model Construction. *Higher-order and Symbolic Computation*, 13(4):315–353, 2000.
8. C.A.R. Hoare. *Communicating Sequential Processes*. Prentice Hall, 1985.
9. J. Hoenicke and P. Maier. Model-checking specifications integrating processes, data and time. In *FM 2005*, volume 3582 of *LNCS*, pages 465–480. Springer, 2005.
10. J. Hoenicke and E.-R. Olderog. CSP-OZ-DC: A Combination of Specification Techniques for Processes, Data and Time. *NJC*, 9(4):301–334, 2002.
11. ISO/IEC. *Enhancements to LOTOS (E-LOTOS) – International Standard 15437:2001*. ISO/IEC – Information technology, 2001.
12. B. Mahony and J.S. Dong. Timed communicating Object-Z. *IEE Transactions on Software Engineering*, 26(2):150–177, 2000.
13. L. Millett and T. Teitelbaum. Issues in Slicing Promela and its Applications to Model Checking. *Software Tools and Technology Transfer*, 2(4):343–349, 2000.
14. A.W. Roscoe. *The Theory and Practice of Concurrency*. Prentice Hall, 1998.
15. G. Smith. *The Object-Z Specification Language*. Kluwer Academic Publisher, 2000.
16. G. Smith and J. Derrick. Specification, Refinement and Verification of Concurrent Systems. *Formal Methods in System Design*, 18(3):249 – 284, 2001.
17. F. Tip. A Survey of Program Slicing Techniques. *Journal of Programming Languages*, 3(3):121–189, 1995.
18. H. Treharne and S.A. Schneider. Communicating B Machines. In *ZB 2002*, volume 2272 of *LNCS*, pages 416–435. Springer, 2002.
19. N. Shankar V. Ganesh, H. Saidi. Slicing SAL. Technical report, SRI International, http://theory.stanford.edu/, 1999.
20. M. Weiser. Programmers use slices when debugging. *Communications of the ACM*, 25(7):446–452, 1982.
21. J.C.P. Woodcock and A.L.C. Cavalcanti. The Semantics of Circus. In *ZB 2002*, volume 2272 of LNCS, pages 184–203. Springer-Verlag, 2002.
22. Fangjun Wu and Tong Yi. Slicing Z Specifications. *SIGPLAN*, 39(8):39–48, 2004.

A Static Communication Elimination Algorithm for Distributed System Verification*

Francesc Babot, Miquel Bertran, and August Climent

Informàtica La Salle, Universitat Ramon Llull, Barcelona
{fbabot, miqbe, augc}@salleURL.edu

Abstract. A schema of communication elimination laws for distributed programs and systems is mathematically justified in a new equivalence, which was introduced in a recent work. A complete set of applicability conditions is derived for them. A formal communication elimination algorithm, applying the laws as reductions, is mathematically justified for an important class of distributed programs and systems, whose communications are outside the scope of selections. The analysis provides the basis for extensions to general statements. State-vector reduction stands as one of the motivations for this static analysis approach. It has already been applied in an equivalence proof of a non-trivial pipelined distributed system, reported in prior works. The state-vector reduction obtained in this proof, yielding a reduction factor of 2^{-607} for the upper-bound on the number of states, is presented in this communication.

1 Introduction

Imperative notations with explicit parallelism and synchronous communication statements provide an intuitive, explicit, and complete framework to express distributed programs and systems with perspective and clarity. OCCAM [1,2,3], the *simple programming language* SPL of Manna and Pnueli [4,5], PROMELA of the SPIN model checker [6], and the *shared-variable language*[++], SVL[++], in [7] are representatives of them.

Automatic verification approaches work on the transition system of the program, defining the semantics of the distributed system. This transition system has often infinitely many states, and always a large size compared to the size of the program modeling the distributed system, which is always finite. For instance, if the number of variables is n, each holding an integer of m bits, the number of states may be of the order of $2^{n \times m}$, whereas the size of the program remains of an order close to n only. These considerations suggest that static automatic verification approaches, avoiding the transition system, working directly on the program would have less computational complexity, in principle. Following this line of work, static analysis methods for state reduction [8,9,10] have been proposed as a step prior to model checking. They reduce the size of the transition system and hence the complexity of model checking.

---

* Work partially supported by the CICYT under project TIC2003-09420-C02-02.

K.-K. Lau and R. Banach (Eds.): ICFEM 2005, LNCS 3785, pp. 375–389, 2005.

Along the same direction, work towards the justification of a static analysis algorithm for formal simplification of a distributed program by eliminating its inner communications, has been undertaken [11,12]. Different static transformation systems were proposed in [13,14,15], without communication elimination. The communication elimination algorithm applies a set of equivalence laws suitable for communication elimination. The resulting inner communication-free program can be transformed interactively, with another set of laws, into a sequential program with less variables than the initial distributed program, but equivalent to it. Altogether, this constitutes a *distributed program simplification* (DPS) proof which can be combined with model checking or interactive verification as a succeeding step, reducing overall proof complexity. In many cases, only an equivalent purely sequential program has to be verified. It is remarked that, within DPS, only communication elimination for selection-free programs (see below) is algorithmic, automatic. This communication reports on substantial state-space reductions obtained in a DPS proof of a pipelined processor model.

The algorithm applies both proper communication elimination and auxiliary laws. The latter, although not eliminating any communication, are necessary in order to transform the program into a form ready for a proper elimination law to be applied. A set of laws for OCCAM was given in [16]. Although a simple communication elimination law was included, rather than communication elimination, the focus there was to obtain normal forms and to define the semantics of the notation. Communication closed layered systems were introduced in [17], and some laws for them are given in [7] in the framework of SVL^{++}. The aim there was formal design by transformation. For instance, sequential-parallelism and iteration unfolding transformations. No communication elimination law was reported. Some laws for SPL are given in [4], with an SPL semantics based on fair transition systems (FTS), but none is for communication elimination.

A set of relations suitable for communication elimination was given and proved sound in [11], showing the necessity of avoiding strong fairness, and where the notion of equivalence was assimilated to congruence, a very strong equivalence. This had the drawback of limiting the formulation of most communication elimination laws to unidirectional refinements. A weaker equivalence, in which all laws are equivalences was presented and studied in [12].

A communication elimination proof of a distributed fast Fourier transform was outlined in [11]. A DPS proof of a pipelined processor model, carried out with the help of a tool which implements a communication elimination algorithm, has been reported in [18]. These proofs used the communication elimination laws. Nevertheless, neither their mathematical justification, with their applicability conditions, nor that of the communication elimination algorithm have been published. This is accomplished in the present work, where the proper communication elimination laws are mathematically justified in the new weaker equivalence and their complete set of applicability conditions is derived. In addition, a communication elimination reduction algorithm is proposed and justified.

The paper is organized as follows. After a section on notation and necessary background notions, a section on bounded communication statements follows.

These are used to define and study communication elimination laws and the algorithm in the following section. Extension to more general statements is given next. After this, substantial results on reduction of an upper bound on the number of states are reported. A section on conclusions and further work ends the paper.

2   Notation and Equivalence

2.1   Basic Notions and Auxiliary Laws

A reduced version of SPL is used. The basic statements are **skip, nil, stop**, the assignment $u := e$, send $\alpha \Leftarrow e$, and receive $\alpha \Rightarrow u$. We limit our work to synchronous channels α, which will be referred to as *channels*. In them both the sender and the receiver wait for each other before exchanging a value and continuing execution. Communication statements will be referred to as *communications*. Both channels and variables are declared globally.

Concatenation is n-ary: $[S_1; \cdots; S_n]$. The iterations are $[\textbf{while } c \textbf{ do } S]$, where c is a boolean expression, and $[\textbf{loop forever do } S]$, which is defined as $[\textbf{while } true \textbf{ do } S]$. The *cooperation* statement is also n-ary: $[S_1 || \cdots || S_n]$. Its substatements S_j are its *top parallel statements*. The cooperation is the *least common ancestor* (LCA) of them. It will be assumed throughout the paper that the S_j's are *disjoint*, in the sense that they only share read variables, and that they communicate values through synchronous channels only. The *regular selection* and the *communication selection* statements are non-deterministic and have, respectively, the forms $[b_1, S_1 \textbf{ or } \cdots \textbf{ or } b_n, S_n]$ and $[b_1, c_1, S_1 \textbf{ or } \cdots \textbf{ or } b_n, c_n, S_n]$, where the b_i's are boolean expressions referred to as *boolean guards*, and the c_i's are synchronous communication statements referred to as *communication guards*. Statement labels, such as l in $l : S$, are used to refer to statements.

Two statements are ordered by the *concatenation ordering* if their LCA is a concatenation statement. This corresponds to the execution order.

Internal channels communicate parallel substatements within a statement S, and are considered to be hidden from the outside. An *external channel* of S is any other channel within S. *Internal communication* and *external communication* will mean communication substatements of S over internal and external channels, respectively. Two internal communications of S form a *matching communication pair* if they are parallel, and one is an output and the other an input over the same channel. Two pairs are *disjoint* when they share no communication. Statements A and B are said to *communicate* when they are parallel and at least a communication in A and another in B form a matching pair.

There are both proper elimination and auxiliary laws. The latter, although not eliminating any communication directly, are needed to transform a statement to a form where a proper communication elimination law can be applied. Some intuitive auxiliary laws are available in [11], where it is shown that many of them do not hold when strong fairness is assumed. Some of them are the congruences **nil**; $S \approx S$, $S||$ **nil** $\approx S$, S; **skip** $\approx S$, $S||$ **skip** $\approx S$. In addition, both sequential and parallel composition are associative. The latter is also commutative.

2.2   Interface Equivalence

The proper communication elimination laws to be presented in this work do not hold for congruence. A weaker equivalence has been introduced in [12] under the name of *input/output equivalence*, which is referred to here as *interface equivalence*. A summary of the related notions is given now. Congruent statements are always interface equivalent but not vice versa. The proper communication elimination laws are interface equivalences.

In the semantics of fair transition systems (FTS) [4,5], a statement S denotes a FTS with states and transitions. A *computation* is a sequence of states of the FTS denoted by S, starting at an initial state with a transition taking any state to its successor. A *reduced behavior*, with respect to a set of observed variables $\mathcal{O}$ is a computation whose components of variables outside this set and whose stuttering steps are deleted. This semantics is extended here by adding to the set $\mathcal{O}$ an auxiliary variable for each channel in S which is not in I, the set of *internal channels*. The extended set $\mathcal{O}$ is referred to as *interface set*.

Auxiliary variables are also named *channel variables*, and record the value passed at the last communication event of the channel. An *interface behavior* is the extension of the notion of reduced behavior to the extended set $\mathcal{O}$. Thus, it records the history of values associated to both variables and channels of the interface. The relative order of value changes of different variables and channels is preserved in interface behaviors. However, interface equivalence, the weaker equivalence which is needed, can neglect this order and still preserve the input/output relation. Then, instead of comparing behaviors, *components* of behaviors are compared. *Components* are lists of values taken by a given variable within the behavior, with independence of those taken by the other variables. The following definitions depend on this notion.

Definition 1 (Equivalence of interface behaviors). *Two interface behaviors are equivalent when they share the same interface set, and for all its variables the two components of both behaviors are equal.*

Definition 2 (Interface equivalent statements). *Two statements S_1 and S_2 are interface equivalent with respect to an interface set $\mathcal{O}$, written $S_1 =_{\mathcal{O}} S_2$, when any interface behavior of any of them is equivalent to an interface behavior of the other.*

3   Bounded Communication Statements

The analysis of communication elimination is started below for some *bounded communication* (BC) statements. This and other required notions are introduced in this section, where S and I denote such a statement and the set of its internal channels, respectively.

Definition 3 (Bounded Communication Statement). *A statement S is said to be of* bounded communication *if it meets the following requirements:*

1. *All its parallel substatements are disjoint, in the sense that they only read their shared data variables, should they have some.*
2. *Any internal communication is outside iteration bodies.*

Execution of a bounded communication statement generates only a finite number of communication events.

Definition 4 (Communication front). *The* communication front *of S, written* ComFront(I,S), *is the subset of minimal elements of the set of communication statements in its concatenation ordering.*

Guards of communication selection statements may be in this set.

Definition 5 (Set of competing pairs). *The set of* competing pairs *of S, written* CompPairs(I,S) *is, by definition,*

$$\{ (l, m) \mid l, m \in \text{ComFront}(I, S) \wedge l \text{ matches } m \}$$

Lemma 1 (Non-Communicating Heading Statements). *Let G be either a communication ℓ over $\alpha \in I$ or a communication selection statement in S one of whose guards is a communication statement ℓ over $\alpha \in I$, and $\ell \in$ ComFront(I, S). Let H be a statement in S which precedes G in its concatenation order. Then, H does not communicate with any substatement P of S which is parallel to G.*

Definition 6 (Selection-free   BC-statement). *A   selection-free BC-statement is a BC-statement all of whose internal communications are outside the scope of both selections and communication selections.*

The execution of a selection-free BC-statement generates a constant finite number of internal communication events. The analysis will be limited to these BC-statements. For any of its matching pairs $(l, m) \in CompPairs(I, S)$, S always has a cooperation substatement which is the LCA of statements l and m. G^l and G^m are the top statements, in this cooperation, corresponding to l and m, respectively.

Lemma 2 (Standard form of pair-embedding top statements). *Symbol x denotes both l and m.*

- *Let $(l, m) \in CompPairs(I, S)$, and α be its channel.*
- *Let G^x, either G^l or G^m, be the top statement, embedding either l or m, of the LCA cooperation of l and m.*
- *For $k = 0, 1, \ldots$, let T_k^x and P_k^x be bounded communication statements, in general with internal and external communications ; and H_k^x be statements which do not have internal communications.*
- *Let G_0^x be either one of the communication statements $\alpha \Leftarrow e$ and $\alpha \Rightarrow u$.*
- *Let $G_k^x = H_{k-1}^x; [G_{k-1}^x \| P_{k-1}^x]; T_{k-1}^x$, for $k = 1, 2, \ldots$, be a sequence of statements.*

> – *Then, S can be transformed into a congruent statement such that the embedding top parallel substatements G^x, for $x = l$ and $x = r$, have been replaced by a statement of the form of $G_{n_x}^x$ for some finite integers n_l and n_r, respectively.*

Justification. The reasoning is made for $x = l$, the other case would be similar. It is clear that the statement G_0^l can be identified within G^l, as either one of its two possible forms in the lemma. Now, since S is selection-free and BC, G_0^l can be neither within the scope of any selection statement nor within any proper alternative of a general communication selection statement. Hence, the LCA of G_0^l is either a concatenation or a cooperation.

In the former case P_0^l is the nil statement, H_0^l and T_0^l correspond to the statements preceding and succeeding G_0^l in the concatenation. Hence, G_1^l can be identified as

$$G_1^l = H_0^l; [G_0^l || \text{ nil }]; T_0^l$$

In the latter case, where the LCA of G_0^l is a cooperation, if one of its top parallel statements is the other G^r, then $n_l = 0$, $G^l = G_0^l$. Otherwise, P_0^l corresponds to all the parallel statements, and G_1^l can be identified as

$$G_1^l = H_0^l; [G_0^l || P_0^l]; T_0^l$$

where H_0^l or T_0^l may be **nil**. In the above cases, where G_1^l has been identified within G^l, the process can be continued. The same reasoning made with G_0^l can be applied now to G_1^l, either terminating or obtaining G_2^l. Hence, an inductive process can be followed. But this process cannot go on forever since G^l is of finite size. Therefore, it will stop at some $G_{n_l}^l$, after a finite number of iterations n_l, as the lemma states. Congruence with the initial G^l follows from the fact that all the nil statements can be introduced by some of the auxiliary laws, always congruences, cited in section 2 and justified in [11]. □

4   Elimination from Selection-Free BC-Statements

The elimination of a single matching pair is considered first. The recursive elimination of all the internal communications of S will be considered later. The simplest case corresponds to $[\alpha \Leftarrow e || \alpha \Rightarrow u] \approx [u := e]$ which we identify with $[G_0^l || G_0^r] \approx G_0$. As it will be shown later, for the more complex forms the elimination law is defined for an arbitrary $k \geq 0$ as

$$\begin{bmatrix} H_k^l; \\ [G_k^l || P_k^l]; \\ T_k^l \end{bmatrix} || \begin{bmatrix} H_k^r; \\ [G_k^r || P_k^r]; \\ T_k^r \end{bmatrix} =_{\mathcal{O}} \begin{bmatrix} [& H_k^l & || & H_k^r &]; \\ [G_k & || & P_k^l & || & P_k^r]; \\ [& T_k^l & || & T_k^r &] \end{bmatrix}$$

where the H statements have no inner communication. When this equivalence is identified with $[G_{k+1}^l || G_{k+1}^r] =_{\mathcal{O}} G_{k+1}$, a recursive definition of G_k^l, G_k^r, and G_k is obtained. For a given value of $k = k_0$, the corresponding law would be constructed recursively, applying the same equivalence to the inner G_k, which stands for $[G^l_{k-1}||G^r_{k-1}]$, for $k = k_0, k_0 - 1, \cdots, 1$. Finally, the last inner parallelism $[G^l_0||G^r_0]$ would be replaced by the corresponding right hand side G_0 of the basic congruence given earlier, and the law for $k = k_0$ would thus be obtained. There is a law for any finite integer $k = 0, 1, \cdots$ which may be applied as a reduction from left to right in order to eliminate a single communication pair.

Observe that some substatements, like T^l_k and P^r_k, are parallel in one side but not in the other. This disordering may introduce deadlock. Nevertheless, there are cases where deadlock is not introduced. For instance, for some communication closed layer systems. These systems, together with their laws, are treated in [7], with a semantics different to the one used here. But the laws also hold in our semantics. The following is an example which we need later.

Lemma 3 (Communication-closed-layers).   *Let   the   statement   pairs*
(A_1, B_2) and (A_2, B_1) be non-communicating, and $[B_1; A_1]$ be disjoint with
$[B_2; A_2]$. Then

$$[[B_1; A_1]||[B_2; A_2]] =_{\mathcal{O}} [[B_1||B_2]; [A_1||A_2]]$$

and either both sides are deadlock-free or none of them is.

Justification.   The only statements which change their concatenation order relation are the pairs which do not communicate. Therefore deadlock can not be introduced, since processes can only wait for internal communications to occur. Also, the same pairs are disjoint as a consequence of the assumptions. This guarantees that variable components do not change. Hence, interface behaviors of both sides remain equivalent. See subsection 2.2.   □

Lemma 4 (G-statement pairing equivalence).   *Let all parallel statements below be disjoint and $\mathcal{O}$ be the union of all variables and channel variables in them, but excluding the variables of internal channels. Let H^l and H^r contain no communication statements over internal channels. Then*

$$\begin{bmatrix} H^l; \\ [G^l || P^l]; \\ T^l \end{bmatrix} || \begin{bmatrix} H^r; \\ [G^r || P^r]; \\ T^r \end{bmatrix} =_{\mathcal{O}} \begin{bmatrix} [\ H^l\ ||\ H^r\ ]; \\ [G^l || G^r || P^l || P^r]; \\ [\ T^l\ ||\ T^r\ ] \end{bmatrix}$$

provided that the following statement pairs do not communicate: (P^l, T^r), (P^r, T^l), (G^l, T^r), (G^r, T^l) . Also, under the same conditions, either both sides are deadlock-free or none of them is.

Justification.   One of the changes of the concatenation order of the substatements of both sides of the equivalence is due to T^l, which is parallel to H^r, G^r, and P^r in the left but in concatenation with the same statements in the right. However, it remains parallel to T^r in both sides. A similar change takes place in relation to T^r. Due to this, the lemma follows by a two-fold application of lemma 3, the communication restrictions of our lemma, and the fact that the H statements do not have internal communications (see lemma 1).   □

The communication elimination law presented earlier, would be derived by the iterative application of the equivalence of lemma 4, from left to right starting at the outermost level $max(n_l, n_r)$ (see lemma 2) . For the moment, it can be assumed that $n_l = n_r$. The general case is treated after theorem 4. The restrictions of lemma 4 should be fulfilled at each application. But in addition, in all the other applications, $[G^l||G^r]$ at the right hand side of the equivalence of lemma 4 is reduced to G with the same equivalence, applying it from left to right. Now, the substatements that change order, considered in the justification of lemma 4 above, have P^l and P^r, at the outer level, in parallel. This may be a further source of deadlock. The following lemma formulates the conditions for deadlock prevention in this new situation. Some notation is introduced before.

Definition 7 (Communication precedence). *Let C be a statement which is clear in a given context, and statements A and B be parallel to C. Then, the symbolism $cw(A) < cw(B)$ will mean that, within C, the communications with A precede, in the concatenation order, all the communications with B.*

Lemma 5 (Reduction of G-statement parallelism). *Let the equivalence of lemma 4 be represented as $\bar{G}^l||\bar{G}^r =_O \bar{G}$, where the substatements of the three $\bar{G}$'s and the statements below satisfy the conditions stated in it. Then*

$$
\begin{bmatrix}
[& \bar{H}^l & || & \bar{H}^r &]; \\
[\bar{G}^l & || & \bar{G}^r & || & \bar{P}^l & || & \bar{P}^r]; \\
[& \bar{T}^l & || & \bar{T}^r &]
\end{bmatrix}
=_O
\begin{bmatrix}
[& \bar{H}^l & || & \bar{H}^r &]; \\
[\bar{G} & || & \bar{P}^l & || & \bar{P}^r]; \\
[& \bar{T}^l & || & \bar{T}^r &]
\end{bmatrix}
$$

provided that, within $\bar{P}^l$ and $\bar{P}^r$,

$$cw(P^l) < cw(T^r), \quad cw(P^r) < cw(T^l), \quad cw(G^l) < cw(T^r), \quad cw(G^r) < cw(T^l)$$

Also, under the same conditions, either both sides are deadlock-free or none of them is.

Justification. In order to obtain the right hand side of the equivalence of this lemma, the equivalence of lemma 4 is applied to the inner parallelism between $\bar{G}^l$ and $\bar{G}^r$. The only statements which are parallel to $\bar{G}^l$ and $\bar{G}^r$ in the left hand side statement are $\bar{P}^l$ and $\bar{P}^r$. Also, they are the only ones which are parallel to $\bar{G}$ in the right hand side statement. But, in the G-statement pairing equivalence, the statements (P^l, T^r), (P^r, T^l), (G^l, T^r), and (G^r, T^l) are parallel in the l.h.s. but concatenated in the above order in the r.h.s., therefore the communications with these statements within $\bar{P}^l$ and $\bar{P}^r$ must have the same order, should they exist. But this holds if the communication order restrictions of the lemma are fulfilled. Finally, the equivalence follows from lemma 4.   □

All the restrictions of lemma 4, that have to be fulfilled in the iterative application to $[G^l_{n+1}||G^r_{n+1}]$ of the equivalence in it, are gathered in the following

Theorem 1 (Non-communication restrictions for eliminability). *A set of necessary conditions to be fulfilled by* $[G^l_{n+1}||G^r_{n+1}]$ *for the eliminability of its communication pair* (l, m) *is that the following substatement pairs do not communicate*

1. (P^l_i, T^r_k) *and* (P^r_i, T^l_k) *for* $k \in [0, n]$ *and* $i \in [0, k]$.

2. (T^r_i, T^l_j) *for* $i, j \in [0, n]$, $i \neq j$.

Justification. In order to obtain the elimination law stated at the beginning of this section, the equivalence of lemma 4 is applied from left to right for $k = n$ first. At this outermost level, its non communication restrictions apply to the pairs $(P^l_n, T^r_n), (G^l_n, T^r_n)$ and the two symmetric ones $(P^r_n, T^l_n), (G^r_n, T^l_n)$. But G^l_n in the second pair can be split, for $n > 0$, into all of its substatements, giving the restrictions $(P^l_i, T^r_n), (T^l_i, T^r_n)$, for $i = n - 1, n - 2, \cdots, 1, 0$. Together with the first pair, these can be re-expressed as

(P^l_i, T^r_n), for $i = 0, \cdots, n$,   and (T^l_i, T^r_n),   for $i = 0, \cdots, n - 1$,   for $n > 0$.

Proceeding similarly with the two symmetric restriction pairs $(P^r_n, T^l_n), (G^r_n, T^l_n)$, the following additional restriction pairs are obtained

(P^r_i, T^l_n), for $i = 0, \cdots, n$,   and (T^r_i, T^l_n),   for $i = 0, \cdots, n - 1$,   for $n > 0$.

However, similar restrictions have to hold at all levels $k = n, n - 1, \cdots, 1$ of application of the above reduction. But for $n = 0$ we have still the restrictions

$$(P^l_0, T^r_0) ,\ \ (G^l_0, T^r_0) ,\ \ (P^r_0, T^l_0) ,\ \ (G^r_0, T^l_0)$$

Putting together all the *P-T* restrictions, we have that, for each $k = 0, 1, \cdots,$ n the following communication restrictions should hold (P^l_i, T^r_k), and (P^r_i, T^l_k), for $i = 0, 1, \cdots, k$, which is restriction 1 of the lemma. Putting together all the *T-T* restrictions, we have: $(T^l_i, T^r_k), (T^r_i, T^l_k)$, for $k = 1, \cdots, n$ and $i = 0, \cdots, k - 1$. But this is equivalent to restriction 2 of the lemma. Restrictions (G^l_0, T^r_0) and (G^r_0, T^l_0) can be ignored since G^l_0 and G^r_0, which form a matching pair, communicate among themselves only. □

In a similar manner, all the restrictions of lemma 5 are gathered in the following

Lemma 6 (Broad communication order restrictions). *A set of communication order restrictions to be fulfilled by* $[G^l_{n+1}||G^r_{n+1}]$ *for the eliminability of its communication pair* (l, m), *without introducing deadlock, is that for* $k \in [1, n]$ *and* $i \in [0, k - 1]$, *within* P^l_k *and* P^r_k

$cw(P^l_i) < cw(T^r_i) ,\ \ cw(P^r_i) < cw(T^l_i) ,\ \ cw(G^l_i) < cw(T^r_i) ,\ \ cw(G^r_i) < cw(T^l_i) .$

Justification. We keep track of the communication order restrictions of lemma 5 in the recursive application to $[G^l_{n+1}||G^r_{n+1}]$ of the equivalence of lemma 4, as a reduction from left to right. Thus, concerning P^l_n and P^r_n , the second outermost application gives the restrictions

and
$$cw(P_{n-1}^l) < cw(T_{n-1}^r) , \;\; cw(P_{n-1}^r) < cw(T_{n-1}^l)$$
$$cw(G_{n-1}^l) < cw(T_{n-1}^r) , \;\; cw(G_{n-1}^r) < cw(T_{n-1}^l).$$

Similarly, the next outermost application gives restrictions on the communications of P_{n-1}^l and P_{n-1}^r but also on those of P_n^l and P_n^r , since the two latter statements are also parallel to P_{n-2} , T_{n-2} and to G_{n-2} , T_{n-2}. These restrictions on the communications within these four P statements are

$$cw(P_{n-2}^l) < cw(T_{n-2}^r) \;\; , \;\; cw(P_{n-2}^r) < cw(T_{n-2}^l) \;\; , \;\; cw(G_{n-2}^l) < cw(T_{n-2}^r) \;\; ,$$
$$cw(G_{n-2}^r) < cw(T_{n-2}^l)$$

Within P_n^l and P_n^r only , and continuing until the last application, at $k = 1$, the following communication restrictions should hold: for $i \in [0, n-1]$,

$$cw(P_i^l) < cw(T_i^r) \;\; , \;\; cw(P_i^r) < cw(T_i^l) \;\; , \;\; cw(G_i^l) < cw(T_i^r) \;\; ,$$
$$cw(G_i^r) < cw(T_i^l) \;.$$

These conditions should also hold within P_k^l and P_k^r , for all $k \in [1, n]$ and $i \in [0, k-1]$, as the lemma states.   □

Theorem 2 (Communication order restrictions for eliminability). *The set of restrictions of lemma 6 to be fulfilled by $[G_{n+1}^l \| G_{n+1}^r]$ for the eliminability of its communication pair (l, m), without introducing deadlock, can be re-expressed as follows: for all $k \in [2, n]$, within P_k^l and P_k^r,*

$$cw(P_j^l) < cw(T_i^r) , \;\; cw(P_j^r) < cw(T_i^l) , \;\; \text{for } i \in [0, k-1] \text{ and } j \in [0, i]$$

$$cw(T_j^l) < cw(T_i^r) , \;\; cw(T_j^r) < cw(T_i^l) , \;\; \text{for } i \in [1, k-1] \text{ and } j \in [0, i-1]$$

and for $k = 1$, within P_1^l and P_1^r

$$cw(P_0^l) < cw(T_0^r) , \;\; cw(P_0^r) < cw(T_0^l) \;.$$

Justification.   The statements G_i^l and G_i^r in the last two conditions of lemma 6 can be replaced by all their substatements Ps and Ts, with the exception of G_0^l and G_0^r, obtaining the equivalent conditions: for $k \in [2, n]$ within P_k^l and P_k^r, and for $i \in [1, k-1]$ and $j \in [0, i-1]$

$$cw(P_j^l) < cw(T_i^r) , \;\; cw(T_j^l) < cw(T_i^r)$$

$$cw(P_j^r) < cw(T_i^l) , \;\; cw(T_j^r) < cw(T_i^l)$$

The case of $i = 0$ gives the restrictions $cw(G_0^l) < cw(T_0^r), cw(G_0^r) < cw(T_0^l)$ within P_k^l and P_k^r for $k \in [2, n]$, which need not be included since (G_0^l, G_0^r) is a pair whose two communications communicate between themselves only. We still have the restrictions for $k = 1$, within P_1^l and P_1^r : $cw(G_0^l) < cw(T_0^r)$, $cw(G_0^r) < cw(T_0^l)$, which can be removed by the same reason as before.

The above P-T restrictions can be put together with the P-T restrictions of lemma 6, holding for $i \in [0, k-1]$. This results in the following conditions: for $k \in [2, n]$ within P_k^l and P_k^r,

$$cw(P_j^l) < cw(T_i^r),\ cw(P_j^r) < cw(T_i^l),\ \text{for } i \in [0, k-1] \text{ and } j \in [0, i]$$

$$cw(T_j^l) < cw(T_i^r),\ cw(T_j^r) < cw(T_i^l),\ \text{for } i \in [1, k-1] \text{ and } j \in [0, i-1]$$

and for $k = 1$, within P_1^l and P_1^r,

$$cw(G_0^l) < cw(T_0^r)\, ,\quad cw(G_0^r) < cw(T_0^l)$$

$$cw(P_0^l) < cw(T_0^r)\, ,\quad cw(P_0^r) < cw(T_0^l)$$

as the lemma states. The G-T restrictions are not in the lemma since they always hold, because G_0^l communicates only with G_0^r only and vice versa. $\qquad\square$

Theorem 3 (Elimination from a standard form binary cooperation).
Let $S = [G_n^l \| G_n^r]$, be selection-free, and its two top statements have the standard form given in lemma 2. Let $\quad G_0 = [u := e]$, and for $k = 1, 2, \ldots$

$$G_k \;=\; [H_{k-1}^l \| H_{k-1}^r];\, [G_{k-1} \| P_{k-1}^l \| P_{k-1}^r];\, [T_{k-1}^l \| T_{k-1}^r]$$

Then $\quad G_n =_{\mathcal{O}} [G_n^l \| G_n^r]$, iff $[G_n^l \| G_n^r]$ satisfies the conditions of theorems 1 and 2. Either both sides are deadlock-free or none of them is.

Justification. The equivalence is obtained applying the following steps:

(1)- Recursive application of the equivalence of lemma 4, starting at $[G_n^l \| G_n^r]$ as above, until the following statement is obtained

$$
\begin{bmatrix}
\begin{bmatrix} H_{n-1}^l \ \| \ H_{n-1}^r \end{bmatrix}; \\
\cdots \\
\begin{bmatrix}
\begin{bmatrix} H_0^l \ \| \ H_0^r \end{bmatrix}; \\
[\ [\ G_0^l \ \| \ G_0^r\ ] \ \| \ P_0^l \ \| \ P_0^r\ ]; \\
\begin{bmatrix} T_0^l \ \| \ T_0^r \end{bmatrix}
\end{bmatrix} \| \cdots ; \\
\cdots \\
\begin{bmatrix} T_{n-1}^l \ \| \ T_{n-1}^r \end{bmatrix}
\end{bmatrix}
$$

(2)- Application, to its inner statement $[G_0^l \| G_0^r]$, of the congruence $[G_0^l \| G_0^r] \approx G_0$, as a reduction from left to right. Thus, the equivalence $G_n =_{\mathcal{O}} [G_n^l \| G_n^r]$ is a direct consequence of lemma 4 and the congruence of step 2. In the present scenario of disjoint processes communicating only via synchronous communications, the only possible cause of deadlock is waiting at communications that can never take place. This can only happen with communications within substatements that change from being parallel in $[G_n^l \| G_n^r]$ to being concatenation ordered in G_n. The possible situations are captured by theorems 1 and 2. Deadlock-freeness follows from the satisfaction of the conditions stated in them. $\qquad\square$

S may be deadlock-free but some of the applicability conditions fail. Given a general selection-free BCS with a non-empty set of competing pairs, the elimination of any pair is feasible under the conditions of the following

Theorem 4 (Elimination from a selection-free BCS). *Let $p = (l, m)$ be one of the pairs in CompPairs(I,S), and the top statements of the LCA parallelism of l and m be G^l and G^r. Then S can be transformed into an interface equivalent statement without p if the standard forms of order $n = max(n_l, n_r)$ of the two top statements satisfy the conditions of theorems 1 and 2.*

In general, the orders n_l and n_r of the standard forms of G^l and G^m will not be equal. Then, if $n_l > n_r$ we make $n = n_l$ and construct G_n^r by inserting $n_l - n_r$ layers of nil H, P, and T statements immediately around G_0^r. One proceeds similarly in the opposite case. The insertion can be done in other ways, but the innermost one leads to maximum parallelism.

Justification. Due to commutativity and associativity of parallelism, S can always be transformed into $S[G^l || G^m]$, where the binary parallelism of the embedding top statements has been isolated. Then $S[G^l || G^m] =_{\mathcal{O}} S[G_n^l || G_n^m] =_{\mathcal{O}} S[G_n]$ by lemma 2, theorem 3, and monotonicity of interface equivalence.   □

Assuming that the conditions of theorems 1 and 2 hold, the term $Elim\{(l,r),S\}$ will represent the statement resulting after elimination of (l, r) from S. Thus, the result of the above theorem may be written as $S =_{\mathcal{O}} Elim\{(l,r),S\}$.

Lemma 7 (Elimination commutativity of disjoint pairs). *Let p_1 and p_2 be two disjoint competing pairs of S. Then*
$$Elim\{p_2, Elim\{p_1, S\}\} =_{\mathcal{O}} Elim\{p_1, Elim\{p_2, S\}\}$$

Justification. One has that $S =_{\mathcal{O}} Elim\{p_1, S\}$ and $S =_{\mathcal{O}} Elim\{p_2, S\}$. But, for the same reason $Elim\{p_2, S\} =_{\mathcal{O}} Elim\{p_2, Elim\{p_1, S\}\}$ and $Elim\{p_1, S\} =_{\mathcal{O}} Elim\{p_1, Elim\{p_2, S\}\}$. The desired result follows, since the left hand sides of the last two equivalences are both equivalent to S.   □

Lemma 8 (Elimination of a set of disjoint competing pairs). *Let n_{cp} be the cardinality of CompPairs(I,S), all of whose pairs $cp_i, i = 1, \cdots, n_{cp}$ are disjoint. Then, $S =_{\mathcal{O}} Elim\{cp_1, Elim\{cp_2, \cdots, Elim\{cp_{n_{cp}}, S\} \cdots\}\}$*
$$=_{\mathcal{O}} Elim\{cp_{p(1)}, Elim\{cp_{p(2)}, \cdots, Elim\{cp_{p(n_{cp})}, S\} \cdots\}\} , \quad where$$
$< p(1), \cdots, p(n_{cp}) >$ is any permutation of $< 1, \cdots, n_{cp} >$.

Justification. This follows by linear induction. The base case, where $n_{cp} = 2$ holds by lemma 7. For the induction step, assume that the result is true for $n_{cp} = k$, then $S =_{\mathcal{O}} Elim\{cp_{p(1)}, Elim\{cp_{p(2)}, \cdots, Elim\{cp_{p(k)}, S\} \cdots\}\}$ for any permutation $< p(1), \cdots, p(k) >$ of the first k integers. But any permutation of the first $k + 1$ integers can be obtained from a suitable permutation of the first k integers by inserting the integer $k + 1$ at a convenient position l. Also,
$$Elim\{cp_{k+1}, S\} =_{\mathcal{O}} S$$
$$=_{\mathcal{O}} Elim\{cp_{k+1}, Elim\{cp_{p(1)}, Elim\{cp_{p(2)}, \cdots, Elim\{cp_{p(k)}, S\} \cdots\}\}\}$$
After some applications of lemma 7, cp_{k+1} can be moved to the l-th position.□

Assuming that all the pairs are mutually disjoint, the following communication elimination algorithm is a consequence of the above results:

$failure := \text{F}$
while $\neg failure \wedge \{\ S$ has a competing pair $p\}$
    do $(failure,S):= PElim(p, S);$
if $\neg failure$
    then if $ComFront(I, S)=\emptyset$
              then terminate with success
              else terminate with deadlock
    else terminate with failure

Procedure *PElim* is the extension of *Elim* which checks applicability conditions. It transforms G^l and G^r into standard form, as in the proof of lemma 2. After structure matching and application of the law, nil statements are eliminated with the basic congruences. When a true boolean result is returned, the applicability conditions were not satisfied. When the loop terminates without failure, *CompPairs(I,S)* of the final statement is empty. When at the same time there is still some communication left in the communication front, this indicates that no match can be found for it. Then the initial statement is not deadlock-free.

5   Extensions

This section summarizes an extension of the communication elimination proof. Its application scope is widened to encompass a very common form of non-BCS.

    Distributed program simplification (DPS) is a proof whose first step is constructed by the *communication elimination* algorithm. The resulting equivalent form has parallelism between disjoint substatements but no internal communications. Its next step, *parallelism to concatenation transformation*, applies permutation laws for transforming the parallel compositions of disjoint processes to interface equivalent sequential forms. A sequential program interface equivalent to the initial one is obtained. The third and last step of DPS is *redundant variable elimination*. State-vector reduction comes with this last step. More details are given in [19].

    Now the DPS proof will be extended to the following very common form of non-BCS: $S = [S_1||\cdots||S_m]$, where the S_k's are of the form $S_k = $ **loop forever do** B_k. The B_k's are BC statements. Since they have communication statements and appear within indefinite iterations, the whole statement is non-BC.

    Assume that we unfold n_k times the loop of each top substatement S_k, thus obtaining the statement $S_u = [B_1^{n_1}; S_1||\cdots||B_m^{n_m}; S_m]$, where the $B_k^{n_k}$'s stand for the concatenation of n_k copies of B_k : $B_k; \cdots; B_k$.

    We can apply DPS to S_u partially, only considering its internal communications in the $B_k^{n_k}$ statements. Assume that we succeed and obtain $B; E$, where B has no internal communication but the ending statement E may be non-BC, it may have both parallelism and inner communication. Assume also that $B; E$ is also reduced by DPS, partially as before, to $B; B; E$. Then, as a consequence of finite induction, $S =_{\mathcal{O}} [B^n; E]$ for any finite integer n, where B^n is both inner parallelism and communication free. In the frequent case where the first elimination yields $B; S$, i.e. $E = S$, then $S =_O$ **loop forever do** B and the right hand side statement has no inner communication. In many practical systems this occurs already for $n_k = 1$; $k = 1, \dots, m$.

6   State-Vector Reduction Example

The DPS equivalence proof of a four stage pipelined processor model [20], with only register to register ALU instructions, but with forwarding circuits and two levels of parallelism, carried out with the help of a tool embedding the communication elimination algorithm, is reported in [18,19,12]. A very clear verification result would be to show that the complex pipelined processor is equivalent to the following simple purely sequential fetch-execute loop

$$reg ::= VNCycle(reg, mem) :: \left[\begin{array}{l} \textbf{for } k := 1..n \textbf{ do} \\ \left[\begin{array}{l} ir := mem(pc); \\ pc := pc + 1; \\ reg(ir.rd) := alures(ir.func, reg(ir.rs1), reg(ir.rs2)) \end{array} \right] \end{array} \right]$$

This is what the DPS proof does. Thus, the state vector was reduced from 1689, for the parallel model, to 1082 bits, for the equivalent sequential model, a reduction of 607 bits. The bits common to both forms were distributed among the following variables: 32 general purpose registers $reg(.)$ of 32 bits each ($32 \times 32 = 1024$), the program counter pc, 32 bits, and the instruction register ir, 26 bits. The *opcode* field was not necessary for the simplified model, the *func* field sufficed. Thus, the reduction ratio of the upper bound on the number of states was 2^{-607}.

7   Conclusions and Future Work

The mathematical justification of proper communication elimination laws in a new distributed system equivalence criterion, published recently, has been carried out. Prior to that work, the laws were justified as unidirectional refinement relations only. This limited their applicability. The detailed mathematical justification of the applicability conditions for the laws has been covered as well. These, together with other results, have lead to the presentation of a communication elimination algorithm for selection-free BC statements. This algorithm generates automatically a communication elimination proof, when applicability conditions hold. The proof may be continued, interactively, into a distributed system simplification proof, eliminating parallelism and redundant variables. Extension of the proof to a very common non-BC statement has been given as well.

Based on these new results, and on other previously published results, a nontrivial distributed system simplification proof of a pipelined processor model has been undertaken. An impressive state number upper bound reduction has been obtained and reported in this communication.

Altogether, this work provides a grounding base for the extension of the algorithm to proper bounded communication statements, whose inner communications may stand under the scope of selections. A general algorithm for communication elimination and distributed program simplification, and its application to distributed algorithms of increasing complexity, is now envisageable.

Acknowledgements

We thank the encouragement received during the last years from Zohar Manna, Bernd Finkbeiner, and Tomas Uribe.

References

1. INMOS-Limited: Occam Programming Manual. Prentice Hall (1985)
2. INMOS-Limited: Occam 2 Reference Manual. Prentice Hall (1988)
3. Jones, G.: Programming in Occam. Prentice Hall (1987)
4. Manna, Z., Pnueli, A.: The Temporal Logic of Reactive and Concurrent Systems. Specification. Springer (1991)
5. Manna, Z., Pnueli, A.: Temporal Verification of Reactive Systems. Safety. Springer (1995)
6. Holtzmann, G.: Design and Validation of Computer Protocols. Prentice Hall (1991)
7. de Roever, W.P., de Boer, F., Hanneman, U., Lakhnech, Y., Poel, M., Zwiers, J.: Concurrency Verification: Introduction to Compositonal and Noncompositional Methods. Cambridge University Press (2001)
8. Yorav, K., Grumberg, O.: Static Analysis for State-space Reductions. Formal Methods in System Design **25** (2004) 67–96
9. Kurshan, R., Levin, V., Minea, M., Peled, D., Yenigun, H.: Static Partial Order Reduction. In Steffen, B., ed.: Proceedings of TACAS'98. Volume 1384 of LNCS., Noordwijkerhout, The Netherlands, Springer (1998) 335–357
10. Clarke, E.M., Grumberg, O., Long, D.: Model Cheking and Abstraction. ACM Transactions on Programming Languages and Systems **16** (1994) 1512–1542
11. Bertran, M., Babot, F., Climent, A., Nicolau, M.: Communication and Parallelism Introduction and Elimination in Imperative Concurrent Programs. In Cousot, P., ed.: Static Analysis. 8th International Symposium, SAS 2001. Volume 2126 of LNCS., Paris, France, Springer (2001) 20–39
12. Bertran, M., Babot, F.X., Climent, A.: An Input/output Semantics for Distributed Program Equivalence Reasoning. Electronic Notes in Theoretical Computer Science **137** (2005)
13. Francesco, N.D., Santone, A.: A Transformation System for Concurrent Processes. Acta Informatica **35** (1998) 1037–1073
14. Schenke, M., Olderog, E.R.: Transformation Design for Real-Time Systems. part i: From Requirements to Program Specifications. Acta Informatica **36** (1999) 1–65
15. Schenke, M.: Transformation Design for Real-Time Systems. part ii: From Program Specifications to Programs. Acta Informatica **36** (1999) 67–96
16. Roscoe, A., Hoare, C.: The laws of OCCAM programming. Theoretical Computer Science **60** (1988) 177–229
17. Elrad, T., Francez, N.: Decomposition of Distributed Programs into Communication Closed Layers. Science of Computer Programming **2** (1982) 155–173
18. Babot, F., Bertran, M., Riera, J., Puig, R., Climent, A.: Mechanized Equivalence Proofs of Pipelined Processor Software Models. In: Actas de las III Jornadas de Programación y Lenguajes, Alicante, Universitat d'Alacant (2003) 91–104
19. Babot, F.X.: Contributions to Communication Elimination Proofs for Distributed Program Simplification. Ph.d. dissertation, Escola Tècnica Superior d'Enginyeria Electrònica i Informàtica La Salle, Universitat Ramon Llull (2005)
20. Hennessy, J.L., Patterson, D.A.: Computer Architecture: A Quantitative Approach. Morgan Kaufmann Publishers Inc., San Mateo, California (1990)

Incremental Verification of Owicki/Gries Proof Outlines Using PVS*

Arjan J. Mooij and Wieger Wesselink

Technische Universiteit Eindhoven,
Department of Mathematics and Computer Science,
P.O. Box 513, 5600 MB Eindhoven, The Netherlands
{A.J.Mooij, J.W.Wesselink}@tue.nl

Abstract. Verifications of parallel programs are frequently based on automated state-space exploration techniques known as model checking. To avoid state-space explosion problems, theorem proving techniques can be used, for example by manually annotating programs with suitable assertions and using these assertions to prove their correctness (e.g. using the Owicki/Gries theory). We propose a method to support assertion-based methods with theorem provers like PVS. Emphasis is on the typical incremental character of assertion-based methods, and on automated strategies for proving correctness of the proof outlines.

1 Introduction

Verifications of parallel programs are frequently based on state-space exploration techniques. A nice property of such techniques is that human input is hardly required, but a serious drawback is the well-known state-space explosion problem. To avoid this, and to be able to prove more general properties of parallel programs, theorem proving techniques can be used. For example, programs can be verified by annotating them with suitable assertions and using these assertions to prove the programs' correctness (e.g. using the Owicki/Gries theory [OG76]). Although human input is required to develop the annotation and to perform the proof, in this way also infinite-state systems can be verified.

In [MW03] we have demonstrated that such methods can be used to analyze (the correctness of) industrial protocol standards. This is illustrated on the distributed spanning tree protocol for dynamic networks from a draft IEEE 1394.1 standard, which could not be verified using model checking. We have reconstructed and proved the correctness of a version of the (not yet proved) algorithm in the draft standard. To this end we have used the assertion-based method of Feijen/van Gasteren [FvG99], that supports the construction of parallel algorithms hand-in-hand with their correctness proof.

Despite this result, the required amount of human effort needs to be significantly reduced to enhance the practical applicability of assertion-based methods.

---

* This research is supported by the NWO under project 016.023.015: "Improving the Quality of Protocol Standards".

K.-K. Lau and R. Banach (Eds.): ICFEM 2005, LNCS 3785, pp. 390–404, 2005.

In this paper we focus on the related proof efforts. Since current theorem provers offer a lot of automatization, we address the integration of automated theorem provers with assertion-based methods. In this way we can also assess the practical usability of current automated theorem provers.

Applications of assertion-based methods (not only [FvG99]) are typically incremental: an initially incomplete annotation is extended repeatedly until all proof obligations can be proved. In contrast to much related work that focuses on formalizations, the emphasis of our approach is on this incremental nature.

To experiment with our approach, we have implemented a tool that uses the PVS [ORS92] theorem prover as a back-end. The effectiveness of the automated proof strategies is illustrated on some case studies, including a handshake register [Hes98] and the spanning tree protocol [MW03] mentioned before.

Overview The remainder of this paper is structured as follows. In Section 2 we discuss some basic techniques that we use. In Section 3 we evaluate related work, after which we describe the main ingredients of our approach in Section 4. Based on these ingredients, in Section 5 we discuss the tool that we have developed and the generated PVS input files. In Section 6 we present the practical results that we have obtained. Finally, in Section 7 we conclude this paper.

2 Preliminaries

2.1 Processes, Actions and Assertions

A parallel system consists of a (possibly dynamic) collection of processes. The execution of the program for a single process results in a sequence of atomic actions; the execution of a parallel program results in an interleaving[1] of these individual sequences. So an atomic action is an action that is guaranteed to be executed without interference of any other action. A control point (or an interleaving point) in a process' program is a location between two subsequent atomic actions of the process. A process is said to be "at a control point" if execution of the process' program so far ended at the control point.

An annotated program is a program that is annotated with assertions. An assertion is a predicate on the state of the system and it is located at a control point. An assertion at a process' control point is correct if the state of the system satisfies the assertion whenever the process is at the control point. A correctly-annotated program (or a proof outline) is a program in which all assertions are correct.

2.2 Running Example: Parallel Linear Search

As a running example we use a parallel linear search algorithm, which solves the following problem: Given a number of boolean functions on the naturals, find a value that is mapped by one of these functions to the value *true*. A collection of

---

[1] Since we ignore progress issues, we do not address fairness of the interleaving.

$$
\begin{array}{|l|}
\hline
\textbf{var } f : [comp \rightarrow [nat \rightarrow bool]], \\
\quad\quad x : [comp \rightarrow nat], \\
\quad\quad b : bool \\
\hline
\end{array}
$$

0: $\{\textbf{inv } b \Rightarrow (\exists_{c:comp} : f_c(x_c))\}$
    par $(c : comp)$:

1:
        do $\neg(b \lor f_c(x_c)) \rightarrow$
2:            $\{\neg f_c(x_c)\}$
            $x_c := x_c + 1$
        od
3:      ; $\{(\exists_{c:comp} : f_c(x_c))\}$
        $b := true$
4:          $\{(\exists_{c:comp} : f_c(x_c))\}$
    rap
5: $\{(\exists_{c:comp} : true) \Rightarrow (\exists_{c:comp} : f_c(x_c))\}$

Fig. 1. Parallel linear search

processes has to be used, such that for each function there is a process that is completely dedicated to the function.

A solution is the annotated program of Figure 1, which is a generalization of the two-process version in [FvG99]. The upper part consists of the declaration of the variables, in which the type $comp$ denotes the set of process identifiers. For each process c, function f_c is the corresponding given function. Variable b is a shared program variable of type boolean, and for each process c, variable x_c is a local program variable of type natural.

The lower part contains the annotated program. The numbers that are followed by a colon are labels that identify the control points. Each assertion P is denoted as $\{P\}$, and each invariant I (i.e. an abbreviation of an assertion that is placed just before the parallel composition and at each control point within) is denoted as $\{\textbf{inv } I\}$. The assertions and invariants at the first control point are also the precondition of the program. What remains are some statements, including a parallel composition (**par**) over the elements of type $comp$, a repetition (**do**), a sequential composition (;) and two assignments (:=).

A brief argument for the correctness of this algorithm is that each process c performs a linear search on its function f_c. Once a value $true$ has been found, the witness index x_c remains unchanged and shared variable b is set to $true$ after which all processes terminate. If termination of the system needs to be guaranteed, it is important to assume that the post-assertion (at label 5) can be established by assignments to x, and that initially $(\forall_{c:comp} : x_c = 0)$ holds.

2.3 Hoare Triples and the Theory of Owicki/Gries

A basic notion for the correctness of assertions is a Hoare triple [Hoa69]. A Hoare triple $\{P\} S \{Q\}$ is a boolean that has the value $true$ if and only if each terminating execution of statement S that starts from a state satisfying predicate P is guaranteed to end up in a final state satisfying predicate Q. This definition expresses *partial correctness*, since termination is not considered.

Hoare triples for atomic statements are usually defined using weakest liberal preconditions. The weakest liberal precondition (*wlp* for short) of a statement S is a predicate transformer, to be denoted by $wlp.S$. The $wlp.S$ of a predicate Q, to be denoted by $wlp.S.Q$, is the weakest precondition P such that $\{P\}\ S\ \{Q\}$ is a correct Hoare triple. More formally $\{P\}\ S\ \{Q\} \equiv [P \Rightarrow wlp.S.Q]$, in which the square brackets are a shorthand for "for all states", i.e. as a universal quantifier binding all free variables. In what follows, the following two properties of Hoare triples $\{P\}\ S\ \{Q\}$ are important: they are anti-monotonic in P, and (universally) conjunctive in Q.

Composite statements are usually flattened into atomic actions using small theorems. E.g., a selection statement $\{P\}$ **if** $B \to \{Q\}\ S$ **fi** $\{R\}$ with inner assertion Q is flattened into an atomic evaluation of guard B (with proof obligation $[P \wedge B \Rightarrow Q]$) and a statement $\{Q\}\ S\ \{R\}$.

Partial Correctness. For the (partial) correctness of an annotation we use the Owicki/Gries theory [OG76] in the terminology of [FvG99]. It states that an assertion P in a process is correct whenever the following two conditions hold:

- local correctness is guaranteed, i.e. if P is an initial assertion then P is implied by the precondition of the program, and if P is preceded by atomic action[2] $\{Q\}\ S$ then P is established by that action, i.e. $\{Q\}\ S\ \{P\}$ is a correct Hoare triple;   and
- global correctness (or maintenance, or interference freedom) under each atomic action $\{Q\}\ S$ in the other processes is guaranteed, i.e. $\{P \wedge Q\}\ S\ \{P\}$ is a correct Hoare triple.

For the running example, global correctness of the assertion at control point 3 of a process c under the assignment at control point 2 of a process $d : d \neq c$ follows from the following (correct) Hoare triple:

$$\{(b \Rightarrow (\exists_{c:comp} : f_c(x_c))) \ \wedge \ (\exists_{c:comp} : f_c(x_c)) \ \wedge \ \neg f_d(x_d)\}$$
$$x_d := x_d + 1$$
$$\{(\exists_{c:comp} : f_c(x_c))\}$$

The *wlp* that is needed to prove this Hoare triple reads as follows:

$$wlp.(x_d := x_d + 1).(\exists_{c:comp} : f_c(x_c)) \equiv (\exists_{c:comp} : c \neq d \wedge f_c(x_c)) \vee f_d(x_d + 1)$$

2.4   Method of Feijen/van Gasteren

Before a program's correctness can be proved using the theory of Owicki/Gries, a full annotation must have been invented. Therefore it was even believed that the theory of Owicki/Gries could not be used for the *design* of programs.

---

[2] Atomic action S with pre-assertion P is denoted as $\{P\}\ S$.

To start verifying an annotation before the full annotated program has been developed, rely-guarantee methods (see e.g. [XdRH97]) have been proposed. These methods allow to verify each single process based on a rely-guarantee abstraction of the other processes. However, during program development it is likely that such abstractions are not available. Others focus on constructing the annotation (together with the program) and on verifying parts of it as soon as possible. In the remainder of this section we illustrate this by describing the recently-developed programming method of Feijen/van Gasteren [FvG99].

Method. The method of Feijen/van Gasteren addresses the construction of parallel programs hand-in-hand with a suitable annotation and correctness proof. Being based on the style of [Dij76], assertions play an important role. We first summarize some conventions. Multiple assertions can be placed at a control point. Such a sequence of assertions denotes their conjunction, and the assertions are called *co-assertions*. Since Hoare triples $\{P\}\ S\ \{Q\}$ are conjunctive in Q, the correctness of individual co-assertions can be proved independently. A *queried assertion* is an assertion which correctness has not yet been proved.

Program development starts by expressing the program's specification in terms of queried assertions and a preliminary program. Then, one-by-one, all queried assertions must become correct assertions (as described below). When all assertions (including those related to the original specification) are correct assertions, the developed program is correct with respect to the specification.

If a queried assertion's correctness (in the current annotated algorithm) cannot yet be proved, there are mainly two solutions (which can also be combined):

- introduce additional queried assertions in the current annotation such that the given assertion is correct in the extended annotation;
- modify the algorithm such that the given assertion is correct in the modified algorithm's annotation.

An important issue is whether these two steps can endanger correctness of the prior assertions. Since Hoare triples $\{P\}\ S\ \{Q\}$ are anti-monotonic in P, introducing additional assertions cannot endanger the correctness of the prior assertions. However, modifying the algorithm may turn all correct assertions into queried assertions again. The typically-used modifications of the algorithm are inserting statements (for local correctness) and changing atomic actions. In the common case that the changes of the atomic actions can only reduce the program's behavior, the correctness of the annotation is maintained.

3   Related Work

Tool support for formal methods is a very active research area. In spite of the enormous interest in techniques related to model checking, some (recent) work addresses axiomatic proofs based on Hoare logic and on the theory of Owicki/Gries. In this overview of related work, we ignore model checking and discuss some work on using theorem provers for the verification of programs.

In [Hoo98] and related publications, there are experiments in modeling proof rules in PVS. The emphasis is on distributed real-time systems, and reusable theories about time have been developed. However, the models of case studies look ad-hoc, and exploiting automatization of PVS is not a key issue.

Other related work originates from formalizations of the Java programming language, e.g. in [Ábr05, JP03]. Distracting complications in such a language are many object-orientation issues. In [JP03] parallelism is excluded, and in [Ábr05] emphasis is on formalization instead of exploiting theorem prover capabilities. Getting closer to our methodological goals, [Fra99] addresses the construction of *sequential* programs and their correctness proofs in the style of [Dij76].

3.1 Theory of Owicki/Gries in Isabelle

The most-related work is [PN02, NPN99], in which the Owicki/Gries theory is formalized in the Isabelle [Pau94] theorem prover. This work has nice theoretical aspects. The formalization does not refer explicitly to control points, which indeed are not contained in the Owicki/Gries theory itself. And because the proof obligations are generated within the Isabelle theorem prover, soundness with respect to operational semantics has been proved.

For practical use, there is a dedicated Isabelle tactic. To prove an annotated program, a user submits a goal of the shape "this given annotated program is correct" to the theorem prover. Then the tactic is applied to conclude that this goal follows from a large proof obligation, consisting of the corresponding Owicki/Gries proof obligations. Afterwards, this large proof obligation needs to be proved using the theorem prover's usual techniques. For effective practical use, this approach has some disadvantages which we discuss in Section 4.

4 Design Points

Although the approach of [PN02] is related to our goals, it does not effectively support incremental assertion-based methods. In what follows we discuss the problems and the way we propose to overcome them. We will not compare the theorem provers in detail, although in Section 6 we briefly address this issue.

4.1 Decomposing the Proof Obligation

To verify an annotated program, the tactic of [PN02] generates one big combined proof obligation, which is related to the fact that the tactic is incorporated in the theorem prover. Afterwards, the theorem prover is used to try to prove the generated proof obligation. Such an approach has two disadvantages.

First, dealing with large proof obligations heavily relies on the capabilities of theorem provers to reduce them into smaller chunks that can easily be proved. As mentioned by [JP03], this easily becomes a bottleneck since there are limits to the size of proof obligations before theorem provers become very time consuming (or running out of memory). In this respect, it is advantageous to split proof obligations into smaller ones before employing a theorem prover.

The second problem origins from the incremental and iterative nature of assertion-based methods. In typical applications, a program and its annotation are repeatedly modified as required for parts of their proof that cannot yet be completed. Since these frequent changes are usually small, many parts of a previous proof attempt can be reused, at least theoretically. So a lot of theorem proving work can be saved by splitting proof obligations into *reusable* parts.

To maximally reuse unchanged parts of the proof obligation, we split the proof obligation such that the typical steps in the methods only affect a minimal number of parts. In correspondence with the structure of the Owicki/Gries theory, this can be achieved by splitting according to the assertion being proved, to local or global correctness and to the particular statement being involved. Thus the individual parts of the proof obligation are identified by a triple ("local/global", assertion, statement).

4.2   Stabilizing the Proof Scripts

A frequently occurring step in assertion-based methods is adding an assertion. Apart from new proof obligations for correctness of the assertion, the assertion also pops up in some existing proof obligations. More specifically, if we consider the *wlp*-versions of the proof obligations, it pops up in the antecedent of the implication. This weakens (or "makes more *true*") the proof obligations, thanks to anti-monotonicity (see Sections 2.3 and 2.4), and hence their correctness is maintained. However, there is no guarantee that the old proof script of the theorem prover is also a proof script for the new proof obligation. In practice this hinders the effective use of theorem provers for incremental methods.

Instead of trying to correct the old proof scripts, we ensure that there are no textual changes in these proof obligations, nor in the ingredients employed by the old proof scripts. To that end, we need to fully decouple the assertions from each other. Consider the typical example $[P \wedge Q \Rightarrow Z]$ (e.g. a proof obligation for local correctness) with predicates P, Q and Z. To decouple Z from P and Q, we use the principle of indirect inequality and obtain $(\forall_X : [X \Rightarrow P \wedge Q] \Rightarrow [X \Rightarrow Z])$, assuming that predicate X is fresh (i.e. not yet in use). Then P and Q can be decoupled using that implication is conjunctive in its consequent:

$$(\forall_X : [X \Rightarrow P] \wedge [X \Rightarrow Q] \Rightarrow [X \Rightarrow Z])$$

In a theorem prover this can be modeled as proof obligation $[X \Rightarrow Z]$, after declaring dummy predicate X as a logical variable and posing the two axioms $[X \Rightarrow P]$ and $[X \Rightarrow Q]$. If (later on) this proof obligation should be weakened into $[P \wedge Q \wedge R \Rightarrow Z]$, then only an axiom $[X \Rightarrow R]$ needs to be added. Hence correctness of the old proof script for $[X \Rightarrow Z]$ cannot be endangered as long as all used axioms are employed explicitly. Note that these introduced axioms cannot cause soundness problems, since dummy X was fresh.

Instead of introducing a fresh predicate X for each proof obligation, we can exploit the structure of the Owicki/Gries theory to reuse some of them. Namely, the antecedent of the implication in each proof obligation is the conjunction of all assertions at one or two control points. We introduce a fresh predicate per control point, relate it to the corresponding assertions using axioms, and use (combinations of) these predicates instead of the dummy predicate explained before. In case there are two control points involved, viz. for global correctness proofs, this can be justified by applying the technique of indirect inequality to $[P \land Q \Rightarrow Z]$ twice, yielding:

$$(\forall_{X,Y} : [X \Rightarrow P] \land [Y \Rightarrow Q] \Rightarrow [X \land Y \Rightarrow Z])$$

4.3 Exploiting Invariants

Often some assertions are located at several control points. Such assertions are typically invariants, and usually many of their proof obligations (and proofs) are almost identical. Instead of treating invariants just as an abbreviation, for effective practical use their redundant proof load must be reduced. To this end we replace their proof obligations by a smaller collection of proof obligations that abstract from the individual control points.

Apart from the well-known repetition invariants supported by [PN02], we also consider invariants of parallel compositions, i.e. assertions that are placed at the control point of the parallel composition and at all control points within. There are three kinds of proof obligations for invariants: *local correctness* at the control point of the parallel composition, *invariance* under each atomic statement within the parallel composition, and *global correctness* under each statement outside the parallel composition. We locate such invariants as a special assertion at the control point of the parallel composition (see e.g. label 0 in Figure 1).

5   Experimental Environment

In this section we describe the experimental environment we have built, which is schematically depicted in Figure 2. Our proof generator reads the annotated program, and recursively decomposes it into atomic actions and assertions. Then internally the corresponding proof obligations are generated independent of the target theorem prover. Finally input files for the specific theorem prover (e.g. PVS) are generated that consist of proof obligations and corresponding proof scripts. Afterwards they are verified by the theorem prover in batch-mode.

In case some proof obligations are not successfully verified by the theorem prover, there are two options:

Fig. 2. Architecture

- the proof obligation does not hold, and hence the annotated program must be adapted (according to the assertion-based method);
- the proof obligation holds, but the generated proof script is not appropriate.

In the latter case, the user can influence the proof scripts by supplying proof guidance. In either case, afterwards our tool is used again to generate the new proof obligations and proof scripts.

In what follows, we first describe how to model the program in PVS, and then we show the generated proof obligations. Finally, we explain the generated proof scripts and the opportunities to influence them using proof guidance. Various illustrations on parts of the running example of Section 2.2 are included.

5.1   Program Model

In this section we discuss our model of atomic statements and assertions in PVS.

Identifiers. For the reuse as discussed in Section 4, we need identifiers for the assertions and statements. We only explicitly assign identifying labels to the control points, and identify the assertions and statements by the label of their control point and some serial number (or character). For example, the invariant at the control point with label 0, and the statement and assertion at the control point with label 2 in the running example are referred to as inv_0a, $stat\_2$ and ass_2a.

Data Types. Elementary data types are standardly available in PVS, so only the additional domain-specific data types need to be modeled. In the running example only a type $comp$ for the process identifiers needs to be defined.

$$\boxed{comp: \textbf{type}}$$

Then a type $state$ can be defined as a record that contains all variables. It will be used to denote states of the entire program.

$$\boxed{\begin{aligned} state: \textbf{type} = [\# \; & f : [comp \rightarrow [nat \rightarrow bool]] \; , \\ & x : [comp \rightarrow nat] \; , \\ & b : bool \\ \#] \end{aligned}}$$

Annotation. The two types of annotation, viz. assertions and invariants, are just predicates on the state.

$$\boxed{\begin{aligned} &\text{inv\_0a: pred}[state] = \\ &\quad \textbf{lambda} \; (s : state): \quad s'b \Rightarrow \textbf{exists} \; (c : comp): s'f(c)(s'x(c)) \\ \\ &\text{ass\_2a}(c : comp): \text{pred}[state] = \\ &\quad \textbf{lambda} \; (s : state): \quad \textbf{not}(\; s'f(c)(s'x(c)) \;) \end{aligned}}$$

Note that in the language of PVS, $s'b$ selects field b from record s.

Statements. Recall that we only need to address the atomic statements, since their composition into larger statements is part of the program's structure (see also Section 2.3). The atomic actions are typically assignments and evaluations of guards. We model the assignments using their *wlp*. Since for a guard of a repetition, evaluation to *true* and evaluation to *false* are two different atomic actions, we do not model them as a predicate transformer *wlp* but as a predicate.

$$
\begin{aligned}
&\text{wlp\_stat\_2}(c : comp)(p : \text{pred}[state]) : \text{pred}[state] = \\
&\quad \textbf{lambda } (s : state): \quad p(s \textbf{ with } [`x(c) := s`x(c) + 1]) \\
\\
&\text{guard\_1a}(c : comp) : \text{pred}[state] = \\
&\quad \textbf{lambda } (s : state): \quad \textbf{not}(s`b \textbf{ or } s`f(c)(s`x(c)))
\end{aligned}
$$

5.2   Proof Obligations

Using these definitions, we can describe the generated proof obligations. We will distinguish between local correctness, global correctness and invariance.

Control Points. Before presenting the proof obligations for correctness of the annotated program, we first address the implementation of the technique as described in Section 4.2. For each control point, say with label i, we introduce a logical variable lab_i, and relate it with axioms to the assertions and invariants that hold at the control point.

$$
\begin{aligned}
&lab\_2: [comp \rightarrow \text{pred}[state]] \\
\\
&\text{lab\_2\_inv\_0a: } \textbf{axiom} \\
&\quad \textbf{forall } (s : state): \textbf{forall } (c : comp): \quad lab\_2(c)(s) \Rightarrow inv\_0a(s) \\
\\
&\text{lab\_2\_ass\_2a}(c : comp): \textbf{axiom} \\
&\quad \textbf{forall } (s : state): \textbf{forall } (c : comp): \quad lab\_2(c)(s) \Rightarrow ass\_2a(c)(s)
\end{aligned}
$$

Similarly for each control point, say with label i, in which a parallel composition starts, we define a logical variable scp_i, and relate it with an axiom to the control points in the scope of the parallel composition.

$$
\begin{aligned}
&scp\_0: \text{pred}[state] \\
\\
&\text{def\_scp\_0: } \textbf{axiom} \\
&\quad \textbf{forall } (s : state): \\
&\qquad scp\_0(s) = (\ lab\_0(s) \\
&\qquad\qquad \textbf{or } (\textbf{exists } (c : comp): lab\_1(c)(s)) \\
&\qquad\qquad ... \\
&\qquad\qquad \textbf{or } (\textbf{exists } (c : comp): lab\_4(c)(s))\ )
\end{aligned}
$$

The main use of this axiom is to prove relations between *scp* variables and invariants, like the relations between control points and assertions above.

$$
\begin{aligned}
&\text{scp\_0\_inv\_0a: } \textbf{lemma} \\
&\quad \textbf{forall } (s : state): \quad scp\_0(s) \Rightarrow inv\_0a(s)
\end{aligned}
$$

Local Correctness. Now we consider the proof obligations for local correctness of the assertions and invariants. We assume that the initial assertion of the program is the precondition of the program. Recall that if an assertion $\{P\}$ is not an initial assertion, then it must be established by the preceding statement $\{Q\}\ S$, i.e. $\{Q\}\ S\ \{P\}$ must be a correct Hoare triple. We directly generate the proof obligations in their *wlp* version.

---
loc_ass_4a_stat_3: **lemma**
    forall $(s : state)$:
        forall $(c : comp)$: $lab\_3(c)(s) \Rightarrow$
            $wlp\_stat\_3(c)(ass\_4a(c))(s)$

Such a lemma "loc_ass_4a_stat_3", for local correctness of assertion ass_4a by preceding atomic statement stat_3, is structured as follows:

- For all states,
- and for all processes (that are about to execute the statement),
- the statement establishes the post-assertion.

Global Correctness. Then we continue with global correctness. Recall that each assertion $\{P\}$ of a process must be maintained under each statement $\{Q\}\ S$ that can be executed by another process, i.e. $\{P \wedge Q\}\ S\ \{P\}$ must be a correct Hoare triple. We directly generate the proof obligations in their *wlp* version.

---
glob_ass_3a_stat_2: **lemma**
    forall $(s : state)$:
        forall $(c : comp)$: $lab\_3(c)(s) \Rightarrow$
            forall $(d : comp)$: $lab\_2(d)(s) \Rightarrow$
                not$(c = d) \Rightarrow$
                    $wlp\_stat\_2(d)(ass\_3a(c))(s)$

Such a lemma "glob_ass_3a_stat_2", for global correctness of assertion ass_3a under statement stat_2, is structured as follows:

- For all states,
- and for all processes that are at the control point of the assertion,
- and for all processes that are about to execute the statement,
- if the processes are different (i.e. in the largest common prefix of the enclosing parallel compositions of the control point and the statement, not all identifying variables are equal),
- the statement (re-)establishes the assertion.

Invariance. Finally we address invariance. In case the statement to be considered is outside the parallel composition of the invariant, invariance is just global correctness (see above) with the first "lab_" replaced by "scp_". If the statement is inside the parallel composition of the invariant, then the invariant must be maintained under executions of the statement in each process.

```
inv_inv_0a_stat_2: lemma
    forall (s : state):
        scp_0(s) ⇒
            forall (c : comp): lab_2(c)(s) ⇒
                wlp_stat_2(c)(inv_0a)(s)
```

Such a lemma "inv_inv_0a_stat_2", for invariance of invariant inv_0a under statement stat_2, is structured as follows:

- For all states,
- and for all processes that are within the parallel composition,
- and for all processes that are about to execute the statement,
- the statement (re-)establishes the invariant.

5.3   Proof Scripts

For these generated proof obligations, proof scripts are generated that rely on the automatization offered by PVS. Such an automated proof might be feasible since atomic actions are typically simple. Furthermore, proving these proof obligations might be easier than proving correctness of the algorithm, since an annotation can be exploited. However, we must be prepared that human intervention in the proof is required, so we also discuss some possibilities for human guidance.

Default Script. The default proof script consists of the following three parts:

```
(skosimp* :preds? t)

(lemma "lab_2_ass_2a")
(inst -1 "s!1" "c!1")
... ...

(branch (grind :if-match nil)
    ((then (try (reduce) (fail) (skip))
        (then (inst? :if-match all) (then (reduce :if-match all) (fail) ) ) )) )
```

The first command decomposes the top-level structure of the proof obligation and introduces skolem constants (and type constraints) for the bound variables, viz. for the state and for the identifying variables of the processes. Then the axioms that relate control points to assertions are *explicitly* employed (as required in Section 4.2), and the known constants are substituted.

From a logical point of view, the order in which the axioms are introduced is irrelevant. However, in our practical experience PVS turns out to prioritize the last introduced axioms, which can have serious consequences for the run-time performance. We exploited the heuristic that for a global correctness proof of an assertion it is usually very important to use that the assertion holds. Hence, we ensured that the corresponding axiom is introduced in the end.

What remains in the script is the real work, consisting of some strategies to automatically complete the proof. It is in fact an extension of the "lazy-grind" strategy. First it applies "grind" without quantifier instantiation, and then it repeatedly tries the normal "reduce" with heuristic quantifier instantiation. If this "reduce" does not complete the proof, then repeatedly all instantiations of a bound variable are substituted and "reduce" is applied again. This proof script does not use induction, since we simply did not need it. The reason is probably that recursion is often encoded in a repetition.

Proof Hints. During execution of the default proof script, the strategies become more time-consuming. In that case, it is often effective to interrupt the prover after a while and to apply proof hints, since usually developers can easily indicate which assertions are not relevant for a proof. Using proof hints, the generated proof script can be improved by reducing the employed collection of assertions. In [GGH05] such proof hints, or dependency relations, were provided as an a-posteriori summary of a huge interactive proof.

Manual Proof. Suppose a generated proof script is very time consuming, or it cannot prove the proof obligation. If the proof obligation does hold, then the user can manually develop a PVS proof script and provide it to our tool. However, for effective verifications manual proofs should not be necessary too often.

6   Experiments

In this section we summarize some experiments to investigate the strength of our method, and in particular of the developed proof scripts. We have applied the environment as described in Section 5 to some fully-annotated algorithms.

6.1   Small Algorithms

We have first experimented with some simple known annotated algorithms from [FvG99, Moo02, PN02]: parallel linear search, wait-free consensus protocol, monitored phase synchronization, mutual exclusion (semaphores, ticket algorithm and Peterson's algorithm for two processes). The parallel linear search example has revealed a peculiarity of the automated strategies of PVS.

The antecedent of the assertion at control point 5 (see Section 2.2), viz. $(\exists_{c:comp} : true)$, is correctly skolemized to $true$ after introducing a skolem constant of type $comp$. However, it turns out that the automated strategies do not use this skolem constant, and hence the antecedent has effectively been weakened to just $true$. The result is that the proof obligation is not automatically provable, although we could finally circumvent this problem using a workaround.

Using our tool environment, correctness of these examples has been proved fully-automatically without using any proof guidance. On a current desktop computer, each example required less than a minute of time. Our results are better than the ones in [PN02, NPN99], e.g. for the ticket algorithm they require human intervention to provide explicit case distinctions.

Since [GH98] rates the automation in Isabelle and PVS as comparably good, we have initiated some experiments with Isabelle as a back-end. The first experiences indicate that from our practical perspective, the automatization in Isabelle performs less effective than the automatization in PVS, especially in treating quantifications. Since quantifications occur frequently, this seriously increases the required amount of manual interaction with the prover.

6.2 Larger Algorithms

We have also verified two larger algorithms. First of all, we have verified the fully-annotated "wait-free handshake register" of [Hes98]. In [Hes98] it is mentioned that it took some eight hours to construct his mechanical proof in the NQTHM prover. Using our default proof script, correctness of this annotated algorithm has been proved within five minutes on a current desktop computer.

The most-complicated algorithm we have verified is the distributed spanning tree algorithm in appendix A of [MW03]. It needs to be mentioned that there is a huge gap in complexity between this algorithm and the other algorithms we have discussed. In particular, dynamic networks play a role and there are complicated assertions and statements. This verification effort has revealed one small error in the manually constructed annotation. After strengthening one invariant in a straightforward manner, the annotated algorithm has been proved.

For this spanning tree algorithm, almost 90% of the generated proof obligations has been proved fully-automatically. The larger part of the remainder has been proved using proof hints, and finally manual proofs have been used for less than 4% of the proof obligations. Some automated proofs have been interrupted after a while in order to save time, so these results might be improved by running the default scripts much longer.

7 Conclusions and Further Work

We have demonstrated that assertion-based methods can be successfully applied in the correctness proof of moderately sized parallel programs. Using our tool that generates proof obligations and proof scripts, and feeds them to PVS, more than 95% of the proof obligations of the real-life case study [MW03] could be handled automatically. By splitting proof obligations into small chunks, and by designing proof scripts that are robust against common program modifications, we have made our approach suitable for incremental methods like [FvG99].

For further work, the proof scripts may be refined, e.g. by including clever case analysis, and by the use of additional theorem provers. Based on these techniques, also experiments need to be done with incremental developments, e.g. in the style of [FvG99]. Thereto suitable interaction between a user and the tool is required, and some additional strategies need to be implemented.

Acknowledgements. We thank Johan Koudijs for carrying out experiments with the Isabelle theorem prover.

References

[Ábr05]   E. Ábrahám. *An Assertional Proof System for Multithreaded Java - Theory and Tool Support.* PhD thesis, Universiteit Leiden, 2005.

[Dij76]   E. W. Dijkstra. *A Discipline of Programming.* Prentice-Hall, Englewood Cliffs, 1976.

[Fra99]   M. Franssen. Cocktail: A tool for deriving correct programs. In *Workshop on Automated Reasoning*, April 1999.

[FvG99]   W. H. J. Feijen and A. J. M. van Gasteren. *On a method of multiprogramming.* Springer-Verlag, 1999.

[GGH05]   H. Gao, J. F. Groote, and W. H. Hesselink. Lock-free dynamic hash tables with open addressing. *Distributed Computing*, 17:21–42, 2005.

[GH98]   D. Griffioen and M. Huisman. A comparison of PVS and Isabelle/HOL. In *Theorem Proving in Higher Order Logics, TPHOLs '98*, volume 1479 of *LNCS*, pages 123–142. Springer-Verlag, 1998.

[Hes98]   W. H. Hesselink. Invariants for the construction of a handshake register. *Information Processing Letters*, 68:173–177, 1998.

[Hoa69]   C. A. R. Hoare. An axiomatic basis for computer programming. *Communications of the ACM*, 12(10):576–580, 1969.

[Hoo98]   J. Hooman. Developing proof rules for distributed real-time systems with PVS. In *Workshop on Tool Support for System Development and Verification*, volume 1 of *BISS Monographs*, pages 120–139. Shaker Verlag, 1998.

[JP03]   B. Jacobs and E. Poll. Java program verification at Nijmegen: Developments and perspective. Report NIII-R0318, University of Nijmegen, 2003.

[Moo02]   A. J. Mooij. Formal derivations of non-blocking multiprograms. Computer Science Report 02-13, Technische Universiteit Eindhoven, October 2002.

[MW03]   A. J. Mooij and W. Wesselink. A formal analysis of a dynamic distributed spanning tree algorithm. Computer Science Report 03-16, Technische Universiteit Eindhoven, December 2003.

[NPN99]   ·T. Nipkow and L. Prensa Nieto. Owicki/Gries in Isabelle/HOL. In *Fundamental Approaches to Software Engineering (FASE'99)*, volume 1577 of *LNCS*, pages 188–203. Springer-Verlag, 1999.

[OG76]   S. Owicki and D. Gries. An axiomatic proof technique for parallel programs I. *Acta Informatica*, 6:319–340, 1976.

[ORS92]   S. Owre, J. Rushby, and N. Shankar. PVS: A prototype verification system. In *Conference on Automated Deduction*, volume 607 of *LNAI*, pages 748–752. Springer-Verlag, 1992.

[Pau94]   L. C. Paulson. *Isabelle: A Generic Theorem Prover*, volume 828 of *LNCS*. Springer-Verlag, 1994.

[PN02]   L. Prensa Nieto. *Verification of Parallel Programs with the Owicki-Gries and Rely-Guarantee Methods in Isabelle/HOL.* PhD thesis, Technische Universität München, 2002.

[XdRH97]   Q. Xu, W.-P. de Roever, and J. He. The rely-guarantee method for verifying shared variable concurrent programs. *Formal Aspects of Computing*, pages 149–174, 1997.

Using Three-Valued Logic to Specify and Verify Algorithms of Computational Geometry

Jens Brandt and Klaus Schneider

University of Kaiserslautern,
Reactive Systems Group, Department of Computer Science,
P.O. Box 3049, 67653 Kaiserslautern, Germany
http://rsg.informatik.uni-kl.de

Abstract. Many safety-critical systems deal with geometric objects. Reasoning about the correctness of such systems is mandatory and requires the use of basic definitions of geometry for the specification of these systems. Despite the intuitive meaning of such definitions, their formalisation is not at all straightforward: In particular, degeneracies lead to situations where none of the Boolean truth values adequately defines a geometric primitive. Therefore, we use a three-valued logic for the definition of geometric primitives to explicitly handle such degenerate cases. We have implemented a three-valued library of linear geometry in an interactive theorem prover for higher order logic which allows us to specify and verify entire algorithms of computational geometry.

1 Introduction

Many applications like motion planning in robotics or collision detection of autonomous vehicles have to consider the positions of physical objects in their environment. For most of these applications, it is sufficient to model the considered objects as polygons (or polyhedra) in an Euclidian plane (or space). This way, these applications directly rely on algorithms of computational geometry [6]. In particular, basic geometric primitives are used to develop software systems for controlling the spatial behaviour of physical objects like autonomous vehicles.

Although these algorithms are not new, their use in upcoming safety-critical embedded systems, used e.g. in automobiles, calls for a more rigorous treatment to guarantee the correctness for all possible inputs. To this end, formal definitions of geometric objects and primitives are required to specify and verify fundamental algorithms of computational geometry. At a first glance, the definition of geometric primitives appears to be easy, since they can be depicted in a natural and intuitive way. However, even definitions of simple geometric primitives are not at all straightforward, since they have to cover all possible cases: For example, what is the intersection point of two line segments, if both line segments are identical or share a common endpoint? Such degenerate cases [6] make clear that consistent definitions, that have to hold for all algorithms, are subtle. In fact, many algorithms only work under certain preconditions on the inputs as e.g. that all input points are pairwise distinct, or that no three input points are collinear.

Even worse, we found that for some primitives, there is no 'good' definition at all. For example, to define whether a point on the edge of a polygon belongs to the interior

K.-K. Lau and R. Banach (Eds.): ICFEM 2005, LNCS 3785, pp. 405–420, 2005.

or not, leads to problems in one or the other algorithm. In our opinion, the best solution is to make these degenerate cases explicit so that definitions and algorithms can directly handle them in a way that is appropriate for the context algorithm. To this end, we employ a three-valued logic to define geometric primitives. In the abovely mentioned example, we can express that a point is inside, outside, or on the edge of a polygon.

Moreover, we propose the use of higher order logics and corresponding theorem provers to consistently reason about the correctness of geometric algorithms. To this end, we extended the HOL theorem prover [10] by a library on two-dimensional analytic geometry that consists of three-valued geometric primitives. This library is not only useful to reason more efficiently about algorithms using two-valued primitives, it may also be viewed as the core of a software library for three-valued computational geometry [2] that is sometimes more concise than the corresponding two-valued version.

Our work deviates from previous work on reasoning about geometric problems with theorem provers in several ways: In particular, Wu's work [18] on translating geometric propositions to an algebraic form, i.e. equations between polynomials, is well-known. Various researchers improved and finally implemented this approach. Several hundred theorems about basic geometric objects like lines, triangles, and circles have been automatically proven with these theorem provers [5]. However, this approach is limited to reason about particular instances of geometric problems, but can not be used to reason about algorithms to solve classes of geometric problems, which is our concern.

The work closest to ours is that of Pichardie and Bertot [15]: Based on the work of Knuth [12], they formalised basic principles of convex hull algorithms. As in our approach, the orientation primitive (see Section 3.3) plays a central role to gain a new level of abstraction. In contrast to our work, they used two-valued logic to formalise geometric primitives. As a consequence of this, they circumvent problems of degenerate cases by modifying the orientation primitive or perturbing the input data. Furthermore, their scope is restricted to convex hull algorithms.

In this paper, we focus on the formalisation of two-dimensional, linear objects like lines, segments and polygons using three-valued geometric primitives. Due to lack of space, we only focus on the definition of the three-valued geometric primitives and show how degenerate cases are handled with appropriate definitions. Detailed definitions, in particular, the code for the HOL library, as well as further case studies like the verification of the Cohen-Sutherland clipping algorithm [9], are available on our website.

This paper is organised as follows: Section 2 describes the formalisation of analytic geometry and discusses the problem of degenerate cases in computational geometry. Section 3 presents our three-valued logic and its use for specifying geometric properties and primitives. Section 4 shows corresponding proof techniques and illustrates them with the help of a small example. Finally, Section 5 draws some conclusions.

2   Prerequisites

In mathematics, geometry is usually formalised in the vector space $\mathbb{R}^n$. However, real computers use floating point arithmetic of a limited precision, so that rounding errors appear as further problems. To circumvent these problems, we use rational numbers of arbitrary precision. The use of rational numbers is motivated by the observation that most algorithms only deal with linear objects like lines and polygons, so that all operations can be performed on rational numbers. As the HOL system does not directly provide rational numbers, we formalised them on our own.

2.1 Formalisation of Basic Analytic Geometry

Since we investigate problems of two-dimensional geometry, a vector is given by an ordered pair of rationals (rat#rat), encapsulated in a new type vec.

Definitions. For this type, we make the following definitions: **0** denotes the zero vector, and **ux** and **uy** denote the unit vectors. The components of a vector v can be accessed by x_v and y_v, respectively. A vector can be mirrored, rotated and multiplied by a scalar. A pair of vectors can be added and subtracted.

$$\text{vec\_mir\_def} \quad \vdash_{\text{def}} \text{mir}(v_1) = (-x_{v_1} \, ; \, -y_{v_1})$$
$$\text{vec\_orth\_def} \quad \vdash_{\text{def}} \text{orth}(v_1) = (y_{v_1} \, ; \, -x_{v_1})$$
$$\text{vec\_scale\_def} \quad \vdash_{\text{def}} r_1 \cdot v_1 = (r_1 \cdot x_{v_1} \, ; \, r_1 \cdot y_{v_1})$$
$$\text{vec\_add\_def} \quad \vdash_{\text{def}} v_1 + v_2 = (x_{v_1} + x_{v_2} \, ; \, y_{v_1} + y_{v_2})$$
$$\text{vec\_sub\_def} \quad \vdash_{\text{def}} v_1 - v_2 = (x_{v_1} - x_{v_2} \, ; \, y_{v_1} - y_{v_2})$$

Multiplication of vectors is not uniquely defined: In addition to the dot product, the cross product is well-known. For the two-dimensional case, it does not exist per se, but a related product that is sometimes called *perp dot product* does exist: This is the dot product where the first vector is replaced by the perpendicular vector. With its help, the linear dependency of two vectors is easily defined.

$$\text{sprod\_def} \quad \vdash_{\text{def}} v_1 \circ v_2 = x_{v_1} \cdot x_{v_2} + y_{v_1} \cdot y_{v_2}$$
$$\text{cprod\_def} \quad \vdash_{\text{def}} v_1 \times v_2 = x_{v_1} \cdot y_{v_2} - y_{v_1} \cdot x_{v_2}$$
$$\text{lindep\_def} \quad \vdash_{\text{def}} \text{lindep}(v_1, v_2) = (v_1 \times v_2 = 0)$$

Theorems. The vectors vec form a vector space over the rational numbers rat. As consequence of this, various arithmetic laws can be derived. For example, the cross product has the following properties (inter alia):

$$\text{CPROD\_RDISTRIB} \quad \vdash \quad (v_1 + v_2) \times v_3 = (v_1 \times v_3) + (v_2 \times v_3)$$
$$\text{CPROD\_RSUM} \quad \vdash \quad v_1 \times (v_1 + v_2) = v_1 \times v_2$$

Clearly, our library also includes important theorems of linear algebra like the two-dimensional case of Cramer's rule for the solution of a system of linear equations.

$$\text{VEC\_CRAMERS\_RULE} \quad \vdash \quad \neg(v_1 \times v_2 = 0) \rightarrow ((v_0 = r_1 \cdot v_1 + r_2 \cdot v_2) =$$
$$(r_1 = (v_0 \times v_2)/(v_1 \times v_2)) \wedge (r_2 = (v_1 \times v_0)/(v_1 \times v_2)))$$

We have also proved that the linear dependency relation is an equivalence relation and that it commutes with various vector operations.

2.2 Degenerate Cases

Most algorithms of computational geometry are designed for the 'general case': Depending on the algorithm, several preconditions are assumed, e.g. no points coincide, given lines are not parallel, or that no three lines intersect in a common point. Thus, so-called *degenerate cases* pose a well-known problem to algorithms in computational geometry [7, 14].

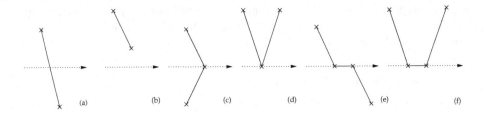

Fig. 1. Cases of the parity algorithm

As an example, consider the *parity algorithm*, which determines whether a point p is inside or outside of a polygon P: It counts the intersections of an arbitrary ray starting in p with edges of the polygon P. If the number of intersections is odd, p is inside; otherwise p is outside P. Figure 1 shows the possible cases, where the ray is drawn with a dotted line and some edges of polygon P are drawn with straight lines: (a) and (b) show simple cases without any problems. (c) to (f) show degenerate cases where either a vertex or an edge of the polygon is on the ray. To make the parity algorithm work correctly, we have to define some of the cases as intersections: cases (c) and (e) are intersections, whereas cases (d) and (f) are not.

Degenerate cases like the above mentioned ones require a substantial amount of additional effort. Since there are numerous degenerate cases, it is not recommended to directly address them in the algorithms as special cases. Instead, some other methods have been proposed that we briefly discuss in the remainder of this section.

Symbolic Perturbations.   A popular method to handle degenerate cases is the symbolic perturbation of degenerate inputs [7], which resolves degeneracies by simply hiding them (black box method). Intuitively, each geometric coordinate is replaced with a symbolically perturbed coordinate, given by a polynomial of an infinitesimal small number ϵ. Substitution of the symbolically perturbed coordinates in a primitive expression results in a polynomial in the variable ϵ with coefficients determined by the original geometric coordinates. The sign of the expression is given by the sign of the first nonzero coefficient, where coefficients are taken in increasing order of powers of ϵ. This resolves all degeneracies of the considered primitive. Programs that use this technique tend to be smaller and more robust: the tedious treatment of many special cases is replaced by a single consistent perturbation scheme.

While this method is certainly a useful tool for the implementation of geometric algorithms, existing perturbation schemes have shown not to be as applicable as desired [4]. First, symbolic perturbations give the programmer a rather unsatisfactory choice: either to find an approximation of the original problem, or to find a precise solution of an approximation of the original problem. In some applications, both choices might be inappropriate, and a post-processing step is then required that determines the exact solution of the original problem. Besides its negative impact on the runtime, the complexity of the solution can be significantly increased. Second, symbolic perturbations need to be worked out in detail, a task that may be very complex. This has been done only for a few geometric primitives. Finally, objects that are constructed by the algorithm (e.g. intersection points) are often forbidden in the computation, because their perturbation function depends on the construction of the object and is much more complicated than the one for a primitive object.

Explicit Treatment of Degeneracies.   The explicit treatment of degeneracies suffers from the enormous number of cases. As an example, consider the intersection of two line segments: In general position, two segments either do not intersect or intersect at a point interior to both segments. Two intersecting segments in special position may overlap, share a common endpoint or have one segment endpoint interior to the other segment – and each case exists in various slightly different variations. Hence, it is obvious that a systematic analysis is indispensable.

As another example, consider the problem to check whether a point is on the edge, inside, or outside a polygon. Assume that the points on the edge are considered to be outside the polygon (i.e. polygons are 'open' point sets). However, if we calculate the difference of two polygons by a set difference, the result is possibly a polygon that contains points on its edge. There are two ways to solve the problem: The first one is to modify the definition of the difference. The second one is not to decide whether points on the edge are inside or outside, and therefore using an undetermined, third value for these points. This naturally motivates the use of a three-valued logic that we explain in the following section. Three-valued logic allows us to describe geometric properties and algorithms more precisely and more compactly without enumerating many tedious cases. Note that although these cases do not disappear, three-valued logic makes it possible to handle them in a systematic and concise way.

3   Using Three-Valued Logics in Analytic Geometry

Classical mathematical logic is bivalent, i.e. there are two possible truth values: *true* and *false*. The law of the excluded middle is one of the foundations of the classical two-valued logic: A proposition P is either true or false, and there is no other choice.

In the early 1920s, the Polish philosopher and logician Jan Lukasiewicz dealt with philosophical problems like Aristotle's paradox of the sea battle. He pointed out that these problems can be solved by introducing a third value. In the following, a lot of mathematicians engaged in this domain of logics, among them Stephen C. Kleene. In the late 1930s, he introduced his three-valued logics for the analysis of partial recursive primitives [11, 1]. Within his work, the third truth value modeled situations where expressions are *undefined*.

Today, many-valued logics have found many applications in computer science. For example, they are applied to solve problems of database systems, artificial intelligence, simulation of hardware circuits, [8, 13], and program analysis [16, 17].

3.1   Three-Valued Logic Operators

Reconsider the example of the *point in polygon* at the end of Section 2.2. The area of a polygon is described by a function that maps each point of the plane to one of the three truth values: *true* (T) is assigned to all points inside, *false* (F) to all outside, while the points on the edge are assigned U (which is interpreted as 'borderline' or generally, *degenerate case*).

$\ddot{\neg}$	
F	T
U	U
T	F

$\ddot{\wedge}$	F	U	T
F	F	F	F
U	F	U	U
T	F	U	T

$\ddot{\vee}$	F	U	T
F	F	U	T
U	U	U	T
T	T	T	T

Fig. 2. Truth tables of basic logical operators

$\ddot{\rightarrow}$	F	U	T
F	T	T	T
U	U	U	T
T	F	U	T

$\ddot{\leftrightarrow}$	F	U	T
F	T	U	F
U	U	U	U
T	F	U	T

$\ddot{\oplus}$	F	U	T
F	F	U	T
U	U	U	U
T	T	U	F

$\ddot{*}$	F	U	T
F	F	F	F
U	F	U	T
T	F	T	T

Fig. 3. Truth tables of $\ddot{\rightarrow}$, $\ddot{\leftrightarrow}$, $txor$ and $\ddot{*}$

These considerations give rise to the definitions of the basic three-valued connectives shown in Figure 2: The negation $\ddot{\neg}$ interchanges the inside and the outside of a polygon, and all points of the edge remain on the edge. The conjunction $\ddot{\wedge}$ represents the intersection of two polygons P_1 and P_2: Points that are both in polygon P_1 and in polygon P_2 belong to the intersection. Points that are either outside P_1 or P_2 are not part of the intersection. Finally, points that are located on the edge of one polygon and not outside the other, are on the edge of the intersection. The disjunction $\ddot{\vee}$ can be derived analogously. Hence, the operators $\ddot{\neg}$, $\ddot{\wedge}$ and $\ddot{\vee}$ correspond to the basic connectives of Kleene's three-valued logic [11].

Definitions. Starting from these definitions, we introduce further operators: implication $\ddot{\rightarrow}$, equivalence $\ddot{\leftrightarrow}$, exclusive-or $\ddot{\oplus}$ and a modified conjuction $\ddot{*}$. Figure 3 gives their truth tables. While $\ddot{\rightarrow}$, $\ddot{\leftrightarrow}$ and $\ddot{\oplus}$ are defined with the help of the basic operators, $\ddot{*}$ (whose meaning will be explained in Section 3.3) is defined by its truth table.

imp3_def $\vdash_{\text{def}} t_1 \ddot{\rightarrow} t_2 = \ddot{\neg} t_1 \ddot{\vee} t_2$
equ3_def $\vdash_{\text{def}} t_1 \ddot{\leftrightarrow} t_2 = t_1 \ddot{\wedge} t_2 \ddot{\vee} \neg t_1 \ddot{\wedge} \neg t_2$
xor3_def $\vdash_{\text{def}} t_1 \ddot{\oplus} t_2 = \neg t_1 \ddot{\wedge} t_2 \ddot{\vee} t_1 \ddot{\wedge} \neg t_2$

We extend the theory by existential and universal quantification. To this end, we recall the disjunctive interpretation of $\exists$ and the conjunctive interpretation of $\forall$ (also known as *substitution interpretation* for finite universes) that defines $\exists x.P(x) = \bigvee_{x \in \mathcal{D}_x} P(x)$ and $\forall x.P(x) = \bigwedge_{x \in \mathcal{D}_x} P(x)$, respectively. For our HOL theory, we chose the following, more feasible definition, which corresponds to the previous one:

exists3_def $\vdash_{\text{def}} \ddot{\exists} P = $ **if** $(\exists x.P(x) = \mathsf{T})$ **then** T **else**
$\qquad\qquad\qquad\qquad$ (**if** $(\forall x.P(x) = \mathsf{F})$ **then** F **else** U)
forall3_def $\vdash_{\text{def}} \ddot{\forall} P = $ **if** $(\forall x.P(x) = \mathsf{T})$ **then** T **else**
$\qquad\qquad\qquad\qquad$ (**if** $(\exists x.P(x) = \mathsf{F})$ **then** F **else** U)

A closer inspection of the truth tables of the basic connectives $\ddot{\neg}$, $\ddot{\wedge}$, and $\ddot{\vee}$ reveals that these operations imply a natural ordering by the degree of truth: F < U < T. In the context of this ordering, $\ddot{\neg}$ just reverses the values, $\ddot{\wedge}$ chooses the least one of its two

$\ddot{\sqsubseteq}$	F	U	T
F	U	T	T
U	F	U	T
T	F	F	U

$\ddot{\sqsupseteq}$	F	U	T
F	U	F	F
U	T	U	F
T	T	T	U

$\ddot{\trianglelefteq}$	F	U	T
F	U	F	U
U	T	U	T
T	U	F	U

$\ddot{\trianglerighteq}$	F	U	T
F	U	T	U
U	F	U	F
T	U	T	U

Fig. 4. Truth tables of $\ddot{\sqsubseteq}$, $\ddot{\sqsupseteq}$, $\ddot{\trianglelefteq}$ and $\ddot{\trianglerighteq}$

$\leq$	F	U	T
F	T	T	T
U	F	T	T
T	F	F	T

$\geq$	F	U	T
F	T	F	F
U	T	T	F
T	T	T	T

$\twoheadrightarrow$	F	U	T
F	T	T	T
U	T	T	F
T	T	F	T

Fig. 5. Truth tables of $\leq$, $\geq$ and $\twoheadrightarrow$

operands and $\ddot{\vee}$ analogously the greatest one. Moreover, existential quantification $\ddot{\exists}x$ computes the maximum of a function $P : \mathcal{D}_x \to \mathbb{T}$, whereas universal quantification $\ddot{\forall}x$ computes the minimum. Hence, we define a relation $\ddot{\sqsubseteq} : \mathbb{T} \times \mathbb{T} \to \mathbb{T}$ that compares two truth values (see Figure 4). Consistently with the other operators, it will return U if both arguments are identical. The relation $\ddot{\sqsupseteq}$ is obtained by swapping the operands. Besides this ordering, there is yet another natural ordering which is given by the amount of knowledge: U < F and U < T. Figure 4 gives the truth tables of $\ddot{\trianglelefteq}$ and $\ddot{\trianglerighteq}$.

Integrating Two-Valued and Three-Valued Propositions. Introducing three-valued formulas into a two-valued environment like HOL poses the problem of integrating both logics. First, how are two-valued terms embedded into three-valued formulas? This direction is rather simple; the definition of the required embedding operator $\ddot{\Delta} : \mathbb{B} \to \mathbb{T}$ is straightforward: *true* is mapped onto T, and *false* is mapped onto F. Second, how are three-valued formulas transformed to the Boolean domain? This depends on the proposition: In some situations, T should be the only designated truth value; in other cases, it suffices that a proposition P is 'at least U'. Although, this can be expressed by $\neg(P = F)$, we introduce two new relations $\leq$ and $\geq$ to improve the readability. By their help, all relevant cases ($P = F$, $P \leq U$, $P \geq U$, $P = T$) can be described concisely (see Figure 5).

3.2 Geometric Objects

The definitions on vectors as given in Section 2.1 are the basis of the formalisation of geometric objects. Vectors are the basic objects of analytic geometry, which are used to define all other objects. With the exception of points (that are represented by their position vectors and thus, are equivalent to vectors), all geometric objects are formed by sets of points that are the solution of a proposition. For example, a line given by two (different) points p and q, consists of all points $(x; y)$ that are a solution of the following equation:

$$\text{line} : \ddot{\exists}\lambda. \, (x; y) = (x_p; y_p) + \lambda \cdot (x_q - x_p; y_q - y_p)$$

Analogously, a square with the vertices $(0; 0)$, $(1; 0)$, $(1; 1)$ and $(0; 1)$ is defined by the following inequations:

$$\text{square} : 0 < x \wedge x < 1 \wedge 0 < y \wedge y < 1$$

Using classical logic, all characteristic propositions are two-valued (as above). Thus, a point is either a solution or not, i.e. it is either part of the object or not. In contrast, we use three-valued propositions to explicitly express degenerate points. These degenerate points are related with the edges and endpoints of objects: Inequations describe two-dimensional objects and degenerates points are located on the edge of the object, i.e. at the transition between the interior and the exterior of an object. Equations generally describe one-dimensional objects with special cases located at the 'end' of these objects. In both cases, the degeneracies are an effect of inequations, which can be seen as the actual source of degeneracies.

Hence, we introduce three-valued inequations between rational numbers. In the case where the left hand side is equal to the right hand side, the validity of the inequation is *undefined*:

$$\texttt{les3\_def} \quad \vdash_{\text{def}} \; r_1 \prec r_2 = \textbf{if}\,(r_1 < r_2)\,\textbf{then}\,\mathsf{T}\,\textbf{else}$$
$$(\,\textbf{if}\,(r_2 < r_1)\,\textbf{then}\,\mathsf{F}\,\textbf{else}\,\mathsf{U})$$

The relation $\prec$ has the following properties:

$$\texttt{RAT\_LES3\_REF} \quad \vdash \; (r_1 \prec r_1) = \mathsf{U}$$
$$\texttt{RAT\_LES3\_ANTISYM} \quad \vdash \; \ddot{\neg}(r_2 \prec r_1) = (r_1 \prec r_2)$$
$$\texttt{RAT\_LES3\_TRANS} \quad \vdash \; (r_1 \prec r_2) \,\ddot{\ast}\, (r_2 \prec r_3) \,\twoheadrightarrow\, (r_1 \prec r_3)$$

Using this relation, we define in the following other geometric objects. We thereby focus on two-dimensional linear objects, i.e. lines, rays, segments and rectangles. Circles, curves, and objects of higher dimensions are not considered, since they are not relevant for most applications. Nevertheless, the principles that are presented in the following can be applied to them, too.

Lines, Rays and Segments. In analytic geometry, a line is usually defined by its parametric equation (see first equation in the previous section). To convert the classic definition of a line to a three-valued one, all two-valued operators are exchanged by their three-valued counterparts:

$$\text{line} : \ddot{\exists}\lambda.\,(x; y) = (x_p; y_p) + \lambda \cdot (x_q - x_p; y_q - y_p)$$

For a line l, there is no difference between the two-valued and three-valued case: l contains all points $(x; y)$ that are a solution of the traditional, two-valued equation. A ray and a line segment can be specified similarly: For the ray, we add the condition that λ must be positive, and for a line segment, λ must be greater than 0 and less than 1. With these restrictions, the starting points of these objects are degenerate points.

$$\text{ray} : \ddot{\exists}\lambda.\,(x; y) = (x_p; y_p) + \lambda \cdot (x_q - x_p; y_q - y_p) \,\ddot{\wedge}\,(0 \prec \lambda)$$
$$\text{segment} : \ddot{\exists}\lambda.(x; y) = (x_p; y_p) + \lambda \cdot (x_q - x_p; y_q - y_p) \,\ddot{\wedge}\,(0 \prec \lambda) \,\ddot{\wedge}\,(\lambda \prec 1)$$

HOL *Theory of Lines.* In our HOL theory, lines, rays, and line segments are represented by the same type `line`. A line is represented by a pair of different vectors, which represent the points in the parametric equation. We use the constructor $\overrightarrow{(v_1, v_2)}$ that converts two vectors v_1 and v_2 to a line (a new data type). After the construction of a line $\ell = \overrightarrow{(v_1, v_2)}$, the points v_1 and v_2 used for the construction of the line, can still be accessed by the following functions: $\text{beg}(\overrightarrow{(v_1, v_2)}) := v_1$ and $\text{end}(\overrightarrow{(v_1, v_2)}) := v_2$.

The following functions define the point sets of a line, a ray or a segment. They correspond to the definitions of the previous paragraph.

on_line_def $\vdash_{\text{def}}$
$\quad \text{onLine}(\ell, v) = \ddot{\exists}\lambda.\, v = \text{beg}(\ell) + \lambda \cdot (\text{end}(\ell) - \text{beg}(\ell))$
on_ray_def $\vdash_{\text{def}}$
$\quad \text{onRay}(\ell, v) = \ddot{\exists}\lambda.\, v = \text{beg}(\ell) + \lambda \cdot (\text{end}(\ell) - \text{beg}(\ell)) \ddot{\wedge} (0 \prec \lambda)$
on_seg_def $\vdash_{\text{def}}$
$\quad \text{onSeg}(\ell, v) = \ddot{\exists}\lambda.\, v = \text{beg}(\ell) + \lambda \cdot (\text{end}(\ell) - \text{beg}(\ell)) \ddot{\wedge} (0 \prec \lambda) \ddot{\wedge} (\lambda \prec 1)$

3.3 Geometric Primitives

Most geometric algorithms rely on a small number of geometric primitives. Among them, there are primitives that take some input and classify it as one of a constant number of possible cases, as e.g.:

- *Position of two points.* A point p is left from a point q iff $\chi_{\text{left}}(p, q) := x_q - x_p > 0$. Analogously, point p is below q iff $\chi_{\text{below}}(p, q) := y_q - y_p > 0$.
- *Orientation of three points.* The points p, q and r define a left turn iff

$$\chi_{\text{lturn}}(p, q, r) := \begin{vmatrix} x_p & y_p & 1 \\ x_q & y_q & 1 \\ x_r & y_r & 1 \end{vmatrix} > 0 \tag{1}$$

Degeneracies with respect to such a primitive P are inputs x that cause the characteristic function to become zero $\chi_P(x) = 0$. Following the approach presented in Section 3, the result U is returned in these cases.

Three-Valued Primitives. To define the primitives, we use the three-valued less-than relation $\prec$ of the previous section. Since all primitives of the previous section compare their result with zero, we additionally introduce the following predicate:

rat_pos_def $\vdash_{\text{def}} \text{pos}(r) = 0 \prec r$

With their help, primitives for determining whether one point is on the left or below of another point are defined as follows:

left_def $\vdash_{\text{def}} \text{left}(v_1, v_2) = \text{pos}(x_{v_2} - x_{v_1})$
below_def $\vdash_{\text{def}} \text{below}(v_1, v_2) = \text{pos}(y_{v_2} - y_{v_1})$

Note that these primitives are three-valued. The following theorems prove some sort of reflexivity, antisymmetry and transitivity laws.

LEFT_REF $\vdash \text{left}(v_1, v_1) = U$
LEFT_ASYM $\vdash \text{left}(v_1, v_2) = \ddot{\neg}\text{left}(v_2, v_1)$
LEFT_TRANS $\vdash \text{left}(v_1, v_2) \ddot{*} \text{left}(v_2, v_3) \twoheadrightarrow \text{left}(v_1, v_3)$

LEFT_TRANS makes use of the connectives $\ddot{*}$ and $\twoheadrightarrow$, which usually appear together in a proposition. They allow a succinct description of the following cases:

- If both left$(v_1, v_2) = \mathsf{T}$ and left$(v_2, v_3) = \mathsf{T}$, then left$(v_1, v_3) = \mathsf{T}$.
- If left$(v_1, v_2) = \mathsf{T}$ and left$(v_2, v_3) = \mathsf{U}$ or vice versa, then left$(v_1, v_3) = \mathsf{T}$.
- If left$(v_1, v_2) = \mathsf{U}$ and left$(v_2, v_3) = \mathsf{U}$, then left$(v_1, v_3) = \mathsf{U}$.
- If left$(v_1, v_2) = \mathsf{F}$ or left$(v_2, v_3) = \mathsf{F}$, then nothing is said about left(v_1, v_3).

The orientation primitives can be defined analogously:

$$\texttt{lturn\_def} \quad \vdash_{\mathrm{def}} \quad \mathsf{lturn}(v_1, v_2, v_3) = \mathsf{pos}((v_2 - v_1) \times (v_3 - v_2))$$
$$\texttt{rturn\_def} \quad \vdash_{\mathrm{def}} \quad \mathsf{rturn}(v_1, v_2, v_3) = \mathsf{lturn}(v_3, v_2, v_1)$$

Again, various properties are proven for the orientation primitive:

$$\texttt{LTURN\_REF} \quad \vdash \quad \mathsf{lturn}(v_1, v_1, v_2) = \mathsf{U}$$
$$\texttt{LTURN\_SYM} \quad \vdash \quad \mathsf{lturn}(v_1, v_2, v_3) = \mathsf{lturn}(v_2, v_3, v_1)$$
$$\texttt{LTURN\_ASYM} \quad \vdash \quad \mathsf{lturn}(v_1, v_2, v_3) = \ddot{\neg}\mathsf{lturn}(v_2, v_1, v_3)$$

$\texttt{LTURN\_TRIAN} \vdash$
$$\mathsf{lturn}(v_1, v_2, v_4) \,\ddot{*}\, \mathsf{lturn}(v_2, v_3, v_4) \,\ddot{*}\, \mathsf{lturn}(v_3, v_1, v_4) \;\twoheadrightarrow\; \mathsf{lturn}(v_1, v_2, v_3)$$
$\texttt{LTURN\_TRANS} \vdash (\mathsf{lturn}(v_1, v_2, v_3) \,\ddot{\wedge}\, \mathsf{lturn}(v_1, v_2, v_4) \,\ddot{\wedge}\, \mathsf{lturn}(v_1, v_2, v_5) \geq \mathsf{U}) \to$
$$\mathsf{lturn}(v_1, v_3, v_4) \,\ddot{*}\, \mathsf{lturn}(v_1, v_4, v_5) \;\twoheadrightarrow\; \mathsf{lturn}(v_1, v_3, v_5)$$
$\texttt{LTURN\_MOD1} \vdash (\mathsf{onRay}(\overrightarrow{(v_2, v_3)}, v_4) = \mathsf{T}) \to \mathsf{lturn}(v_1, v_2, v_3) = \mathsf{lturn}(v_1, v_2, v_4)$
$\texttt{LTURN\_MOD2} \vdash (\mathsf{onRay}(\overrightarrow{(v_4, v_3)}, v_2) = \mathsf{T}) \to \mathsf{lturn}(v_1, v_2, v_4) = \mathsf{lturn}(v_1, v_3, v_4)$

These theorems are three-valued reformulations of the ones that can be found in [15]. The first three theorems (LTURN_REF, LTURN_SYM and LTURN_ASYM) state that a sequence in which a point appears at least twice is a degenerate case. Moreover, a sequence can be rotated without changing the orientation, and two points can be interchanged with negating the orientation of the sequence. LTURN_TRIAN describes the situation depicted in Figure 6 (a): If a point is on the positive side of three pairwise connected segments, they form a triangle with positive orientation. LTURN_TRANS proves the transitivity of the left-turn primitive under the condition that the three points v_3, v_4 and v_5 lie on the positive side of a segment from v_1 to v_2 (see Figure 6 (b)). The last

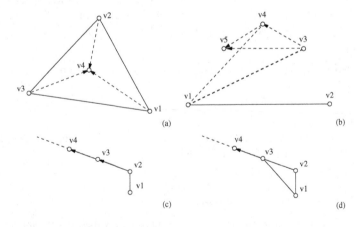

Fig. 6. Properties of left orientation primitive

two theorems (Figure 6 (c) and (d)) are used in [15] to handle degenerate cases. Actually, they are not needed in our approach, since LTURN_TRIAN already covers these cases. This illustrates the advantages of our approach: We always address general and degenerate cases at the same time, which makes the description succinct and readable. The same holds for later implementations that are made with three-valued data types.

4   Proof Techniques

In the previous section, we presented a way to specify geometric properties and algorithms with the help of three-valued logic. If a geometric algorithm is verified and all decisions of the algorithm depend on three-valued primitives, it can be analysed systematically. The following section presents theorems, conversions, and tactics to simplify this task.

4.1   Three-Valued Logic

Ternary Algebra.   The system $\langle \mathbb{T}, \ddot{\vee}, \ddot{\wedge}, \ddot{\neg}, \mathsf{F}, \mathsf{T}, \mathsf{U} \rangle$ is a ternary algebra [3]: In addition to the laws of commutativity, associativity, distributivity, absorption and de Morgan as known from a Boolean algebra, the following theorems can be used for the transformation of three-valued terms:

CONJ_TERNARY $\vdash\ a \ddot{\wedge} \ddot{\neg} a \ddot{\wedge} \mathsf{U} = a \ddot{\wedge} \ddot{\neg} a$

DISJ_TERNARY $\vdash\ a \ddot{\vee} \ddot{\neg} a \ddot{\vee} \mathsf{U} = a \ddot{\vee} \ddot{\neg} a$

Variations of Two-Valued Tactics.   For interactive proofs, the theory offers several tactics that are adapted from the two-valued domain.

- LOG3_GEN_TAC strips the outermost universal quantifier from the conclusion of a goal. When applied to $A \vdash^? \ddot{\forall} x.\, P$, it reduces the goal to $A \vdash^? P[x'/x]$ where x' is a variant of x chosen to avoid clashing with any variables free in the assumption list of the goal. This tactic reduces both $\ddot{\forall} x.\, P(x) = \mathsf{T}$ and $\ddot{\exists} x.\, P(x) = \mathsf{F}$, since both express universal goals.
- LOG3_EXISTS_TAC reduces an existentially quantified goal to one involving a specific witness. When applied to a term u and a goal $\ddot{\exists} x.\, P$, LOG3_EXISTS_TAC reduces the goal to $P[u/x]$ (substituting u for all free instances of x in P, with variable renaming if necessary to avoid free variable capture).
- LOG3_DISCH_TAC moves the antecedent of a (three-valued) implicative goal into the assumptions.
- LOG3_CONJ_TAC reduces a conjunctive goal to two separate subgoals. When applied to a goal $A \vdash^? t_1 \ddot{\wedge} t_2$, the tactic reduces it to the two subgoals corresponding to each conjunct separately.
- LOG3_EQ_TAC reduces a goal of equivalence of three-valued terms to forward and backward implication. When applied to a goal $A \vdash^? t_1 \ddot{\leftrightarrow} t_2$, the tactic EQ_TAC returns the subgoals $A \vdash^? t_1 \ddot{\rightarrow} t_2$ and $A \vdash^? t_2 \ddot{\rightarrow} t_1$.
- Given a term u, LOG3_CASES_TAC applied to a goal produces three subgoals, one with $u = \mathsf{T}$ as an assumption, one with $u = \mathsf{U}$, and one with $u = \mathsf{F}$. A simple and very effective tactic to automatically prove simple theorems about the three-valued

logic is LOG3_EXPLORE_TAC: It performs a case distinction on all free variables of the type $\mathbb{T}$ and then uses the simplifier of the theory.

Reduction to Two-Valued Terms.   A powerful tactic to prove goals specified in three-valued logic is the transformation to two-valued terms with a subsequent application of the traditional tactics for two-valued goals. For this purpose, a number of rewrite rules are provided that split up a three-valued proposition into positive atomic sub-proposition of the form $P = c$, $P \leq c$ or $P \geq c$ (where $c \in \{F, U, T\}$) connected by two-valued operators. The complete reduction step is implemented by the tactic LOG3_CALC_TAC and involves the following steps:

- Elimination of non-constant expressions on the right hand side of equations and inequations:

  LOG3_CASES_EQ $\vdash (a = F) \wedge (b = F) \vee (a = U) \wedge (b = U) \vee$
  $\qquad\qquad (a = T) \wedge (b = T) = (a = b)$

  LOG3_CASES_LEQ $\vdash (a = F) \wedge (b = F) \vee a \leq U \wedge (b = U) \vee (b = T) = a \leq b$

  LOG3_CASES_GEQ $\vdash (b = F) \vee a \geq U \wedge (b = U) \vee (a = T) \wedge (b = T) = a \geq b$

  In order to eliminate non-constant expressions on the right hand side, these rules must be applied from the right to the left. Of course, unconditional rewriting with these rules does not terminate.

- Elimination of proposition of the form $P = U$: As the following theorems only consider the cases $P = F$, $P = T$, $P =\leq U$ and $P =\geq U$, rewriting (from right to left) with the following theorem eliminates propositions of the form $P = U$.

  LOG3_LEQ_GEQ_UU $\vdash a \leq U \wedge a \geq U = (a = U)$

- Elimination of depending connectives: By rewriting with the definitions of $\overset{\cdot\cdot}{\rightarrow}$, $\overset{\cdot\cdot}{\leftrightarrow}$, $\oplus$ and $\overset{\cdot\cdot}{\exists}$, all terms only consist of basic connectives.

- Elimination of basic connectives: All basic three-valued connectives can be reduced to two-valued connectives by the rewriting with theorems of the following form:

  LOG3_NOT_CALC $\vdash ((\overset{\cdot\cdot}{\neg}t = F) = (t = T)) \wedge ((\overset{\cdot\cdot}{\neg}t = T) = (t = F)) \wedge$
  $\qquad\qquad (\overset{\cdot\cdot}{\neg}t \leq U = t \geq U) \wedge (\overset{\cdot\cdot}{\neg}t \geq U = t \leq U)$

  LOG3_AND_CALC $\vdash (a \overset{\cdot\cdot}{\wedge} b = F) = (a = F) \vee (b = F)) \wedge$
  $\qquad\qquad (a \overset{\cdot\cdot}{\wedge} b = T) = (a = T) \wedge (b = T)) \wedge$
  $\qquad\qquad (a \overset{\cdot\cdot}{\wedge} b) \leq U = a \leq U \vee b \leq U) \wedge$
  $\qquad\qquad (a \overset{\cdot\cdot}{\wedge} b) \geq U = a \geq U \wedge b \geq U$

  LOG3_EXT_CALC $\vdash ((\overset{\cdot\cdot}{\Delta} a = F) = \neg a) \wedge ((\overset{\cdot\cdot}{\Delta} a = T) = a) \wedge$
  $\qquad\qquad (\overset{\cdot\cdot}{\Delta} a \leq U = \neg a) \wedge \overset{\cdot\cdot}{\Delta} a \geq U = a$

  LOG3_FORALL_CALC $\vdash ((\overset{\cdot\cdot}{\forall}x. P(x) = F) = \exists b. P(b) = F) \wedge$
  $\qquad\qquad ((\overset{\cdot\cdot}{\forall}x.P(x) = T) = \forall b. P(b) = T) \wedge$
  $\qquad\qquad ((\overset{\cdot\cdot}{\forall}x.P(x) \leq U) = \exists b. P(b) \leq U) \wedge$
  $\qquad\qquad (\overset{\cdot\cdot}{\forall}x.P(x) \geq U) = \forall b. P(b) \geq U$

- Elimination of negative terms: All two-valued negations in front of subterms can be eliminated, leaving better understandable expressions.

  LOG3_NOT2_CALC $\vdash (\neg(a = F) = a \geq U) \wedge (\neg(a = T) = a \leq U) \wedge$
  $\qquad\qquad (\neg(a = U) = (a = F) \vee (a = T)) \wedge$
  $\qquad\qquad (\neg(a \leq U) = (a = T)) \wedge \neg(a \geq U) = (a = F)$

  LOG3_ABS_NOT $\vdash (\overset{\cdot\cdot}{\Delta} \neg a) = \overset{\cdot\cdot}{\neg}(\overset{\cdot\cdot}{\Delta} a)$

4.2   Vectors and Rational Numbers

Conversions and tactics that calculate vector and rational number expressions are provided. VEC_CALCTERM_TAC applies the calculation rules to a term, VEC_CALC_TAC to all terms of the type $\mathbb{Q}^2$. With the help of these tactics and the two theorems VEC_EQ and RAT_EQ, the equality of two vectors is reduced to the equalities between integers, which can be solved by the integer decision procedures of the HOL system. In this way, a lot of simple theorems can be automatically proven.

4.3   Example

We illustrate our approach by the convex hull algorithm presented in [6]. It divides the computation of the convex hull into two parts: the upper part and the lower part of the hull (see Figure 7 (a)). In this section, we focus on the construction of the lower part.

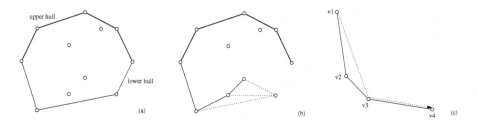

Fig. 7. Computation of the convex hull

Formalisation. The algorithm takes a list of points $\mathcal{L}$, which is sorted in lexicographic order (denoted as lexSorted$(\mathcal{L})$), i.e. points are first sorted by their x-coordinates and if the x-coordinates should be the same, then the y-coordinates determines the ordering. The points are iteratively added to the lower part of the convex hull. After each addition, it is checked whether the last three points make a left turn. If this is not the case, the middle point is deleted. These steps are repeated until the last three points make a left turn, or there are only two points left (the leftmost point and the added point). Figure 7 (b) illustrates this procedure. Formally, the construction of the lower hull can be described by the following functions[1]:

normalise_lower $\vdash_{\text{def}}$ $(\text{normLow}([\,]) = [\,]) \wedge$
$(\text{normLow}([e_1]) = [e_1]) \wedge$
$(\text{normLow}([e_1; e_2]) = [e_1; e_2]) \wedge$
$(\text{normLow}((e_1 :: e_2 :: e_3 :: \mathcal{L})) =$
    if lturn$(e_1, e_2, e_3) = \text{T}$ then $e_1 :: e_2 :: e_3 :: \mathcal{L}$
    else normLow$((e_1 :: e_3 :: \mathcal{L})))$

hull_lower $\vdash_{\text{def}}$ $(\text{hullLow}([\,]) = [\,]) \wedge$
$(\text{hullLow}(e :: \mathcal{L}) = \text{normLow}(e :: \text{hullLow}(\mathcal{L})))$

---

[1] [ ] denotes the empty list, $[e_1; e_2]$ a list containing the two elements e_1 and e_2, and $e :: \mathcal{L}$ denotes the concatenation of a new leftmost element e to an existing list $\mathcal{L}$.

If $\mathcal{L}$ has at least three elements, normLow($\mathcal{L}$) deletes the second element if the first three elements should not form a left turn, and hullLow applies this function to all sublists of a list $\mathcal{L}$.

Specification. A sequence of points is part of the convex hull if for two consecutive points, all other points lie on the left hand side of the line passing those points. We define the corresponding predicate lconvex recursively: A sequence of no elements or one element is always convex. Each additional point that is added must lie on the left of all former edges of the constructed convex hull (lpoint), and all points must lie on the left side of the edge that is created by the insertion of the new point (ledge).

$$
\begin{aligned}
\text{left\_edge} \vdash_{\text{def}} \ & (\text{ledge}(e_1, e_2, [\,])) \wedge \\
& (\text{ledge}(e_1, e_2, e :: \mathcal{L}) = (\text{lturn}(e, e_1, e_2) = \mathsf{T}) \wedge \text{ledge}(e_1, e_2, \mathcal{L})) \\
\text{left\_point} \vdash_{\text{def}} \ & (\text{lpoint}(e, [\,])) \wedge \\
& (\text{lpoint}(e, [e_1])) \wedge \\
& (\text{lpoint}(e, e_1 :: e_2 :: t) = \\
& \quad (\text{lturn}(e, e_2, e_1) = \mathsf{T}) \wedge \text{lpoint}(e, e_2 :: \mathcal{L})) \\
\text{left\_convex} \vdash_{\text{def}} \ & (\text{lconvex}([\,])) \wedge \\
& (\text{lconvex}([e_1])) \wedge \\
& (\text{lconvex}(e_1 :: e_2 :: \mathcal{L}) = \\
& \quad \text{ledge}(e_1, e_2, \mathcal{L}) \wedge \text{lpoint}(e_1, e_2 :: \mathcal{L}) \wedge \text{lconvex}(e_2 :: \mathcal{L}))
\end{aligned}
$$

Verification. The verification is done in several steps. First, by applying the definitions, it is proven that every sublist of three points in the result make a left turn.

$$
\begin{aligned}
\text{left\_chain} \vdash_{\text{def}} \ & (\text{lchain}([\,])) \wedge \\
& (\text{lchain}([e_1])) \wedge \\
& (\text{lchain}([e_1; e_2])) \wedge \\
& (\text{lchain}(e_1 :: e_2 :: e_3 :: \mathcal{L}) = \\
& \quad (\text{lturn}(e_1, e_2, e_3) = \mathsf{T}) \wedge \text{lchain}(e_2 :: e_3 :: \mathcal{L})) \\
\text{LEFT\_CHAIN\_HULL\_LOWER} \vdash \ & \text{lchain}(\mathcal{L}_0) \Rightarrow \text{lchain}(\text{hullLow}(\mathcal{L}_0)\mathcal{L}_1)
\end{aligned}
$$

Then, under the condition of a lexicographic ordering a kind of transitivity (see Figure 7 (c)) is derived. To prove this, the lexicographic conditions are translated to left turn conditions before the transitivity of the left-turn predicate LTURN_TRANS is used. With the help of this lemma, an induction results the desired theorem CVX_LOWER.

$$
\begin{aligned}
\text{CVX\_TRANS\_LOWER} \vdash \ & (\text{lturn}(v_1, v_2, v_3) = \mathsf{T}) \wedge (\text{lturn}(v_2, v_3, v_4) = \mathsf{T}) \wedge \\
& (v_1 \prec_{\text{lex}} v_2 = \mathsf{T}) \wedge (v_2 \prec_{\text{lex}} v_3 = \mathsf{T}) \wedge (v_3 \prec_{\text{lex}} v_4 = \mathsf{T}) \\
& \Rightarrow (\text{lturn}(v_1, v_3, v_4) = \mathsf{T}) \\
\text{CVX\_LOWER} \vdash \ & \text{lexSorted}(\mathcal{L}) \wedge \text{lchain}(\mathcal{L}) \Rightarrow \text{lconvex}(\mathcal{L})
\end{aligned}
$$

Note that in the proofs, we do not have to address the degenerate cases explicitly. We exploit that theorems like LTURN_TRANS subsume many cases. Thus, the correctness of the algorithm is guaranteed for all cases: in particular for the situation that two subsequent input points have the same y-coordinate or there are collinear points in the input set.

5 Conclusions

In this paper, we addressed the problem of specifying and verifying algorithms of computational geometry. Starting from applications like motion planning or collision detection, we formalised basic geometric objects and primitives used in analytic geometry. The main contribution of this paper is to consistently use three-valued logic for this purpose. To this end, we defined a three-valued logic in the theorem prover HOL and used it for the formalisation of geometric primitives in the presence of degenerate cases. Using the HOL theorem prover, we proved numerous theorems and provided various tactics for automating parts of proofs. In particular, we use efficient tactics to translate three-valued goals to two-valued ones. In this way, conventional tactics and proof tools can be used for automated reasoning.

We evaluated our approach by small examples. They all show that our approach is very suitable: The specifications are both precise and compact; the integrated consideration of degenerate cases with the help of three-valued logic makes both algorithms and proofs simpler and clearer. At the same time, all advantages of traditional proof techniques are preserved due to the possible reduction to two-valued expressions.

Our next and more ambitious verification project is the development of a formally proven map overlay algorithm [6] that is suited for applications in safety-critical embedded systems. For this algorithm, some more foundations are required, as e.g. an appropriate formalisation of plane graphs [19].

References

1. L. Bolc and P. Borowik. *Many-Valued logics*. Springer, 1992.
2. J. Brandt and K. Schneider. Dependable polygon-processing algorithms for safety-critical embedded systems. In *International Conference on Embedded And Ubiquitous Computing (EUC)*, LNCS, Nagasaki, Japan, 2005. Springer.
3. J. Brzozowski and C.-J. Seger. *Asynchronous Circuits*. Springer, 1995.
4. C. Burnikel, K. Mehlhorn, and S. Schirra. On degeneracy in geometric computations. In *Symposium on Discrete Algorithms (SODA)*, pages 16–23, Arlington, Virginia, USA, 1994. ACM.
5. S. Chou, X. Gao, and J. Zhang. *Machine Proofs in Geometry*. World Scientific, Singapore, 1994.
6. M. de Berg, M. van Kreveld, M. Overmars, and O. Schwarzkopf. *Computational Geometry*. Springer, 2000.
7. H. Edelsbrunner and E. Mücke. Simulation of simplicity: a technique to cope with degenerate cases in geometric algorithms. *ACM Transactions on Graphics*, 9(1):66–104, 1990.
8. E. Eichelberger. Hazard detection in combinational and sequential switching circuits. *IBM Journal of Research and Development*, 9:90–99, 1965.
9. J. Foley, A. van Dam, S. Feiner, and J. Hughes. *Computer Graphics: Principles and Practice*. Addison Wesley, 2000.
10. M. Gordon and T. Melham. *Introduction to HOL: A Theorem Proving Environment for Higher Order Logic*. Cambridge University Press, 1993.
11. S. Kleene. *Introduction to Metamathematics*. North Holland, 1952.
12. D. Knuth. *Axioms and Hulls*, volume 606 of *LNCS*. Springer, 1992.
13. S. Malik. Analysis of cycle combinational circuits. *IEEE Transactions on Computer Aided Design*, 13(7):950–956, July 1994.

14. K. Mehlhorn and S. Näher. *The LEDA Platform of Combinatorial and Geometric Computing.* Cambridge University Press, 1999.

15. D. Pichardie and Y. Bertot. Formalizing convex hull algorithms. In R. Boulton and P. Jackson, editors, *Higher Order Logic Theorem Proving and its Applications (TPHOL)*, volume 2152 of *LNCS*, pages 346–361, Edinburgh, Scotland, UK, 2001. Springer.

16. T. Reps, M. Sagiv, and R. Wilhelm. Static program analysis via 3-valued logic. In R. Alur and D. Peled, editors, *Conference on Computer Aided Verification (CAV)*, volume 3114 of *LNCS*, pages 15–30, Boston, MA, USA, 2004. Springer.

17. T. Schuele and K. Schneider. Three-valued logic in bounded model checking. In *Formal Methods and Models for Codesign (MEMOCODE)*, Verona, Italy, 2005. IEEE Computer Society.

18. W.-T. Wu. On the decision problem and the mechanization of theorem proving in elementary geometry. *Scientia Sinica*, 21:157–179, 1978.

19. M. Yamamoto, S. Nishizaki, and M. Hagiya. Formalization of planar graphs. In E. Schubert, P. Windley, and J. Alves-Foss, editors, *Higher Order Logic Theorem Proving and its Applications (TPHOL)*, volume 971 of *LNCS*, pages 369–384, Aspen Grove, Utah, USA, September 1995. Springer.

An Automated Approach to Specification-Based Program Inspection[*]

Shaoying Liu[1], Fumiko Nagoya[1], Yuting Chen[1],
Masashi Goya[1], and John A. McDermid[2]

[1] Department of Computer Science,
Faculty of Computer and Information Sciences, Hosei University, Tokyo, Japan
[2] Department of Computer Science, University of York, UK

Abstract. In this paper, we describe how formal specification is adopted to improve the commonly used verification and validation technique known as *program inspection*, in order to establish a more rigorous, repeatable, and efficient inspection process than the conventional practice. We present a systematic approach to inspecting program code on the basis of the relation between functional scenarios defined in a specification and execution paths implemented in its program. We report a prototype tool for the approach to support both *forward* and *backward* inspection strategies, and a case study of inspecting an Automatic Teller Machine system to evaluate the performance of the approach and the tool.

1 Introduction

Program inspection has become a commonly used technique for verification of programs in industry since it was developed by Michael E. Fagan at IBM in the 1970s [1]. The essence of the technique is to detect errors in programs by *human* inspectors through *reading* and *analyzing* programs, based on some criteria. Many researchers have contributed to the progress of the technology by establishing various reading techniques [2, 3, 4, 5] and inspection processes [6, 7, 8], but most of the existing techniques do not take formal specification into account in program inspection, simply because formal specification is not available in most industrial software development projects. With the continual development of formal methods, however, many industrial sectors have gradually adopted formal specification techniques [9, 10, 11, 12]. Although formal specifications are becoming more widely used, formal proof has achieved less industrial acceptance, due to cost and limitations of tools. However, inspection can be a practical approach for verification and validation, especially when the application domain is not safety-critical; even in safety critical applications inspection has an importance. The problem is how to make inspection techniques rigorous so that they can be applied effectively and repeatedly in practice.

---

[*] This work is supported by the Ministry of Education, Culture, Sports, Science, and Technology of Japan under Grant-in-Aid for Scientific Research on Priority Areas (No. 16016279).

K.-K. Lau and R. Banach (Eds.): ICFEM 2005, LNCS 3785, pp. 421–434, 2005.

In this paper, we describe an automated approach to program inspection that utilizes the power of formal specification to tackle the problem. Our inspection approach shares Parnas' idea described in [13] in that the use of formal specification is advocated, but develops the idea further to establish precise and detailed instructions on how a formal specification can be used to help systematic program inspection.

Specifically, a functional specification is treated as a document to define a collection of *functional scenarios*. Each scenario defines a specific functional requirement or service in terms of taking input and generating output. A scenario can be defined by a predicate expression in the model-oriented specification languages at the unit level (e.g., operation) or a series of state transitions at the system level. Our inspection approach suggests that the program be examined to ensure that every functional scenario defined in the specification is implemented correctly by a set of *execution paths* in the program. An execution path is a sequence of operations and/or conditions in a program, starting from one of the start operations or conditions and terminates at one of the end operations or conditions of the program. The case study described in Section 6 shows that derivation of both functional scenarios in a specification and necessary execution paths in a program can be automatically performed by a software tool, hence inspection can be performed systematically and efficiently.

Our major contributions in this paper include (1) the establishment of the principle and strategies for program inspection based on the relation between functional scenarios and their corresponding execution paths, (2) the design of the algorithms and rules for automating the activities involved in our inspection approach, (3) the implementation of a prototype software tool to support the activities involved in an inspection process, and (4) the presentation of a case study of inspecting an Automated Teller Machine (ATM) system to evaluate the performance of the approach and the tool.

The remainder of this paper is organized as follows. Section 2 describes the principles underlying the inspection approach. Section 3 discusses the issues of how to derive functional scenarios from a specification and execution paths from a program, respectively. Section 4 discusses the process of inspecting execution paths in a program. Section 5 reports a prototype tool for our inspection approach, while Section 6 presents a case study using the tool. Finally, in Section 7 we conclude the paper and point out future research.

2   The Principle of Specification-Based Inspection

To facilitate the discussion of the principle, we first need to define all the related notions concerned with both specifications and programs. This paper focuses on the description of how our inspection approach is applied to an operation defined with pre- and postconditions, and will discuss the extension of the approach to software integration level in a future publication.

2.1   Basic Concepts in Specification

Without losing generality in model-oriented specifications (e.g., VDM, Z, B, SOFL), we can assume that an operation is defined by pre- and postconditions.

Definition 1. *An operation OP is a five tuple $[OP_{iv}; OP_{ov}; OP_{ev}; OP_{pre}; OP_{post}]$, where OP_{iv} denotes the set of all the input variables, OP_{ov} the set of all the output variables, and OP_{ev} the set of all the related external variables (state variables), OP_{pre} and OP_{post} represent the pre- and postconditions of OP, respectively, and it satisfies the following condition:*

$$Variables(OP_{pre}) \cup Variables(OP_{post}) \subseteq (OP_{iv} \cup OP_{ov} \cup OP_{ev}).$$

where $Variables(C)$ denotes the set of all variables occurring in predicate C (such as OP_{pre} and OP_{post}). For example, let $C = x > 0 \wedge y < x + 1$. Then $Variables(C) = \{x, y\}$.

All the other concepts concerned with operations defined below are based on the structure of an operation defined in Definition 1.

Definition 2. *Let OP_{eviv} denote the set of all 'rd' external variables and decorated 'wr' external variables (e.g., $\tilde{x}$) of OP. Let OP_{evov} denote the set of all 'wr' undecorated external variables of OP. Then $OP_{ev} = OP_{eviv} \cup OP_{evov}$.*

An 'rd' (readable) external variable of operation OP provides an unmodifiable input value to the operation. A 'wr' (writable) external variable (e.g., x) provides both an input value, represented by the decorated variable (e.g., $\tilde{x}$), and represents an output value, denoted by the undecorated variable (e.g., x) of operation OP. We call the variables of OP_{eviv} *input external variables* and the variables of OP_{evov} *output external variables* of OP, respectively.

Definition 3. *A predicate C in OP_{post} is called a* guard condition *if and only if it contains neither output variables of OP_{ov} nor output external variables of OP_{evov} (part of OP_{ev}).*

Note that an implication of this definition is that both the boolean values *true* and *false* if they appear in OP_{post} are guard conditions.

Definition 4. *A predicate expression D in OP_{post} is called a* defining condition *if and only if it does not contain any guard condition as its constituent expression.*

For example, let the operation *Search* be defined as follows:
$$Search = [\{x\}; \{index\}; \{list\}; true;$$
$$x \in elems(list) \wedge (\exists_{i \in inds(list)} \cdot list(i) = x \wedge index = i) \vee$$
$$\neg x \in elems(list) \wedge index = 0],$$
where x (input variable) denotes an integer, *index* (output variable) a natural number, and *list* (a readable external variable) a sequence of integers; $elems(list)$ denotes the set of all elements on the sequence *list*, and $inds(list)$ represents the index set of *list*.

If input x is a member of $list$, its index (location) in the list will be represented by the variable $index$ as the result of the operation; otherwise, $index = 0$ will be the result. In this specification, the conditions $x \in elems(list)$ and $\neg x \in elems(list)$ are both guard conditions, while $(\exists_{i \in inds(list)} \cdot list(i) = x \wedge index = i)$ and $index = 0$ are both defining conditions.

Definition 5. *Let OP be an operation and $OP_{post} = C_1 \wedge D_1 \vee C_2 \wedge D_2 \vee \cdots \vee C_n \wedge D_n$, where C_i ($i \in \{1, 2, ..., n\}$) is a guard condition and D_i is a defining condition. Then, a* functional scenario f_s *of OP is a conjunction $C_i \wedge D_i$, and such a form of postcondition is called a* functional scenario form *or FSF for short.*

Consider the operation $Search$ above as an example. Its postcondition is in a FSF in which the two functional scenarios $x \in elems(list) \wedge (\exists_{i \in inds(list)} \cdot list(i) = x \wedge index = i)$ and $\neg x \in elems(list) \wedge index = 0$ are included. Since any predicate can be converted into an equivalent disjunctive normal form (if quantified expressions are treated as atomic predicates) and any postcondition in a disjunctive normal form can be converted into an equivalent FSF using **Algorithm 1** described in Section 3, the postcondition of any operation can be converted into an equivalent FSF. Note that simply treating a disjunctive clause in the disjunctive normal form of a postcondition as a functional scenario is not necessarily correct in supporting our inspection approach. For example, let $x > 0 \wedge (y = x \vee y = -x) \vee x \leq 0 \wedge y = x + 1$ be the postcondition of an operation, where x is the input and y is the output. It states that when $x > 0$, y is defined either as x or as $-x$ (the specifier does not care which definition will be implemented). In this case, if we convert it into the disjunctive normal form $x > 0 \wedge y = x \vee x > 0 \wedge y = -x \vee x \leq 0 \wedge y = x + 1$, and treat each of the two disjunctive clauses $x > 0 \wedge y = x$ and $x > 0 \wedge y = -x$ as an individual functional scenario, and require the existence of corresponding execution paths in the program to implement both of them, we may not find a satisfactory answer in the program, since the programmer may (legitimately) have decided to implement only clause $x > 0 \wedge y = x$ as a refinement of $x > 0 \wedge (y = x \vee y = -x)$.

If the testing of the precondition of an operation is enforced in its implementation (in case it is not tested by the environment before the operation is called), we must take the precondition into account as well in forming the FSF of the operation; that is, we need to convert the conjunction $OP_{pre} \wedge OP_{post}$ rather than merely OP_{post} into an equivalent FSF. Since this does not increase technical difficulties compared to the conversion of OP_{post}, for simplicity we only consider OP_{post} in deriving functional scenarios discussed in this paper.

2.2   Basic Concepts Relating to Programs

In this section, we define all the necessary concepts relating to programs, such as program graph and execution path. The program graph of a program is intended to be a syntactically alternative representation of the program that only involves conditions and basic operations, and it offers the base for deriving execution paths in our inspection approach.

Definition 6. *A program graph is a directed graph, represented by a four tuple* (V, S_o, R, E_o), *where* V *is a set of vertices, each representing either an operation or a condition;* $S_o \subseteq V$ *is the set of start vertices;* $R \subseteq V \times V$ *is a relation over* V; *and* $E_o \subseteq V$ *is a set of end vertices.*

A program graph contains a set of vertices denoted by V. Each vertex can be either an operation or a condition. Each operation is defined by a basic statement (assignment or method call) in a programming language, say Java, and each condition is represented by a logical expression. Note that we deliberately disallow operations in V that are defined by compound statements (e.g., *if-else*, *while*, *for* statements) in Java, because each of them can be decomposed into either a single execution sequence or a set of execution sequences of basic statements. There is a unique set of vertices, denoted by S_o, whose elements are contained in V; each element of S_o represents a starting point of an execution of the program. There is also a set of end vertices, denoted by E_o, whose elements are included in V; each element of E_o represents a terminating point of an execution of the program. In addition to the individual vertices in V, a program defines behaviors resulting from either conditional or unconditional executions of operations in V in certain orders. The relation R defines the order of execution of vertices. If a vertex is an operation, by execution of the vertex we mean the execution of the operation; but if it is a condition, by execution of the vertex we mean the evaluation of the condition. Let the pair $(x, y) \in R$ represents a sequential execution of vertex x, then vertex y. Note that $(x, y) \neq (y, x)$ holds in general.

A program graph can be depicted graphically. For example, the program graph $Search_g$, which implements the operation $Search$ described in Section 2, is defined as follows:

$$
\begin{aligned}
Search_g = (&\{i = 1, i <= len(list), \neg i <= len(list), x == list(i), \\
&\quad \neg x == list(i), i = i + 1, index = i, index = 0\}, \\
&\{i = 1\}, \\
&\{(i = 1, i <= len(list)), (i = 1, \neg i <= len(list), \\
&\quad (i <= len(list), x == list(i)), (i <= len(list), \neg x == list(i)), \\
&\quad (x == list(i), i = i + 1), (\neg x == list(i), index = i), \\
&\quad (i = i + 1, i <= len(list)), (i = i + 1, \neg i <= len(list)), \\
&\quad (\neg i <= len(list), index = 0)\}, \\
&\{index = i, index = 0\}) \, .
\end{aligned}
$$

The program graph contains eight vertices, one start vertex ($i = 1$), nine edges, and two end vertices ($index = i$ and $index = 0$). It can be represented graphically by a control flow diagram, as shown in Figure 1, so that each operation vertex is represented by an operation node (rectangle) and each pair of a condition and its negation vertices are represented by a single condition node (elongated hexagon) with 'T' and 'F' marks. Thus, the node containing the condition $i <= len(list)$ in Figure 1, for example, actually represents two condition vertices of the program graph: the one containing the condition $i <= len(list)$ and the one containing $\neg i <= len(list)$, where $len(list)$ yields the length of $list$. The character 'T'

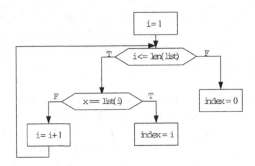

Fig. 1. The graphical representation of a program graph

denotes the boolean value *true* and 'F' denotes *false*. Note that the directed line from the vertex $i = i+1$ to the vertex containing the condition $i <= len(list)$ actually describes two relationships ($i = i + 1$, $i <= len(list)$) and ($i = i + 1$, $\neg i <= len(list)$). In the program graph, we try to use the same syntax as Java, so operator $<=$ means $\leq$, $==$ denotes equality, and $i = i + 1$, for example, represents an assignment.

To facilitate the presentation of rules and algorithms in this paper, we use $P.V$, $P.S_o$, $P.R$, and $P.E_o$ to denote the set of vertices, the set of start vertices, the relation, and the set of end vertices of program graph P, respectively.

Definition 7. *Let* $P = (V, S_o, R, E_o)$ *be a program graph. An execution path of* P *is a path of the graph starting from any vertex in* S_o *and ending at any vertex in* E_o.

An execution path, or simply path, of a program graph can be represented by a sequence of vertices: $[v_1, v_2, ..., v_n]$, where $v_1 \in S_o$ and $v_n \in E_o$, and each v_i ($i \in \{1, 2, ..., n\}$) is a member of V. For example, the program graph $Search_g$ given above includes the following three paths (in addition to many others):

$[i = 1, \neg i <= len(list), index = 0]$
$[i = 1, i <= len(list), x == list(i), index = i]$
$[i = 1, i <= len(list), \neg x == list(i), i = i + 1, \neg i <= len(list), index = 0]$

2.3   The Principle of Specification-Based Inspection

Having defined the necessary concepts previously, we can now describe the principle of specification-based inspection by formally defining the two inspection strategies: *forward inspection* and *backward inspection*.

Definition 8. *Let* $F_s = \{f_1, f_2, ..., f_n\}$ *be the set of all the functional scenarios defined in specification* S *and* $E_p = \{p_1, p_2, ..., p_m\}$ *be the set of all the possible execution paths of program* P. *Then,* P *satisfies* S *if and only if there exists a mapping* $M : F_s \rightarrow power(E_p)$ *that satisfies the following condition:*

$$\forall_{f \in F_s} \exists_{q \in power(E_p)} \cdot M(f) = q \ ,$$

where $power(E_p)$ denotes the power set of E_p, and $M(f) = q$ ($q \subseteq E_p$) means that the set of execution paths q implements correctly the functional scenario f defined in specification S.

Definition 9. *Let f be a functional scenario and q be a set of execution paths. Then $M(f) = q$ iff the following condition holds:*

$$\forall_{s,s' \in \Sigma_{abs}} \cdot f(s,s') \Rightarrow \exists_{p \in q} \exists_{t \in \Sigma_{con}} \cdot s = \Psi(t) \wedge s' = \Psi(p(t))$$

where Σ_{abs} and Σ_{con} denote the set of states on which the operation is defined in the specification and the set of states of its corresponding program, respectively; $\Psi : \Sigma_{con} \rightarrow \Sigma_{abs}$ is a function that yields an abstract state (e.g., s) in the specification for a given concrete state (e.g., t) in the program; and an execution path is treated as a state transformer (e.g., path p transforms state t to state $p(t)$).

A set of execution paths q satisfies functional scenario f if and only if the existence of any pair of initial and final abstract states s and $s\prime$ satisfying f (note that f may contain both initial and final state variables) ensures that the final state $s\prime$ is generated by executing one of the paths in q at the initial concrete state t representing s in the program. We call inspection for verifying whether there exist paths to satisfy any given functional scenario 'forward inspection', indicating the intuition of 'moving' forward to a program from its specification in an inspection.

Although it may not be ideal, a program in practice may often implement more functions than required in its specification. This point is not difficult to understand if we consider the situations of software development in industry. A specification for a program may not be completed due to some possible constraints (e.g., time, difficulties in formalization of requirements) or may not be updated timely to keep the consistency with the implemented program due to limited time and/or budget. For this reason, we propose a backward inspection strategy to ensure that every path in the program will be inspected.

Definition 10. *Let $F_s = \{f_1, f_2, ..., f_n\}$ be the set of all the functional scenarios in operation specification S and $E_p = \{p_1, p_2, ..., p_m\}$ be the set of all the possible execution paths of program P. Then, P is defined by S if and only if there exists a mapping $H : E_p \rightarrow F_s$ that satisfies the following condition:*

$$\forall_{p \in E_p} \exists_{f \in F_s} \cdot H(p) = f$$

where $H(p) = f$ means that the execution path p *contributes* to the implementation of the functional scenario f. Inspection based on this principle is called 'backward inspection'.

Definition 11. *A specification S is consistent with a program P if and only if P satisfies S and P is defined by S.*

The aim of inspecting a program with both the forward and backward inspection strategies is to verify whether the program is consistent with its specification. In the case of an inspection failing to establish the consistency between a specification and its corresponding program, the inspection result is expected to provide useful information to the developers (e.g., designer, programmer) for either completing their specification and program or paying more attention to those incorrectly defined functional scenarios or incorrectly implemented execution paths.

3   Derivation of Functional Scenarios and Execution Paths

The derivation of both functional scenarios and execution paths are two fundamental activities involved in our inspection approach. In this section, we focus on the discussion of algorithms and/or rules for deriving functional scenarios from an operation specification and for deriving execution paths from a program in Java, respectively.

3.1   Derivation of Functional Scenarios

As before, we let operation $OP = [OP_{iv}; OP_{ov}; OP_{ev}; OP_{pre}; OP_{post}]$. Then we use **Algorithm 1** to derive the functional scenario form for the OP_{post} in which all the functional scenarios are included. To describe the algorithm, the following notation is needed.

1. $OUTP_v(OP)$ represents the collection of all output and final external (undecorated) variables of the operation OP.
2. $INP_v(OP)$ denotes the collection of all input and initial external (decorated) variables of the operation OP.
3. $V_{oe}(OP, E)$ denotes the set of variables from $OUTP_v(OP)$ which occur in the predicate E.
4. $V_{ie}(OP, E)$ denotes the set of variables from $INP_v(OP)$ which occur in the predicate E.

Algorithm 1

No.1 Express the postcondition OP_{post} in disjunctive normal form: $P_1 \vee P_2 \vee \cdots \vee P_n$, each P_t ($t \in \{1, 2, ..., n\}$) being a conjunction of atomic predicates and/or quantified expressions.

No.2 For each $P_t = R_1 \wedge R_2 \wedge \cdots \wedge R_m$, construct the partition $\{B_1, B_2\}$ for the set $\{R_1, R_2, ..., R_m\}$ that satisfies the conditions:

    (1) $R_i \in B_1 \Rightarrow V_{oe}(OP, R_i) = \emptyset$, $i \in \{1, 2, ..., m\}$

    (2) $R_i \in B_2 \Rightarrow V_{oe}(OP, R_i) \neq \emptyset$.

No.3 For each predicate set B_k where $k \in \{1, 2\}$, form the conjunction $Q_k = \bigwedge_{i \in s} R_i$, where $s = \{i \in \{1, 2, ..., m\} \cdot R_i \in B_k\}$ and it can be empty for B_1 or B_2 (e.g., when $P_t = true$).

No.4 Express P_t as the conjunction of every such Q_k: $P_t = Q_1 \wedge Q_2$ (Q_1 corresponds to the *guard condition*, while Q_2 corresponds to the *defining condition* given in Definitions 3 and 4, respectively).

No.5 Construct the partition $\{A_1, A_2, ..., A_w\}$ for the set $\{P_1, P_2, ..., P_n\}$ obtained from Step 4 that satisfies the conditions: $P_i, P_j \in A_k \Rightarrow Q_1^i = Q_1^j$, assuming $P_i = Q_1^i \wedge Q_2^i$, $P_j = Q_1^j \wedge Q_2^j$, $i, j \in \{1, 2, ..., n\}$, $k \in \{1, 2, ..., w\}$.

No.6 For each A_k, produce a predicate $P_{A_k} = Q_1 \wedge (\bigvee_{l \in \{1,2,...,u\}} Q_2^l)$, assuming $P_1, P_2, ..., P_u$ are members of A_k; $u \leq n$; and each $P_l = Q_1 \wedge Q_2^l$, where Q_1 is a common guard condition and Q_2^l is a defining condition.

No.7 Express OP_{post} in the functional scenario form: $P_{A_1} \vee P_{A_2} \vee \cdots \vee P_{A_w}$, where each A_k denotes a functional scenario defined in Definition 5.

The essential idea of this algorithm is to convert the disjunctive normal form of a postcondition to an equivalent FSF by reorganizing all the disjunctive clauses with the same guard condition as a single functional scenario while maintaining the structure of the rest of the postcondition.

3.2 Derivation of Execution Paths

The derivation of execution paths from a Java program is performed in two steps: first a program is analyzed by a parser to generate its program graph and then the paths are produced based on the program graph. We apply a constrained depth-first searching algorithm for traversing a program graph to discover all the *necessary* paths of a program graph. A necessary path indicates that either itself needs to be inspected or a set of similar paths together implementing the same functional scenario needs to be inspected. For example, the algorithm generates only two execution paths for each loop: (1) the execution path that covers the loop condition and the loop body once and (2) the path that covers the negation of the loop condition but no loop body. Although not all the paths representing all the possible executions of the loop body are generated by the algorithm due to the difficulty in determining them based only on the syntax of the loop statement, the generated paths related to the loop statement are intended to remind the inspector to consider all the possible cases based on the inspector's intellectual analysis and engineering judgement. Since the algorithm for path generation results from only a slight modification to the standard algorithm for searching paths in a directed graph [14], we omit it for brevity.

4   Inspection of Execution Paths

To inspect the execution paths against their functional scenarios, we take two steps. The first step is to link scenarios to their corresponding paths and the second step is to analyze the paths to detect errors. The linking of scenarios to paths can be automatically performed if all the variables and the logical expressions used in the specification are preserved directly in the program; otherwise, it can be performed manually with tool support. The reading of paths can be done by taking the two strategies described in Definitions 8 and 10, respectively. Taking the forward strategy, the inspector concentrates on the examination of whether or not every scenario defined in the specification is implemented correctly by a single or set of paths in the program. While using the backward strategy, the inspector can focus on checking whether every path in the program contributes to the implementation of any scenario defined in the specification. The discovery of any inconsistency between the specification and the corresponding program will indicate the existence of potential errors, either in the specification or in the program, and the nature of the discrepancy can be determined based on a rigorous analysis. The analysis may be conducted only by the inspector, but to be more effective in practice, it is better to be carried out by a group of people together, including the inspector, the specifier, and the programmer, if they are available within the allowed timetable.

Our tool, described in Section 5, effectively supports the inspection of each path by automatically highlighting every statement or condition under examination, providing a well-designed graphical user interface to enable the inspector to input his or her comments on any detected errors or any issue concerned with the statement or condition, and automatically recording and categorizing the comments. After the inspection of a path is finished, a systematic inspection result report will be displayed in appropriate forms.

5   A Prototype Tool

We have constructed a prototype tool, called *SBPIT* (Specification-Based Program Inspection Tool) to support our inspection approach with three person-year efforts. The tool was designed using SOFL [15] and implemented in Java. It is an integration of two sub-tools and it supports SOFL as the specification language and Java as the programming language. One sub-tool supports the forward inspection strategy, while another supports the backward strategy. To support an inspection using the forward strategy, the tool displays the content of a selected specification in a window, and then automatically generates a list of all its functional scenarios. To link each scenario to its corresponding execution paths in the program, the tool will switch to display the content of the corresponding program on a specific area in the GUI (graphical user interface), and automatically generate its program graph so that it is displayed on an adjacent window, and automatically generate all the necessary execution paths based on the program graph. Then, the tool supports the inspector to link each scenario to some execution paths in the program by automatically highlighting the current scenario, and recording the association between scenarios and the corresponding paths. Once a specific scenario is selected, its corresponding paths will be displayed based on the recorded association relation obtained previously. The inspector can carry out the inspection of each path based either on the program graph (which is represented by a control flow diagram) or the source code of the program. The source code and the program graph are connected by hyperlinks. Figure 2 shows a snapshot of the GUI of the tool supporting the forward inspection strategy for an operation (we call it *process* in SOFL) Withdraw in the ATM system used in our case study. The left pane of the GUI shows the list of generated paths from the program displayed in the middle pane. The program graph shown in the right pane of the GUI is automatically

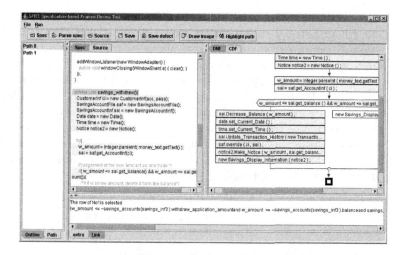

Fig. 2. A snapshot of the inspection tool supporting forward strategy

generated from the program. The bottom-right pane of the GUI displays a single scenario for the current inspection.

Taking the backward strategy for an inspection needs to go through the same process, but the starting point is the source code of the program rather than its specification. For the sake of brevity, we omit the detailed descriptions of this and other features of the tool.

6   A Case Study

The goal of our case study of inspecting an ATM system is to assess the effectiveness of the inspection approach in detecting errors and the efficiency of the tool in supporting the inspection approach. The selection of the ATM system for the case study was made mainly based on the consideration of its critical nature, commercial impact, and the availability of its formal specification in SOFL. The specification is implemented in Java and the corresponding program is organized in a package including eleven Java files, and the interfaces of the related methods in the classes are similar to those of their operation specifications.

We started the case study by inserting eighty-one errors in the program independently of the inspectors. Those errors are divided into three categories by the person who inserted them (the third author of the paper), which are *component redundancy*, *component scarcity*, and *component distortion*. A component redundancy error means that some extra function or variable is inserted into the program. A component scarcity error implies that some original component of the program is deleted from the program. A component distortion error means that some component in the program is modified so that it may not provide the correct functions. We choose those types of errors because they are concerned with the consistency between the specification and the program.

The inspections were conducted by three different inspectors (the first, second, and fourth authors). Two inspections were conducted using our tool, while another one was performed manually (without using the tool at all), in order to find out how useful the tool is. In the case of using the tool, one inspector, called A, used the forward inspection strategy and another, called B, used the backward strategy. In the case of manual inspection, the inspector, called C, mainly took the forward inspection strategy, but also took the backward strategy for the inspection of the paths not covered during the forward inspection. Table 1 shows the inspection result of inspector A. The overall effectiveness of error detection in this case is $Effectiveness_A = 71.6\%$, where the effectiveness is calculated using the following formula.

$$Effectiveness = \frac{Number\ of\ inserted\ errors\ detected}{Total\ number\ of\ inserted\ errors}$$

Table 1. Inspection result of inspector A

Error Type	Number	Detected	Effectiveness
Component redundancy	12	9	0.750
Component scarcity	32	21	0.656
Component distortion	37	28	0.757
Total	81	58	0.716

In addition to the effectiveness, we also evaluate the inspection efficiency with the formula

$$Efficiency = \frac{Effectiveness\ of\ the\ inspection}{Time\ to\ inspect\ the\ program} \times 100\ .$$

Inspector A spent seven hours for the inspection, the inspection efficiency is therefore $Efficiency_A \approx (0.716\ /\ 7) \times 100 \approx 10.23$, that is, the average effectiveness per unit time ('hour' in our case).

Table 2 shows the inspection result of inspector B. The inspection effectiveness in this case is $Effectiveness_B \approx 55.6\%$. Since inspector B took eight hours to perform the inspection, the inspection efficiency is $Efficiency_A \approx (0.556\ /\ 8) \times 100 \approx 6.95$.

Table 2. Inspection result of inspector B

Error Type	Number	Detected	Effectiveness
Component redundancy	12	5	0.417
Component scarcity	32	16	0.500
Component distortion	37	24	0.649
Total	81	45	0.556

In contrast to the above two inspections using the tool, the inspection result of inspector C without using the tool indicates a lower effectiveness of error

Table 3. Inspection result of inspector C

Error Type	Number	Detected	Effectiveness
Component redundancy (type 1)	12	5	0.417
Component scarcity (type 2)	32	10	0.313
Component distortion (type 3)	37	16	0.432
Total	81	31	0.383

detection ($Effectiveness_C \approx 38.3\%$), as shown in Table 3, and a much lower inspection efficiency, which is $Efficiency_C \approx (0.383/13) \times 100 \approx 2.92$. The reason for the much lower efficiency is that inspector spent a much longer time (thirteen hours) than the other two inspectors.

Our experience in the case study suggests that ease of understanding of the program structure based on the functional scenarios in the specification contributed considerably to the higher effectiveness and efficiency of the inspection with the forward inspection strategy, though it may be extremely difficult to assert in general that the forward strategy is superior to the backward strategy. Furthermore, the automation provided by the tool made many activities (e.g., derivations of scenarios and paths) much more efficient than those in the manual inspection, it helped the inspectors using the tool to easily and quickly analyze paths against their scenarios and to detect errors. Of course, we understand that these preliminary results require further validation through more extensive case studies and ultimately industrial-scale application. For the sake of space, we omit the explanation of other more detailed issues concerned with the case study.

7   Conclusions and Future Research

This paper introduced a specification-based inspection approach to detecting errors in programs. The essential principle of the approach is to check whether every functional scenario in a specification is implemented by some execution paths in its program and whether every execution path contributes to the implementation of some functional scenario. Two inspection strategies, known as forward and backward strategies, are proposed for inspections. We have built a prototype tool to support the inspection approach and conducted a case study to evaluate the effectiveness of the approach and the efficiency of the tool. The result shows that both forward and backward strategies are rather effective for finding errors, and the tool is effective in efficiently supporting the inspection approach. Meanwhile, our experience in the case study also indicated the potential challenge in the application of the method in practice. The reason is that specifications may often be incomplete and their structures may be quite different from those of their programs, thus linking scenarios in specifications to paths in their programs would be difficult and time-consuming.

More research is needed to enhance the practicality, efficiency, and capability of our inspection approach for verification and validation of program systems in general. We are interested in investigating more effective methods for linking scenarios in a specification to paths in its program and in extending the approach to deal with architecture level verification and validation. We are also interested in investigating potential benefits in extending these techniques to safety-critical code, where the use of inspection is often a precursor to other forms of verification [16].

Acknowledgements. We would like to thank Tomoya Sano for his contribution to the building of the prototype tool.

References

[1] M. E. Fagan. Design and Code Inspections to Reduce Errors in Program Development. *IBM Systems Journal*, 15(3):182–211, 1976.

[2] A. A. Porter, H. P. Siy, and L. G. Votta. A Review of Software Inspections. *Advances in Computers*, 42:39–76, 1996.

[3] O. Laitenberger and J-M. DeBaud. An Encompassing Life-Cycle Centric Survey of Software Inspection. *Journal of Systems and Software*, 50(1):5–31, 2000.

[4] T. Gilb and D. Graham. *Software Inspection*. Addison-Wesley, 1993.

[5] NASA. *Software Formal Inspection Process Standard*. NASASTD-2202-93, 1993.

[6] D. L. Parnas and D. M. Weiss. Active Design Reviews: Principles and Practice. In *8th International Conference on Software Engineering*, pages 132–136, 1985.

[7] J. C. Knight and E. A. Myers. An Improved Inspection Technique. *Communications of the ACM*, 36(11):51–61, 1993.

[8] D. L. Parnas and M. Lawford. The Role of Inspection in Software Quality Assurance. *IEEE Transactions on Software Engineering*, 29(8):674–676, August 2003.

[9] Peter Gorm Larsen, John Fitzgerald, and Tom Brookes. Applying Formal Specification in Industry. *IEEE Software*, 13(3):48–56, May 1996.

[10] C. L. Heitmeyer. Applying the SCR Requirements Method to a Weapons Control Panel: an Experience Report. In *Proceedings of the Second Workshop on Formal Methods in Practice*, pages 92–102. ACM Press, 1998.

[11] G. Babin and F. Lustman. Application of Formal Methods to Scenario-based Requirements Engineering. *International Journal of Computers and Applications*, 23(3):141–151, 2001.

[12] S. Sahara. An Experience of Applying Formal Method on a Large Business Application (in Japanese). In *Proceedings of 2004 Symposium of Science and Technology on System Verification*, pages 93–100, Osaka, Japan, Feb. 4-6 2004. National Institute of Advanced Industrial Science and Technology (AIST).

[13] D. L. Parnas, J. Madey, and M. Iglewski. Precise Documentation of Well-Structured Programs. *IEEE Transactions on Software Engineering*, 20(12):948–976, December 1994.

[14] Michael T. Goodrich and Roberto Tamassia. *Data Structures and Algorithms in Java*. John Wiley & Sons, Inc, 2001.

[15] S. Liu. *Formal Engineering for Industrial Software Development Using the SOFL Method*. Springer-Verlag, 2004.

[16] F.O. Iwu, A. Galloway, I. Toyn, and J.A. McDermid. Practical Formal Specification for Embedded Control Systems. In *INCOM'04: 11th IFAC Symposium on Information Control Problems in Manufacturing*, page 6pp, April 2004. Special session on formal methods: promising solutions to improve industrial controllers' dependability.

Visualizing and Simulating Semantic Web Services Ontologies

Jun Sun[1], Yuan Fang Li[1], Hai Wang[2], and Jing Sun[3]

[1] School of Computing, National University of Singapore
{sunj, liyf}@comp.nus.edu.sg
[2] Department of Computer Science, University of Manchester
hai.wang@cs.man.ac.uk
[3] Department of Computer Science, The University of Auckland
j.sun@cs.auckland.ac.nz

Abstract. The development of Web Services has transformed the World Wide Web into a more application-aware information portal. The various standards ensure that Web Services are interpretable and extensible, opening up possibilities for simple services to be combined to build complex ones. The Semantic Web presents a new mechanism for users and software agents to discover, describe, invoke, compose and monitor Web services. For these purposes the Semantic Web Services (OWL-S) ontologies have been developed to provide vocabularies to describe Web Services in a precise and machine-understandable way. It is necessary to ensure the ontological descriptions of the services capture the intended meaning as erroneous description may cause invocation of wrong services, with wrong parameters, resulting in undesired outcome. In this paper, we propose to apply software engineering method and tools to visualize, simulate and verify OWL-S process models. Namely, Live Sequence Charts (LSCs) is used to model services, capturing the inner workings of services, and its tool support Play-Engine is used to perform automated visualization, simulation and checking.

Keywords: Semantic Web Services, OWL-S, LSC, Play-Engine.

1 Introduction

The World Wide Web has evolved from a static information repository to a current dynamic distributed information sharing and processing source. Web Services [2,3] are one of the latest endeavors in this evolution. Together with layers of XML-based open standards [19,18,3], Web Services provide a framework for automated service advertisement, discovery, invocation, composition & inter-operation and execution monitoring. Web applications can be dynamically discovered, invoked and simple services can be composed to build more complex ones.

The Semantic Web [1] is another frontier of the Web development that is believed by many as the future of the Web, in which software agents can cooperate to accomplish tasks without human supervision. Web resources are given

K.-K. Lau and R. Banach (Eds.): ICFEM 2005, LNCS 3785, pp. 435–449, 2005.

well-defined meaning so that they are readily available to human users as well as machines to understand and process. Resources on the Web are expressed in terms of ontologies, which define concepts and relationships of a particular domain. Based on description logics, OWL (Web Ontology Language) has been published by W3C as a Proposed Recommendation.

A Semantic Web Services ontology, the OWL-S [17], is currently being developed to *semantically* specify Web services. Expressed in OWL, it is a meta-ontology aimed at supplying the service producers/consumers with a core set of machine-interpretable vocabularies for precisely describing the properties and capabilities of Web services. It can be foreseen that the blending of OWL-S and various Web Services standards will present a more automated, effective approach to developing, deploying and utilizing Web services. As OWL-S ontologies define what a service (sometimes referred to as a process) does, how it works and what are its inputs, outputs, preconditions and effects (IOPEs), it is necessary that they capture the correct information. Erroneous definition of preconditions, for example, may make a service invoked when it should not be. Hence, tool support, especially reasoning and simulation tool support is highly desirable for Semantic Web Services developers.

A number of reasoning engines have been developed for ontology languages RDF, DAML+OIL and OWL, such as FaCT [11] and RACER [5]. All these tools are concentrated on deducing subsumption relationship (deducing whether one OWL class is a "sub class" of another class) and checking consistency of static Semantic Web ontologies. We foresee that, since OWL-S emphasize on service description, forthcoming tool support ought to efficiently capture the dynamic aspects of services.

In this paper, we propose to use the software engineering language Live Sequence Charts (LSCs) [4] and its tool support Play-Engine [8] to visualize and simulate OWL-S process model ontologies, which capture the essential information about how a service is to be invoked, executed and the expected result and outputs. LSCs are a broad extension of the classic Message Sequence Charts (MSCs [13]). They capture communicating scenarios between system components rigorously. LSCs distinguish scenarios that must happen from scenarios that may happen, conditions that must be fulfilled from conditions that may be fulfilled, etc. Together with various high-level operators like bounded loop, if-then-else, LSCs may well be used to specify complicated inter-object system requirements. One of the novel aspects of LSCs is that they allow a "play-in/play-out" approach to simulate and verify the requirements without implementing the underlying object systems [7], which is realized in Play-Engine. It allows users to interactively introduce a set of LSCs as behavioral requirements and automatically drive the execution of the requirements by employing formal verification techniques.

The essential idea of capturing OWL-S process models using LSCs is that a OWL-S process model may be perfectly viewed as describing a scenario of the interactions between a service-using agent and the service-providing agent. The benefits of modeling OWL-S process models as LSCs are many-fold:

- Allowing service designers to enjoy the visual power of LSCs by visually designing OWL-S process models in Play-Engine. As LSCs are expressed in XML, they can be easily transformed back to OWL-S ontologies when a service designer is satisfied with the simulation runs in Play-Engine.
- Using Play-Engine to simulate services without implementing them. By smart playing-out [6] OWL-S process models in Play-Engine, unwanted scenarios may be discovered early in the design stage.
- Tapping Play-Engine's ability of interacting with dynamic linked libraries (.dlls) such as COM, COM+, ActiveX Controls, service designers can more easily write LSCs specifications by directly calling functions from Web services defined as these libraries, therefore integrate existing Web services with OWL-S process models.

Moreover, we believe that mature development of the synthesis and verification techniques of LSCs and MSCs offers helpful guidance on designing and verifying Web Services.

The rest of the paper is organized as follows. In Section 2, an overview of Web Services, the Semantic Web, ontology languages RDF, OWL and OWL-S, the language LSC and tool Play-Engine is briefly presented. In Section 3, we present the transformation rules from OWL-S process model ontology to LSCs. The air ticket search and booking case study is introduced in Section 4. It is the running example of the paper. In this section, we also demonstrate how Play-Engine can be used to run automatic simulation of services and verify properties dynamically. Finally, Section 5 concludes the paper and discusses future work directions.

2   Overview

This section is devoted to a brief introduction of Semantics Web and Web Services, LSCs and Play-Engine. Interested readers are referred to [17] and [8] for detailed features of OWL Web Services and LSCs, respectively.

2.1   Semantic Web and Web Services

Web Services is a W3C coordinated effort to define a set of open and industry-supported specifications to provide a standard way of coordination between different software applications in a variety of environments. A Web service is defined as "a software system designed to support interoperable machine-to-machine interaction over a network. It has an interface described in a machine-processable format (specifically WSDL). Other systems interact with the Web service in a manner prescribed by its description using SOAP messages, typically conveyed using HTTP with an XML serialization in conjunction with other Web-related standards" [2].

The various specifications in the Web services domain are all based on XML, making information processing and interchange easier. However, as XML Schema only defines the syntax of a document, it is hard for software agents to understand the *semantics* of a Web service described using these specifications. A language that is both syntactically well-formed and semantical is therefore desirable.

The Semantic Web [1] is an envisioned extension of the current Web, in which resources are given machine-understandable, unambiguous meaning so that software agents can cooperate to accomplish complex tasks without human supervision. Resources in Semantic Web are marked up using ontologies, defining concepts of and relationships between resources. Ontology languages give basic vocabularies for expressing ontologies. The Web Ontology Language (OWL) [15] is the de-facto ontology language. Given a particular domain, OWL uses *classes* to represent abstract knowledge, use *properties* to relate different classes and use *individuals* to represent concrete entities that belong to various classes. It lays the foundation on which other ontologies can build.

OWL-S is an OWL-based Web service ontology, which supplies Web service producers/consumers with a core set of markup language constructs for describing the properties and capabilities of their Web services in an unambiguous, computer-interpretable form. OWL-S was expected to enable the tasks of 'automatic Web service discovery', 'automatic Web service invocation' and 'automatic Web service composition and inter-operation'. OWL-S consists of three essential types of knowledge about a service: the profile, the process model and the grounding. Figure 1 shows the high-level architecture of an OWL-S ontology. A ServiceProfile tells what the service does. It is the primary construct by which a service is advertised, discovered and selected. The ServiceGrounding tells how the service is used. It specifies how an agent can access a service by specifying, for example, communication protocol, message format, port numbers, etc.. The primary concern of our work in this paper is the OWL-S ServiceModel (also called process model), which tells how the service works. Thus, the class Service is described By a ServiceModel. It includes information about the service's inputs, outputs, preconditions and effects. It also shows the component processes of a complex process and how the control flows between the components.

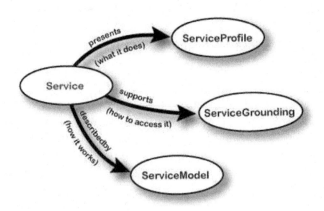

Fig. 1. Architecture of OWL-S Ontology

The OWL-S process model is intended to provide a basis for specifying the behavior of a wide array of services. There are two chief components of an OWL-S process model – the process, and process control model. The process describes a Web Service in terms of its input, output, precondition, effects and, where appropriate, its component subprocess. The process model enables planning, composition and agent/service inter-operation. The process control model – which describes the control flow of a composite process and shows which of various inputs of the composite process are accepted by which of its sub-processes – allows agents to monitor the execution of a service request. The constructs to specify the control flow within a process model include Sequence, Split, Split+Join, If-Then-Else, Repeat-While and Repeat-Until. The full list of control constructs in OWL-S and its semantics can be found in the latest version of OWL-S [17].

2.2   LSC and Play-Engine

LSCs are a powerful visual formalism which serves as an enriched requirements specification language. There are two kinds of charts in LSCs. Existential charts are mainly used to describe possible interactions between participants in early stages of system design. At a later stage, knowledge becomes available about when a system run has progressed far enough for a specific usage of the system to become relevant. Universal charts are then used to specify behaviors that should always be exhibited. A universal chart may be preceded by a pre-chart, which serves as the activation condition for executing the main chart. Whenever a communication sequence matches a pre-chart, the system must proceed as specified by the main chart. A chart typically consists of multiple instances, which are represented as vertical lines. Along with each line, there are a finite number of locations (i.e. the joint points of instances and messages). A location carries the temperature annotation for progress within an instance. Message passing between instances is represented as horizontal lines. Cold conditions are used to assistant specifying complex control structures like guarded-choice, do-while. Hot conditions are asserted to assure critical properties at certain point of execution. Typically, a system is described by a set of LSCs, both universal charts and existential charts. LSCs support advanced MSC features like co-region, hierarchy and etc. For details on features of LSCs, refer to [7]. LSCs are far more expressive than MSCs, which makes them capable of expressing complicated inter-objects system requirements.

An interaction-based model specifies the desired inter-object relationships before a system is actually constructed. It is beneficial if the model can be simulated and tested so as to detect inconsistencies and under-specification. One of the significance of LSCs is that descriptions in the LSC language can be executed by Play-Engine without implementing the underlying object system. Play-Engine is a tool recently developed to support an approach to the specification, validation, analysis and execution of LSCs, called "play-in" and "play-out". Behavior is "played in" directly from the system's user interface, and as this is being done the Play-Engine continuously constructs LSCs. Later, behavior can be "played out" freely from the user interface, and the tool executes the LSCs directly, thus driving the system's behavior. When "playing out", Play-Engine computes a "maximal response" to a user-provided event, called a super-step. During the computing of a super-step, hot conditions are evaluated. If any hot condition evaluates to false, a violation is caught. Otherwise, simulation continues with the user provided events. This way, users may detect undesired behaviors allowed by the specification early in the development. The basic play-out engine arbitrarily explores a single super-step, hence possibly running into problems. The smart play-out approach uses model checking to compute a valid super-step if it exists. Alternatively, test case may be supplied by the users as existential charts so that Play-Engine may guide the system accordingly to verify a scenario of interactions between the user and system is possible.

3 Modeling OWL-S with LSCs

In this section, we concentrate on the process model of OWL-S and abstract away the service grounding details. The key idea of using LSCs to visualize and simulate the OWL-S process models is to use an LSC universal chart capturing a process model. In other words, each process is viewed as describing a possible communicating scenario between a service-using agent and the service-providing agent. For each process model, we assume there is a pre-service request from the service-using agent to the service-providing agent that identifies the service to perform, which corresponds to the service grounding phase that we ignore in this work. For instance, the *request*() message in Figure 3 is a pre-service request from a *HolidayBookingAgent* to a *BdgtChker*. Once a pre-service request is exchanged between the service-using agent and the service-providing agent, subsequent interactions follow precisely as defined in the service definition (the process model).

The classes of processes of a OWL-S ontology are categorized into three groups: atomic, composite and simple. An atomic process corresponds to the actions that a service can perform by engaging it in a single interaction, i.e. a one-step service that expects a bundle of inputs and produces a bundle of outputs. An atomic process is a "black box" representation; that is, no description is given of how the process works (apart from inputs, outputs, preconditions, and effects). The following are a list of process features of atomic processes.

- *process.hasInput*: It specifies one of the inputs of the service.
- *process.hasLocal*: It specifies one of the local parameters. Local parameters are only used in atomic processes.
- *process.hasOutput*: It specifies one of the outputs of the service.
- *process.hasPrecondition*: It specifies one of the pre-conditions of the service. Preconditions are evaluated with respect to the client environment before the process is invoked.
- *process.hasResult*: It specified one of the effects of the service. Result conditions are effectively meant to be 'evaluated' in the server context after the process has executed.

Basically, a service defined by an atomic process is translated to an LSC universal chart preceded by a pre-chart containing only the pre-service request. An atomic process has always two participants, i.e. service-using agent and service-providing agent if the participants are skipped in the OWL-S ontology. Otherwise, participants in an ontology are translated to instances in the chart. According to [17], "inputs and outputs specify the data transformation produced by the process", hence they are identified with communication between different participants in the main chart. If a process has a precondition, it cannot be performed successfully unless the precondition is true. Pre-condition of a service is, therefore, identified with a shared cold condition (among all participants) at the very beginning of the main chart. Thus, if the condition is violated, the chart terminates and hence the process (service) is not performed. Post-condition of the *inCondition* properties in *process.hasResult* are conjoined and identified with a shared hot condition at the end of the chart so that if the post-condition is violated, an error is raised by Play-Engine. The *withOutput* properties are then identified with communications after the hot condition.

The data bindings are analyzed to identify the correspondence between different inputs and outputs and local variables (if there are). Besides, built-in functions in the process models are translated to external functions in LSC (Play-Engine) and local variables are identified with variables associated with the instances in the chart.

Composite processes are composed of sub-processes, and specify constraints on the ordering and conditional execution of these sub-processes. These constraints are captured by the "composedOf" property. Composite processes are constructed using control constructs and references to processes called *PERFORMs*. These are analogous to function calls in procedural language function bodies. *PERFORM* itself is a kind of control construct specifying where the client should invoke a process provided by some server. *PERFORM* may be references to atomic or other composite processes. *PERFORM* are composed using other control constructs. The minimal initial set includes *Sequence, Split, Split+Join, Any-Order, Condition, If-Then-Else, Iterate, Repeat-While* and *Repeat-Until*. We summarize the list of control constructs in Table 1 (according to OWL-S 1.1).

In the following, we discuss how composite services are systematically transformed to LSCs. We present the transformation in the following as transformation rules for each and every control construct in Table 1.

- *Sequence*: It is naturally translated to sequential communications along the vertical lines in a chart. If a sub-process itself is composed by other processes, the sub-process is transformed to a sub-chart or a pre-service request in case the sub-process is reused in other processes. Variables in the output bindings are parameterized with the message so that they are unified with the variables in the invoked processes.
- *Split*: Because no specification about waiting or synchronization is made among the bag of process components, processes in *Split* correspond to multiple pre-service requests grouped as a co-region so that the ordering of the

Table 1. A Partial Summary of the OWL-S constructs

OWL-S Constructs	Description
process:Sequence	Executes a list of processes in order.
process:Split	Executes a bag of processes concurrently.
process:Split+Join	Executes a bag of processes concurrently with barrier synchronization.
process:Any-Order	Execute a bag of processes in any order but not concurrently.
process:Choice	Chooses between alternatives and executes.
process:If-Then-Else	Tests the *if-condition*. If *true* executes the "Then" branch, if *false* executes the "Else" branch.
process:iterate	Serves as the common superclass of *Repeat-While* and *Repeat-Until* and potentially other specific iteration constructs.
Repeat-While	Iterates execution of a bag of processes until the *while* Condition becomes true.
Repeat-Until	Iterates execution of a bag of processes until the *until* Condition becomes true.
timeout	Interval of time allowed for completion of the process component (relative to the start of process component execution).

execution of the components are not constrained. Each pre-service request will in term activate an LSC modeling the corresponding service.

- *Split-Join*: Because of the possible barrier synchronization, it is transformed to LSCs similarly as *Split* with additional 0-buffered communication corresponding to the barrier synchronization. The 0-buffered communication events are shared by all LSCs modeling the invoked services. Therefore, the synchronization is made among all sub-processes. Moreover, the location where the co-region is is set to be hot so that completion of all components are guaranteed.
- *Unordered*: All components must be executed. This is transformed to LSCs exactly as *Split* except all locations in LSCs corresponding to the components are set to be hot so that completion of all components are guaranteed.
- *Choice*: This corresponds to the *SELECT-Case* construct in LSCs. Thus, a choice in OWL-S is transformed to a *SELECT-Case* sub-chart with equally distributed possibility.
- *If-Then-Else*: The exact same construct *if-then-else* is available in LSCs. The *If-condition* and *Else-condition* are mapped to cold conditions in the respective sub-chart. The only problem is to syntax-rewrite the logical ex-

pression used in OWL-S (represented in DRS[1] or SWRL [12] or perhaps KIF[2]) properly to logical expression in LSCs.

- *Repeat-While and Repeat-Until*: Whether the test occurs at a fixed place within the iteration or runs asynchronously varies from subclasses to subclass of these classes. The former is transformed to a looping sub-chart in LSCs with a shared cold condition (corresponding to the condition in the service definition) at the end of the sub-chart. The latter is transformed to a looping sub-chart in LSCs with a cold condition (corresponding to the negation of the condition in the service definition) at the end of the sub-chart.
- *timeout*: It is mapped to a timer set event followed by a timeout event in LSCs containing the respective process components.

The transformation rules for composite processes are applied inductively. One of the difficulties of using LSCs to simulate the OWL-S process models is to do the correct data binding and data computation. We assume that a simple underlying data and functional model of the system is supplied by the users, i.e. the underlying system variables and the implementation of the external functions and so on. To simulate the set of process models interactively, we may build a simple user interface to trigger environmental events manually. A simple user-interface is built with a button for triggering every process model. Play-Engine supports such user-interface built with Visual Basic, and plays-out the corresponding LSCs according the user interaction through the interface.

4   Case Study

This section illustrates the approach with an example of an online holiday booking system.

4.1   System Scenario

The holiday booking system is a Web portal offering access to information about air tickets and hotels. This Web portal provides automated air ticket and hotel booking services to users who are planning their holidays.

In the course of operation, the customer submits a request, which includes the information about the destination, travelling time and maximum budget, to the holiday booking agent. Upon receiving the request, the holiday booking agent tries to find the most suitable air ticket and hotel based on information in the customer's preferences, which have been obtained from his online, OWL-encoded profile. The preferences may include the preferred airlines, hotels, etc. Following that, the holiday booking agent calculates if the total cost overruns the budget limit. If the total cost is more than customer's budget, the holiday booking agent tries to find another cheaper hotel or ticket. If there is no ticket and hotel combination that can be found within the budget,

---

[1] cf. http://www.daml.org/services/owl-s/1.0/conditions.html
[2] cf. http://logic.stanford.edu/kif/dpans.html

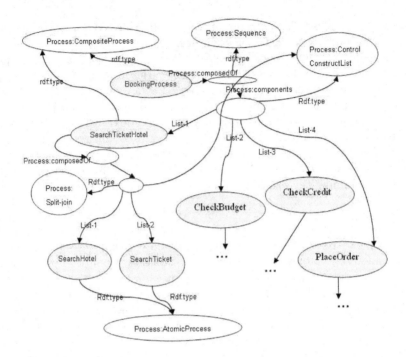

Fig. 2. Holiday booking System

the customer will be notified. Otherwise the booking agent shows the information about the matched ticket and hotel to the customer. If the customer is satisfied, he/she submits his/her credit card information to the holiday booking agent. The holiday booking agent asks a third-part credit checking agent to check if the card is valid with sufficient credit. If it is, the book will be made.

Figure 2 is a RDF graph of the service ontology. It shows part of the OWL-S process model for the holiday booking agent[3]. The holiday booking service has a composite process *BookingProcess* which sequentially performs four sub-processes – *SearchTicketHotel*, *CheckBudget*, *CheckCredit* and *PlaceOrder*. *SearchTicketHotel* is a composite process as well, which performs two atomic process, *SearchHotel* and *SearchTicket*, in parallel. The complete OWL-S process model can be found at http://www.cs.man.ac.uk/~hwang/booking.xml.

Being part of our case study, the following is the process model of an atomic OWL-S service ontology that checks whether the current air ticket and hotel prices are within user budget, given as inputs the air ticket price (variable X1), hotel accommodation cost (variable X2) and the user's budget (variable X3)[4]. As output, this atomic service returns true for variable Check_Budget_result if

---

[3] The diagram has been slightly revised for presentation purpose.

[4] These variables are represented as budget_ticket_Cost, budget_hotel_Cost and budget_total_Cost in the ontology, respectively.

X3 ≤ X1 + X2, and false otherwise. For atomic processes, the inputs must come from the service-using agent.

```
<process:AtomicProcess rdf:ID="CheckBudget">
  <process:hasInput><process:Input rdf:ID="budget_hotel_Cost">
    <process:parameterType rdf:datatype="&xsd;#nonNegativeInteger"/>
  </process:Input></process:hasInput>
  <process:hasInput><process:Input rdf:ID="budget_ticket_Cost">
    <process:parameterType rdf:datatype="&xsd;#nonNegativeInteger"/>
  </process:Input></process:hasInput>
  <process:hasInput><process:Input rdf:ID="budget_total_Cost">
    <process:parameterType rdf:datatype="&xsd;#nonNegativeInteger"/>
  </process:Input></process:hasInput>
  <process:hasOutput><process:Output rdf:ID="Check_Budget_result">
    <process:parameterType rdf:datatype="&xsd;#anyURI">&xsd;#boolean
  </process:parameterType></process:Output></process:hasOutput>
  <process:hasResult>
   <process:Result rdf:ID="Within_budget">
     <process:withOutput>
       <process:OutputBinding>
         <process:toParam rdf:resource="#Check_Budget_result"/>
         <process:valueData rdf:datatype="&xsd;#boolean">true
         </process:valueData></process:OutputBinding></process:withOutput>
       <process:inCondition>
        <expr:KIF-Condition>
          <expr:expressionBody>
             (>= ?budget_total_Cost
                 (+ ?budget_ticket_Cost ?budget_hotel_Cost))
          </expr:expressionBody>
        </expr:KIF-Condition>
       </process:inCondition>
     </process:Result>
  </process:hasResult>
  <process:hasResult>
    <process:Result rdf:ID="beyond_budget">
      ...
    </process:Result>
  </process:hasResult>
</process:AtomicProcess>
```

Figure 3 shows an LSC universal chart capturing the necessary interactions between a service-using agent and a budget-checking agent cooperating in the above atomic service. Once the service-using agent requests the service *CheckBudget* (after determining whether the service meets its needs by exploring the service profile), necessary information like budget_ticket_Cost and budget_hotel_Cost is supplied by the service-using agent. The budget-checking agent replies with true, if the budget is at least as much as the sum of the air ticket and hotel prices, and false otherwise.

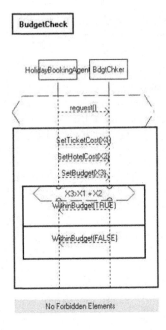

Fig. 3. LSC Example: Budget checking

4.2 Simulation

Figure 4 shows in Play-Engine part of the LSC of the *HolidayBooking* process model. Given a set of inputs including departure and destination cities, outbound and inbound dates, budgets, etc., the service will search for valid air tickets and hotels. Finally if such flights and hotel accommodation are available, it will proceed to book the flight and room.

Our simulation begins with building a simple Graphical User Interface (GUI) for interactively introducing external events. A systematic approach is to build one GUI component for each user-accessible Web service. In our example, only one Web service is accessible to service-using agents, namely *HolidayBooking*. The simple GUI is shown in the left bottom corner of Figure 4. Play-Engine allows user-defined variables and external function through ActiveX DLLs. For the purpose of simulation before actual implementation, an abstract "implementation" capturing only necessary details of the system is sufficient. However, if the underlying data and functional system is implemented using techniques compatible with ActiveX DLLs, e.g. ASP, .NET, Play-Engine may import the actual implementation of the underlying system and perform the simulation.

From our experiences, symbolic messages and instances are very helpful for capturing the OWL-S process models compactly. After building the LSC model, a user may interactively play out the system by initiating an (or a series of) external event and check how the system proceeds step-by-step. Assertion can be inserted freely by introducing hot conditions in the LSCs. During simulation, a violation of the hot condition will be caught by Play-Engine. This way, inconsis-

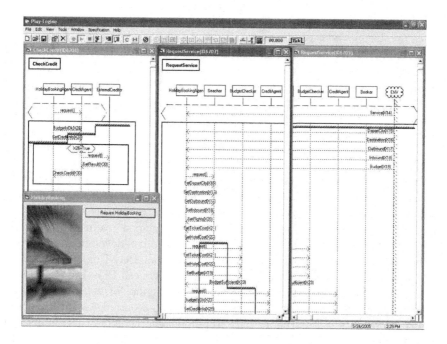

Fig. 4. Simulation Screen Shot

tency and under-specification is detected intuitively. In case an external process (to be offered by third party) is assumed, the user may specify the possible output of the process manually or Play-Engine would use model-checking techniques to automatically find a valid value (if the variables have finite domain). In our example, during simulation, windows are popped up for the user to specify the ticket price and the hotel price. Alternatively, a user may build a test case of the system as an existential chart (with assertions) and let Play-Engine do the guided play-out according the existential chart.

In Figure 4, the *HolidayBooking* process is invoked by two different service-using agents. Hence, two copies of the chart *HolidayBooking* (according to the *HolidayBooking* process) are monitored. With simulation run of this scenario, where a number of service-using agent are using the ticket-booking service, we gain confidence that the same shared resource (e.g. ticket vacancy) are accessed exclusively.

5 Conclusion

In this paper, we propose to use LSCs and Play-Engine to visualize and simulate OWL-S process models. The significance and novel aspects can be summarized as follows. Firstly, by transforming an OWL-S service model ontology into an LSC, service developer can design the services in a more visual and intuitive manner. In XML format, the LSCs can be easily transformed back to OWL-

S. Secondly, we may simulate the interactions without implementing the Web service (exploring the service grounding), and be able to gain confidence of the service models. The key point of this approach is that a Web service can be naturally viewed as a desired usage of the web agent, i.e., a scenario of the interaction between the service-using agent the service-providing agent. Thirdly, as Play-Engine supports dynamic linked libraries such as COM and ActiveX Controls, Web services written in these libraries can be more easily transformed to LSCs, from which the OWL-S service model may be derived. Hence, our approach also facilitates the integration of Web services with OWL-S. Moreover, we presented a travel booking case study to demonstrate our approach.

There are a number of future work directions that we deem as worthwhile to pursue. First of all, it is necessary to develop programs to automatically construct LSCs from the OWL-S process models to make this approach more practical. Recently an OWL-S editor has been developed[5] as a plug-in for the Protégé OWL Editor [14]. It will be valuable for OWL-S developers if they can obtain feedback, in terms of simulation results, from Play-Engine simulations directly to the editor. Hence, such a deep linking between Play-Engine and the OWL-S editor is desirable. Besides LSC and Play-Engine, formal languages such as CSP [9] can also be considered to represent OWL-S ontologies and their tool support, such as the FDR [16] or SPIN [10] model checkers, may also be used to perform verification tasks.

We foresee that Web Services will be a new and fruitful application domain of Software Engineering (SE) methods and tools. Our approach, along with other approaches on applying SE methods to the Web domain, offers both experience and possible tool supports for developing Web services languages and techniques.

Acknowledgement

The second author would like to thank Singapore Millennium Foundation[6] for the financial support. This work was supported in part by HyOntUse Project (GR/S44686) funded by the UK Engineering and Physical Science Research Council.

References

1. T. Berners-Lee, J. Hendler, and O. Lassila. The Semantic Web. *Scientific American*, 284(5):35–43, 2001.
2. D. Booth, M. Champion, C. Ferris, F. McCabe, E. Newcomer, and D. Orchard. Web Services Architecture. `http://www.w3.org/TR/2004/NOTE-ws-arch-20040211/`, Feb. 2004.
3. E. Christensen, F. Curbera, G. Meredith, and S. Weerawarana. *Web Services Description Language (WSDL) 1.1*. W3C, 1.1 edition, March 2001. `http://www.w3c.org/TR/wsdl`.

---

[5] cf. `http://owlseditor.semwebcentral.org/index.shtml`

[6] cf. `http://www.smf-scholar.org/`

4. W. Damm and D. Harel. LSCs: Breathing Life into Message Sequence Charts. In *Proceedings of the IFIP TC6/WG6.1 Third International Conference on Formal Methods for Open Object-Based Distributed Systems (FMOODS)*, page 451. Kluwer, B.V., 1999.

5. V. Haarslev and R. Möller. *RACER User's Guide and Reference Manual: Version 1.7.6*, Dec. 2002.

6. D. Harel, H. Kugler, R. Marelly, and A. Pnueli. Smart play-out. In *OOPSLA Companion*, pages 68–69, 2003.

7. D. Harel and R. Marelly. Specifying and Executing Behavioral Requirements: The Play-In/Play-Out Approach. Technical Report MCS01-15, The Weizmann Institute of Science Rehovot, Israel, 2002.

8. D. Harel and R. Marelly. *Come, Let's Play: Scenario-Based Programming Using LSCs and the Play-Engine*. Springer-Verlag, 2003.

9. C. A. R. Hoare. *Communicating Sequential Processes*. Prentice-Hall International, 1985.

10. G. Holzmann. The model checker spin. *IEEE Trans. on Software Engineering*, 23(5):279–295, May 1997. Special issue on Formal Methods in Software Practice.

11. I. Horrocks. The FaCT system. *Tableaux'98, LNCS*, 1397:307–312, 1998.

12. I. Horrocks, P. F. Patel-Schneider, H. Boley, S. Tabet, B. Grosof, and M. Dean. SWRL: A Semantic Web Rule Language Combining OWL and RuleML. http://www.w3.org/Submission/2004/SUBM-SWRL-20040521/, May 2004.

13. ITU. *Message Sequence Chart(MSC)*, Nov 1999. Series Z: Languages and general software aspects for telecommunication systems.

14. H. Knublauch, R. W. Fergerson, N. F. Noy, and M. A. Musen. The Protégé OWL Plugin: An Open Development Environment for Semantic Web Applications. In *Proceedings of the Third International Semantic Web Conference (ISWC 2004)*,, Hiroshima, Japan, Nov. 2004.

15. M. K. Smith and C. Welty and D. L. McGuinness (editors). OWL Web Ontology Language Guide. http://www.w3.org/TR/2004/REC-owl-guide-20040210/, 2004.

16. A. W. Roscoe. *Theory and Practice of Concurrency*. International Series in Computer Science. Prentice-Hall, 1997.

17. The OWL Services Coalition. OWL-S: Semantic Markup for Web Services. http://www.daml.org/services/owl-s/, 2004.

18. UDDI. *Universal Description, Discovery, and Integration of Business for the Web*, October 2001. http://www.uddi.org.

19. W3C. *Simple Object Access Protocol (SOAP) 1.1*, 2000. http://www.w3c.org/TR/SOAP.

A Model-to-Implementation Mapping Tool for Automated Model-Based GUI Testing

Ana C.R. Paiva[1], João C.P. Faria[1,2], Nikolai Tillmann[3], and Raul A.M. Vidal[1]

[1] Engineering Faculty of the University of Porto
[2] INESC Porto,
Rua Dr. Roberto Frias, s/n, 4200-465 Porto, Portugal
(apaiva, jpf, rmvidal)@fe.up.pt
[3] Microsoft Research, One Microsoft Way, Redmond, WA 98052, USA
nikolait@microsoft.com

Abstract. This paper presents extensions to Spec Explorer to automate the testing of software applications through their GUIs based on a formal specification in Spec♯. Spec Explorer, a tool developed at Microsoft Research, already supports automatic generation and execution of test cases for API testing, but requires that the actions described in the model are bound to methods in a .Net assembly. The tool described in this paper extends Spec Explorer to automate GUI testing: it adds the capability to gather information about the physical GUI objects that are the target of the user actions described in the model; and it automatically generates a .Net assembly with methods that simulate those actions upon the GUI application under test. The GUI modelling and the overall test process supported by these tools are described. The approach is illustrated with the Notepad application.

1 Introduction

Today's software systems usually feature Graphical User Interfaces (GUIs). GUIs have become an important and accepted way of interacting with today's software. GUIs get more and more established in daily lives, and this makes us more dependent on their correct functioning. However, testing of GUIs is difficult because very few tools and techniques are available to aid the testing process. Currently used GUI testing methods are almost ad hoc and require the test designer to manually develop test cases, identify the conditions to check during test execution, determine when to check these conditions, and evaluate whether the GUI software is adequately tested.

There have been efforts to automate GUI testing. Some tools, called Capture/Replay tools (www.testingfaqs.org/t-gui.html), are commercially available. They record user interactions to replay them later.

Other approaches exist to automate test case generation. Given expected outputs for certain inputs, existing code can be analyzed for conformance. However, this can only be done after the code has been written. An approach that can be applied in earlier phases of the software development process is specification-based (or model-based) testing. Here, a GUI model must be constructed and,

K.-K. Lau and R. Banach (Eds.): ICFEM 2005, LNCS 3785, pp. 450–464, 2005.
© Springer-Verlag Berlin Heidelberg 2005

depending on the nature of the model, different techniques can be used to generate test cases [1] which in turn can be used to verify conformance between an implementation and the specification. Some formal models allow automatic generation of test inputs and expected outputs. During the process of writing a specification, inconsistencies and usability problems are often found. This results in time and money savings. Also, the construction of models enables the analysis of alternative designs without having to code them.

Spec Explorer (research.microsoft.com/SpecExplorer), from Microsoft Research, is an example of an advanced model-based testing tool. It fully automates the generation and execution of test cases from an annotated model, and it provides an easy way to relate specification actions and implementation methods. However, when used to test GUIs, significant effort is required to map the user actions described in the model to real actions in the GUI under test.

The main contributions of this paper are a modelling pattern for GUIs and the GUI mapping tool:

- It reduces the manual work required to test an application through its GUI.
- It bridges the gap between a model written in a high-level modelling language and the simulation of user events.
- It promotes a modelling pattern in which GUI components can be specified as reusable classes controlled by a window manager.

The tool is implemented as an extension to Spec Explorer.

The paper is organized along the activities of the proposed GUI test process: the next section presents an overview; section 3 explains how GUIs can be modelled adequately with Spec♯; section 4 describes how Spec Explorer automatically generates test cases; the main contributions are in section 5, where the new GUI mapping tool is described; and section 6 describes test execution. Related work is discussed in section 7 and the last section summarizes the results achieved and points out future work. The Notepad application is used as a running example.

2   Overview of the Model-Based GUI Testing Process

The goal of model-based testing is to check if an implementation of a software system conforms to its specification. The specification captures the requirements and enables checking if those requirements are fulfilled by an implementation. Given an implementation and a specification of a software system, the generic activities involved in model-based testing are (1) test case generation (from the specification), (2) test case execution, and (3) comparison of the actual results obtained from the implementation with the expected results described by the specification (which plays the role of a test oracle). A formal specification is necessary to automatically generate test cases and expected results. If the specification is also executable (as is the case for Spec♯), and test inputs are given, expected results can be obtained by executing the specification.

2.1   Automated Model-Based Testing with Spec Explorer

Spec Explorer[2] is a software modelling and testing tool from Microsoft Research. Formal executable models are written in the abstract state machine language (AsmL) (research.microsoft.com/fse/AsmL) or Spec♯ [3], a superset of C♯.

Some of the methods in the specification are annotated as actions representing possible transitions of a transition system. Actions can have pre-conditions, written as "requires" clauses that define the states in which actions are enabled.

From the model, a Finite State Machine (FSM) is derived, from which test cases (sequences of actions with actual inputs) are automatically generated.

Conformance between the model and an implementation can be established by binding the model actions to implementation methods, executing the test cases in "lock-steps" on both the model and the implementation, and comparing their results. The implementation can be written in any .Net language.

Spec Explorer also supports "on-the-fly" testing. In this case, the test generation and test execution are combined in a single algorithm.

2.2   Automated Model-Based Testing of GUI Applications with Spec Explorer and the GUI Mapping Tool

Fig. 1 presents the main activities and artefacts involved in testing GUI applications with Spec Explorer extended with our GUI mapping tool.

As already mentioned, to perform conformance tests with Spec Explorer, a binding or mapping between the model actions and implementation methods in a .Net assembly must be provided. For APIs exposed by other means, some glue code might be needed to map forth and back the data and method calls. For instance, when the applications functionality is only exposed through its GUI, then the application must be driven through the GUIs abstraction layer, by simulating the actions of a user interacting with it. That is the role of the GUI mapping code in Fig. 1.

In previous experiences of using Spec Explorer to model and test GUI applications [4], the authors realised that, even in the case of simple applications such as Notepad, the manual building of the GUI mapping code was unpractical and required too much effort. To solve that problem, we developed a GUI mapping tool integrated with Spec Explorer.

The GUI mapping tool assists the user in relating the ("logical") model actions to "physical" actions on "physical" GUI objects. A major difficulty that is solved by the tool is the identification of the physical GUI objects that the model actions refer to. The mapping code is automatically generated from high-level mapping information. See section 5 for further information.

3   GUI Modelling with Spec♯ and Spec Explorer

The behaviour of GUIs can be modelled by state machines, with transitions triggered by user actions. State machines can be useful to guide the testing of software systems [5], although they suffer from the state explosion problem.

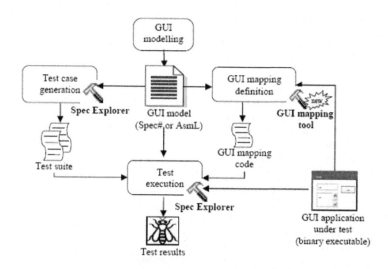

Fig. 1. Overview of the GUI modelling and testing process

The way of modelling with Spec Explorer has been inspired by Abstract State Machines (ASMs). ASMs [6] provide a way to model any system at any level of abstraction. This is adequate for GUI modelling, because, depending on the context, one may want to model user actions at different levels of abstraction: at operating system level (where a click event is the sequence of pressing and releasing the mouse button); at API level (where a click event is seen as an atomic action); at user task level; etc.

Independently of the abstraction level considered (lower level messages, or higher level messages constructed from sequences of lower level messages), a GUI implementation places the messages in a queue and processes those messages in order. This behaviour can also be adequately modelled as an ASM with guarded actions which fire only when appropriate messages are fetched from the queue.

A model written in Spec♯ describes a possibly infinite state transition system. States are modelled by state variables. Some of the methods in the specification are annotated as actions that represent the possible transitions of a transition system. These actions can have pre-conditions, written as "requires" clauses that define the states in which they are enabled. Thus, actions can be seen as the guarded update rules of an ASM. It is important to note that the states can have a very rich structure. In the case of GUIs, this allows to model the GUIs state faithfully from a user perspective. For example, a state variable can hold the textual content of a field. Methods annotated as actions can be used to model complex user actions (enter a string into a field, issue a command, loading content from a file, etc.) and describe their effects on the state of the system.

A simplified excerpt of a Spec♯ model of the Notepad application is shown in Spec. 1. An extensive model can be found in www.fe.up.pt/~apaiva/MyNotepad.pdf. It covers the behaviour of the Open, Save, Find, and Replace dialogs.

It consists of 35 actions, and 32 helper methods. The window manager consists
of 6 methods. The model was written within one week. To complete the model,
less than one week's time would be needed.

```
namespace MyNotepad;
// State variables
string text="",selText=""; bool dirty=false; int posCursor=0;
// Start and close the Notepad application
[Action] void LaunchNotepad()
requires !IsOpen("Notepad"); {
  AddWindow("Notepad","",false);
  //... state variables initialization ...
}
[Action] void Close()
requires IsEnabled("Notepad"); {
  if (dirty) AddWindow("MsgClose","Notepad",true);
  else { RemoveWindow("Notepad");
         //... reset variables to initial values }
}
[Action] void MsgSaveChangesBeforeClose(string option)
requires IsEnabled("MsgClose"); {
  RemoveWindow("MsgClose");
  switch (option){
    case "No": RemoveWindow("Notepad"); return;
    case "Yes": AddWindow("Save"); return;
    case "Cancel": return;
    default: return;}
}
// change and query the content of the main window
[Action] string GetText()
requires isEnabled("Notepad"); { return text;
}
[Action] void InsText(string typedTxt)
requires IsEnabled("Notepad"); {
  text = text.Substring(0,posCursor-selTxt.Length) + typedTxt
       + text.Substring(posCursor,text.Length-posCursor);
  posCursor = posCursor  selTxt.Length+typedTxt.Length;
  selTxt = ""; dirty = true;
}
```

Spec. 1. Excerpt of a Spec♯ model of the Notepad application

We discuss the modelling techniques illustrated in the Spec♯ excerpt above.

For modularity reasons, except for trivial applications, the top-level windows
of the application are better modelled in separate namespaces or classes. In
the example shown, the MyNotepad namespace refers to the main window of the
Notepad application. The complete model has other namespaces corresponding
to the Save, Open, Find and Replace dialog windows.

Inside each module (namespace or class) corresponding to a top-level window,
we model its abstract state with state variables, and we model the possible

user actions on that window with methods annotated as actions. To enable conformance testing of the outputs displayed to the user, methods annotated as actions should also be provided to observe the state of the GUI that is exposed to the users' eyes. A query method can be provided for each observable state variable, with the name of the variable and a suitable prefix (e.g. `GetText` in the example above). Spec Explorer allows designating such actions as probes. A probe only observes the current state and does not change it. Probes are treated differently from ordinary actions during test case generation, as we will see later.

All the actions inside each module, except the one that launches the application, have at least one pre-condition: that the corresponding window is enabled. A window is enabled when it is open and does not have a child modal window on top. When a modal window is open (e.g. the Save and Open windows in the Notepad application), the other windows of the application are disabled. Since this is a common feature of GUIs, a separate reusable module - a window manager - was created to handle it.

The window manager provides the following self-explanatory helper methods. We omit modifiers like `public` in the presentation.

```
AddWindow(windowName, parentWindowName, isModal)
RemoveWindow(windowName)
IsEnabled(windowName)
IsOpen(windowName)
```

When a method opens/closes a window it should add/remove that window to/from the window manager. When a window is removed, all its child windows are also removed. Message boxes are also registered in the window manager but need not be modelled as separate modules (e.g. `MsgClose` in the example above).

The window manager methods and its state are part of the model.

4   Test Case Generation with Spec Explorer

Spec Explorer automatically generates test cases in two steps (Fig. 2) from a Spec♯ or AsmL specification. In the first step, a FSM is generated from a Spec♯ or AsmL specification. In the second step, test cases that fulfill certain coverage criteria are generated from the FSM.

The FSM is generated by bounded exploration of the state space of the model. Some techniques available to prune the exploration are:

1. **state filters** - boolean expressions that determine which states to explore;
2. **restriction of the domains** - the domains of the parameters are bounded to a finite set of possible values;
3. **equivalence classes** - this technique partitions states into equivalence classes and prevents further exploration from any state of such a class once a specified number of representatives has been reached;
4. **reduction based on hierarchical structure** - this technique was developed by the authors to reduce the size of the FSM obtained from a GUI

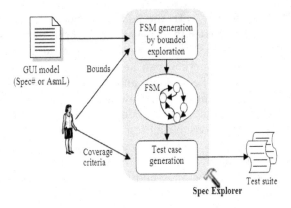

Fig. 2. Test case generation

model [4]. The FSM is organized in a hierarchical model and that structure is the input to the FSM reduction algorithm. In our experiences, a reduction by around 50% of the number of states can usually be achieved.

The pruning of exploration becomes crucial when modelling and testing GUIs. That is because testing an application through its GUI by simulating user events entails a significant overhead resulting in much slower test execution than testing an application through its API. The main challenge is to generate a test suite of manageable size while still guaranteeing adequate testing.

As soon as the FSM is constructed, and the coverage criteria chosen, a traversal engine is used to unwind the resulting FSM to produce behavioural tests that fulfil the coverage criteria. The coverage criteria can be set to full transition coverage, shortest path to a set of user-defined states, or a random walk. Actions designated as probes are checked in every state of the resulting tests, and do not take part in coverage considerations.

In the Notepad example, the full transition coverage criterion was used to generate the test cases. Other coverage criteria, more adapted to GUI testing [7], can be easily added to the Spec Explorer tool through its API.

5   Model-to-Implementation Mapping with the GUI Mapping Tool

The aim of the GUI mapping tool is to reduce the manual work involved in model based testing of software applications through their GUI.

As already mentioned in the overview, the GUI mapping tool assists the user in relating the logical actions described in the model to physical actions on physical GUI objects of the application under test (AUT).

The GUI mapping tool (Fig. 3) has a front-end (Fig. 4) that shows the mapping information gathered so far and gives access to the GUI Spy tool and the GUI Mapping Code Generator. The Spy tool is used to get information about

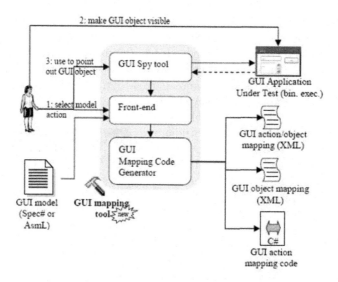

Fig. 3. Architecture of the GUI mapping tool

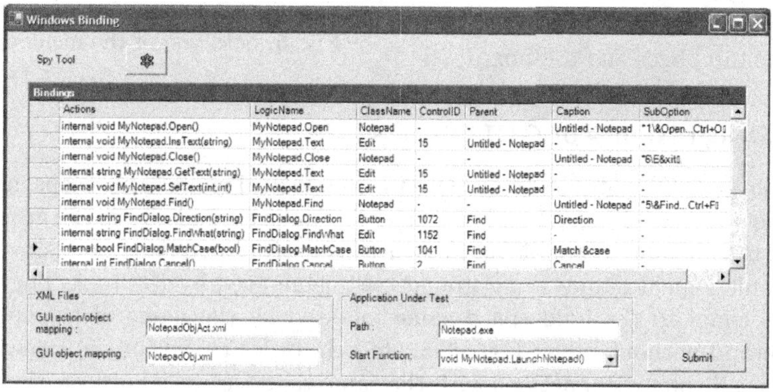

Fig. 4. Front-end of the GUI mapping tool

physical GUI objects in the AUT, in a way similar to the Spy++ tool that ships with Microsoft Visual Studio. The code generator exports to XML files and C♯ the mapping information gathered. The C♯ code generated is based on calls to a reusable GUI Test Library. Further details will be provided in the next sections.

5.1   The GUI Spy Tool

The GUI Spy Tool is accessible from the font-end of the GUI mapping tool (see Fig. 4). It allows the user to point out the physical GUI object that is the target of each logical action specified in the model.

After selecting the logical action in the main grid (first column), the user drags and drops the Spy icon on top of the corresponding physical GUI object in the AUT. If the desired GUI object is not visible, the user will have to interact also with the AUT in order to make it visible. The physical properties of the GUI object selected, as well as a logical name inferred by the tool (as will be explained in the next section), are then displayed in the grid (see Fig. 4). The Spy++ tool that is shipped with Microsoft Visual Studio can only gather information about proper windows (or GUI objects with a window handle). Our tool goes a bit further: it can also gather information about window menus. So, when the tester wants to establish a relation between a specification method and an item inside a menu, he can drag and drop the mouse on top of the window that contains the menu at which time another window (see Fig. 5) is opened with all the submenu options, allowing him to choose the submenu option he wants. A similar option exists for controls like tab pages and toolboxes.

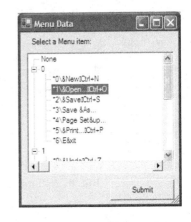

Fig. 5. Selection of the menu options

5.2   Logical Names of GUI Objects

Every physical GUI object is associated with a logical name. This keeps independence between specification and implementation levels and allows the generation of code that is more readable and easier to construct manually, if desired.

Default logical names are automatically generated by the tool. The logical name is equal to the namespace name followed by the name of the specification method without prefix (Set, Get, etc.). In order to obtain the same logical name for all the logical actions with the same target physical object, the names of those actions should be constructed with a different prefix and the same suffix.

5.3   XML Files Generated

The mapping information captured is saved into two XML text files:

1. a file with the mapping between model actions and the logical names of the target GUI objects (GUI action/object mapping file in Fig. 3);

   ```
   <Action id="internal void MyNotepad.Open()">
     <LogicalName>MyNotepad.Open</LogicalName>
   </Action>
   ```

2. a file with the mapping between logical names and physical properties of GUI objects (GUI object mapping file in Fig. 3).

```
<GUIObject logicalName="MyNotepad.Open">
  <ClassName>Notepad</ClassName>
  <Caption>Untitled - Notepad</Caption>
  <SubClassName>menu</SubClassName>
  <SubOption>&Open...Ctrl+O</SubOption>
</GUIObject>
```

The mapping information needs to be gathered just once for each application. But if the specification is changed and the mapping information has to be updated, the XML files can be loaded by the GUI mapping tool for update. The XML files can also be changed directly by the user.

These XML files are also used for code generation and test execution as is explained in subsequent sections.

5.4   GUI Test Library

The C♯ code generated is based on calls to a reusable GUI test library that provides methods to simulate the actions of a user interacting with a GUI application and observe the content of GUI objects. This library was constructed in C♯ extending a previous existing library to best fit our needs.

The GUI test library provides three kinds of methods (Code. 1):

- methods that act upon GUI objects simulating the user, like sending text to a control that accepts text input (SendText). The target GUI object is identified by its logical name. Each method may have additional parameters with information needed to perform the action.
- methods that observe properties of GUI objects, like the text (GetText), insertion point (GetInsertionPoint), and selected text (GetSelectedText) of a text box. The target GUI object is also identified by its logical name. The return value conveys the information requested.
- methods that provide physical information about GUI objects identified by their logical names in order to identify those objects in the real AUT. This information may be loaded from a XML file.

```
// To act upon GUI objects
void Click(string GUIObjName);
void SendText(string GUIObjName, string txt);
void SelectText(string GUIObjName, int start, int end);
void SelectSubOption(string GUIObjName, string option);
void SelectCheckBox(string GUIObjName, bool check);
void SelectMsgBoxOp(string GUIObjName, string option);
// To observe properties of GUI objects
string GetText(string GUIObjName);
string GetSelectedText(string GUIObjName);
int GetInsertionPoint(string GUIObjName);
bool GetCheckBox(string GUIObjName);
```

Code. 1. Examples of methods implemented in the GUI test library

5.5   Rules for Mapping Logical Actions in the GUI Test Library

Besides identifying the physical GUI object that is the target of each model action, it is also necessary to select the appropriate method from the GUI test library, which will simulate a physical action of the user on that GUI object.

The GUI mapping tool automatically infers the appropriate library method based on the type of the GUI object, and the signature of the model action.

Some of the rules that are applied are:

- When the sub option is filled in the mapping information, we assume that the logical action is modelling the action of a user selecting a sub menu option, a tab option, or a tool button inside a toolbox (SelectSubOption method in the test library). This is the case for Open, Close, and Find in Fig. 4.
- When a logical action with string parameter is mapped to a textbox, we assume that the action is modelling an event sending text (SendText method in the test library). This is the case for InsText and FindWhat in Fig. 4.
- When the logical action is an inspection method, has a string as return value and is mapped to a textbox, we assume that it is modelling the eyes of the user looking at the content of the textbox, thereby retrieving the text (GetText method in the test library). This is the case for GetText in Fig. 4.
- When the logical action has neither parameters nor return values, and is mapped to a button, we assume that physical action is to click the button (Click method in the test library). This is the case for Cancel in Fig. 4

5.6   Code Generation

Spec Explorer requires that the actions in the model are bound to implementation methods (in a .Net assembly) with identical signatures (identical return type, number of parameters, and parameters' types). To fulfil this requirement, the tool generates C♯ code with methods with the same signature as the model actions, as illustrated in Code 2. For each logical action, a method is generated with the same signature, calling the method of the GUI Test Library inferred according to the rules described before, with the logical name of the target GUI object as an additional parameter.

```
#region automatically generated code
class GeneratedCode{
  void LaunchNotepad(){
    LoadXMLObjMapping("C:\\temp\\Notepad.xml");
    new App(@"Notepad.exe"); }
  void Open() { UserEvents.SelectOption("Notepad.Open"); }
  void InsText(string p0) { UserEvents.SendText("Notepad.Text",p0); }
  string GetText() { return UserEvents.GetText("Notepad.Text"); }
  //...
} #endregion
```

Code 2. Excerpt of the code generated automatically for the Notepad example

The start function launches the application and reads the information mapping logical to physical objects from the GUI object mapping file (in Fig. 3).

6   Test Execution

As soon as the mapping code is constructed, compiled into a library, a reference
to this library added to the Spec Explorer project, and the test cases are generated, the test cases can be executed autonomously without user intervention.

Lets assume we have a deterministic model. Then, each test case consists of
a sequence of steps. For each step, a specification action and its related implementation method are executed in locked step mode (e.g. the Close() method
in Fig. 6). At the implementation level, each method makes a call to a method
defined in the generic GUI test library (e.g. Click() in Fig. 6) that interacts
with the GUI AUT simulating the user actions. The probe actions (with the Get
prefix) get information about interaction objects properties that are compared
with the expected values obtained from the specification. The execution stops
when inconsistencies are detected.

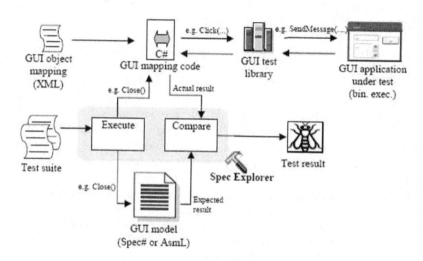

Fig. 6. Test execution

In GUI testing, inconsistencies between the specification and the implementation can arise for several reasons:

1. the model is trying to act on a control that is not enabled or cannot be
   found; or
2. the model is trying to act on a window that is not reachable or is not opened
   (e.g., a modal dialog is open and the window we want to reach is behind
   that dialog);
3. the expected result was not displayed (e.g., expected content of a text box).

During the testing of Notepad, we discovered one sequence of actions which
leads to an inconsistency between our intuitive model and the actual Notepad
application:

1. Type text.
2. Search for text using the find dialog (Ctrl-F). Close the dialog.
3. Open the replace dialog (Ctrl-H). Close the dialog.
4. Press the F3 key (shortcut for "Find Next").

Then Notepad will search backwards instead of forwards. This is a sequence of events that manual test would probably miss since it is not a common scenario.

7   Related Work

Today, many tools exist to develop GUI applications visually, but they do provide neither support for specifying or modelling GUIs including their functional behaviour on a higher abstraction level nor for testing them in an effective way. Yet, testing GUIs represents a significant amount of overall testing efforts. To overcome this discrepancy, several kinds of testing tools were developed. These tools can be classified into capture/replay, random input testing, unit testing frameworks, and model-based.

With capture/replay tools, the tester builds a test script by interacting with the GUI while his actions are recorded for later replay. This kind of tools shifts the testing activity to the final phases of the software development process since they can be only used when the GUI, or part of the GUI, is already constructed. Also, these tools do not provide any support to evaluate the test script constructed according to coverage criteria. Examples of these tools are WinRunner (www.mercury.com) and Rational Robot (www.ibm.com). Changes to the implementation may require the recapturing of all affected test scripts.

The goal of random input testing tools is to crash the system under test. They generate test cases randomly and ignore any unexceptional outputs of the system. These tools cannot detect incorrect behaviour, but they are the most cost-effective for finding defects that crash the system. Panorama C/C++ (www.softwareautomation.com) is an example of this category.

Another possible approach is to program the test cases. Frameworks like JUnit (www.junit.org) and NUnit (www.nunit.org) are of great help in organizing and executing test cases, particularly for API testing, but not in generating those tests. In the case of GUI testing, many bugs can only be uncovered through particular sequences of actions, which might arise in the daily use of the GUI. Unit tests however are usually a few hand-written sequences of actions, which tend to be very short. Thus, there is a high probability to miss these kinds of errors. Another disadvantage of these tools is the required extra programming effort.

Model-based testing tools can be used to test conformity between an implementation and the specification. A high level of automation can be achieved with these tools since the test case generation, the test case execution, and the comparison of the expected results with actual results can all be automated.

The model is used to generate test cases that fulfil a given coverage criterion. The techniques used to do it depend on the kind of specification used.

Belli, in [1], uses FSMs and regular expressions to model GUIs. He expands the original model with illegal behaviour and generates test cases that can bring the system into legal or into faulty states.

Shehady et al., in [8], use Variable Finite State Machines (VFSM) to model GUIs and to cope with FSM scaling problems. VFSMs are FSMs with an added condition associated to each transition. The VFSM is converted into a FSM to generate test cases using the partial W algorithm [9]. The test cases are applied to the GUI and the results obtained are compared with the results expected. The comparison is performed at the end of the test case execution so that, even if the inconsistencies are found at the beginning of the test cases, the execution of an entire case is required.

Memon et al., in [10], use hierarchical structures to model GUIs. They define operators corresponding to user actions. Such low level operators can be combined to form upper levels. A technique based on Artificial Intelligence gets a set of operators, and an initial and a goal states, to produce a sequence of operators.

In general, when the source code of the software application is available, white-box testing can be applied by analysing the source code and applying coverage criteria on the implementation to measure the quality of tests. However, often source code is not available, and black-box testing must be performed. In these cases, using model-based testing allows to apply coverage metrics on the model as a quality measurement. Although model-based testing can have many advantages like the automatic generation of test cases, it also often suffers from the gap between the modelling paradigm and the implementation interface. In addition to absent source code, often the access to the actual functionality of the software application is barred, in our case by a GUI that represents the only interface to the software.

The tool presented in this paper overcomes these limitations of black-box testing GUIs with the automatic generation of the mapping code that allows interacting with a software application.

8   Conclusions and Future Work

We have presented a tool which reduces the effort to test applications through their GUI based on a formal specification in Spec♯. This tool is an extension of the Spec Explorer tool, developed by Microsoft Research that already supports the modelling, test case generation, and test case execution. An overview of the GUI model and test process is provided and the components of Spec Explorer as well as the components of the tool extensions are described.

Our tool has some limitations: it doesn't deal with internationalization i.e. variable name mappings; it only addresses Windows applications; and it is not possible to test external effects like output of a printer.

Spec Explorer together with the GUI mapping tool can be used to test existing software applications, or it can be used to assist the development of new software applications and to test them through their GUI. In the former case, a reverse engineering process could be useful to construct a model, or part of the model, of an arbitrary application exhibited by its GUI. In the latter case, the specification of the application (or part of the application) is constructed and afterwards the application is implemented and tested using automatically generated mapping code.

We used the Notepad application as a running example to illustrate our approach, and we found an inconsistency with the intuitive model.

Our future work will be to derive a technique to reverse engineer an existing GUI application by automatic exploration through the application's GUI and automatic generation of a Spec♯ model, in a way similar to the one presented by Memon in [11]. Such a model will usually not be complete and only capture the coarse structure of the application; nevertheless, it can serve as a starting point for further manual modelling. This will allow us to apply our approach to bigger application without the effort of constructing their entire models from scratch.

References

1. F. Belli, "Finite State Testing and Analysis of Graphical User Interfaces", ISSRE 2001 - The 12th International Symposium on SW Reliability Engineering, Hong Kong, 2001.
2. C. Campbell, W. Grieskamp, L. Nachmanson, W. Schulte, N. Tillmann, and M. Veanes, "Model-Based Testing of Object-Oriented Reactive Systems with Spec Explorer", Microsoft Research MSR-TR-2005-59, May 2005.
3. M. Barnett, K. R. M. Leino, and W. Schulte, "The Spec♯ Programming System: An Overview", CASSIS'04 - International workshop on Construction and Analysis of Safe, Secure and Interoperable Smart devices, Marseille, 2004.
4. A. C. R. Paiva, N. Tillmann, J. C. P. Faria, and R. F. A. M. Vidal, "Modeling and Testing Hierarchical GUIs", ASM 2005 - 12th International Workshop on Abstract State Machines, Paris - France, 2005.
5. Y. Gurevich, "Evolving Algebras 1993: Lipari Guide," in Specification and Validation Methods, E. Brger, Ed.: Oxford University Press, 1995, pp. 9-36.
6. W. Grieskamp, Y. Gurevich, W. Schulte, and M. Veanes, "Generating Finite State Machines from Abstract State Machines", ISSTA 2002, International Symposium on SW Testing and Analysis, 2002.
7. A. M. Memon, M. L. Soffa, and M. E. Pollack, "Coverage Criteria for GUI Testing", 8th European SW Engineering Conference (ESEC) and 9th ACM SIGSOFT International Symposium on the Foundations of SW Engineering (FSE-9), 2001.
8. R. K. Shehady and D. P. Siewiorek, "A Method to Automate User Interface Testing Using Variable Finite State Machines", 27th International Symposium on Fault-Tolerant Computing, 1997.
9. S. Fujiwara, G. v. Bochmann, F. Khendek, M. Amalou, and A. Ghedamsi, "Test selection based on finite state models", IEEE Transactions on SW Engineering, vol. 17, pp. 591-603, 1991.
10. A. M. Memon, M. E. Pollack, and M. L. Soffa, "Hierarchical GUI Test Case Generation Using Automated Planning", IEEE Transactions on SW Engineering, vol. 27, 2001.
11. A. Memon, I. Banerjee, and A. Nagarajan, "GUI Ripping: Reverse Engineering of Graphical User Interfaces for Testing", WCRE2003 - The 10th Working Conference on Reverse Engineering, Victoria, British Columbia, Canada, 2003.

ClawZ: Cost-Effective Formal Verification for Control Systems

M.M. Adams and P.B. Clayton

Systems Assurance Group, QinetiQ
m.adams@eris.qinetiq.com, p.clayton@eris.qinetiq.com

Abstract. Control system software now plays a key role on many platforms, including aircraft and automobiles. However, as control system software has been performing increasingly complex tasks, the associated software development, maintenance and certification costs have escalated significantly. The ClawZ toolset is dedicated to the formal verification of control system software. By using some novel ideas, it achieves the highest levels of assurance whilst not suffering from the prohibitively high costs normally associated with applying formal verification. It has been successfully used in the certification of the Flight Control Computer of the Eurofighter Typhoon aircraft. This paper outlines the toolset, and explains how the approach used to build it enables formal verification costs to be dramatically reduced whilst not compromising on soundness.

Keywords: industrial formal verification, refinement, formal proof, Z, ProofPower, safety-critical software, real-time software, control systems, Simulink, Ada, Eurofighter Typhoon.

1 Introduction

1.1 Control Systems

A *control system* is a mechanism for controlling physical attributes of a platform, according to user inputs and measured physical attributes of the platform and its environment. Control systems occur in a wide range of platform domains, from higher-end domains such as aircraft, automobiles and nuclear and chemical plant, down to simpler lower-end domestic domains such as central heating systems and washing machines.

Over the past 30 years, digital control systems have replaced analogue electronic control systems in virtually all domains. This has given considerable scope for making control systems more sophisticated, and control systems in higher-end domains have indeed been getting increasingly complex. For example, Flight Control Computers (FCCs), that control an aircraft's flight surfaces to give it stability and manoeuvrability in the air, have become increasingly sophisticated in fighter aircraft, to achieve improved manoeuvrability and a reduction in the pilot's workload.

K.-K. Lau and R. Banach (Eds.): ICFEM 2005, LNCS 3785, pp. 465–479, 2005.

However this increased complexity comes at a cost. Many of these higher-end domains, such as aircraft and nuclear plant, are safety-critical and thus platforms have to be developed to high standards and then certified to be safe. The costs of developing, maintaining and certifying control system software for these platforms have escalated so much that together they can now represent a large proportion of overall platform costs. Other domains, such as automobiles, involve high-volume products, and reliability problems with safety-related features are requiring expensive product recalls, that are cutting deep into manufacturers' low profit margins.

1.2 Simulink

The use of graphical control system design tools is helping to improve the situation. Instead of designing control systems on paper and then only finding problems further down the line during software testing, control system design engineers are able to simulate the behaviour of the control system at the design stage, finding problems with the functionality and performance. This saves on expensive iterations of the software development cycle. The most widely used graphical control system design tool is Simulink [1].

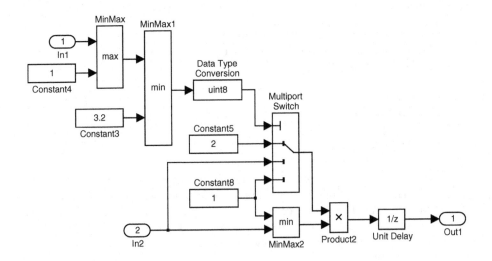

Fig. 1. The Simulink diagram for Pump

In Simulink, a control system specification is expressed in a graphical form called a *Simulink diagram*. A Simulink diagram consists of a collection of inputs, outputs and blocks, all connected by wires. Each block also has its own inputs and outputs, and is either a basic block, corresponding to a primitive operation such as sum or multiplication, or a subsystem block, corresponding to a sub-diagram. Opening a subsystem block will reveal the sub-diagram and its internal blocks and wires. See Figure 1 for a simple example of a Simulink diagram.

1.3   Formal Verification

Formal verification often plays an important role in the certification of safety-critical platforms. This is used because it provides very high levels of assurance for finding certain important classes of software error. However, the tools required for performing formal verification are normally prohibitively expensive to use. This is due to two main factors: they require highly-skilled expert analysts, and they require a high degree of user interaction. The costs of using formal verification tools are so high that formal verification, despite the useful extra assurance it can offer, is rarely performed outside safety-critical domains, and, even within safety-critical domains, mainly only for the certification of software.

ClawZ is a toolset for the formal verification of software[1]. It differs from other formal verification toolsets in that it is dedicated to a specific verification domain. In particular, it is dedicated to the verification of control system software that has been specified in Simulink and implemented in Ada. By taking advantage of this fact, the toolset enables analysts to interact with it at a more abstract level than with most formal verification toolsets. This enables the analyst's expertise to be reduced, whilst at the same time considerably reducing the amount of user interaction required. This can result in dramatically reduced formal verification costs. Despite the cost savings, the assurance gained by using ClawZ has in no way been compromised, and in fact it achieves even higher assurance than many existing formal verification toolsets. In principle, the approach used to build the toolset is equally applicable to other verification domains.

ClawZ has been successfully used in the certifications of three successive versions of Eurofighter Typhoon's FCC, one of the most advanced FCCs yet produced. Its core control system functionality is implemented in 35,000 non-comment, non-blank lines of Ada source code. Analysts were typically able to formally verify around 50 to 80 lines of source code per day each. Although an accurate comparison is difficult due to the differing nature of individual verifications, this clearly compares favourably with a typical 10 to 15 lines of source code per day for using other toolsets in other industrial formal verifications (for example, see [2, Overview, page 16]).

1.4   Overview

This paper outlines the ClawZ toolset, and explains how the approach used to build the toolset enables formal verification costs to be dramatically reduced, whilst not compromising on soundness. Rather than by appealing to a theoretical framework, this claim about cost savings is backed up by pointing to industrial, albeit anecdotal, experience of using the toolset.

In Section 2, an overview is given of how a ClawZ analysis is performed from the perspective of the analyst. In Section 3, the architecture of the ClawZ toolset is explained, as well as how this architecture ensures a high level of assurance. Conclusions are drawn in Section 4.

---

[1] The name ClawZ was previously used to refer to one component of the toolset, which is now called Z Producer.

```
procedure PUMP (COND  : in     REAL_T;
                STATE : in out REAL_T;
                GO    :    out REAL_T)
is
   TMP : REAL_T;
begin
   GO := STATE;
   if COND > 1.0 then
      TMP := 1.0;
   else
      TMP := COND;
   end if;
   if PUMPS_GO < 2.0 then
      STATE := 2.0 * TMP;
   elsif PUMPS_GO < 3.0 then
      STATE := COND * TMP;
   else
      STATE := TMP;
   end if;
end PUMP;
```

Fig. 2. The Ada subroutine implementation for Pump

2   Using ClawZ

In this section, an overview is given of how a ClawZ analysis is performed from the perspective of the analyst. The intention is to give an impression of the analyst tasks involved in using the toolset, and of the required degree of analyst interaction and expertise. This should give the reader an understanding of how formal verification costs are so significantly reduced when compared with traditional formal verification toolsets.

Throughout this section, statistics and screen shots are used to help give a feel for the degree of analyst interaction required in a typical analysis. The quoted statistics are for the analysis of a typical subroutine of 80 non-comment, non-blank lines of Ada source code. Any references to computer execution time relate to using a 2.2GHz Pentium IV processor with 1GB of RAM. The statistics are rough figures, intended as a guide only, and are based on experiences from the industrial analyses of Typhoon's FCC as well as numerous other smaller analyses. The true figures will vary, depending on the peculiarities of the system being analysed. The screen shots are from the analysis of a non-trivial implementation of the Simulink diagram in Figure 1. See Figure 2 for this implementation, written in 20 lines of Ada. Note that the reader is not expected to understand the detail of these screen shots.

A ClawZ analysis verifies that a Simulink specification of a control system is correctly implemented in Ada, and involves performing a separate analysis for each Ada subroutine that implements part of the Simulink diagram (called a *control system subroutine*). Note that the Ada source code may contain some subroutines that only perform tasks outside the scope of what is specified in the Simulink diagram. Such subroutines are not covered by a ClawZ analysis. Also note that a ClawZ analysis just covers core functional correctness of the source code, and does not cover classes of error such as run-time errors (e.g. overflow or divide-by-zero) or program termination.

The analysis of a given subroutine breaks down into three principal stages: specification, witnessing and interactive proof. The analyst skills required differ between the stages, and analysts should be assigned to stages according to their skill sets. The underlying mathematical model used in ClawZ is expressed in the Z notation [3], and all analysts are required to be familiar with reading this notation.

The graphical user interface to the ProofPower theorem prover [4], called xpp, is used throughout an analysis, for viewing and editing Z, and for giving interactive feedback during the witnessing and interactive proof stages. It also helps to use Simulink, in conjunction with the toolset, to view Simulink diagrams, although strictly speaking this is not necessary if a printout can be obtained.

2.1 The Specification Stage

In the specification stage, the Ada subroutine's specification components are created. These capture the intended behaviour of the subroutine in terms of the Simulink diagram and the input and output parameters of the Ada subroutine.

Firstly, the analyst produces the subroutine's *block list*, that lists exactly those blocks in the Simulink diagram that are intended to be implemented by the Ada subroutine. An Ada subroutine will often correspond to a single Simulink subsystem block, in which case it is sufficient for the analyst simply to identify just this one Simulink block, although sometimes it is necessary to identify numerous blocks. The collection of the parts of the Simulink diagram that correspond to the block list is called an *artificial subsystem block*, since it can be considered to have its own inputs, outputs and internal blocks although it does not itself necessarily correspond to an actual Simulink subsystem block. The process of identifying the subroutine's blocks can be helped by examining the software's design documentation.

Secondly, the analyst defines a data refinement retrieve relation between all of the artificial subsystem's inputs and outputs, and corresponding input and output parameters of the Ada subroutine. This will often be a simple one-to-one mapping. See Figure 3 for an example data refinement relation. The left-hand sides of the equalities in the data refinement relation refer to Simulink wires, and the right-hand sides refer to Ada variables.

Finally, the analyst may have to identify a precondition for the Ada subroutine. Usually a subroutine will assume nothing about the variables it reads. However, some subroutines make assumptions, and these need to be explicitly identified as preconditions in order to complete the subroutine's verification. These usually only become apparent during the witnessing stage, and need to be justified once identified. Often a subroutine's precondition will be established

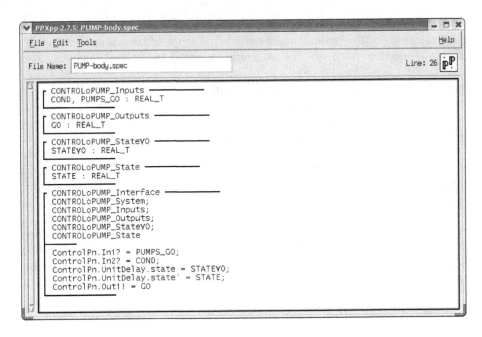

Fig. 3. *CONTROLoPUMP_Interface*, the data refinement relation for Pump

in another control system subroutine. Such a precondition will then become a postcondition of the subroutine that establishes it.

The specification stage will typically require a total of around 30 to 70 lines of input from the analyst. This will typically take around half an hour to an hour. The analyst performing the specification stage needs to be able to read Simulink diagrams and to be aware of the subtleties of writing a formal specification.

The important point to note about this stage is that there is no need for the analyst to laboriously construct a detailed specification of an Ada subroutine's behaviour. The analyst just provides the key components of the specification, and the toolset will fill out the details automatically (see Section 3.1).

2.2   The Witnessing Stage

The witnessing stage takes up the bulk of the analysis effort. In this stage, the analyst constructs a *witness script*, which justifies in detail how the Ada subroutine body correctly implements its specification. This is done by identifying correspondences between wires in the Simulink diagram and the values of Ada variables at specific points in the subroutine's body.

The analyst constructs the witness script by interacting with a tool called RSG, via the xpp interface. See Figure 4 for an example of an interactive RSG session. The witness script is edited in the upper window, and is entered for interactive RSG feedback, which appears in the lower window.

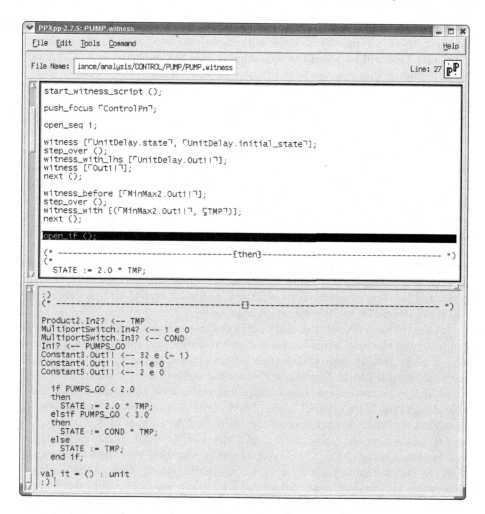

Fig. 4. The interactive session from the witnessing stage for Pump. The *open_if* command is about to be entered, for witnessing the second Ada *if* statement in Figure 2.

A witness script needs to account for every Simulink wire in the subroutine's artificial subsystem in terms of values of Ada variables, called *witnesses*. RSG ensures that this is done by maintaining a wavefront of wires in the Simulink diagram, where wires behind the wavefront have already been accounted for. The user is prompted to supply a witness for any wire on the current wavefront. RSG enables the analyst to step through the subroutine body to reach an appropriate point for supplying a given witness. When a wire's witness has been supplied, the wavefront advances along that wire. A witness script is complete when the wavefront has crossed the entire diagram, from inputs to outputs.

Often, a suitable witness is self-evident because the Ada source code closely mirrors the detail of the Simulink diagram, in which case RSG will supply an appropriate suggested witness, derived by symbolic execution of the specfication. However, there will usually be a few witnesses that the analyst has to construct manually. This will be when the Ada source code has departed from the detail of the Simulink diagram, perhaps in order to achieve greater efficiency.

A witness script for a typical 80 line subroutine will be around 100 to 150 lines long. This will typically take around two to three hours to construct. However, note that the witnessing stage is not necessarily complete once a witness script has first been completed.

Once a witness script has been completed, the analyst then submits it to the toolset for processing and waits for the results. During this time, the toolset is generating a set of Z conjectures to be proved, called *verification conditions*, and attempting to prove them automatically. If all these verification conditions are provable, then the Ada subroutine meets its specification. The proof side of the processing is carried out by a tool called Supertac. After a wait of typically around a minute or two, the toolset reports back the results in the form of the total number of verification conditions generated and the total number that have been proved automatically. There tends to be almost one verification condition generated per line of source code analysed, and so a typical 80 line subroutine will have around 50 to 70 verification conditions.

If all have been proved automatically, then the analysis for that subroutine is complete and the subroutine has been shown to correctly implement its specification. If there are any unproved verification conditions, the analyst must examine the proof output file. In this file, any unproved verification conditions have been simplified. Supertac ensures that a simplified verification condition will be provable if and only if its original unsimplified verification condition is provable. A simplified verification condition will typically be 5 to 15 lines of Z.

On examining the proof output file, the analyst must grade each simplified verification condition. If every verification condition is graded as provable, then the subroutine is passed on to the interactive proof stage of the analysis. Otherwise, the analyst must determine why there are unprovable verification conditions. This may be due to an analyst error, either in constructing the subroutine's specification components or its witness script. If this is the case, then the analysis is iterated from the relevant stage. However, if a verification condition is unprovable, but this is not due to an analyst error, then a genuine error has been found, either in the Simulink diagram or its Ada implementation.

In practice, most unproven verification conditions will be due to an error in the witness script. The simplified verification condition will contain information about the part of the witness script it relates to, to help the analyst locate the error. The next most common explanation for an unproven verification condition is that it is provable, but Supertac has not managed to prove it completely. Supertac will complete the proof of around 95% to 98% of provable verification conditions. A typical 80 line subroutine will have all but one or two of its provable verification conditions completely proved by Supertac.

There will typically be two to four iterations before all the witnessing errors are ironed out, typically taking half an hour each. The most complex subroutines to analyse will be those that deviate from the structure of the Simulink diagram in many ways, and it will usually take many more iterations to reach a correct witness script for these.

To perform the witnessing stage effectively, the analyst needs to be able to read Simulink diagrams and Ada programs, and to have a good knowledge of how to interact with RSG. These are all skills that are quickly picked up by university software engineering graduates. However, the analyst also needs to be able to assess the provability of Z conjectures, which is a less common skill.

There are two important points to note about this stage. Firstly, due to the relatively abstract level of interaction with RSG, it involves considerably less effort than with the corresponding activity in other formal verification toolsets. The analyst does not have to construct a detailed refinement script, or be familiar with all the subtleties of algorithmic program refinement. Secondly, due to Supertac's high level of proof automation, there can be an easy separation of duties between the witnessing analyst and the interactive proof analyst. The analyst performing the witnessing stage does not have to be familiar with the highly-skilled and time-consuming task of interactive formal proof, and can usually produce a correct witness script, albeit after a few iterations, before any remaining unproved verification conditions are passed on for interactive proof.

2.3   The Interactive Proof Stage

The interactive proof stage involves using the xpp interface to construct an interactive proof script for every remaining unproved verification condition for the subroutine. These verification conditions will already have been graded as provable during the witnessing stage.

The verification conditions are proved using the ProofPower theorem prover. Interactive proofs are carried out within a proof environment that closely corresponds to HOL's subgoal package [5]. A proof involves the analyst applying a series of proof tactics to a proof goal. The analyst can make the proof branch into several parts, called *subgoals*. A proof is complete when all subgoals have been reduced to true. As well as having access to ProofPower's tactics for reasoning about Z, the analyst also has access to specialised tactics used in the implementation of Supertac. Occasionally, the analyst performing the interactive proof will notice that a verification condition has been wrongly graded as provable, in which case it will be passed back to the witnessing stage for regrading.

This stage is the most skilled stage to perform, and a thorough knowledge of ProofPower's proof tactics is required. It typically takes 15 to 30 minutes to prove each simplified verification condition, although some can take several hours. However, because 95% to 98% of the verification conditions have been automatically proved, and those that have not have been largely simplified, interactive proof takes up the smallest proportion of the overall analysis effort.

The important point to note about this stage is that, due to Supertac's high level of proof automation, very little of the highly-skilled activity of performing interactive proof is necessary. The amount of interactive proof required is less than a tenth of what is typically required in other formal verificaiton toolsets.

3   The ClawZ Approach

In this section, the components of the ClawZ toolset and how they fit together are described in more detail. As well as explaining how the toolset works, the intention is to give an understanding of how the approach used to build the toolset can be applied to other verification domains.

3.1   The ClawZ Architecture

The ClawZ toolset is composed of six tools: Z Producer [6,4], RSG, DAZ[2] [7,4], Supertac, ProofPower [4] and CPS. The central tool in the toolset is DAZ. This is a tool for performing formal refinement between a Z specification and Ada source code. All the other tools revolve around DAZ. Z Producer translates a Simulink diagram into a Z specification, ultimately used by DAZ. RSG is used as an interactive tool for creating a witness script, but its main role is to translate the witness script into a DAZ refinement script. The Supertac and ProofPower theorem provers are used to prove verification conditions that are output from DAZ as a result of processing a refinement script. Finally, CPS is ClawZ's Unix command line environment, and acts as a front end for much of the analyst interaction with the toolset, as well as performing house keeping tasks. See Figure 5 for a diagram illustrating the architecture of the toolset.

The refinement supported by DAZ is loosely based on Carroll Morgan's algorithmic refinement calculus [8]. A refinement script starts with a *specification statement* for a block of source code. The specification statement defines what the source code block is supposed to do. It consists of three parts: a frame, that lists the variables that are allowed to change in the source code block; a precondition, that can be assumed about the values of variables on entry to the block; and a postcondition, that must be upheld on exiting the block. The pre- and postconditions are expressed in Z.

The specification statement can then be refined to source code under a series of refinement steps. In intermediate refinement steps there will be a mixture of source code and specification statements. Each refinement step results in verification conditions being generated by DAZ. DAZ can output the set of verification conditions and the Ada source code resulting from the refinement. Every verification condition of every refinement step must be proved in order to establish that the source code meets its specification.

Before a subroutine can undergo interactive witnessing with RSG, it requires a specification statement. This is constructed using the components supplied by the analyst during the specification stage (see Section 2.1). The subroutine's block list is read in by CPS, which uses it to construct an input command for Z Producer. Z Producer then outputs a Z translation of the artificial subsystem corresponding to these blocks. CPS then combines this Z artificial subsystem with the subroutine's data refinement relation and any preconditions and post-

---

[2] DAZ has also been known as the Compliance Tool and the Compliance Notation Tool.

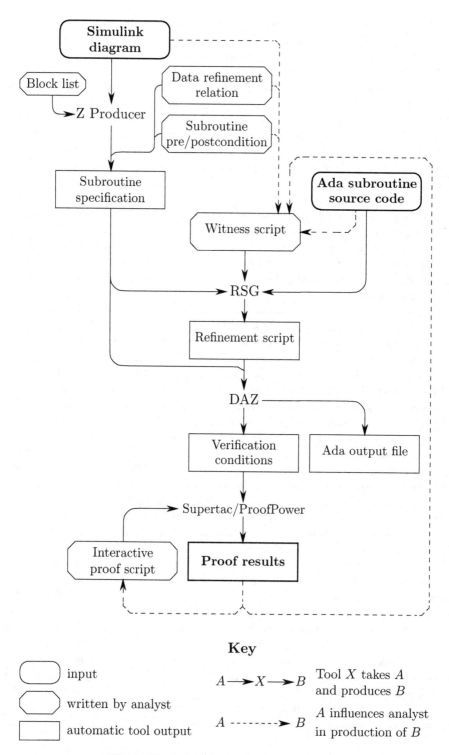

Fig. 5. The architecture of the ClawZ toolset

conditions associated with the subroutine to form a specification statement for the subroutine. This is all done in the execution of one CPS command.

Once a witness script has been produced by the analyst (see Section 2.2), CPS passes it, the subroutine's specification statement and the subroutine's Ada source code to RSG, which results in a DAZ refinement script being generated. For reasons explained in Section 3.2, this refinement script outputted by RSG has the starting point, i.e. the subroutine's specification statement, missing. CPS then combines the subroutine's specification statement with RSG's output to form a complete refinement script. This complete refinement script is then submitted to DAZ, which results in a set of verification conditions and an Ada output file being generated. For reasons explained in Section 3.2, CPS then checks that the Ada subroutine output from DAZ is syntactically equivalent to the original Ada subroutine source code. Supertac is then run on every verification condition generated. Finally, CPS summarises the results of the Supertac run to the screen. Again, this is all done in the execution of one CPS command.

Before the ClawZ toolset was invented, a few parts of control systems were analysed by manually writing DAZ refinement scripts and performing all formal proofs interactively by using ProofPower (but still using Z Producer to translate Simulink), and so it is possible to compare the times taken. The speed up achieved by using ClawZ is impressive. The refinement script for a typical subroutine would take around one month to produce, and the verification conditions would take around one month to prove. Using ClawZ this is all done in about a day, and can mostly be performed by an analyst with considerably less expertise. This speed up of 50 times is not wholly representative, since there was probably considerable scope for improving the manual process. However, it gives an idea of the order-of-magnitude improvement that has taken place.

The sizes of the intermediate objects passed between the tools can vary considerably, but tend to be large. For a typical 80 line Ada subroutine, the refinement script outputted by RSG tends to range from 1,000 to 10,000 lines. Note that, in terms of numbers of lines, the witness script written by the analyst is around 10 to 50 times shorter than the resulting refinement script. Also note that the witness script is considerably more abstract than the refinement script, and so less susceptible to tedious errors in detail. Individual verification conditions tend to range from 100 to 1,000 lines of Z.

For the examples that can be compared, these objects tend to be around 4 times the size of those produced in the pre-ClawZ days. The reason for the increase in size is ultimately due to the systematic way in which RSG works, where automation is introduced at the expense of some conciseness. Raw refinement scripts and verification conditions are never seen by the analyst, and so conciseness is not an issue unless it impacts significantly on execution time.

The success of Supertac in being able to prove such huge verification conditions automatically is down to two main factors. The first is that the verification conditions are rarely as complicated as they might first seem, and much of the proof of a verification condition involves relatively trivial reductions. However, it would be insufficient for Supertac to only perform such trivial reductions, since the proofs of most verification conditions would still require some complex reasoning taking several hours to perform interactively.

The second main factor is that Supertac is designed with the context in which these verification conditions are generated in mind. Z Producer creates Z specifications that follow a well defined structure, computer programs for control systems tend to be written in similar ways, RSG generates refinement scripts in a highly systematic way and DAZ generates verification conditions according to a strict set of rules. It was possible to take all of these conventions into account when designing Supertac.

So, in summary, the architecture of ClawZ revolves around the classic formal verification toolset model of using a translator, a formal refinement tool and a theorem prover. The way that ClawZ differs is that it incorporates additional tools, in particular RSG and Supertac, that shield the analyst from tedious details normally associated with formal verification, and so enable analyst input and expertise to be dramatically reduced. These additional tools are able to achieve this by being dedicated to a specific verification domain.

3.2 Soundness

Formal verification tools are useful for providing positive evidence that software correctly meets its specification, as well as for finding errors. This positive evidence is very important if a toolset is being used for the certification of safety-critical software. Thus it is important that there is a high degree of confidence in the soundness of a formal verification toolset.

The success of ClawZ in being able to analyse software at relatively low cost is almost entirely due to the RSG and Supertac tools. However, equivalents of these tools do not exist in other formal verification toolsets, and they are implemented in several thousand of lines of source code. A concern might be that errors in RSG or Supertac may compromise the soundness of the toolset.

RSG, however, cannot introduce unsoundness to ClawZ. This is because all that RSG does, ultimately, is produce a refinement script. The way in which the refinement script was constructed does not affect soundness. If we assume that DAZ itself is sound, then it is impossible for anything, including RSG or the witnessing analyst or someone manually writing a refinement script, to fool it. DAZ will only produce verification conditions that are all provable if the initial specification statement in the refinement script is correctly implemented by the refined source code in the refinement script.

It might be possible to fool the analyst, however, by feeding DAZ a refinement script that has an initial specification statement that does not reflect the analyst's specification, or a refinement script that refines to source code different from the original. To give a pathological example, regardless of the analyst input in the specification and witnessing stages, DAZ could be presented with an initial specification statement that has a postcondition of "true" that is refined to a "null" Ada statement. This would result in all the verification conditions being provable, regardless of whether the original source code met its intended specification. However such situations cannot happen due to RSG, since it is

CPS, and not RSG, that inserts the initial specification statement, and since CPS checks that the Ada source code resulting from the refinement is syntactically (and thus semantically) equivalent to the original source code. Thus RSG, by the way that it is used, cannot introduce unsoundness to ClawZ.

Supertac, too, cannot affect the soundness of ClawZ, but for different reasons. Supertac is built on top of the ProofPower theorem prover, which is an LCF-style theorem prover [9]. A theorem prover is said to be sound if it is only possible to prove conjectures that are true. Great care is taken to make theorem provers sound. However, they are large programs that perform highly complex manipulations. Given the subtleties of mathematics, it is very difficult to ensure that nowhere in the large theorem prover program is a mistake that introduces unsoundness. There are numerous steps that can be taken to reduce the risk of this, but the most effective is to make the theorem prover LCF-style [10].

In the implementation of an LCF-style theorem prover, a special data type is reserved for theorems, i.e. conjectures that have been proved. Strong data typing of the programming language is then used to ensure that theorems can only be constructed from a kernel of operations, called *primitive inference rules*. New operations to prove conjectures can be defined outside the kernel, but they must ultimately be implemented in terms of the primitive inference rules. Thus an LCF-style theorem prover is sound so long as its primitive inference rules are sound and the small amount of source code implementing these is correct.

ProofPower's primitive inference rules are based on the HOL logic system [5]. This is the most widely used logic system used for LCF-style theorem provers, and is one of the simplest, and so it is perhaps the best logic system to use to minimise the risk of unsoundness. Thus ProofPower, being a HOL-based, LCF-style theorem prover, has a very high pedigree for soundness. Also, any new proof operations built on top of ProofPower cannot introduce unsoundness, because they must ultimately be defined in terms of primitive inference rules. So, since Supertac is built on top of ProofPower, which is an LCF-style theorem prover, it cannot introduce unsoundness.

Thus the additional tools incoporated into ClawZ, i.e. RSG and Supertac, that differentiate ClawZ from traditional formal verification toolsets and enable it to be used so much more cost-effectively, are incorporated in such a way that cannot compromise soundness of the overall toolset.

4   Conclusions

Control systems play an important role in modern society, and the increasing complexity of their software is causing the associated development, maintenance and certification costs to escalate. The ClawZ toolset is dedicated to the formal verification of control system software, and has been successfully applied to the industrial formal verification of Eurofighter Typhoon's FCC at much reduced certification costs when compared with other formal verification toolsets. ClawZ adapts the classic formal verification toolset architecture by including two novel components, RSG and Supertac, that are key to achieving its effectiveness.

RSG enables the analyst to construct a relatively abstract witness script instead of the refinement script that is required with existing formal verification toolsets. This enables the costly task of manual program refinement to be replaced by a much simpler, although still non-trivial, task. Supertac highly automates the formal proof, completing over 95% of verification condition proofs entirely automatically, and simplifying the remainder for interactive proof. This greatly reduces the costly task of interactive formal proof, and enables the witness script construction and interactive proof roles to be easily separated.

By being tailored to a specific verification domain, namely the verification of control system software specified in Simulink and implemented in Ada, these two components dramatically reduce the amount of analyst input and expertise required to perform formal verification. Furthermore, they are incorporated into the toolset in such a way that guarantees they cannot introduce unsoundness.

Although the toolset enables highly productive verification as it stands, there is still significant scope for improvement to help further reduce analyst time and expertise. Both RSG and Supertac could provide more feedback to the analyst to help in tracking down analyst errors more quickly. Also, Supertac could be enhanced to further automate verification condition proof.

There is nothing about this approach to building a formal verification toolset that limits it to this specific verification domain. Such an approach could equally be used to verify systems implemented in other programming languages, or specified in other design notations. Also, the scale of the cost reductions brought about by ClawZ opens up the prospect of much wider use of formal verification, including during development, and perhaps even for non safety-critical code. This approach could therefore have a profound impact on the use of formal verification in industrial applications.

References

1. The Mathworks Inc.: Using Simulink. 5th edn. (2002)
2. TA Consultancy Services Ltd.: MALPAS Training Course Notes. 2nd edn. (1995)
3. J.Woodcock, J.Davies: Using Z: Specification, Refinement and Proof. 1st edn. Prentice Hall (1996)
4. Lemma 1 Ltd. website: www.lemma-one.com.
5. M.J.C.Gordon, T.F.Melham, eds.: Introduction to HOL: A Theorem Proving Environment for Higher Order Logic. Cambridge University Press (1993)
6. C.O'Halloran, A.Smith: Verification of Picture Generated Code. In: 14th IEEE ASE, IEEE Computer Society Press (1999)
7. C.O'Halloran, A.Smith: Don't Verify, Abstract! In: 13th IEEE ASE, IEEE Computer Society Press (1998)
8. C.Morgan: Programming from Specifications. 2nd edn. Prentice Hall (1994)
9. M.Gordon, A.Milner, C.Wadsworth: Edinburgh LCF – A Mechanical Logic of Computation. In: LNCS 78, Springer-Verlag (1979)
10. J.Harrison: Metatheory and Reflection in Theorem Proving: A Survey Critique. Technical report, University of Cambridge Computer Laboratory (1995)

SVG Web Environment for Z Specification Language

Jing Sun[1], Hai Wang[2], Sasanka Athauda[1], and Tazkiya Sheik[1]

[1] Department of Computer Science,
The University of Auckland, New Zealand
j.sun@cs.auckland.ac.nz
{sath002, fshe009}@ec.auckland.ac.nz
[2] Department of Computer Science,
The University of Manchester, United Kingdom
hai.wang@cs.man.ac.uk

Abstract. This paper presents a web environment for the Z formal specification language using the Scalable Vector Graphics (SVG) technology. The Z Specification Web Editor (ZSWE) is the first prototype of a web based graphical editor for the Z specification language. It not only supports graphical editing and global accessibility for the Z formal specifications, but also provides model comprehension facilities such as schema expansion, specification navigation and model querying. This paper outlines the requirement, design and implementation of the tool and its future improvements.

Keywords: Z formal specification language, Web based tool support, Scalable Vector Graphics.

1   Introduction

Formal methods is defined as mathematically based techniques for the specification, development and verification of software and hardware systems [1]. The well-defined semantics and syntax of formal specification languages make them suitable for precisely capturing and formally verifying system requirements. Z is a formal specification language based on set theory and predicate logic [2]. It has been widely used in both industry and academic research for the specification and verification of software systems. The World Wide Web (WWW) acts as a promising environment for software specification and design because it allows sharing design models and providing hyper textual links among the models. Formal methods like the CafeOBJ system [3] have included an environment supporting formal specification over the Internet. Schemas using pure Z notation on the web based on HTML and Java Applet have also been investigated by Bowen et al. [4] and Ciancarini et al. [5]. Although HTML has been successful in presenting information on the Internet, the lack of content information and the overburdened use of the display tags have made the efficient retrieval and exchange of information content more difficult to achieve. In 2001, Sun et al. proposed an XML/XSL approach in presenting the Z/Object-Z languages

K.-K. Lau and R. Banach (Eds.): ICFEM 2005, LNCS 3785, pp. 480–494, 2005.

on the web [6]. It uses the XSL Transformation language to translate the XML form of Z/Object-Z models into HTML for automated browser display. In their approach, XML has been introduced as an interchange format for document- ing Z specifications. However, the graphical support of the resulting Z model display was still restricted on using HTML only. In this paper, we present an approach of using the Scalable Vector Graphics (SVG) to implement a web based environment for the Z specification language[1]. SVG is a World Wide Web Con- sortium (W3C) recommended language for describing two-dimensional graphics and graphical applications in XML. It can overcome the poor graphical support in using HTML for displaying Z specifications on the web. The Z Specification Web Editor (ZSWE) prototype tool presented in the paper uses the standard Z Markup Language (ZML) format defined by Utting et al. in 2003 [7]. The ZSWE tool not only supports true graphical editing for the Z formal specifications, but also provides model comprehension facilities such as schema expansion, specifi- cation navigation and model querying. There is some related work in providing editing facility for the Z notation, such as the functions in Z/EVES, ZETA and CADiZ. From an editing support point of view, most of those tools only provide limited editing facility of Z specifications. Compared to our approach, they are lack of additional model comprehension functions such as specification naviga- tion and model querying. In comparison with other approaches in presenting Z models on the web, our SVG prototype tool also provides a better graphical display and editing supports for Z models over the internet.

The remainder of the paper is organized as follows. Section 2 introduces background information on Z, ZML and SVG. In section 3, we discuss the var- ious aspects regarding a specification environment for the Z language. Section 4 presents the architecture design of the web based specification prototype tool - ZSWE. In section 5, we present some implementation issues of the ZSWE. Section 6 gives an overview of the prototype tool. Section 7 concludes the paper and discusses future improvements.

2   Background

2.1   The Z Formal Specification Language

Z [2] is a state-based formal language based on ZF set theory and first-order predicate logic. It is specially suited to model system data and state changes. A Z specification typically includes a number of state and operation schema defi- nitions. A state schema encapsulates variable declarations and related invariant predicates. An operation schema defines the relationship between the 'before' and 'after' states corresponding to one or more state schemas. Complex schema definitions can be composed from the simple ones using the schema calculus. Z has been widely adopted to specify a range of software systems. The following is a state schema example of a Birthday Book specification taking from [2].

---

[1] This work was supported in part by HyOntUse Project (GR/S44686) funded by the UK Engineering and Physical Science Research Council.

```
┌─ BirthdayBook ─────────────────────────────────────────
│ known : ℙ NAME
│ birthday : NAME ↦ DATE
├────────────────────────────────────────────────────────
│ known = dom birthday
└────────────────────────────────────────────────────────
```

The above defines a basic structure of a birthday book. The variable **known** represents the set of people in the birthday book; and the variable **birthday** is a partial function that associates the people's names with their birth dates. The state invariant imposes that the **known** set is set of the people who already had their birthday recorded. Other operations such as 'add' or 'find' a birthday record can be defined accordingly. In this paper, we will be using this Birthday Book example to illustrate the requirements of a Z specification editor.

2.2   The Z Markup Language

EXtensible Markup Language (XML) is a global standard for representing information in a textual format. The Z Markup Language (ZML) is defined to serve as an XML interchange format for documenting Z specifications by Utting et al. in [7]. Its syntax was based on the Z ISO International Standard format [8]. It is recommended by the Community Z Tools Initiative (CZT) group that future tool development on Z should follow this XML convention. In addition, a library of Java classes has been developed for the parser support of the ZML files. The following denotes a partial ZML representation of the variable declaration '*known* : ℙ *Name*' in the Birthday Book state schema example.

```
<VarDecl>
  <DeclName>
    <Word>known</Word>
  </DeclName>
  <PowerExpr>
    <RefExpr Mixfix="false">
      <RefName>
        <Word>NAME</Word>
      </RefName>
    </RefExpr>
  </PowerExpr>
</VarDecl>
```

We can see from the above example that ZML has a complex syntax structure and it is intended for machine (tool) interpretation only.

2.3   Scalable Vector Graphics

Scalable Vector Graphics (SVG) is a language for describing two-dimensional graphics on the web using a standard XML format [9]. It supports three types of graphic objects:

- **Vector graphic shape**: SVG provides pre-defined graphical shapes and a path element which can be used to create any arbitrary two-dimensional shape.
- **Text**: SVG has several elements that displays text in different layouts.
- **Image**: SVG supports other types of graphical images to be embedded in SVG documents.

The data representation of conventional images is quite different to SVG. Conventional images are broken into small pixels and the description (e.g., color of the pixel) of each of these pixels has to be stored. Therefore, these images hold a large file size. On the other hand, SVG provides the type of shape required to be drawn, the coordinates, and the style of the shape in XML format. This information can be translated by the SVG plug-in on the web browser as the shape is displayed. An example of an SVG file that generates a simple rectangle is shown below:

```
<svg width="100" height="100">
  <rect x="10" y="10" width="50" height="50" style="fill:red"/>
</svg>
```

As shown in this example, the 'rect' tag informs the browser that the shape is a rectangle with the coordinates and style of the rectangle provided. SVG also supports the following aspects, which we found useful in developing the ZSWE prototype tool:

- **Animation support**: SVG provides animation support on graphical shapes. Such animation support includes dynamically changing the location, size, style of a shape.
- **Zoom-in and zoom-out**: SVG supports zoom in/out features on its graphical shapes. The graphical quality of the shape is maintained during the zoom-in and zoom-out.
- **Unicode support**: SVG provides support to display Unicode symbols.
- **DOM functionality**: Since SVG is in XML format, other programming languages can use the DOM functions to create the SVG DOM which can be used to locate and access SVG content information.

3   Aspects of a Z Specification Editor

In this section we describe some of the key issues related to a web based editor for the Z specification language. We summarize our requirements into five different aspects, i.e., graphical display, schema expansion, specification navigation, model querying, and specification validation.

3.1   Graphical Display

A Z specification consists of schema boxes and mathematical expressions. Z is a language based on set theory and predicate logic, which consists of a rich set of mathematical symbols. The following defines the *AddBirthday* operation schema in the Birthday Book example.

```
┌─ AddBirthday ─────────────────────────────────────────
│ ΔBirthdayBook
│ name? : NAME
│ date? : DATE
├───────────────────────────────────────────────────────
│ name? ∉ known
│ birthday' = birthday ∪ {name? ↦ date?}
└───────────────────────────────────────────────────────
```

The `AddBirthday` operation allows the users to add new birthday records into the system based on the pre-condition that the person has not been recorded before. From the above example, we can see that the first requirement of a Z specification editor is to support elegant graphical display of Z schema box drawings and the usage of mathematical symbols such as '∉','∪', '↦' and so on.

3.2   Schema Expansion

In a Z specification, the full definition of a schema can be obtained by expanding the inclusion section of the schema. For example, the expanded view of the *AddBirthday* schema in the previous subsection is as follows.

```
┌─ AddBirthday ─────────────────────────────────────────
│ known, known' : ℙ NAME
│ birthday, birthday' : NAME ⇸ DATE
│ name? : NAME
│ date? : DATE
├───────────────────────────────────────────────────────
│ known = dom birthday
│ known' = dom birthday'
│ name? ∉ known
│ birthday' = birthday ∪ {name? ↦ date?}
└───────────────────────────────────────────────────────
```

The above gives the full definition of the `AddBirthday` schema by expanding the definitions inside the '*ΔBirthdayBook*' expression. Another form of expansion is the Z schema calculus. In a Z specification, complex operations can be constructed by using schema calculus operators such as '∧', '∨' and so on. For example, a 'robust' version of the `RAddBirthday` operations can be specified by using the conjunction and disjunction operators on the `AddBirthday`, `Success` and `AlreadyKnown` schemas in the Birthday Book example as follows.

```
┌─ Success ──────────────────┐      ┌─ AlreadyKnown ─────────────┐
│ result! : REPORT           │      │ ΞBirthdayBook              │
├────────────────────────────┤      │ name? : NAME               │
│ result! = ok               │      │ result! : REPORT           │
└────────────────────────────┘      ├────────────────────────────┤
                                     │ name? ∈ known              │
                                     │ result! = already_known    │
                                     └────────────────────────────┘
```

$$RAddBirthday \mathrel{\widehat{=}} (AddBirthday \wedge Success) \vee AlreadyKnown$$

The `RAddBirthday` operation will insert a new record into the birthday book or report the record has already been stored. The full definition of the `RAddBirthday` schema can be obtained by expanding the definitions in the `AddBirthday`, `Success` and `AlreadyKnown` schemas as follows.

RAddBirthday _____

$known, known' : \mathbb{P}\, NAME$
$birthday, birthday' : NAME \nrightarrow DATE$
$name? : NAME$
$date? : DATE$
$result! : REPORT$

$known = \mathrm{dom}\ birthday$
$known' = \mathrm{dom}\ birthday'$
$(name? \notin known \wedge birthday' = birthday \cup \{name? \mapsto date?\} \wedge result! = ok)$
$\vee\ (name? \in known \wedge birthday' = birthday \wedge result! = already\_known)$

Other forms of schema operators include schema composition '$\mathbin{\raise.5ex\hbox{$\scriptscriptstyle 9$}}$', implication '$\Rightarrow$', negation '$\neg$' and piping '$\gg$', which have been discussed in many Z books [2]. The schema expansion is useful for analysis, review and reasoning about Z specifications. For instance, in the case of calculating the pre-/post-conditions related to a particular scheme operation, it is necessary to expand (unfold) the full definition of schema before the calculation. Thus, the second requirement of the Z specification editor is to support automatic schema expansions to display a full definition of a schema as needed.

3.3 Specification Navigation

In a large Z model that contains quite a number of schemas, it is sometimes hard for the users to keep track of all the definitions. In this case, it is desirable for the users to be able to navigate from one point of definition to another by referring to a schema name or a variable type. For example, in the following `FindBirthday` schema, if the users would like to refer to the original definition of the `BirthdayBook`, they should be able to navigate to its point of definition by referring to the `BirthdayBook` schema name inside the operation. Similarly, variable types, such as `NAME`, `DATE`, etc., should have the navigation facility as well.

FindBirthday _____

$\Xi BirthdayBook$
$name? : NAME$
$date! : DATE$

$name? \in known$
$date! = birthday(name?)$

As mentioned earlier, this kind of navigation feature is very useful when the user is dealing with a large Z specification that contains quite a number of schema definitions. It will not only help the user to obtain a good understanding of the relationships among the schemas, but also provide easy accessibility for all the definitions in the specification. Thus, the third requirement of a Z specification editor is to support specification navigation that allows the users to navigate from one point of the definition to another inside a Z model.

3.4   Model Querying

The idea of querying a Z model comes from the concept of specification comprehension, i.e., to obtain a better understanding of what has been modeled in the specification. In general, specification comprehension is analogous to program understanding. But the former is more complicated than program understanding because programs are executable, while specifications are not necessarily to be so [10]. Thus it is desirable for a specification tool to provide means for the users to enhance the understanding of the static properties of a formal model it represents. The query of a Z model is to fulfill such a comprehension facility. We summarized four types of query functions on a Z model as follows.

- **Schema query**: provides information on the schemas in a Z model, such as where this schema is used and how it is used, i.e., being included in or modified in other schemas.
- **Variable query**: provides information on the variables in a schema, such as the type of variables (state/input/output), in which schema or operation the variable is defined or used, etc.
- **Operation query**: provides information on the operations in a Z model, such as the variables and predicates that an operation has and so on.
- **Reference query**: provides cross-reference information on the schemas in a Z model.

Querying is considered as a usability function. It is not an implicit element of a Z specification. For example, Z schemas, functions, and its variables and predicates can be considered as containing implicit elements of the Z model. But model querying is search functionality for locating these implicit elements and providing a better understanding of the underlying Z specification. Thus, the fourth requirement of the Z specification editor is to support model querying functions that allows the users to explore the static properties inside a Z model.

3.5   Specification Validation

Specification validation denotes the process of determining whether the specification is correct and a true reflection of the requirements that is meant to capture. We summarized three levels of validation associated to a particular Z model.

- **Syntax checking**: to check whether a Z expression is written properly according the Z language syntax.
- **Type checking**: to check whether an expression is correct according to the type checking rules of the Z language. For example, we could define a syntactically correct expression such as 'x : $\mathbb{N}_1$' where 'x' takes values from the positive nature number set. But if we later assign a value of negative integer to 'x', this is where a type inference error is occurred. Type checking [11] techniques are usually applied for validating these kind of errors in a specification.
- **Semantic checking**: to check the logical correctness of a Z specification. Even if a Z specification is syntactically and type correct, there are still possibilities that the logical statements in the model might conflict each other or the dynamic behaviors of the model does not truly reflects the requirement. These errors are related to the semantic meanings of the Z model. Semantic checking usually requires more complicated techniques than that of syntax and type checking. In general, theorem proving and specification animation [12] are two approaches that can be used for the semantic checking process.

We believe that a Z specification editing tool should provide some mechanism to allow the users to validate whether their specifications are correct. Thus, our last requirement of a Z specification editor is to support specification validation for checking the correctness of a Z model. In this section, we discussed some general aspects related to a Z specification editing tool. And our prototype implementation should closely follow some of these requirements.

4   Architecture Design of the ZSWE

Software architecture is an important level of description for the development of software systems. It represents the high level structure of a system, which comprise the definitions of software components involved, the external visible properties of those components, and the communications among the components. When consider the architecture of a web based application, there are two major type of approaches, i.e., client-side based architecture and server-side based architecture. Client-side applications are loaded from server and reside in memory of the client machines. Complicated computations are done on the client machines without having to request them from the server. Although this lessens the overburdens on the server, the initial loading and response times of client-side applications are slow. This is one of the major drawbacks of the approach. On the other hand, server-side architecture handles all the complex computations on the server and sends the results back to the client. Therefore, the client machine is not under heavy load and acts as a simple web browser that posts requests and display the results. This also provides the use of less bandwidth and gaining faster web responses, as all processing is done on the server and web pages are dynamically presented. In nowadays, as the web servers become increasingly powerful in terms of the computational capability, more and more web based softwares choose the server-side architecture to provide an easy accessible and 'thin client' application. We decided to implement our ZSWE prototype tool on the server side for the same reason. Figure 1 shows an overview of the sever-side component architecture of the tool.

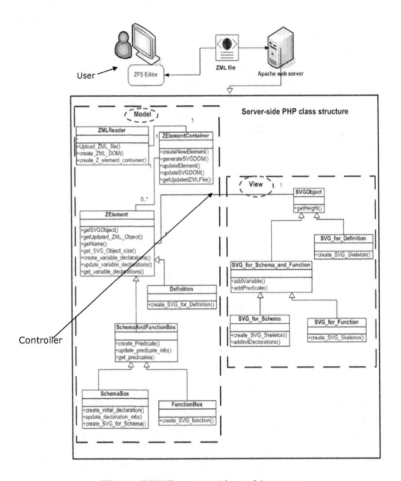

Fig. 1. ZSWE server-side architecture

As shown in the diagram, the client-side consists of the web browser, SVG plug-in, and the client requests. It is the communication point between the server and the actual client. The user can create/upload a Z specification to the server, modify the information in the Z specification, or download an updated Z specification from the server. Note that the standard ZML syntax mentioned in section 2.2 is chosen as the input/output interchange format for documenting the Z specification in our tool. The server-side of the tool consists of components that handles the corresponding computation of SVG elements. When a ZML file is uploaded to the server, the 'ZMLReader' component on the server processes the file and generates the ZML-DOM representation of the specification. This DOM is then passed to the 'ZElementContainer' component which creates the 'ZElement' objects according the information presented in the ZML-DOM. The users can add new Z definitions, or update the existing definitions of a Z model. This is also performed by sending the updating information to the server, the 'ZElementUpdater' component on the server finds the corresponding 'ZElement' object from the 'ZElementContainer' and performs the update. Once each of the 'ZElement' objects has been created or updated, a SVG representation of the specification is generated through the 'SVGGenerator' component. After the server creates the graphical representation of the Z model in SVG format, it is sent back to the client as a SVG file. The SVG plug-in which runs inside the web browser identifies this file as a SVG document, and translates its tags into proper graphical elements. Finally, these graphical elements are displayed in the web browser.

Figure 1 also describes the architecture in a Model View Controller (MVC) structure. MVC is a common architecture used by the modern software developers to increase modularity of the code. It divides the code into three modules: Model, View, and Controllers, which enables data flow between the Model and View via the Controller. Each of these three modules acts independently to maintain consistency. MVC architecture is commonly used in server-side development because it enables the maintenance of multiple views of the same system. As highlighted in the above diagram, the class structures is divided in to major sub-components: Model, View and Controller. The Model contains the components such as 'ZMLReader', 'ZElementContainer', 'ZElement' and so on, to read the ZML file, creates its DOM, breaks the ZML-DOM into Z elements such as schemas, functions, definitions etc. The View can be considered as all the SVG content related components such as the 'SVGObject', and the server-side PHP script that generates them because these SVG files contain the graphical interface of the tool. Finally, the data updating components such as the 'ZElementUpdater' and the PHP script that maps the user actions to model updates can be considered as the Controller elements of the MVC model. And the updater script that performs the updates of SVG representation and the Z element object also act as a Controller element.

5   Implementation Issues of the ZSWE

The main techniques involved in the implementation of the ZSWE prototype tool are Scalable Vector Graphics (SVG), Hypertext Pre-processor (PHP) and ECMA scripting.

5.1   SVG and ECMA Scripting

Our main issue in the implementation was to combine data information between SVG and HTML. Since both HTML and SVG support web scripting functions,

ECMA scripting is used for the implementation. ECMA scripting is a standard for describing a web scripting language that can create a rich environment for a web site. It provides built-in methods and classes to support XML-DOM. A web browser allows ECMA scripting for client-side computing and also provides for events such as mouse events, change of focus, image and page loading, selection and form submission etc. It can be embedded in HTML and PHP to allow for animation of objects and events. This scripting language is very useful in web application as it provides the functionalities of object oriented programming that cannot be achieved by using plain HTML. The following is an example that uses ECMA scripting to perform dynamic updates on SVG elements by catching the events triggered by these elements:

```
<svg width="100" height="100" onload=init(evt)>
 <desc>
  <script language="text/ecmascript">
   <![CDATA[
   var svgdoc;
   function init(evt){
     svgdoc=evt.getTarget().getOwnerDocument();
   }
   function mousePress(name){
     var element=svgdoc.getElementById(name);
     element.setAttribute ("height", "40");
   }
   ]]>
  </script>
  <rect id="rectangle" x="10" y="10" width="40" height="100"
   style="fill:red" onmouseclick="mousePress('rectangle')"/>
 </desc>
</svg>
```

As show in the above code segment, the ECMA functions are embedded inside the SVG content. When these SVG content is loaded onto a web browser, the 'onload' event calls the 'init' method in the ECMA script. This method assigns the SVG-DOM root object to a variable. As highlighted above, the SVG 'rect' element has an unique ID and a mouse-click event. When the user clicks on the rectangle, the 'onmouseclick' event calls the 'mousePress' method in the ECMA script, and sends the rectangle ID as its input. This method uses the ID to get the rectangle object from the SVG-DOM. Then it changes the height attribute of the rectangle object, which dynamically effects on the graphical display.

5.2   SVG and PHP

When developing web based applications on the server-side, there are special programming languages to handle the computation mechanism. We chose the Hypertext Pre-processor (PHP) script language in our implementation. PHP provides a good set of functions that are used for extracting and modifying information from XML documents. PHP version 4 and above includes functions that can generate XML documents using XML-DOM. Therefore, the SVG code can be generated by creating the XML nodes that represent the SVG pages. The following is a segment of PHP code for generating the SVG example shown in section 2.3.

```php
$root = $doc->create_element("svg");
$root = $doc->append_child($root);
$root->set_attribute ("width", "100");
$root->set_attribute ("height", "100");
$rect = $doc->create_element("rect");
$rect = $root->append_child($rect);
$rect->set_attribute ("x", "10");
$rect->set_attribute ("y", "10");
$rect->set_attribute ("width", "50");
$rect->set_attribute ("height", "50");
$rect->set_attribute ("style", "fill:read");
```

The code segment displayed above first creates a new SVG canvas and set its size, then create a SVG rectangle element and appends it to SVG canvas as a child node. The position, size and the style attributes of the SVG rectangle are set accordingly. From the above example, we can see that by using PHP we are able to easily generate and modify SVG representations of Z models and sent them back to the web browser for displaying.

6   ZSWE in Action

The ZSWE prototype tool consists of three main pages, i.e., the index page, the SVG display page and the Z schema editing page[2].

6.1   SVG Z Model Display

The SVG display page provides the main functionalities of the tool, such as model display, schema expansion, navigation and querying. Figure 2 illustrates the SVG display page of the ZSWE tool. The Z specification model is displayed on the left hand side of the page. Navigation points are provided for each of the schema names and type declarations to allow quick references among the definitions. The down arrows represent expansion points inside the specification to allow the user to view the full definition of a schema. The schema expansion function was implemented using the SVG animation technique. In addition, a zoom in/out feature was provided for the display page to allow the user to zoom in and out on the Z models. On the right hand side of the page are the button panel and the query panel. The button panel contains buttons for creating new schema, give type, axiom definition and so on. There are two additional buttons

---

[2] The Z Specification Web Editor (ZSWE) prototype tool is available at http://www.cs.auckland.ac.nz/~jingsun/ZFSE/pages/index.php

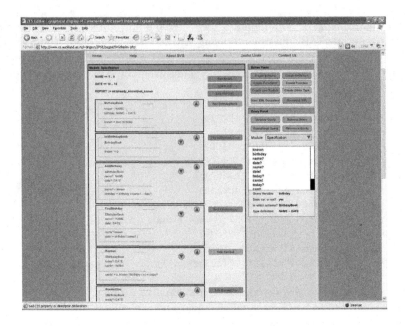

Fig. 2. The SVG display page

on bottom of the button panel where one is used to view the ZML document of the current Z specification, and the other to download the ZML file.

Model querying is an important functionality that has been implemented in the ZSWE tool. The query panel consists of four types of querying buttons, i.e., variable query, schema query, operational query, and reference query. Each of the query functions provides model comprehension facilities described in section 3.4. For example, in the case of a schema query, when the user click on the 'Schema Query' button, a list of all the schema names in the Z model are displayed on the query panel. After one of these listed schema names is selected, the query panel provides the names of other schemas that has extended or used the selected schema.

6.2   Z Schema Editing

By clicking on the editing the Z definitions button in Figure 2, a Z schema editing page can be invoked to allows the user to make changes to the schema definitions. The schema editing page can also be opened by the create new definition buttons on the SVG display page. Figure 3 shows the functionality provide by the ZWSE schema editing page. New variables and predication definitions of a schema are input on the right panel and updated to the SVG display panel on the left. A mathematics symbol panel is provided to assist the user for inputting Z mathematical expressions. It uses the SVG Unicode representations for the displaying of the mathematical symbols. Note that our mathematics symbol panel

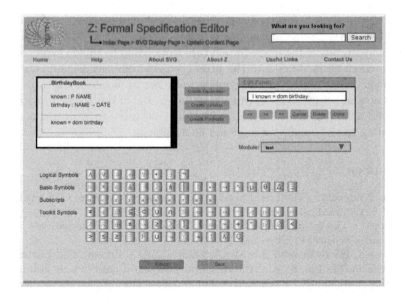

Fig. 3. Z schema editing page

adopts some of the symbol layout from the Z/EVES tool. After the modifications have been made, new updates on the specifications are displayed on the main SVG display page. The user can download an updated version of the ZML file of the Z specification. As we mentioned in section 3.5, a Z specification editor should provide some mechanism for checking the correctness of the Z model. In our ZSWE prototype tool, we have implemented a syntax checking facility for validating whether the Z specification is written according to a proper Z syntax. The syntax checking is based on XML schema validation mechanism. Every time when a Z specification is uploaded, its XML representation is validated against the ZML schema definition.

7   Conclusion

In this paper, we presented a web environment for the Z formal specification language. Different aspects of a Z specification editor were discussed. The design and implementation of the Z Specification Web Editor (ZSWE) prototype tool using the SVG technology was presented. Our ZSWE tool not only supports graphical editing and global accessibility for the Z formal specifications on the internet, but also provides model comprehension facilities such as schema expansion, specification navigation and model querying. In addition, the ZSWE tool also provides a basic Z syntax checking facility.

For the future extensions, firstly, our idea of the Z web environment can be easily adopted to other formal specification languages such as Object-Z [13], TCOZ [14] and so on. Both Object-Z and TCOZ have XML representations of their langauge syntaxes, thus such extensions should be straightforward. Secondly, as our ZSWE tool only supports syntax checking facility of the Z language at the moment, one of the immediate future work could be to add type and some semantic checking facilities into the prototype environment. Finally, our Z web environment is currently an anonymous web user application. By providing a login name and password for each user, online saving of the Z specification models can be achieved. This would enable different users to work on a same Z specification model collaboratively and continuously.

References

1. From Wikipedia: (The Free Encyclopedia) Available at: http://en.wikipedia.org/wiki/Formal_methods.
2. Spivey, J.: The Z Notation: A Reference Manual. 2nd edn. International Series in Computer Science. Prentice-Hall (1992)
3. Futatsugi, K., Nakagawa, A.: An Overview of CAFE Specification Environment. In Hinchey, M., Liu, S., eds.: the IEEE International Conference on Formal Engineering Methods (ICFEM'97), Hiroshima, Japan, IEEE Computer Society Press (1997)
4. Bowen, J.P., Chippington, D.: Z on the Web using Java. [15] 66–80
5. Ciancarini, P., Mascolo, C., Vitali, F.: Visualizing Z notation in HTML documents. [15] 81–95
6. Sun, J., Dong, J.S., Liu, J., Wang, H.: Object-Z Web Environment and Projections to UML. In: WWW-10: 10th International World Wide Web Conference, ACM Press (2001) 725–734
7. Utting, M., Toyn, I., Sun, J., Martin, A., Dong, J.S., Daley, N., Currie, D.: ZML: XML Support for Standard Z. In: 3nd International Conference of Z and B Users (ZB'03). LNCS, Springer (2003)
8. Developed by members of the Z Standards Panel, Project Editor: Toyn, I.: Z Notation: Final Committee Draft, CD 13568.2 (1999) Available at: http://www.cs.york.ac.uk/~ian/zstan/.
9. World Wide Web Consortium (W3C): (Scalable Vector Graphics (SVG)) Available at: http://www.w3.org/Graphics/SVG/.
10. Hayes, I., Jones, C.: Specifications are not (necessarily) executable. Software Eng. Journal 4 (1989) 330–339
11. Dong, J.S., Li, Y.F., Sun, J., Sun, J., Wang, H.: XML-based static type checking and dynamic visualization for TCOZ. In: 4th International Conference on Formal Engineering Methods, Springer-Verlag (2002) 311–322
12. Sun, J., Dong, J.S., Liu, J., Wang, H.: A XML/XSL Approach to Visualize and Animate TCOZ. In: The 8th Asia-Pacific Software Engineering Conference (APSEC'01), IEEE Press (2001) 453–460
13. Smith, G.: The Object-Z Specification Language. Advances in Formal Methods. Kluwer Academic Publishers (2000)
14. Mahony, B., Dong, J.S.: Timed Communicating Object Z. IEEE Transactions on Software Engineering 26 (2000)
15. Bowen, J.P., Fett, A., Hinchey, M.G., eds.: ZUM'98: The Z Formal Specification Notation, 11th International Conference of Z Users, Berlin, Germany, 24–26 September 1998. Volume 1493 of Lect. Notes in Comput. Sci., Springer-Verlag (1998)

Author Index

Lecture Notes in Computer Science

For information about Vols. 1–3677

please contact your bookseller or Springer

Vol. 3721: A. Jorge, L. Torgo, P. Brazdil, R. Camacho, J. Gama (Eds.), Knowledge Discovery in Databases: PKDD 2005. XXIII, 719 pages. 2005. (Subseries LNAI).

Vol. 3720: J. Gama, R. Camacho, P. Brazdil, A. Jorge, L. Torgo (Eds.), Machine Learning: ECML 2005. XXIII, 769 pages. 2005. (Subseries LNAI).

Vol. 3719: M. Hobbs, A.M. Goscinski, W. Zhou (Eds.), Distributed and Parallel Computing. XI, 448 pages. 2005.

Vol. 3718: V.G. Ganzha, E.W. Mayr, E.V. Vorozhtsov (Eds.), Computer Algebra in Scientific Computing. XII, 502 pages. 2005.

Vol. 3717: B. Gramlich (Ed.), Frontiers of Combining Systems. X, 321 pages. 2005. (Subseries LNAI).

Vol. 3716: L. Delcambre, C. Kop, H.C. Mayr, J. Mylopoulos, O. Pastor (Eds.), Conceptual Modeling – ER 2005. XVI, 498 pages. 2005.

Vol. 3715: E. Dawson, S. Vaudenay (Eds.), Progress in Cryptology – Mycrypt 2005. XI, 329 pages. 2005.

Vol. 3714: H. Obbink, K. Pohl (Eds.), Software Product Lines. XIII, 235 pages. 2005.

Vol. 3713: L. Briand, C. Williams (Eds.), Model Driven Engineering Languages and Systems. XV, 722 pages. 2005.

Vol. 3712: R. Reussner, J. Mayer, J.A. Stafford, S. Overhage, S. Becker, P.J. Schroeder (Eds.), Quality of Software Architectures and Software Quality. XIII, 289 pages. 2005.

Vol. 3711: F. Kishino, Y. Kitamura, H. Kato, N. Nagata (Eds.), Entertainment Computing - ICEC 2005. XXIV, 540 pages. 2005.

Vol. 3710: M. Barni, I. Cox, T. Kalker, H.J. Kim (Eds.), Digital Watermarking. XII, 485 pages. 2005.

Vol. 3709: P. van Beek (Ed.), Principles and Practice of Constraint Programming - CP 2005. XX, 887 pages. 2005.

Vol. 3708: J. Blanc-Talon, W. Philips, D.C. Popescu, P. Scheunders (Eds.), Advanced Concepts for Intelligent Vision Systems. XXII, 725 pages. 2005.

Vol. 3707: D.A. Peled, Y.-K. Tsay (Eds.), Automated Technology for Verification and Analysis. XII, 506 pages. 2005.

Vol. 3706: H. Fuks, S. Lukosch, A.C. Salgado (Eds.), Groupware: Design, Implementation, and Use. XII, 378 pages. 2005.

Vol. 3704: M. De Gregorio, V. Di Maio, M. Frucci, C. Musio (Eds.), Brain, Vision, and Artificial Intelligence. XV, 556 pages. 2005.

Vol. 3703: F. Fages, S. Soliman (Eds.), Principles and Practice of Semantic Web Reasoning. VIII, 163 pages. 2005.

Vol. 3702: B. Beckert (Ed.), Automated Reasoning with Analytic Tableaux and Related Methods. XIII, 343 pages. 2005. (Subseries LNAI).

Vol. 3701: M. Coppo, E. Lodi, G. M. Pinna (Eds.), Theoretical Computer Science. XI, 411 pages. 2005.

Vol. 3699: C.S. Calude, M.J. Dinneen, G. Păun, M. J. Pérez-Jiménez, G. Rozenberg (Eds.), Unconventional Computation. XI, 267 pages. 2005.

Vol. 3698: U. Furbach (Ed.), KI 2005: Advances in Artificial Intelligence. XIII, 409 pages. 2005. (Subseries LNAI).

Vol. 3697: W. Duch, J. Kacprzyk, E. Oja, S. Zadrożny (Eds.), Artificial Neural Networks: Formal Models and Their Applications – ICANN 2005, Part II. XXXII, 1045 pages. 2005.

Vol. 3696: W. Duch, J. Kacprzyk, E. Oja, S. Zadrożny (Eds.), Artificial Neural Networks: Biological Inspirations – ICANN 2005, Part I. XXXI, 703 pages. 2005.

Vol. 3695: M.R. Berthold, R. Glen, K. Diederichs, O. Kohlbacher, I. Fischer (Eds.), Computational Life Sciences. XI, 277 pages. 2005. (Subseries LNBI).

Vol. 3694: M. Malek, E. Nett, N. Suri (Eds.), Service Availability. VIII, 213 pages. 2005.

Vol. 3693: A.G. Cohn, D.M. Mark (Eds.), Spatial Information Theory. XII, 493 pages. 2005.

Vol. 3692: R. Casadio, G. Myers (Eds.), Algorithms in Bioinformatics. X, 436 pages. 2005. (Subseries LNBI).

Vol. 3691: A. Gagalowicz, W. Philips (Eds.), Computer Analysis of Images and Patterns. XIX, 865 pages. 2005.

Vol. 3690: M. Pěchouček, P. Petta, L.Z. Varga (Eds.), Multi-Agent Systems and Applications IV. XVII, 667 pages. 2005. (Subseries LNAI).

Vol. 3689: G.G. Lee, A. Yamada, H. Meng, S.H. Myaeng (Eds.), Information Retrieval Technology. XVII, 735 pages. 2005.

Vol. 3688: R. Winther, B.A. Gran, G. Dahll (Eds.), Computer Safety, Reliability, and Security. XI, 405 pages. 2005.

Vol. 3687: S. Singh, M. Singh, C. Apte, P. Perner (Eds.), Pattern Recognition and Image Analysis, Part II. XXV, 809 pages. 2005.

Vol. 3686: S. Singh, M. Singh, C. Apte, P. Perner (Eds.), Pattern Recognition and Data Mining, Part I. XXVI, 689 pages. 2005.

Vol. 3685: V. Gorodetsky, I. Kotenko, V. Skormin (Eds.), Computer Network Security. XIV, 480 pages. 2005.

Vol. 3684: R. Khosla, R.J. Howlett, L.C. Jain (Eds.), Knowledge-Based Intelligent Information and Engineering Systems, Part IV. LXXIX, 933 pages. 2005. (Subseries LNAI).

Vol. 3683: R. Khosla, R.J. Howlett, L.C. Jain (Eds.), Knowledge-Based Intelligent Information and Engineering Systems, Part III. LXXX, 1397 pages. 2005. (Subseries LNAI).

Vol. 3682: R. Khosla, R.J. Howlett, L.C. Jain (Eds.), Knowledge-Based Intelligent Information and Engineering Systems, Part II. LXXIX, 1371 pages. 2005. (Subseries LNAI).

Vol. 3681: R. Khosla, R.J. Howlett, L.C. Jain (Eds.), Knowledge-Based Intelligent Information and Engineering Systems, Part I. LXXX, 1319 pages. 2005. (Subseries LNAI).

Vol. 3680: C. Priami, A. Zelikovsky (Eds.), Transactions on Computational Systems Biology II. IX, 153 pages. 2005. (Subseries LNBI).

Vol. 3679: S.d.C. di Vimercati, P. Syverson, D. Gollmann (Eds.), Computer Security – ESORICS 2005. XI, 509 pages. 2005.

Vol. 3678: A. McLysaght, D.H. Huson (Eds.), Comparative Genomics. VIII, 167 pages. 2005. (Subseries LNBI).